THE SPANISH WAR

THE
SPANISH
WAR

An American Epic – 1898

B Y

G. J. A. O'TOOLE

W · W · N O R T O N & C O M P A N Y

New York   London

Published simultaneously in Canada by Stoddart, a subsidiary of
General Publishing Co. Ltd., Don Mills, Ontario.

Printed in the United States of America.

The text of this book is composed in Electra, with
display type set in Perpetua. Composition and
manufacturing by The Haddon Craftsmen, Inc.
Book design by Christine Aulicino.

FIRST EDITION

Library of Congress Cataloging in Publication Data
O'Toole, G. J. A. (George J. A.), 1936–
The Spanish War, an American epic.
Includes index.
1. United States—History—War of 1898. I. Title.
E715.O76   1984   973.8'9   83-19355

ISBN 0-393-01839-3

W. W. Norton & Company, Inc.
500 Fifth Avenue, New York, N. Y. 10110
W. W. Norton & Company Ltd.
37 Great Russell Street, London WC1B 3NU

1 2 3 4 5 6 7 8 9 0

For Mary Ann

CONTENTS

ACKNOWLEDGEMENTS   9

CHRONOLOGY   1 1

INTRODUCTION   1 7

Chapter One: "THIS MEANS WAR!"   1 9

Chapter Two: THE PEARL   3 5

Chapter Three: CUBA LIBRE   46

Chapter Four: MARCHING AS TO WAR   9 0

Chapter Five: SIXTY-SIX DAYS   1 2 4

Chapter Six: MANILA   1 7 4

Chapter Seven: A DREAM OF SPRING   1 9 4

Chapter Eight: THE ARMADAS   2 2 2

Chapter Nine: TO WAR   2 4 6

Chapter Ten: THE ROAD TO SANTIAGO   2 5 4

Chapter Eleven: WHEN HEROES MEET   2 9 8

Chapter Twelve: THUNDER ON THE SEA   3 2 3

Chapter Thirteen: THE HONOR OF ARMS   340

Chapter Fourteen: PUERTO RICO   353

Chapter Fifteen: YELLOW JACK   358

Chapter Sixteen: THE FALL OF MANILA   364

Chapter Seventeen: VERSIONS OF PEACE   372

Chapter Eighteen: THE WHITE MAN'S BURDEN   383

Epilogue: THE WAKE OF THE *MAINE*   397

NOTES   401

BIBLIOGRAPHY   431

INDEX   437

PHOTOGRAPHS   151–158
                                                     257–264

MAPS   23, 175
                                                     247, 283

ACKNOWLEDGEMENTS

For decades the prevailing view of our war with Spain in 1898 was that it was no more than a colorful episode of the Ragtime Era, a chapter in the biographies of Theodore Roosevelt and William Randolph Hearst, a slightly ridiculous and somewhat discreditable affair, but a matter of little historical consequence. As a corrective against such notions stand the works of several recent writers, most notably Charles H. Brown, Jack Cameron Dierks, Philip S. Foner, Walter LaFeber, Ernest R. May, H. G. Rickover, and David F. Trask. The author wishes to acknowledge his special indebtedness to these works, which are listed in full in the bibliography. It should be understood, however, that this book is not an attempt to represent the views of anyone but the author.

The author wishes to express his special gratitude to Mrs. Betty Bruce, the Local and State History Department, Monroe County Public Library, Key West, Florida, and Mr. Wright Langley of the Key West Historical Preservation Commission, for their assistance in tracking down some of the details of the Key West part of the story; to Ms. Alice Critchley and the Western Union Corporation for permission to review old telegraph publications in which useful details were found; to the staff of the U.S. Army Communication Systems Center Electronics Museum Library, Fort Monmouth, N.J., for access to the files of The U.S. Veteran Signal Corps Association, Spanish War Division.

Special thanks are also due to the staff of the Manuscript Division of the Library of Congress, the staff of the Army and Old Navy Records Division, and the Central Reference Division of the U.S. National Archives.

CHRONOLOGY

1895	FEBRUARY 24	Second Cuban revolution against Spanish rule begins.
1896	JANUARY 1	Cuban insurgents cross into Havana Province.
	FEBRUARY 16	Governor General Weyler issues first of the *reconcentrado* orders; thousands of Cubans herded into concentration camps.
	APRIL 7	Cleveland administration proposes Cuban reforms to Spain, offers to act as mediator.
	AUGUST 9	Great Britain sabotages Spanish diplomatic efforts to form a European coalition to counter American interference in Cuba.
	AUGUST 26	Philippine revolution against Spanish rule begins.
	DECEMBER 7	President Cleveland, in his last annual message to Congress, declares American patience with Cuban problem to be limited.
1897	MARCH 4	President McKinley inaugurated.
	APRIL 6	McKinley names Theodore Roosevelt as Assistant Secretary of the Navy.
	JUNE 30	U.S. Navy adopts plans for Spanish War.
	AUGUST 8	Spanish Prime Minister Cánovas assassinated by anarchist.
	OCTOBER 4	Ministry of Spanish Prime Minister Sagasta comes to power.
	OCTOBER 31	Sagasta recalls Governor General Weyler, replaces him with Blanco.
	DECEMBER 6	Hundreds of thousands of Cuban *reconcentrados* have died from famine and disease. President McKinley denounces

		Spanish concentration policy as "extermination," threatens to "intervene with force."
1898	JANUARY 1	Limited political autonomy under Spanish rule instituted in Cuba.
	JANUARY 12	Spanish militants, led by army officers, riot in Havana against autonomy policy.
	JANUARY 25	U.S.S. *Maine* arrives at Havana ostensibly on "friendly visit."
	FEBRUARY 9	Personal letter by Spanish ambassador, critical of McKinley, is published in American newspapers. Spanish ambassador resigns.
	FEBRUARY 15	U.S.S. *Maine* destroyed by explosion in Havana harbor; 268 American lives lost.
	MARCH 17	Senator Redfield Proctor of Vermont reports to Senate on conditions in Cuba; prowar feeling spreads to American business community.
	MARCH 28	Finding of Naval Court of Inquiry that *Maine* destroyed by a submerged mine given to Congress; prowar feeling grows.
	APRIL 11	President McKinley asks Congress for authority to use American military force to end Spanish rule in Cuba.
	APRIL 22	U.S. North Atlantic Squadron blockades Cuba; state of war exists between the United States and Spain.
	MAY 1	U.S. Asiatic Squadron under Commodore Dewey attacks and destroys Spanish fleet in Manila Bay and blockades Manila.
	MAY 11	First American combat fatalities in naval actions at Cuban ports of Cárdenas and Cienfuegos.
	MAY 15	Lieutenant Colonel Theodore Roosevelt arrives in San Antonio, Texas, to train with the Rough Riders.
	MAY 28	Spanish squadron under Admiral Cervera blockaded in harbor of Santiago de Cuba by U.S. Flying Squadron.
	JUNE 22	Sixteen thousand American troops begin to land on Cuban coast for advance on Santiago de Cuba.
	JUNE 24	Roosevelt and Rough Riders encounter Spanish troops at Battle of Las Guásimas.
	JULY 1	Major American advance on Santiago de Cuba; battles of San Juan Heights and El

		Caney; Roosevelt leads charge up Kettle Hill.
	JULY 3	Spanish squadron under Admiral Cervera attempts to run American blockade. All Spanish ships destroyed.
	JULY 17	Spanish surrender Santiago de Cuba.
	JULY 25	American invasion of Puerto Rico begins.
	AUGUST 12	Spanish and American officials sign peace protocol to end fighting.
	AUGUST 13	Commodore Dewey and General Wesley Merritt, unaware of peace protocol, attack Manila; Spanish surrender Philippines.
	NOVEMBER 8	Spanish War hero Theodore Roosevelt elected governor of New York State.
	DECEMBER 10	Treaty of Paris officially ends Spanish War. Spain agrees to cede Puerto Rico and Guam to the United States, to sell the Philippines to the United States for $20 million, and to grant independence to Cuba.
1899	FEBRUARY 4	Fighting erupts between Filipinos and U.S. occupation forces; the Philippine War begins.
1901	MARCH 4	President McKinley inaugurated for second term. His new vice-president is former New York Governor Theodore Roosevelt.
	MARCH 23	Filipino revolutionary leader Emilio Aguinaldo captured by U.S. forces.
	SEPTEMBER 14	President McKinley dies from gunshot wounds sustained in attack by anarchist on September 6. Theodore Roosevelt sworn in as president.
1902	JULY 4	President Roosevelt proclaims Philippine War ended.

THE SPANISH WAR

INTRODUCTION

Could we regard the Spanish War as calmly as if it were a thing of the past, we should doubtless perceive that it formed a link in a long chain of events which, when complete, would represent one of those memorable revolutions wherein civilizations pass from an old to a new condition of equilibrium. The last such revolution ended with Waterloo; the one now at hand promises to be equally momentous.

Brooks Adams, 1898

FOR 113 days during the spring and summer of 1898, the United States was at war with Spain. Neither the president of the United States, nor his cabinet, nor the queen regent of Spain, nor her ministers wanted the war. It happened despite their best efforts to prevent it. It happened because forces set in motion decades before had become too powerful to resist. It happened because of ambition, miscalculation, and stupidity; and it happened because of kindness, wit, and resourcefulness. It happened because some were indifferent to the suffering of the world's wretched and others were not. And it happened because history is sometimes the plaything of chance.

For Spain it was the bottom of a centuries-long slide from imperial power. For the United States it was a metamorphosis; the shell of isolation was broken, and a new American dominion suddenly stretched from the Caribbean to the Far East.

It was the most popular of all our wars. Never before or since has grass-roots America been so ready to fight. God seemed to have taken our side for, despite some monumental military blunders, we never lost a battle on land or sea. When it was over we reckoned the cost. Killed in action: 369 soldiers, 10 sailors, 6 Marines. Some two thousand more died from disease, bad food, and other causes. As wars go this was a cheap one.

"It has been a splendid little war," wrote the American ambassador in

London, "begun with the highest motives, carried on with magnificent intelligence and spirit, favored by that fortune which loves the brave."

It was more. It was a national rite of passage, transforming a former colony into a world power. Almost unconsciously, the United States had taken the road to empire, and there was no turning back, not even had some prophet foreseen that Pearl Harbor, the Bay of Pigs, and Vietnam had been made inevitable. The twentieth century was waiting in the wings.

This is how it happened.

CHAPTER ONE

"THIS MEANS WAR!"

FEBRUARY 15, 1898

A HEAVY RAIN had been falling on Key West for several hours. Tom Warren stood at the second floor window of the International Ocean Telegraph Company's office and looked down at Greene Street, wet and empty. He glanced at the clock. Nine P.M. It had been a quiet evening. The telegraph sounder on his desk began to clatter. He sat down and transcribed the incoming message:

> To Burgin, The Herald, New York City:
>   Tranquillo.
>
> Meriwether, Havana.

Ninety miles to the south, Domingo Villaverde arose from his telegraph key in the Havana cable office. *Tranquillo,* he thought; it was so. The city was quiet, although the streets were crowded for this time of the evening. It was the start of the pre-Lenten fiesta. It hardly seemed possible there had been rioting here only a month ago. He waited for the American newspaperman and his translator to leave, then locked the door behind them. The cable office closed at nine. The Spanish military censor had gone off duty, and no more messages could be sent until tomorrow. Villaverde returned to his key and tapped out a personal message to his old friend Warren at Key West.

.   .   .

WALTER SCOTT MERIWETHER of the New York *Herald* stood on the steps of the Palace and lit a cigar. The rich fragrance of the local leaf mixed with the special perfume of the tropics. The night was warm, the air almost oppressive but for a faint breeze blowing from the east. Overhead a million stars adorned a nearly cloudless sky. The great ships riding at their buoys in the harbor were barely visible through the darkness. He made out the Spanish cruiser *Alfonso XII*, and another, the Ward Line steamer *City of Washington*. A third vessel was moored between them, and the dim glow of Havana and the tropical starlight was cast back by the white luster of her freshly painted hull. He felt a quick thrill of patriotic pride. It was the U.S.S. *Maine*.

Meriwether had served for ten years in the U.S. Navy before leaving the service in 1892 to become navy editor of the New York *Times*. Three years later he was hired away by James Gordon Bennett, Jr., to work for the New York *Herald*. The Navy was still his beat.

Early in December the Navy announced that the North Atlantic Squadron would go to the Gulf of Mexico for winter exercises. For the past two years the fleet had abandoned its traditional winter drill grounds near the Dry Tortugas off Key West in deference to Spanish sensibilities. Tensions between the two nations were already high.

There was a revolution going on in Cuba, a war for the island's independence. Many Americans supported the insurgents, sent them arms and supplies, even fought beside them. Officially the U.S. government opposed such intervention, but in Spanish eyes it had not taken the proper steps to prevent it.

The Spanish had resorted to the most ruthless measures to crush the revolution, transporting almost the entire rural population of the island into the coastal cities, where it was confined in concentration camps. Famine and disease had killed hundreds of thousands. There was a public outcry in the United States against Spain's action, and the sensational press further inflamed public opinion. The U.S. government made repeated protests to Madrid over the human rights violations, but Madrid rejected all such protests as unwarranted interference in Spain's internal affairs.

Behind the scenes, both governments worked hard to avert a war over Cuba, but American sympathy toward the rebels sparked as much indignation among Spaniards as did the Spanish outrages on the island among Americans. Public opinion in the two nations was pulling in opposite directions, straining the slender thread of Spanish–American relations dangerously near the breaking point. On both sides of the Atlantic the popular demand for war was increasing, threatening to sweep away the peacemakers.

Late the previous year a new government had come into power in Madrid. It sought peace in Cuba through compromise, instituting a new policy of limited political autonomy for the island. The move satisfied no one. The Cuban revolutionaries continued to insist on full independence, while the hard-liners in the Spanish Army resented the new policy, seeing it as a dishonorable acquiescence to Cuban mutiny and American meddling. They especially objected to Madrid's recall of General Valeriano Weyler, the tough governor general of Cuba, who was responsible for the former harsh counterinsurgency policies. On January 12 a mob of the militants, led by nearly a hundred army officers, rioted in Havana, sacking the offices of four newspapers that supported the autonomy program.

The administration of President William McKinley was concerned for the thousands of Americans living in Cuba and the millions of American dollars invested on the island. For months, the American consul general at Havana had been urging McKinley to send a warship to the port, believing the presence of a tangible symbol of American military strength would keep the Spanish dissidents in line. After the riots, the McKinley administration began to take the same view.

On the night of January 24 the U.S.S. *Maine* left the North Atlantic Squadron at the Dry Tortugas and steamed south. At nine o'clock the next morning she dropped anchor in Havana harbor, as her guns roared a salute to the Spanish flag flying over Morro Castle. A friendly visit, the Americans blandly proclaimed; a welcome one, the Spanish replied with frigid propriety. Neither side expected the other to believe its declaration, of course, but no matter. American fears had been eased with a minimum of injury to Spanish pride. For the next three weeks Havana remained *tranquillo.* There had been little news to report from the Cuban capital.

Meriwether and his translator got into a cab in front of the palace and told the driver to take them downtown. The correspondent took out his watch. It was ten past nine.

.   .   .

CORPORAL NEWTON, U.S. Marine Corps, raised the bugle to his lips and blew taps. The notes carried throughout the U.S.S. *Maine* and across the placid waters of Havana harbor. Aft, in the spacious and richly appointed admiral's cabin, Captain Charles Sigsbee paused for a moment. He had been writing a letter to his wife.

> I laid down my pen to listen to the notes of the bugle, which were singularly beautiful in the oppressive stillness of the night. Newton, who was rather given to fanciful effects, was evidently doing his best. During his pauses the echoes floated back to the ship with singular distinctness, repeating the strains of the bugle fully and exactly.

Most of the *Maine*'s 328 enlisted men were already in their bunks and hammocks in the forward part of the battleship. Some of the officers had gone to their cabins; others smoked, read, or otherwise passed the time in the wardroom near the ship's giant after turret. The men of the quarter watch stood duty on the deck. As the last echo of the bugle faded away, Captain Sigsbee picked up his pen and resumed his letter.

Charles Dwight Sigsbee was fifty-two years old. A graduate of Annapolis, class of 1863, he had seen action during the Civil War in the Battle of Mobile Bay and the attacks on Fort Fisher. Sigsbee had a flair for science and engineering; after the war he had served with the Navy's Hydrographic Office. He commanded the survey ship *Blake* and made extensive explorations of the Gulf of Mexico, discovering the Sigsbee Deep, the deepest spot in the gulf. He invented several deep-sounding and sampling devices for studying the ocean floor.

In March 1897 he was promoted to the rank of captain; a few weeks later he was given command of the *Maine*.

The *Maine* was one of the first two modern steel battleships built by the U.S. Navy. She marked the end of the days of fighting sail and the dawn of the era of the steam-driven battlewagon. Her keel was laid in the Brooklyn Navy Yard in 1888, and her original plans called for a canvas and coal-powered armored cruiser—a steel steamship carrying over seven thousand yards of square sails and topgallants. But it was six years before she sailed out of New York harbor, and during that time she was overtaken by the progress of naval technology. The era of wind, wood, and canvas had passed; now steam and steel would rule the seas. In the Brooklyn shipyard the plans for the *Maine* were redrawn and the construction modified. At 10 A.M. on November 5, 1895, she stood out to sea for the first time. No crowded yards of canvas rose above her decks. Instead, a pair of tall stacks poured twin streams of black smoke into the wind. More than nine thousand horsepower drove her through the water; spray flew from her bows, and her wake boiled and foamed in the maelstrom of twisting screws.

She drove through the sea at better than seventeen knots. Her overall length was 319 feet. She was 57 feet broad at the beam and displaced 6,683 tons. She was armed with four ten-inch guns—two mounted in each of a pair of armored steel turrets fore and aft—six six-inch guns, and seven rapid-fire six-pounders. She also carried torpedos and had four launching tubes. Three hundred and fifty-four officers and men operated this floating steel fortress. For all that, she was rated by the Navy as a second-class battleship; four larger and more powerful vessels had joined the fleet during the two years since she had left her Brooklyn berth.

If the *Maine* was not the most formidable battleship in the American fleet, that fact did not seem to trouble Captain Sigsbee. Her importance as an element of U.S. naval might had been confirmed four months earlier when she was ordered to Port Royal, South Carolina, to stand by in case of trouble at Havana. And two months later, after Spanish–American tensions had mounted further, it was the *Maine* that was sent to Key West, just five hours and ninety miles north of Havana. Sigsbee told his wife, "In certain events the *Maine* is to be the chosen of the flock; it being so ordered by the department."

Those events came to pass. On the night of January 24 the *Maine* was riding at anchor with the other ships of the North Atlantic Squadron some sixty miles from Key West. At about 9 P.M. the torpedo boat *Dumont* was sighted speeding toward the fleet from the direction of the Keys.

As Sigsbee watched the swift little boat approach, it occurred to him it might be bringing a dispatch ordering the *Maine* to Havana: "It was an intuition, but without waiting for orders, I directed that fires be spread and preparations made for getting under way."

Sigsbee's intuition proved correct. By 11 P.M. the *Maine* had gotten up a full head of steam. From the bridge Captain Sigsbee issued a string of orders. The anchor was raised, and the *Maine*'s great triple expansion engines began to turn. The helmsman spun his wheel, and the battleship swung to a heading of south by southeast. The *Maine* was on her way to Havana.

Dawn found the warship steaming slowly off the Cuban coast, well west of

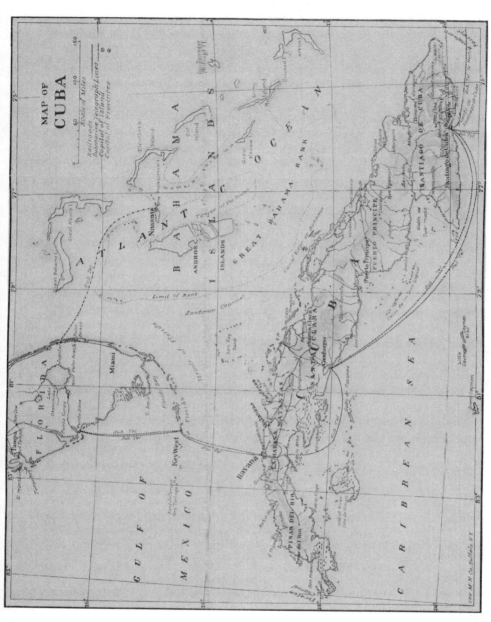

Cuba and south Florida. Dotted lines show submarine telegraph cables in use in 1898.

Havana: "I did not desire to reach Havana at early daylight, but rather to steam in when the town was alive and on its feet."

Sigsbee knew that the desired effect of the *Maine*'s visit was to be psychological rather than military, and he intended to make an entrance. When he judged the Cuban port to be fully awake, he steamed past the harbor entrance, the Stars and Stripes flying from the *Maine*'s peak and a jack from her foremast head, a signal to the Havana port authorities that an American man-of-war wished to enter the harbor. Presently a Spanish pilot boat came out of the harbor and fell in beside the battleship. The pilot came on board and guided the *Maine* through the narrow channel to a buoy in the middle of the harbor. She dropped anchor and fired a salute, which was answered by a Spanish man-of-war anchored nearby.

There were formal visits to and from the *Maine*, the ranks of the visitors and the order of the visits dictated by the rigid precepts of naval courtesy and protocol, culminating in a call by Sigsbee upon the Spanish admiral aboard the cruiser *Alfonso XII*. If the Spanish did not greet the Americans with warmth, they displayed elaborate civility. At least there was no shooting. At the American Consulate, Consul General Lee breathed a sigh of relief.

Fitzhugh Lee—portly, mustachioed, and sixty-two years old—was a nephew of General Robert E. Lee. A soldier himself, Lee had graduated in the West Point class of 1856, seen action against the Indians, then later against the Yankees. He was a veteran of Second Manassas, Kelly's Ford, Chancellorsville, and other Civil War battles. He rose to the rank of brigadier general, senior cavalry commander of the Army of Northern Virginia.

He was appointed consul general at Havana in 1896 by President Cleveland. Now, in one of the little ironies of history, he found himself reporting to a secretary of state who was the brother of General William Tecumseh Sherman. Like many other former Confederates, he had put aside old enmities in the face of the growing hostility between the United States and Spain.

Months ago Lee had urged Washington to send a battleship to the Cuban port. In mid-December, when the *Maine* was stationed at Key West, he was given the authority to summon her if and when he considered it necessary. But in the event it was not Lee but President McKinley who took that step, and he did it against the consul general's advice. Since the mid-January riots, the situation at Havana had been so tense that Lee feared the arrival of the *Maine* might touch off worse violence. As the battleship was made fast to her mooring buoy, he cabled the State Department:

Ship quietly arrived 11 A.M. to-day. No demonstrations so far.
                                                                    Lee

There were no demonstrations that day, or the next. Lee realized he had been overanxious. There had been no trouble, and now there was the American naval presence he had wanted for so many months. He wrote to the assistant secretary of state, "I . . . am so happy that we have reached and quietly crossed over the bridge which for a long time we have seen in front of us."

He thought the crisis was over. Events seemed to bear this out.

More formalities were observed that week, more courtesies exchanged. Two days after the *Maine*'s arrival Sigsbee and Lee called on General Parrado, the Spanish officer who had been left in charge of the city during the governor general's temporary absence. The visiting Americans were treated to a lavish, if stiffly formal, reception. Next Parrado visited the *Maine* and was given a seventeen-gun salute, exactly the same honor prescribed in naval regulations for the visit of an American state governor.

There was to be a bullfight on Sunday in the ring at Regla, a small community across the harbor from Havana. Mazzantini, the famous "gentleman bullfighter of Spain," was to appear. Captain Sigsbee said he'd like to attend; General Parrado sent him box seat tickets.

Despite the Spaniard's courteous gesture, he probably hoped Sigsbee would change his mind and stay aboard the *Maine* on Sunday. If there was to be trouble over the American warship's visit, he knew, it would probably begin among the excited crowds at the bullfight. As an American resident of Havana told Sigsbee, "If they [the Spanish] will allow you there, they will allow you anywhere."

But as Sigsbee, Lee, and a group of the *Maine*'s officers waited for the ferryboat to take them across the harbor to Regla that Sunday, they were given some evidence that the Spanish might not allow them there. Someone handed Sigsbee a circular. It was printed in Spanish. Translated, it read as follows:

SPANIARDS!
LONG LIVE SPAIN WITH HONOR!
What are you doing that you allow yourselves to be insulted in this way? Do you not see what they have done to us in withdrawing our brave and beloved Weyler,* who at this very time would have finished this unworthy, rebellious rabble who are trampling on our flag and on our honor?

Autonomy is imposed on us to cast us aside and give places of honor and authority to those who initiated this rebellion, these lowbred autonomists, ungrateful sons of our beloved country!

And, finally, these Yankee pigs who meddle in our affairs, humiliating us to the last degree, and, for a still greater taunt, order to us a man-of-war of their rotten squadron, after insulting us in their newspapers with articles sent from our home!

Spaniards! The moment of action has arrived. Do not go to sleep! Let us teach these vile traitors that we have not yet lost our pride, and that we know how to protest with the energy befitting a nation worthy and strong, as our Spain is, and always will be!

Death to the Americans! Death to autonomy!
Long live Spain! Long live Weyler!

Captain Sigsbee, unimpressed, put the circular in his pocket and boarded the ferryboat.

The Americans were tolerated at the bullfight, but they were clearly unwel-

*General Valeriano Weyler, the harsh ex-governor general, had recently been replaced by the milder General Ramón Blanco.

come. General Parrado bowed politely as Sigsbee, Lee, and the others entered
their box, but the Americans could not fail to notice the armed troops among
the crowd. A guard of twenty soldiers had been stationed directly in front of their
box, while others had been posted at regular intervals around the ring. The
atmosphere was tense, but nothing worse than dirty looks were thrown at the
visitors. Still, Sigsbee may have thought he had pushed matters a bit too far. The
American party left before the last bull was killed in order to avoid the crowds
outside the stadium and on the ferry. Later, from the deck of the *Maine*, Sigsbee
watched as the ferryboat carried throngs of Spaniards back to Havana. There
were hoots and catcalls as the boat passed the American warship.

The tension and hostility he saw did not keep Sigsbee from returning to the
bullring the following Sunday. This time things seemed more relaxed, and the
American party stayed to see all six bulls killed. Sigsbee was there to make a point,
for he did not enjoy the spectacle.

> The Spanish bull-fight should be considered as a savage spectacle passed
> down from generation to generation from a remote period when human
> nature was far more cruel than at present. . . . During the progress of
> the last bull-fight that I attended, several poor, docile horses were killed
> under circumstances that were shocking to the American mind. In a
> box near that which my friends and I occupied, a little girl of ten or
> twelve years of age sat apparently unmoved while a horse was prostrate
> and dying in prolonged agony near the middle of the ring.

But Sigsbee also reflected that "similar considerations might be thought to apply
to our own prize-fights."

Another copy of the Spanish circular was sent anonymously to Sigsbee. He
guessed the sender was "some American who judged it important." Sigsbee may
not have considered it important, but he was not inclined to be careless. He kept
a quarter watch on the ship at night, instead of the usual anchor watch, and he
made sure the sentries had live ammunition in their guns. Artillery rounds were
kept handy, and steam was kept up in the boilers at all times, so the massive gun turrets could be operated immediately. The master-at-arms was ordered to have all visitors to the ship watched closely, and any who went below were to be escorted.

But there were no further incidents. Havana was indeed *tranquillo*. By the
beginning of February the Navy was considering withdrawing the *Maine* from Havana in response to a request from the New Orleans city fathers that the battleship be sent there for the Mardi Gras on the seventeenth. Consul General Lee objected. "We are the masters of the situation now and I would not disturb or alter
it," he advised. The Spanish seemed to have gotten used to the idea of the ship
being at Havana. Removing it might stir things up; sending another ship was certain to do so. The Navy agreed. The *Maine* would stay at Havana indefinitely.

.   .   .

IN A VILLA on a quiet residential street overlooking the harbor, Clara Barton and
her assistant worked late into the evening clearing away some of the paperwork

that had accumulated since their arrival at Havana a week earlier. The seventy-six-year-old Barton, founder and president of the American National Red Cross, was in Cuba to oversee the distribution of American aid to the *reconcentrados*, the sick and starving Cubans whom the Spanish had forcibly removed from their homes in the countryside and crowded into coastal concentration camps. Two months earlier the U.S. State Department had arranged with the Spanish authorities for the duty-free import of food and other materials collected by American charities for Cuban relief. At President McKinley's request, Barton and the Red Cross were to manage things on the Cuban end of the relief pipeline.

She arrived at Havana on February 9 and immediately visited the city hospitals, where some of the worst cases had been taken. They were living skeletons, beyond hope. Infants with swollen stomachs and bulging eyes clung to the milkless breasts of their dying mothers. Outside the door of every hospital there was a waiting pile of empty coffins.

Barton pleaded with the Spanish authorities to ease the plight of the *reconcentrados*. The officials were polite, even friendly, but only knew the reasons why nothing could be done. They were, she wrote, "perplexed on both sides; first by the Spanish soldiery, liable to attack the [relief] workers, likewise the Cuban guerrillas, who were equally as dangerous."

She did what she could, despite official Spanish indifference, remaining in almost constant motion since her arrival, organizing food distribution centers throughout Havana and some of the nearby towns where the *reconcentrados* were confined.

She paused in her labors once, to accept Captain Sigsbee's invitation to lunch aboard the *Maine*. Tonight, as she looked down at the white shape of the battleship in the harbor, she recalled "the lunch at those polished tables, the glittering china and cut glass . . . his officers . . . his crew, strong ruddy and bright."

          —   •   •

As the last echoes of Corporal Newton's bugle faded into the stillness of Havana harbor, Father Chidwick, chaplain of the *Maine*, climbed into his bunk. It was a quarter past nine, and Chidwick decided to read for a while before turning out the light. He took down a copy of *Facts and Fakes About Cuba* by George Bronson Rea.

Rea was a newspaper correspondent who reported on Cuba for the New York *Herald*. Unlike most of his colleagues, Rea was not content to stay in Havana and base his stories on covert interviews with spokesmen for the Cuban rebels. He had worked as an engineer on Cuban sugar plantations, and he knew his way around the countryside. It was there he gathered his information, despite the danger of stopping a Spanish or Cuban bullet. Rea differed in another way from most of his colleagues; he was sympathetic to the Spanish side. In his book, published a few months earlier, he had criticized many of the reports filed by American reporters whose travels in Cuba had been limited to trips between the bar at the Inglaterra Hotel and the cable office. Rea had traveled the length and breadth of the island and had visited the insurgents in their mountain and jungle hideouts. There may have been deliberate Spanish atrocities in Cuba, he said, but he had seen no evidence of them.

If Father Chidwick thought that Rea may have overstated his case, he would have been interested to know that the author of the book he was reading was, at that moment, almost near enough to defend it in person. Rea was seated in a cafe near Havana's Central Park, together with Sylvester Scovel, of the New York *World,* and Scovel's wife.

Rea and the Scovels chatted and watched the masked and costumed revelers on their way to the pre-Lenten festivities. The three Americans were, in all likelihood, discussing the Cuban revolution. And if any American was as well informed on that subject as Rea, it was Sylvester Scovel.

Like Rea, Scovel had slipped out of Havana and made his way to the rebel strongholds in the eastern provinces. He made contact with General Máximo Gómez, the insurgent leader, and spent six months living with the rebels. After his return to Havana, he was expelled from Cuba by the authorities and was immediately hired by the *World.* He slipped back into Cuba and rejoined Gómez. But this time, while filing a report from the southern port of Las Tunas, he was caught by the Spanish Army and imprisoned.

Overnight Scovel became a *cause célèbre.* Led by the *World,* other newspapers, civic groups, state legislatures, and city councils across America protested his imprisonment and demanded action by the State Department. The Spanish minister to Washington warned Madrid that, if anything happened to Scovel, the U.S. government might not be able to resist the ensuing public pressure for military action. Scovel was released and once again expelled from Cuba, but within a few months he was back again. He found General Gómez in time to interview him regarding the new Spanish autonomy policy. It was too little and too late, Gómez told him. The rebels would settle for nothing less than full independence, and they expected to achieve it soon.

Scovel was not arrested when he returned to Havana. The Spanish apparently now believed it better to ignore the reporter's repeated breaking of their laws. Tonight he was at large and enjoying the company of his wife and his friend.

It was 9:40 P.M.

.   .   .

WALTER SCOTT MERIWETHER and his translator, Felipe Ruíz, had taken a horse-drawn cab from the cable office at the palace and were riding toward the Hotel Inglaterra. They passed a cafe, one frequented by the American press corps (perhaps the same one where Rea and the Scovels were now sitting), and Meriwether signaled the driver to stop. He got out, paid the cabman, and entered the cafe.

He had just stepped through the door when he felt the impact: "The city shook to a terrific explosion. Amid a shower of falling plaster every light in the place went out, as did every other electric light in the city."

He heard a confused jumble of voices in the darkness. Someone said the insurgents had blown up the palace. Someone else said it must have been the arsenal at Regla, across the harbor. Meriwether turned and left, hurrying to the vantage of his topfloor room at the Inglaterra. He looked toward the harbor. He could see nothing but a great glare.

Clara Barton and her assistant were still at work when the blast struck:

> The house had grown still; the noises on the street were dying away, when suddenly the table shook from under our hands, the great glass door opening on to the veranda, facing the sea, flew open; everything in the room was in motion or out of place. The deafening roar was such a burst of thunder as perhaps one never heard before. And off to the right, out over the bay, the air was filled with a blaze of light, and this in turn filled with black specks like huge specters flying in all directions. Then it faded away, the bells rang, the whistles blew, and voices in the street were heard for a moment; then all was quiet again.

Rea and the Scovels looked out through the shattered windows of the cafe. The harbor "was lit up with an intense light, and above it could be seen innumerable colored lights, resembling rockets."

From the cable office at the palace, Domingo Villaverde looked toward the mooring in the harbor where the *Maine* had been riding at anchor. He could not see the battleship; a great cloud of smoke covered the place where she had been a few moments before. The echo of the explosion rang in his ears.

Rea and Sylvester Scovel hailed a cab and told the driver to head toward the harbor. Near the docks they got out and joined an excited crowd gathered before the custom house, held back by Spanish guards. Elbowing their way forward, they told the guards they were officers from the *Maine* and they were admitted. They rushed through the baggage inspection room and out onto the dock, where they found Havana police chief Colonel José Paglieri climbing into a boat. He said they could come with him if they wished.

Across the harbor, the British bark *Deva* was moored at the Regla wharf. Her master, Captain Frederick G. Teasdale, was in his cabin when he felt the explosion. He thought some other ship had collided with his own, and he rushed on deck. The concussion had been so great he was stunned, thinking momentarily he might have been shot through the head. As he emerged from the shattered doors of his cabin, there was a second explosion. He saw a great cloud of debris hurled high into the air over the harbor and a huge, slate-colored cloud of smoke rising after it. Lights, like fireworks, flashed up through the cloud.

Sigmund Rothschild, a passenger aboard the *City of Washington*, had gone on deck about half past nine to enjoy the tropical evening. He had just adjusted his deck chair and sat down when he heard the first blast.

> I looked around, and I saw the bow of the *Maine* rise a little, go a little out of the water. It couldn't have been more than a few seconds after that noise . . . that there came in the center of the ship a terrible mass of fire and explosion, and everything went over our heads, a black mass. We could not tell what it was. It was all black. Then we heard the noise of falling material on the place where we had been, right near the smoking room. One of the life boats, which was hanging, had a piece

go through it and made a big hole in it. After we saw that mass go up, the whole boat [the *Maine*] lifted out, I should judge about two feet. As she lifted out, the bow went right down. . . .

There were screams from the water.

"Help! Lord God, help us! Help! Help!"

Captain Frank Stevens, master of the *City of Washington*, ordered the liner's boats lowered. Two were found to have been riddled by falling debris, and the rescue efforts were delayed.

·   ·   ·

CAPTAIN SIGSBEE GROPED his way forward through the blackness. He knew from the slope of the deck beneath his feet that the *Maine* was listing to port. At a turn in the passageway, he collided with Marine Private William Anthony. Sigsbee and Anthony emerged onto the main deck, forward of the superstructure. An immense dark mass loomed up amidships.

"The explosion took place at nine-forty, sir," said Private Anthony, as though the sudden chaos might be vanquished through military precision. There was no need to add that the ship was sinking; the main deck was already awash. Sigsbee and the Marine private climbed to the poop deck, where they found Lieutenant Commander Wainwright and several others. Sigsbee went to the starboard rail and tried to see forward. A fire had broken out amidships, and he ordered the forward ammunition magazine flooded. He was informed the forward part of the ship was already under water. There was no need to worry about the after magazines; they too would be submerged before the fire could reach them. The *Maine* was settling rapidly. The rising water drove the air from the ship's compartments. There was a strange whistling moan as it escaped through the seams of doors and hatches.

Sigsbee's eyes gradually became accustomed to the darkness, and he could make out white forms in the water. He heard the cries for help and knew these were the men of the *Maine*. Only three of the ship's boats could be reached; Sigsbee ordered two of them lowered, and the uninjured officers and men set out to rescue the living from the water. Other boats were already lifting the wounded from the harbor. The undamaged boats of the *City of Washington* had arrived, as well as those of the *Alfonso XII*. The Spanish seamen spared no effort to help the Americans, despite the danger. There was small-arms ammunition and six-pound shells in the fire amidships, and the shooting lights seen by observers ashore were live rounds detonated by the flames.

As Scovel and Rea approached the scene in the boat with Colonel Paglieri, projectiles whistled past them and over their heads. The police chief had to beat the boatman with his cane to force them to proceed toward the burning wreck. The two American reporters looked at the scene in horror. Rea later recalled it:

Great masses of twisted and bent iron plates and beams were thrown up in confusion amidships. The bow had disappeared; the foremast and smoke stacks had fallen and to add to the horror and danger, the mass of wreckage amidships was on fire.

Scovel also remembered the scene:

> The superstructure alone loomed up, partly colored by the red glare of flames glancing upon the black water. At first it appeared as if her bow was totally demolished. Then the mass of beams and braces was seen that was blown forward by the awful rending.

Clara Barton rushed to the San Ambrosio Hospital, where some thirty or forty of the wounded had been taken. She described the scene:

> They had been crushed by timbers, cut by iron, scorched by fire, and blown sometimes high in the air, sometimes driven down through the red hot furnace room and out into the water, senseless, to be picked up by some boat and gotten ashore. Their wounds were all over them —heads and faces terribly cut, internal wounds, arms, legs, feet and hands burned to the live flesh.

There was little to do for them that was not already being done by the Spanish doctors and nurses. Barton began taking down the names of the survivors. The first she approached gave his name and address, then pulled the bandage away from his face so he could see her.
"Isn't this Miss Barton?"
"Yes."
"I thought it must be. I knew you were here, and thought you would come to us. I am so thankful for us all."

> I passed from one to another, till twelve had been spoken to and the names taken. . . . Their expressions of grateful thanks, spoken under such conditions, were too much. I passed the pencil to another hand and stepped aside.

Walter Scott Meriwether found more of the wounded at the Havana City Hospital:

> Most of the victims were either dead or dying and only one was able to talk coherently. All he knew was that he was asleep in his hammock when he was hurled high in the air by a terrific explosion, had struck the water, and someone had rescued him.

Throughout the night Meriwether watched a seemingly endless line of stretchers carried into the hospital bearing the burned and broken bodies of the *Maine* crewmen. In the dispatch filed the next day he reported:

> Men that I took by the hand and with the best voice I could command spoke cheerful words to are this morning dead or will be helpless

cripples the rest of their lives. . . . In adjoining cots were a sailor with his face half blown away and another with both legs so badly fractured that he must lose them.

At the end of the ward was a lusty Marine crying, "For God's sake, let me die!"

With all possible tenderness and care the Spanish doctors were dressing the face of a fireman. "There is something in my eyes," he said. "Wait and let me open them."

Both eyes were gone.

THE POOP DECK of the *Maine* was now nearly awash. Lieutenant Commander Wainwright advised Sigsbee that all the wounded that could be found had been rescued from the harbor. In a whisper Wainwright added that he thought the forward ammunition magazine had been thrown amidships by the blast and might now be in the midst of the flames. Sigsbee directed the others to get into the boats and cast off. Then he climbed into the gig, and the men pulled on their oars. The three boats drew away toward the *City of Washington*.

.   .   .

NINETY MILES to the north the torpedo boat *Cushing* rode quietly at her moorings at the Key West Naval Station. At 10 P.M. her commander, Lieutenant Albert Gleaves, was below, preparing to turn in, when the quartermaster came to his cabin and announced that there was a gentleman on deck who wished to see him on a very important matter.

"I went on deck immediately," Gleaves later recalled, "and found our secret agent."

"I have a most important message from our agent in Havana," the visitor said. By the light of an oil lantern on the dock he read Gleaves the message. The *Maine* had been blown up by her powder magazine. Crowds of people on the marina were watching as the American man-of-war sank in the harbor.

Gleaves was skeptical. There had been rumors in Key West almost every day that either the American Consulate in Havana had been attacked or Consul General Lee had been assassinated. But the visitor was adamant. The report, he said, came from a source "who has never failed us."

The secret agent was Martin L. Hellings, manager of the Key West telegraph office. Hellings, a longtime friend of Captain Sigsbee, had been performing secret intelligence missions for the Navy for months. His Cuban source was the Havana telegraph operator, Domingo Villaverde, the only person able to get a message out of the Cuban port after the cable office closed and the Spanish military censor went off duty at 9 P.M.

Gleaves and the agent went to the U.S.S. *Fern*, also moored at the naval station, and conferred with her skipper, Lieutenant Commander W. S. Cowles. Cowles happened to be the most senior officer at Key West at that moment.* Hellings repeated his information to him. The three immediately went to the

*Cowles was the brother-in-law of the assistant secretary of the Navy, Theodore Roosevelt.

telegraph office on Greene Street, where the night operator, Tom Warren, was on duty. The telegraph instruments stood silent.

It was not possible to telegraph to Villaverde, asking for confirmation of his report and additional details. The Spanish censor might have already returned to the Havana cable office. Such an inquiry from Key West would reveal that Villaverde had sent an unauthorized dispatch in the censor's absence, perhaps leading to the discovery of his role as an American spy. They would have to wait for Villaverde to send another report. The four men sat staring at the silent telegraph instrument.

. . .

ON BOARD THE *City of Washington*, Captain Sigsbee's first concern was the *Maine's* wounded. Some of the injured men were below in the liner's dining saloon, which had been turned into a makeshift hospital. Sigsbee visited them and satisfied himself they were given every possible care. Then he went back on deck and looked across the harbor, where his ship still burned, occasional explosions of ammunition rending the air. He turned and went to the captain's cabin. Taking a pen and a sheet of Ward Line stationary, he wrote a dispatch for Washington:

> Secnav, Washington, D.C.
> *Maine* blown up in Havana harbor at nine forty to-night and destroyed. Many wounded and doubtless more killed or drowned. Wounded and others aboard Spanish man-of-war and Ward Line steamer. Send Light House Tenders from Key West for crew and the few pieces of equipment above water. No one has clothing other than that upon him. Public opinion should be suspended until further report. All officers believed saved. Jenkins and Merritt not yet accounted for. Many Spanish officers, including representatives of General Blanco, now with us to express sympathy.
> Sigsbee

Sigsbee had not yet met with the Spanish officials. He emerged from the cabin and found them waiting for him on the deck. Among them was Secretary General Congosto, chief of the Havana censor's office. Sigsbee handed him the dispatch he had just written; the Spaniard read it and handed it back.

The message was "very kind," he said, with some emotion.

It was nearly 11 P.M. Rea and Scovel had arrived aboard the *City of Washington*, hoping to interview Sigsbee. Sigsbee handed his dispatch to Rea, whom he knew, and asked him to see that it was sent immediately. General Congosto had ordered the cable office opened and put two extra censors on duty. Rea put Sigsbee's telegram in his pocket and climbed down into the waiting boat.

. . .

AT 11 P.M. the telegraph instrument in the Key West cable office began to clatter. Tom Warren began taking down the words as they came across the wire from Havana. Lieutenant Gleaves and Lieutenant Commander Cowles waited anxiously. Halfway through the message, Warren suddenly glanced up at Martin Hellings. The cable office manager had been reading the message by ear and knew what Warren had scribbled on his pad. Gleaves saw the grim exchange of silent glances between the two. He knew for certain the first report had been true.

The *Maine* had been blown up.

.   .   .

HELEN LONG, the daughter of the secretary of the Navy, returned home from a dance at 1:30 A.M. to find a messenger waiting outside with a telegram. It was, the man said, a dispatch of great urgency. She awakened her father.

"It was almost impossible to believe that it could be true, or that it was not a wild and vivid dream," he recalled. He quickly scribbled a message to Commander Francis W. Dickens, acting chief of the Navy's Bureau of Navigation, ordering the rescue ships Sigsbee had asked for be sent to Havana immediately.

After he had seen to the rescue ships, Commander Dickens walked the several hundred feet from the Navy Department building to the White House. He roused the night watchman and sent him upstairs to the family quarters to awaken President McKinley.

.   .   .

IN NEW YORK CITY William Randolph Hearst found a messenger from his office waiting for him when he got home from the theater. He was to call the editor of his newspaper, the New York *Journal*. There was important news, he was told. He picked up the telephone.

"Have you put anything else on the front page?" he asked, after he was told of the explosion in Havana harbor.

"Only the other big news," the editor replied.

"There is not any other big news," Hearst said. "Please spread the story all over the page."

"This means war!"

CHAPTER TWO

THE PEARL

HE SAW IT the first time one morning in October, a vision rising up from the sea beyond the bows of the *Santa María*. Between heaven and the sea it stood, beyond the lines of snowy breakers and the palm-fringed beach, beneath the sun-filled clouds crowning the sierra.

"Everything is green as April in Andalusia," Columbus reported. "The singing of the birds is such that it seems as if one would never desire to depart. There are flocks of parrots that obscure the sun. There are trees of a thousand species, each having its particular fruit, and all of marvelous flavor."

He wondered at first if it might be China or Japan. Later, when he knew it was not, he called it la Isla Juana in honor of the young prince of Castile. Yet later it would be called Fernandina, and then Santiago, and finally it would be called by the name given it by the Tainos Indians before Columbus, Colba. The Spanish would pronounce it Cuba.

The Spanish came looking for gold; they found little on the island. There were other treasures: tobacco, which they did not know, and smoking, which they learned from the Tainos. And on the northwest coast of the island there was one of the finest deep-water harbors in the world. It was in a region the Indians called Avan, so the Spanish called the port Havana.

Their great fleet was based there. Philip's galleons rode at anchor in the harbor, waiting for the carracks from Vera Cruz and Portobello laden with Indian treasure, to escort them on their dangerous journeys home to Cádiz. In time the port grew from a garrison to a cosmopolitan city with a university and a cathedral. A seventeenth-century visitor called Havana "the boulevard of the New World."

The garrison was not impregnable. The British seized it in 1762 and used it as a bargaining chip to end the Seven Years' War. Next year the Spanish returned, resolved that history should not repeat itself, and built a new fort to guard the harbor entrance. The project required the importation of a great many African slaves. After the construction was finished, the slaves were sold to work the plantations in the countryside.

Slaves already worked the tobacco plantations, but this sudden surplus of labor prompted the planters to try a new crop. Labor-intensive, sugar was well suited to the institution of slavery, and it was very profitable. Tens of thousands more slaves were imported. By 1817 the Cuban slave population had swelled to 199,000. By the late 1820s Cuba was the largest sugar producer and the richest colony in the world.

·   ·   ·

SOMETHING HAPPENED in 1808 that marked the beginning of the end of the Spanish Empire: Napoleon invaded Spain and put his brother, Joseph, on the Spanish throne. The Spanish colonies in the Americas refused to recognize the usurper, and some declared their independence. The Spaniard Ferdinand VII was restored to the throne after Napoleon's fall in 1814, but the events set in motion in Latin America could not be reversed. By 1825 the Spanish Empire in America, from Mexico to the Straits of Magellan, was gone. Only Cuba and Puerto Rico remained Spanish.

Cuba's loyalty to Spain was tinged with self-interest. A few decades earlier the slaves of the neighboring French island of Saint Domingue, inspired by the French Revolution, had risen up under Toussaint L'Overture and created the black republic of Haiti. The Cuban planters feared the same might happen on their island; a break with Spain might lead to a slave revolt and a black republic of Cuba. The presence of Spanish troops in Cuba insured both the planters' safety and their prosperity.

But prosperity was threatened in 1820, when Britain prevailed upon Spain to end the slave trade. The Cortes—the Spanish parliament—even considered momentarily the total abolition of slavery in Cuba and Puerto Rico. The planters faced a dilemma: independence was dangerous, but continued Spanish rule seemed to threaten the very basis of Cuban prosperity. The planters looked north toward the United States, where the U.S. government had already begun to look south, toward Cuba.

·   ·   ·

"THESE ISLANDS [Cuba and Puerto Rico] . . . are natural appendages to the North American continent," wrote Secretary of State John Quincy Adams in 1823, "and one of them, Cuba, . . . has become an object of transcendent importance to the political and commercial interests of our Union."

The island was of immense strategic importance to the United States, commanding the sea lanes of the Caribbean and the Gulf of Mexico and blessed with Havana harbor, the finest deep-water port in the region. Of no less importance was the commercial value of the rich colony as a U.S. trading partner. These assets, Adams said, gave Cuba "an importance in the sum of our national interests, with which that of no other foreign territory can be compared, and little inferior to that which binds the different members of this Union together."

As Adams saw it, the immediate danger in 1823 was that Spain might cede the island to Great Britain, twice the armed enemy of the United States in the preceding fifty years and now a potential ally of Spain in a new war with France.

"The transfer of Cuba to Great Britain would be an event unpropitious to the interests of this Union," he told the American minister to Madrid. "The question both of our right and our power to prevent it, if necessary, by force, already obtrudes itself upon our councils, and the administration is called upon, in the performance of its duties to the nation, at least to use all the means within its competency to guard against and forefend it."

In the long run, Adams said, there seemed but one acceptable future for the island: "In looking forward to the probable course of events for the short period of half a century, it is scarcely possible to resist the conviction that the annexation of Cuba to our federal republic will be indispensable to the continuance and integrity of the Union itself."

.   .   .

NEITHER ADAMS'S DREAM of American annexation nor his nightmare of cession to another European power came to pass, although both seemed on the point of doing so at times. In 1825 the mysterious visit of a powerful French naval squadron to Cuban waters caused new uneasiness in Washington. Secretary of State Henry Clay declared that the United States could not consent to the acquisition of Cuba "by any other European power than Spain under any contingency whatever."

American apprehensions over Cuba were fueled by unrest in Spain. The reign of the restored Spanish monarch, Ferdinand, was interrupted by a revolt of the army in 1820. He was restored to the throne a second time, three years later, when France sent an army into Spain to suppress the revolution. After his death in 1833, a dispute over succession to the throne between his brother, Don Carlos, and supporters of his three-year-old daughter, Isabella, precipitated a five-year civil war. Once again stability was restored through foreign intervention, this time by the Quadruple Alliance of England, France, Spain, and Portugal, which defeated the Carlists and installed Ferdinand's widow as regent. But Spanish domestic tranquility was elusive, and the next forty years were marked by a series of forced abdications, military coups, provisional governments, and revolutions. The prospect of one such tremor shaking loose the colony of Cuba from Spanish dominion and into other European hands continued to worry Washington.

"You are authorized," Secretary of State John Forsyth told the American minister in Madrid in 1840, "to assure the Spanish government, that in case of any attempt, from whatever quarter, to wrest from her this portion of her territory [i.e., Cuba], she may securely depend upon the military and naval resources of the United States to aid her in preserving or recovering it."

But, in the event, the quarter from which came the most earnest efforts to wrest the island from Spain was the United States.

·   ·   ·

IN 1848, President Polk authorized the American minister to Spain to offer as much as $100 million to purchase Cuba. The Spanish foreign minister declined the offer and declared that "sooner than see the island transferred to any power, [Spain] would prefer seeing it sunk in the ocean."

In 1851 an invasion force of five hundred men—mostly Americans—sailed from New Orleans and landed at Bahía Honda on the northern Cuban coast. The tiny army was led by Venezuelan adventurer Narcisco Lopez, who had led two earlier abortive invasions of the island, and by W. S. Crittenden, a young West Point graduate and Mexican War veteran. The invasion was mounted on the theory that the arrival of the expeditionary force would inspire a general Cuban uprising against the Spanish, resulting in independence and a request for American annexation. The uprising failed to materialize, however. The invaders were captured by Spanish troops, and Lopez, Crittenden, and about fifty others were executed.

In 1854, while Great Britain and France were preoccupied with the Crimean War, the administration of President Pierce thought the time ripe for another bid to purchase Cuba from Spain. The American ministers to Spain, Great Britain, and France met at Ostend, Belgium, to plan a strategy for making the proposal and drafted a dispatch to the secretary of state containing their recommendations.

"Our past history forbids that we should acquire the Island of Cuba without the consent of Spain," they wrote, "unless justified by the great law of self-preservation." But the so-called Ostend Manifesto went on to imply very clearly that such action was indeed justified, if only to guard against the possibility of Cuba following in the footsteps of Haiti and the danger of a black revolt spreading across the Florida Straits to the slaves in the American South. If it came down to a fight, the manifesto said, "we ought neither to count the cost, nor regard the odds which Spain might enlist against us."

The manifesto was leaked to the American press, perhaps to test public opinion regarding the proposals, or as a means of intimidating the Spanish government into selling. American public opinion proved decidedly negative on the idea of acquiring the island by conquest, and the Spanish foreign minister declared that "to part with Cuba would be to part with the national honor." The U.S. government quickly repudiated the manifesto and assured Spain that it had no intention of taking the island by force of arms.

The American minister to Great Britain who signed the manifesto was James Buchanan. Buchanan did not finally abandon all idea of a Cuban purchase, and after he became president in 1857 he again proposed it, requesting an appropriation for the purpose in his annual message of 1860. This time the idea was overtaken by other events. Keeping the South safe for slavery was no longer a national goal. Fort Sumter was but months away.

.   .   .

HALF A CENTURY was the period of John Quincy Adams's 1823 prophecy of inevitable Cuban annexation. but the year 1873 found the island yet a Spanish colony. With the abolition of slavery in the United States, interest in annexation had dwindled on both sides of the Florida Straits; Cuban sugar planters no longer could look to America to preserve slavery on the island, while Southern cotton growers no longer feared that a black uprising in Cuba might spread to their own plantations. But if the Cubans no longer wished to become Americans, neither were they content to remain Spaniards.

Continued unrest in Spain, misrule of the island by the government in Madrid, taxation without representation, and a realization by the sugar planters that the days of slavery were numbered all encouraged Cuban aspirations toward nationhood. In October 1868 a poorly armed band of whites and free mulattos took up arms in the mountains of Oriente Province. Within a month the insurgent force had swelled to twelve thousand and captured the towns of Bayamo and Holguín. A war for Cuban independence was underway, a protracted guerrilla struggle against Spanish rule. It would be known to history as the Ten Years' War.

The administration of President Grant kept a proper official distance from the rebels, shunning any temptation to help them break loose the island from Spain and accepting Madrid's position that the conflict was a mutiny and purely an internal Spanish matter. But in New York the so-called Cuban Junta—a rebel legation without U.S. government recognition—spread pro-Cuban propaganda and raised funds from sympathetic Americans. The money was used to finance filibustering expeditions—illegal expeditions bringing men and arms to the Cuban insurgents—and it was one of these that nearly fulfilled Adams's prophecy in its fiftieth year by bringing about a Spanish–American war over Cuba.

.   .   .

ON THE AFTERNOON of October 31, 1873, the side-wheeler *Virginius*, flying the American flag, steamed about twenty miles off the Cuban coast. Aboard were more than a hundred rebels led by Cuban General Oscar Varona and William A. C. Ryan, a Canadian soldier of fortune who had served in the Union Army during the Civil War. The ship had aboard some five hundred Remington rifles, a large number of swords and revolvers, plus a quantity of ammunition, clothing, medicine, and provisions. The passengers and cargo were on their way to join the Cuban rebels in the mountains of eastern Cuba.

At about 2 P.M. smoke was sighted on the horizon as a Spanish warship came into view. The *Virginius* came about and headed out to sea, and the Spanish ship gave chase. As the afternoon wore on the two vessels rocked and plunged through the sea on a southward course toward the British island of Jamaica.

By the standards of the day the *Virginius* was a swift ship, having started life as a Civil War blockade runner, built for the Confederacy in a Scottish shipyard on the banks of the Clyde. The combined power of her sails and paddle wheels drove her through the water at more than eight knots, a speed that had enabled her repeatedly to slip through the Union blockade while running between Mobile and Havana with cargos of cotton to help finance the Confederate war effort. But her Spanish pursuer, the *Tornado,* was also a former Confederate blockade runner and had been built in the same Scottish shipyard. And today she seemed to have the advantage of a few knots over her former sister ship. As the afternoon wore into evening the Spanish ship slowly overhauled the filibuster.

Night fell, but bright moonlight illuminated the sea as the *Tornado* continued to narrow the gap, while the dark outline of the Jamaican coast climbed over the southern horizon. The British sanctuary was no less than twenty miles off, but the Spaniard had come into cannon range of the *Virginius.* Her gun spoke, and a fountain erupted from the sea ahead of the fleeing ship.

The scene aboard the *Virginius* was wild confusion as the insurgents hastily threw the cargo of arms over the side. A second shot from the *Tornado* struck her smokestack, and the fugitive ship hove to. Although their Jamaican refuge was so agonizingly near at hand, the crew and passengers of the *Virginius* could do nothing but wait for the Spaniard to overtake and board her.

The captain of the *Virginius* was Joseph Fry, an Annapolis graduate who had fought for the Confederacy and, since the Civil War, had sailed as a merchant officer. As he waited for the Spanish boarding party, he reviewed his situation and tried to muster his indignation.

The *Virginius* was an American ship with American registry papers and flying the American flag, and Fry and most of his crew were American citizens. He probably knew that the ship's owner of record—a John F. Patterson of New York City—was merely acting as a front, that the true owner of the *Virginius* was the Cuban Junta, and that the ship's American registry was therefore invalid. And he certainly knew that filibustering expeditions were a violation of U.S. neutrality laws. Nonetheless, the most significant fact at that moment may have seemed to be that the ship was in international waters (and was, in fact, just eighteen miles off the Jamaican coast), and therefore the Spanish had no legal right to stop and board her. As Captain Castillo of the *Tornado* came on deck with the boarding party, Fry presented his American papers and protested the Spanish action.

Castillo brushed aside the protest. The *Virginius* was well known to the Spanish Navy in these waters, having carried recruits and weapons to the Cuban insurgents several times in the past two years. Word that the ship was again on a filibustering voyage to Cuba had been the reason the *Tornado* had been patroling the coast that afternoon. As to the American flag flying from the ship's mast, Castillo ordered it hauled down and the Spanish colors raised in its place. The *Virginius* was a "pirate ship," he said, and he was taking her and all aboard to the port of Santiago de Cuba.

General Juan Burriel, the Spanish governor of Santiago, was delighted to see the *Virginius* steam into the harbor the following afternoon, and he wasted no time in demonstrating the way he believed filibusters should be dealt with. A summary court-martial was held the following day, and the passengers and crew of the captured ship were sentenced to death.

E. G. Schmidt, the American vice-consul at Santiago, attempted to intervene. He tried to send telegrams to the American consuls in Havana and Kingston, Jamaica, inquiring about the status and registry of the *Virginius*, but the messages were embargoed on orders of General Burriel. Burriel ignored Schmidt's protests for several days, then explained that he had been occupied "in the meditation of the divine mysteries of All Saints', and the commemoration of All Souls' day, as prescribed by our holy religion."

At dawn on November 4, four of the rebels were executed, including General Varona and William Ryan. The men were shot and decapitated, and their heads were displayed on spikes. George W. Sherman of the New York *Herald* was thrown into jail for trying to sketch the execution scene.

Two days later a New York *Times* correspondent in Havana wired his newspaper: "The public rejoicings last night over the capture of the steamer Virginius were most enthusiastic. The Governor's palace, all public buildings, and many private houses were illuminated. Torchlight processions passed through the principal streets, which were thickly hung with flags and tapestry."

It was among the first reports of the capture to reach the outside world. There had yet been no announcements of the court-martial and executions. In Madrid Emilio Castelar, president of the newly formed Spanish Republic (the monarchy had been turned out in 1863), read the official report of the capture with some concern and immediately cabled Havana ordering that none of the captives be executed pending a thorough review of the situation by the government. He was unaware that four of the men had already been shot and that more executions were scheduled for the following day.

Among those now due to be shot was the captain of the *Virginius*, Joseph Fry. As he passed his final hours aboard a Spanish warship in the harbor, Fry wrote a farewell letter to his wife:

Dear, dear Dita,
    When I left you I had no idea that we should never meet again in this world, but it seems strange to me that I should to-night, and on Annie's birthday, be calmly seated, on a beautiful moonlight night, in a most beautiful bay in Cuba, to take my last leave of you my own dear, sweet wife! and with the thought of your own bitter anguish, my only regret at leaving.

President Castelar's orders reached Havana, but there was no way to relay them immediately to Santiago, hundreds of miles away in the remote southeastern end of Cuba and isolated from the rest of the island by a break in the telegraph lines. There was nothing to stay the sentence of General Burriel's military tribunal. The following afternoon Fry and thirty-six others were shot.

There was mounting concern in Washington, although no word of the executions had yet been received. Secretary of State Hamilton Fish cabled the American minister at Madrid: "The capture on the high seas of a vessel bearing the American flag presents a very grave question, which will need investigation.

. . . And if it prove that an American citizen has been wrongfully executed, this government will require most ample reparation."

Twenty-six of the *Virginius*'s crew and twelve of the passengers were British subjects, and the British vice-consul at Santiago had succeeded in sending word of the executions by cable to Jamaica. On November 7 the British warship *Niobe* arrived. Her commander, Sir Lambton Lorraine, protested the summary executions to General Burriel. Burriel curtly replied, "I am not in the habit of allowing myself to be overawed by anyone, and I will not take notice of any petition unless [Havana] orders me to."

Twelve more of the prisoners were shot the following day, bringing the total to fifty-three.

By November 12 reports of the massacre had reached Washington. Secretary Fish cabled the American minister at Madrid:

> If the report be confirmed, you will protest, in the name of this government and of civilization and humanity, against the act as brutal, barbarous, and an outrage upon the age, and will declare that this government will demand the most ample reparation of any wrong which may have been committed upon any of its citizens, or upon its flag.

The American minister was Civil War hero General Daniel Sickles. Those who had followed his career questioned Sickles's fitness for a diplomatic post, if only because he had once escaped a murder conviction through a plea of temporary insanity.* But the forty-eight-year-old New Yorker seemed to have mellowed with middle age. At this stage of the crisis, his tone in dealing with the Spanish government was conciliatory.

It was obvious that General Burriel had acted without the approval of Madrid or even the Spanish governor general in Havana. At first Sickles postponed making any official protests or demands on the Spanish Foreign Ministry, believing Spanish–American relations would be better served if Madrid, on its own initiative, apologized for the incident, paid reparations to the families of the victims, and punished the officer responsible. He was confident that such measures would soon be forthcoming, but they were not. Much as Madrid deplored Burriel's actions, it realized that they were very popular in Spain and among the Spanish in Cuba. Rather than deal promptly and firmly with a difficult political problem, the Foreign Ministry temporized.

On the fourteenth there were huge rallies in New York City at Steinway Hall and Tammany Hall. Other indignation meetings were held in other American cities. Demands were made for military action against Spain. Secretary Fish was condemned for his inaction. In Washington the Grant administration responded to the political pressure. A New York *Times* correspondent reported:

> The session of the Cabinet today continued over two hours, and was the most important which has taken place under President Grant's

---

*Discovering that Philip Key (son of Francis Scott Key) was enjoying a dalliance with his wife, Sickles dispatched the man with a pistol in Lafayette Park, across the street from the White House.

Administration. The capture of the *Virginius* and the shocking barbarities perpetrated by the Spanish authorities at Santiago de Cuba formed the subject of serious consideration, and definite action toward maintaining the dignity of the United States in the existing complication was taken. . . .

One member of the Cabinet, when approached on the subject, replied: "As to the matter of the action agreed upon to-day, I can say nothing, but you may rest assured the people of the country will be satisfied."

The action agreed upon was the instruction of General Sickles to demand an apology, reparations, and the punishment of Burriel, and if such were not forthcoming within twelve days (i.e., by November 26), Sickles was to close the American legation and leave Spain. At a minimum the Grant administration was threatening to break off diplomatic relations over the incident. Implicitly, the next step might be war.

When Sickles conveyed Fish's note to Foreign Minister Carvajal, the Spaniard fired back an angry rejection to the American, taking particular offense at "the harshness of style, and . . . the heated and improper words you used to qualify the conduct of the Spanish authorities." Carvajal mistakenly believed the language, if not the ultimatum itself, had originated with the notoriously hot-headed Sickles. Sickles now abandoned his uncharacteristic forbearance and permitted his dander to rise to the occasion. He sent a scathing note to the foreign minister which began by informing Carvajal that "the language of the protest to which he takes exception" was not his own but an exact transcript of his instructions from Washington and ended by declaring that American patience had reached its limit.

After three days of dismayed silence, Carvajal sent the American minister a long-winded and argumentative note which boiled down to the declaration that Spain would do nothing to rectify matters unless and until a minute and leisurely review of the incident proved that a wrong had really been done.

"Regarding this as a refusal within the sense of your instruction," Sickles cabled Secretary Fish, "I propose, unless otherwise ordered, to close this legation forthwith and leave Madrid." But Fish replied that the minister should remain where he was and await further instructions. Unknown to Sickles, negotiations were continuing. Carvajal now understood that war was a real possibility, and he desperately hoped to avert it, but his angry exchanges with Sickles a few days earlier made further discussion in Madrid difficult. The foreign minister had solved the problem by going around Sickles and using the Spanish minister in Washington as the intermediary between the two governments. Fish was willing to continue talking on that basis, but he held Carvajal to the November 26 deadline he had already established.

In the event, Spain agreed to the American demands, but not without further foot-dragging. Sickles had actually begun the first formalities of closing the legation on the afternoon of the twenty-sixth before the Spanish government agreed in principle to the settlement. The final terms included the release of the

Virginius and the survivors, payment of an $80,000 indemnity to the U.S. government to be distributed to the families of the victims, and the punishment of General Burriel.* Sickles, thoroughly outraged at having been excluded from the negotiations, resigned his post and left Spain.

American public opinion was somewhat mollified by the outcome of the affair, although further outrage followed the publication in several newspapers of Captain Fry's touching farewell letter to his wife. Cooler heads were grateful that the incident had not led to war and praised the Grant administration for its moderate response to the Spanish provocation. Few realized that the U.S. government had had no alternative to a peaceful resolution.

At the height of the crisis Secretary of the Navy George Robeson had tried to mobilize a flotilla of warships at Key West, Florida, "for possible punitive action," but the best the Navy could assemble was an assortment of rusty old hulks, most of which had not been to sea since the close of the Civil War eight years earlier. One officer recalled:

> The force assembled at Key West was the best, and indeed about all, we had. We had no stores or storehouses to speak of at this so-called base of supplies, and if it had not been so serious it would have been laughable to see our condition. We remained there several weeks, making faces at the Spaniards ninety miles away at Havana, while two modern vessels of war would have done us up in thirty minutes. . . . We were dreadfully mortified over it all, but we were not to blame; we did the best we could with what Congress gave us.

The *Virginius* incident brought home to American policy makers the danger of military weakness and the need to rebuild the Navy. Among the American public the affair left a lasting residue of anti-Spanish feeling and sympathy with the cause of Cuban independence. These seeds would bear fruit a generation later.

.   .   .

THE WAR IN Cuba continued in a desultory fashion. The poorly armed and equipped insurgents could not drive the Spanish from their stronghold in the western end of the island, while the Spanish, preoccupied with civil wars and rebellions at home, could not muster the numerical superiority in Cuba necessary to crush the insurgents in the mountains and jungles of eastern Cuba. For several years the situation remained a standoff.

Late in 1874 a group of army generals and conservative politicians in Spain engineered the restoration of the monarchy. Alfonso, the sixteen-year-old royal heir, was called home from the British military academy at Sandhurst. The power behind the restored throne was a wily conservative politician, Antonio Cánovas del Castillo.

---

*Spain made good on the first two conditions but managed to avoid satisfying the third. Through the expedient of yet more foot-dragging, Madrid managed to defer justice for four years, until Burriel saved his government further embarrassment by dying.

Having established a measure of domestic tranquility at home, Prime Minister Cánovas turned his attention to ending the insurrection in Cuba. He dispatched 25,000 fresh troops under the energetic young General Arsenio Martínez Campos to the island, increasing Spanish strength there by more than a third. By early 1878 the insurgent leaders were ready to negotiate an end to the war.

The peace treaty was signed in the town of Zanjón in the eastern province of Camagüey. Martínez Campos made several concessions on behalf of Spain: freedom for the rebel leaders who agreed to leave Cuba; liberation of all slaves who had fought on the rebel side; and political representation of Cuba in the Cortes. For their part, the rebels dropped their demands for independence from Spain and total abolition of slavery.

Exhausted by the long war, both sides were prepared to compromise for the moment. But it was much less than a permanent solution. Cuba had paused on the path to independence, but she had not turned back. Independence was inevitable, and none could have doubted that the force that would ultimately end Spanish rule would come from the north, beyond the Florida Straits. The destinies of Cuba and the United States seemed forever entwined.

CHAPTER THREE

CUBA LIBRE

THE NEW YORK OF 1884 was a metropolis of six-story skyscrapers, a city of cobbled streets choked with horse-drawn traffic The wonderful new Brooklyn Bridge had been in service for a year. For the past four years the lights of Broadway had been electric, and thick cobwebs of wire shrouded the streets of lower Manhattan. Trains of the new elevated railway roared above the avenues, making a rapid transit of the island between Harlem and the Battery. Daily consignments of new arrivals from every quarter of the compass paused upon the wharfs and ferry slips to marvel at the bustling prodigy. Among them on that day in early October was a thin, wiry man of sixty-one years with a snow-white goatee. General Máximo Gómez left no record of his private thoughts on that occasion, but if he chanced to pass through Madison Square, if he was told by a passerby that the great right arm and torch temporarily erected there were part of a statue that would some day stand in the harbor and be called Liberty, then he might have taken this to be a favorable portent to his own errand, for Gómez had come to New York to build the foundation of a second Cuban revolution.

He was, in the words of one who knew him, "a stern, hard-hearted man, with a violent temper, but had in his nature some streaks of human kindness that shone luminously by contrast." Another, who fought beside him some years later, recalls him in his jungle headquarters:

> He is a gray little man. His clothes do not fit well, and, perhaps, if you saw it in a photograph, his figure might seem old and ordinary. But the moment he turns his keen eyes on you, they strike like a blow from the shoulder. You feel the will, the fearlessness, and the experience of men that is in those eyes, and their owner becomes a giant before you.

He was born in Santo Domingo, the son of a prosperous planter, and he served in the Spanish Army. He rose to the rank of major before resigning to work a farm of his own near Bayamo in Cuba. When the Ten Years' War began he was among the first to offer his services to the revolution. After the Peace of Zanjón he returned to his native Santo Domingo and resumed his life as a farmer. From the vantage of his prosperous plantation at Montecristi he watched events in nearby Cuba.

He believed the war had accomplished nothing. The "shameful peace of Zanjón," as he called the treaty, had failed to achieve the promised political reforms. True, forty Cuban delegates now sat in the Spanish Cortes, but the right to elect them was limited to those Cubans likely to see things Madrid's way— employees of the government and the Spanish trading companies and wealthy Creoles able to pay the heavy annual poll tax. Political power remained in the hands of the *peninsulares,* the Spanish-born elite.

He saw the once bountiful Cuban economy fall into a long postwar depression. Many of the mills had been destroyed in the fighting, and high interest rates prevented the full rebuilding and mechanization of the sugar industry. In Europe beet sugar thrived on government subsidies. Germany had replaced Cuba as the world's leading sugar producer. The United States, once Cuba's best customer, had begun to produce much of her own sugar. Poverty had driven thousands of Cubans from the island, but many had found a new prosperity in the American cigar-making colonies. It was among these, the so-called Cubans of the Emigration, that Gómez hoped to found the second revolution.

The Ten Years' War had failed from a want of will and wherewithal. Had there been enough guns, ammunition, and supplies, had there been the determination to use these things to break out of the rebel strongholds in Oriente and Camaguey and spread devastation into the western end of the island, then, Gómez firmly believed, the Spaniards would have been driven out. Instead there had been hesitancy, timidity, meanness—and the revolution had failed. But Cuba could have a second chance, if the Cubans of the Emigration were ready and willing to turn away from their prosperous complacency, dig deeply into their pockets, and follow a strong and determined leader. Gómez had come to see for himself whether or not the moment had arrived.

Early in 1884 Gómez wrote to his old friend and comrade, Antonio Maceo, "the Bronze Titan," as the Negro cavalry leader was called, who was living quietly in Costa Rica. Gómez proposed that they visit some of the Cuban colonies in the United States to gauge the emigres' readiness to support a second revolution. By October the pair had visited New Orleans and Key West. Their next stop was New York.

New York—center of commerce, crossroads of the New and Old Worlds, bustling with enterprise, babbling in a hundred tongues, a sanctuary for refugees, a way station on the routes of immigration. It was home to natives of every Spanish American nation; a year before, on the centennial of Simón Bolívar, the New York Hispanic community had gathered in fashionable Delmonico's, just off Madison Square. It was a festival of eloquence, and the last of the orators, a thin young man with an air of passionate intensity, was considered to be the best of all. He offered a toast "to free peoples and to those in bondage," and then delivered a magnificent eulogy to the Latin American Liberator. His peroration brought the room to its feet: "Gentlemen, let him who has a country honor it; and let him who has no country conquer it!"

His name was José Martí, and he had a way with words. He was only fifteen when the Ten Years' War began, but the anti-Spanish letters he wrote and published in his native Havana landed him in prison, sentenced to six years' hard labor in a Cuban rock quarry. Through the intercession of his father, a Spanish artillery sergeant, he was transferred to easier imprisonment in Spain and eventually released. Forbidden to return to Cuba, he enrolled in the University of Madrid and studied law and literature. Later he lived the life of an exile, earning his living as a journalist in Mexico, Guatemala, and Venezuela. Finally he settled in New York. It was there that Martí and Gómez met for the first time.

There was much more to separate the young José Martí and the elderly Máximo Gómez than the thirty years' difference in their ages. Martí was an ideologist, a statesman in the making. He looked at the class differences and the racial animosities dividing the Cubans of the Emigration and saw a reflection of all that was wrong with Spanish rule in Cuba. The ultimate goal of the revolution was to end such things on the island; the first step must be to end them among the emigres. Cubans needed something more to unify them than a hatred of Spain. To Martí, the words and the ideas that could accomplish that were far more important than the guns and ammunition Gómez sought.

Gómez was a professional soldier. He saw revolution as a form of warfare, nothing else. Wars were won with courage, determination, adequate logistics, and obedience. To him, the most important item on the Cuban revolutionary agenda at that moment was filling the army's coffers. A collision between the two men was inevitable. It came in mid-October, two weeks after Gómez arrived in New York.

The scene was Madame Griffous's boardinghouse, a favorite stopping place for visiting Cubans. Gómez, already furious over the meager financial response of the New York Cubans, decided to dispatch Maceo and Martí to Mexico in hope that more enthusiastic support might be found among the emigres living there. He announced his plan to the other two, then indicated that the meeting was over.

Martí was delighted at the prospect of returning to Mexico. He began to speak animatedly, offering a dozen ideas about what might be accomplished during the Mexican visit. General Gómez, who had thrown a towel over his shoulder and was preparing to withdraw to his bath, interrupted the young man.

"Limit yourself to obeying orders," he said. "For the rest, General Maceo will do what is to be done."

Without waiting for a reply he turned and left the room.

"The Old Man considers the Cuban War almost as if it were his exclusive property," said Maceo with a conciliatory smile. "He does not permit anyone to interfere."

Hurt and angry, Martí left. Two days later he had convinced himself that there was more to the incident than a personal affront. He saw in Gómez's manner an autocratic and militaristic attitude that threatened the democratic ideals of the revolution. He sent the general a letter:

> A nation is not founded, General, the way one commands a military camp. . . . If war and its noble and legitimate prestige are possible, it is because there was first that painfully wrought spirit that demands it and makes it necessary. It is that spirit we must heed, and to that spirit we must show the most profound respect in every public and private act.

Martí declared he was withdrawing from the movement, that he refused to take part in "changing the present political despotism in Cuba for a personal despotism, a thousand times worse."

General Gómez read the letter and was more surprised than angered. Giving and obeying commands was the natural order of things. He had not intended his words as an insult. That Martí should find them subversive to the spirit of the revolution he found a very curious idea. Moreover, he genuinely liked the young man, despite his irritating preoccupation with political rhetoric.

"This man carelessly insults me," Gómez wrote on the back of the letter before filing it away. "If the great friendliness I felt for him were known, it would give an idea how the reading of his judgement has affected me."

But it was not known, certainly not by Martí. And the peppery old soldier could not find it in himself to tell him, to take the first step toward reconciliation. It may have seemed fruitless to Gómez in any case. The Cubans of New York —prosperous, complacent, and divided—had contributed a grand total of fifty dollars to the general's war chest. If ever there was to be a moment to mount the second revolution, clearly this was not it. Angry and discouraged, Gómez returned to his Santo Domingo home.

José Martí did not forsake the cause that had become so close to his heart. He resumed writing, speaking, and traveling to the Cuban emigre centers throughout the country. He preached unity to the emigres, convinced them to put aside the differences of black and white, rich and poor. He organized them, welding the local Cuban social clubs into a secret revolutionary network reaching into Cuba itself. He raised funds, persuading the cigar makers to contribute 10 percent of their wages to the cause. He found allies for the movement among such men as Charles A. Dana of the New York *Sun*, Civil War veteran and former American minister to Spain, General Daniel Sickles, labor leader Samuel Gompers, and the colorful old gunrunner and friend of Latin American liberation, Captain "Dynamite Johnny" O'Brien. By 1892 the movement had taken on a formal existence—the Cuban Revolutionary party, with headquarters in New York City.

The party was run from a tiny office on the fourth floor of a dingy old brick building at 120 Front Street. A forest of masts rising above the nearby rooftops marked the busy waterfront, and the bells and horns of the harbor could be heard day and night.

As Martí intended, it was not a one-man show. There was "Don Tomás," the venerable, white-maned Tomás Estrada Palma, who had served as president of the embryonic Cuban Republic during the Ten Years' War and now ran a school for the sons of prosperous Hispanic families in Central Valley, New York. There was Gonzalo de Quesada, a young writer and man about Washington, who courted powerful senators and congressmen on behalf of the cause. There was Horatio S. Rubens, a young graduate of New York City College and Columbia Law School, who served as the party's legal counsel. And there was Carlos Roloff, a Polish-Jewish exile and soldier of fortune who adopted the Cuban cause as his own and had fought in the Ten Years' War. There were Carlos Balino and Diego Vincente Tejera, union organizers of the Cuban cigar workers. The party reached even into Havana, where the Negro journalist and intellectual Juan Gualberto Gómez coordinated the secret revolutionary network throughout the island.

If there was democratic diversity among them, there was also a militant unity regarding the ultimate ends of their work and the means necessary to achieve them. It was true that some big planters on the island still saw annexation by the United States as the ideal solution to their business problems, and some segments of the American business community still entertained the old idea of purchasing Cuba from Spain. But to the Cubans who regularly met with Martí in the tiny office on Front Street, such ideas were unacceptable. The only goal was independence, the only possible way of getting it was armed revolution. They saw that a second war was inevitable. The only question was when it would begin.

.   .   .

ON THE NIGHT OF April 10, 1895, the German freighter Nordstrand hove to in the midst of a violent tropical storm off the southeastern coast of Cuba, just beyond the three-mile limit. Despite the heavy seas and the warnings of the ship's master, the six men who had boarded at the Haitian port of Inagua lowered a small boat and pushed off into the darkness. The German captain shook his head, shrugged, and gave the order to get underway. In a moment the Nordstrand was again steaming out to sea, leaving the six to whatever fate awaited them.

Four of the travelers bent to the oars, while a fifth crouched in the bow and tried to make out the distant coastline through the tropical downpour. The sixth, a small elderly man, sat in the stern and worked the rudder. General Máximo Gómez was now seventy-two but not in anyone's estimate too old to take the field and lead a new revolution against the Spanish.

That he was the best possible commander-in-chief was not doubted by the other five in the boat, certainly not by José Martí, who labored at one of the oars, for it was Martí who, three years before, had traveled to the general's Santo Domingo home and invited him "without fear of refusal, to undertake this new task, although I have no other remuneration to offer you than the pleasure of sacrifice and the probable ingratitude of men." Martí was far too dedicated a patriot and far too able a conciliator to founder on his own personal bygones. He knew that Gómez was the best man for the job. And Gómez now had nothing but admiration for the young man and the miracles he had worked.

"From this moment you can count on my services," Gómez had quietly replied.

But hard times had delayed the revolutionary timetable. There had been a financial panic in the United States in May 1893, followed by a depression that shut down the cigar factories, throwing thousands of Cuban emigres out of work and drying up the party's income. But the following year the crisis spread to Cuba, when the U.S. Congress passed the Wilson-Gorman tariff, which put a 40 percent duty on Cuban sugar imports. In New York the price of sugar dropped to a record low of 3.25 cents per pound. Thousands of Cuban millworkers and plantation hands were idled, and unrest was on the increase throughout the island. By the end of January 1895, Martí, Gómez, and the other party leaders had decided that the moment for a new revolution had arrived.

The date of the new uprising was set by the underground in Cuba for February 24. Simultaneous insurrections in both the western and eastern provinces were planned, but at the last moment the Spanish authorities discovered the rebels' plans and captured two of the underground leaders in Havana, forestalling any action in the west. Still, the uprising went as scheduled in the east. The first shots were fired at Baire, a village about fifty miles from Santiago de Cuba. On March 31 General Antonio Maceo and his brother José, accompanied by twenty other rebels, landed on a beach near the town of Baracoa. It was the first of many expeditions that would bring men and arms to the revolution.

Although he was completely lacking in military experience, Martí was now unwilling to continue his political and organizational work in New York. He believed he could not serve the revolution as "one who preached the need of dying without beginning by risking his own life."

"I called up the war," he wrote. "My responsibility begins rather than ends with it. . . . For me the hour has come."

.   .   .

To ALL SIX OCCUPANTS of the tiny boat that April night it may well have seemed their final hour had arrived. A heavy following sea washed over the stern and tore away the rudder. Gómez grabbed an oar and tried to steer with it, but none of the party was any longer certain of the direction of the beach. Without moon or stars to steer by, they might easily be heading further out to sea. After a desperate quarter-hour the sky cleared and the storm abated. A few minutes later a bright red tropic moon shone down as the rebels dragged their boat onto a rocky beach.

They wasted no time but immediately set out to link up with the rebel forces, navigating by Gómez's compass and hacking their way through the dense jungle growth with their machetes. Later Gómez would remember with fondness Martí stumbling happily along beneath the weight of a heavy pack, "radiant with pride and satisfaction . . . because he was able to hold his own in all this with five rugged men."

His contentment was that of a man who knows his personal destiny is at last near at hand. He found it some five weeks later in a cavalry skirmish near the tiny village of Dos Ríos. When the Spanish bullet ended his life he was just forty-two years old.

.   .   .

Second Lieutenant Winston S. Churchill of Her Majesty's Fourth Hussars marched with the Spanish column as it picked it way along the jungle trail near the Cuban village of Arroyo Blanco in Santa Clara Province. Later he recalled:

> There was a low mist as we moved off in the early morning, and all of a sudden the rear of the column was involved in firing. In those days when people got quite close together in order to fight, and used—partly, at any rate—large-bore rifles to fight with, loud bangs were heard and smoke puffs or even flashes could be seen. The firing seemed about a furlong away and sounded very noisy and startling.

They were, in fact, the first shots the recent Sandhurst graduate had ever heard fired in anger. The date was November 30, 1895, Churchill's twenty-first birthday. He had come to Cuba because he wanted to see a war.

Two months earlier, with some time on his hands while his unit prepared to embark for India, the young subaltern had prevailed upon the British ambassador in Madrid, a family friend, to pull some strings so that he could visit "the seat of war" in Cuba. On November 20 Churchill and another subaltern arrived in Havana aboard the Plant Line steamship *Olivette*. Churchill carried letters from the Spanish ministers of foreign affairs and war introducing him to the governor general of the island, as well as press credentials from the London *Daily Graphic* and a discreet request from General E. F. Chapman, director of British military intelligence, to collect some information regarding points of Spanish military procedure about which her majesty's government was especially curious.

Traveling by rail and coastal steamer, Churchill set out in search of the war. After several days he located a large Spanish force commanded by General Suares Valdés at the town of Sancti Spíritus. After presenting his credentials, he was assigned by the general to serve on his staff so that he might get a close look at some action. Valdés, having received word that a large insurgent force under Máximo Gómez was camped a few miles east of the village of Iguara, set out at 5 A.M. on November 30. The Spanish column did not take the rebels by surprise.

> A long distance away the approach of a Spanish column sounds like the coming of a large herd of belled cattle (a New York *Sun* correspondent reported). In addition, the flock of vultures above the column, which in Cuba, as throughout the tropics, always follows crowds of men moving through the country, is infallible evidence that the Spaniards are near at hand.

Chronically short of rifles and ammunition, completely lacking in artillery, and vastly outnumbered by the Spanish Army, Gómez avoided large pitched battles. His assets were the classical advantages of the guerrilla: mobility, familiarity with the terrain, strongly motivated troops, superior tolerance of hardships and the local diseases, and the sympathetic cooperation of the civilian populace. Gómez was a master of hit-and-run warfare.

For the next three days General Valdés's column was harassed day and night by the rebels. On the afternoon of December 1 Churchill sought relief from the tropical heat by swimming in a stream and suddenly came under fire. Hurriedly grabbing up his clothes, he beat a hasty retreat as rebel bullets rustled through the jungle foliage all around him. That night a round passed through the hut in which he was sleeping, and another wounded a Spanish orderly stationed outside.

If young Churchill was disappointed by the scale of the fighting he had thus far witnessed, he must have been better satisfied two days later, when he took part in one of the few big actions of the war. Attracted by the prospect of capturing the well-supplied convoy General Valdés was escorting near the village of Iguara, Gómez departed from his usual policy and joined a major engagement with the Spanish. Beginning as a typical rebel ambush, it soon developed into a full-scale pitched battle. Churchill found himself advancing with the Spanish across open ground and under very heavy fire. Several days later he recounted the scene in a letter to his mother:

> The General, a very brave man—in a white and gold uniform on a grey horse—drew a great deal of fire on to us and I heard enough bullets whistle and hum past to satisfy me for some time to come. He rode right up to within 500 yards of the enemy and there we waited till the fire of the Spanish infantry drove them from their position. We had great luck in not losing more than we did—but as a rule the rebels shot very high. We stayed by the General all the time and so were in the most dangerous place in the field. The general recommended us for the Red Cross—a Spanish decoration given to Officers.

But the battle could hardly have been claimed as a Spanish victory. Valdés retreated to the safety of the fort at Iguara, leaving behind fifty-four rifles, eight hundred cartridges, twenty heavily laden pack mules, and eighteen Spanish dead. Churchill, his thirst for warfare temporarily slaked, returned to England. He brought home with him a taste for Cuban cigars—a habit he would retain for the rest of his life—and a burden of unshakable opinion that might have overwhelmed anyone but a twenty-one-year-old second lieutenant fresh from Sandhurst.

The insurgents, he wrote, in a published account of his adventures, "neither fight bravely nor do they use their weapons effectively. They cannot win a single battle or hold a single town. Their army, consisting to a large extent of coloured men, is an undisciplined rabble." But apparently he did not entirely discount the possibility that this rabble might win the war, and he was horrified by that prospect:

> A grave danger represents itself. Two-fifths of the insurgents in the field, are negros. These men, with Antonio Maceo at their head, would, in the event of success, demand a predominant share of the govern-

ment of the country. Such a claim would be indignantly resented by the white section and a racial war, probably conducted with bitter animosity and ferocious cruelty, would ensue, the result being, after years of fighting, another black republic.

However, other Englishmen suspected that the whole affair might be none of their business. "Sensible people," observed the Newcastle *Leader*,

will wonder what motive could possibly impel a British officer to mix himself up in a dispute with the merits of which he had absolutely nothing to do. Mr. Churchill was supposed to have gone to the West Indies for a holiday, he having obtained leave of absence from his regimental duties at the beginning of October for that purpose. Spending a holiday in fighting other peoples' battles is rather an extraordinary proceeding even for a Churchill.

The highly visible young aristocrat, finding himself the subject of an embarrassing national controversy, hastily backpedaled. "I have not even fired a revolver," he declared. "I am a member of General Valdés's staff by courtesy only, and am decorated with the Red Cross only by courtesy." A year later, a slightly older and wiser Churchill confided in a letter to his mother from India:

I reproach myself somewhat for having written a little uncandidly and for having perhaps done injustice to the insurgents. I rather tried to make out, and in some measure succeeded in making out, a case for Spain. It was politic and did not expose me to the charge of being ungrateful to my hosts, but I am not quite clear whether it was right.

· · ·

GÓMEZ MOVED WEST. For twenty years he had cherished the certainty that in this direction lay victory, that the Spanish could be driven from the island only after the war was carried into the rich provinces of Matanzas, Havana, and Pinar del Río. Overmatched by the Spanish in numbers of men and arms, Gómez knew there was no hope of a decisive military victory. But while he could not conquer the Spanish Army, he could destroy that thing which kept it in Cuba—sugar.

"The chains of Cuba have been forged by her own richness," he proclaimed, "and it is precisely this which I propose to do away with soon." On November 6 he issued this order to the rebels:

Article 1. That all plantations shall be totally destroyed, their cane and outbuildings burned and railroad connections destroyed.

Article 2. All laborers who shall aid the sugar factories—these sources of supplies that we must deprive the enemy of—shall be considered as traitors to their country.

Article 3. All who are caught in the act, or whose violation of Article 2 shall be proven, shall be shot. Let all chiefs of operation of the Liberating Army comply with this order, determined to unfurl triumphantly, even on ruin and ashes, the flag of the Republic of Cuba.

Gómez was resolved to render the island worthless to Spain, and the Spanish soon discovered they could not stop him. A Spanish military expert described the rebels' tactics:

> They ride incessantly here and there, and when their horses are tired, they seize any they come across. They frequently rest during the day, and march at night, in as light order as possible, carrying only a hammock, a piece of oilcloth, cartridges, machete, and rifle. They live by marauding. The country people feed them, and help them so far as they can, and where these insurgents don't find sympathy, the machete, the torch, and the rope are good arguments. In the woods they find good shelter, places for storage and for hospitals. . . . They place themselves in ambush, selecting narrow passages in the woods, fords and lagoons. They always run after firing, and if pursued, they leave a small body charged with firing on their pursuers, while the main body advances rapidly and then stops, and by circling around, get to the rear of our troops and harass them. When they go a long distance, they divide into small parties, make the journey at night in the woods, and then several groups assemble, until necessity compels them to part again, and meet anew at a preconcerted spot. Their infantry is always in loose order, hiding among the bushes, and always protected by the cavalry. At times a group separates from the main body, the mission being to attract the attention of the government troops, while the main body charges '*al machete.*" Such are the insurgents of Cuba, and their ways of fighting.

Throughout the latter half of December the rebel army marched back and forth across the province of Matanzas, burning cane fields and sugar mills, dynamiting railroad trestles, and cutting telegraph wires. On January 1 the army crossed into Havana Province, bringing the war almost to the suburbs of the capital. Meeting almost no Spanish opposition, the invading army left a smoldering swath in its wake as it marched across some of the most valuable property in Cuba. By January 22 a column of fifteen hundred insurgents led by General Antonio Maceo reached Mantua in Pinar del Río Province, the westernmost village on the island. A great path of scorched earth and devastation now reached into every corner of Cuba, and Máximo Gómez repeated his terrible benediction, "Blessed be the torch!"

.   .   .

NINE MONTHS EARLIER, on April 15, 1895—just five days after Máximo Gómez and José Martí waded onto a deserted beach in Oriente Province—a new governor general arrived in Havana, sent by the Madrid government to deal with the new Cuban insurrection. He was Arsenio Martínez Campos, the same officer who had successfully concluded the Ten Years' War in 1878. The Spanish government expected him to repeat his miracle, but it was soon apparent to him that this might prove impossible. Seventeen years earlier he had faced a weary and divided rebel army, and he had resorted to conciliation, promises—even bribery —to obtain the peace treaty of Zanjón. But now it was clear to him that these same measures could not work a second time. He was sixty-four years old; Gómez was seventy-two. Between the two old enemies there was too much respect to resort to such foolishness.

The guerrilla is the fish; the people are the water in which he swims. Mao Tse-tung's maxim was as true in Cuba in 1895 as it was in China a half-century later. Martínez Campos understood this. There was only one way to defeat Gómez: isolate him from the *pacíficos*, the peasant farmers of the island who sheltered and supported the rebels. But the way to do this and the consequences of doing it were things Martínez Campos did not like to contemplate. In July, three months after his arrival in Cuba, he wrote to Prime Minister Cánovas in Madrid and outlined what was later to become the infamous *reconcentrado* policy: forcing the peasants to leave their homes in the countryside and crowd into designated towns where they could neither feed themselves nor expect the government to feed them.

"The misery and hunger would be horrible," he wrote, and he permitted himself to wonder if it all would be worth the terrible price.

> Even if the insurgents are beaten in the field or forced into submission, my loyal and sincere opinion is that, . . . with or without reforms, offering pardon or extermination, we will have another war within ten years; and if we still did no more than shed our blood, there would be another and another. Can Spain afford to go on like this?

As to the *reconcentrado* plan: "Perhaps I may arrive at such measures, but only as a last resort, and I do not think that I have the qualities for such a policy. In Spain, only Weyler has them."

General Valeriano Weyler y Nicolau—a tough, even ruthless man; an ascetic who neither drank nor smoked; a battle-scarred veteran of Spain's civil and colonial wars. He had earned a sobriquet none dared speak to his face: the Butcher.

"Reflect, my dear friend, "Martínez Campos wrote to Prime Minister Cánovas, "and if, talking with him, you prefer his system, do not hesitate to replace me. We are dealing with the fate of Spain, but I have scruples that come before everything else and forbid shootings and analogous acts."

On January 7, 1896, while Gómez marched across Havana Province, Martínez Campos cabled his resignation to Madrid. One month later the next governor general arrived. He was General Valeriano Weyler.

He was, according to the New York *Journal* of February 23, a "fiendish despot . . . a brute, the devastator of haciendas . . . pitiless, cold, an exterminator of men. . . . There is nothing to prevent his carnal, animal brain from running riot with itself in inventing tortures and infamies of bloody debauchery."

In his own defense, General Weyler demanded, "How do they want me to wage war? With bishops' pastorals and presents of sweets and money?" A Spanish military attaché in Washington during the American Civil War, he understood war in the terms of a Union general he had come to admire—William Tecumseh Sherman.

He was the descendant of German emigres who settled in the Balearics generations before. Short, wiry. Spartan, energetic, possessed of a stern Prussian countenance and steel blue eyes, he had a reputation for efficiency and a disregard for personal hardship and danger. Unlike much of the Spanish officer corps, he had advanced more through performance than politics. He was neither heartless brute nor cold-blooded murderer. He was a professional soldier prepared to carry out with complete single-mindedness the only policy that had any chance of defeating the rebels. But to hundreds of thousands of Cuban peasants, this distinction was to be of absolutely no importance.

The advantages of the reconcentration program were obvious to Weyler. Herded into fortified towns, the peasants could no longer furnish the rebels with food and other material support, and the rebels would also be deprived of a very effective intelligence system for keeping track of Spanish military movements. The peasants would no longer be exposed to revolutionary propaganda, and young men would be prevented from joining the rebels. And finally, since the rebels would have relatives and loved ones among the *reconcentrados,* the program would work as a sort of hostage system, demoralizing the rebels and encouraging them to end hostilities.

Within days of his arrival Weyler issued the first of a series of reconcentration orders. The rural population had eight days to move into the designated reconcentration areas in the fortified towns. Food products could not be removed from the fortified areas, and the owners of cattle were required to herd them into the reconcentration zones. Any person failing to obey would be considered as a rebel and treated accordingly, i.e., shot.

On paper, Weyler had made provision to house and feed the *reconcentrados,* even designating adjacent areas of land for them to farm. The reality was very different. The housing usually consisted of abandoned and decaying warehouses without toilet facilities, interior partitions, and often even roofs. Even these accommodations were limited and inadequate to the numbers of *reconcentrados,* and many were forced to sleep in doorways or courtyards, or anywhere else the slightest shelter could be found.

Weyler's promise to feed the *reconcentrados,* or at least enable them to feed themselves, also proved illusory, and the effects of famine were soon apparent. Starving beggars fought over scraps of garbage in the streets, and the sight of children with bodies swollen by starvation became commonplace. Some Spanish commanders unofficially permitted *reconcentrados* to visit the countryside to forage for food, reasoning that if they were caught by the troops and shot as rebels, this would at least be a more merciful death than the end they faced in the towns.

At first Weyler put the *reconcentrado* program into effect only in the eastern provinces, but he soon extended it to the entire island. No one knows how many Cuban peasants died of hunger and disease during the next twenty-four months, but according to a Spanish estimate, "at least a third of the rural population, this is to say, more than four hundred thousand human beings," perished.*

.   .   .

THE Great CUBAN-AMERICAN FAIR was held in New York's Madison Square Garden during the last week of May 1896. "Cuba Appreciates Sympathy—She Must Have Assistance," was the fair's slogan, and the public turnout was not disappointing.

"Between the military uniforms, the gay trappings of the stalls, and the bright decorations of the roof and boxes, the fair looked at its best last night," the New York *Times* reported on the morning after the day the fair had been due to close. "The arena was thronged with persons anxious to buy sugar cane, green cocoa, nuts, cigars, and other native products of the Queen of the Antilles." So successful was the fair, it was extended for a second week. A "grand naval and military night" was proclaimed; Troop C of Brooklyn's National Guard Cavalry, the Twenty-third Regiment, and one thousand members of the Irish Volunteers joined the festivities. One highlight was staged in a hospital tent—the marriage of Dr. A. Sidney Angle and Mrs. Leo Villard Hill, who declared their intention shortly to go to Cuba to serve as doctor and nurse with the rebel army. Among the guests of honor who spoke to the assembled fairgoers was General Daniel E. Sickles, the former American minister to Madrid whose sympathy for the Cuban insurgents and enmity toward Spain dated back twenty-three years to the *Virginius* incident.

Sickles was but one of many prominent Americans sympathetic to the Cuban cause or, at least, somehow interested in seeing the end of Spanish rule on the island. Charles A. Dana, the editor of the respected New York *Sun*, had long been a personal friend of José Martí and an ally of Cuban independence. Samuel Gompers, who had apprenticed as a cigar maker in his native London, had come to sympathize with the aspirations of Cuban Americans as he rose to the post of president of the Cigar Makers Union in America; by 1895, when he was president of the American Federation of Labor, that organization formally adopted a resolution sympathizing with the Cuban rebels. The Cuban cause was generally popular with American organized labor; the *Journal of the Knights of Labor* proclaimed, "The revolution is one of the most righteous ever declared in any country and should be supported by every lover of liberty and free government in this country."

William O. McDowell, a New York businessman who had befriended Martí, founded the Cuban League of the United States, an affiliation of pro-

*A few writers place the *reconcentrado* toll at "only" 200,000 or even 100,000 deaths, attributing the higher figures to contemporary anti-Spanish propaganda in the United States. Millis (p. 76) cites a 1899 U.S. government estimate that the population of Cuba was only 200,000 less than what might have been expected from a projection of earlier Cuban census figures. However, the last preceding Cuban census was compiled twelve years earlier, and the population had fluctuated up and down in the years immediately prior to it; a modern statistician might therefore judge the extrapolation of the population curve over twelve years as, at best, somewhat dubious. The 400,000 figure (cited in Levy and Peterson, 2: 166) seems the most reliable one available, since the Spanish were best able to estimate the toll and certainly had no reason to exaggerate the tragedy.

Cuban clubs throughout the country devoted to providing material and moral support to the rebels. The breadth of American support for the revolution was demonstrated in Chicago late in September 1895, when four thousand people jammed into the Central Music Hall for a mass rally and an overflow crowd of nearly two thousand assembled in Association Hall. The rally had been organized initially by a local Cuban American club, but it swiftly gained the support of such diverse groups as the Chicago Trades Assembly, the Illinois Federation of Labor, the Union League Club, and veterans groups such as the Grand Army of the Republic, the Loyal Legion, and the Sons of the Colonial Wars. The German-American Committee, the Civil Service Reform Association, and an assortment of clergymen also joined the rally. Similar fairs and rallies were held in Philadelphia, Kansas City, Cleveland, Akron, Cincinnati, and Providence.

American sympathy was rooted deep in our own traditions. The grievances set forth in our own Declaration of Independence were still able to quicken the pulse and arouse indignation against colonial monarchies across the seas. Republican government was still considered something of a radical new departure from the status quo, an American innovation over which we still exercised a near monopoly; most of the nations of Europe were still ruled by crowned heads. More than any other European power, Spain represented the medieval despotism of the Old World. Catholic Spain—the land of the Inquisition and the Armada, the ancient nemesis of Anglo-Saxon, Protestant liberalism, the home of the conquistadores who raped and plundered from Mexico to Peru—this was the image that fueled popular sentiment in the United States. Indignation over Spain's Cuban policy was already high in 1896, when the first reports were received of the terrible consequences of General Weyler's *reconcentrado* program.

. . .

AMONG THE THOUSANDS who gathered in Madison Square Garden that early June day to hear General Sickles's speech was an adventurous young man named Frederick Funston. A dropout from the University of Kansas, Funston had searched for excitement in the wilds of Death Valley and the Yukon. As he listened to the fiery and eloquent Sickles tell of the Cuban struggle, Funston began to form what he later described as "a vague sort of idea that I would like to take part in it, I fear as much from a love of adventure and a desire to see some fighting as from any more worthy motive." Two days later he went round to Sickles's house, presented himself to the general, and made known his aspiration. After a brief chat he departed, bearing a letter of introduction to Señor Tomás Estrada Palma, the leader of the Cuban Junta.

After José Martí departed on his fateful trip to Cuba eighteen months earlier, the elderly and distinguished Estrada Palma succeeded him as chief of the Cuban Revolutionary party and its propaganda and fund-raising arm, the Cuban Junta. Funston found Estrada Palma cordial but cautious. In his letter, General Sickles noted that, although he was favorably impressed by the young man, he did not know him personally; Estrada Palma realized Funston might be something other than what he claimed to be, perhaps a fugitive from justice, or simply an irresponsible thrill-seeker, or even a Spanish spy. Caution was essential because the Junta's activities were skating perilously close to a violation of the U.S. neutrality laws.

Filibustering—the dispatching of private military expeditions to foreign countries for the purpose of revolution—was a violation of section 5286 of the Revised Statutes of the U.S. Code, and the Cuban Junta was forced to resort to some elaborate maneuvers to stay within the letter of the law. For its part, the administration of President Grover Cleveland did not wish to find a second *Virginius* affair on its hands and was beginning to enforce the spirit, as well as the letter, of the statutes. The Danish steamer *Horsa* was a case in point.

Seven months earlier, on November 9, 1895, the *Horsa* cleared the port of Philadelphia bound for Port Antonio, Jamaica, to pick up a cargo of fruit. However, the ship dropped anchor that night off Barnegat, New Jersey, just beyond the three-mile limit, and was joined by a lighter, which transferred to her a load of arms, supplies, and upward of forty Cubans. The *Horsa* then proceeded to Jamaica, stopping off the Cuban coast to unload the men and weapons. On her return to the United States the ship's captain and two officers were tried and convicted of filibustering. The case went to the Supreme Court, which upheld the convictions, finding that the maneuver of taking aboard the military expedition beyond the territorial waters of the United States did not obviate the fact that the defendants had taken part in a criminal conspiracy hatched within American jurisdiction. Even as Funston and Estrada Palma spoke, President Cleveland was preparing a proclamation warning that all similar violations of the U.S. neutrality laws would be similarly prosecuted.

But if Estrada Palma harbored any suspicion that the young volunteer was actually an *agent provocateur* of the Spanish, he must also have considered it unlikely. For one thing, Funston was far too modest in claiming qualifications to fight for the Cuban cause. Asked whether he had any military experience, Funston admitted he had none, adding somewhat feebly that he "had read considerably along military lines and felt I had it in me to make good." As to his knowledge of Spanish, Funston claimed only "a fair reading but not a speaking acquaintance with that language."

Estrada Palma remained cautious, however. It was not possible, he said, for him to enlist the young man in the Cuban Liberation Army because to do so would violate American neutrality laws. But it might be possible for Funston to go along with the next shipment of supplies to Cuba. When he reached the island he would be free to do whatever he liked, including joining the rebels. Exactly when the next supply ship might depart was information Estrada Palma was not inclined to announce very much in advance. He suggested Funston go home and wait, checking back at the Junta's office once a week.

Funston did as he was told. On one of his weekly visits to the Junta an assistant discreetly suggested that the Cuban Army might find especially valuable a recruit with some knowledge of field artillery, a subject and a commodity in which the rebels were severely lacking. Funston took the hint and a note of introduction from the Cuban and presented himself at the firm of Hartly & Graham, arms dealers to the revolution. There he received instruction in the care and operation of the Hotchkiss twelve-pound breech-loading field piece. Soon he had mastered the manufacturer's instruction manual, had learned to strip and reassemble the weapon, and had done everything but actually fire it. This meager expertise was more than any of the Cubans knew of artillery, so Estrada Palma arranged for Funston to teach what he had learned to a group of fifteen young Cubans in a makeshift classroom above a Third Avenue saloon. A week or so later, in his new and unofficial role of ordnance advisor to the Cubans, Funston accompanied several of the Junta to a remote point on the shores of Long Island Sound to witness a demonstration of the new Sims-Dudley dynamite gun, a strange-looking device that fired a projectile loaded with high explosive. The exhibition, which involved firing the piece into the waters of the sound, produced hundred-foot-high geysers and succeeded in terrifying the passengers and crew aboard a passing excursion boat. Such exploits marked Funston's gradual accept-ance by the Junta, and one August afternoon he received a telegram notifying him to present himself at the Cortland Street ferry at seven o'clock that evening, ready to leave for Cuba.

Aboard the ferry to Jersey City, Funston met a Junta official and was introduced to his fellow soldiers of fortune: a former Canadian Northwest mounted policeman, a veteran of the British Royal Marines, another Englishman, and a young American. The party boarded a Pennsylvania Railroad train in Jersey and a few days later arrived in Charleston, South Carolina.

The group stopped at a hotel in the city, joining some thirty Cubans who were already registered. Among the other guests were fifteen or twenty quiet, well-dressed gentlemen, whom the Junta official identified as U.S. deputy mar-shals, Secret Service agents, and Pinkerton detectives employed by the Spanish government, all intently surveillant of the Cuban party. The undercover men hoped to discover the Cubans' intended port of embarkation and the name of their vessel so that the expedition could be intercepted by a U.S. revenue cutter in American waters, or by a Spanish gunboat off the Cuban coast. Their plan was thwarted, however, through the good offices of one of the most powerful friends of the Cuban cause, Henry B. Plant, an elderly Connecticut Yankee who owned a vast system of railroads, hotels, and steamship lines. The Plant System's Charleston agent, a Mr. Fritot—conveniently, a nephew of a Junta official— devised and executed an operation that effectively separated the hounds from their prey.

Funston, his fellow adventurerers, and the Cubans boarded a Plant Line train in Charleston; the undercover men did the same. When some of the detectives tried to take seats in the same car as the Cuban group, the conductor insisted they leave, explaining the car had been chartered by a party of sightseers. The train sped on through the afternoon and evening, and stopped briefly during the night by a sidetrack in the middle of the Georgia woods. The Cubans' car was quietly detached, and the train, carrying the detectives and government agents, continued on its way.

A locomotive backed from the sidetrack, coupled to the Cubans' car, backed a few miles to a switch, then proceeded off on a branch line. At dawn the one-car train stopped at the tiny station of Woodbine on the banks of the Saltilla River in southern Georgia. As Funston and the rest of the party climbed out, the engineer leaned from the locomotive cab and called out, "Goodby and good luck! Don't let them Spanions git you!"

As the train pulled away, Funston surveyed the scene. Three boxcars stood on a siding; the bill of lading said they contained "saw mill machinery"; in fact, they held a shipment of guns, ammunition, and military supplies, including the Hotchkiss twelve-pounder Funston had so often stripped and assembled in the classroom above the Third Avenue saloon. Beneath the railroad bridge lay a large, ocean-going tug—the legendary filibuster, *Dauntless*. On her bridge stood the equally legendary and dauntless Captain "Dynamite Johnny" O'Brien.

Nearing sixty, a mild-mannered, thickset man with an iron-gray mustache, O'Brien was a native New Yorker, born in the Dry Dock section of Manhattan. He spent much of his life on the sea or in the port of New York, where he was a harbor pilot, but his avocation was Latin American revolutions. He acquired his nickname during one of his exploits in 1888, when he carried a dangerous cargo of explosives to the insurgents in Panama, and since the outbreak of the second Cuban revolution, he had made more than a dozen filibustering trips to Cuba. The Pinkerton men who lurked about his New Jersey home learned to avoid the bear traps he set for them and were careful not to stray too close to the house, lest Mrs. O'Brien douse them with a pot of boiling water. Their efforts to shadow him on his frequent trips into New York to meet with Junta agents were frustrated by elaborate maneuvers worked out by the captain and his son, Fisher. "Dynamite Johnny" proved equally elusive away from home; after General Weyler put a price on his head, he slipped into Havana, left his calling card for the governor general, and departed.

O'Brien's talent for wily evasiveness was put to good use now as the *Dauntless*, with its military expedition aboard, steamed down the Saltilla to Brunswick, Georgia, and stood out to sea. None of the fleet of federal revenue cutters was about, for the *Commodore*, another notorious filibuster, which had been lying in Charleston harbor, had left port the night before. Convinced the *expedicionarios* were aboard her, the federal cutters were now in hot pursuit of the *Commodore* some 150 miles to the north as she steamed innocently toward Hampton Roads.

After four days of rolling and pitching on the long Atlantic swells, the *Dauntless* made land on August 16 and put into a tiny inlet just east of the port of Nuevitas on the northeast coast of Cuba. The seasick *expedicionarios* were landed on the low, mangrove-covered coast without mishap, although one of the small boats foundered in the surf, and the Spanish torpedo gunboat *Galacia* stumbled upon the midnight disembarkation and chased the *Dauntless* out to sea, where "Dynamite Johnny," true to form, gave her the slip.

After an anxious four-day wait, a train of Cuban pack mules escorted by six hundred rebels arrived on the beach to recover the expedition. A day's march of thirty miles into the interior brought them to the camp of General Máximo Gómez.

The day after their arrival, Gómez sent for the newcomers. Speaking through an interpreter, he began by stating his appreciation for the spirit that had moved them to leave their homes and cast their lot with a people struggling for independence. Then, turning to Funston, he bluntly inquired what the young man knew about artillery. Funston answered that his knowledge of the subject was limited.

"Well," said Gómez, "you cannot know any less than another American who came down here and said he knew it all." Without further discussion Gómez put Funston in charge of the newly arrived Hotchkiss gun and another fieldpiece that had arrived with an earlier expedition. It was some time before the thirty-one-year-old adventurer realized he had been made commander of artillery of the Cuban Army.

.   .   .

OFFICIAL WASHINGTON could not ignore the groundswell of public sympathy for the Cuban rebels. Indeed, the Cuban Junta, resolving that it would not be ignored by the U.S. government, sent the talented young writer, Gonzalo de Quesada, to Washington to lobby for the cause. Operating out of a suite of offices in the Hotel Raleigh and using the good offices of Matias Romero, the Mexican ambassador to the United States, Quesada cultivated sympathetic senators and congressmen. His specific goal was the same one sought but never attained by the rebels during the Ten Years' War—American recognition of Cuban belligerency.

It was a fine point of international law, but it had important consequences. To recognize the belligerency of the Cuban rebels would not mean American recognition of Cuban independence, nor would it ally the United States with the revolution. But it would recognize the rebels as something more than outlaws, bandits, or mutineers, and it would permit the United States to treat them as it would a sovereign nation engaged in a war with Spain, to conduct U.S. relations with both Spain and the rebels as a third and neutral party, governed by the international rules of war. In concrete terms it would permit American arms merchants to sell guns and other war material to the rebels with the same freedom from official interference as they enjoyed when they sold the same commodities to Spain. Such a step could not reasonably be considered by Spain as a *casus belli* —a provocation to war—for the United States would only be following the precedent of Spain, England, and other European nations that had granted belligerent rights to the Confederacy during the American Civil War.

There were some drawbacks, however. Recognition would give Spain the right to stop and inspect American ships on the high seas, a consequence that might actually make it more difficult for the rebels to receive supplies. More importantly, American recognition of rebel belligerency would absolve the Spanish from any obligation to protect American property in Cuba. Since the economic depression on the island that followed the Ten Years' War, American investors had bought up large numbers of sugar plantations and mills in Cuba and were heavily invested in the Cuban railroad system. American investment in Cuba now amounted to forty or fifty million dollars, an enormous sum in 1896.

American owners of large Cuban plantations, such as Edwin F. Atkins, a Boston sugar millionaire, were as opposed to the belligerency proposal and wished as fervently for a return to the prerevolutionary status quo as the most conservative *peninsulare* in Havana. When Atkins learned that Tomás Estrada Palma was due to pay a call on the American secretary of state, Richard B. Olney, to lobby for belligerency, he made it a point to see Olney first and state the American investors' case. Atkins made his point. When Estrada Palma, Quesada, and another representative of the Cuban Junta visited Olney, the secretary began the conversation by inquiring whether the three were American citizens. They were, in fact, naturalized citizens, as were many other Cuban emigres, and they promptly affirmed this. Olney next asked whether they endorsed Gómez's policy of burning sugar plantations, including those owned by American citizens, and Estrada Palma answered that he approved the policy as a necessity of war.

"Well, gentlemen," Olney said brusquely, "there is but one term for such action. We call it arson." With that he terminated the interview.

The Cleveland administration could not as easily dismiss demands for belligerency originating on Capitol Hill, however. On January 28, just a few weeks after the meeting between Olney and the Cubans, the Senate Foreign Relations Committee reported out a resolution stating,

> In the opinion of Congress a condition of public war exists between the government of Spain and the government proclaimed and for some time maintained by the force of arms by the people of Cuba; and . . . the United States should maintain a strict neutrality between the contending powers, according to each all the rights of belligerents in the ports and territories of the United States.

The resolution was reported by Senator John T. Morgan, Democrat of Alabama, and one of the senators who had warmly responded to Gonzalo de Quesada's lobbying. A second resolution was reported for the committee's Republican minority by Senator Donald Cameron of Pennsylvania: "Resolved, further, that the friendly offices of the United States should be offered by the president to the Spanish government for the recognition of the independence of Cuba."

On February 20, Cameron's friend and colleague, the Boston Brahmin Henry Cabot Lodge, arose to speak in support of the belligerency resolution. Noting that Cuba was "one of the richest spots on the face of the earth" and that American pecuniary interests on the island were very great and were being destroyed, Lodge predicted that "free Cuba would mean a great market for the United States; it would mean an opportunity for American capital, invited there by signal exemptions; it would mean an opportunity for the development of that splendid island." Perhaps aware of the rather crass tone of his observations, he added that he was prepared "to put our duty on a higher ground . . . common humanity. No useful end is being served by the bloody struggle that is now in progress in Cuba, and in the name of humanity it should be stopped." Lodge's specific proposal was "to offer our good offices to mediate between Spain and the Cubans in order to restore peace and give independence to the island which Spain can no longer hold."

On April 6, after two months of debate, the Congress passed by an overwhelming majority the Morgan–Cameron resolution. As a concurrent resolution of the Senate and House, it did not have the status of a law but was merely an expression of congressional opinion. Still, the Cleveland administration did not fail to get the message: something must be done about Cuba.

Secretary of State Olney had already taken a first step aimed at defusing the Cuban issue. On March 20 he met with the Spanish ambassador, Enrique Dupey de Lôme, and tentatively offered a proposal: If Spain would put into effect some new political reforms on the island, the Cleveland administration might make a public declaration that it was satisfied with that progress and, in the words Dupey de Lôme used to report the meeting to Madrid,

> In that case the insurrection would be shorn of the moral support it now has in this country, and the task of suppressing it would be easier, because public opinion in the United States would be arrayed against it and would force abandonment of arms by the Cubans, or facilitate their complete rout.

On April 7 Olney followed up this conversation with a formal note (predated to April 4, at President Cleveland's suggestion, to avoid the appearance of having been prompted by the just-passed congressional resolution). The note, which was drafted with the help of sugar magnate Atkins, began with a long recapitulation of the state of affairs in Cuba: things were bad, getting worse, and the end was not in sight; the United States could not tolerate another Ten Years' War in her back yard. The United States therefore proposed a pacification plan: Spain would retain her rights of sovereignty over the island, but the Cubans would be granted a reasonable degree of local self-government. The United States offered to mediate the issue between Spain and the rebels. If the rebels refused to accept the arrangement, then American public sympathy would swing against them.

The Spanish foreign minister was Carlos O'Donnell y Abreau, duke of Tetuán, the son of an Irish family long resident in Spain and involved in Spanish politics. If he recognized the Olney note for what it really was—a move to appease American public opinion rather than a realistic plan to bring autonomy and peace to Cuba—he must not have believed it was going to work. O'Donnell and his boss, Prime Minister Cánovas, had a public opinion problem of their own. Reports of the speechifying in the American Congress during the recent Cuban debate had reached Spain, and the unflattering terms that had sometimes been applied to things Spanish had inflamed passions throughout the country. There had been anti-American demonstrations in Madrid. In Barcelona a mob of fifteen thousand angry Spaniards stoned the American Consulate, tore down both the American and Spanish flags, and fought a pitched battle with the police. In such an atmosphere, official Spanish acceptance of American mediation might well bring down the government.

The monarchy, restored by Cánovas in 1876, was not as firmly established as he might have wished. The young Alfonso XII had done his duty, wedding María Cristina of Austria and fathering an heir, but the young king died the same year his son was born, 1885. Until little Alfonso XIII came of age in 1902, María

Cristina would have to rule as queen regent. But having an Austrian woman on the throne was not the perfect fulfillment of the Spanish idea of monarchy. Spanish politics remained fully as tumultuous as they had been throughout the century; the pretender, Don Carlos, still waited patiently somewhere in Europe; and the possibility of a *coup d'état* seemed very real to Cánovas and, especially to his foreign minister—O'Donnell's uncle had led the army in deposing the last queen regent, Cristina, in 1854.

O'Donnell replied to the Olney note on June 4. The lengthy diplomatic response boiled down to this: thanks, but no thanks; the United States can best help the situation by letting Spain handle Cuba without outside interference. But O'Donnell also realized that, if eventual American intervention was to be avoided, he would have to do something more than simply ask the United States please to mind her own business. While President Cleveland had shown no inclination toward intervention, his term of office had nearly expired, and 1896 was an election year. William Jennings Bryan, Cleveland's Democratic successor, was running against Republican William McKinley. And whoever succeeded Cleveland in the White House was likely to be more responsive to American public sympathy for the rebels. If a confrontation with the United States over Cuba was to be avoided, O'Donnell would have to do something soon. He believed he knew what thing that might be.

.   .   .

"What If Spain Should Declare War?" asked a headline in the American *Review of Reviews* of May 1896, and posed three "very serious practical questions":

> First, is a war between the United States and Spain among the possibilities of the near future? Second, in case of such a contest would Spain be able to secure an ally among the great powers? Third, in the case of Spain's obtaining the aid of a strong naval power could we expect any assistance, and if so, from what quarter?

The *Review* found the answers in an interesting and prescient article recently published by Mayo W. Hazeltine, literary editor of the New York *Sun*. Hazeltine's piece was quoted and summarized at length.

Hazeltine seems to have had good diplomatic sources; he correctly forecast both Olney's proposal and O'Donnell's refusal. American mediation "could not, in the existing state of public feeling in Spain, be accepted by the Madrid government without exciting a popular uprising, which not only would cause the downfall of the present ministry, but would endanger the monarchy." But Hazeltine noted the mood in Congress to recognize Cuban independence and estimated that a resultant war with Spain had become very likely. In that case, he asked, would Spain be able to find an ally among the great powers?

Germany, with a rapidly growing navy and powerful imperialistic cravings, seemed one likely candidate.

Spain could afford to gratify the hunger of the German emperor for colonial possessions by a cession of the Caroline Islands in the Pacific and of the Canaries in the Atlantic. Sooner than abandon Cuba to the United States, Spain might be willing to sell or give Cuba to a European ally.

But Hazeltine doubted that even the kaiser's lust for colonies could induce him to accept the bargain and join a war against the United States. "The millions of German-Americans would make such a conflict second only in fratricidal horror to a war between the United States and England."

France seemed a more likely Spanish ally, Hazeltine thought. The Chamber of Deputies was controlled by capitalists who were heavily invested in Spanish securities, and an alliance with Spain over the Cuban issue might be seen as a means of protecting that investment. France might be restrained from intervening by Russia, friendly toward the United States since Lincoln's administration and France's partner in the so-called Dual Alliance. But if that restraint failed, if France joined Spain in an American war, could the United States look for its own European ally? Hazeltine thought she could, and might find it in England. "Three months ago," Hazeltine admitted, "such a supposition would have seemed absurd."

The idea of an Anglo–American alliance would indeed have seemed absurd in December 1895, which marked the climax of a long-simmering dispute between the United States and Great Britain over the latter's policies in Latin America. In November 1894 three British warships steamed into Corinto, a port on the west coast of Nicaragua, to demand immediate payment of a sum of $75,000 England claimed was owed her. When the authorities replied that they could not raise that sum, the British blockaded the harbor, landed a force of Marines, seized the customs house, occupied the town, forcibly suppressed local resistance, and sat down to wait for the money to be paid.

In the United States the high-handed British action caused a wave of outrage. Bellicose voices were raised in Congress, and the New York *Tribune* saw the incident as a violation of the Monroe Doctrine, although it admitted that it was giving that hallowed policy a rather broad interpretation. The British managed to collect their money from Nicaragua and leave before the crisis reached full boil, but Anglo–American relations were not destined to return to tranquility just yet.

In July 1895 Secretary Olney sent Britain an official note regarding the longstanding dispute between Britain and Venezuela over the location of the boundary line separating that Latin American nation from the colony of British Guiana. Venezuela had some time before requested American arbitration of the dispute, but the British rejected the American offer to mediate. Now, however, the United States was insisting on doing it. In the tone of his note, Olney matched the impudence and pugnacity of the recent British adventure in Nicaragua:

Today the United States is practically sovereign on this continent, and its fiat is law upon the subjects to which it confines its interposition.

Why? . . . It is because, in addition to all other grounds, its infinite resources combined with its isolated position render it master of the situation and practically invulnerable as against any or all other powers.

In closing, Olney invoked the Monroe Doctrine, "which entitles and requires the United States to treat as an injury to itself the forcible assumption by an European power of political control over an American state."

Olney's note was, of course, fully endorsed by President Cleveland, who declared in an address to Congress his intention "to resist by every means . . . the appropriation by Great Britain of any lands . . . which after investigation we have determined of right belongs to Venezuela."

Britain bluntly refused to accept American mediation, and both nations prepared to settle the question by other means. The U.S. North Atlantic Squadron was put on alert, while a British flying squadron of twelve warships prepared to sail for the Caribbean. The British War Office made plans to send its Sikh and Ghurka regiments to fight in the South American jungles, while an Irish American organization offered President Cleveland a hundred thousand volunteers to fight the English. The Washington *Post* commented, "Let but a drum tap be heard from the White House grounds, and in every city of the land a host will rise, and in every rural neighborhood and countryside battalions will start up."

The prospect of war between Britain and the United States was real, but as suddenly as it had sprung up, the crisis was defused by the unlikely combination of an event in the distant Transvaal and an imprudent act by Germany's impulsive kaiser.

On December 29 Dr. Leander Starr Jameson, a hotheaded administrator for Cecil Rhodes's South Africa Company, led some six hundred armed men into the Boer South African Republic. An expected uprising against Boer President Paul Kruger failed to materialize, however, and Jameson and his men were taken prisoner. On January 3, Kaiser Wilhelm II telegraphed Kruger: "I express to you my sincere congratulations that without appealing to the help of friendly powers, you and your people have succeeded in repelling with your forces armed bands which had broken into your country and in maintaining the independence of your country against aggression."

The implication was clear: Had Kruger looked to "friendly powers" for assistance in the affair, Germany would have been ready to come to his aid. The British government viewed the Kruger telegram as a belligerent act, a deliberate provocation, and interference in a British matter and correctly inferred that it was part of Wilhelm's campaign to frighten Great Britain into the Triple Alliance of Germany, Austria, and Italy.

Queen Victoria took pen in hand to chastise the kaiser, who happened to be her grandson:

My dear William,
    As your Grandmother . . . I feel I cannot refrain from expressing my deep regret at the telegram you sent President Kruger. It is consid-

ered very unfriendly towards this country . . . and has, I grieve to say, made a very painful impression here.

Other British reaction was less restrained. Angry mobs attacked German sailors in the streets of London. As anti-German feeling increased, British attitudes toward the United States underwent an abrupt about-face. The feeling seemed to be that, if there was to be trouble with Germany, Britain's best allies might be her transatlantic cousins.

"War between the two nations [England and the United States] would be an absurdity as well as a crime," declared the British foreign minister.

The two nations are allied and more closely allied in sentiment and in interest than any other nations on the face of the earth. While I should look with horror upon anything in the nature of a fratricidal strife, I should look forward with pleasure to the possibility of the Stars and Stripes and the Union Jack floating together in defence of a common cause sanctioned by humanity and justice.

As to the Venezuelan boundary dispute, the British government was now ready to settle the matter on whatever terms the Americans wished. A historic corner had been turned. Remarkably, in the space of a week, the lingering animosities of two wars and a century of veiled hostility had been swept away. As Henry Adams observed, "The sudden appearance of Germany as the grizzly terror . . . effected what Adamses had tried for two hundred [years] in vain— frightened England into America's arms."

A few weeks after the Venezuelan crisis ended, the first secretary of the American legation called on Lord Salisbury. What would be the attitude of Great Britain, he asked hypothetically, were the United States to annex Cuba?

"It is no affair of ours," the prime minister replied. England would of course be reluctant to see Spain humiliated, but he did not "consider that we have anything to say in the matter, whatever . . . course the United States may decide to pursue."

And so, a month or so later in the *Review of Reviews,* it was not at all absurd for Mayo Hazeltine to write:

It is at least conceivable that we may be threatened by a hostile European coalition, because we have determined to discharge our debt to civilization by insisting that to the Cuban revolutionists shall not be refused the rights secured to belligerents by the rules of modern warfare. Let us suppose that in a crisis of that kind the message should be flashed under the Atlantic that in the cause of humanity and liberty England would not suffer us to stand alone.

.   .   .

EACH AUGUST the Spanish government fled the heat of Madrid and repaired to the seaside town of San Sebastian on the Bay of Biscay. The foreign diplomatic corps went along, and this year, 1896, as in each of the past three, the American minister was Hannis Taylor. Taylor was a forty-four-year-old native of South

Carolina, a lawyer, and a scholar who had written the two-volume *Origin and Growth of the English Constitution.*

On August 8, a Saturday, Taylor received a visitor at his hotel, an English reporter named Houghton from the London *Standard.* The interview was unusual, for Houghton had come to convey information rather than acquire it, and what he had to say was of the utmost interest to the American diplomat.

A certain document had been drafted by the foreign minister, Señor O'Donnell, Houghton said. It was a diplomatic memorandum intended to be conveyed through the Spanish embassy of every major European capital. Its purpose was to urge mediation by the European powers "through the medium of friendly recommendations, with the object of causing the government of the United States to bring about a more strict observance of the neutrality laws." The draft document had been circulated to every member of the foreign diplomatic corps, except Taylor, for the purpose of comment.

Where had Houghton gotten such a story, Taylor demanded. The journalist replied that he had been told it by the British ambassador, the distinguished veteran diplomat, Sir Henry Drummond Wolff. In fact, Wolff had made a curious stipulation when giving the story to Houghton—that he not publish it without Taylor's permission. But Taylor had known absolutely nothing of the mysterious Spanish memorandum until Houghton asked him about it. Stunned by the disclosure, Taylor immediately called on Sir Henry at his home.

Sir Henry could not have been surprised by Taylor's visit or by the subject the American immediately broached. Very well, said the British ambassador. Since Taylor seemed to know part of the story, he no longer felt obliged to withhold the details from him.

O'Donnell had been searching desperately for a plan to forestall American intervention in Cuba when the idea struck him. For almost a century America's policy regarding Cuba turned on a cardinal rule: As long as things remained relatively peaceful and quiet on the island, there was no objection to continued Spanish rule; but the prospect of Cuba passing into the hands of another European power was absolutely unacceptable. Thus there seemed one thing that might prevent American intervention—the threat that it might result in European intervention. O'Donnell looked about for something that he could use to involve the other European powers in the affair, and he found it: the monarchical principle. He spelled out the idea in his instructions to the Spanish envoy in London:

It is requisite that you stress the effects which the Cuban insurrection may have on the monarchy in Spain, on the Regency, and on the monarchical principle in general. You should stress also the consequences of a war with the United States, which may be forced upon us in defending our rights and our national honor.

O'Donnell beat the same drum in the draft memorandum: Under the circumstances, the Government of Her Majesty would regard themselves as faithless to their duty, if they did not place before the consideration of the cabinets of the Great Powers of Europe, the special dangers which they see looming in the near future, and which, though especially affecting Spain, hold also a threat to colonial and maritime nations in general, and may even compromise other very important European interests. . . . There is inherent in the Cuban question a problem supremely European, affecting not only the development and future of Spain, but also the general interest of Europe, because very grave international consequences may result from the Cuban insurrection, and the daily more absorbent and expansive Monroe Doctrine.

Thus, O'Donnell had formulated a kind of "domino theory." If America intervened, Cuba would be lost. If Cuba were lost, the monarchy would fall. If the monarchy fell, then what of Czar Nicholas, Kaiser Wilhelm, Emperor Franz-Joseph, Queen Victoria, and the other crowned heads? Would their own thrones remain secure? Or would the republican elements in their kingdoms seize on the first opportunity to follow the Spanish example? And what of their colonies? Did not even republican France have cause to fear for her possessions in Guiana and the West Indies if the Americans continued to broaden the interpretation of their Monroe Doctrine?

The European sky was falling, O'Donnell declared, and disaster could be averted only if the great powers joined Spain in pressing certain specific demands upon the United States: the president of the United States must publicly condemn filibustering and warn American citizens that they would have no American protection if they conducted such expeditions; the U.S. Congress must enact more effective laws preventing filibustering; the U.S. government must cease granting citizenship to Cubans who wished to use it as a shield to their insurrectionist activities in Cuba; the U.S. government must begin interpreting its existing laws more favorably to Spain's interests; American officials negligent in their duty to prevent filibustering must be severely punished; the U.S. government must "harass the Cuban Junta in New York" and frustrate its efforts to aid the rebels; the U.S. government must cease making declarations that give moral support to the rebels. The memorandum also specified that "the Minister of Spain in Washington receive, in his dealings with the Government of the United States, the willing assistance and the support of his colleagues, the diplomatic envoys of the Great Powers."

Hannis Taylor listened to Sir Henry's words with growing dismay. The century-old American fear of intervention in Cuba by other European powers seemed on the brink of realization.

·　　·　　·

IT WAS SUNDAY AFTERNOON and Carlos O'Donnell was attending the bullfights in San Sebastian. Hannis Taylor visited him in his box, but the American minister displayed no hint of agitation and limited his conversation to courteous amenities. The first indication the Spanish foreign minister received that anything was amiss was the note from Sir Henry Drummond Wolff he found waiting for him when he returned home. Sir Henry had urgently requested an audience, and O'Donnell sent word for him to come by at 10:30 that night.

When the Englishman arrived, he told O'Donnell that he had received a visit from a very excited Hannis Taylor. Somehow, said Sir Henry, the American had learned of the draft memorandum. Taylor had said that the affair was an insult to President Cleveland and the U.S. government that would seriously affect Spanish–American relations and result in tremendous domestic repercussions when the American press learned of it. Sir Henry said he had been able to calm Taylor only by offering to mediate between the American and O'Donnell.

On the following evening O'Donnell met with Taylor. The foreign minister began by offering his assurance that he had complete confidence in the honorable intentions of President Cleveland and Secretary Olney, that the draft memorandum only reflected his concern over the possible policies of the next American administration. Taylor replied that nonetheless the memorandum would inspire the greatest anti-Spanish feeling among Americans. He added that the ambassadors of the great powers were as disturbed as he by the project, to which O'Donnell replied that he was surprised to hear that, that none of the European ambassadors had said that to him.

O'Donnell did not add that they, in fact, had greeted the plan with approval; one of the most enthusiastic proponents of the memorandum had been the Austrian ambassador, which was perhaps understandable, since the queen regent had been a princess of the Austrian royal house. Another early supporter of the plan had been none other than Sir Henry Drummond Wolff. All of this O'Donnell kept to himself.

Taylor suggested that not every member of the diplomatic corps had been entirely candid with the foreign minister, and that, in any case, any European intervention in American affairs would certainly be offensive to the United States. He asked O'Donnell to reconsider the memorandum project.

O'Donnell returned to the theme of his confidence in the Cleveland administration and his fears for the future. Picking up on this note, Taylor ventured his estimate that William Jennings Bryan would be the next president of the United States and Senator John T. Morgan the next secretary of state, and that both were hostile toward Spain. That was all the more reason, he argued, why Spain ought to accept Cleveland's offer to mediate the crisis now and bring it to an end before his successor took office. O'Donnell sadly agreed with Taylor's forecast but foresaw that the Cuban crisis could not possibly be solved before the presidential inauguration next March 4. In the end he agreed to reconsider the memorandum and convey the American's objections to the cabinet. He promised that in any case the memorandum would not be delivered without his advising Taylor in advance.

After Taylor left, O'Donnell reflected on the affair with angry bewilderment. It was obvious the British ambassador had betrayed the memorandum project to Taylor through clever indirection, thus nipping it in the bud. Yet Sir Henry had been one of the earliest advocates of the plan. New instructions must have been sent from London, he concluded. He was right.

O'Donnell's plan for a joint European initiative against American intervention was a shambles. As a measure of its failure, Britain, France, and Germany, before the year was out, submitted a joint note to Spain urging her to accept the American mediation offer.

.   .   .

As AUGUST WORE ON, Spain's troubles multiplied. On the twenty-sixth a force of Filipino insurgents attacked the Spanish fort at Caloocan and four days later fought a pitched battle at San Juan del Monte. An uprising was underway in the Philippines, and Spain had a second colonial insurrection on her hands.

.   .   .

THROUGHOUT THE SUMMER and fall Cuba remained on the front pages, but it was not an issue in the presidential campaign. The Republicans directed a nod toward the island, including in the party platform their "best hopes . . . for the full success of [the insurgents'] determined contest for liberty," while the Democrats expressed sympathy for the Cubans in "their heroic struggle for liberty and independence." Having dispensed these platitudes, the two parties turned to the important issue of the campaign: the economy, and the question of free silver versus gold as a monetary standard. In November William McKinley, advocate of the gold standard, defeated William Jennings Bryan, champion of free silver. Northeastern business interests breathed a sigh of relief. They believed they could look forward to four years of economic recovery, nurtured by a sound monetary policy. And war, which they viewed as bad for business, had no place in that recovery.

.   .   .

REPORTS FROM CUBA continued to be grim. In July a correspondent had written to sugar magnate Edwin Atkins from Cienfuegos, telling him of small pox in the city, pernicious fevers, and many fatalities, especially among children. "I am informed that a large trench has been dug in the cemetery, where the dead are thrown in during the night and covered with quick lime. . . . Yellow fever is very epidemic and of an alarming type and many of the troops are dying."

.   .   .

IN THE VIEW OF General Valeriano Weyler, if there was one man in the world more dangerous than Máximo Gómez, it was Antonio Maceo. Weyler had a high regard for blacks as soldiers; he was opposed to racial discrimination in the army, and his own cavalry escort during the Ten Years' War was made up of Negroes, a fact that reflected, he said, his "esteem for them as soldiers." Thus the fact that the Bronze Titan had been operating freely with his cavalry in the western provinces for most of the year was especially disquieting to the governor general.

If the cumbersome Spanish Army could not match the Cubans' mobility, Weyler could at least find a way to counter it. The means he used was the *trocha*, a long fortified ditch cut through the jungle, a barrier to the easy passage of the rebels. The *trocha* had been used in the Ten Years' War, a single barrier stretching the fifty miles between Morón on the north coast and Júcaro on the south, which effectively confined the insurgents within Oriente Province. Weyler restored the old Morón–Júcaro *trocha* and constructed a second one between Mariel and Majana to contain Maceo in the western end of the island.

An American correspondent who visited the Morón–Júcaro *trocha* described it this way:

> The trocha is a cleared space one hundred and fifty to two hundred yards wide, which stretches for fifty miles through what is apparently an impassable jungle. The trees which have been cut down in clearing this passageway have been piled up at either side of the cleared space and laid in parallel rows, forming a barrier of tree-trunks and roots and branches as wide as Broadway and higher than a man's head. It would take a man some time to pick his way over these barriers, and a horse could no more do it than it could cross a jam of floating logs in a river.
>
> Between the fallen trees lies the single track of a military railroad, and on one side of that is the line of forts, and a few feet beyond them a maze of barbed wire. Beyond the barbed wire again is the other barrier of fallen trees and jungle. . . . The forts are of three kinds. They are best described as the forts, the block-houses, and the little forts. A big fort consists of two stories, with a cellar below and a watch-tower above. It is made of stone and adobe, and is painted a glaring white. One of these is placed at intervals of every half-mile along the trocha, and on a clear day the sentry in the watchtower of each can see three forts on either side.
>
> Midway between the big forts, at a distance of a quarter of a mile from each, is a block-house of two stories, with the upper story of wood overhanging the lower foundation of mud. These are placed at right angles to the railroad, instead of facing it, as do the forts.
>
> Between each block-house and each fort are three little forts of mud and planks, surrounded by a ditch. . . . They hold five men, and are within hailing distance of one another. Back of them are three rows of stout wooden stakes, with barbed wire stretching from one row to another, interlacing and crossing and running in and out above and below like an intricate cat's cradle of wire.
>
> One can judge how closely knit it is by the fact that to every twelve yards of posts there are four hundred and fifty yards of wire fencing.
> . . .
> As a further protection against the insurgents, the Spaniards have distributed a number of bombs along the trocha, which they show with great pride. These are placed at those points along the trocha where the jungle is less thickly grown, and where the insurgents might be expected to pass.
>
> Each bomb is fitted with an explosive cap, to which five or six wires are attached and staked down on the ground. Any one stumbling over one of these wires explodes the bomb and throws a charge of broken iron to a distance of fifty feet.

The Mariel–Majana *trocha*, which ran along the border of the western province of Pinar del Río, was even more formidable, having been equipped with electric lights and artillery and manned by some fourteen thousand troops. Maceo had easily crossed this barrier during the early stages of its construction, but after its completion he found it impassable. Weyler had succeeded in trapping the Bronze Titan in the western end of the island.

But the rebels were faced with an obstacle far more formidable than General Weyler's *trochas;* the divisive forces of jealousy and racism threatened to do what the Spanish could not accomplish.

From its earliest days the second revolution strived to appear to the world as something more than an armed band of insurgents. Soon after the first military expeditions landed in 1895, the leaders met in the tiny village of Jimaguayú in Camagüey Province to organize a civilian government, replete with a provisional constitution, president, vice-president, and cabinet. The trappings of the "Republic of Cuba" extended even to publishing a newspaper, which was printed on secret presses hidden in the jungle and distributed free of charge throughout the island. All of this was in keeping with the plans of the late José Martí to emphasize civilian control of the revolution, and it served the additional purpose of lending credibility to the insurgents' pleas for official recognition by the U.S. government. But in practice it saddled the revolution with a top-heavy bureacracy that remained comfortably ensconced in the relative safety of the eastern provinces with little to do while Gómez and Maceo did all the fighting.

The seeds of dissension began to grow. The provisional president was Salvador Cisneros Betancourt, an aristocratic Creole of about the same age as Gómez and also a veteran of the Ten Years' War. A simmering enmity between the two old men dating back to the earlier war now began to boil. Cisneros was offended by Gómez's brusque autocratic style, while for his part, Gómez had no intention of permitting Cisneros and his aristocratic clique to meddle in military matters and repeat the errors that had cost the rebels victory twenty years earlier. The situation was exacerbated by a degree of racism among Cisneros and the other Creoles in the government. The spectacular successes of Antonio Maceo in the west and his brother José in the east inspired fears that the brothers might create the dreaded black republic after the Spanish were driven out. Cisneros demanded that Gómez replace José Maceo as commander in Oriente Province and cease sending supplies to Antonio Maceo. When Gómez refused both orders, he was dismissed from his post of general-in-chief.

Gómez wrote to Maceo and urged him to return to the east to help deal with the situation, a thing more easily said than done because of the Mariel–Majana *trocha*. Maceo tried to cross the line near Mariel but encountered a Spanish force totaling some six thousand men under the personal command of General Weyler, who had taken the field in search of the Bronze Titan. Maceo, with little more than two hundred men in his escort, sustained heavy losses on November 9 in the Tapia Valley.

Finding the *trocha* impassable, Maceo decided to go around it by boat at the Mariel end. On the night of December 4, Maceo and a small force successfully made the trip. Among the seventeen men he picked to accompany him was Francisco "Panchito" Gómez Toro, the young son of Máximo Gómez.

Before returning to the east, Maceo planned one last battle. He believed that a successful assault on the town of Mariano on the very outskirts of the city of Havana might so humiliate Weyler that Madrid would be forced to recall him.

The attack was planned for the night of December 7. Maceo and his band were waiting in the nearby village of San Pedro de Hernandez when they were surprised by a Spanish infantry force. The rebels quickly mounted and charged the attackers. After a brief fight the Spanish retreated with the rebels in pursuit. Maceo leaned toward a companion and shouted, "This is going well!" At that moment a bullet struck him in the face. Panchito Gómez rushed to the fallen man's side and was himself shot in the leg. As he tried to drag Maceo's body away he received a second bullet and fell dead.

On December 28 Gómez announced the death of General Maceo in a general order: "The army is in grief and with the army its general-in-chief." Gómez made no public reference to Panchito's death, but in a personal letter to Maceo's widow he wrote, "Weep, weep, Maria, for both, for you and for me, since for this unhappy old man, the privilege of relieving his innermost grief by letting go a flood of tears, is not possible."

.   .   .

ON DECEMBER 7, the day Maceo died, President Cleveland delivered his last annual message to Congress. He presented a long summary of the situation on the island and noted that American concern "is by no means of a wholly senti-mental or philanthropic character. . . . Our actual pecuniary interest in Cuba is second only to that of the people and government of Spain." Thirty to fifty million dollars of American capital were invested on the island, and the annual volume of Cuban–American trade had been about one hundred million dollars immediately before the revolution.

Cleveland recalled the congressional demands for Cuban belligerency rights and noted that those demands had escalated to calls for recognition of Cuban independence, and even armed American intervention, "even at the cost of a war between the United States and Spain." But the United States believed, Cleve-land said, "that right and not might should be the rule of its conduct," and he urged once again that Spain pacify the island by offering political autonomy to the Cubans. The friendly offices of the United States would continue to be available to mediate such a settlement.

The affair of the O'Donnell memorandum apparently had made a strong impression on the president: "Whatever circumstances may arise, our policy and our interests would constrain us to object to the acquisition of the island or an interference with its control by any other power."

The patience of the United States was not unlimited, Cleveland warned. Events might "fix a limit to our patient waiting for Spain to end the contest. . . . When the inability of Spain to deal successfully with the insurrection has become manifest . . . a situation will be presented in which our obligations to the sovereignty of Spain will be superseded by higher obligations, which we can hardly hesitate to recognize and discharge."

The warning was clear: Spain must pacify Cuba soon if she hoped to prevent American intervention.

· · ·

THE PEANUT CLUB met every afternoon in an office at 66 Broadway. The members were reporters from the more than forty daily newspapers then flourishing in New York City. The presiding officer was Horatio Rubens, a twenty-seven-year-old graduate of Columbia Law School, legal counsel to the Cuban Junta, and its de facto press officer. A large box of peanuts Rubens kept on his desk fortified the press corps and gave the informal gathering its name.

It was the golden age of the newspaper, the only news medium available. The wire services that instantly reported events from distant corners of the world by telegraph and ocean cable were innovations of recent memory, and the luxury of reading about what happened yesterday half a world away was still a savored novelty. There were as yet no photographs in the daily papers; only a few square inches of line cuts and engravings competed with the columns of print, but newspaper prose made up for the deficiency with vivid descriptions. The "yellow journals" of the day served up large portions of blood, thunder, and scandal to a public that had acquired a taste for such sensations. This segment of the press found much good copy in the Cuban revolution, and it was well represented each day when the Peanut Club met to receive Rubens's handouts on the latest rebel victory or Spanish atrocity.

The most constant members of the Peanut Club were the reporters from two of the yellowest of New York's yellow journals, the *World* and the *Journal*. The *World* was owned by Joseph Pulitzer, a Hungarian-born newspaperman who purchased the paper from Jay Gould in 1883 and proceeded virtually to invent yellow journalism and amass a fortune in the process. Now a near-blind and ailing recluse, he continued to run the *World* through a staff of secretaries.

Among the host of Pulitzer's imitators, his sincerest admirer was the thirty-three-year-old William Randolph Hearst, owner of the *Journal*. Hearst was the son of a rough old sourdough who had struck it rich in the Comstock Lode, pyramided his fortune through crafty investments in land, and bought himself a seat in the U.S. Senate before he died. Young Hearst was a shy, gentle, and soft-spoken lad, but he had a talent for mischief; he was expelled from Harvard in his junior year after presenting several of the distinguished faculty chamber pots with their own names ornamentally inscribed inside. Hearst had already settled on his life's calling; he planned to follow in the footsteps of his idol, Joseph Pulitzer. He persuaded his father to give him the San Francisco *Examiner*, one of the old man's few unprofitable investments. But before taking charge of the paper, Hearst spent a year's apprenticeship as a reporter on Pulitzer's New York *World*.

Putting into practice the lessons he learned on Pulitzer's paper, Hearst soon turned the *Examiner* into a profitable enterprise, and in 1895 he decided to go into direct competition with his mentor in the New York market; he bought the New York *Journal*. He lowered the paper's price, increased its size, and served up to an eager public a diet of accidents, disasters, murders, suicides, criminal trials, love triangles, and such feature items as, "Why Young Girls Kill Themselves," and "Strange Things Women Do for Love."

The yellow press found a rich vein of lurid tales in the Peanut Club handouts, and soon the *Journal*, the *World*, and the others were printing accounts
of beautiful young Cuban Amazons fighting alongside the rebels and Catholic
priests roasted alive by the Spanish. Many of these stories were total fabrications,
not even based on the naturally biased press releases handed out by Rubens or
Estrada Palma. Hearst constantly drove the *Journal*'s staff to new flights of lurid
fantasy, completely unrestrained by any considerations of accuracy. He was first
and foremost out to sell more papers than Joseph Pulitzer. And quite apart from
this, he was not adverse to spreading anti-Spanish propaganda; he nursed a real
dislike for the Spanish monarchy, and he was sincerely sympathetic toward the
Cuban rebels.

Hearst engaged a fashionable Fifth Avenue jeweler to create a presentation
sword, its gold-plated hilt encrusted with diamonds, and its blade engraved with
the inscription, "To Máximo Gómez, Commander-in-Chief of the Army of the
Cuban Republic—Viva Cuba Libre." He kept it in his office in a fine mahogany
case and waited for a chance to send it to the general by the hand of one of the
Journal's correspondents. That event, whenever it occurred, would make wonderful copy. In a way, the sword symbolized Hearst's attitude toward the Cuban
revolution: His heart was with the rebels, but his eye was on the main chance.

.   .   .

None of them knew the colour of the sky. Their eyes glanced level, and
were fastened upon the waves that swept toward them. These waves
were of the hue of slate, save for the tops, which were of foaming white,
and all of the men knew the colours of the sea.

The twenty-six-year-old Stephen Crane, who would soon begin the most
famous of his short stories with these lines, sat in the open boat of the tale's title
as it plunged between mountainous seas some twenty miles east of New Smyrna,
Florida. The *Commodore* had begun taking on water soon after she left Jacksonville late on New Year's Day, 1897, and about midnight it was obvious that the
steamer's pumps couldn't handle the leak. The captain changed course, hoping
to make Mosquito Inlet before she sank, but he soon gave the order to abandon
her. Most of the crew, the fifteen Cuban passengers, and the writer made it to
the small boats before the *Commodore*, her decks awash, gave a final lurch and
dove into the sea. Crane, the captain, and two of the crew were in a ten-foot
dinghy.

The oiler, steering with one of the two oars in the boat, sometimes
raised himself suddenly to keep clear of water that swirled in over the
stern. It was a thin little oar, and it seemed often ready to snap.

The correspondent, pulling at the other oar, watched the waves
and wondered why he was there.

He was there because there was a war in Cuba, because it had become
fashionable for newspapers to send famous writers and journalists to the island,
and because the Bacheller Syndicate of papers wanted the well-known novelist

to report the war from the insurgents' side. Perhaps he was also there because *The Red Badge of Courage*, judged one of the finest war novels in the language, was the product of his research and imagination. Perhaps he had suspended his own judgement of the work and hoped that in Cuba he could measure his art against reality. But now he met a different reality—the sea.

> As each slaty wall of water approached, it shut all else from the view of the men in the boat, and it was not difficult to imagine that this particular wave was the final outburst of the ocean, the last effort of the grim water. There was a terrible grace in the move of the waves, and they came in silence, save for the snarling of the crests.

The ordeal went on for thirty hours. Finally, after the boat was swamped just off Mosquito Inlet, Crane and some of the others were pulled from the surf by bystanders on the beach. It would be some months before he would get to see a war, but he had made the acquaintance of sudden death on that Florida beach.

> In the shallows, face downward, lay the oiler. His forehead touched the sand that was periodically, between each wave, clear of the sea.

THAT SAME DAY another novelist-reporter tried to reach General Gómez and was thwarted by the sea. The *Vamoose*, a yacht purchased by William Randolph Hearst to use as a dispatch boat, met heavy weather in the Florida Straits and returned to Key West. Aboard were Richard Harding Davis and Frederic Remington, who had been waiting for nearly a month for the chance to slip across and join the rebels in Santa Clara Province.

Davis was a celebrity. His clean-cut, square-jawed countenance was familiar to the public; Charles Dana Gibson used him as a model, judging him a suitable match for the illustrator's popular Gibson Girl. He was very much the handsome young man about town, moving easily between the glamorous realm of New York society and the slightly disreputable world of big city journalism.

He was from Philadelphia, where his father edited a newspaper and his mother—Rebecca Harding—wrote uplifting novels. He had worked as a reporter on the New York *Sun* and as managing editor of *Harper's Weekly*. He had written many short stories and several novels, often with the theme of a Latin American revolution (he had traveled in Venezuela and Central America). His most popular work, *Soldiers of Fortune*, which concerned an insurrection in a mythical South American republic, was written in Santiago de Cuba, while he was a guest at the home of Jennings Cox, an American expatriate distinguished to history as the inventor of the daiquiri cocktail.

Davis's air of wholesome, upper-class respectability attracted William Randolph Hearst quite as much as the young writer's sharp reportorial eye and clear, direct prose style, and Hearst thought nothing of paying Davis five hundred dollars to cover the most recent Harvard–Yale game. Davis was getting three

thousand dollars per month, plus expenses, to go to Cuba for the *Journal*, plus
another six hundred dollars for an article on the war for *Harper's*.

The other member of the team was equally famous. Frederic Remington's
drawings of cowboys, cavalrymen, Indians, horses and Southwestern landscapes
were familiar to every reader of *Harper's* and *The Century*. The small, fast cam-
eras used to record the action of more recent wars were still unknown, and besides,
there was not yet a practical means of printing photographs in a daily newspaper,
so Remington's pictorial skills were a valuable complement to Davis's stories. The
two men were splendidly qualified to cover the war, if only they could find it.

The war was not in the city of Havana, although the great majority of the
American press corps tried to cover it from there. The correspondents would
sometimes interview General Weyler, or more often the American consul general, Fitzhugh Lee, but they spent most of their time in the bar of the Hotel
Inglaterra trading scraps of rumor or fabrication, and when they tried to file their
dispatches at the cable office, they were required to submit them first to the
Spanish military censor, who often revised the copy, transforming cruelty into
benevolence, defeat into victory, and generally replacing one lie with another.

Still, Havana was closer to the war than Key West, where Davis and Remington had wasted a month waiting for the timorous skipper of the *Vamoose* to
sail. On January 9, a week after the abortive attempt to cross to Santa Clara, the
pair booked passage for Havana on the steamship *Olivette*.

Soon after he arrived, Davis managed to obtain permission from General
Weyler to leave Havana and travel in the countryside, although the *Journal's*
front-page announcement of January 17 that he had reached the rebels was a
complete fabrication, resulting in close surveillence by the Spanish, which further
reduced his freedom of movement. Still, he reached the Júcaro–Morón *trocha*
and was given an officially escorted tour of it. He saw no action as he traveled
about the island, but the devastation of the war was apparent everywhere.

> I always imagined that houses were destroyed during a war because they
> got in the way of cannon balls or they were burned because they might
> offer shelter to the enemy, but here they are destroyed with the purpose
> of making the war horrible and hurrying up the end. The insurgents
> began first by destroying the sugar mills, some of which were worth
> millions of dollars in machinery, and now the Spaniards are burning the
> homes of the people and herding them in around the towns to starve
> out the insurgents and to leave them without shelter or places to go for
> food or to hide the wounded. So all day long wherever you look you see
> great heavy columns of smoke rising into this beautiful sky above the
> magnificent palms.

On January 19 Davis was in Santa Clara and witnessed the predawn execution of a rebel by a Spanish firing squad. The condemned was twenty-year-old
Adolfo Rodriguez, the only son of a Cuban farmer, who had joined the insurgents
and was captured and found guilty of bearing arms against the government. Davis
wrote a long and moving account of the execution, "The Death of Rodriguez,"
which became a classic of its kind.

He had a handsome, gentle face of the peasant type, a light, pointed beard, great wistful eyes, and a mass of curly black hair. He was shockingly young for such a sacrifice. . . .

The officer of the firing squad hastily whipped up his sword, the men . . . leveled their rifles, the sword rose, dropped, and the men fired. At the report the Cuban's head snapped back almost between his shoulders, but his body fell slowly, as though some one had pushed him gently forward from behind and he had stumbled. . . .

He sank on his side in the wet grass without a struggle or sound, and did not move again. . . .

At that moment the sun, which had shown some promise of its coming in the glow above the hills, shot up suddenly from behind them in all the splendor of the tropics, a fierce red disk of heat, and filled the air with warmth and light. . . .

. . . The whole world of Santa Clara seemed to sir and stretch itself and to wake to welcome the day just begun.

But as I fell in at the rear of the procession and looked back, the figure of the young Cuban, who was no longer part of the world of Santa Clara, was asleep in the wet grass, with his motionless arms still tightly bound behind him, with the scapular twisted awry across his face, and the blood from his breast sinking into the soil he had tried to free.

.   .   .

Davis's Cuban tour ended on a ridiculous note. Aboard the *Olivette* on his return to the United States, he met Señorita Clemencia Arango, one of three young Cuban women who had been exiled by the Spaniards for having aided the insurgents.

"She was a well-bred, well-educated young person who spoke three languages and dressed as you see girls dress on Fifth Avenue after church on Sunday," he wrote in his dispatch to the *Journal*.

This is what the Spaniards did to these girls: After ordering them to leave the island on a certain day, they sent detectives to their houses on the morning of that day and had them undressed and searched to discover if they were carrying letters to the junta at Key West and Tampa. They then, an hour later, searched them at the custom house as they were leaving for the steamer. They searched them thoroughly, even to the length of taking off their shoes and stockings, and fifteen minutes later, when the young ladies stood at last on the deck of an American vessel with the American flag hanging from the stern, the Spanish officers followed them there and demanded that a cabin should be furnished them to which the girls might be taken, and they were then undressed and searched for the third time.

From the tenor of Davis's story, it was almost as though his Victorian sensibilities had been more outraged by this supposed affront to feminine modesty than by any of the horrors he had witnessed in the last few weeks. The *Journal* put the report on the front page February 12, beneath the headline: "Does Our Flag Shield Women? Indignities Practiced by Spanish Officials on

Board American Vessels. Richard Harding Davis Describes Some Startling Phases of the Cuban Situation. Refined Young Women Stripped and Searched by Brutal Spaniards While Under Our Flag on the *Olivette.*" Frederic Remington, who had already returned to New York, was commissioned to illustrate the story. Not unreasonably, he executed a drawing showing a young woman standing naked while three bearded detectives looked on.

The relevant fact omitted by Davis (if he knew it) was that the strip searches had been performed by matrons out of the view of any males. When she arrived at Tampa, an embarrassed Señorita Arango set the record straight, and Pulitzer's *World,* smarting under its recent defeat by Hearst in the circulation war, gloated ostentatiously over the *Journal's* mistake. Davis, feeling he'd been made to appear a sensation-monger by Hearst, resigned from the *Journal.*

The *Olivette* incident has often been cited as emblematic of the distortions published by Hearst and the rest of the yellow press during the Cuban revolution, but it seems to have been founded in an honest mistake. In fact, the tale was far from preposterous; the day after the story appeared, Consul General Lee reported to the State Department, documenting two other instances of the searching of women aboard American steamers by the Spanish authorities, and in these cases the searchers were, in fact, men.

Among the most cherished lore of the role of the yellow press in those days is a story, published some years later, of an alleged exchange of telegrams between Frederic Remington and William Randolph Hearst. Remington, wishing to leave Havana, supposedly cabled Hearst:

"Everything is quiet. There is no trouble. There will be no war. I wish to return."

To which Hearst is said to have replied:

"Please remain. You furnish the pictures and I'll furnish the war."

Hearst denied the exchange ever took place. Whether it did or not is of little importance. William Randolph Hearst did not furnish the war. Nor, had he wished to try with all his might, could he have prevented it. The war, when it came, was furnished by forces more powerful than yellow journalism.*

·   ·   ·

THE LARGEST ARMY ever to cross the Atlantic Ocean had been sent to Cuba— 160,000 Spanish troops since the revolution began in 1895. The *trochas*—feats

---

*Regarding the belief that the yellow press caused the Spanish War, LaFeber (p. 401) notes: "In areas where this press supposedly was most important, such as New York City, no more than one-third of the press could be considered sensational. The strongest and most widespread prowar journalism apparently occurred in the Midwest. But there were few yellow journals there. The papers that advocated war in this section did so for reasons other than sensationalism; among these reasons were the influence of the Cuban Junta and, perhaps most important, the belief that the United States possessed important interests in the Caribbean area which had to be protected. Finally, the yellow press obviously did not control the levers of American foreign policy. . . . An interpretation stressing rabid journalism as a major cause of the war should draw some link to illustrate how these journals reached the White House or the State Department. To say that this influence was exerted through public opinion proves nothing; the next problem is to demonstrate how much public opinion was governed by the yellow press, how much of this opinion was influenced by more sober factors, and which of these two branches of opinion most influenced McKinley."

of military engineering comparable to the Great Wall of China—now girded the island. The rural population—some half-million people—had been herded into concentration camps where they died by the tens and hundreds of thousands. And Antonio Maceo was dead. General Valeriano Weyler was beginning to see the light at the end of the tunnel.

On February 26 he cabled Madrid that the provinces of Havana, Matanzas, and Pinar del Río had been pacified, an announcement that was somewhat premature. Maceo's successor, Major General José María Rodriguez, and a large force of rebels still operated freely in Pinar del Río, and the insurrection continued in the other western provinces. And Máximo Gómez still controlled virtually all of the eastern end of Cuba, with the exception of a few Spanish strongholds, such as the city of Santiago. These facts notwithstanding, Weyler's mood of optimism spread to Madrid, where Prime Minister Cánovas announced certain constitutional reforms to take effect "as soon as the state of war in Cuba will permit."

Cánovas hoped eventually to end the crisis by granting the island autonomy, the same solution Cleveland and Olney had proposed, but Máximo Gómez would have none of it. On January 19 the New York *World* published Sylvester Scovel's interview with Gómez in which the general flatly rejected the autonomy idea. A month later Consul General Lee reported the same thing to Secretary Olney, adding that the other rebels "in the hills" were not interested in the proposed Spanish reforms.

      .   .   .

ON THE MORNING of March 2, a special six-car train, festooned with patriotic bunting, arrived in Washington carrying the president-elect and his party. Arm in arm, William and Ida McKinley led the retinue of dignitaries through the Baltimore and Potomac depot to the line of carriages waiting on Sixth Street. The procession started down Pennsylvania Avenue toward the Ebbitt House, where the McKinleys were to stay until the inaugural two days later. That evening McKinley went to the White House for an informal dinner with President and Mrs. Cleveland; the semi-invalid Mrs. McKinley, fatigued by the trip from Ohio, sent her regrets.

The evening was marked by warmth and cordiality. McKinley was in closer accord with Cleveland's views on the major issues than the Democratic standard-bearer, Bryan, had been, and the outgoing Democrat considered McKinley's victory a public vindication of his own policies. In the matter of Cuba, the two men were in nearly perfect agreement.

"Mr. President," said McKinley, "if I can only go out of office at the end of my term, with the knowledge that I have done what lay in my power to avert this terrible calamity, with the success that crowned your patience and persistence, I shall be the happiest man in the world."

William McKinley had seen war. At seventeen he had enlisted as a private in the Union Army, had served in the Twenty-third Ohio Volunteers under Rutherford B. Hayes, and had seen action at Antietam, Kernstown, and Cedar Creek before mustering out in the brevet rank of major. His short stature and facial features reminded some political cartoonists of Napoleon Bonaparte, but any similarity ended there; McKinley was the least bellicose of men.

He had served two terms as a Republican congressman from Ohio and had become identified with the protective tariff, a favorite issue of Republican business interests. With the financial support of his friend Marcus Hanna and other Ohio businessmen, he was elected governor of the state in 1891 and served two terms before running for the presidency.

He was not quick-witted, nor was he a brilliant speaker, but he compensated with a personal style that bespoke a calm and kindly heart. In the presidential race, faced by the most eloquent orator of the day, he abandoned the campaign trail to William Jennings Bryan and retired to the front porch of his home in Canton, where he read prepared speeches to visiting delegations standing on his lawn. The unlikely strategy worked; he was the first presidential candidate to receive a popular majority since 1872.

He was a devoutly religious man, a member of the Methodist Episcopal church, and he often deflected wrath with a soft answer, meeting angry visitors at his office door with a disarming smile and sending them away a quarter-hour later beaming and wearing the red carnation he had placed in their lapels.

But how such qualities would serve in the Cuban crisis was problematical. To Grover Cleveland, the prospect of averting a war with Spain through kindliness, generosity, turning the other cheek, or, in fact, anything else, seemed more a matter of hope than faith. He was personally convinced a war was all but inevitable, and he later recalled that his conversation that night with McKinley was marked by a "settled sadness and sincerity."

·   ·   ·

THROUGHOUT MARCH the new president completed the task of selecting his cabinet, and the Cuban problem was never far from his mind. He offered the secretary of the interior slot to New York attorney John J. McCook, partly to discharge a political debt to New York Republican leaders who had helped deliver the state. But McCook held out for the job of attorney general, and McKinley balked.

"I do not understand Colonel McCook's interest in Cuban affairs," he said, explaining his refusal. McCook had close ties to the Cuban Junta and was involved in a syndicate attempting to purchase Cuba from Spain. Instead McKinley appointed as attorney general Judge Joseph McKenna of California, a man more likely to prosecute filibusters and enforce American neutrality laws.

McKinley offered the post of secretary of state to Senator John Sherman of Ohio, and the seventy-four-year-old Sherman, feeling too old and ill to defend his seat in the next election, accepted. The appointment was a political maneuver, a means of vacating Sherman's Senate seat; McKinley would reward his old friend and supporter, Marcus Hanna, by arranging to have him appointed to fill it. The president had no qualms about putting the feeble (and notoriously anti-Spanish) Sherman in the all-important cabinet post; the day-to-day running of the State Department would be left to the assistant secretary, the able Judge William R. Day of Ohio, McKinley's trusted confidant.

As secretary of war, McKinley named Michigan lumber magnate and former Civil War general Russell A. Alger, a distant cousin of the "luck and pluck" boys' novelist, Horatio Alger, Jr. Alger was generally considered completely unqualified for the job. His choice may have reflected McKinley's faith that war would be averted or just that he shared the general belief that any war over Cuba would be fought by the Navy.

The post of secretary of the Navy went to John D. Long, the former governor of Massachusetts, who readily admitted to a total ignorance of naval affairs. McKinley apparently agreed with Long's theory that the principal requirement of the secretary was that he be an able administrator, there being an abundance of technical expertise already on hand in the admirals and other officers.

Choosing the assistant secretary of the Navy was more of a problem. Senator Henry Cabot Lodge had visited McKinley while the president-elect was still in Canton to urge the appointment of the young New York City police commissioner, Theodore Roosevelt. McKinley was not so sure Roosevelt was a wise choice. He suspected he might be a "jingo," as the war advocates were called; the Navy Department was the last place McKinley wanted to put such a fellow.

Lodge continued to push for the appointment, enlisting the aid of his father-in-law, Commander Charles H. Davis, superintendent of the Naval Observatory and former chief of the Office of Naval Intelligence, as well as other allies. He wrote to Roosevelt, explaining the problem: "The only, absolutely the only thing I can hear adverse is that there is a fear that you will want to fight somebody at once."

Secretary Long was opposed to Roosevelt on slightly different grounds: "If he becomes Assistant Secretary of the Navy he will dominate the Department within six months!"

But Roosevelt managed to soothe such fears, and the issue swung in his favor after he received the endorsement of Senator Thomas C. Platt. Platt was the New York party leader and no friend of the young police commissioner, but he believed Roosevelt would cause him far less trouble if he were in Washington. On April 6 McKinley yielded and sent Roosevelt's name to the Senate.

·　　　·　　　·

THE PLIGHT OF the *reconcentrados* continued to get worse. Descriptions of the wretchedness and desolation throughout Cuba were carried not only in the press but in official U.S. consular reports. This, more than any other aspect of the Cuban crisis, must have been painful to the gentle-natured McKinley. The State Department estimated that between six and eight hundred of the homeless were naturalized American citizens who had returned to Cuba, and on May 6 the president sent Congress a special request for an appropriation of fifty thousand dollars for their relief and evacuation to the United States. The bill was passed on May 24, 1897.

On June 26 Secretary of State Sherman, momentarily taking the initiative away from his deputy, sent a note to the Spanish ambassador:

No incident has so deeply affected the sensibilities of the American people or so painfully impressed their government as the proclamations of General Weyler, ordering the burning or unroofing of dwellings, the destruction of growing crops, the suspension of tillage, the devastation of fields, and the removal of the rural population from their homes to suffer privation and disease in the overcrowded and ill-supplied garrison towns. . . .

If the friendly attitude of this government is to bear fruit it can only be when supplemented by Spain's own conduct of the war in a manner responsive to the precepts of ordinary humanity.

Sherman's note was forwarded to Foreign Minister O'Donnell, who replied on August 4 with a lengthy justification of Weyler's policies.

All civilized countries which, like Spain at present, have found themselves under the harsh necessity of resorting to arms to crush rebellions, not always so evidently unjustifiable as that of Cuba, proceed and have proceeded in the same manner.

O'Donnell cited the American Civil War as an example and offered a detailed recitation of similar scorched earth policies employed by the Union Army in the South, including "the expedition of General Sherman, that illustrious and respected general, through Georgia and South Carolina." O'Donnell's Celtic irony was not inhibited by diplomatic tact: The late William Tecumseh Sherman was the secretary of state's elder brother.

.   .   .

MAJOR FREDERICK FUNSTON of the Cuban Army supervised the emplacement of the six artillery pieces behind the low ridge that lay just to the south of the town. It was just over a year since he had landed with the expedition from the *Dauntless* and marched into the jungles of Oriente Province to join General Gómez. He had taken part in the brief siege of Cascorra, the capture of Guaimaro, the futile and costly attack on Jiguaní, as well as a host of lesser engagements. He had been transferred to the command of General Calixto García, who, late in August, began to concentrate his forces for a siege of one of the most heavily fortified towns in Oriente, Victoria de las Tunas.

In the wake of the Maceo tragedy the previous December, the rebels managed to put aside their differences and continue fighting. The peripatetic Cuban Republic had even managed to hold islandwide elections during the summer, and General Bartolomé Masó succeeded Cisneros as president. But the U.S. Revenue Cutter Service had reduced the flow of war materiel and medical supplies to the rebels, and Weyler's *reconcentrado* program succeeded in denying them food. Like most of his Cuban comrades, Funston was ragged, hungry, and occasionally delirious with malaria. As the rebels assembled around Las Tunas on August 27, they all knew that great stores of supplies lay within the fortified walls.

As dawn broke on the twenty-eighth, Funston looked over the parapet his men had constructed during the night. Five hundred yards off there was a maze of trenches and barbed wire entanglements. Seven hundred yards beyond that stood the thick masonry walls of one of the forts, and another fort lay twelve hundred yards to the right. There was not a sound or any other sign of life in the Spanish lines. Funston pulled the lanyard on the Sims-Dudley dynamite gun; he had seen it fired only once before, that day more than a year ago when it was demonstrated to the Junta on the shore of Long Island Sound.

> There was no little uneasiness as to what would happen when this uncanny weapon was fired, and there was not much of a tendency to stand too close to it. When the lanyard was pulled the gun gave what sounded like a loud cough, and jumped a little. We were in some doubt as to whether it had gone off or not, but looking toward the *Cuartel de la Caballería* saw a most astounding spectacle. A section of the brick wall was blown in, making a hole large enough to have admitted a good-sized truck, while the sound of a dull explosion was borne to our ears. A cloud of dust and fragments of the wall rose fifty feet in the air and descended in a shower on the roof. We raised a great cheer, which was taken up and re-echoed by our people all about the town. . . . The dust was still settling down over the scene of the explosion when every man rushed to his place, and the other three guns crashed out, making a wall of smoke in front of our position. Then we heard the cracks of Jones's two-pounders to our right. In no time the battle was fairly on.

The battle raged for two days and two nights. One after another of the Spanish forts and blockhouses fell before the Cuban onslaught. Before dawn on the thirtieth a Spanish soldier crept across to the Cuban lines and surrendered. He said his comrades had been completely demoralized by the dynamite shells and were ready to throw down their arms regardless of their officers' orders. At sunrise Funston and several Cuban officers carefully approached the fort.

> The door swung open and the haggard and wasted men, barely able to stand, threw down their arms, while their officers looked on in helpless astonishment. But they accepted the inevitable and made no resistance.
> I was so hungry that I had pretty nearly lost all regard for the proprieties, and made a quick run for the kitchen, a Spanish soldier showing me where the officers' provisions were kept. The first thing I found was some sausages in cans, and cutting one of these open by one blow of my machete, began to get at the contents in the most primitive way imaginable. I saw two Spanish officers looking at me with disgust plainly evident on their features, but feeling sure that I would never meet them socially, went on appeasing my hunger.

. . .

AUGUST 8 was a Sunday. Prime Minister Cánovas had returned from mass in the town of Santa Agueda, a spa in the western Pyrenees not far from the summer capital of San Sebastian. He was sitting with his wife in a public gallery reading the morning paper when he glanced up to see a young man standing before him. Without a word the stranger drew a pistol and fired three shots into Cánovas. The prime minister was dead within an hour.

The assassin was Miguel Angiolillo, an Italian anarchist. He had come to Spain and stalked Cánovas to avenge the torture and death of Spanish anarchists in the notorious Montjuich Prison.

.   .   .

PRÁXEDAS MATEO SAGASTA seated himself behind the desk and looked around at the familiar office. During the past twenty years he had occupied the prime minister's chair as often and as long as had his late predecessor, Antonio Cánovas. He had left it last in March 1895, soon after the second revolt broke out in Cuba.

Sagasta and Cánovas had been partners in an informal political coalition that brought Alfonso to the Spanish throne in 1876 and had supported the restoration in the ensuing years. They were, respectively, the leaders of the two important political parties, the Conservatives and the Liberals, and their tacit partnership, the willingness of each to serve as prime minister for a time, then yield the post to the other, had shielded the monarchy from threats from the other centers of power—the Army, the Carlists (supporters of the exiled royal pretender, Don Carlos), and the Church. But now the long-established coalition had been dissolved by an assassin's bullet, and Sagasta found himself heir to a situation he might have preferred to let his late colleague handle.

The prime minister took up his pen and scrawled across a file folder on his desk, "The situation at our entry into power." He reread the report from the Spanish official in Cuba before placing it in the folder:

> The administration has reached the last stage of disarray and disorder; the army, exhausted and bloodless, filling the hospitals, without the power to fight or hardly even to lift their arms; more than three hundred thousand *concentrados* suffering or starving, dying of hunger and misery all around the towns; the people frightened, in the grip of real terror, obliged to abandon their homes and properties in order to suffer under even more terrible tyranny, with no opportunity to escape this fearful situation except by going and joining the ranks of the rebels.

.   .   .

ON OCTOBER 17 *The Nation* summed up the situation for American readers:

> Sagasta before taking office declared that the financial situation was deplorable if not desperate. . . . It is confessed that the troops in Cuba are six months in arrear in their pay and there is no money to send them. . . . Between November, 1895, and May, 1897, no less than 181,738 men, 6,261 officers, and 40 generals have been sent to Cuba. Counting the garrisons already in the island, the total fighting force must have been hard on 225,000 men. In addition and during the same period, Spain has had to send 28,000 men to the Philippines. . . . Sagasta's task will be the difficult one of inducing the Spanish people to submit to the inevitable. He may be aided or he may be hampered

by the attitude of our own government. At present, we must confess, a diplomatic collision and a rupture appear the most probable.

. . .

In Madrid, a prominent member of the Cortes granted an interview to a reporter from the Paris *Revue de deux mondes*. Conservatives, Liberals, Carlists, and all other Spaniards, regardless of politics, were united on the Cuban issue, he said. "Understand this well," he said. "We *cannot* give up Cuba; we absolutely cannot."

CHAPTER FOUR

MARCHING
AS TO WAR

THE BRISK YOUNG MAN with the conspicuous eyeglasses and the mouth full of large white teeth arrived in Washington in April. The new assistant secretary of the Navy was no stranger to the city; he had served there for over five years as a civil service commissioner. Nor was Theodore Roosevelt ignorant of naval affairs; at the precocious age of twenty-two he had written *The Naval War of 1812*, considered by military historians as the definitive account of the subject, and he had long been a public advocate of a bigger and more modern fleet. Nor was he innocent of the political labyrinth of Washington, for it was only a replica on a grander scale of the politics of Albany, where he had served a term as a Republican member of the New York State Assembly.

Roosevelt's carefully tailored suit, his precise enunciation, his upper-class nasalization that echoed the Harvard Quad, might have misled the casual observer. A two-gun barroom bully once made that sort of mistake in a Dakota saloon; the Eastern dude took away his guns, knocked him cold, and dumped him in a shed until he could come to and get out of town. People better acquainted with the thirty-eight-year-old aristocrat knew him to be as much a man of action as of words, a practicing advocate of the strenuous life, and someone not content merely to write history but resolved to make it as well.

Roosevelt arrived in Washington without impedimenta; his wife, Edith, the five children of their marriage, and a daughter by his first wife (who died in childbirth) had been temporarily left behind at their Oyster Bay, Long Island, home. Meanwhile Roosevelt stayed in Washington with his longtime friend, Senator Henry Cabot Lodge, and the senator's lovely wife, Nannie.

Lodge was eight years older than Roosevelt and also a man of both letters and politics. Before standing for Congress from the Lynn-Nahant district of

Massachusetts, he had been editor of the *North American Review*, author of biographies of George Washington, Daniel Webster, Alexander Hamilton, and other great figures from the American past, and teacher of history at Harvard. Now, as junior senator from Massachusetts, he was a power in the Republican party. Roosevelt had known him since 1884, when the two joined forces unsuccessfully to block their party's nomination of James G. Blaine for president. To his wife, Roosevelt, and a handful of his closest friends he was "Cabot." To all others, Senator Lodge.

Leadership of Washington's social life was shared by Nannie Lodge and Mrs. Elizabeth Cameron, the wife of Senator Donald Cameron, Lodge's Republican colleague from Pennsylvania. An invitation to the salon of Mrs. Lodge or Mrs. Cameron was a thing to be envied, for there one might hope to meet the best and the brightest—Henry Adams or his brother Brooks, William Dean Howells or Rudyard Kipling, John Hay, Charles Bonaparte—men of politics, letters, and wealth.

John Hay called them the Pleasant Gang. They shared the attitudes of the Northeastern establishment. In spirit they stood midway between London and Chicago, viewing with equal disdain the decadence of the Old World and the vigorous greed of the nouveau riche Midwest. They regarded the new president and his coterie of Ohio millionaires with mixed emotions, consoling themselves with the thought that McKinley was, at least, neither a Democrat nor William Jennings Bryan.

The Pleasant Gang gathered in the Washington salons and talked about expansion. Later Roosevelt defined the word: "not only the extension of American influence and power, [but] the extension of liberty and order, and the bringing nearer by gigantic strides of the day when peace shall come to the whole earth." Building an American empire was not just a privilege, or even a duty. It was the New Manifest Destiny.

They had all read the historian Frederick Jackson Turner. Turner said that everything good in America was a result of the frontier; the vigor of American ideals and institutions sprang from the arduous task of pushing the boundary of civilization across a wild and inhospitable continent. But in 1890 the Census Bureau had declared the frontier closed; there were no longer any large western territories that needed settling. Turner saw that as the end of an era, but he predicted that "American energy will continually demand a wider field for its exercise." In other words, Americans needed a frontier, even if they had to go overseas to find it. He set down his theory in a paper he called "The Significance of the Frontier in American History," and Roosevelt had read it three years earlier, when he was working on the third part of his own four-volume *Winning of the West*. He wrote to Turner, telling him, "I think you have struck on some first class ideas."

Expansionism was in the American air. Josiah Strong, an evangelical preacher, believed that Anglo-Saxon Americans had been chosen by God and Darwin's natural selection to go forth and rule Latin America and Africa. His theories were a curious blend of Social Darwinism, the *Ubermensch*, and That Old Time Religion and were immensely popular, especially among Anglo-Saxon

Americans. His book, *Our America,* was a best seller, but the holy roller flavor of his exhortations was not much to the taste of the Brahmin literati who frequented the Lodge and Cameron salons. Strong's influence on the Pleasant Gang was indirect, by way of a writer Roosevelt, Lodge, and the others took quite seriously, naval officer and historian Alfred Thayer Mahan.

Seven years before, Roosevelt had spent a weekend reading Mahan's *Influence of Sea Power Upon History* and had immediately written the author to tell him, "It is a *very* good book—*admirable."* Roosevelt elaborated his admiration at length later that year in an *Atlantic Monthly* review:

> Captain Mahan's effort is to show the tremendous effect which sea power has had upon the development of certain of the great nations of the world. . . .
> . . . He shows . . . the wonderful extent of the influence of the sea power of the various contending nations upon their ultimate triumph or failure and upon the futures of the mighty races to which they belonged.

What lessons did Mahan's work offer America? Mahan answered the question during the next few years as he further elaborated his sea power thesis and set it before the public.

America, he said, had moved from agriculture to industry, and her ability to produce manufactured goods would soon outstrip her capacity to consume them. When that time came, America's survival as an industrial nation would depend absolutely on foreign markets. But, he noted, other nations, especially Germany, were in the identical position. In head-to-head competition for world markets, "neither the sanctions of international law, nor the justice of a cause can be depended upon for a fair settlement of difference." There was, in fact, only one thing that America could depend on—sea power.

To Mahan, modern American sea power consisted of three elements: a large fleet, with powerful battleships and cruisers; a canal across the Central American isthmus; and overseas colonies to serve as distant coaling stations for the fleet. "Whether they will or no," he wrote, "Americans must now begin to look outward."

Even before publication of his first book, Mahan had become the intellectual voice of the "New Navy," which had come into being on the heels of the humiliating *Virginius* incident. A new shipbuilding program had been started by the administration of President Arthur. Three steel warships and an armed dispatch steamer were authorized. In 1886 Congress ordered the construction of two armor-clad battleships, the *Texas* and the *Maine.* By 1897 the fleet had grown to include four first-class battleships, two second-class battleships, two armored cruisers, and thirteen protected cruisers. In total the American fleet numbered 111 serviceable naval vessels of all types.

In 1884 a Naval War College was established at Newport, Rhode Island, as a place where officers could pursue postgraduate studies and naval doctrine could be developed and taught. In 1886 Mahan was made president of the college. *The Influence of Sea Power on History* grew out of a series of lectures he presented there.

Mahan was the son of a West Point professor, but he had taken no particular interest in military history until the War College assignment was offered. Then he took a year's leave to prepare himself for the job, spending most of 1885 in New York City's Astor Library, where, coincidentally, Roosevelt had researched and written his *Naval War of 1812* just five years earlier. Indeed, Roosevelt's book profoundly impressed Mahan as he began to develop his sea power thesis. Through this curious turn of events, the sea power theories that were to influence Roosevelt so greatly a few years later had been, in turn, inspired and nurtured by his own early work.

It is not surprising, then, that Mahan and Roosevelt saw eye to eye in their view of history, and were well acquainted both professionally and personally. By the spring of 1897, as the new assistant secretary of the Navy took office, he had long since digested the sea power philosophy. At that moment a new and different theory of history was uppermost in Roosevelt's mind, but he could not digest this one so easily.

.   .   .

ALMOST EVERY AFTERNOON in May, Roosevelt left his office in the Navy Department and crossed Lafayette Park to the massive four-story Romanesque building that stood on the corner of H and Sixteenth streets. The great pile of dark red bricks was actually two residences; the portion of the structure that opened onto Sixteen Street was the home of John Hay, once secretary to Abraham Lincoln and this moment the newly appointed ambassador to London. The other residence, which faced across H Street and the park to the White House, was the home of Henry Adams, and it was to this that the assistant secretary of the Navy daily directed his footsteps at the luncheon hour. Just before or after his arrival, a carriage would deliver Cabot Lodge from his office or the Senate chamber a mile and a half away.

It was not Henry Adams who hosted these luncheons; he was traveling in Europe at the time. The temporary resident of 1603 H Street was his younger brother Brooks. Like Henry, Brooks Adams was an old friend of both Lodge and Roosevelt. All four were members of the exclusive Porcellian Club of Harvard. Lodge and Adams also had in common their father-in-law, Admiral Davis, the officer who had helped persuade President McKinley to appoint Roosevelt to the Navy post.

Now forty-seven, Brooks Adams had left the practice of law fifteen years earlier to devote himself to the study of history. The fruit of his labors thus far was two books: *The Emancipation of Massachusetts*, and *The Law of Civilization and Decay*. Both were essays in the philosophy of history, and both were examples of Social Darwinism. Like Strong, Mahan, and many other historians of the day, Brooks Adams believed that societies obeyed the law of the survival of the fittest.

In his most recent book, *The Law of Civilization and Decay*, Adams had gone a step further, attempting to apply to history not only the laws of evolutionary biology but the principles of physics as well; he believed human society obeyed

the same inexorable laws that govern the decay of physical energy. Roosevelt
found the result both depressing and unsettling: depressing because Adams
offered a bleak outlook for the future of America and Western civilization;
unsettling because Roosevelt esteemed him too formidable an intellect simply to
dismiss as a crank. He published a review of the work the previous January in
The Forum.

> Few more powerful and more melancholy books have been written than
> Mr. Brooks Adams's "Law of Civilization and Decay." . . .
>   It is a rare thing for a historian to make a distinct contribution to
> the philosophy of history; and this Mr. Adams has done. . . .
>   The life of nations, like any other form of life, is but one manifes-
> tation of energy; and Mr. Adams's decidedly gloomy philosophy of life
> may be gathered from the fact that he places fear and greed as the two
> forms of energy which stand conspicuously predominant; fear in the
> earlier, and greed in the later stages of evolution from barbarism to
> civilization.

According to Adams, mankind progressed through the accumulation and
concentration of wealth. The early stages of this development were marked by
a certain predominant type of human being; Adams called him the Imaginative
Man. Typified by the soldier and the artist, the Imaginative Man was characterized by fear of a priesthood, and so society was ruled by the Church. As time
passed and wealth became concentrated, this type was gradually supplanted by
Economic Man—the man of industry, trade, and capital. Now greed ruled and
two subtypes emerged: "the usurer in his most formidable aspect, and the peasant
whose nervous system is best adapted to thrive on scanty nutriment."

Plutocrats and proles, then, were the heirs of progress, and Adams clearly
believed America and Europe had reached that stage. Roosevelt continued:

> These two very unattractive types are in his belief the inevitable final
> products of all civilization, as civilization has hitherto been developed;
> and when they have once been produced there follows either a station-
> ary period, during which the whole body politic gradually ossifies and
> atrophies, or else a period of utter disintegration.
>   This is not a pleasant theory.

Roosevelt found it an appalling theory. Yet, as he looked around, he wondered if it might not be true. America was at the height of the Gilded Age. It
was, to a great extent, controlled by coarse, self-made millionaires and other
money men who counted business and commercial success above all else—even,
Roosevelt believed, national honor and "manliness." It was these people who had
been too timid to fight the British over Venezuela, they who were too stingy to
give the country the navy he and Captain Mahan believed was needed. Had
Brooks Adams's Economic Man appeared on the American scene? Was the
whole body politic now to ossify and atrophy according to Adams's formula? Was
a period of utter disintegration at hand?

That there is grave reason for some of Mr. Adams's melancholy forebodings, no serious student of the times, no sociologist or reformer, and no practical politician who is interested in more than momentary success would deny. . . . There is a certain softness of fibre in civilized nations which, if it were to prove progressive, might mean the development of a cultured and refined people quite unable to hold its own in those conflicts through which alone any great race can ultimately march to victory. . . .

With his scorn of what is ignoble and base in our development, his impatient contempt of our deification of the stock market, the trading counter, and factory, all generous souls must agree. When we see prominent men deprecating the assertion of national honor because it "has a bad effect upon business," or because it "impairs the value of securities"; . . . it is no wonder that a man who has in him the stuff of ancestors who helped found our government, and helped to bring it safely through the civil war, should think blackly of the future.

But the most disturbing element in Adams's theory was this:

Mr. Adams does not believe that any individual or group of individuals can influence the destiny of a race for good or evil. All of us admit that it is very hard by individual effort thus to make any alteration in destiny, but we do not think it is impossible.

This was the crux of the matter. Theodore Roosevelt believed that history is made by heroes. It was not just a matter of intellectual conviction, or even faith; heroism was his vocation. He tried mightily to reject Adams and his work, confiding to a friend:

I would have written my review very much more brutally than I did, but really I think the trouble is largely that his mind is a little unhinged. All his thoughts show extraordinary intellectual and literary dishonesty; but I don't think this is due to moral shortcomings. I think it really is the fact that he isn't quiet straight in his head. For Heaven's sake don't quote this, as I am very fond of the family.

But, he added,

It certainly is extraordinary that just at this time there seems to be a gradual failure of vitality in the qualities, whatever they may be that make men fight well. . . . I have a very uneasy feeling that this may mean some permanent deterioration.

Try as he might, Roosevelt could not convince himself that Brooks Adams was simply the eccentric sport of an illustrious American family. Every afternoon in May he returned with Lodge to the house on H Street and listened to the gloomy philosopher. What did they talk of, those three historians, as they sat round the luncheon table and looked across the park at the White House where

William McKinley, crony of the Midwest money men, was enthroned?

A year before, Adams and Roosevelt had corresponded when the latter was still in New York. Adams told him:

> I have watched your career with deep interest. . . . You are an adventurer and you have but one thing to sell—your sword. You can take your wages like Nelson and Clive, and fight where you are sent, just as every soldier must in a commercial age, or you can lie and rot. Capital will not employ you if you have a conscience, a heart, patriotism, honesty or self-respect. . . .
>
> In this world we must all live if we can—what is hardest is to be so made that you cannot sell. If you can sell, do. If you don't, others will. The world will be no better and you much the worse.

And now Roosevelt, having soothed McKinley's fears of his bellicosity, had won himself a senior position in the administration. Brooks Adams must have believed the young man had taken his advice and sold out to the money men. And Roosevelt may have reflected in his heart of hearts that, like Adams's *Civilization and Decay*, the belief was not without some supporting evidence.

.   .   .

ON JUNE 2 Roosevelt was at the Naval War College in Newport, Rhode Island, to deliver a speech to the student body and faculty. The speech was intended for public consumption and was a plea for a bigger and better Navy. Roosevelt took as his text George Washington's maxim, "To be prepared for war is the most effectual means to promote peace," and developed the theme along the familiar lines time-honored by proponents of increased military budgets—strength deters aggression. But the tone of the speech was so bellicose and bloody-minded it must have startled the professional naval officers in the audience.

> All the great masterful races have been fighting races; and the minute that a race loses the hard fighting virtues, then . . . it has lost its proud right to stand as the equal of the best. . . .
>
> No triumph of peace is quite so great as the supreme triumphs of war . . . It may be that at some time in the dim future of the race the need for war will vanish; but that time is yet ages distant. . . .
>
> Diplomacy is utterly useless when there is no force behind it; the diplomat is the servant, not the master of the soldier. . . .
>
> . . . There are higher things in this life than the soft and easy enjoyment of material comfort. It is through strife, or the readiness for strife, that a nation must win greatness. We ask for a great navy partly because we feel that no national life is worth having if the nation is not willing, when the need shall arise, to stake everything on the supreme arbitrament of war, and to pour out its blood, its treasure, and its tears like water, rather than submit to the loss of honor and renown.

It was a paen to the god of war. It was also a reply to Brooks Adams and his "melancholy forebodings." And it was a rebuke to that small, dismaying voice within himself that whispered, "Brooks Adams may be right."

.   .   .

THE NAVAL WAR COLLEGE was established on Coaster's Harbor Island at Newport in 1884 in a building that had formerly been the city poorhouse. These modest premises contrasted to the grand ambition of the founder, Admiral Stephen B. Luce, whose objective was "to teach officers the science of their own profession—the science of war." There were, he observed, "certain fundamental principles underlying a military operation which it were well to look into; principles of general application whether the operations were conducted on land or sea."

Sea warfare was changing. Lessons learned in the great naval battles of the past were not easily applied to present operations and future war plans. Since the first ironclads met in battle off Hampton Roads in 1862, the rapid progress of naval technology changed the rules of the game at an accelerating rate. Steam-driven warships swiftly crossed great stretches of ocean independent of the wind. Big, breech-loading guns fired with a range, a rapidity, and an accuracy unknown a generation earlier. Steel armor sheathing protected ships and crews from all but the mightiest blows. Small, swift torpedo boats raced into battle at speeds in excess of twenty knots to loose "automobile fish torpedos" that could sink massive battleships.

Every great industrial nation had such weapons in their naval inventories, but they had rarely been used in battle. In 1866 the Austrian and Italian fleets met in the Adriatic to fight the Battle of Lissa; it lasted only ninety minutes, but it was the first fleet action between ironclads in history. More recently, in 1894, twelve Japanese cruisers attacked a Chinese fleet of two battleships and ten cruisers at the Battle of the Yalu.

Tacticians from the world's navies studied such actions minutely, but they offered a very limited fund of experience. To supplement the lessons of real battles, naval theorists and planners turned to imaginary ones. They resorted to a device that had been used for centuries in the study of land warfare—the war game. Commanders gathered around long, broad tables at the Naval War College and moved miniature fleets across painted oceans. The object of the game was to answer a question that began, What if . . . ?

What if the United States went to war with Spain?

The question was first asked in 1894, months before Gómez and Martí landed in Oriente Province. It was then still a purely hypothetical and academic problem. One student, Lieutenant Commander Charles J. Train, worked out a war plan to meet the situation.

The war would be fought in the Caribbean, he said, and to whichever side established control of those waters would go victory. Most of the Spanish Navy would be located at Cádiz, he assumed, and would have to cross the Atlantic. Meanwhile the U.S. Navy would blockade the major ports of Cuba, seizing some to use as coaling stations. Train foresaw a major engagement between the Spanish fleet—its coal depleted by the long transatlantic voyage—and the fresh American fleet and estimated the advantage was with the latter.

The following year—Gómez had begun his hit-and-run attacks in the eastern provinces but had not yet undertaken his major move westward—the Naval War College again considered the problem of a Spanish war. The new scenario differed from Lieutenant Commander Train's plan in an important respect: it proposed spreading the war beyond the Caribbean by attacking Spain's possessions in the Pacific. This might divert some of the Spanish Navy away from the Caribbean, which continued to be the center of the war planners' interest.

The planners estimated that Spain would require thirty days to send any substantial reinforcements to Cuba, and during that period the United States would land an invasion force of some 280,000 men on the northwest coast of the island and prepare to seize Havana. The eastern half of Cuba would be left to the insurgents. The objective would be to liberate Cuba from Spain and obtain from the newly independent Cuban republic a naval station on the Isle of Pines off the south coast. The planners noted that "the strategic relation of Cuba to the Gulf of Mexico is so close and intimate that the value of that island to the United States in a military and naval way is invaluable."

The next year a war with Spain was again considered at the college. By this time—1896—Weyler's *reconcentrado* program was burying the first of its victims and Spanish–American relations had begun a real deterioration. The Office of Naval Intelligence sent Lieutenant William W. Kimball to serve as staff intelligence officer at the college during the war gaming exercises. On June 1 Kimball authored a document containing the latest strategic ideas on the plans for a Spanish war.

According to the Kimball plan, the United States would fight entirely on the sea, leaving a land war in Cuba to the insurgents. This would permit "the establishment of the Cuban Republic through the efforts of its own citizens within its own borders, aided only by the exteriorly applied sea power of the United States, instead of a conquest and invasion of Spanish territory by an organized army of invasion from this country." Kimball cited the "diplomatic or sentimental" advantage of this course, which he expected to benefit postwar Cuban–American relations.

As in the earlier plans, the principal theater of operations would be the Caribbean, but Kimball proposed two supplementary campaigns. A naval squadron would be sent to Spanish waters to harass commerce, raid coastal cities, and keep the Spanish Navy tied down at home. The U.S. Asiatic Squadron would capture and hold Manila as a bargaining chip to be used in negotiating peace after Cuba was liberated.

By the end of 1896 the question of war with Spain was of more than theoretical concern. The Kimball plan, as well as competing Spanish war plans authored by War College president Captain Henry C. Taylor and his faculty, was evaluated by an ad hoc Navy Department board that produced its own version in December. The board compiled yet another edition of the war plan early in 1897, and it was officially adopted on June 30.

The official plan for a Spanish war was a synthesis of the earlier papers. It called for a blockade of Cuba. At the same time the Asiatic Squadron would attack and try to capture Manila. During the thirty days the planners estimated the Spanish would require to send reinforcements to the Caribbean, a force of thirty thousand men would be assembled in Tampa for invasions of Cuba and Puerto Rico. The Cuban landings would be in the northwest part of the island, where the invasion force would be assembled for an assault on Havana. The Cuban insurgents in the eastern provinces would be furnished with supplies of arms and materiel to step up their harassment of the Spanish forces.

As 1897 wore on, further refinements and variations of the war plan were considered, but the essentials remained unchanged. In the event of war, Cuba would be blockaded, Manila captured, and an invasion of Cuba and Puerto Rico launched from Tampa before Spanish reinforcements could reach the Caribbean. The Spanish war plan was in place.

.   .   .

THERE WAS NO MORE AVID reader of the Navy's war plan papers than the assistant secretary. Roosevelt was consumed by the geopolitics of the day. In May he told his colleague Captain Mahan:

> I suppose I need not tell you that as regards Hawaii I take your views absolutely, as indeed I do on foreign policy generally. If I had my way we would annex those islands tomorrow. . . . I believe we should build the Nicaraguan canal at once . . . I am fully alive to the danger from Japan, and I know that it is idle to rely on any sentimental good will towards us.
>   . . . But there are big problems in the West Indies also. Until we definitely turn Spain out of those islands (and if I had my way that would be done tomorrow), we will always be menaced by trouble there.
> . . . by turning Spain out [we] should serve notice that no strong European power, and especially not Germany, should be allowed to gain a foothold by supplanting some weak European power. I do not fear England; Canada, is a hostage for her good behavior but I do fear some of the other powers.

Japan, a rapidly growing naval power in the Pacific, was casting covetous glances at the Hawaiian Islands, which the United States was on the point of annexing. But Roosevelt's bête noire was Germany. "At the moment Japan is a more dangerous opponent than Spain," he wrote a colleague in August, "but I entirely agree with you that Germany is the Power with which we may very possibly have ultimately to come into hostile contact."

Roosevelt's phobia was not rooted in personal animosity toward Germans. He told his English friend Cecil Arthur Spring-Rice that he advocated

> keeping our Navy at a pitch that will enable us to interfere promptly if Germany ventures to touch a foot of American [i.e., Latin American] soil. . . . I am absolutely sure that it is the proper course to follow, and

I should adopt it without in the least feeling that the Germans who advocated German colonial expansion were doing anything save what was right and proper from the standpoint of their people. . . . We are all treading the same path.

Theodore Roosevelt and Kaiser Wilhelm were kindred spirits indeed. The kaiser shared Roosevelt's admiration for Captain Mahan's theories.

"I am just now not reading but devouring Captain Mahan's book and am trying to learn it by heart," the kaiser told a friend in 1894. "It is a first-class book and classical in all points. It is on board all my ships and constantly quoted by my Captains and officers." He invited Mahan, who was then traveling in Europe, to dine with him aboard his yacht the *Hohenzollern* and was mightily impressed by the American and his sea power theory.

As Mahan himself had pointed out much earlier, his theory applied to Germany equally well as it did to the United States. Like America, Germany was a growing industrial nation whose capacity to produce exceeded her capacity to consume, and so her survival seemed to depend on foreign markets. And like America, Germany had few overseas colonies to service the far-flung naval force Mahan deemed essential to the protection of commerce. German longing for new colonies was made more acute by her burgeoning population, which could no longer be contained within her European borders; vast numbers of Germans had been forced to emigrate to the United States in search of land and *lebensraum.* But the most promising areas in which to search for colonies were Latin America and the Pacific, the two regions Americans like Mahan and Roosevelt considered special American spheres of influence. And there was also the Monroe Doctrine, of course.

A German legislator, speaking in the Reichstag in favor of a bill to increase the size of the navy, observed:

> The United States . . . undoubtedly wishes to protect itself against our exports, but matters are coming to such a pass that other American republics are joining the United States in order to form a *Zollverein* [union].
> . . . European states will in the coming century be obliged to cooperate in order to support each other in the struggle for existence with America. Germany . . . must take care that when the hour comes she is in a position to take her part.

To Roosevelt, an armed struggle with Germany seemed likely to take place much sooner than the next century. He told Secretary Long, "Germany shows a tendency to stretch out for colonial possessions which may at any moment cause a conflict with us."

·　　·　　·

ON AUGUST 2 Navy Secretary Long fled the sweltering Washington summer for the cooler weather of his native Massachusetts, leaving Roosevelt in the capacity of acting secretary of the Navy. Nothing could have pleased the younger man more. "I am having immense fun running the Navy," he told a friend. On August 26 he wrote to Long, telling him, "Now, stay there just exactly as long as you want to. There isn't any reason you should be here before the 1st of October, unless something unexpected turns up. Everything is running quietly now, and there is nothing of importance on hand . . . and September is sometimes not a pleasant month in Washington." Long took Roosevelt's advice and extended his vacation.

On September 14 President McKinley invited the acting secretary for a carriage ride. Roosevelt was flattered and delighted with the opportunity to present some of his thoughts to the top man.

Cuba and Hawaii were on the president's mind. He said there might be trouble with Spain or Japan, although he hoped to avoid it.

The Navy Department ought to be given some warning if trouble was about to develop, Roosevelt answered. It was no good keeping the fleet at full readiness all the time. Ships and men were like horses; if you kept them ready minute after minute for twenty-four hours, they wouldn't be worth much when they were needed. But if there was to be a war, he added, he would guarantee the Navy would be in the best shape possible.

Of course, Roosevelt added, he did not intend to sit out a war in Washington; if there were to be one, he would insist on seeing action. What would Mrs. Roosevelt think of that, the president asked. Roosevelt replied that, in this one matter, he would not consult his wife, or even the president.

McKinley laughed. Very well, he said. He thought he could guarantee Roosevelt the chance to see some action if there was a war.

Two days later Roosevelt was invited to dinner at the White House, and the following week he took another carriage ride with the president. Roosevelt took the opportunity to discuss the Navy's Spanish war plans. He recalled the discussion in a letter to Cabot Lodge:

> I gave him a paper showing exactly where all our ships are, and I also sketched in outline what I thought ought to be done if things looked menacing about Spain, urging the necessity of taking an immediate and prompt initiative if we wished to avoid the chance of some serious trouble, and of the Japs chipping in. If we get Walker* with our main fleet on the Cuban coast within forty-eight hours after war is declared —which we can readily do if just before the declaration we gather the entire fleet at Key West; and if we put four big, fast, heavily armed cruisers under, say, [Captain Robley D.] Evans, as a flying squadron to harass the coast of Spain until some of the battleships are able to leave Cuba and go there, and if at the same time we throw, as quickly as possible, an expeditionary force into Cuba, I doubt if the war would last six weeks so far as the active phase of it was concerned. Meanwhile, our Asiatic Squadron should blockade, and if possible take, Manila.

---

*Roosevelt may have meant Rear Admiral John Grimes Walker. However, Walker had retired in March. Possibly Roosevelt was actually thinking of the officer then in command of the North Atlantic Squadron, Rear Admiral Montgomery Sicard.

As Roosevelt rehearsed the Spanish war plans for the president, he was aware that the critical post of commander of the Asiatic Squadron was soon to be vacant. Whoever the new commander was to be, he would find himself in a uniquely demanding situation in the event of war.

Telegraphic communication with the Far East was slow. While orders could be sent to the naval stations along the Atlantic coast or in Florida in a matter of minutes, or at most an hour or so, a cable might take up to a day or longer to reach the Asiatic Squadron at Yokohama or Hong Kong. Whoever was to be in command there, he would have to be a man of extraordinary judgement and responsibility, ready and able to act on his own initiative, if necessary, should orders from Washington be delayed or interrupted.

A week after his carriage ride with McKinley, Roosevelt intercepted a letter Senator William E. Chandler of New Hampshire sent to Secretary Long recommending Commodore John A. Howell for the Asiatic command. Roosevelt was appalled by the idea. He immediately wrote to Senator Chandler and tried to talk him out of it:

> Before you commit yourself definitely to Commodore Howell I wish very much you would let me have a chance to talk with you. I have seen a good deal of him . . . He is an honorable man . . . but I have rarely met one who strikes me as less fit for a responsible position. To take a definite case I hardly know a man of high rank in the Navy whom I should be more reluctant to see entrusted with a squadron or fleet under peculiar circumstances, such as actual or possible hostilities with Spain. He is irresolute; and he is extremely afraid of responsibility.

But Roosevelt failed to talk the senator out of the idea. Chandler had himself served a tour as secretary of the Navy during the Arthur administration and was not willing to subordinate his own judgement in the matter to that of the young assistant secretary.

Roosevelt had his own candidate for the Asiatic command—Commodore George Dewey. The fifty-nine-year-old Civil War veteran seemed the ideal man for the job, as Roosevelt recalled in his *Autobiography:*

> I was already watching him, for I had been struck by an incident in his past career. It was at a time when there was a threat of trouble with Chile. Dewey was off the Argentine, and was told to get ready to move to the other coast of South America. If the move became necessary, he would have to have coal, and yet if he did not make the move the coal would not be needed. In such a case a man afraid of responsibility always acts rigidly by the regulations and communicates with the Department at home to get authority for everything he does; and therefore he usually accomplishes nothing whatever, but is able to satisfy all individuals with red-tape minds by triumphantly pointing out his compliance with the regulations. In a crisis, the man worth his salt is the man who meets the needs of the situation in whatever way is necessary. Dewey purchased the coal and was ready to move at once if need arose.

This was Roosevelt's own style, and he decided to meet the needs of this situation in a way that suddenly had become necessary. He sent for Dewey, explained the problem, and asked if he knew any member of the Senate who might champion his own candidacy. To Roosevelt's satisfaction, Dewey answered that he was acquainted with Senator Redfield Proctor of Vermont, a Republican, a good friend of the president and a man of expansionist disposition. Roosevelt suggested that Dewey seek Proctor's help. Dewey saw Proctor, Proctor visited McKinley, and when Secretary Long returned from his vacation the next morning, he found a memorandum from the president on his desk suggesting Commodore George Dewey for the Asiatic command. As added insurance of the success of his machinations, Roosevelt saw to it that Senator Chandler's nomination of Commodore Howell was not seen by Long until after he had acted on McKinley's recommendation and appointed Dewey.

Secretary Long's feathers were a little ruffled by the Roosevelt–Dewey subterfuge, but this seemed to Roosevelt a small price. The critical Asiatic Squadron was now in the hands of a self-starter who could be relied on to act on his own initiative in the event of a Spanish war.

·   ·   ·

ON SEPTEMBER 13 the new American minister to Spain presented his credentials in San Sebastian. He was General Stewart L. Woodford, sixty-two-year-old Civil War commander, former congressman, and former lieutenant governor of New York. Woodford had departed for his post in mid-July, stopping en route in London and Paris to consult with the American ambassadors to England, France, and Germany regarding their estimates of European response to such eventualities as American recognition of Cuban belligerency or annexation of Cuba. He had reported back to McKinley that there was little real European interest in the Cuban situation. While in London he received the news of Prime Minister Cánovas's assassination, and he delayed the final leg of his trip to give the Spanish government time to sort itself out. As of his arrival a new ministry was yet to be appointed, and Carlos O'Donnell continued in the post of foreign minister. At 5 P.M. on the eighteenth, Woodford met with O'Donnell.

During their three-hour meeting, Woodford made an oral presentation of his instructions. The message was a familiar one: American patience was nearly exhausted; Spain must resolve the Cuban problem very soon. The United States asked the Spanish government to give "before the first of November next, such assurance as would satisfy the United States that early and certain peace can be promptly secured, and that otherwise the United States must consider itself free to take such steps as its government should deem necessary to procure this result, with due regard to our interests and the general tranquility.' Once again, the United States offered her good offices to help resolve the crisis. Five days later Woodford presented O'Donnell with a formal note to the same effect.

The events of the past year had made O'Donnell much more receptive to the idea of using America's good offices, and he conveyed Woodford's message to the cabinet in terms suggesting the proposal might be given serious consideration. Before any action could be taken, however, the new ministry of Prime Minister Sagasta was appointed, and once again the American offer was politely declined.

Sagasta had his own formula for Cuban peace—fire General Weyler and establish political autonomy on the island. On October 6 he recalled Weyler, replacing him with the more moderate General Blanco. Blanco arrived in Havana on October 31. The same day, Weyler departed for Spain aboard the mail steamer *Montserrat.* He told a group of *peninsulares* (the militant, Spanish-born loyalists) who had come to see him off, "I had expected my release from the time of the death of Señor Cánovas, not believing that any political leader would be strong enough to sustain me when the United States and the rebels were together constantly demanding that Spain should come to a settlement." When he arrived in Barcelona a few days later he was mobbed by sympathetic supporters. His popularity was suddenly at a peak, and dissidents from both ends of the political spectrum rallied to him. Prime Minister Sagasta realized too late that Valeriano Weyler in Spain would be much more of a problem than ever he had been in Cuba.

.   .   .

EVER SINCE he had inherited the German throne nine years earlier, at the age of twenty-nine, Wilhelm II had thoroughly enjoyed being the kaiser. He was a volatile, hyperactive personality, with powerful enthusiasms for diplomacy and warfare, two activities he seemed to regard as one. He loved to meddle in the details of military and foreign affairs that his generals and ministers might have wished were left to their more sober deliberations. His sudden enthusiasms in such matters could have sent the German ship of state on a zany and often dangerous course but for the fact that those who served him had learned that such whims were usually evanescent and that a little studied foot-dragging often permitted prudent policy to outlast the kaiser's attention span.

On September 28 the kaiser read a dispatch from the German ambassador to Madrid reporting on the arrival of General Woodford and predicting that the American would soon deliver to Spain an ultimatum regarding Cuba with which the Spanish government would have to comply. Wilhelm was outraged by "the insolence of the Yankee, who will be secretly supported by John Bull," and he scribbled in the margin of the dispatch instructions to the new foreign minister, Bernhard von Bülow:

> I believe it is now high time that we other monarchs . . . agree *jointly* to offer our help to the Queen in case the American-British Society for International Theft and Warmongering looks as if it seriously intends to snatch Cuba from Spain. A common note which all of us Continentals sent to Uncle Sam and John Bull with the statement that we would mutually stand together and not allow Cuba to be stolen from H[er] M[ajesty] could not fail to have . . . effect. . . . Feeling in this connection among the great monarchs should be tested at once and reported to me.

Von Bülow replied to the kaiser that he would take the necessary steps immediately but cautioned that the United States provided a rich market for German exports. In carrying out the instructions, he said, he assumed he should "endeavor to prevent England and France from using a German action in behalf of Spain in order to embroil us in quarrels with America from which they themselves abstain or at our expense secure economic advantages."

Von Bülow proposed that Austria—the country of María Cristina's birth—take the lead in encouraging the Spanish queen regent to appeal to France, Russia, and Britain in the matter. Germany would thus be spared the exposed position at the head of the parade. After obtaining the kaiser's consent to this, von Bülow instructed the German chargé d'affaires in Vienna that "Germany cannot for practical reasons anticipate the Western powers in taking a positive stand on the Cuban question, though she will be ready to give the most earnest consideration to any appropriate proposals which come to us from London or Paris." Thus the kaiser's whim to meddle in the Spanish–American situation was effectively sidetracked for the moment.

If Wilhelm's appetite for foreign adventures went unsated by von Bülow's artifice, it remained so for only a few weeks. On October 31 the German High Command received a report from Hankow, China, that the officers and men of a German warship had been "insulted" by a mob of Chinese. The kaiser had long been eager for a coaling station in China, but the area was considered by Wilhelm's cousin, Czar Nicholas, to be within the Russian sphere of influence. Wilhelm's chief of staff now suggested that "the incident might offer a suitable occasion for more serious negotiations with China and a new approach to Russia." The kaiser agreed and raised the matter with von Bülow, speaking "very indignantly about the flaccid policy of the Foreign Ministry, which had not understood how to exploit the favorable opportunities which had repeatedly presented themselves in recent years."

Before von Bülow could invent an appropriate evasion, a report arrived in Berlin on November 5 that two German missionaries had been murdered in Shantung Province. The kaiser immediately dispatched his Asiatic squadron to the scene, instructing its commander, Admiral Otto von Diedrichs, "I am thoroughly resolved, with full severity and at need with the most brutal regardlessness to show the Chinese at last that the German emperor does not allow himself to be played with; and that it is bad to have him for an enemy." Diedrichs arrived in Kaichow Bay on November 14, landed a force of several hundred Marines, and announced the German seizure of the bay and the province of East Shantung. Four additional companies of Marines arrived two weeks later, bringing the total force to 4,566 men, the largest German military expedition ever sent beyond European waters.

As the world watched the kaiser's land-grab in the Far East, another German incident began to unfold, offering the prospects of an outcome similar to the Kaichow invasion. This one was of considerably greater interest to Washington observers because it was much closer to home and only a few miles from the troubles in Cuba.

On September 20 Emile Lüders, a half-Haitian German national who kept a livery stable in Port-au-Prince, Haiti, became involved in a fray with the local police over the arrest of one of his hostlers. When Lüders was fined and thrown in jail, the German minister, Count Kurt Christoph von Schwerin—by all accounts, a loud-mouthed, overbearing, and generally unpleasant man—intervened, and Lüders was released and deported. Not content with this, von Schwerin demanded the dismissal of the police and the judges involved in the case. The German bypassed the customary channel of the Haitian Foreign Ministry and pursued the Haitian president personally, in the words of one observer, "like a process server." When he failed to obtain satisfaction by this means, he escalated the German demand to include the payment of an indemnity and referred the matter to Berlin.

On November 30 the Haitian government replied to a stiff German note: Haiti was prepared to discuss the merits of the Lüders controversy but objected to Germany deciding the matter and demanding an indemnity without any discussion whatsoever. Moreover, Count von Schwerin was *persona non grata;* any settlement of the Lüders case would have to be negotiated in Berlin by the Haitian minister and the German Foreign Office.

Rumors were abroad in Haiti that a German warship was on its way. Washington watched the situation uneasily and dispatched the cruiser *Marblehead,* which was at Annapolis, to Port-au-Prince to protect American interests.

On December 3, the Haitian minister to Washington, Jacques Nicolas Leger, called at the State Department with a report that two German warships had cleared Kingston, Jamaica, bound for Port-au-Prince. Apprehensions were somewhat eased when it was learned that the ships in question were the *Stein* and the *Charlotte,* school ships manned by German naval cadets. Nonetheless, they were armed ships of the German Navy, and Minister Leger believed they were not on any peaceful mission. The same day, Roosevelt issued orders for a battleship currently on its way to dry dock at Norfolk to be ready to depart for Key West in one week. It was the U.S.S. *Maine.*

It was probably no coincidence that the following day the Navy Department announced that the North Atlantic Squadron was to go on winter maneuvers off the Florida coast, farther south than it had been in some time. For the past three years, since the Cuban revolution began, the fleet had forsaken its regular winter drill ground in the Gulf of Mexico in deference to the sensitive diplomatic situation between the United States and Spain and conducted its winter exercises in the Atlantic off Virginia.

The announcement prompted speculation that something more than routine exercises was planned, because Spanish–American tensions certainly had not eased since the previous winter. But a Navy spokesman insisted,

> They are not to be sent [to southern waters] now for the purpose of making any demonstration, but purely for drills. Heretofore the squadron was sent South every year. We cannot get the best results either from the men or ships while they are kept on our coast North. The weather is treacherous, and often the drills have to be discontinued on account of severe cold weather.

AT DAWN on December 6, the German training ships *Charlotte* and *Stein* anchored off Port-au-Prince. Kapitan-zur-See August Theile, commander of the schoolship fleet, sent a message ashore. On behalf of Kaiser Wilhelm II, he was making the following demands: a twenty thousand-dollar indemnity must be paid to Herr Lüders, and he must be readmitted to Haiti; the government of Haiti must submit a formal apology to the government of Germany; a twenty-one-gun salute must be made to the imperial German colors flying above his ships; there must be a reception at the palace for Count von Schwerin. If the Haitian government failed to haul down the Haitian colors and hoist a white flag over the Palais National, signifying its agreement to all these demands, by 1 F.M., he would sink all Haitian warships in the harbor, destroy the Palais National, and bombard the city.

The Haitian president contacted the American minister, William F. Powell, and urgently inquired whether any help might be expected from the U S Navy. The *Marblehead* was still at sea, steaming south from Annapolis, and Powell, who had for more than a week been warning Washington of an impending German action and begging for warships, was forced to reply that no American aid was available at that moment.

Shortly before 1 P.M. the Haitian colors came down and the white flag was raised. By four o'clock the indemnity had been raised, and shortly thereafter Herr Lüders came ashore to receive it. The twenty-one-gun salute was fired at sunset while the Haitian Navy Band played the German national anthem. That evening a sneering Count von Schwerin attended the reception held in his honor at the Palais National. Minister Powell sent a report of the day's events to Washington, closing with the declaration, "This is the first time in my life I have ever had cause to be ashamed of being an American, or to have to blush for the flag that protects me."

.   .   .

IN BERLIN, Wilhelm commented on the Haitian affair:

"They are a contemptible crowd of Negroes, slightly inoculated with French civilization. My school ships, even though only manned by boys, will teach them manners."

In Port-au-Prince, the Haitian president issued a proclamation to his people. Haiti had yielded to a superior military force. The government had intended to resist to the last, but, "owing to the the lack of promised moral influence," it had been obliged to accept the German ultimatum.

In Paris, the *Revue des deux mondes* offered a theory to explain U.S. docility in the affair. American "designs on Cuba and Spain," the paper said, had precluded antagonizing Germany.

On December 9, the *Marblehead* arrived at Port-au-Prince without incident. The same day, the German armored cruiser *Geier* departed the port of Kiel, bound for the West Indies.

Throughout the United States, newspaper front pages carried side-by-side accounts of the German adventures in China and Haiti. There was a strong impression that the kaiser was on the march in search of new colonies. On the seventeenth Roosevelt remarked in a letter to Lieutenant Kimball, the naval war-planner, concerning the Cuban situation, "I doubt if those Spaniards can really pacify Cuba, and if the insurrection goes on much longer I don't see how we can help interfering. Germany is the power with whom I look forward to serious difficulty.

·   ·   ·

On December 10 the U.S.S. *Maine* cleared Norfolk bound for Key West. In July, Consul General Fitzhugh Lee had urged the government to station an American warship at Havana to protect American lives and property. On October 8, Secretary Long had detached the *Maine* from the North Atlantic Squadron and stationed it at Port Royal, South Carolina—near enough to Cuba to be available there within a day or so if necessary; far enough away from the island to avoid seeming a provocation.

Early in December, Lee received reports of an anti-American plot being fomented by militant *peninsulares* in Matanzas, and he again urged the dispatch of a battleship to Havana. The administration compromised by moving the *Maine* to Key West, ninety miles and about five hours away from Havana. Lee was granted the authority to summon the battleship if he considered it necessary, without submitting his request to Washington. The *Maine*'s captain, Charles Sigsbee, was ordered to proceed immediately to Havana if he received a telegram from Lee containing a prearranged code.

The *Maine* arrived at Key West on December 15. Lee remained uneasy and continued to propose a ship be stationed at Havana. On December 22 he wrote to the State Department:

> A large German national steamer arrived from Hayti a few days ago— one of their training ships. It now floats in the harbor without comment of any sort. Germany is not more at peace than the United States is with Spain. . . . If these vessels [the *Marblehead* and the U.S.S. *Wilmington*, which was now also at Port-au-Prince] are no longer required at Port-au-Prince, they might stop here en route to Key West as it were.

But the administration knew that the Spanish would see a great deal of difference between the visit of a German naval vessel and the visit of an American warship. The *Maine* remained at Key West.

·   ·   ·

On December 23, Roosevelt wrote to Lieutenant Commander Richard Wainwright, the executive officer of the *Maine* and, coincidentally, the former chief intelligence officer who had authored the June 1897 Spanish war plan: "I wish there was a chance that the *Maine* was going to be used against some foreign power; by preference Germany—but I am not particular, and I'd even take Spain if nothing better offered."

The following day he wrote to the adjutant general of the New York National Guard, C. Whitney Tillinghast II. The prospect of seeing some fighting was on his mind: "As I said before, if there is trouble I shall go down in the New York contingent, whether it is to be Cuba, or Canada, or Haiti."

.   .   .

THE MILITARY CLUB OF PALMA on the island of Majorca gave a luncheon in honor of General Weyler on December 4. As Weyler entered the banquet hall the band struck up the Royal Hymn. The general raised his hand signaling the band to stop. In the ensuing silence he proposed a toast to King Alfonso XIII and his mother, the queen regent.

"So long as their majesties are heads of the state," he said, with deliberate ambiguity, "they will be the heads of the country and the army."

During the few weeks since his return from Cuba, Weyler had become a loose gun crashing around the Spanish ship of state. Events had suddenly cata-pulted him into an extraordinarily powerful political position. At the point of his recall by Prime Minister Cánovas, the ultimate success of the *reconcentrado* program in crushing Gómez was very much in doubt; had he remained in Cuba it is likely he would have been held solely responsible for the eventual military failure on the island. But having been recalled by Sagasta, he was completely absolved of any blame. At the same time, that large segment of the Spanish nation that disapproved of the new, milder Cuban policy, saw Weyler as a martyr, a victim of a dishonorable compromise with American meddling in Spanish affairs. The possibility of a military *coup d'état* was real.

Political dissidents of both the left and right hoped to enlist Weyler and ride into power on his coattails. Two generals of republican leanings, Augustín Luque and Paez Jaramillo, were already planning a conspiracy to overthrow the regency, and they hoped Weyler would join them. He declined the invitation, however.

The Carlists also hoped to capitalize on the situation. The exiled pretender, Don Carlos, publicly denounced Weyler's recall, and the leading Carlist ideo-logue, Vasquez de Mella, proclaimed on December 14 that the Carlists were "in substantial agreement" with the general. The Carlists had, in fact, organized an extensive conspiracy throughout the country and believed they could make it work if Weyler would join them. Weyler agreed to meet with Don Carlos to discuss the idea, and the pretender secretly sailed from Ostend aboard the yacht of an English aristocrat for a rendezvous with the general on the high seas off the coast of Majorca. The meeting did not take place, however. Weyler had stipulated an absolutely private meeting with Don Carlos, but the pretender's wife, a strong-willed French woman named Berthe de Rohan, insisted on being present. When the general was advised of this he refused to participate.

Clearly, Weyler was in so strong a position he could dictate any terms he wished with any political faction that wished to court him. He could afford to wait because the situation in Cuba was certain to get worse. Time was on his side.

.   .   .

ON JANUARY 3 Roosevelt assigned seven warships to the upcoming exercises of the North Atlantic Squadron in the Gulf of Mexico: the *New York, Indiana,*

Massachusetts, Iowa, Maine, Texas, the monitor *Terror,* and one additional cruiser. It was the largest and most powerful American fleet to be assembled since the Civil War.

On January 7 the American ambassador to Berlin cabled Washington, "On the Continent there has never been a time, probably, when ill will towards the United States has been so strong as at present." He added that, nevertheless, he did not expect the powers to overcome their differences and form an anti-American coalition.

On January 9, the German warship *Geier* arrived at Port-au-Prince. Unlike the two school ships that had been sent to Haiti to enforce the German demands, the *Geier* was a substantial naval vessel, an armored cruiser of some 1,700 tons and a complement of 160 men, and carrying twelve rapid-fire guns and two torpedo tubes. It had been launched three years earlier as part of the kaiser's new fleet.

The following day Commander Chapman C. Todd, captain of the cruiser *Wilmington* reported from St. Thomas in the Danish West Indies:

> I learn on inquiry from various sources that this port has not been left without a German ship close by during the past four months. There exists here among the people a spirit of unrest, based upon the belief that the national allegiance may shortly be changed.

The general feeling in the Danish colony was that the islands were to come under American domination, Todd reported, but "some of the more intelligent people residing in and near here" believed that Germany intended to acquire the colony. Todd added that "the Commanding Officer of the 'Charlotte' has mentioned to me more than once that Germany was anxious to acquire a coaling station in the West Indies."

The next day Secretary Long ordered the commander of the European Squadron to retain in service those men whose enlistments might be about to expire.

On January 12 Consul General Lee reported to Washington,

> The German Consul General informed me last night that two more of his Government's ships were coming here—one on the 25th and one on the 27th. It occurred to me that if one or two of our ships were cruising about watching for filibusters and should get out of coal and the commanding officer came in here about that time after it or entered the harbor to send some dispatches to the Navy Department or in any other way it might be a good thing.

While the sudden appearance of a German fleet in the Caribbean may have caused alarm in Washington, Lee did not seem disposed to seek a hidden motive in the visit of the warships. Perhaps because of his concern over the immediate situation in Cuba he saw no similarity, no connection, between the recent German adventures in China and Haiti and the forthcoming visit of the German ships to Havana. The German consul's announcement suggested nothing more to him than a pretext for the visit of an American battleship to Havana:

I am sure the majority—great majority—of all classes here would welcome the event with great pleasure and feel better satisfied that life and property would be protected in this city. However I make no request for a ship or ships but mention this matter simply for consideration in connection with pertinent subjects.

.   .   .

"IT WAS A Wednesday morning, the morning of January 12, when the rioting began," Charles M. Pepper, the Havana correspondent of the Washington *Star*, later recalled.

There was a lull during the midday, but in the afternoon the mob rallied. It made little demonstration, and was content with throwing stones and breaking windows. . . . It was known that the authorities had been unravelling several supposed conspiracies, and that at all the recent bull-fights extraordinary precautions had been taken to prevent an outbreak. In Spain the popular uprisings usually begin at the bull ring.

Prime Minister Sagasta's compromise policy of political autonomy for Cuba had gone into effect on the first of the year. For nearly two weeks resentment had simmered among the *peninsulares*. The Spanish-born loyalists saw the move as a surrender to the insurgents and American meddling. Today, feelings had finally boiled over.

Shops were closed, doors locked and shutters drawn. The mob chanted, "Long live Weyler! Down with Autonomy! Death to Blanco [the new governor general]!" At 6 P.M. Captain Sigsbee at Key West received a telegram from Consul General Lee containing the words "two dollars," the preestablished code meaning the *Maine* was to get ready to depart for Havana immediately. Fires were spread to build up steam pressure in the battleship's boilers. To avoid giving public evidence of the preparations, Sigsbee continued with his planned attendance at a dance ashore in the company of a party of ship's officers. If a second telegram from Lee was received, and if it contained the second code phrase summoning the battleship, one of the ship's guns was to be fired to signal the officers and crew to return. Sigbee listened expectantly throughout the evening, but the gun was not fired.

There was more rioting during the night and the next day. Pepper recalls:

During the days of rioting it was observed that the rioters seemed to be incited by persons not taking part, and the presence of the fraternal spirit between them and the military forces was also manifest.

It was a political demonstration of the Army against autonomy, and it served its purpose. Three or four score of the officers who participated in the rioting were placed under military arrest, but they were never punished. Not one was court-martialed. Pretexts were found for releasing them within a few days of their arrest, and they were returned to their commands.

Consul General Lee told the New York *Herald*, "If American interests are further imperiled, warships will be called down for protection."

.   .   .

THE HEIGHTENED WAR FEVER drove Roosevelt into a frenzy of activity. On January 14 he presented Secretary Long with a memorandum of several thousand words on the subject of naval preparedness, detailing the steps he considered essential to ready the fleet.

> I feel, sir, that I ought to bring to your attention the very serious consequences to the Government as a whole, and especially to the Navy Department (upon which would be visited the national indignation for any check, no matter how little the Department was really responsible for the check) if we should drift into a war with Spain and suddenly find ourselves obliged to begin it without preparation, instead of having at least a month's warning, during which we could actively prepare to strike. In addition to this, when the blow has been determined upon we should defer delivering it until we have had at least three weeks or a month in which to make ready. The saving in life, money, and reputation by such a course will be very great.
>   Certain things should be done at once if there is any reasonable chance of trouble with Spain during the next six months.

The fleet was scattered, Roosevelt said. It must be concentrated at Key West to be ready for a Cuban blockade. Commodore Dewey seemed to have sufficient warships to "overmaster" the Spanish fleet in the Philippines, but the margin of superiority was uncomfortably thin; three more warships should be sent to join the Asiatic Squadron. A flying squadron should be ready to steam to Spanish waters to harass the Spanish fleet and keep it from crossing the Atlantic and threatening the Eastern seaboard. There was a shortage of ammunition; steps should be taken immediately to acquire additional supplies. The fleet was under-manned; the Navy should draw upon the naval militia, the Revenue Marine, and the Coast Survey for additional seamen.

For page after page, Roosevelt spelled out his urgent recipe for readiness.

> Some of the steps above advised should be taken at once if there is so much as a reasonable chance of war with Spain. The others it is not necessary to take now, but they should be taken well in advance of any declaration of war. In short, when the war comes it should come finally on our own initiative, and after we had had time to prepare. If we drift into it, if we do not prepare in advance, and suddenly have to go into hostilities without taking the necessary steps beforehand, we may have

to encounter one or two bitter humiliations, and we shall certainly be forced to spend the first three or four most important weeks not in striking, but in making those preparations to strike which we should have made long before.

Roosevelt was also making his own personal preparations for war. The day before he composed his lengthy memo for Secretary Long, he wrote a letter to General Tillinghast of the New York National Guard and another to Colonel Francis Greene, one of the guard's commanders. Both letters were on the same subject—Roosevelt obtaining a commission as major or lieutenant colonel and going along with the New York Guard to see action in Cuba.

·   ·   ·

JANUARY 15 was a Sunday. In Madrid Ambassador Woodford presented the young ladies of his family to the queen regent. As the reception ended, her majesty asked the American diplomat to stay for a talk.

The queen regent said she understood that Woodford was a personal friend of President McKinley. He confirmed that he was. She then asked to speak in confidence. She said she had done all that McKinley had asked regarding Cuba that it was in her power to do, referring to the recall of Weyler and the autonomy policy. Woodford replied candidly:

> The mutiny in Havana does not look as if Marshal Blanco can control his own army. If he cannot control his own army, how can he hope to crush the rebels? And besides, I hear every day of mutinies and conspiracies that are threatened here in Madrid.

In his confidential report of the conversation to McKinley, Woodford recalled,

> She drew herself up and looked every inch a queen as she said:
> "I will crush any conspiracy in Spain. Upon this you may rely. I believe that my government will keep peace in Havana and reduce Army officers to obedience. I want your President to keep America from helping the rebellion until the new plan of autonomy has had a fair chance."

The following day, Segismundo Moret, the new Spanish minister for colonies, called on Woodford at his residence. Woodford reported:

> I asked him if he believed that Marshal Blanco could restore complete order in Havana and Moret replied that order would be promptly and finally re-established. I then asked him what truth there was in the rumors of mutinies and conspiracies here in Spain. He replied that Weyler, Romero Robledo [a dissident politician], the ultra Conservatives, the Carlists, the Socialists and the Republicans were combining

to demand that the present Cortes should not be dissolved; that the Liberal Ministry should be dismissed; autonomy rescinded; and Weyler sent back to Cuba. But that he had no present fear that any such conspiracy could succeed.

Woodford warned that, if Weyler were sent back, the United States would intervene. Moret dismissed the possibility. "We shall crush Weyler and his fellow conspirators," he said.

Woodford closed his report of the meeting with an observation: "When it becomes clear that [Blanco] cannot succeed or that the United States must intervene, the Queen will have to chose between losing her throne or losing Cuba at the risk of war with us."

That same day, the Spanish ambassador to Washington, Enrique Dupuy de Lôme, received the city editor of the New York *Herald*. Dupuy de Lôme regarded Mr. William C. Reick as "a person of importance" in Washington and someone "generally well informed." Reick, despite his modest title, actually ran the newspaper for its expatriate owner, James Gordon Bennett, Jr. Moreover, he was influential in New York Republican circles and a confidant of the McKinley administration. Dupuy de Lôme was not disposed to consider the visit the routine call of a New York journalist.

Reick seemed to have come to the Spanish Embassy at the unofficial behest of President McKinley to sound out the ambassador on a particularly sensitive proprosal—the sending of an American ship to Havana. He told Dupuy de Lôme that McKinley was very concerned over the recent anti-autonomy rioting in Havana and believed Sagasta's autonomy program was destined to fail. The president feared that more serious disorders would soon take place; if they did, he intended to land troops from warships to protect the American Consulate. Reick asked what the Spanish response would be if that happened.

Dupuy de Lôme answered categorically that Spain would not submit to such an action. After Reick left, he fired off a cable to the Spanish foreign minister in Madrid, reporting the conversation.

> [The conversation] indicates a state of things that would have been impossible a week ago. The danger is that the President or public may be persuaded that a riot in Spain or Cuba could overthrow the Spanish Government and change its policy, in which case [the United States] may believe that it will succeed by a move of force as the shortest way out of the difficulty. Without wishing to alarm, I believe it my duty to state this.

As Dupuy de Lôme's ciphered dispatch was being telegraphed over the Atlantic cable, the North Atlantic Squadron formed at Hampton Roads and headed south toward the Caribbean.

·   ·   ·

ON JANUARY 20 Ambassador Dupuy de Lôme called on Assistant Secretary of State Day. He had received a sharp response from the Spanish foreign minister

to his report of his conversation with Reick: "your excellency will endeavor
. . . to speedily make known there, possibly by conference with Day, in order to
set the matter clear, that the extreme and inadmissable opinions given to your
excellency by the chief of the *Herald* lacks even the pretext of reason."

Dupuy de Lôme reaffirmed to Day his faith in the autonomy policy but
expressed misgivings about the attitude of the United States, which was the only
thing keeping the insurrection alive, he said. A "courageous act of statesmanship"
by President McKinley—i.e., a public denunciation of the rebels and the Cuban
Junta—was necessary if a break was to be averted between Spain and the United
States.

Regarding the American naval activity near Cuba, Dupuy de Lôme said
he was disturbed by newspaper speculation that the United States was preparing for an emergency in the area, rather than simply conducting routine exercises.

Day replied that, if Consul General Lee needed warships, he would have
them. He did not see how Spain could object to the United States exercising its
right to protect the lives and property of its citizens.

Sending naval vessels to Havana would be regarded by Spain as an unfriendly
act and the first step toward intervention, Dupuy de Lôme answered. Landing
American troops anywhere in Cuba would be considered a cause of war. Dupuy
de Lôme asked Day to make sure that message was given to the president.

·   ·   ·

THE NEXT DAY Secretary Long sent a brief note to the president, apparently in
reply to a request from him for information about the German fleet:

> I find upon inquiry that the Office of Naval Intelligence is not informed
> as to the presence of German ships of war in the harbor of Havana.
> To ascertain this, inquiry would have to be made through the State
> Department of their officials on the ground [i.e., the consular officers
> in Havana].

There is no recorded explanation of McKinley's reason for asking about
German ships at Havana at this moment. Two days earlier, William F. Powell,
the American minister at Port-au-Prince, reported to the State Department that
the large German armored cruiser *Geier* was leaving for "other Haitian ports"
with the arrogant Count von Schwerin aboard.

McKinley was, of course, aware of the recent events in China and Haiti. He
may have read the report of the kaiser's desire for a coaling station in the West
Indies. He knew of the recent efforts by Spain to enlist the support of the
European powers against the United States and may have been advised of the
kaiser's disposition toward the Spanish–American difficulties. He certainly had
heard the speculation that Spain might prefer to turn Cuba over to a European
power rather than lose it to America. All of this may have served to put a very
sinister cast on the presence of a formidable German fleet (four warships, including the big armored cruiser *Geier*) in the Caribbean at this moment. On the other

hand, he may have heard and come to share Fitzhugh Lee's view that the friendly and routine visit of a German warship to Havana would be an excellent pretext for an American naval visit there; that if the Spanish permitted a German cruiser to visit, they could hardly object to a U.S. vessel. What seems even more likely is that McKinley had both thoughts in mind when he made his inquiry of Secretary Long.*

The day following Long's note to the president, Assistant Secretary Day sent a ciphered cable to Fitzhugh Lee: "Wire number and character naval vessels other countries now in the port of Havana."

Lee immediately replied:

"None. Two German naval vessels are expected this month."

Day also cabled the American minister at Port-au-Prince for a report on the movements of the German fleet. The next day Powell replied: "I respectfully report to the Department that there are four German war vessels in Haitian waters. Charlotte (school ship) at Jacomel; Stein at Port de Pax; Geier, which returned yesterday, here, and one, name unknown,† at the Cape, reached there Saturday."

Whatever his reasons, the kaiser had assembled a very significant naval force just outside Cuban waters.

Within twenty-four hours of Minister Powell's dispatch, President McKinley ordered the *Maine* to Cuba.

      •   •   •

"GENERALLY SPEAKING, President McKinley did not write letters on important government matters," McKinley's personal secretary recalled many years later. "When occasion arose, members of Congress or others interested were asked to call at the White House, where the matter would be discussed."

Thus there is no detailed record of the process by which McKinley arrived at the decision to send the *Maine* to Havana, so the story must be pieced together from the differing accounts of several persons. There seems no doubt, however, that the decision was made some time on Monday, January 24.

Ambassador Dupuy de Lôme called at the State Department at 10 A.M. and met with Assistant Secretary Day. The purpose of his visit was to reiterate the theme he had struck at their last meeting four days earlier: the president must take a more positive role in supporting the autonomy program. According to Day, the assistant secretary turned the conversation to another subject, informing Dupuy de Lôme that McKinley intended sending American naval vessels on friendly visits to Cuban ports very soon and pointing out that Spain could hardly object, since the two nations were at peace. Day said Dupuy de Lôme quietly

---

*This is exactly the explanation offered by James Rankin Young for both the decision to send the North Atlantic Squadron on winter exercises in the Gulf of Mexico and the sending of the *Maine* to Havana. Young was a Republican congressman from Pennsylvania. He was also the brother of John Russell Young, the librarian of Congress, former confidential agent of the State Department, and a McKinley administration insider likely to be consulted by the president in sensitive foreign policy matters. See James Rankin Young, pp. 46–47.

†Probably the *Gniesenau*, another German school ship.

conceded the point. However, immediately upon his return to the Spanish Embassy, Dupuy de Lôme sent a report to the foreign minister in Madrid recounting the "long and important conference" he'd just had with Day, but making no mention of an American naval visit to Cuba.

After the Spanish ambassador departed, Day went to the White House. The Washington *Evening Star* picks up the story at that point:

> The most significant conference of the day at the White House was that participated in by the President, Secretary Long and Judge Day, assistant Secretary of State. The presence of these men together was sufficient to indicate the discussion of Cuban affairs, and at a phase of more than ordinary interest. Justice McKenna* joined the conference later and these men talked over the situation, while senators and representatives of prominence waited in adjoining rooms. Gen. [Nelson A.] Miles was sent for before the conference was concluded and was present for a short time. His branch of the service has not been largely considered heretofore in connection with the situation in Cuba.

General Miles was the commander-in-chief of the Army. If he was called to join in a discussion of Cuba, the question of the Army's readiness to take part in the Navy's June 1897 Spanish war plan may have been raised.

There are no minutes of the White House meeting. Virtually all that is recorded of it is what Secretary Long confided to his diary that night:

> I have favored, for some time, suggesting to the Spanish Minister here that his government recognize the wisdom of our sending a ship in a friendly way to Havana . . . to exchange courtesies and civilities with the Spanish authorities there, and thus to emphasize the change and the improved condition of things which have resulted from the new Spanish policy. Today the Spanish Minister assented to this view, in conversation with the State Department. Judge Day and I called on the President, and we arranged that the *Maine* should be ordered at once to Havana; notice having been given by the Spanish Minister to his people, and by our Department to our Consul.

Long makes no mention of the presence of General Miles or Justice McKenna at the meeting.†

After the meeting, Day returned to the State Department and cabled

---

*Recently appointed by McKinley to the Supreme Court, Joseph McKenna had been the president's attorney general; his presence suggests that the legal questions of the *Maine*'s visit may have been discussed.

†Long may have written this account without the complete candor one usually expects of diarists. At the close of his January 24, 1898, entry he notes that some newspapers have tried "to discover some hidden meaning" in the sending of the *Maine*, but that what he has written in his diary on the subject "happens to be the truth, the whole truth, and nothing but the truth," which certainly seems an excessive reassurance for someone to offer himself concerning his own veracity. His daughter, Margaret, seems to have felt it was; when she edited the diary for publication in 1956 (214), she truncated this line to, "happens to be the truth."

Fitzhugh Lee at Havana, advising him the *Maine* would be sent "in a day or two."
Next he cabled Ambassador Woodford in Madrid and quoted his cable to Lee:

> Have just cabled Consul-General of the United States at Havana:
>   It is the purpose of this Government to resume friendly naval visits
> at Cuban ports. In that view the *Maine* will call at the port of Havana
> in a day or two. Please arrange for a friendly interchange of calls with
> authorities.
>
> Day
>
> Please advise foreign minister of friendly visit as above indicated.
>
> Day

While Day was informing Lee and Woodford, Secretary Long announced
the visit to the press. According to the New York *Times:*

> Washington, Jan. 24. Orders to the battleship Maine to go to Havana
> were made known about noon to-day at the Navy Department. . . .
> Following the bare news that the Maine was to go to Havana, not at
> once, but as soon as she could be made ready to leave Key West and
> after the announcement of her intended visit could be made at Madrid,
> Secretary Long gave out a statement.

Long's statement denied rumors that had appeared in the press over the
weekend to the effect that the consulate at Havana had come under attack and
that Fitzhugh Lee may have been assassinated. Long also said, "The *Maine* will
go in a day or two." The *Times* continues:

> Late in the afternoon, as if by pre-arrangement, Minister de Lome [sic]
> reappeared at the Department of State and was for an hour or more
> in company with Asst. Sec. Day, during which the statement of Secre-
> tary Long was read to him. He departed, leaving behind him the
> authorized statement that he believed the explanation of the purpose
> of the Maine's visit would be entirely satisfactory to the Madrid govern-
> ment.

What actually was said at the meeting is unclear. According to Day, "I told
him [Dupuy de Lôme] the President had dispatched the *Maine* to Cuba." But
on his return to the Spanish Embassy, Dupuy de Lôme sent this cable to Madrid:
"Since my conference of this morning with Day, the latter went to see the
president and by telephone appointed three o'clock P.M. for me to call. I have
just seen him, and he told me . . . that the president has determined to send the
Maine to Havana as a mark of friendship."
     According to Day's version of events, he told Dupuy de Lôme in the
morning of a planned naval visit, then in the afternoon told him the *Maine* was
actually on her way. But Dupuy de Lôme's cables seem to imply the subject of
naval visits was not discussed in the morning and that only in the afternoon was
he told of McKinley's decision to send the *Maine* (presumably "in a day or two,"
and after receiving Spanish consent). The discrepancy is important because the

evidence suggests that the decision to send the *Maine*, not "in a day or two," but immediately, was suddenly made late in the afternoon, sometime after the second meeting between Day and Dupuy de Lôme.

The *Maine* was, of course, ready to leave for Havana on a few hours notice, as it had been since December 15. In fact, the day before, the battleship had left Key West to join the North Atlantic Squadron's maneuvers in the Gulf. Orders could reach it in a matter of two or three hours via telegraph to the Key West Naval Station and fast torpedo boat across the forty or so nautical miles to the Dry Tortugas, where the fleet was presently exercising. The "day or two" of the administration's midday announcement was the interval calculated to permit Ambassador Woodford in Madrid to advise the Spanish Ministry of the visit and Consul General Lee in Havana to make advance arrangements with the local Spanish authorities for the exchange of formal courtesies after the ship arrived. In view of the tense situation in Havana, this was not only a matter of formal diplomatic etiquette, but simple prudence. In fact, when Lee received Day's cable notifying him of the visit "in a day or so," he immediately replied:

> Advise visit be postponed six or seven days to give last excitement more time to disappear. Will see authorities and let you know the result. Governor General away for two weeks. I should know day and hour of visit.
>
> Lee

Lee's cable arrived at the State Department at 6:15 P.M., possibly after the sailing orders had been sent to the *Maine*, but certainly not too late to send another order canceling them. Instead, Day replied with this message: "*Maine* has been ordered. Will probably arrive at Havana some time tomorrow. Cannot tell hour; possibly early. Cooperate with authorities for her friendly visit. Keep us advised by frequent telegrams."

But this cable did not reach Lee until the *Maine* was already riding at anchor in Havana harbor. The battleship's arrival early in the morning of January 25 came as a complete surprise to both Fitzhugh Lee and the Spanish authorities. The Havana authorities granted the battleship permission to enter the harbor on their own authority: The Foreign Ministry in Madrid had not yet received any notice of the visit for the excellent reason that Day's telegram of the previous day had not yet reached Ambassador Woodford.

It was indeed fortunate that the Spanish authorities, acting in the absence of Governor General Blanco from the city, and without any guidance from Madrid, did not refuse the *Maine* entrance to the harbor, because Captain Sigsbee had been given no orders to cover such a contingency. Indeed, he was unaware that all the arrangements for his arrival had not already been made. "It became known to me afterward," he wrote, "that the *Maine* had not been expected, not even by the United States Consul General." Had he steamed back to Key West, the political repercussions for the McKinley administration would have been awesome. Had he shot his way into the harbor, the Spanish War would have begun, then and there.

.   .   .

THE DECISION to send the *Maine* was made by the McKinley administration sometime during the late morning of January 24, and the ship was obviously to go only after the Spanish government had been informed. But sometime during the afternoon the timetable was abruptly moved up, and the battleship was sent immediately. American lives and property were in no special danger at the moment. Fitzhugh Lee had advised a delay of six or seven days. Governor General Blanco was out of touch in the Cuban countryside, having left matters in the hands of a deputy. Only four days earlier Ambassador Dupuy de Lôme had relayed his government's position that sending an American warship to Havana at the moment would be regarded as an unfriendly act. No one in either Madrid or Havana knew that the ship was actually on her way. And the *Maine*'s captain was proceeding under the mistaken belief that the visit was expected and approved by the Havana authorities.

Short of deliberately attempting to provoke a war, what could have prompted the McKinley administration to such an action? The answer may possibly be found in another cable Fitzhugh Lee sent from Havana earlier in the day, which arrived at the State Department at 4:25 P.M. The telegram concerned several rather routine matters, but ended with this news: "One German vessel in port—two others expected."

.   .   .

THE GERMAN SHIP was the square-rigged training steamer *Gniesenau*. The day after the *Maine*'s arrival, another German school ship, the *Charlotte* (one of the vessels that threatened Port-au-Prince in the Lüders incident), entered the harbor. Routine courtesies were exchanged between Captain Sigsbee and officers from the visiting German ships. The German presence at Havana proved to be entirely innocent. The kaiser appeared to have no immediate plans to intervene in Cuba.

With the arrival of the *Maine* at Havana without incident, a mood of relief swept through the McKinley administration. But no one thought the essential situation had actually improved. War preparations continued. On the twenty-seventh the Navy Department cabled Commodore Dewey at Yokohama, instructing him to hold in service those men of the Asiatic Squadron whose enlistments were due to expire.

.   .   .

THE RECENTLY APPOINTED commander of the Spanish naval squadron based at Cádiz was Rear Admiral Pascual Cervera y Topete, a fifty-nine-year-old nobleman and Spain's foremost sailor, who had served in the Navy since the age of twelve. He was a much decorated veteran of the wars of the past half-century and had been Prime Minister Sagasta's minister of marine—the Spanish equivalent of secretary of the Navy—until he resigned that post when he failed to receive support for his naval reform policies. Now, as war with the United States looked increasingly likely, he considered the relative strengths of the Spanish and American navies, and he was not optimistic. On January 30 he wrote to his cousin:

> To-day we find ourselves again in one of those critical periods which seem to be the beginning of the end . . . The relative military positions of Spain and the United States have grown worse for us, because we are reduced, absolutely penniless, and they are very rich. . . .
> But my purpose is not to accuse, but to explain why we may and must expect a disaster. But as it is necessary to go to the bitter end, and as it would be a crime to say that publicly today, I hold my tongue, and go forth resignedly to face the trials which God may be pleased to send me. I am sure that we will do our duty, for the spirit of the Navy is excellent; but I pray God that the troubles may be arranged without coming to a conflict, which, in any way, I believe would be disastrous to us.

Two weeks later Cervera wrote to the minister of marine requesting intelligence data regarding the American fleet and details of any war plans the Spanish Navy had made.

> If I had information on these matters I could go ahead and study and see what is best to be done, and if the critical day should arrive we could enter without vacillations upon the course we are to follow. This is the more needful for us, as their squadron is three or four times as strong as ours, and besides they count on the alliance of the insurgents in Cuba, which will put them in possession of the splendid Cuban harbors, with the exception of Havana and one or two others, perhaps. The best thing would be to avoid war at any price; but, on the other hand, it is necessary to put an end to the present situation, because this nervous strain can not be borne much longer.

Cervera knew perfectly well that no amount of intelligence data or war planning could offset the essential military imbalance, but he may have hoped the act of compiling this information might bring home to the government the absolute hopelessness of the situation. Still, as a former cabinet minister, he understood the cold equations of Spanish policy and politics: a military defeat would be a blow to national pride, but Spanish honor would remain intact; but the simple expedient of yielding Cuba to the Yankees and the insurgents would be regarded as a monstrous national disgrace. The Sagasta government would fall, and probably the monarchy along with it. It seemed a sacrifice on the altar of national honor might soon be required. Cervera understood that he had been ordained to be the victim.

·   ·   ·

ON FEBRUARY 7 Ambassador Woodford reported a conversation with a Madrid correspondent of the New York *Herald:*

> . . . He tells me today, confidentially, that the Spanish Ministry have decided that they have made all the concessions to the United States

that they can make, without endangering both their own power and the continuance of the present Dynasty; that they will do no more; and will fight if what they have done does not secure our neutrality. He says that he gets this information from a source so high and so reliable that he is not at liberty to print it.

·   ·   ·

ON THE MORNING of February 9, Assistant Secretary Day received two unexpected callers at the State Department. They were Horatio Rubens, the Cuban Junta's legal counsel, and John J. McCook, the prominent New York attorney whose Cuban sympathies cost him the appointment as attorney general in the McKinley administration. They presented Day with a handwritten letter, in Spanish, and bearing the signature of Enrique Dupuy de Lôme, the Spanish ambassador to Washington.

It appeared to be a personal and unofficial letter addressed to Dupuy de Lôme's friend, Don José Canalejas, editor of the Madrid *Heraldo*. From its contents, it seemed to have been written some time in the latter half of the previous December.

In the letter, Dupuy de Lôme implied a cynical disdain for the Cuban autonomy policy and characterized proposed negotiations with the insurgents as "a waste of time." Next he turned to President McKinley's (December 6) address to Congress, in which the president had discussed the Cuban problem:

> Besides the natural and inevitable coarseness with which he repeats all that the press and public opinion of Spain have said of Weyler, it shows once more that McKinley is weak and catering to the rabble and, besides, a low politician who desires to leave a door open to himself and to stand well with the jingos of his party.

The letter had been written by Dupuy de Lôme in Washington and was intended to reach Canalejas in Havana, where the editor happened to be at that time. Somehow it fell into the hands of the Junta instead.

Day's first reaction was to question the authenticity of the document. He called in the second assistant secretary, Alvee Adee, and after some discussion, reluctantly acknowledged that the letter seemed genuine, and the signature seemed to be that of the Spanish ambassador. To remove any last doubt, Day called on Dupuy de Lôme, showed him the letter and asked him if he had written it. The Spaniard quietly confirmed that he had. He told Day he had already cabled his resignation to Madrid. He was not surprised by Day's visit. A facsimile of the letter, together with an English translation, had appeared that morning on the front page of Hearst's New York *Journal* under the headline, "The Worst Insult to the United States in Its History." All the other dailies also carried the text of the letter. By afternoon it was making the front pages of every newspaper in the country.

The waves of editorial indignation that followed release of the letter took no notice of the simple facts of the matter: the letter contained Dupuy de Lôme's personal opinion, expressed privately and confidentially, and its disclosure was the result of theft. Under the pressure of the public outcry, however, President McKinley felt he could do no less than instruct the State Department to demand an official Spanish apology, an act which, in itself, offered some evidence to support Dupuy de Lôme's accusation of weakness. The Spanish government, perhaps reluctant to accentuate its own domestic image of weakness, was slow to apologize for something for which it was not actually responsible. However, on February 14 the foreign minister informed Ambassador Woodford that Spain "with entire sincerity lamented the incident."

The administration quickly accepted the apology and hoped the affair would be forgotten as speedily. In view of the circumstances, Dupuy de Lôme did not wait for the arrival of his replacement, Luís Polo de Bernabe, but set out immediately to return to Spain, leaving the Embassy temporarily without a senior diplomat in residence.

In the event, the Dupuy de Lôme letter was destined to be forgotten much sooner than anyone could have expected. Dupuy de Lôme was in New York on February 16, waiting for a ship to Spain, when he was awakened by reporters in the early hours of the morning and asked for comment.

They informed him that the *Maine* had exploded and sunk in Havana harbor.

CHAPTER FIVE

SIXTY-SIX DAYS

FEBRUARY 16, WEDNESDAY.

THE REGULAR CITY EDITION of the New York *World* was on the streets a little after 3 A.M. carrying the four-column headline, "U.S.S. *Maine* Blown Up in Havana Harbor," over an Associated Press dispatch:

> Havana, February 15—At a quarter of ten o'clock this evening a terrible explosion took place on board the United States battleship *Maine* in Havana harbor. Many were killed and wounded. . . . As yet the cause of the explosion is not apparent. The wounded sailors of the *Maine* are unable to explain it.

But a new note was sounded in the 5 A.M. special edition of the newspaper: "*World* Staff Correspondent Cables It Is Not Known Whether Explosion Occurred on or Under the *Maine*."

Under the *Maine*. In other words, a submerged mine. The *World* had asked the question that was to become paramount in the days and weeks ahead:

Accident or sabotage?

In Washington, the lights burned through the night at the White House. There was no further word from Havana beyond a dispatch from Consul General Lee containing little that had not been in Captain Sigsbee's telegram. At dawn a crowd of silent onlookers watched from Pennsylvania Avenue as the flag over the Executive Mansion was raised, then lowered to half-mast. Shortly after 9 A.M. President McKinley met with Secretary Long. Later that day Long wrote in his diary:

There is an intense difference of opinion as to the cause of the blowing up of the *Maine*. In this, as in everything else, the opinion of the individual is determined by his original bias. If he is a conservative, he is sure that it was an accident; if he is a jingo, he is equally sure that it was by design.

The conservative McKinley instinctively resisted the idea of a mine. As he told a friend:

I don't propose to be swept off my feet by the catastrophe. My duty is plain. We must learn the truth and endeavor, if possible, to fix the responsibility. The country can afford to withhold its judgement and not strike an avenging blow until the truth is known. The Administration will go on preparing for war, but still hoping to avert it.

But events were moving rapidly to a point beyond the president's ability to shape them. If it were proved that the *Maine* had been destroyed by a Spanish mine, McKinley would indeed be swept off his feet by the clamor for war. It would be up to a Naval Court of Inquiry to establish the cause of the explosion. Secretary Long telegraphed Rear Admiral Montgomery Sicard, commander of the North Atlantic Squadron, instructing him to keep the *Maine* survivors at Key West, where they would be available to testify. Sicard had already begun to compile a list of officers who could serve on the court.

The dangerous turn of events was not lost on the Spanish government. Segismundo Moret, the minister of colonies, cabled Governor General Blanco, advising him "to gather every fact you can to prove the *Maine* catastrophe cannot be attributed to us." At Havana, Admiral Vincente Manterola was establishing a Spanish Naval Board of Inquiry.

.   .   .

AT 2 A.M. Captain Sigsbee went to a stateroom on the *City of Washington* to catch a few hours of fitful sleep. He was up again before dawn, checking on the condition of the wounded aboard the Ward liner. At daylight he went on deck and looked toward the wreckage of his ship.

The *Maine* had sunk in some forty feet of water and settled into the muddy bottom. The battleship's hull was almost completely submerged, but part of the torn and twisted superstructure protruded above the surface. Some of the debris was still burning, and a pillar of smoke rose above the wreckage. The black cloud cleared momentarily, revealing mute evidence of the force that had ripped the vessel. Sigsbee describes the scene:

The forward part of the central superstructure had been blown upward and somewhat to starboard, and had folded back on its after-part, carrying the bridge, pilothouse, and six-inch gun and conning tower with it, and completely capsizing them. The broad surface that was uppermost was the ceiling of the berth deck, where many men had swung from beam to beam in their hammocks the night before. On the

white paint of the ceiling was the impression of two human bodies—
mere dust.

The explosion had occurred in the forward part of the ship, almost directly
under the enlisted men's quarters. Later Sigsbee would know the grim totals: 230
sailors, 28 Marines, and 2 officers had been killed or were missing and presumed
dead; 8 of the survivors would later die of their injuries.

About midday the Plant Line steamer *Olivette* arrived from Key West to
take back the uninjured survivors. Sigsbee and five officers remained behind to
handle matters at Havana. Later in the day Consul General Lee telegraphed the
State Department:

> Profound sorrow expressed by Government and Municipal authorities,
> consuls of foreign nations, organized bodies of all sorts, and citizens
> generally. Flags at half-mast on Governor-General's Palace, on shipping
> in harbor, and in city. Business suspended; theatres closed. . . . Suppose
> you ask that Naval Court of Inquiry be held to ascertain cause of
> explosion. Hope our people will repress excitement and calmly await
> decision.

But in some quarters of Washington the stunned disbelief that marked the
early hours of the morning had given way by late afternoon to angry suspicion.
That night, in a personal letter to a friend, Roosevelt wrote, "The *Maine* was
sunk by an act of dirty treachery on the part of the Spaniards I believe."

The press had already taken up the cry. Hearst's *Evening Journal* proclaimed, "Crisis at Hand . . . Growing Belief in *Spanish Treachery.*"

FEBRUARY 17, THURSDAY.

AT 3 P.M. a procession of nineteen hearses left the Governor General's Palace
and made its way through the crowded streets of Havana. A Spanish military
escort ordered by the authorities led the cortege on its route to Colón Cemetery
in the suburbs. A line of carriages brought up the rear, bearing Sigsbee, Lee, and
a party of American naval officers and Spanish officials. Father Chidwick, the
chaplain of the *Maine,* and the bishop of Havana presided at the burial. No
Protestant clergyman could be found in the city; Sigsbee read the burial service
from an Episcopal prayer book.

Sigsbee had reluctantly agreed to the immediate burial of the dead at
Havana; it was not possible to ship the bodies home without some delay, and
embalming facilities were limited in the Cuban port. In any case, identification
of the dead often was impossible; even many of the wounded were difficult to
recognize.

After the burial of the nineteen bodies, Sigsbee was informed that forty
more had been recovered from the harbor. Most of the dead were still down in
the wreck. He made arrangements for divers to begin recovering them the next

day. And there was an even more pressing need to send divers down into the *Maine*. New York *World* correspondent Sylvester Scovel wrote in a story appearing that morning:

> The cause of the blowing up of the ship will not be known until divers go down and examine the wreck. If their investigation shows that the indentation of the hull is inward, the conclusion that the magazine was exploded by a bomb or torpedo placed beneath the vessel is inevitable. If the indentation is outward, it will be indicated that the first explosion was in the magazine.

In the absence of any evidence, theorizing about the cause of the disaster had become a national preoccupation. There was no doubt that the *Maine's* forward ammunition magazine had exploded, but whether that explosion was caused by a mine, an accident, or some other event, remained a topic of speculation. The Washington *Evening Star* surveyed an assortment of naval officers and found that most leaned toward the accident theory. The proximity of one of the battleship's coal bunkers to an ammunition magazine seemed especially significant. Bituminous coal was likely to ignite by spontaneous combustion, and there had been more than a dozen coal bunker fires aboard U.S. naval vessels during the past three years. Recently, spontaneous bunker fires aboard the battleship *New York* and the cruiser *Cincinnati* had nearly caused explosions in nearby ammunition stores. Officers of the Navy's Bureau of Ordnance were certain this was what had happened to the *Maine*, while those of the Bureau of Equipment —which was responsible for the quality of the Navy's coal—held otherwise. The Bureau of Equipment chief, Rear Admiral Royal B. Bradford, told the *Star* he was certain the *Maine's* coal had been of good quality.

The matter was no longer in doubt in the editorial offices of Hearst's *Journal*, where the suspicions of the previous day had been turned into graphic conviction. The early morning editions of the paper carried the headline, "Destruction of the Warship *Maine* Was the Work of an Enemy," and a page-wide drawing showing how a submerged mine had been anchored beneath the battleship. The illustration bore the caption, "The Spaniards, it is believed, arranged to have the *Maine* anchored over one of the harbor mines. Wires connected the mine with a powder magazine [sic] and it is thought the explosion was caused by sending an electric current through the wire."

At least one knowledgeable naval officer agreed with the *Journal's* theory and telegraphed his belief to Secretary Long that day: "Probably the *Maine* destroyed by mine, perhaps by accident. I surmise that her berth was planted previous to her arrival, perhaps long ago. I can only surmise this."

The sender of the telegram was Captain Charles D. Sigsbee.

FEBRUARY 18, FRIDAY.

THE VULTURES CAME, wheeling high above the wreck of the *Maine*, resting now and then in the twisted remains of her superstructure. There were bodies in the harbor, and the tide had washed many of them against the sea wall that ran along the Havana waterfront.

A team of American divers from the North Atlantic Squadron had arrived aboard the coastal steamer *Bache* but were turned back when they approached the wreck. The Spanish had posted a cordon of patrol boats around the site; the Americans were told that no American diver could go down without a Spanish diver. Captain Sigsbee went to the site to investigate. He too was turned back by the Spanish guards.

Sigsbee and Lee went to the palace to protest. They were received by General Blanco. Secretary General Congosto acted as interpreter.

With elaborate civility Captain Sigsbee instructed his Spanish hosts in the provisions of international law. The *Maine* had come to Havana on a legitimate errand, he said, and had entered the harbor with the consent of the local authorities. Therefore, even the wreck must be regarded as American territory, and the American master of the vessel could not be denied access to her.

General Blanco did not dispute the point; instead he raised a different question: Spanish law required that the disaster receive a Spanish investigation. Furthermore, Spanish honor was involved in this case. Blanco proposed a joint Spanish–American investigation of the sinking.

Spain surely had a moral right to investigate, Sigsbee answered, but that was a matter that must be raised directly with the U.S. government. He doubted Washington would consent to a joint investigation, he said, but he thought there would be no objection to a separate Spanish investigation. General Lee agreed.

The interior of the *Maine* might be subject to American control, Blanco countered, but the exterior was a matter of Spanish jurisdiction. Sigsbee replied that the Americans didn't plan to explore the bottom of Havana harbor, making an implicit reference to the submerged mine theory. Dr. Cognostino quickly retorted that the Americans were free to inspect the harbor bottom if they wished. Blanco said he would see that they were no longer refused access to the wreck. The interview was over.

The grim work of recovering the bodies began shortly. The Stars and Stripes now flew at half-mast above the wreck, a reminder to the Spanish that the *Maine* was U.S. territory.

FEBRUARY 19, SATURDAY.

AFTER THE PREVIOUS DAY'S MEETING with Blanco, Lee cabled the State Department, reporting the Spanish proposal for a joint investigation, and the matter was taken up with the Navy Department. Roosevelt opposed the idea, and today, after conferring with Assistant Secretary of State Day, he put his objections on record in a memorandum to Secretary Long:

. . . Let me again earnestly urge that you advise the president against our conducting any examination in conjunction with the Spaniards as to the *Maine*'s disaster. I myself doubt whether it will be possible to tell definitely how the disaster occurred by an investigation; still it may be possible, and it may be that we could do it as well in conjunction with the Spaniards as alone. But I am sure we never could convince the people-at-large of this fact. There is of course a very large body of public opinion to the effect that we some time ago reached the limit of forebearance in our conduct toward the Spaniards, and this public opinion is already very restless, and might easily be pursuaded to turn hostile to the administration.

Roosevelt's political counsel was accepted, and Day cabled Lee informing him that the Navy's investigation was already in progress and would continue independently. The United States would cooperate with any independent Spanish investigation, however.

At Key West, Admiral Sicard was naming the officers who would serve on the Court of Inquiry. The president of the court was to be Captain William T. Sampson, commander of the *Iowa*. Sampson had served as chief of the Bureau of Ordnance and as commandant of the torpedo station at Newport, Rhode Island, positions that qualified him with some knowledge of explosives.

Captain French E. Chadwick and Lieutenant Commander William P. Potter were named as members of the court. Chadwick, commander of the *New York*, was a seasoned intelligence officer who had served a long hitch as naval attaché in London and another as chief of the Office of Naval Intelligence. Chadwick also had been chief of the Bureau of Equipment. Thus, neither sabotage nor spontaneous combustion were unfamiliar matters. Potter was considered to be an officer of technical experience and calm judgement.

Lieutenant Commander Adolph Marix was named as the court's judge advocate. Marix knew the *Maine;* he had served as her executive officer until only a few months earlier.

Admiral Sicard detailed the duties of the court. It would "diligently and thoroughly inquire into all the circumstances attending the loss . . . report whether or not the loss . . . was . . . in any respect due to fault or negligence on the part of the officers or members of the crew," and "report its opinion as to the cause of the explosion, or other incidents that bore directly or indirectly on the loss of the *Maine*."

Sicard fixed the time and place for the court to begin its work: two days hence, at Havana.

. . .

THE SPANISH BOARD OF INQUIRY was already in being. Admiral Vicente Manterola, commander of the naval station at Havana, had appointed Captain Don Pedro del Peral y Caballero to head the investigation. Lieutenant Don Francisco Javier de Salas y Gonzales would serve as secretary. As yet the Spanish investigation had involved nothing more than a visual inspection of the wreck from the surface of the harbor; Captain Peral could do little else while the question of the proposed joint Spanish–American investigation remained open. Informed by Lee of Washington's refusal of the joint probe, Admiral Manterola called on Captain Sigsbee at his rooms in the Hotel Inglaterra. The desk clerk served as interpreter.

"The admiral assumed from the first that the explosion was from the interior of the vessel," Sigsbee later recalled.

Had not the dynamo-boilers exploded? the admiral inquired.

There were no dynamo-boilers on the *Maine*, Sigsbee answered.

The published plans of the ship showed the guncotton magazine forward, near the point of the explosion, did they not?

They did, but the plans had been changed. The guncotton was stowed aft, under the captain's cabin. It hadn't exploded.

The gunpowder, then. Modern gunpowders tended to be unstable.

True, Sigsbee replied, but there hadn't been any modern gunpowder aboard the *Maine*. It had all been the safe, old-fashioned kind.

But what about those boilers near the forward coal bunkers? the admiral asked.

They had not been lighted in three months, said Sigsbee. The ship had spent most of that time in one port or another, and only the aftermost boilers had been used.

The admiral heaved a sigh. Very well, what did the American captain believe had caused the explosion.

Sigsbee chose his words carefully. A few persons of evil disposition *could* have blown up the *Maine* from outside the ship, he said, adding that there were bad men as well as good men to be found everywhere.

Admiral Manterola's face clouded as Sigsbee's reply was translated. He spoke sharply in Spanish, but before the interpreter could translate, the admiral's aide said a few words of caution to his chief. The interpreter remained silent and Sigsbee continued.

Any investigation that did not consider all possible causes, exterior as well as interior, could not be considered as exhaustive, he said. Until the official investigation had been completed, the United States could reach no conclusions as to the cause of the disaster.

Admiral Manterola listened to the translation, then politely expressed his agreement. He arose and, with the exchange of a few courtesies, he and his aide departed.

.   .   .

THE PLANT LINE steamer *Olivette* arrived from Key West, bringing more Navy divers to work on the wreck. Sigsbee went to the cable office near the palace and filed his report to Washington: "One hundred and twenty-five coffins, containing one hundred and twenty-five dead, now buried; nine ready for burial tomorrow."

FEBRUARY 20, SUNDAY.

CAPTAIN SIGSBEE WENT from bed to bed in the San Ambrosio Hospital ward where seven of the *Maine's* injured crewmen were being cared for. He listened to each man tell his recollection of that night, where he had been at the moment of the explosion, whatever he could remember of what it had been like. Sigsbee heard each of them, offered words of encouragement, and wished them well. He stopped at the bed of Frederick C. Holzer, ordinary seaman from Brooklyn, New York.

"Captain, I'm sorry such bad luck has come upon you," said Holzer.

"Thank you, Holzer; I fear you have sailed with the wrong captain this time."

Nearby, Apprentice First Class George Koebler, also from Brooklyn, cried out. Sigsbee went to his bed and saw that the young man was delirious.

"It's not right to leave me here, captain. I'm able to go on board. Take me along to New Orleans."

The *Maine* had been due to visit New Orleans for the Mardi Gras on February 17.

"Don't worry, Koebler. The *Maine* shall never leave Havana without you."

The young sailor lay back quietly. He died two days later. Seaman Holzer lived until February 25.

.   .   .

CAPTAIN PERAL COMPOSED an interim report of his investigation for Admiral Manterola. He had studied the reports of three officers who had inspected the wreck, a naval artilleryman, an engineer, and a torpedo expert. Thus far, he reported, all evidence pointed to an internal explosion.

FEBRUARY 21, MONDAY.

THE NAVAL COURT OF INQUIRY convened at 10 A.M. aboard the U.S. lighthouse tender *Mangrove* in Havana harbor. After a few preliminary formalities the first witness took the stand. The court's judge advocate, Lieutenant Commander Marix, conducted the examination.

Q: What is your name, rank and present station?
A: Charles D. Sigsbee; captain, United States Navy; commanding the U.S.S. *Maine.*
Q: When did you take command of the *Maine?*
A: On the tenth day of April, 1897.
Q: When did the *Maine* arrive at Havana the last time?
A: On the twenty-fifth day of January, 1898.
Q: At what time?
A: About half past nine in the morning.
Q: Do you know, or have you any reason to believe, that the authorities of Havana knew of the *Maine's* coming?

A: Yes; I understand that they were notified by the United States consul general.

Sigsbee next recounted his arrival outside the harbor, where he took aboard a Spanish pilot who guided the *Maine* to an anchorage off the Machina section of the Havana waterfront.

Q: Do you know if you were placed in the usual berth for men-of-war?
A: No. I can only state that by remarks I have heard since the explosion.
Q: State what you heard.
A: I have been informed by Captain Stevens, who is temporarily in command of the steamer *City of Washington*, of the Ward Line of steamers, that he had never known in all his experience, which covers visits to Havana for five or six years, a man-of-war to be anchored there, and that it was the least used buoy in the harbor.

There was no need for Sigsbee to spell it out. The members of the court knew it would have been nearly impossible for the Spanish to have placed a submerged mine beneath the *Maine* after she arrived without being detected. The implication of the question and the answer was that a mine could have been in place before the *Maine* entered the harbor. Lieutenant Commander Marix turned to the question of spontaneous combustion of coal. Sigsbee testified that the *Maine* had coaled twice at Key West.

Q: Was the coal regularly inspected?
A: My recollection is that it was. It was from the government coal pile, and we had the usual men on shore; and while I cannot now state specifically, it was our invariable custom on board the *Maine* to inspect all coal before it was brought on board.
Q: Into what bunkers was the coal placed at these coalings?
A: Generally in the forward bunkers, because it was customary to use coal from the forward bunkers first. These bunkers naturally, therefore, were replenished with new coal.
Q: There is a peculiar bunker under the forward turret, abreast of the ten-inch magazine. Do you know when it was last emptied?
A: I cannot personally recollect that particular bunker.
Q: Did you ever receive any report from the chief engineer of your ship that any coal had been too long in any bunker?
A: Never that I can recollect.
Q: Did the fire alarms in the bunkers work?
A: They were sensitive. They worked occasionally when there was no undue heat in the bunkers, on which occasions we invariably examined the bunkers and got a report.

Methodically, Marix directed his examination of Sigsbee to each of the possible causes of an accidental explosion—the storage of paints and flammables on board, the discharge of ashes, the condition of the ship's electrical system, the temperatures of the ammunition magazines. Sigsbee's testimony always came down to the same thing: to the best of his recollection he had been unaware of any problems. If the court was dissatisfied with such qualified assurance, it did not reflect it in its questions.

At 1 P.M., after a few questions regarding the amount of coal in the forward bunkers, the court adjourned for the day.

.   .   .

THE NAVY DIVER grouped his way through the blackness of the passageway and entered the captain's cabin. He had been there before and recovered the Navy cipher code and signal books, but he had failed to locate the keys to the shell room and ammunition magazine. Captain Sigsbee had been shaken when he was told the keys were missing from their hooks at the foot of his bunk. Could someone have stolen them, unlocked the magazines, and planted a bomb? It seemed impossible; the security precautions aboard the *Maine* had been excellent, he believed. But where were the keys? The diver was sent down again.

The water of Havana harbor was foul; it was impossible to see more than a few inches through the murk. And no light at all reached inside the wreck. The diver moved his hands over the bulkhead and found the hooks. He hadn't been mistaken—the keys were gone. He was about to turn away when he felt something soft and yielding floating above him. He reached up and discovered the mattress from the captain's bunk. He pulled it down and felt along the top. The keys were there. In addition to the keys, the divers recovered Sigsbee's silverware, his typewriter, his bicycle, and a file of confidential letters sent by General Lee when the *Maine* was at Key West. As of this date 143 bodies had been recovered from the wreck and the waters of the harbor. In Washington Congress appropriated $200,000 for the salvage of the wreck and the burial of the dead.

FEBRUARY 22, TUESDAY.

THE COURT OF INQUIRY convened at 11 A.M. aboard the *Mangrove*. The *Maine*'s ordnance officer, Lieutenant George F. M. Holman, testified regarding the safety precautions that had been in force in the ship's ammunition magazines. After a midday break the court heard executive officer Lieutenant Commander Richard Wainwright testify about security regulations in force aboard the *Maine* while at Havana. Next, naval cadets W. T. Cluverius and J. H. Holden were examined regarding the ship's electrical system.

None of the testimony pointed to any accidental cause of the explosion.

.   .   .

IN WASHINGTON, President McKinley and his cabinet waited for some news from Havana. Naval regulations forbade Captain Sampson or any other member of the court from disclosing any hint of their findings until the investigation was complete. For the moment the president chose not to exempt himself from this fiat, instead relying on others close to the scene for their estimates of what was taking place aboard the *Mangrove*. Late in the day the State Department received a telegram from Lee reporting that divers had recovered some intact ammunition cases from the *Maine*'s ten-inch magazine, evidence that the magazine had not exploded. Lee said the discovery indicated the explosion had been the result of a mine.

FEBRUARY 23, WEDNESDAY.

AN ACCIDENTAL COAL BUNKER fire as an explanation remained a real possibility in the minds of the court members. Today the man best qualified to speak to this theory testified. He was Charles P. Howell, chief engineer of the *Maine*, the officer most immediately responsible for preventing such a fire.

The judge advocate's examination of Howell was lengthy and minute, centering on the coal bunkers in the forward part of the ship, the area where the explosion had taken place. There had been no evidence of heating, the chief engineer testified; the temperature in the coal bunkers had been normal. But then Howell made a surprising disclosure concerning bunker A16.

Coal bunker A16 was forward and on the port side of the ship. Only a metal bulkhead separated it from the six-inch reserve ammunition magazine. The coal in A16 at the time of the explosion had been taken on at Newport News, Virginia, Howell testified.

Captain Sigsbee had testified that all the coal taken on at Key West had been stowed in the forward bunkers; the court may have assumed therefore that all the coal in the forward part of the ship was newly stored Key West coal. But now it realized that one forward bunker had been filled with coal from Newport News, and the *Maine* had not been at Newport News since the middle of November. The coal in A16 had lain undisturbed for at least three months, more than enough time for spontaneous combusion to have taken place.

Captain Sigsbee was present during Chief Engineer Howell's testimony. Now, at his own request, he returned to the stand to speak to the question of bunker A16.

Spontaneous combustion is not an instantaneous process; it involves a gradual increase in temperature over a period of days or weeks. Had the interior of A16 been hot enough to have been dangerous, Sigsbee explained, the heat would have been felt on the outside plating of the bunker. But three sides of A16 shared common bulkheads with a wing passageway in the forward part of the ship. The passageway was narrow, and passersby usually touched the bulkheads as they went through it. Sigsbee himself had passed through it the day before the explosion. He said he remembered that the outside plating of A16 had been cool to the touch.

The Court of Inquiry had reached a most difficult juncture in its unenviable task. The members, naval officers themselves, could not doubt that Captain

Sigsbee believed what he had testified to; it would have been nearly impossible for any man to believe anything else. The rules he lived by through a lifetime upon the sea were the Navy's rules, and they said a captain was responsible for everything that happened on his ship. If the *Maine* had been destroyed by an accident, or even by an act of sabotage *on board*, then Charles Dwight Sigsbee must hold himself responsible for the deaths of 268 friends and comrades. And if the court fixed that responsibility on Captain Sigsbee, it should certainly call down upon itself the wrath of an outraged American public that needed to believe such tragedies can only result from malice, never from chance. But to say otherwise, to say the *Maine* had been blown up by a submerged mine, amounted to nothing less than a declaration of war against Spain. And the truth, were it to be found at all, lay hidden in the murky waters of Havana harbor.

For this brief moment, three officers of the U.S. Navy held the fate of two nations in their hands. What they might have done with it shall never be known, for now another man stepped forward and took their burden from them.

Ensign Wilfred Van Nest Powelson took the stand immediately after Sigsbee stepped down. Powelson was a young man, less than four years out of the Naval Academy. He had not served aboard the *Maine* but had arrived at Havana the day after the explosion aboard the lighthouse tender *Fern*. He brought with him a particular kind of expertise that proved of great value to the investigation; Powelson had studied naval architecture at Glascow, Scotland, before attending Annapolis.

The Navy divers who had been exploring the wreck for nearly a week were enlisted men, gunner's mates from the *New York* and *Iowa*. They were experts in underwater salvage, but they were neither engineers nor naval architects. After groping beneath the murky waters of the harbor they could report that some particular section of plating was ruptured, or that some frame was bent upward or downward, but the court badly needed someone to interpret such reports into a coherent and comprehensive picture of the damaged hull. Ensign Powelson was on hand to fill that need.

Powelson had been working with the divers for most of a week, interviewing them as they came up from the wreck, and relating their reports to a set of plans of the *Maine*. Today he would testify as to what had been learned thus far.

The forward part of the ship was completely destroyed, he said. The forward superstructure had been turned upside down by the blast, and the steel frames in the area were bent upward.

Had there been any important discoveries? Lieutenant Commander Marix asked.

Powelson hesitated. There was one, he said. Gunner Charles Morgen of the *New York*, while walking along the harbor bottom on the port side of the wreck, had fallen into a deep hole in the mud. The diver had climbed out and examined the hull in the vicinity of the pit. Everything seemed bent upward.

The deep depression in the mud and the upward bending of the metal suggested that a tremendous explosion had taken place *outside* the hull—a submerged mine.

Q: What weight do you give to the statement by Mr. Morgen as to his falling in the hole on the port side?
A: No weight, sir.
Q: You give no weight to that?

Lieutenant Commander Marix must have been incredulous.

A: No sir; because I think he may be mistaken about it.

Ensign Powelson was a careful young man, not inclined to jump to conclusions. His caution now would lend even more credibility to the testimony he would give later.

FEBRUARY 24, THURSDAY.

THE COURT HEARD the testimony of eyewitnesses who had been ashore or aboard other ships in the harbor at the time of the explosion. Most recalled two explosions—a sharp, gunlike report, followed a second or so later by a more massive and prolonged blast. Several witnesses said the forward part of the *Maine* was lifted up in the water by the first explosion.

FEBRUARY 25, FRIDAY.

SECRETARY LONG TOOK the afternoon off, leaving the assistant secretary in charge.
"Whenever I was left as Acting Secretary," Roosevelt later recalled, "I did everything in my power to put us in readiness." As the afternoon wore on, a stream of orders issued from the assistant secretary's office.
Ten six-inch guns and twenty-two five-inch guns were removed from storage in the Washington Navy Yard and shipped to New York, where they could be used to arm merchant ships as auxiliary cruisers. Cables went out to American squadron commanders around the world, ordering them to keep their ships coaled and ready to sail immediately. Roosevelt's most audacious action involved the Asiatic Squadron.
"All that was needed with Dewey was to give him the chance to get ready, and then to strike, without being hampered by orders from those not on the ground," Roosevelt explained. On his own initiative, Dewey had taken his flagship, the *Olympia,* to Hong Kong on February 11.
"It was evident that in case of emergency Hong Kong was the most advantageous position from which to move to the attack," Dewey observed many years afterward. Hong Kong was only some six hundred miles from Manila. However, most of the remainder of the squadron remained at Nagasaki, twelve hundred miles from the Philippines. Now Roosevelt seized the chance to remedy that with a cable to Dewey:

Order the squadron, except the *Monocacy*, to Hong Kong. Keep full of coal. In the event of declaration of war Spain, your duty will be to see that the Spanish squadron does not leave the Asiatic coast, and then offensive operations in Philippine Islands. Keep *Olympia* until further orders.

Roosevelt

It was sheer audacity. Later it would be seen as one of the most propitious acts of Theodore Roosevelt's career. But the next day a stunned Secretary Long would tell his diary that his assistant had "come very near causing more of an explosion than happened to the *Maine* . . . the very devil seemed to possess him yesterday afternoon."

But the orders to Dewey were not revoked. The first phase of the Spanish war plans the Navy had compiled during the past four years had now been put into effect.

.   .   .

ABOARD THE *Mangrove* in Havana harbor the Court of Inquiry heard again from Ensign Powelson. The young officer had taken the stand to report a somewhat puzzling discovery. Using plans of the *Maine* and drawings of the wreck, Powelson explained what he had found.

The shattered keel of the battleship appeared to have been bent in the form of an inverted V about fifty-nine feet back from the bow, where the explosion had been centered. The bottom of the ship rested in the mud some forty feet down, but a section of bottom plating had been twisted up to within four feet of the surface.

For the moment it seemed no more than another mystery. It would soon be seen as the answer to the question of what had destroyed the *Maine*.

FEBRUARY 26, SATURDAY.

SENATOR REDFIELD PROCTOR arrived at Havana aboard the *Olivette*. Proctor, a Republican from Vermont and former secretary of war, was the same senator who had interceded on behalf of Commodore Dewey in the Asiatic Squadron appointment. He had not come to Cuba to inquire into the *Maine* disaster. Ostensibly he had come to investigate the plight of the *reconcentrados*, but the real significance of his visit was a matter of conjecture. Some observers recalled that he was a close political ally of President McKinley and assumed he shared the president's aversion to a war with Spain. Others remembered he was also a close friend of several prominent expansionist senators and congressman and believed the opposite. Like McKinley, Proctor was inclined to be noncommittal. He offered no clue to the real motive for his trip.

.   .   .

IN THE PORT OF Cartagena on the Mediterranean coast of Spain, Admiral Pascual Cervera composed a report for Segismundo Bermejo, the minister of marine.

Three days earlier he had advised Bermejo, "We must not indulge in any illusions relative to our situation, although we are ready and willing to bear whatever trials God may be pleased to send us." Today, at the close of a technical discussion of artillery cartridge casings, he appended this:

> Do we not owe to our country not only our life, if necessary, but the exposition of our beliefs? I am very uneasy about this. I ask myself if it is right for me to keep silent, make myself an accomplice in adventures which will surely cause the total ruin of Spain. And for what purpose? To defend an island which was ours, but belongs to us no more, because even if we did not lose it by right in the war we have lost it in fact, and with it all our wealth and an enormous number of young men, victims of the climate and the bullets, in the defense of what is now no more than a romantic idea.

Cervera asked Bermejo to convey his words to the queen regent and the Council of Ministers.

.   .   .

ENSIGN POWELSON RETURNED to the *Mangrove* to testify further about the inverted V shape of the *Maine*'s keel. He illustrated his testimony with plans of the battleship, showing the positions of the frames, the steel ribs of the vessel. The frames were spaced three to four feet apart and were numbered in ascending sequence fore to aft. The apex of the inverted V was located just forward of frame 17. In his earlier testimony about the strange formation, Powelson had offered no theory to explain it, but today he would.

> Q: What do you deduce from this information?
> A: I think the explosion occurred on the port side somewhere about frame 18 . . . I should say . . . between frames 16 and 18 was the center of the impact, and that this was under the ship, a little on the port side.
> Q: How far from the keel?
> A: . . . I should say . . . fifteen feet in a horizontal line.

An explosion under the ship, fifteen feet from the keel, had hurled the battleship upward, bending the hull into the inverted V shape the divers had found, according to the young officer. Ensign Powelson had given the Court of Inquiry the first solid evidence that the *Maine* had been sunk by a submerged mine.

FEBRUARY 28, MONDAY.

FROM THE HAVANA CAFES where they gathered, the American newspaper correspondents could look out at the harbor and see the lighthouse tender *Mangrove* and the wreck of the *Maine*, twin symbols of their bafflement and frustration.

A reporter from the New York *Herald* sent home this dispatch: "Never in the history of similar proceedings have such precautions been taken to guard the facts from public scrutiny. Never have officers of either arm of the service remained more consistently reticent under the orders of their chief."

But fifteen hundred miles away, the commander-in-chief remained almost as ignorant of the proceedings aboard the *Mangrove* as did the reporters on the scene at Havana. Virtually the only source of information available to the White House was Consul General Fitzhugh Lee. The witnesses who testified before the Court of Inquiry were forbidden to discuss their testimony with anyone, but some may have broken their vow of silence in the presence of the senior American official on the scene. Today President McKinley had a report from Lee offering his best estimate of the court's probable findings. At the White House the president called a meeting to discuss Lee's report. Present were Secretary Long, Assistant Secretary of State Day, and the Navy's chief of ordnance, Rear Admiral Charles O'Neil.

Lee believed the court would find there had been a mine but that the mine had been a makeshift device, a wooden barrel filled with a few hundred pounds of guncotton and planted in the harbor where the *Maine* would drift against it. Such an amateurish device would have to have been planted by a few malicious individuals and could not be attributed to the Spanish authorities. A makeshift mine planted by dissidents was a theory favored by Captain Sigsbee, who may have been Lee's source. Technically it was a very dubious idea, but politically it was enormously attractive to President McKinley, for it absolved the Spanish government of any complicity. Spain could be charged with nothing more than negligence in failing to protect the battleship.

"I believe that war will be averted," Secretary Long wrote in his diary that night, "for I am satisfied that the Spanish Government is not responsible for the disaster."

Secretary Long's serenity was founded in ignorance. The Court of Inquiry had heard no testimony to support Lee's theory of a makeshift mine.

. . .

THEODORE ROOSEVELT was annoyed. An interview with Lieutenant Philip Alger, published more than a week earlier in the Washington *Evening Star,* had come to his attention. Alger, a professor of mathmatics at the Naval Academy and the Navy's leading ordnance expert, told the newspaper he knew of no submerged mine that could have caused the explosion on the *Maine.* Alger stated that, in seeking the cause of the disaster, it was not necessary to look beyond the same hazard which had nearly caused similar explosions in the past—coal bunker fires.

Roosevelt fired off a snappish letter to Admiral O'Neil sharply criticizing the lieutenant's statements:

> Mr. Alger cannot possibly know anything about the accident. . . .
> When we have a court sitting to find out these facts it seems to me
> . . . inadvisable for any person connected with the Navy Department
> to express his opinion publicly in the matter, and especially to give

elaborate reasons for one side or the other. The fact that Mr. Alger happens to take the Spanish side, and to imply that the explosion was probably due to some fault of the Navy . . . has, of course, nothing to do with the matter.

Roosevelt believed absolutely that the Spanish had blown up the *Maine*. To suggest anything else was to side with the enemy.

MARCH 2, WEDNESDAY.

JUST AFTER 2 P.M. the Court of Inquiry convened in the army barracks of Fort Zachary Taylor at Key West. All the *Maine* survivors not still at Havana were assembled, and they listened as Lieutenant Commander Marix read the prescribed questions from the Navy regulations.

Is there present any officer or man who has any complaint to make or fault to find with any officer or man belonging to the *Maine* on the night of the destruction of that ship at Havana, February 15 of this year? If so, let such officer or man step to the front.

Marix paused and looked around at the assembly before continuing.

Is there present any officer or man who has any complaint to make or fault to find with any officer or man belonging to the *Maine* as to the care and guarding of that ship in the harbor of Havana previous to her destruction on February 15, 1898? If any such officer or man has any such complaint to make or fault to find, let him step to the front.

No one moved. Marix adjourned the court.

MARCH 4, FRIDAY.

IN MADRID, Minister of Marine Bermejo, having overcome his anger at Admiral Cervera's latest letter, wrote a reply. Cervera had greatly overestimated American naval strength, he said. In gauging the force the United States could marshal in the Caribbean, Bermejo discounted the U.S.S. *Oregon*, one of the four first-class battleships of the American fleet. The *Oregon* was on the West Coast, Bermejo pointed out, and it could be expected to remain there. The Spanish Asiatic Squadron in the Philippines constituted a threat to San Francisco, San Diego, and other West Coast ports, as well as to American shipping in the Pacific and the Hawaiian Islands, which the United States was at this moment on the point of annexing. Furthermore, Bermejo argued, even if the Americans wished to bring the *Oregon* to the Caribbean, it would mean sending the warship some sixteen thousand miles around the southern tip of South America, a long and difficult voyage.

Bermejo accentuated the positive. The American fleet was manned by "mercenaries," he said, while the Spanish seamen were well trained and disciplined. While it was true there were some deficiencies in the Spanish fleet, he was confident they would be completely corrected by the end of April. By then, Spain would have concentrated her naval forces at Havana to defend Cuba.

"I will close," he wrote, "never doubting for one moment that you and all of us will fulfill the sacred duty which our country imposes upon us, and in giving you my opinions in answer to yours there is nothing that I desire more than peace."

Apparently Bermejo had not conveyed Cervera's warnings to the queen regent or the cabinet, and he had no intention of doing so.

MARCH 6, SUNDAY.

"We are certainly drifting toward, and not away from, war," Roosevelt confided to a friend. "In a week or so we will get that report; if it says the explosion was due to outside work, it will be very hard to hold the country."

President McKinley was beginning to think much the same thing. That morning he met with Secretary Long and Admiral O'Neil. He authorized O'Neil to order an additional four million dollars' worth of ammunition for the Navy.

"I must have money to get ready for war," McKinley told Congressman Cannon and other members of the House Appropriations Committee that afternoon.

"Who knows where this war will lead us," he wondered, perhaps thinking of the German fleet that had so recently threatened the Caribbean. "It may be more than war with Spain."

He asked for a fifty-million-dollar appropriation.

MARCH 7, MONDAY.

Cervera drafted a long reply to Bermejo, answering the minister of marine point by point.

> It would be foolish to deny that what we may reasonably expect is defeat, which may be glorious, but all the same defeat, which would cause us to lose the island in the worst possible manner. . . .
>   Only in case we could count on some powerful ally could we aspire to obtain a satisfactory result.

Cervera was not alone in resorting again to the elusive hope of countering American strength through a European alliance. The Foreign Ministry had already renewed its appeal to the great powers for a diplomatic intervention. Germany, France, Austria, Italy, and Russia had all expressed their willingness to go along with some such move, but none was ready to take the first step.

And all were waiting to see if England could be persuaded to join the coalition.

MARCH 9, WEDNESDAY.

"IF THERE IS a war I want to get away from here and get to the front if I possibly can," Roosevelt confided in a personal letter to Admiral Davis, the retired officer who had helped obtain Roosevelt's Navy Department appointment a year earlier. "I inflict so much advice on the Secretary that I fear I become *persona non grata.*"

Roosevelt next wrote to General Tillinghast of the New York National Guard:

> I have been in a great quandary . . . I don't want to be in an office during war, I want to be at the front; but I should rather be in this office than guarding a fort and no enemy within a thousand miles of it. . . . Do you think the Governor would give me a chance to start in and raise that regiment in New York were war declared?

THE SENATE MET to vote on the fifty-million-dollar appropriations bill that the House had passed unanimously the day before. The Senate vote was also unanimous.

From Madrid, Ambassador Woodford reported the psychological effect of the vote, which, he said, "has not excited the Spaniards—it has simply stunned them. To appropriate fifty millions out of money in the treasury, without borrowing a cent, demonstrates wealth and power. Even Spain can see this."

In New York Hearst's *Journal* exulted:

"For War! $50,000,000!"

MARCH 10, THURSDAY.

SINCE IT RETURNED to Havana from Key West the Court of Inquiry had heard several times from Ensign Powelson and the divers exploring the wreck. Powelson's testimony confirmed his earlier explanation of the V shape of the keel. Today the court heard no witnesses but spent the day in the harbor at the site of the wreck.

MARCH 11, FRIDAY.

IN MADRID, the queen regent called in Count Viktor Dubsky, the Austrian ambassador. María Cristina, a daughter of the Austrian royal house, had resolved to make a personal appeal to Franz-Joseph.

"I have thus far carefully avoided causing His Majesty the Emperor the least concern for my affairs," she said. "At this moment, however, the agony which presses on the heart of this mother is so great as to overcome any fear of seeming importunate."

France and Germany had already agreed to take part in a joint declaration on behalf of Spain if someone else would take the lead, she explained.

> It is not at all improbable that McKinley, who, I would like to believe, maintains a properly pacific attitude, would also welcome the opportunity to be able to point out to certain groups that my fate was not a matter of indifference to the rest of the world.
> In any event, I leave it up to the Emperor and his heart.

However, María Cristina was not ready at that moment to leave matters entirely in Austrian hands. That same day she sent her private secretary to call on Ambassador Woodford and raise a matter of the utmost secrecy and sensitivity —selling Cuba to the United States.

The very unpopular idea of selling the island had lately received support from an unexpected quarter: the Church. Realizing that, in one way or another, Spain seemed likely soon to lose Cuba, some Spanish clerics favored the alternative of a sale whose terms would protect Catholic interests on the island and prevent it from becoming a Protestant domain. Political dissident Romero Robledo, courting Church support for his own aspirations, had published an editorial in favor of the idea on March 5 in his newspaper, *El Nacional*.

Woodford reported to Washington that the queen regent wished to meet with him privately to open negotiations for the sale. The news could not have been more welcome to President McKinley.

·   ·   ·

AT HAVANA, the court returned to the wreck site. In the afternoon it heard the testimony of Commander George A. Converse, an officer with considerable knowledge of ordnance and the effects of underwater explosions.

Converse said he believed there had been two explosions. The first, a submerged mine, could have bent the keel into the V form reported by Powelson and the divers. The second explosion had been the detonation of one or more of the *Maine*'s powder magazines.

Was there any other possible explanation? he was asked. Could the explosion of the ship's powder magazines, and not a mine, have caused the upward bending of the keel?

Converse replied that it seemed very unlikely.

MARCH 12, SATURDAY.

THE NEWLY REVIVED HOPE for peace through purchasing Cuba proved short lived. This morning Woodford was informed that the queen regent did not wish to see him after all. Church approval of the proposed sale notwithstanding, there was not sufficient political support for the idea in the Cortes. Woodford informed

McKinley, adding, "The Queen evidently lost courage between Friday afternoon and Saturday noon."

MARCH 13, SUNDAY.

A FLOTILLA OF three torpedo boats and three torpedo boat destroyers under command of Captain Fernando Villaamil departed Cádiz, its destination Cuba, by way of the Canary Islands. Ambassador Woodford reported the movement in a cable to Washington.

MARCH 14, MONDAY.

"WE SHOULD FIGHT this minute in my opinion, before the torpedo boats get over here," Roosevelt wrote in a letter to Captain Mahan. "But we won't. We'll let them get over here and run the risk of serious damage from them, and very possibly we won't fight until the beginning of the rainy season, when to send an expeditionary force to Cuba means to see men die like sheep."

The small, swift torpedo boat was one of the many unknowns in the military equation. Some naval strategists believed the little craft were a major threat to the large armored battleship and cruiser. There was little combat experience to prove or disprove the idea.

But the real threat to American forces in the Caribbean was not Spanish torpedo boats or any other man-made weapon. It was the tropical disease that accompanied the rainy season.

In Cuba, the rains came in June.

MARCH 15, TUESDAY.

THE COURT OF INQUIRY adjourned at Havana and prepared to return to Key West to begin its deliberations. In a letter to his wife, Captain Sigsbee wrote, "I have no knowledge as to what the findings of this court will be but I do not fear anything which will reflect on the Maine."

In other words, Sigsbee was confident the court would rule out an accidental explosion.

.   .   .

ROOSEVELT RECEIVED a disappointing reply to his request of Colonel Francis Vinton Greene of the New York National Guard. Greene was unable to arrange a commission for Roosevelt and suggested he would be more valuable right where he was.

"I don't want to be in an office instead of at the front," Roosevelt protested, "but I daresay I shall have to be, and I shall try to do good work wherever I am put."

Yet he was far from being resigned to the idea. He dashed off a letter to New York Congressman William Astor Chanler, another Guard commander, asking to go "in any capacity, in any regiment that goes to the front."

Roosevelt also put in the same request on behalf of his friend Leonard Wood. Wood was a young Army surgeon who had seen action against the Apaches and was now serving as President McKinley's personal physician. Like Roosevelt, Wood did not wish to sit out the war in Washington.

MARCH 16, WEDNESDAY.

AT CARTAGENA, Admiral Cervera continued to argue for peace while he prepared for war. Again he wrote to Minister Bermejo, urgently pleading that his assessment of the situation be presented to the cabinet.

> I am afraid that there may be some minister who, while believing that we are not in favorable conditions, may have been dazzled by the names of the vessels appearing in the general statement, and may not realize how crushing a disproportion really exists, especially if he is not thoroughly aware of our lack of everything that is necessary for a naval war, such as supplies, ammunition, coal, provisions, etc. We have nothing at all.
>
> . . . I think it is of the greatest importance that the whole council of ministers, without exception, be fully and clearly informed of our terrible position . . .
>
> . . . Perhaps there is nothing left for us to do but to settle the dispute through arbitration or mediation, provided the enemy accepts.
> . . .
>
> Perhaps it would be well for me to inform the members of the cabinet myself. If this is deemed expedient I am ready to start at the first intimation.

Secretary Long had appointed Roosevelt to an ad hoc panel to plan the Navy's response to the growing crisis. The other members of the group, soon to be known as the Naval War Board, were Captain Arent S. Crowninshield, chief of the Bureau of Navigation, Admiral Montgomery Sicard, recently commander of the North Atlantic Squadron, and Captain Albert S. Barker. Captain Mahan had been recalled from retirement and was on his way home from Europe to serve as the fifth member of the board. Today the board stated its concern to Long over the Spanish torpedo flotilla now en route to Cuba.

Roosevelt had already advised the president that the movement ought to be treated "exactly as a European power would the mobilization of a hostile army on its frontiers." Captain Sampson, president of the Court of Inquiry, had proposed notifying Spain that the U.S. Navy would sink any torpedo boat sent to Cuban waters. Today Roosevelt, speaking for the board, urged that the Court of Inquiry be ordered to make its report at once in order that appropriate plans could be made for countering the flotilla if necessary.

President McKinley rejected the proposals. He would not rush the court to judgement; nor would he make the Spanish torpedo boats a cause for war.

.   .   .

"WHAT THE ADMINISTRATION will ultimately do I don't know," Roosevelt told his sister, whose husband was commander of the *Fern*, currently at Havana.

"McKinley is bent on peace, I fear."

MARCH 17, THURSDAY.

SENATOR REDFIELD PROCTOR arose to address a packed Senate chamber after his return from Cuba.

"It has been stated that I said there was no doubt the *Maine* was blown up from the outside," he began. "This is a mistake. . . . In fact, I have no opinion about it myself, and carefully avoided forming one."

He said that the members of the Court of Inquiry were competent to find the truth, and he recommended waiting until they had made their report. Then he turned to the subject of the conditions in Cuba.

Speaking dispassionately, almost pedantically, he said what he had seen.

"There are six provinces in Cuba," he began, and proceeded to name and describe them. It was a grammar school lecture in geography.

"Everything seems to go on much as usual in Havana. Quiet prevails . . . one sees little signs of war."

Then, almost imperceptibly, his tone changed.

"Outside Havana all is changed. It is not peace, nor is it war. It is desolation and distress, misery and starvation."

He told of the *trochas*, the desolated and empty countryside, the fortified towns, the *reconcentrados*.

Torn from their homes, with foul earth, foul water and foul food or none, what wonder that one-half have died and one quarter of the living are so diseased that they cannot be saved? A form of dropsy is a common disorder resulting from these conditions. Little children are still walking about with arms and chest terribly emaciated, eyes swollen and abdomen bloated to three times the natural size. The physicians say these cases are hopeless.

Deaths in the streets have not been uncommon. I was told by one of our Consuls that they have been found dead about the markets in the morning, where they had crawled, hoping to get some stray bits of food.

Flatly, clinically, unemotionally, Senator Proctor continued to recount the tragic details to the stunned, silent chamber.

I went to Cuba with a strong conviction that the picture had been overdrawn. I could not believe that out of a population of one million six hundred thousand, two hundred thousand had died within these Spanish forts. . . . My inquiries were entirely outside of sensational sources. . . . Several of my informants were Spanish born, but every time the answer was that the case had not been overstated.

What I saw I cannot tell so that others can see it. It must be seen with one's own eyes to be realized.

"To me," he concluded, "the strongest appeal is not the barbarity practiced by Weyler, nor the loss of the *Maine* . . . but the spectacle of a million and a half people, the entire native population of Cuba, struggling for freedom and deliverance from the worst misgovernment of which I ever had knowledge."

Proctor's quiet outrage had more effect than the noisiest yellow journals. Prowar feeling now appeared in a quarter from which it previously had been absent, the business community—the political base of conservative Republican McKinley. Two days later the *Wall Street Journal* noted, "Senator Proctor's speech converted a great many people in Wall Street who had heretofore taken the ground that the United States had no business to interfere in a revolution on Spanish soil."

.   .   .

"FULL OF TRUST IN YOU, I am writing to explain my difficult position, convinced that you will support me with your powerful help and good advice."

María Cristina was writing to her aunt, Queen Victoria. She had something more in mind than good advice.

We should long ago have brought the war in Cuba to an end, had America remained *neutral,* but she continually sent money, munitions, and weapons to the rebels; and now, when the insurrection is nearly over, the Americans intend to provoke us and bring about a war, and this I would avoid at all costs. But there are limits to everything, and I cannot let my country be humbled by America. . . .

Until now I have not troubled anybody with my affairs, and I only do so now in order to preserve peace. I have applied to the Emperor of Austria, who promised to approach the other powers in order that the common action be taken for the preservation of peace; but I wished to address myself to you at the same time, to beg you not to deny me your powerful protection. I know how, with the greatest kindness, you always interest yourself in my poor fatherless son—for *his* sake I beg you to help me. It would so distress me if England were not at one with the other Great Powers in this matter!

Had the queen regent written more candidly, she would have said what she now understood: none of the European powers would agree to take the lead in an anti-American coalition until England declared her intentions. And without England's participation, there would be no coalition.

.   .   .

THE COURT OF INQUIRY convened aboard the U.S.S. *Iowa* at Key West, ostensibly to begin its final deliberations. In fact, the court's only remaining task was drafting a formal report. The court had already reached a verdict, and a team of four officers was en route to Washington to brief Secretary Long.

The court had found that the *Maine* was destroyed by a submerged mine. It had been unable to fix responsibility for the placing of the mine.

The verdict, then, was mass murder by a person or persons unknown.

MARCH 19, SATURDAY.

THE LARGE, TWIN SCREW, triple-expansion engines of the U.S.S. *Oregon* turned over, churning the water aft as the twelve thousand-ton battleship began to move through San Francisco Bay. The vessel was a familiar sight from the city's hills; she had been built there at the Union Iron Works and launched five years earlier. San Franciscans looked upon her with something akin to civic pride and claimed she was the mightiest warship afloat. They were probably right.

She was girded at the water line with belts of armor eighteen inches thick. Her sides were protected by five inches of steel. She bristled with four thirteen-inch guns, eight eight-inch, and four six-inch, any of which could pierce the armor of most modern warships at a range of two miles. Additionally, she carried twenty six-pound rapid-fire guns, two Gatlings, and six torpedo tubes.

Her crew consisted of some 30 officers and 438 men. Her commander was Captain Charles E. Clark, a fifty-five-year-old Civil War veteran. One of the two engineering cadets aboard was twenty-two-year-old William D. Leahy, destined to rise to the rank of five-star admiral and serve as President Franklin Roosevelt's chief of staff during World War II.

She rode low in the water as she passed through the Golden Gate; she was carrying sixteen hundred tons of coal, five hundred tons of ammunition, and enough stores for six months. As she cleared San Francisco Bay, all divisions reported secure for sea. The engine room telegraph clanged. Her throbbing rhythm quickened. The frothing bow wave she pushed grew, and she swung to a southern heading.

The Spanish minister of marine had been wrong. The *Oregon* had begun the sixteen thousand-mile voyage to the Caribbean.

MARCH 20, SUNDAY.

THOSE CLOSE TO President McKinley had seen the change that had come over him during the last two days.

"He appeared to me careworn," his secretary, George Cortelyou, wrote in his diary. "He did not look well, and his eyes had a far-away, deep-set expression in them."

Little time remained—a week at most—before the formal report of the Court of Inquiry would be received from Key West, and the president would have to place it before Congress. The only hope for peace lay in some major concessions by Spain. Assistant Secretary Day cabled Woodford in Madrid, notifying him of the most recent developments:

> Confidential report shows naval board will make unanimous report that *Maine* was blown up by submarine mine. This report must go to Congress soon. Feeling in the United States very acute. . . . President has no doubt Congress will act wisely and immediately if there be certainty of prompt restoration of peace in Cuba. *Maine* loss may be peacefully settled if full reparation is promptly made . . . but there remains general conditions in Cuba which can not be longer endured, and which will demand action on our part unless Spain restores honorable peace which will stop starvation of people and give them opportunity to take care of themselves. . . . Relations will be much influenced by attitude of Spanish Government in *Maine* matter, but general conditions must not be lost sight of. It is proper that you should know that, unless events otherwise indicate, the President, having exhausted diplomatic agencies to serve peace in Cuba, will lay the whole question before Congress.

Thus, the *Maine* was no longer the single, central issue. The mood of the country had passed beyond the initial shock and suspicion that followed the disaster and had entered a new phase, marked by Senator Proctor's speech three days earlier. The issue of Spanish misrule in Cuba had acquired an importance equal to the question of responsibility for the explosion. Day's dispatch formalized the new American position: Spain must accept responsibility for the loss of the *Maine*, make reparations to the United States, *and* grant Cuba independence.

Otherwise President McKinley would not be able to resist the popular demand for war.

MARCH 23, WEDNESDAY.

IN MADRID, Ambassador Woodford met with Pío Gullón, the Spanish foreign minister, and Segismundo Moret, the minister for colonies.

"We ask patience of your government," Gullón said. "You must indulge us until the rainy season begins in Cuba. By then we shall have reached an accommodation with the Cuban insurgents that will be acceptable to all parties and then there will be peace."

"That is impossible," Woodford replied. "My government wishes an immediate and honorable peace on the island. Unless it is achieved in a very few days,

President McKinley must submit the entire question to the Congress."

The Spanish cabinet met later in the day, and Gullón repeated the American ultimatum.

MARCH 24, THURSDAY.

ROOSEVELT MET WITH Captain Charles F. Shoemaker, chief of the Revenue Cutter Service* to arrange for the turnover of ten cutters to the Navy. The ships were to receive extra armament and be sent to Key West to join the North Atlantic Squadron. Roosevelt hoped they could be used to counter the threat of the Spanish torpedo boats to the American battleships.

"These craft will be from one-half to two-thirds as fast as the torpedo boats against which they will be pitted," he informed Captain Mahan. "They will not be as noiseless or as invisible, and they will have fewer guns, and only here and there a torpedo tube. It is not necessary to say that they will constitute far from an ideal flotilla, but it will be the best we can improvise."

Today Roosevelt repeated his advice to McKinley that the sailing of the Spanish torpedo boat flotilla be regarded as a hostile act. "I do not think it will be regarded," he told Mahan.

.   .   .

LIEUTENANT COMMANDER MARIX and four officers of the *Maine* arrived at the Baltimore and Potomac Railroad station at the foot of Capitol Hill at 9:35 P.M. Lieutenant John Hood carried the locked canvas pouch containing the final report of the Court of Inquiry. The five men pressed through the crowd of reporters and onlookers and got into a waiting cab.

MARCH 25, FRIDAY.

PRESIDENT MCKINLEY MET with his cabinet at 10:30 A.M. to consider the report of the Naval Court of Inquiry. The document contained no surprises, unfortunately; the administration had known the essence of the report for a week. But now that the formal document was in the president's hands, he must send it to Congress. After that it would be almost impossible to hold back the tide.

The cabinet met through the morning and into the afternoon. It was decided to delay sending the report to Congress until Monday. That would give the administration the weekend to attempt some last-minute diplomatic resolution of the Cuban issue with the Spanish government.

The meeting adjourned at 4 P.M. McKinley and his secretary, George Cortelyou, walked in Lafayette Park across from the White House.

.   .   .

*The seafaring branch of the Treasury Department, predecessor to the U.S. Coast Guard.

TOP LEFT: *General Máximo Gómez, Cuban insurgent leader. Source: Author's Collection.* TOP RIGHT: *General Antonio Maceo, "the Bronze Titan." Source: Author's Collection.* BOTTOM LEFT: *José Martí. Source: Author's Collection.* BOTTOM RIGHT: *William Randolph Hearst. Source: Library of Congress.*

RIGHT: *Governor General Valeriano Weyler y Nicolau, "the Butcher." Source: Author's Collection.* CENTER: *The U.S.S. Maine entering Havana harbor, January 25, 1898. Source: National Archives.* BOTTOM: *Captain Charles D. Sigsbee, commander of the Maine (shown here aboard the St. Louis). Source: Library of Congress.*

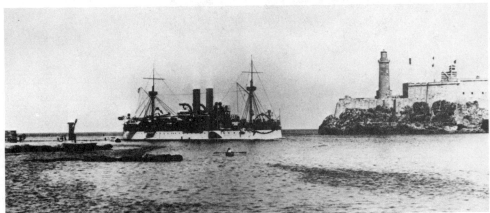

LEFT: *Contemporary artist's conception of the final moments of the Maine, February 15, 1898. Source: Author's Collection.* BOTTOM: *Wreckage of the Maine, Havana harbor. Source: National Archives.*

TOP LEFT: *President William McKinley. Source: Library of Congress.* TOP RIGHT: *Clara Barton, founder of the American Red Cross. Source: Author's Collection.* BOTTOM: *Funeral of the* Maine *victims, Havana, February 17, 1898. Source: Author's Collection.*

TOP: *Naval Court of Inquiry on Maine disaster meeting aboard the U.S. Light House Tender Mangrove. Left to right: Captain French E. Chadwick, Captain William T. Sampson, Lieutenant Commander William F. Potter, Ensign Wilfred V. N. Powelson, Lieutenant Commander Adolph Marix, Stenographer. Source: Author's Collection. Rear Admiral George Dewey and friend aboard U.S.S. Olympia. Source: Library of Congress.*

TOP: *Russell A. Alger, Secretary of War* (left), *and Brigadier General Henry C. Corbin, Adjutant General* (right). *Source: Library of Congress.* BOTTOM LEFT: *Rear Admiral Alfred T. Mahan, naval historian and sea power advocate. Source: Library of Congress.* BOTTOM RIGHT: *Colonel Theodore Roosevelt. Source: Library of Congress.*

TOP: *Gatling gun crew at practice, Tampa. Source: National Archives.* BOTTOM: *Operating room in the White House. Lieutenant Colonel B. F. Montgomery is seated at left. Source: Library of Congress.*

TOP: *Troops on transports waiting to sail from Port Tampa. Source: Library of Congress.* RIGHT: *Richard Harding Davis. Source: Library of Congress.*

In Madrid, Ambassador Woodford thought he saw a way out of the dilemma. He believed Spain could be persuaded to grant a truce with the insurgents, then negotiate with them. If no permanent peace had been achieved by mid-September, the United States and Spain would impose a joint settlement.

Woodford cabled McKinley that the plan had "the advantage of immediate truce and of practical recognition by Spain of an insurgent government." He believed the move had but two possible results: "The one will be independence of Cuba. The other may be annexation to the United States. Truce and negotiations in Cuba mean, in my respectful judgement, that the Spanish flag is to quit Cuba."

MARCH 26, SATURDAY.

Assistant Secretary Day cabled Woodford with the president's response to the ambassador's proposal: the United States did not want Cuba; it wanted peace. If Spain was prepared to grant the Cubans full self-government, the United States would help out in any way it could.

Woodford had proposed a gradual solution. McKinley knew he needed an immediate one to prevent war.

.   .   .

Queen Victoria had not replied to María Cristina's plea. The silence of the English had become unbearable in Madrid. Foreign Minister Gullón cabled the Spanish ambassador in London:

> I wish . . . Your Excellency should learn if Great Britain actually has made any agreement with the United States in the event of war, or if Britain's silence is due solely to the wish to keep her hands free, and not to be bound in advance by any commitment.

In Berlin, von Bülow cabled the German minister at the Vatican and instructed him to explore the idea of papal arbitration between Spain and the United States. Although he doubted the United States would accept the plan because "the Catholic element is not very strong in the American Congress," he believed it was worth a try.

.   .   .

Roosevelt reported to Secretary Long that the Spanish torpedo gunboat *Temerario*, which had been based at Montevideo, Uruguay, for the past two years, had left port on the previous day, destination unknown. He believed she might be on her way to the Straits of Magellan to intercept the *Oregon* or the *Marietta*, an American gunboat also en route to the Caribbean from the West Coast. The big battleship would be at a tactical disadvantage in the narrow waters of the straits. Roosevelt suggested that it might be safer to reroute the *Oregon* around Cape Horn to avoid encountering the Spanish vessel.

·   ·   ·

"THINGS LOOK as if they were coming to a head," Roosevelt exulted in a letter to Congressman Chanler. "Now, can you start getting up that regiment when the time comes? Do you want me as lieutenant-colonel?"

That evening he gave a rousing prowar speech after dinner at the Gridiron Club. "We will have this war for the freedom of Cuba," he said, despite "the interests of the business world and of financiers [which] might be paramount in the Senate." McKinley's millionaire crony, Senator Mark Hanna, was seated nearby. As the thunderous applause that followed his speech died away, Roosevelt turned to Hanna.

"Now, senator, may we please have war?"

·   ·   ·

PRESIDENTIAL SECRETARY CORTELYOU took the handwritten report of the Court of Inquiry home with him and spent the evening typing ten copies.

MARCH 27, SUNDAY.

THERE WAS AN unusual flurry of activity at the State Department in Washington and at the American Ministry in Madrid. Day cabled Woodford, following up on the president's proposal of yesterday. He proposed an immediate revocation of the *reconcentrado* policy and an armistice until October 1. During that period arrangements for Cuban self-government would have to be made.

Woodford cabled back. The Spanish wanted to know what McKinley specifically meant by "self-government."

Day responded, spelling it out: "Self-government means Cuban independence from Spain."

·   ·   ·

FOREIGN MINISTER GULLÓN RECEIVED some good news from the Spanish ambassador at St. Petersburg. Russia would go along with any joint action agreed upon by the other great powers. But each of the powers was still waiting for someone else to take the lead. Queen Victoria had not yet replied to María Cristina's letter.

·   ·   ·

SOMEWHERE IN THE PACIFIC, about midway between San Francisco and Callao, Peru, the *Oregon* plowed southward at twelve knots. With a full head of steam in three of the battleship's four boilers, the consumption of the supply of fresh water on board was high, but salt water in the boilers would mean scale and a reduction of speed. As the ship entered the tropics, the crew accepted the limitation of drinking water without complaint.

Sometime during the afternoon, smoke was seen coming from one of the coal bunkers. After four hours of furious digging the burning coal was reached and extinguished.

The cause of the fire was spontaneous combustion.

MARCH 28, MONDAY.

THERE WAS NO SUSPENSE in Congress as the report of the Court of Inquiry was read. The senators, the congressmen, and the rest of America had already read the gist of it over breakfast in the morning papers. In a minor mystery destined never to be solved, the Associated Press had obtained an accurate summary of the report. But if the report itself offered no surprises, there was shock, disbelief, and outrage at President McKinley's message of transmittal, which was framed in the mildest language and asked for "deliberate consideration."

The angry reaction was not limited to those already on record for war; loyal Republicans who had supported McKinley's conciliatory policy before now deserted him. Leaders of both the Senate and House rushed to the White House to warn the president it might be impossible to stop a "Cuban outbreak," a declaration of war against Spain without the president's initiative.

As the White House tried to quell the revolt within the Republican party on the Cuban issue, the diplomatic dialogue continued. Woodford cabled Day, reporting the Spanish government's response to the American weekend proposal. It said it could not recognize Cuban independence as McKinley requested without the concurrence of the Cortes, which was not due to meet until Aprl 25.

Day could only reply that a delay was unacceptable. The administration must have an immediate promise of Cuban independence.

·   ·   ·

AMBASSADOR POLO PRESENTED the results of the Spanish inquiry into the *Maine* disaster to the State Department. The Spanish report argued that no evidence of a mine had been found and that the explosion was probably the result of spontaneous combustion in one of the battleship's coal bunkers. Perhaps to the surprise of no one, the Spanish report was virtually ignored.

MARCH 29, TUESDAY.

PROWAR HYSTERIA CONTINUED to grow in Congress. It was now certain that if the president did not take the initiative he would lose it. A presidential message had become a necessity. But McKinley was reluctant to make any moves while there still seemed any small hope of negotiating peace.

Time was running out. Day cabled Woodford setting a deadline for Spain. The negotiations for an armistice must be completed within forty-eight hours, by March 31.

·   ·   ·

ROOSEVELT WAS IN a strangely introspective mood. It was unlike him to be reflective, but the realization that the war was soon to be a reality rather than a distant goal seemed to have turned his thoughts inward.

It had been a sad and difficult winter for him. A month earlier he had told his sister, "I have not felt the loss of the *Maine* nearly as much as I would if I had not had so much to worry over in my own home." His eldest son had been sick, and his wife, Edith, gravely ill. The Johns Hopkins specialist he called in told him she must undergo surgery or die. It was the recurrence of a nightmare; fourteen years earlier his first wife, Alice, and his mother had both died within hours of each other in different rooms of their New York home. Indeed, the national events of recent weeks must have been a welcome distraction from his personal situation.

Edith had come through the operation and was recovering, but the recent proximity of death must have been on his mind. He poured out his thoughts in a letter to his old friend, William Sturgis Bigelow, who had joined Lodge in urging against Roosevelt's plan to leave his post in the Navy Department and seek a combat role:

> If I should consult purely my own feelings I should earnestly hope that we would have peace. I like life very much. I have always led a joyous life. I like thought, and I like action, and it will be very bitter to me to leave my wife and children; and while I think I could face death with dignity, I have no desire before my time has come to go out into the everlasting darkness. Moreover, I appreciate thoroughly that in such a war disease, rather than the enemy's rifles will be what we shall have to fear, and that it will not be pleasant to die of fever in some squalid hospital without ever having seen an armed foe. So I shall not go into a war with any undue exhilaration of spirits or in a frame of mind in any way approaching recklessness or levity; but my best work here is done. . . . Whatever influence I have exerted . . . was . . . due simply to the fact that I took upon myself the responsibility of interfering with what was not my business . . . the things that I have done have usually been done when I was Acting Secretary. I shouldn't be allowed to be Acting Secretary in time of war.
>
> Moreover, a man's usefulness depends upon his living up to his ideals in so far as he can. . . . One of the commonest taunts directed at men like myself is that we are armchair and parlor jingoes who wish to see others do what we only advocate doing. . . . my power for good, whatever it may be, would be gone if I didn't try to live up to the doctrines I have tried to preach. . . . it seems to me that it would be a good deal more important from the standpoint of the nation as a whole that men like myself should go to war than that we should stay comfortably in offices at home and let others carry on the war that we have urged.

MARCH 31, THURSDAY.

THE COURT OF INQUIRY having delivered its verdict, Captain Sigsbee was now free to go public with his own theory of the *Maine* disaster. Today he testified before the Senate Foreign Relations Committee, venturing his belief that the ship had been blown up by a submerged mine detonated electrically from some position ashore.

Mr. Frye of the Committee questioned him:

> Q: If that [an electrically detonated mine] was the condition, who would be likely to have charge of the electric battery which exploded the mine?
> A: I am unable to say that; I infer the Navy.
> Q: An official?
> A: I have a certain reason for believing this, which perhaps it would be injudicious to disclose.

The senators did not pursue it. They had heard Sigsbee's charge that the destruction of the *Maine* was an official act of Spain, but they did not insist on hearing the presumably privileged information on which he based his accusation.

· · ·

THERE WAS BOTH good and bad news at the State Department. Spain had revoked the *reconcentrado* policy. But she refused to initiate an armistice; the insurgents must be the first to request a cease-fire. It was, as Ambassador Woodford noted, "a question of punctilio."

> Spanish pride will not permit the ministry to propose and offer an armistice; which they really desire because they know that armistice now means certain peace next autumn. I am told confidentially that the offer of armistice by the Spanish government would cause revolution here. Leading generals have been sounded within the last week and the ministry have gone as far as they dare go to-day. I believe the ministry are ready to go as far and as fast as they can and still save the dynasty here in Spain. They know that Cuba is lost. Public opinion in Spain has steadily moved toward peace. No Spanish ministry would have dared to do one month ago what this ministry has proposed to-day.

The Spanish government needed time; McKinley had little time to offer. Wednesday, April 6, had been set as the date he would send his Cuban message to Congress.

· · ·

THE FOREIGN MINISTRY distributed a dispatch to each of its European legations:

> If [the latest concessions] are to be accepted at Washington, the valued good offices of the sovereign (or president of the republic) and govern-

ment to which you are accredited ought to be immediately determined upon and put into effect at once, if, as we hope by the reports from your excellency, they desire to co-operate to effect the preservation of peace and the reasonable protection of our rights.

If there were to be a European coalition on behalf of Spain, it was now or never.

APRIL 1, FRIDAY.

QUEEN VICTORIA WAS not disposed to act in the Spanish–American matter contrary to the advice of her prime minister, Lord Salisbury. Today, Salisbury (writing in the third person, as was customary) sent a note to the queen:

> The Spanish question is very grave; and Lord Salisbury would not like to advise your Majesty to give any undertaking to assist the Queen of Spain, without consulting his colleagues; for any communication from this country to the United States, in the way of remonstrances, might arouse their susceptible feelings, and produce a condition of some danger, without any corresponding advantage. At the same time, Lord Salisbury thinks that your Majesty would not refuse to join in any course taken by all the other Great Powers. But he doubts the expediency of action by them. It is more likely to help the war party in the United States than to weaken them.
>   The position of the Queen Regent of Spain is most lamentable and grievous. It is impossible not to feel the deepest sympathy for her.

Sympathy, then, and lukewarm consent to a European coalition, was the extent of the aid Britain was prepared to offer Spain.

．　　　．　　　．

THE SPANISH FIRST-CLASS armored cruisers *Vizcaya* and *Almirante Oquendo*, each of some seven thousand tons and thirty guns, were at this moment in Havana harbor. Roosevelt begged Long and McKinley for permission to send the North Atlantic Squadron to blockade the port and prevent the warships from leaving. His request was denied.

APRIL 2, SATURDAY.

THE SPANISH AMBASSADOR to the Vatican reported to Madrid that Pope Leo XIII was prepared to request an armistice. The news was not welcome. Foreign Minister Gullón believed it would be used as an excuse by the great powers not to intervene. However, if the United States accepted papal intervention, there seemed no alternative for Spain but to do likewise.

APRIL 3, SUNDAY.

PUBLIC ENTHUSIASM FOR the coming war was sweeping the country. The New York *World* reported that "Buffalo Bill" Cody had declared that thirty thousand Indian fighters could clear the Spanish out of Cuba in sixty days. Frank James, brother of Jesse, volunteered to lead a company of cowboys to liberate Cuba. It was said that six hundred Sioux were ready to go on the warpath and collect Spanish scalps. And Hearst's *Journal* proposed a regiment of American athletes who "would overawe any Spanish regiment by their mere appearance. They would scorn Krag-Jorgensen and Mauser bullets."

. . .

THE VATICAN HAD designated Archbishop John Ireland of St. Paul, Minnesota, as its unofficial representative to Washington in the Cuban matter Today Ireland called at the White House to sound out President McKinley on the idea of a papal plea for an armistice. He reported back to Rome that McKinley seemed well disposed toward the idea. The Spanish ambassador to the Vatican reported the development to Madrid in such optimistic terms Foreign Minister Gullón drew the mistaken inference that McKinley had actually asked Pope Leo to intervene. He immediately called on Woodford.

Gullón told Woodford that McKinley had requested papal intervention for an armistice and that Spain would go along with the proposal on that basis. However, he made the condition that the United States withdraw the North Atlantic Squadron from Key West. Woodford cabled a report of the meeting to Washington.

McKinley could not simply let the mistake stand and use it to advantage. The idea of an American president invoking the intervention of the Roman Catholic church in these circumstances would simply have provoked outrage in the country. It surely would not have helped McKinley hold back the tide of war. Day replied immediately to Woodford:

> The President has made no suggestions to Spain except through you He made no suggestions other than those which you were instructed to make for an armistice to be offered to Spain and insurgents, and which Spain has already rejected. . . . The disposition of our fleet must be left to us. . . The President cannot hold his message [to Congress] longer than Tuesday.

APRIL 4, MONDAY.

AFTER A CONTINUOUS RUN of sixteen days and 4,112 nautical miles, the *Oregon* arrived at Callao, Peru. Nine hundred tons of coal had been burned. The ship proceeded to recoal while the chief engineer and his assistant overhauled the engines. A double watch was posted and the ship's steam launches patrolled day and night to guard against any actions by Spanish sympathizers in the port.

Captain Clark received a dispatch from Washington containing Roosevelt's warning about the Spanish torpedo gunboat *Temerario*. Among the crew the word was that Clark intended to sink the *Temerario* if she was sighted, war or no war.

·   ·   ·

"I WOULD GIVE a large sum," Roosevelt told a friend, "to have the running of our national affairs for just three days to come!"

·   ·   ·

AN UNEXPECTED REPRIEVE arrived at the State Department in the form of a cable from Fitzhugh Lee at Havana. If war should come, Lee warned, the Americans still in Cuba would be in danger. Some time was needed to arrange their evacuation to the United States. President McKinley sent copies of Lee's cable to congressional leaders, who quietly passed it along to the most outspoken prowar senators and congressmen.

McKinley had bought a few more days. Monday, April 11, was now set as the date for his Cuban message.

APRIL 5, TUESDAY.

IN BERLIN, Foreign Minister von Bülow met with the Spanish ambassador.

"I have no advice to give you, officially," he said. "It would be acting disloyally if I should allow Your Excellency to believe there was any real prospect of active intervention by the powers in Spain's favor. I admire the courage Spain has shown, but I would admire more a display of practical common sense."

·   ·   ·

IN LONDON, Ambassador John Hay wrote to his friend, Henry Cabot Lodge:

I do not know whether you especially value the friendship and sympathy of this country [England]. . . . it is the only European country whose sympathies are not openly against us. . . . If we wanted it—which, of course, we do not—we could have the practical assistance of the British Navy.

In Washington, Secretary Long sent a dispatch to Commodore Dewey at Hong Kong:

"War may be declared. Condition very critical."

APRIL 6, WEDNESDAY.

AMBASSADOR HAY CALLED on British Foreign Secretary Arthur Balfour to ask that Britain handle American consular affairs in Spain in the event of a break in

Spanish–American diplomatic relations. Balfour said he saw no problem in that, then brought up the matter of the European coalition.

Sir Julian Pauncefote, the British ambassador to Washington, had been instructed, he said, to be guided by the wishes of President McKinley in "any collective representation of the diplomatic body in Washington." It happened, he went on, that some such representation was to be made today.

There was indeed that same day a meeting in the White House Blue Room between President McKinley and Assistant Secretary Day and a delegation of European envoys. The delegation was comprised of the ambassadors of France, Germany, Austria, Italy, Russia, as well as British Ambassador Pauncefote, who served as spokesman and presented their joint note.

The note contained "a pressing appeal to the feelings of humanity and moderation of the President and the American people in their existing differences with Spain." It expressed the hope "that further negotiations will lead to an agreement which, while securing the maintenance of peace, will afford all necessary guaranties for the reestablishment of order in Cuba."

"We hope for humanity's sake you will not go to war," said Pauncefote.

"We hope, if we do, you will understand it is for humanity's sake," McKinley replied.

The European coalition Spain had so long hoped for had resulted in nothing more than this meaningless diplomatic minuet. Pauncefote had participated in the joint initiative only after first clearing the matter with the White House and revising an earlier draft of the note to meet State Department objections.

·   ·   ·

AT CÁDIZ, Admiral Cervera had received a letter from Minister Bermejo explaining that, due to the international crisis, "nothing can be formulated or decided" in the way of naval war plans.

"It is precisely on account of the general anxiety prevailing that it is very important to think of what is to be done," Cervera now replied. He was especially concerned about the Canary Islands, which he knew the American forces could easily capture and use as a base of operations against the Spanish peninsula.

"It is therefore absolutely necessary to decide what we are going to do," he wrote. "If the case arises, we may act rapidly and with some chance of efficiency and not be groping about in the dark, or, like Don Quixote, go out to fight windmills and come back with broken heads."

APRIL 8, FRIDAY.

THE BOILERS OF the armored cruisers *María Teresa* and *Cristobal Colón* were fired as the two Spanish warships prepared to sail from Cádiz. Yesterday Minister Bermejo ordered Cervera to rendezvous with the torpedo boat flotilla, which had proceeded no farther than the Cape Verde Islands off the African coast. Cervera immediately telegraphed Bermejo. What was he supposed to do after he reached

Cape Verde? Bermejo replied that there was not enough time to explain. He promised to send Cervera's orders after him by steamer.

As Cervera prepared to sail, he wrote Bermejo, "I regret very much to have to sail without having agreed upon some plan, even on general lines."

At 5 P.M., Don Pascual, the reluctant Quixote, sailed out into the Atlantic.

APRIL 9, SATURDAY.

TWO DAYS OUT of Callao, fully coaled and overhauled, the *Oregon* steamed south toward the Straits of Magellan. Today the battleship's fourth boiler was fired, increasing her speed to thirteen knots.

· · ·

AT THE VATICAN, the Spanish ambassador sent a dispatch to Madrid. "The Pope begs the Government of Her Majesty to consider the grave consequences that war might have for many interests. . . . The urgent need is that an armistice be declared."

In Madrid, the ambassadors of the great powers called on Foreign Minister Gullón, presenting a joint request that Spain agree to the Vatican's cease-fire plea.

It was, of course, a well-orchestrated move to make it politically possible for Spain to take the initiative in declaring an armistice. Woodford was called to the Foreign Ministry and informed of the Spanish agreement. He rushed back to his office and reported the development to Washington. Woodford said that, if McKinley could pursuade Congress to be patient, he was sure the entire Cuban question could be resolved by August 1 through some form of autonomy acceptable to the insurgents, independence, or cession of Cuba to the United States.

"I hope that nothing will now be done to humiliate Spain, as I am satisfied that the present Government is going . . . as fast and far as it can."

APRIL 10, EASTER SUNDAY.

AT THE WHITE HOUSE, President McKinley received a stream of visiting congressional leaders. Assistant Secretary of State Day called to report a meeting earlier in the day with Spanish Ambassador Polo, who had asked for an American response to the cease-fire. The cabinet met twice. The president's Cuban message was due to go to Congress the next day.

It came down to this: Spain had agreed to arbitrate the matter of the *Maine;* she had revoked the *reconcentrado* policy; and now she had declared an armistice. She had acceded to all of the American demands but one: independence for Cuba.

Woodford forecast that independence, too, was forthcoming, that it would be achieved by August 1. Yet even if the ambassador's prediction was well founded, it could not be made public now, could not be offered to the Congress and the American public tomorrow.

McKinley wished to revise the Cuban message he had already written, to propose deferring matters until the results of the armistice had been seen. Everyone urged him against this. The Spanish concessions were too little and too late, they said. The prowar forces in Congress were too powerful. If McKinley did not yield to them, he was told, they would sweep him away.

In the end the president agreed to deliver his Cuban message as it was written, although he would append to it an acknowledgement of the latest Spanish concession.

·   ·   ·

FITZHUGH LEE and most of the remaining Americans left Havana.

APRIL 11, MONDAY.

THE PRESIDENT'S MESSAGE was read to Congress.

It began with a catalog of the sufferings of the Cuban people under the *reconcentrado* policy, "an inhuman phase happily unprecedented in the modern history of civilized Christian peoples." Next it recounted the damage to American business interests in Cuba. The issue of the *Maine* had shrunk to no more than an illustration of the "danger and disorder" in Cuba, which Spanish military efforts had failed to remedy. There was no implication that the Spanish had destroyed the battleship. To the Spanish offer to submit the question of reparation for the *Maine* to arbitration, the president said he had made no reply.

Regarding the Cuban republic established by the insurgents, McKinley did not favor recognition.

> To commit this country now to the recognition of any particular government in Cuba may subject us to embarrassing conditions of international obligations toward the organization so recognized. In case of intervention our conduct would be subjected to the approval of that government.

The message concluded:

> In the name of humanity, in the name of civilization, in behalf of endangered American interests which give us the right and the duty to speak and to act, the war in Cuba must stop. In view of these facts and these considerations, I ask the Congress to authorize and empower the President to take measures to secure a full and final termination of hostilities between the government of Spain and the people of Cuba, and to secure in the island the establishment of a stable government . . . and to use the military and naval forces of the United States as may be necessary for these purposes. . . .

The issue is now with the Congress. It is a solemn responsibility.

I have exhausted every effort to relieve the intolerable conditions of affairs which is at our doors. Prepared to execute every obligation imposed upon me by the Constitution and the law, I await your action.

The president's message did not receive unqualified approval in Congress. Many members were shocked and outraged that McKinley proposed not to recognize the existing Cuban republic. Congressman Dinsmore of Arkansas was speaking for many of his colleagues when he said:

We talk about liberty. Then let us give the Cubans liberty. We talk about freedom. Let us give to them the right to establish a government which they think will be a free government, and which does not reserve to us, the Government of the United States, the right to say, after it is established, "Ah, this is not a 'stable' government; we can not turn it over to you yet; we must look after this thing."

Senator Joseph Foraker of Ohio voiced the fear that "this intervention is to be deliberately turned from intervention on the ground of humanity into an aggressive conquest of territory."

But there seemed little real support for the idea of annexing Cuba. Even the outspokenly expansionist Roosevelt had told a friend two weeks earlier,

I am perfectly willing to follow the policy of intervening without recognizing independence, although I think it a mistake; for I should be very doubtful about annexing Cuba in any event, and should most emphatically oppose it unless the Cubans wished it. I care nothing about recognizing the present government if only we emphatically state that we will recognize the independence of Cuba.

Thus the Congress, embroiled in the debate over recognition, was unable to act immediately on the president's message. Peace had received an unexpected temporary reprieve.

APRIL 14, THURSDAY.

THE *María Teresa* and the *Cristobal Colón* arrived at St. Vincent in the Cape Verde Islands. The engines and boilers of the two warships had not been working well, and the voyage had consumed a large amount of coal. Cervera discovered that the U.S. consul on the islands had already bought up almost all the coal available there. With much difficulty he managed to buy seven hundred tons at a greatly inflated price. The two ships had burned nine hundred tons in the voyage from Cadiz.

Cervera cabled Bermejo: "Arrived here safely. Am anxious to know instructions. I beg for daily telegram. Need 1,000 tons of coal to refill bunkers."

.   .   .

AFTER MUCH DEBATE, the House Foreign Affairs Committee sent to the floor a resolution for U.S. intervention to establish "by the free action of the people [of Cuba] a stable and independent government of their own on the island." McKinley favored the resolution because "intervention" could be taken to include diplomacy, rather than immediate military action.

Roosevelt was worried. He told Lodge: "I earnestly hope that it will not be passed by the Senate, and that you will stick to your own resolution; otherwise we shall have more delay and shilly-shallying."

APRIL 16, SATURDAY.

THE SENATE, debating its own resolution, passed an amendment to recognize the Cuban republic. Later that day it passed another amendment, this one offered by Senator Henry M. Teller of Colorado. The Teller Amendment stipulated that "the United States hereby disclaims any disposition or intention to exercise sovereignty, jurisdiction, or control over [Cuba] except for the pacification thereof, and asserts its determination when that is accomplished to leave the government and control of the island to its people."

·   ·   ·

FOREIGN MINISTER GULLÓN sent a request to the Vatican that the pope suggest "to the Great Powers that one of the best ways of preventing war would be for them to make a naval demonstration" against the United States. Pope Leo declined.

·   ·   ·

THE *Oregon*, running before a moderate gale, plowed through the heavy winter seas off the coast of Chile. Just before dark Captain Clark made out the Evangelistas and Cape Pillar, marking the western entrance to the Straits of Magellan. The battleship anchored for the night off Tamar Island.

APRIL 19, TUESDAY.

AFTER MORE THAN a week of debate, the House and Senate, at 3 A.M., passed a joint resolution

> for the recognition of the independence of the people of Cuba, demanding that the government of Spain relinquish its authority and government in the island of Cuba and Cuban waters, and directing the President of the United States to use the land and naval forces of the United States to carry these resolutions into effect.

All that remained was for the president to sign it. After that a state of war between the United States and Spain would be in effect.

APRIL 20, WEDNESDAY.

THE SQUADRON OF Admiral Cervera rode at anchor in the harbor of St. Vincent, in the Cape Verde Islands. Besides the *Infanta María Teresa* and the *Cristobal Colón,* there were the three torpedo boat destroyers *Plutón, Furor,* and *Terror,* three torpedo boats, the *Rayo,* the *Ariete,* and the *Azor,* and the armored cruisers *Vizcaya* and *Almirante Oquendo,* which had arrived from Cuba on the nineteenth.

It would have been a formidable assemblage of sea power had it been in a better state of repair and readiness. But the guns of three of the four cruisers had defective breech mechanisms and no reliable ammunition for their 5.5-inch guns. The *Colón* lacked her main 10-inch battery, which had not been mounted on the warship. The boilers and engine of the *Ariete* were in such bad condition she could no longer make way, but had to be towed. The *Azor* was in similar condition. The *Vizcaya,* long overdue for dry-docking, had a keel encrusted with barnacles, which sharply cut her speed and increased her coal consumption. Coal was generally in short supply, and the bunkers of the ships were half empty.

Minister Bermejo had ordered the squadron to sail to the West Indies and defend the island of Puerto Rico.

Cervera assembled his captains for a meeting aboard the *Colón.*

"Under the present circumstances," he asked, "is it expedient that this fleet should go at once to America, or should it stay to protect our coasts and the Canaries and provide from here for any contingency?"

After nearly four hours the officers of the squadron reached a consensus. It was, first of all, an open question as to whether the squadron could even reach Puerto Rico. Assuming that it did, and that it might be of some use in defending the island, what of Cuba? The inevitable result of an American landing in Cuba would be a public outcry in Spain resulting in the sending of the squadron into battle against the American fleet, an engagement whose outcome could not any more be in question.

If the squadron were lost or stranded in the West Indies, Spanish home waters would be left virtually defenseless. An American squadron could raid the peninsula and take the Canaries with impunity.

The officers concluded that the only rational alternative was to return to the Canaries. They sent a joint message to Bermejo to that effect.

·   ·   ·

AT THE WHITE HOUSE, President McKinley signed into law the joint congressional resolution for Cuban intervention.

APRIL 21, THURSDAY.

THE *Oregon,* recoaled and overhauled, left Sandy Point on the eastern end of the Straits of Magellan and headed north into the Atlantic.

. . .

"WAR SEEMS hopelessly declared and the respective Spanish and United States Ministers have left their posts!" Queen Victoria wrote in her diary. "It is monstrous of America."

APRIL 22, FRIDAY.

FROM HAVANA, Governor General Blanco cabled Madrid:

> Public spirit very high; great enthusiasm among all classes. But I must not conceal from your excellency that if people should become convinced that squadron is not coming, disappointment will be great, and an unpleasant reaction is possible. Beg that your excellency will advise me whether I can give them any hope of more or less immediate arrival of squadron.

MINISTER BERMEJO CABLED Cervera. The Canaries were perfectly safe, he said. He ordered the squadron to proceed to Puerto Rico as soon as possible.

"Though I persist in my opinion, which is also the opinion of the captains of the ships, I shall do all I can to hasten our departure," Cervera replied, "disclaiming all responsibility for the consequences."

. . .

AT 6:30 A.M. the North Atlantic Squadron under command of Admiral Sampson formed off Key West and headed for Havana. The fleet included the battleships *Iowa* and *Indiana,* the armored cruiser *New York,* three monitors, five gunboats, three cruisers, and seven torpedo boats. At about 3 P.M. the dark, medieval towers of Morro Castle rose above the horizon. The blockade of Havana was in place.

The Spanish War had begun.

CHAPTER SIX

MANILA

THE NINE SHIPS of the Asiatic Squadron swung at their moorings in Mirs Bay, a small inlet on the Chinese coast. It was Monday, April 25.

Two days earlier word of the Cuban blockade had reached Hong Kong. Major General Wilsone Black, the governor of the British enclave, immediately sent an official notice to Commodore Dewey. A state of war existed between the United States and Spain, it said, and Great Britain had proclaimed her neutrality. All Spanish and American warships must leave the waters of the colony as soon as possible and no later than 4 P.M. on Monday.

Beneath the official message Black had penned a personal note: "God knows, my dear Commodore, that it breaks my heart to send you this notification."

But it was not unexpected. Dewey had already made his plans, knowing that the Chinese government would be less punctilious in its interpretation of the Occidental rules of war and neutrality. Before noon on the twenty-fifth, he had assembled the squadron in Mirs Bay, thirty miles from the British colony.

Late that afternoon smoke was sighted down the coast. By early evening the approaching vessel was identified as the *Fame*, a Hong Kong tug Dewey had chartered to carry dispatches back and forth from the cable head in the British colony. Aboard was Lieutenant H. H. Caldwell, who had stayed behind to await cabled orders from Washington.

At 7 P.M. Caldwell entered the commodore's cabin on the *Olympia* and delivered a dispatch that had been received that afternoon: "War has commenced between the United States and Spain. Proceed at once to Philippine Islands. Commence operations particularly against the Spanish fleet. You must capture vessels or destroy. Use utmost endeavour."

Dewey's squadron now consisted of seven warships: his flagship, the

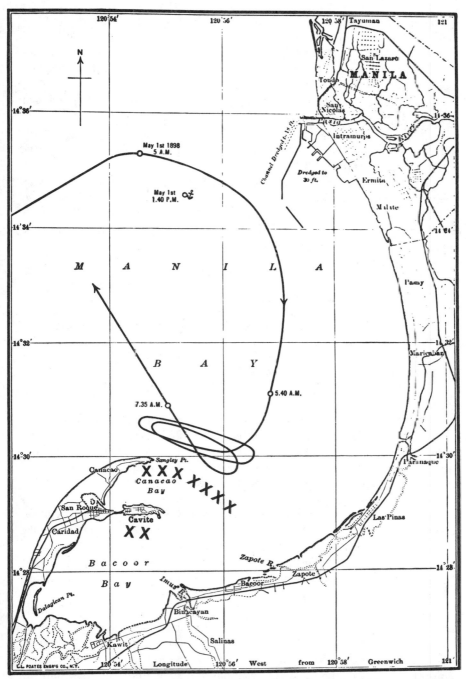

Manila Bay, showing the track of Dewey's squadron during the battle of May 1, 1898. The Xs indicate the approximate positions of the Spanish warships, which remained at anchor during the battle.

Olympia; three other protected cruisers, the *Raleigh,* the *Baltimore,* and the *Boston;* two gunboats, the *Petrel* and the *Concord;* and the *McCulloch,* a Revenue Service cutter that had been in the midst of a round-the-world shakedown cruise when it was pressed into service with the Navy's Asiatic Squadron.

In addition to the warships, two unarmed colliers, the *Zafiro* and the *Nanshan,* completed the fleet. During March and early April, Dewey had purchased the two ships and their cargoes of coal from their British owners.

"The English crews, including the officers, with the spirit of true seamen, agreed not only to stand by their ships, but welcomed the prospect of an adventurous cruise," Dewey recalled.

But the English tars may have wondered whether the voyage with the Yanks might not prove a bit too adventurous. There had been frequent reports in the Hong Kong newspapers that the fortifications at Manila, the Spanish squadron in the harbor, and the mine fields at the mouth of the bay made the place impregnable. "The prevailing impression among even the military class in the colony," Dewey recalled,

> was that our squadron was going to certain destruction.
> In the Hong Kong Club it was not possible to get bets, even at heavy odds, that our expedition would be a success, and this in spite of a friendly predilection among the British in our favor. I was told, after our officers had been entertained at dinner by a British regiment, that the universal remark among our hosts was to this effect: "A fine set of fellows, but unhappily we shall never see them again."

Dewey was not impressed by such forebodings, but he acknowledged that there was much uncertainty in the matter of Spanish defenses in the Philippines. Official U.S. intelligence advice on the subject was so deficient that the commodore was reduced to buying his own charts of the islands in Hong Kong. To reduce doubts about the Spanish strength he instituted his own informal intelligence system weeks before the outbreak of hostilities.

Dewey's primary source of information was O. F. Williams, the American consul at Manila. But although Williams was on the spot and his espionage activities were protected by the cloak of diplomatic immunity, he lacked the technical expertise to make sense of what he saw. Moreover, he had been at Manila only since January, far too short a time to have gained much knowledge of the place or cultivated many local sources of information.

To supplement Williams's reports, Dewey's aide, Ensign F. B. Upham, posing as a civilian traveler with an interest in nautical matters, interviewed the crews of steamers arriving at Hong Kong from Manila. Additionally, an American businessman living in Hong Kong—his name is lost to history—made frequent visits to Manila and reported his observations to Dewey. From this makeshift spy system, Dewey was able to construct a better estimate of the reception he was likely to meet.

There were some forty Spanish naval vessels in and around Manila, a numerically superior force. However, most of these were gunboats and other small vessels of negligible value in a modern sea battle. The largest vessels were the cruisers *Reina Cristina* and *Castilla,* and the latter was constructed of wood. There were four smaller cruisers, each less than twelve hundred tons and none armed with more than four 4.7-inch guns in its main battery.

The coastal defenses sounded more formidable. The island of Corregidor stood in the broad entrance to Manila Bay, dividing it into two channels: Boca Chica, which was two miles wide; and Boca Grande, four miles wide. The tiny island of El Fraile stood in the Boca Grande, subdividing it into a pair of channels one and three miles wide, respectively. There were reports that a battery of five or six six-inch guns had recently been installed on Corregidor, commanding the entire entrance to the bay. There was a smaller battery at the naval station at Cavite and small batteries at or near the city of Manila.

There was also the question of submerged mines. Williams reported that Boca Grande had been mined, and this was confirmed by the accounts of merchant captains who had recently been at Manila and who had been instructed by the Spanish authorities to enter and leave the bay by way of special zigzag courses, presumably to avoid the mines.

Dewey was skeptical. Mining a deep-water channel like the Boca Grande was a difficult undertaking; he doubted the Spanish could do it. Even if they had, he believed the mines were probably now useless; submerged mines deteriorated rapidly in tropical waters. As to the Spaniards' ostentatious zigzag courses, Dewey snorted, "A specious bluff!"

He was confident, but he was not precipitous. The Navy's orders said "proceed at once," but at that very moment Consul Williams was en route to Hong Kong aboard the steamer *Esmeralda.* Dewey decided to wait and see whether Williams had any last-minute advisories on the situation at Manila.

For two days and nights the restless and impatient squadron marked time in Mirs Bay. On the morning of the twenty-seventh the little tug *Fame* arrived, carrying Williams. As steam was gotten up in the ships' boilers, the commanders gathered on the *Olympia* for a final conference.

At 2 P.M. the Asiatic Squadron steamed out of Mirs Bay and set a course for the island of Luzon in the Philippines. The sea was calm, the sky clear. From the bridge of the *Olympia,* Dewey could look back along his flagship's foaming wake. The *Baltimore,* the *Raleigh,* the *Petrel,* the *Concord,* and the *Boston* followed in line astern. The *McCulloch* and the two colliers, *Zafiro* and *Nanshan,* were in a second column about 1,200 yards back. The force totaled more than 19,000 tons of fighting ships, over 100 guns, and some 1,456 officers and men.

The cruisers were modern ships—not the Navy's newest, but far from antiquated. They were the product of a shipbuilding program of some dozen years past in the last twilight of the days of fighting sail, when men-of-war still were propelled by a combination of canvas and steam. Tall masts and broad yards rose above the black smoke billowing from their stacks and swayed steeply over the water with every quartering sea.

The fleet was a hybrid creature born of a past already gone and a future not fully arrived, commanded by a veteran who had served under Farragut and seen action at New Orleans and Fort Fisher, manned by seamen who would live to remember Pearl Harbor. Their sons would learn the names of Guadalcanal, Iwo Jima, and Inchon. Their grandsons would know Chu-lai, Plei-me, and the Iadrang Valley.

A sudden explosion of brass and percussion shook the quarter deck of the *Olympia,* where the Marine band, resplendent in white tropical uniform, broke into "El Capitán." The music drifted out over the water to the other ships of the squadron. A cheer went up: "Remember the *Maine!*"

The powerful rhythms of Sousa quickened their pulse. In the passion of that instant a momentous die had been cast and went unnoticed. Above the ships the Stars and Stripes snapped in the wind. They were carrying it on a voyage from which it would be a long time coming home.

The U.S. Asiatic Squadron steamed out into the South China Sea.

.   .   .

"CONSUL WILLIAMS, when he came on board just before our departure from Mirs Bay, had brought news which was anything but encouraging," Dewey recalled. "It upset my preconceived ideas, as I had counted upon fighting in Manila Bay. Just as the consul was leaving Manila he had learned of the sailing of the Spanish squadron for Subic Bay."

Subic Bay lay thirty miles north of Corregidor along the route the American squadron would traverse on its way to Manila. It was smaller and narrower than Manila Bay, hence more easily defended against a naval attack. Dewey considered it an "invaluable aid" to the defense of Manila: "With this strategic point effectively occupied, no hostile commander-in-chief would think of passing it and leaving it as a menace to his lines of communication. But with it unoccupied the way was clear."

Unfortunately, Dewey reflected, the Spanish commander "at the last moment seemed to have realized the strategic advantage of Subic over Manila, which we hoped he would fail to do."

Dewey continued to prepare to engage the Spanish squadron, wherever it was. There were frequent drills. At midnight on the first day out, "quarters for action" was sounded and the crew tumbled out of their hammocks and went to battle stations. The commodore, observing the exercise from the bridge, watch in hand, noted with satisfaction that the *Olympia* had cleared for action in just seven minutes.

The squadron proceeded southward at a stately eight knots in deference to the two colliers, heavily laden and riding low in the water. Its wake was marked by tables, chairs, wall panels, and every imaginable piece of wood not deemed absolutely necessary to combat operations. "Essential to comfort in time of peace," Dewey observed later, "[wood] might become ignited in an engagement. Had the Spaniards disposed of their wood-work their ships would have burned less fiercely."

On the second day out officers and crewmen crowded around ship's bulletin boards to read an unusual notice. It was a proclamation by the Spanish governor general of the Philippines, dated five days earlier. A copy had reached Mirs Bay just as the squadron was sailing. Dewey had it posted in each of the ships without comment.

Spaniards:
Between Spain and the United States of North America hostilities have broken out.
The moment has arrived to prove to the world that we possess the spirit to conquer those who, pretending to be loyal friends, take advantage of our misfortunes and abuse our hospitality, using means which civilized nations count unworthy and disreputable.
The North American people, constituted of all the social excrescences, have exhausted our patience and provoked war with their perfidious machinations, with their acts of treachery, with their outrages against the law of nations and international conventions. . . .
A squadron manned by foreigners, possessing neither instructions nor discipline, is preparing to come to this archipelago with the ruffianly intention of robbing us of all that means life, honor, and liberty. Pretending to be inspired by a courage of which they are incapable, the North American seamen undertake as an enterprise capable of realization the substitution of Protestantism for the Catholic religion you profess . . . to take possession of your riches as if they were unacquainted with the rights of property, and to kidnap those persons who they consider useful to man their ships or to be exploited in agricultural or industrial labor.
Vain designs! Ridiculous boastings! . . . The aggressors shall not profane the tombs of your fathers, they shall not gratify their lustful passions at the cost of your wives' and daughters' honor, or appropriate the property that our industry has accumulated as a provision for your old age. . . .
Filipinos, prepare for the struggle. . . .

And so on.
The crewmen read the proclamation and were fully as indignant as Dewey expected. Whatever the effect the Spaniard's words may have had on his own people, they served to make the Americans fighting mad. That evening the *Olympia*'s band serenaded the squadron with "Yankee Doodle," "Marching Through Georgia," and several Sousa favorites. But the selection enjoyed most may have been a popular song of the day that was on its way to becoming the hit of the Spanish War—"There'll Be a Hot Time in the Old Town Tonight!"

· · ·

ADMIRAL PATRICIO MONTOJO Y PASARÓN was dismayed. Montojo, commander of Spanish naval forces in the Philippines, had been pressing Madrid for additional arms and supplies for the past six weeks, ever since war with the Americans had begun to appear inevitable.
"I am without resources, or time," he declared on April 11. But his entreaties of the minister of marine had no more effect than those of Admiral Cervera.

Bermejo advised him to make up for his deficiencies of materiel with an excess of "zeal and activity."

But enthusiasm was no substitute for submarine mines, which Montojo needed to seal the entrance to Manila Bay. Bermejo promised that a shipment of seventy mines was on its way to the Philippines from Spain, but on April 25 it appeared to Montojo that the American fleet would arrive before the mines. He moved the six largest ships of his squadron to Subic Bay.

The short voyage up the coast was not without mishap. The cruiser *Castilla* sprung a leak in a propeller shaft housing and began taking on water. The leak was sealed with cement at Subic, stopping the water, but making the propeller immobile; the *Castilla* now could move only by means of her sails or a tow rope.

The situation at Subic Bay was not encouraging either. Montojo discovered that only five of the fourteen underwater mines available had yet been put in place. Worse, the four 5.9-inch guns he believed to be guarding the bay entrance were still lying on the beach. And his last hopes that there might still be time to complete the bay's defenses vanished on April 28, when he received a telegram from the Spanish consul at Hong Kong sent on the previous day: "The enemy's squadron sailed at 2 P.M. from Mirs Bay, and according to reliable accounts they sailed for Subic to destroy our squadron and then will go to Manila."

The water of Subic Bay was forty meters deep. Montojo decided that, if he was going to be sunk, he'd prefer it to happen in a shallower place ("What a strange conclusion for a naval officer!" Dewey later observed). With the crippled *Castilla* in tow, Montojo's squadron made its way back to Manila Bay.

．　　　．　　　．

THE AMERICAN FLEET moved through the darkness off the coast of Luzon. Except for a single light at the stern to guide the next ship in line, the squadron was in total blackout. "The presence of the squadron on the waters was denoted alone by the dark forms of the ships and the breaking of phosphorescence at their bows and in the wake of their propellers," Dewey remembered. In the predawn of April 30, Cape Bolinao on the northwest coast of Luzon was sighted. Lieutenant Calkins, the *Olympia*'s navigator, recalled:

> A dark mass and a rank tropical odor revealed the great island. Daylight showed leagues of mangrove swamp backed by ridges of rock, covered with scrubby timber, with lofty peaks farther inland. Rather barren for the tropics it seemed, but the coast is bold with landmarks for safe navigation.

Subic Bay lay some hundred miles to the south. Dewey signaled the *Boston* and *Concord* to steam ahead of the squadron and reconnoiter. The rest of the squadron followed in their wake at a cautious eight knots, keeping three or four miles off the Luzon coast.

Shortly after daybreak several Filipino fishing boats were sighted. The collier *Nanshan* was sent to overhaul some of them and question their crewmen about the location of the Spanish fleet. Some of the fishermen professed to know nothing; others claimed there were only two gunboats at Manila Bay. The reports seemed doubtful and worthless.

Some of the *Olympia*'s officers believed they heard the sounds of gunfire from the south. Dewey heard nothing but dispatched the *Baltimore* to steam ahead in case the *Boston* and *Concord* needed help. The remainder of the squadron followed slowly.

At 3:30 P.M. the squadron rounded the southwestern cape of Luzon and found the three advance ships lying peacefully off the entrance to Subic Bay. The Spanish fleet had abandoned the strategically important point. Dewey was deeply relieved. He turned to Commander B. P. Lamberton, his chief of staff.

"Now we have them," he said.

The squadron continued south. Manila Bay lay thirty miles further. Now fast approaching was the critical moment when they would steam through the expected minefields in the Boca Grande beneath the Spanish artillery on Corregidor. As darkness approached the squadron halted. The commanders came aboard the *Olympia* for a final meeting with the commodore.

"We shall enter Manila Bay tonight and you will follow the motions and movements of the flagship, which will lead," Dewey announced.

As the meeting broke up, Lieutenant William Winder of the *Baltimore* approached the commodore and saluted smartly.

"Commodore, I have always made it a policy never to take advantage of our being related," Winder began. He was Dewey's nephew. "But in this instance I should like to make an exception."

Winder wanted to take the *Zafiro* through the Boca Chica ahead of the squadron. The heavily laden collier had the deepest draught of all of the ships; if she passed through the entrance to the bay without mishap, the others could follow in her wake secure from the danger of mines. And if she struck a mine —well, the ship was unarmed, hence of no value in the coming battle with the Spanish fleet.

"Sir," Winder stammered, "this is one chance I have to become famous."

Dewey smiled and shook his head.

"Billy, I have waited sixty years for this opportunity. And much as I like you and know you are a fine officer—mines or no mines, I am leading the squadron in myself."

The mines were a possibility—Dewey considered it a remote one; the artillery on Corregidor was a certainty.

> If the guns commanding the entrance were well served, there was danger of damage to my squadron before it engaged the enemy's squadron. If the Spaniards had shown enterprise in the use of the materials which they possessed, then we might have expected a heavy fire from the shore batteries.

As to the matter of fame, if he considered it at all at that moment, Dewey might have noted that Lieutenant Winder would have the rest of his life to pursue it. For him, the Spanish War was probably to be his last campaign.

.   .   .

NIGHT DESCENDED OVER the squadron as it steamed toward the Boca Grande. Darkness was to be the best shield against the guns of Corregidor. The black masses of islands and headlands were dimly visible against the lighter backgrounds of sea and sky. Lieutenant Calkins had no difficulty picking up his cross-bearings and keeping the squadron on the track he had laid out.

"No local knowledge was needed to arrange these details," he recalled, "and no degree of darkness could have disturbed our navigation."

The moon made efforts to break through the clouds, but on the whole the night was dark, in spite of the dancing pillars of cloud pulsing with tropical lightning among which we cruised. There were light showers which dampened hundreds of suits of white duck, but nobody noticed such trifles.

As night fell, we began to realize that we were preparing to force an entrance into a guarded bay with hostile batteries and ships lying in wait for us. . . . Having reason to suspect that the batteries of Corregidor were placed to command both channels, we had chosen the wider one and had shaped courses to pass that stronghold at a distance of three miles and a half,—not out of range, but too far off to be checked in a resolute advance. . . . Small islands showed clearly on the horizon, though black shadows lay under the land. La Monja, or the Haystack, was left to port, and El Fraile showed a jagged lump nearly ahead.

The Americans did not know that the best of the Spanish artillery, including three of most modern pieces, had been placed amid the rocks of El Fraile.

Ten miles off the entrance to the bay, the lookouts saw a signal light flashing on Corregidor and knew they had been sighted. A rocket soared into the night sky. But there were no shots, no dash of torpedo boats, no sign of life beyond the Spanish signals.

Dewey recalled: "As we watched the walls of darkness for the first gun-flash, every moment of our progress brought its relief, and now we began to hope that we should get by without being fired on at all."

The *Olympia* was now inside Manila Bay. The flagship swung to a northeast by north heading. The cruisers and gunboats astern did the same. Only the revenue cutter *McCulloch* and the two colliers remained in the channel. Suddenly a tall pillar of flame erupted from the *McCulloch*'s stack. Accumulated soot had caught fire, giving the Spanish gunners a target. The battery on El Fraile opened up. An artillery round whistled and tumbled through the air over the revenue cutter.

The guns of the *Boston*, *Concord*, and *Raleigh* returned the fire. Even the *McCulloch* answered with her little six-pounder. The El Fraile battery fired twice more, then went silent. A round from the *Boston* had found its mark. The cutter and the two colliers continued unmolested. The Asiatic Squadron had safely run the gauntlet of Boca Grande.

"The moon set shortly after the firing ceased," Lieutenant Calkins recalled, "and we crept onward through the darkness at slow speed."

Manila lay ahead, twenty-five miles across the broad expanse of the bay. The Spanish naval station was located at Cavite, on a hook of land some five miles closer.

"As . . . I did not wish to reach our destination before we had sufficient daylight to show us the position of the Spanish ships, the speed of the squadron was reduced to four knots, while we headed toward the city of Manila," Dewey remembered.

A white glow in the northeast marked the city. As the squadron approached the electric lights of the streets and avenues became visible. At 4 A.M. coffee and cold breakfast was served to the crew. The mood was a mixture of nervousness and raillery. In a soft falsetto, someone began to sing, "Just Before the Battle, Mother." Someone else poured a pot of coffee over him. On the navigator's platform above the forward bridge of the *Olympia*, Lieutenant Calkins stood at Dewey's side and watched the sky grow light.

Daylight came out behind Manila and revealed long ranges of white houses and gray fortifications with domes and towers breaking the dim outlines. Eager eyes were turned to the anchorage off the breakwater. The binoculars showed a cluster of black hulls and lofty spars; sixteen sailing ships were counted. There were no men-of-war, no steamers of any sort. . . . It was almost five o'clock and the dawn was spreading.

The squadron was now within a mile or so of the city's waterfront, which lay almost directly to the west. Shortly after five o'clock, as the growing early light revealed more of the coastline, a lookout sighted ships about five miles to the south, where a hook of land protruded into the bay. Calkins swung around and thumbed the knob on his binoculars, bringing Sangley Point and the Cavite naval station into sharp focus. A line of gray and white vessels stretched eastward from the point. Above them flew the flame-colored flags of Spain. Dewey turned and spoke an order to the *Olympia*'s commander, Captain Charles V. Gridley. The flagship swung to starboard. The *Baltimore* following astern did the same, and in a few moments the six warships of the squadron were bearing south, the distant Spanish fleet on their starboard bows. The pulse of the warships quickened as their speed was increased to eight knots.

"Take her close along the five-fathom line, Mr. Calkins," Dewey ordered, "but be careful not to run her aground." The *Olympia* was drawing more than four fathoms, but Dewey wanted to get close enough to the Spanish ships to insure sinking them with his limited ammunition. A leadsman sang a slow litany of soundings as the city slipped past to port.

Calkins remembered:

A white cloud with a heart of fire rose from Sangley Point and a shell soared toward our line. The plunge of the projectile was followed by the roar of the gun. . . . One shell was seen dropped beyond us describing a trajectory of more than six miles. They were ready for us then, and meant to fight. But a moment later two harmless fountains sprang up miles ahead of our column, and it was plain that the defense was flurried.

The batteries along the Manila waterfront also began firing, their shots passing well over the American squadron, some falling into the bay seven miles off. The *Boston* and *Concord* replied with two shells apiece, then ceased firing. Ammunition was too precious to be spent on anything but the principal target —the Spanish fleet. The squadron continued to bear down on Cavite. Dewey remembered the strange stillness of the moment:

> All the guns were pointed constantly at the enemy, while the men were at their stations waiting the word. There was no break in the monotone of the engines save the mechanical voice of the leadsman or an occasional low-toned command by the quartermaster at the conn, or the roar of a Spanish shell.

The squadron continued to advance at eight knots, its guns silent. At 5:40 A.M. the *Olympia* had approached to within two and a half-miles of the Spanish ships (navigator Calkins estimated 5,400 yards). Dewey turned to the warship's commander.

"You may fire when you are ready, Gridley."

.   .   .

"THE AMERICANS FIRED most rapidly," Admiral Montojo recounted. "There came upon us numberless projectiles, as the three cruisers at the head of the line devoted themselves almost entirely to fight the *Cristina,* my flag ship."

But at least the excruciating wait was over. Since 7 P.M. the previous evening, when he received a telegram from the base at Subic Bay reporting that the Americans had been there and gone on, there had been little to do but wait. At midnight he had heard the firing from Corregidor, and at 2 A.M. he had a telegram reporting the exchange of fire in Boca Grande. Then he knew the American admiral would come at dawn. At 4 A.M. he signaled the squadron to prepare for action. Now the action was underway. It was a relief.

.   .   .

THE FIRE FROM THE eight-inch guns in the *Olympia*'s forward turret was slow and deliberate. Each roar marked the launch of a 250-pound mass of steel and high explosive at the Spanish fleet. A shell struck the *Cristina*'s forecastle, knocking out the flagship's four rapid-fire cannon and splintering the forward mast. A second shell struck and the ship began burning, but the Spanish sailors managed to put out the flames.

The American squadron, still following the five-fathom line that ran roughly parallel to the shore, had now come to a westerly heading, putting Cavite and the Spanish fleet to port. The heavy gun turrets swung round, and the squadron's port batteries joined in. The ships were now running parallel to the line of the Spanish fleet and at a distance of three thousand yards.

"The enemy shortened the distance between us, and, rectifying his aim, covered us with a rain of rapid-fire projectiles," Montojo recounted.

A Spanish torpedo boat suddenly appeared steaming out from Cavite and across the American squadron's path. It was spotted by Joseph Stickney, a newspaperman who had joined the fleet at Hong Kong and was now serving in a combat role as Dewey's aide. Stickney pointed out the Spanish boat to the commodore.

"You look after her," Dewey replied. "I have no time to bother with torpedo boats. Let me know when you've finished with her."

The *Olympia*'s rapid-fire guns and six-pounders turned on the newcomer. Even the Marines aboard began firing their rifles at her. The boat was quickly crippled and driven ashore.

The *Olympia* had now completely passed the Spanish fleet and was abeam of Sangley Point. She heeled over and executed a 180-degree turn, steaming eastward and passing the Spanish ships once more. The other ships of the squadron quickly followed suit, the massive gun turrets of the cruisers swinging around from port to starboard. As the squadron again passed abeam of the Spanish fleet, its starboard batteries opened up. Lieutenant Calkins tried to see the results of the first pass.

With some exasperation we noted a large percentage of misses from our well-aimed guns. It was hard to be sure of the fall of any particular shell, but many splashed ineffectually. Yet our batteries kept hammering away, straining and jarring the ship in the shock of their recoil.

But the American shells were finding their marks. Admiral Montojo recalled the damage aboard his flagship:

Another shell exploded on the poop, and put out of action nine men. Another destroyed the mizzen-mast head, bringing down the flag and my ensign, which were replaced immediately. A fresh shell exploded in the officers' cabin, covering the hospital with blood and destroying the wounded who were being treated there. Another exploded in the ammunition-room astern, filling the quarters with smoke . . . As it was impossible to control the fire, I had to flood the magazine when the cartridges were beginning to explode.

Amidships several shells of smaller caliber went through the smoke-stack, and one of the large ones penetrated the fire-room, putting out of action one master-gunner and twelve men serving the guns. Another rendered useless the starboard-bow gun. While the fire astern increased, fire was started forward by another shell which went through the hull and exploded on the deck.

But the battle was far from being one-sided. The guns of the Spanish fleet were augmented by the batteries on Cavite. The *Olympia*, flying the commodore's ensign and leading the American line, drew much of the fire. Stickney recalled some of the results:

> Shots from their ship and shore guns came through the air in a screaming shower; time-fuse shells were constantly bursting about the American fleet, and their fragments, scattering in all directions, would strike the water like shrapnel or cut the hull and rigging of the ships.
> . . . One shell struck close by a gun in the ward room. The signal halyards were cut from Lieutenant Brumby's hand, as he stood on the after bridge. One great projectile, with almost human intuition, came straight toward the forward bridge, but burst less than a hundred feet away. A fragment cut the rigging directly over the heads of Commander Lamberton and myself. Another struck the bridge railings in line with us, and still another, about as large as a flat iron, gouged a hole in the deck a few feet below the commodore.
> The *Baltimore*'s crew had several narrow escapes. One shot struck her and passed through her, but fortunately hit no one. Another ripped up her main deck, disabling one six-inch gun, and exploded a couple of 3-pounder shells, wounding eight men. . . .
> The *Boston* received a shell in her port quarter. It burst in Ensign Doddridge's stateroom and caused a hot fire, as did also one that burst in the port hammock netting; but both these fires were quickly extinguished. One shell passed through the Boston's foremast, just in front of Captain Wildes on the bridge.

The American squadron steamed past the Spanish line, amid the clouds belched from its own guns and the erupting geysers of incoming shells. Once again the ships came about and steamed westward, while turrets swung round and gun crews readied the port batteries. The *Olympia* led a third pass along the Spanish line. Again the thunder of artillery shook the walls and windows of Manila and echoed from the hills beyond.

"There was some natural impatience for visible results," Calkins remembered. But there was no shortage of visible results—thick billows of black smoke rolled up from the burning Spanish ships and drifted out over the bay. Yet there was no sign of surrender. The red and yellow flag of Spain still flew above the shattered, burning hulks, and their broadsides flashed defiantly. The American squadron completed its third pass, turned around to begin a fourth, and was met by an astonishing sight. Admiral Montojo's flagship, the *Reina Cristina*, had left the Spanish line and was limping out into the bay. From her course it was clear she intended to attack the *Olympia*. Calkins watched the Spaniard's approach from the elevated platform of the American flagship.

> The two flagships drew together as if for a duel, but the *Olympia* was covering more ground than her opponent, who was exposed to the concentrated fire of several broadsides. The slow advance continued until the *Cristina* was within 1,200 yards and we could see our shells

strike home. Dark clouds of smoke poured up from the bow and stern and a plume of white steam made another signal of distress. A shell had pierced the superheater, the ship was on fire in two places, the steering-engine was shot away and most of the guns were disabled. So the ship turned inshore and sought refuge in shoal water close to the Arsenal.

Admiral Montojo described the situation aboard:

The ship being beyond control, the hull, smokepipe, and mast riddled with shot, the confusion occasioned by the cries of the wounded, half the crew out of action, among whom were seven officers, I gave the order to sink and abandon the ship before the magazine should explode, making signal at the same time to the *Isla de Cuba* and *Isla de Luzon* to assist in saving the rest of the crew, which they did.

But the losses aboard the *Cristina* were terrible. "When she was raised from her muddy bed, five years later," Dewey wrote in his *Autobiography*, "eighty skeletons were found in the sick-bay . . . Her loss was one hundred and fifty killed and ninety wounded. . . . Among the killed was her valiant captain, Don Luís Cadarso, who, already wounded, finally met his death while bravely directing the rescue of his men from the burning and sinking vessel."

At 7:35 A.M., just after the squadron had begun its fifth pass of the Spanish line, Captain Gridley informed Dewey there remained only fifteen rounds per gun for the flagship's five-inch battery, or, in other words, enough to last another five minutes at the rate it was being used. If this was indicative of the situation on the other ships, then the Asiatic Squadron was in the middle of a hostile bay seven thousand miles from home and almost out of ammunition. Dewey looked toward the Spanish line. He could see nothing but smoke, but the last time the smoke had cleared the Spanish flag was still flying and the Spanish gunners still firing.

"It was a most anxious moment for me. So far as I could see, the Spanish squadron was as intact as ours. I had reason to believe that their supply of ammunition was as ample as our was limited."

Dewey ordered the squadron to withdraw into the bay and redistribute the remaining ammunition. As the ships steamed north beyond the range of the Spanish guns, the smoke near Cavite cleared for a few moments, disclosing the devastation. "It was clear that we did not need a very large supply of ammunition to finish our morning's task," Dewey wrote. And, in fact, Captain Gridley had been wrong; plenty of ammunition remained.

Dewey took advantage of the break in the battle to call a meeting of the captains aboard the *Olympia*, directing that the crews should have breakfast meanwhile. The impression immediately spread throughout the squadron that breakfast had been the reason for the pause.

"For God's sake, captain," one gunner cried, "don't let us stop now! To hell with breakfast!" Dewey noted that the idea of a breakfast break in the middle of a naval battle seemed to indicate "a nonchalance that had never occurred to me."

Dewey turned at once to the serious question of his own losses. An observer aboard one of the colliers, seeing the punishment the American squadron had taken, had estimated that there were no fewer than four hundred dead. But when Dewey told his captains to report their casualties he was delighted to learn that there had been only six wounded and none killed. The only fatality was the *McCulloch*'s chief engineer, who had succumbed to heat prostration the night before, while the squadron was passing through Boca Grande.

Breakfast was served. Calkins climbed down from the navigator's platform of the *Olympia*. "There were sardines, corned beef, and hardtack on a corner of the wardroom table, still encumbered by the surgeons' ghastly gear, which was all unstained, however." The half-dozen slightly wounded were all on the *Baltimore*.

The crewmen began to drift on deck to smoke and pass the time. Calkins observed that the smoke of the battle and the heat in the turrets and boiler rooms had taken a toll of white duck uniforms. "Golf caps and pith helmets were seen in high places; officers and men came on the bridge in obsolescent pajamas or inadequate undershirts; the turret crews were frankly primeval in their attire."

The strange interlude in the battle was punctuated now and then by exploding ammunition aboard the burning Spanish ships. In the city of Manila, curious onlookers climbed to the tops of roofs and church steeples to stare in dismay. The lull continued for three and a half hours. Then the American warships got underway once again.

"At 11:16 A.M. we stood in to complete our work," Dewey recalled. "There remained to oppose us, however, only the [shore] batteries and the gallant little [*Don Antonio de*] *Ulloa*. Both opened fire as we advanced."

It did not take long. By 12:30 the *Ulloa* had been sunk, and a white flag was raised over the naval station at Cavite. Dewey ordered the gunboat *Petrel* into the shallow water near Sangley Point to finish off the abandoned and burning Spanish warships. Meanwhile he took the rest of the squadron to an anchorage off the city.

The batteries along the waterfront had been firing intermittently at the American squadron since dawn, but Dewey had not answered the fire. Now he sent a message ashore to the Spanish captain general of Manila. If another shot was fired by the batteries he would destroy the city. The Spanish commander quickly agreed to cease firing. Dewey had also told him that "if we were allowed to transmit messages by the cable to Hong Kong, the captain general would also be permitted to use it." The Spaniard balked at this and refused the Americans the use of the cable. On Dewey's instructions, the *Zafiro* dredged up the cable from the bottom of the bay and cut it. Manila was now cut off from the outside world.

"From the moment the captain-general accepted my terms [to silence the batteries] the city was virtually surrendered," Dewey recalled. "I had established a base seven thousand miles from home which I might occupy indefinitely."

As the sun dropped below the distant heights of Corregidor and the Bataan Peninsula, crowds of Spaniards and Filipinos came down to the waterfront to look upon their new conquerors. Dewey remembered the scene:

They climbed on the ramparts of the very battery that had fired on us in the morning. The *Olympia*'s band, for their benefit, played "La Paloma" and other Spanish airs, and while the sea-breeze wafted the strains to their ears the poor colonel of artillery who had commanded the battery, feeling himself dishonored by his disgraceful failure, shot himself through the head.

.   .   .

THE SILENCE FROM Manila was alarming. The first week of May passed without any word from Dewey. The only news of the battle came from Madrid, where the Spanish government had received a report sent by the captain general of Manila during Dewey's breakfast-time pause:

> Our fleet engaged the enemy in brilliant combat, protected by the Cavite and Manila forts. They obliged the enemy, with heavy loss, to maneuver repeatedly. At 9 o'clock the American squadron took refuge behind the foreign merchant shipping, on the east side of the bay.
> Our fleet, considering the enemy's superiority, naturally suffered severe loss. . . .
> There was considerable loss of life.

The American newspapers chose to interpret this optimistically. The New York *Herald* of May 2 ran the report beneath the headline: "Spain's Asiatic Fleet Destroyed by Dewey."

Hearst's *Journal* proclaimed: "Victory, Complete! . . . Glorious! . . . The *Maine* Is Avenged." In Washington, a jubilant Senator Redfield Proctor reminded McKinley that it had been he who had recommended Dewey for the Asiatic Squadron post.

But as the days passed without any word from Dewey, the phrase "heavy loss" in the Spanish dispatch began to take on an ominous significance. There were unconfirmed reports from Europe that five American ships had been sunk. By the morning of the seventh the *Journal* was reporting, "Great Nervousness Is Felt in Washington Because Nothing Is Heard from Dewey." "Not a Word from Dewey," said the New York *Sun*. "Still No News from Dewey," echoed the *Tribune*.

A similar headline had been printed in the early editions of the New York *World,* but at 3 A.M. a poker game in the newspaper's office was interrupted by the arrival of a dispatch from Edwin Harden, a *World* correspondent who had wangled a berth on the *McCulloch*. Harden's dispatch was from Hong Kong:

> I have just arrived here on the United States revenue cutter *McCulloch* with my report of the great American triumph at Manila. The entire Spanish fleet of eleven vessels was destroyed. Three hundred Spaniards were killed and four hundred wounded.* Our loss was none killed and but six slightly wounded. Not one of the American ships was injured.

*According to Admiral Montojo's report to Madrid, Spanish casualties, including both those aboard the ships and those ashore at Cavite, totaled 381 men killed and wounded. Quoted in Dewey, p. 307.

Harden's dispatch beat the official Navy report by some five hours; the official report, sent in cipher, had to be repeated back at each relay point along the route to insure accuracy. The first word the Navy Department received came from a correspondent of the Chicago *Tribune,* who awakened the duty officer in Washington at 6:15 A.M.

A one-word dispatch was received from the American consul at Hong Kong: *"McCulloch."* The *McCulloch* had indeed arrived. Presumably Commodore Dewey's report would soon follow. Secretary Long hurried to his office to find there was nothing to do but wait. Meanwhile, word had spread rapidly through Washington, and the secretary's anteroom was filled with newsmen and officials.

At 8:45 the first page of Dewey's dispatch was put in Secretary Long's hand; it was still in cipher, a maddening array of meaningless symbols. More delay while the clerks down the hall busied themselves with the code books. At 10 A.M. the complete dispatch had been received and deciphered. Long read it through quickly, picked up the telephone, and asked for the president.

A few minutes later Secretary Long emerged from his office and beamingly stepped into the crowded anteroom holding a slightly censored version of Dewey's message; President McKinley had authorized its release minus some details believed to be of military significance. But as he read it out he was aware that a certain mood of expectant tension seemed lacking. In fact, the full, uncensored text of the dispatch was already in the pockets of messengers pedaling their bicycles at breakneck speed to newsrooms across the city. In searching for the culprit Long needed to look no further than his assistant secretary.

It was Roosevelt's final act of official insubordination in the Navy Department. He had just been commissioned a lieutenant colonel in the U.S. First Volunteer Cavalry, an outfit that was soon to be known as the Rough Riders.

·   ·   ·

Dewey! Dewey! Dewey!
Is the hero of the day!
And the *Maine* has been remembered
In the good old fashioned way.

That was the opening to just one of the many Dewey songs that were immediately composed and sung.

The Chicago *Journal*'s Mr. Dooley claimed the commodore for Hibernia in general and the Dooley clan in particular: "Dewey or Dooley, 'tis all the same. We dhrop a letter here and there . . . but we're th' same breed iv fightin' men. Georgy has th' thraits iv th' fam'ly."

"Every American is in your debt," Roosevelt cabled.

Secretary Long's congratulations were more substantial: "You are assigned to command the U.S. Naval force on the Asiatic Station with the rank of Rear Admiral. Hoist the flag of a rear admiral immediately."

American jubilation was matched by European incredulity. The truth, of course, was that Spain's failure to make even minimal defensive preparations at Manila had been a major factor in Dewey's victory, but such gross negligence was beyond belief. It was easier to accept the idea that the United States had suddenly become one of the world's major naval powers, in the same league as England, France, and Germany. But only in England was that conclusion drawn with pleasure.

"The state of feeling here is the best I have ever known," Ambassador Hay told Cabot Lodge from London on May 25.

> From every quarter, the evidences of it come to me. The royal family, by habit and tradition, are most careful not to break the rules of strict neutrality, but even among them I find nothing but hearty kindness, and—so far as is consistent with propriety—sympathy. Among the political leaders on both sides I find not only sympathy, but a somewhat eager desire that "the other fellows" shall not seem the more friendly.

"What is our next duty?" asked Colonial Secretary Chamberlain, speaking to a political gathering two weeks after the Battle of Manila Bay, and he proceeded to answer his own question:

> It is to establish and to maintain bonds of permanent amity with our kinsmen across the Atlantic. There is a powerful and generous nation. They speak our language. They are bred of our race. Their laws, their literature, their standpoint upon every question, are the same as ours. Their feeling, their interests in the cause of humanity and the peaceful developments of the world are identical with ours. I don't know what the future has in store for us; I don't know what arrangements may be possible with us; but this I do know and feel, that the closer, the more cordial, the fuller, and the more definite these arrangements are, with the consent of both peoples, the better it will be for both and for the world—and I even go so far as to say that, terrible as war may be, even war itself would be cheaply purchased if, in a great and noble cause, the Stars and Stripes and the Union Jack should wave together over an Anglo-Saxon alliance.

On May 24, Americans and Englishmen joined in gatherings on both sides of the Atlantic to celebrate the seventy-ninth birthday of Queen Victoria. At one, a British regimental surgeon toasted the two flags, which were displayed side by side.

"Their colors never run," he proclaimed.

· · ·

A FEW DAYS AFTER the battle the German warships began arriving in Manila Bay. The cruiser *Irene* arrived on May 6, steaming past the *Olympia* without stopping and dropping anchor without consulting Dewey. "I regarded this as an oversight which was a breach of naval etiquette, of course, but not to be taken seriously unless I were inclined to insist on punctiliousness," Dewey remembered "It was only natural to reason that the captain of the *Irene* might not be familiar with the customs and the laws of blockades."

But when the German cruiser *Cormoran* did the same thing at 3 A.M. on

the ninth, ignoring the hail from the *Olympia's* steam launch, which Dewey had
sent to board her, he had had enough.

> In order to get the attention of the *Cormoran,* the *Raleigh* fired a shot
> across her bows. Then she promptly came to. Her captain was surprised
> at our action, but our boarding officer explained the law, and also the
> risk that a man-of-war was running in coming into the harbor at night.

The cruisers were from the German Asiatic Squadron, commanded by the
kaiser's younger brother, Prince Henry of Prussia. Dewey had encountered the
young prince during his stay in Hong Kong. Henry seemed to have been going
out of his way to be irritating. "Upon one occasion," Dewey recalled, "in discussing the possible outcome of our complications with Spain, Prince Henry remarked that he did not believe that the [European] powers would ever allow the
United States to annex Cuba."

"We do not wish to annex Cuba, Your Highness," Dewey answered, "but
we cannot suffer the horrible condition of affairs which exists at present in that
island at our very doors to continue, and we are bound to put a stop to it."

"And what are you after?" the prince inquired of Dewey on another occasion. "What does your country want?"

"Oh, we need only a bay," Dewey laughed, in a pointed reference to
Germany's recent seizure of Kaichow Bay.

A few weeks, later, as Dewey was preparing to leave Hong Kong, Prince
Henry bid him farewell:

"Well, commodore, good luck. I may send some ships to Manila—to see
that you behave."

"I should be delighted to have you do so, Your Highness," Dewey retorted.
"But permit me to caution you to keep your ships from between my guns and
the enemy."

Dewey feared that Germany might be about to come to Spain's aid, offering
materiel or military assistance to the blockaded force at Manila. In fact, the kaiser
had something else in mind. A few days after the Battle of Manila Bay, Prince
Henry had advised Berlin that "the [Filipino] natives would gladly place themselves under the protection of a European power, especially Germany."

Shortly thereafter the German consul at Manila offered the kaiser his estimate that the Filipinos believed themselves incapable of establishing a republic
and might prefer to be ruled by a German prince. Back in Berlin Wilhelm
scribbled enthusiastic *jas* in the margins of such dispatches, while von Bülow
urged him to proceed cautiously. But the kaiser made it clear: he did not intend
to let the Philippines change hands without getting something out of the transac-
tion.

·   ·   ·

DEWEY CONTINUED to maintain the blockade, painfully aware that his squadron
consisted of a handful of unarmored cruisers and gunboats at the end of a very
long line of supply. He had advised Washington that, while he could take Manila

whenever he wished, he had not the land force necessary to hold it. He estimated that five thousand troops would be needed for the task. On May 7 the Navy Department informed him that the cruiser *Charleston* would be sent soon, together with a contingent of troops on the *City of Pekin*. Some disturbing news followed on the twentieth. Naval intelligence sources in Europe had turned up a report that a Spanish task force was being assembled at Cádiz, including the big armored battleship *Pelayo*, the armored cruiser *Carlos V*, several auxiliary cruisers, plus armed troop transports. The force was to be commanded by Admiral Manuel de la Cámara.

Its destination was reported to be Manila.

CHAPTER SEVEN

A DREAM
OF SPRING

TWO DAYS BEFORE the Battle of Manila Bay, and half a world away from it, the squadron of Admiral Cervera departed the Cape Verde Islands. For a full week after the opening of hostilities Cervera's ships had lain at anchor in the harbor of St. Vincent while coal was laboriously transferred from a Spanish transport to their bunkers and the admiral continued to try to change the mind of Minister Bermejo. But on April 29 the Portugese harbor officials explained that their country had declared her neutrality, and so the Spanish fleet must leave.

"Am going north," Cervera cabled Madrid as he got underway. It was a preestablished code that could not disguise the fact that his fleet was sailing due west. An enterprising correspondent of the New York *Herald* chartered a small steamer and followed the warships out of the harbor. At dawn the next day he was back at St. Vincent cabling his paper that Cervera had continued to sail west through the day and until darkness hid the ships from view. He guessed they were bound for Puerto Rico and estimated they would arrive in twelve to fourteen days.

Admiral Cervera would have been astonished had he known of the panic this news produced along the East Coast of the United States.

"The Governor of one State actually announced that he would not permit the National Guard of that State to leave its borders," Roosevelt indignantly recalled,

the idea being to retain it against a possible Spanish invasion. So many of the business men of the city of Boston took their securities inland to Worcester that the safe deposit companies of Worcester proved unable to take care of them. In my own neighborhood on Long Island clauses were gravely put into leases to the effect that if the property were destroyed by the Spaniards the lease should lapse. . . . Congress-men . . . Chambers of Commerce and Boards of Trade of different coast cities all lost their heads for the time being, and raised a deafening clamor and brought every species of pressure to bear on the Administra-tion . . . to distribute the navy, ship by ship, at all kinds of points and in all kinds of ports with the idea of protecting everything everywhere.

With special outrage Roosevelt remembered a Georgia congressman who wanted a ship to protect Jekyll Island "because it contained the winter homes of certain millionaires" and an influential woman who "came to insist that a ship should be anchored off a huge sea-side hotel because she had a house in the neighborhood."

After assuring himself that Secretary Long and the president understood that dispersing the Navy in this way would permit even the poor squadron of Admiral Cervera to pick it off one ship at a time, he was content to leave such matters in their hands, busying himself with his preparations to depart for San Antonio, Texas, where the Rough Riders were training. On May 2 he fired off a telegram to his New York haberdasher, Brooks Brothers: "Ordinary cavalry lieutenant colonel's uniform blue Cravenette."

Another secretary of the Navy might have viewed Roosevelt's departure with pleasure, hoping to enjoy the war in relative peace and quiet, but the generous John D. Long was distressed at what he considered a terrible mistake, and he confided to his diary:

> My Assistant Secretary, Roosevelt, has determined upon resigning, in order to go into the army and take part in the war. He has been of great use; a man of unbounded energy and force, and thoroughly honest, which is the main thing. He has lost his head to this unutterable folly of deserting the post where he is of most service and running off to ride a horse and, probably, brush mosquitoes from his neck on the Florida sands. His heart is right, and he means well, but it is one of those cases of aberration—desertion—vainglory; of which he is utterly unaware. He thinks he is following his highest ideal, whereas, in fact, as without exception every one of his friends advises him, he is acting like a fool.

But with a sudden flash of prescience, Long added: "And, yet, how absurd all this will sound if, by some turn of fortune, he should accomplish some great thing. . . ."

        •   •   •

ON APRIL 23, the day after the Cuban blockade was put in place, President McKinley sent out a public call for 125,000 volunteers. The Army needed young men, healthy enough to pass the physical and willing to put on a uniform, carry a rifle and follow orders, which would probably include sailing off to some tropic place where there was a good chance of stopping a Spanish bullet and a better one of dying from yellow fever. In consideration of these services, such volunteers would be paid thirteen dollars per month.

The response was overwhelming. A million men wanted to enlist.

They lined up at the recruiting stations that seemed to have blossomed across the country overnight in vacant stores, post offices, tents pitched in public parks, or simply desks placed on sidewalks. They were given the jumping test (heart), the coughing test (hernia), and the eyesight test.

Some might have done better had there been a test for ingenuity or resourcefulness. One applicant tried to make the minimum weight by drinking a gallon of water before the physical. Another, three-eights of an inch short of the required height stayed in bed for three days in hope that this respite from vertical gravity might permit him to stretch his frame to government standards. But such measures usually failed. The Army could afford to be choosy: 77 percent of the applicants for enlistment were rejected, as were 90 percent of those seeking commissions.

.   .   .

As WILLIAM McKINLEY PREPARED to lead the country in a war he had not wanted, he saw a chance to put adversity to good use. The Spanish War was uniting the American people in a way they had not known in more than a generation. It promised to erase the last scars of the Civil War and Reconstruction. McKinley hoped to make this new unity a permanent condition by appointing prominent ex-Confederates to senior positions in the Army.

Commissioning Fitzhugh Lee as a major general of volunteers was reasonable on other grounds, as well. Although the portly sixty-three-year-old West Pointer had not worn a uniform since that day in April 1865 when he led the last Confederate charge at Farmville, Virginia, he had for the past two years been acquiring a comprehensive knowledge of the Cuban situation. But the choice of "Fighting Joe" Wheeler was probably made on entirely political grounds, although he was to play one of the most important combat roles in the war.

Joseph Wheeler, West Point class of 1859, distinguished Confederate cavalry leader who ended the war in the rank of lieutenant general at the age of twenty-eight, was lately a Democratic congressman from Alabama and chairman of the House Ways and Means Committee. On April 26 he received an invitation to stop at the White House that evening at 8:30.

"General, I have sent for you to ask if you want to go," President McKinley told his visitor, then added, "and if you feel able to go."

Wheeler looked like a frail little old man. He was sixty-one, stood five feet five inches in his bare feet, was slightly built, and had hair and a full beard that were snow-white. With Southern courtliness he replied that he felt quite capable and should welcome the chance to serve his country.

As events would soon prove, Wheeler was as tough as old rawhide and one of the most capable commanders to serve in the Spanish War. He was about to don a blue army uniform for the first time in thirty-eight years, and this time he would keep it. Long after the Spanish War he would be buried in it. When that day came, an old comrade would stand by his coffin and exclaim, "Jesus, General, I hate to think of what old Stonewall's going to say when he sees you arrivin' in that uniform!"

. . .

As of April 1, 1898, the U.S. Army consisted of 2,143 officers and 26,040 enlisted men. Most of the service was scattered at posts in the West between the Mexican and Canadian borders. Three weeks later it was directed to recruit, select, equip, train, and organize 125,000 new men, or, in other words, instantly quintuple in size. The inevitable consequence was an administrative nightmare and chaos.

On April 20 President McKinley met with the secretaries of war and the Navy and senior officers of the two services. General Nelson Miles, the Army's commanding general, advised that the Army could not be ready to land a large invasion force in Cuba for two months. That meant the end of June—the start of the rainy season and the period of greatest jeopardy from yellow fever.

"The sanitary objections to a campaign in Cuba during the summer season were well understood," Miles later recalled. He pointed out that the last time Cuba had been invaded—by the British in 1762—the invading force had picked the rainy season and lost thousands of men as a result. He was also worried about Admiral Cervera and was reluctant to send a fleet of transports into the Florida Straits while the Spanish squadron was still at large.

Miles proposed that the Cuban invasion be postponed until the fall, when the fever season had passed. Meanwhile the Navy would continue blockading the island and the Army would carry out small-scale expeditions to supply the insurgents and harass the Spanish, a policy that might of itself force Spain to capitulate and so save the human cost of a large invasion. Impressed by Miles's arguments, McKinley decided to adopt this plan.

Cape Tunas on the southern coast of Cuba, about seventy miles east of Cienfuegos, was selected as the landing point for the first raiding party. A force of six thousand men under General Rufus Shafter was to land there and move inland, link up with Máximo Gómez's army, deliver supplies, then return to the coast and reembark. Miles's orders to Shafter were sent April 29, the same day Cervera sailed from Cape Verde. The next day, when reports of the Spanish squadron's departure were received, the Tunas expedition was canceled.

The impoverished and uncertain squadron of Admiral Cervera had acquired a surprising measure of naval power, disrupting American plans through its mere existence somewhere, perhaps in the Atlantic, perhaps en route to the Caribbean, or even, by some accounts, Manila. It had taken on the role of a *fleet in being,* which, Captain Mahan later explained in his analysis of the Spanish War,

> is one the existence and maintenance of which, although inferior
> . . . is a perpetual menace to the various more or less exposed interests
> of the enemy, who cannot tell when a blow may fall, and who is
> therefore compelled to restrict his operations . . . until that fleet can
> be destroyed or neutralized.

It was a pungent irony. The reluctant Quixote and his sad squadron had become the most important unknown in the American military equations. The

"Cape Verde fleet," as anxious Washington planners now called it, would continue to disrupt American plans just as long as it remained out of sight. Admiral Cervera had unwittingly acquired the most fearsome of martial qualities—he was invisible.

.   .   .

GENERAL NELSON A. MILES was not a West Pointer; he had been commissioned as a captain in a Massachusetts volunteer regiment at the outbreak of the Civil War and through distinguished and heroic service quickly rose to the rank of brigadier general. He stayed in the Army and fought against the Indians in the Southwest during the next few decades. In 1895 he was appointed commanding general of the Army.

At fifty-nine, he was a big, athletic man. He had the imperious countenance of a Roman proconsul, decorated with an ostentatious iron gray mustache, in its size, shape, and ferocity suggestive of a Texas longhorn. He was the ablest of commanders, and he had succeeded in the Army because fighting Confederates, Comanches, and Apaches did not require tact or diplomacy, perhaps the only qualities he lacked. But in ascending to the post of commanding general he may have exceeded his competency. By all accounts General Miles was a hard man to get along with.

It was his fixed opinion that, in war, the only civilian who might have any business meddling in military matters was the president of the United States. This view was in sharp divergence from that of the secretary of war, Russell A. Alger.

From his appearance one would not have taken Alger to be a lumber magnate, former Civil War general of volunteers, former governor of Ohio, or a mover and shaker in Republican political circles, all of which he had been before McKinley appointed him to his cabinet in 1897. His fine profile and carefully trimmed, snow-white goatee were more suggestive of a college professor or clergyman. He was pleasant of temperament, tended to be impulsive, was more than a little vain, and had a skin much too thin for public life. One of his subordinates remembered the sixty-three-year-old secretary of war as "the most egotistic man with whom I have ever come in contact."

Whatever their individual qualities may have been, Miles and Alger presented an unpromising combination locked together by bureaucratic bonds neither could do anything about. Miles had been appointed commanding general by President Cleveland entirely on the basis of rank. As the Army's senior officer he would hold that post until retirement; the secretary of war could neither fire nor transfer him. For his part, Miles had seen secretaries of war come and go; since the Civil War only one secretary had served more than one four-year term, and several had served less than four years. As a rule, secretaries were not in office long enough to establish much control over the workings of the Army. Miles would much have preferred that Alger confine himself to the legal and financial concerns of the War Department and leave the running of the Army to the commanding general. But Alger was not so inclined, and there was little Miles could do about it.

Within the cabinet, Alger was embarrassed and defensive. The chaotic condition of the Army was accentuated by the Navy's high state of readiness, a contrast heightened further by the euphoria following news of Dewey's victory at Manila. Of course, the condition of both services was largely the result of past congresses and administrations, and Alger was as little to blame for the state of the Army as Secretary Long was to be praised for the readiness of the Navy. But this neither comforted Alger nor deterred Long from an attitude of smug superiority. Long argued the Navy's point of view: there should be an immediate invasion of Cuba; the longer it was delayed, the greater the danger to the blockading fleet from the approaching hurricane season.

On May 2, Alger, Long, Miles, and Admiral Sicard met in a counsel of war with President McKinley. McKinley now advocated immediate invasion of Cuba. Alger took the optimistic stance that the new volunteers would soon be ready for such an operation. Miles demurred, continuing to cite the fever season, the lack of training of the new recruits, and the mystery of Cervera's whereabouts. But the Navy prevailed, and it was decided to land a force of forty thousand to fifty thousand troops at Mariel, a port some twenty-six miles west of Havana that would become a staging area for an attack on Havana. The operation was to commence without regard to the rainy season, but as soon as the Army was ready. Alger estimated that would be in three or four weeks.

Four days later Long chose a cabinet meeting as the occasion to convey to Alger a Navy report that the Army could not meet its scheduled commitments to the Mariel operation. Alger was understandably offended and, in effect, told Long to mind his own business, i.e, the Navy, not the Army. Long reported to his diary:

He [Alger] intimates that the War Department will take care of itself without any interference from the Navy. I meet this with good nature, and simply suggest that my purpose is to show the readiness of the Navy, as I do not wish the impression to go abroad that there is any delay on our part.

Alger smarted over the incident for three days. He was in an unenviable situation, between Long who demanded immediate action and Miles who insisted on delay. Finally, on May 9, he sought sweet bureaucratic revenge on both in a single blow by ordering Miles to take seventy thousand men and immediately undertake the capture of Havana.

Long was caught off balance, protesting to his diary: "I learn to my utter amazement that [the landing] is to be made tomorrow, and not a word has been said to me about furnishing a convoy. Our ships are ready, but we must have at least some notice when and where they are wanted."

Alger had tried to put the ball in the Navy's court, but it was General Miles who actually canceled the operation by going directly to McKinley and notifying him that, apart from all other considerations, there just wasn't enough ammunition available for a force of seventy thousand men. The president directed that the invasion be postponed until May 16.

·   ·   ·

THE OCEANGOING TUG, *The Three Friends*, rocked and plunged through the sea midway between Havana and Key West. Stephen Crane sat in his bunk, the valise across his knees serving as a writing table. He bent over to retrieve the bottle of beer he held between his heels. When he had taken a long pull, he returned it to its place and resumed his dispatch for the New York *World*.

A day on the Cuban blockade.

The coast of Cuba, a high, wooded bank, with ranges of hills in the background, lay ten miles to the south. The flagship New York lifted her huge slate-colored body moodily over the quiet waves, disclosing from time to time a bit of blood-red hull below the water-line. Some officers in various degrees of white duck were grouped on the quarter-deck and on the after bridge. The signal men were sending aloft the line of flags, holding talk with a faint gray thing far away, the only other ship on the sweeping expanse of sea.

To those who imagine the blockade of Cuba to be a close assembling of ships about the mouth of Havana Harbor this would be confusing. It does not represent the popular idea of the blockade; but, nevertheless, on six days out of eight and twenty-two hours out of twenty-four this is the appearance of the Cuban blockade. . . .

The details of Havana grew slowly out of the mist. Morro Castle, low to the water, bared an outline which, strangely enough, was exactly like a preconception of it conceived from pictures. On the sides of the hills to its right were two long, straight yellow scars, modern batteries.

With immense dignity the New York steamed at a distance of six miles past the Havana fortifications. . . .

Over a brilliant sea she swung again to the northeast. The bugle for the regular call to quarters pealed through the ship, even when the houses of Havana could be counted, and, as usual, the marines and a division of blue jackets formed on the quarter deck. After inspection they took their trot about the deck in perfect rhythm to the music of the band, which played a rollicking, fascinating melody.

It was a peaceful scene. In fact it was more peaceful than peace, since one's sights were adjusted for war.

THE BLOCKADE WAS a thin gray line of warships stretching along the northern coast of Cuba from Bahía Honda to Cárdenas, and another off the port of Cienfuegos on the southern coast. It was there to turn away neutral vessels attempting to enter Cuban ports and to capture any Spanish vessels encountered. The first Spanish prize was captured on April 22, within sight of Key West. It was the *Buenaventura*, a merchantman carrying a cargo of lumber from Pascagoula, Mississippi, to Rotterdam. Captain Lazarraga of Bilbao, Spain, did not know there was a war in progress when the ships of the North Atlantic Squadron came into view.

"Behold!" he exclaimed to his crew. "The courtesy of my race requires that

I salute these beautiful warships." The red and yellow colors of Spain were hoisted.

The *Buenaventura* was shortly delivered to Key West by a prize crew. The shot the *Nashville* fired across her bow was reckoned to have been the first of the war.

·   ·   ·

THE BLOCKADING FLEET was ordered to stay clear of Cuban coastal defenses; it was there not to attack Cuban ports but to interdict supply ships and wait for Admiral Cervera. But on April 27 the *New York* shelled Matanzas, and several days later it returned fire from the shore at Cabañas. Richard Harding Davis was aboard and reported:

> The four-inch gun was aimed . . . and as it spoke the deck of the flag-ship heaved as suddenly as an elevator starts when it rises with a jerk, and for a few moments the gun continued to hurl flashes of flame and clouds of hot smoke and volleys, that shook the leaves of the palms and echoed among the hills of Cuba.
>
> It was just at sunset, when the sky was blazing with a gridiron of red and gold. On the decks and on the superstructure, in the turrets and on the bridges, the blue-jackets and the marines crowded together, leaning forward and peering into the fading light. As each shell struck home they whispered and chuckled as though they were seated in the gallery at a play . . .
>
> The ship ran up nearer to the shore, and as she did so a troop of cavalry galloped into view across the fields and formed a cordon under a great tree.

The cavalrymen dismounted and began firing their rifles at the ship, which answered with seven rounds from a deck gun.

> Meanwhile from below came the strains of the string band playing for the officers' mess, and the music of Scheur's "Dream of Spring" mingled with the belching of the four-inch gun.
>
> This is not a touch of fiction, but the reporting of cold coincidence, for war as it is conducted at the end of the century is civilized.

So a troop of cavalry engaged a battleship while a string quartet played on. It was a war the likes of which would not be seen again. An old century rubbed against a new one. It was indeed a dream of spring.

·   ·   ·

THE DIRTY MAN ran up and down the beach near Guanabacoa, a few miles east of Havana. He had torn off his shirt and tied the sleeves to a stick, which he frantically waved over his head. From the deck of the *Wilmington* Commander Chapman C. Todd watched the apparition through binoculars. Presently he sent a boat in toward shore flying a flag of truce.

Near hysterical with joy, the dirty man waded out through the breakers. From the boat an officer hailed him, asking who he was and what he wanted.

"I'm Charles Thrall of the *World*," the derelict panted as the seamen hauled him into the boat.

The next morning, May 4, Thrall, bathed, fed, and shaved, was aboard the *New York*, reporting his experiences to Admiral Sampson. His story, published a few days later in the New York *World*, began on April 22, the day the blockade began.

> I reached Havana proper that night. On the train from Marianao I first heard that the American fleet was off Havana. When I reached the city crowds were running about the streets in a state of frenzy. Women were wringing their hands and calling upon the saints to save them. Children clung to their skirts, wild with fright and terror of incomprehensible dangers that beset them.
>
> Jumping into a coach, I went to the vicinity of the shore batteries in the neighborhood of the Reina Battery. Everything was in confusion —not a single thing in readiness. Havana could have been taken at that moment without a struggle.
>
> After that quiet was restored, and next day every man inhabitant of the city who could be impressed was set at work in batteries and defenses. All theatres and places of amusement closed their doors. Everybody that had ready money took passage on foreign ships that were in the harbor.

Thrall soon discovered he was a wanted man with a two-thousand-dollar price on his head. With the help of the insurgents he made his way to Guanabacoa. After a night of fruitless attempts to signal the blockading ships, he returned to Havana.

> When I got back to Havana I found they were taking the guns out of the Alfonso XII. They could not get her boilers repaired, so they took her heavy battery of six-inch guns and mounted them on shore.
>
> I hung about the fortifications from La Punta to Vedado all that day. They [were] mounting a new battery on La Punta of two six-inch breech-loading rifles.
>
> On all the other batteries large forces of men were at work piling up sand in front of the emplacement.

Thrall made two more attempts to leave Cuba before finally attracting the attention of the *Wilmington* on May 3. He described the situation of the populace of Havana when he last saw the city:

> The distress in Havana is already severe. Food and clothing sent there by the Americans for the relief of the reconcentrados have been appropriated by the Spaniards, and not a particle of them will ever reach those for whom they were intended.

OTHER ADVENTURERS TRAVELED to and from Cuba. Lieutenant Andrew S. Rowan of the Army's fledgling intelligence unit, the Military Information Division, was sent by General Miles to establish contact with the insurgent forces of Calixto García. Rowan left on his mission two weeks before the war began, traveling by way of Jamaica with the help of Cuban insurgents, and finally reached García at Bayamo on May 1. García furnished him with maps and other needed information and sent a delegation of Cuban officers along on his return to Washington to help coordinate strategy with the U.S. Army and Navy.*

Similar liaison missions to Máximo Gómez were made by New York *Herald* correspondent Fred O. Somerford for the Army and Lieutenant Victor Blue for the Navy. Gómez, who was now encamped in the central province of Las Villas, was informed of American plans to make an amphibious landing somewhere on the northwestern coast in the vicinity of Havana. He accordingly detached a large part of his army and sent it west and arranged with García to do the same.

The Army promised to supply the insurgents. On May 10, Captain J. H. Dorst of the Fourth U.S. Cavalry left Tampa with a consignment of arms and ammunition aboard the *Gussie*, a side-wheeled riverboat that might have paddled right out of the pages of Mark Twain's *Life on the Mississippi.* The shipment was intended for General Pedro Díaz, commander of the insurgents in Pinar del Río Province. Two companies of the First Infantry came along to guard the expedition after it landed in Cuba.

The *Gussie* was towed out of Port Tampa by the New York *World's* chartered tugboat, then proceeded south under her own power. She rode out a squall and managed to pass through the Navy's blockade with only seven shots fired across her bow by commanders who had not been informed of her mission. By dawn on the twelfth the startled residents of Havana were greeted by the sight of the big red steamboat churning westward.

"It was apparent that the whole country was apprised of our coming and knew the purpose of it," one correspondent who came along on the voyage reported. "The heliograph stations upon the low mountains near the coast were signaling our presence."

At Mariel several hundred Spanish soldiers, some on horseback, overcame their astonishment and began shooting at the steamboat. The *Gussie* continued west and put into a bay near Point Abolitas. As two boatloads of troops headed toward the beach, a pair of chartered newspaper tugs appeared on the scene, their whistles blowing madly. It seemed the correspondents aboard needed the name of the soldier in the bow of the first boat for their copy. A regiment of twelve hundred Spanish troops hiding in the brush opened fire, and a sudden thunderstorm drenched the scene with a tropical downpour.

The American troops ran up the beach, formed a skirmish line, and entered

---

*Rowan's rather modest exploit caught the fancy of businessman-dilettante Elbert Hubbard, who celebrated it as an example of pluck in his "A Message to Garcia," which he published in his magazine, the *Philistine.* The essay, which scrambles most of the facts, became a best seller when a half-million reprints were ordered by the New York Central Railroad for distribution to its own employees and other workers who might benefit by Rowan's example. Pizer, pp. 468–472.

the jungle. A contingent of reporters stumbled through the surf and followed after them. Indifferent to the rifle bullets flying past, an artist from *Harper's Weekly* sketched the scene for his publication. A Cuban scout, sent out by the Army to learn the whereabouts of the place, returned with the news that the expedition had landed within two miles of the Cabañas fortress, where two thousand Spanish troops were stationed.

The Americans fell back through the brush and reappeared on the beach, permitting the *Gussie's* naval escort, the *Manning* and the *Wasp*, to drop some artillery rounds into the jungle, forcing the Spaniards to withdraw. The expedition went back aboard the steamboat, which set out along the coast once more in search of the Cuban insurgents. Miraculously, the only American casualty was James F. J. Archibald of the San Francisco *Post*, who sustained a slight wound to the left arm.

After another day of trying, the *Gussie* returned to Key West with its cargo of arms, having been unable to find any insurgents. The mission was a failure, but it had the distinction of being the first land action of the war.

.   .   .

CÁRDENAS MARKED the easternmost end of the blockade. Three Spanish gunboats lay in its broad, shallow harbor. The *Wilmington* stood outside, kept out by the shoals and her ten-foot draft. On the afternoon of May 11, Commander Todd tried to take her inside, guided by the revenue cutter *Hudson* and the torpedo boat *Winslow*, which went ahead to sound out a channel.

The three American ships approached the waterfront, the *Winslow* in the lead. The Spanish opened fire at a range of 1,200 yards. A six-pound shell entered the bow of the *Winslow*, smashing the forward conning tower and disabling the steering gear. Before the steering could be switched to the aft tower, that was destroyed by a second round. The rudder was jammed hard over, and the boat now could be steered only by stopping, reversing, or steaming ahead with either the starboard or port engines.

The Spanish fire was returned by the torpedo boat's three one-pound deck guns and the larger guns of the *Wilmington* and *Hudson*, but the Spanish fire continued. The torpedo boat sustained several more hits; one disabled the forward engine. A shell fragment tore into the thigh of the boat's commander, Lieutenant John B. Bernadou.

Ensign Worth Bagley was stationed at the engine room hatch to relay instructions as the boat alternately steamed ahead and astern, trying to reach the deeper water where the *Hudson* could take her in tow and pull her safely out of the bay. After many tense minutes this was accomplished, but a shell parted the towing hawser, and the *Winslow* was again forced to back and steam ahead while efforts were made to rig another tow line.

Lieutenant Bernadou was limping aft to speak to Ensign Bagley when he heard a sharp report and saw Bagley and four crewmen sink to the deck. A shell had struck the deck and exploded, raining fragments.

The *Hudson* received a second line and took the crippled *Winslow* in tow. The American ships withdrew, leaving two of the Spanish gunboats sunk at the wharf and a large section of Cárdenas in flames.

Ensign Worth Bagley was dead, as were John Barberes, oiler, G Deneefe and George B. Meek, firemen, and E. B. Tunnell, cook. The day had brought the first American combat fatalities of the war.

The dream had ended. The war went on.

.   .   .

LIEUTENANT CAMERON WINSLOW STOOD on the bridge of the *Marblehead* and focused his binoculars on the shoreline. The white stone lighthouse stood on Punta de la Colorados, just to the east of the mouth of Cienfuegos Bay. Winslow swung his glasses slowly to the right. He could see men digging in the tall grass and dense chaparral fifty feet from the water's edge, and marked the location of the Spanish rifle pits. Further to the right he saw a low white cubical building apparently constructed from the same stone as the lighthouse. This was the cable house, the landing point of the two submarine cables that stretched east and west from Cienfuegos along the ocean floor south of Cuba. All telegraph messages between Havana and Madrid passed through this building.

A telegram originating in Havana was sent south over land lines, across the island to the port of Batabanó. From there it was relayed along a submarine telegraph cable that looped along the south coast to Santiago de Cuba, where it was again relayed over the transatlantic cable system to Spain. The Cuban submarine cable came ashore here at Cienfuegos. If it could be cut in the shallow waters outside the bay, then Havana would be left with only a land line route to the transatlantic cable head at Santiago that linked the island with Madrid, and the land line, stretching through hundreds of miles of jungle and mountains, was easy prey for the insurgents.

The plan, then, was to take two of the ship's boats, row into the shallows near the cable house, dredge up the cables, cut them, and drag them out into the deeper water where the Spanish could not easily recover and splice them. A pair of steam launches carrying Marine sharpshooters, a one-pound Hotchkiss cannon, and two Colt machine guns would keep the Spanish soldiers in the rifle pits busy. The guns of the *Marblehead*, the gunboat *Nashville*, and the revenue cutter *Windom* would provide covering artillery fire. The operation began shortly before 7 A.M.

The *Marblehead* and the *Nashville* opened fire as the little flotilla of boats headed inshore. Lieutenant Winslow recalled:

A moderate breeze was blowing on shore from the southward and eastward, and the long ocean swell rolling in from the Caribbean Sea broke heavily on the rocks and coral-lined shore, making a long ribbon of white foam and spray, which marked clearly the reefs awash and formed the dividing line between land and sea.

The ships were now firing on the cable-house, and after a few shots found the range. Soon the shells were busting all about the cable-house and the rocky bluff in its rear. In a few minutes the house was struck, the shells apparently piercing both the front and rear walls and bursting against the rocks of the bluff beyond. Again and again the shells found their mark, bursting and sending clouds of stone and mortar into the air, demolishing wall after wall, until one shot, striking the tottering structure, burst, and brought it down, leaving nothing but a disordered pile of masonry covering the wreck of electrical instruments. As the boats neared the land, the ships slackened their fire, and the steam-cutters began firing on the rifle-pits. . . .

The deep water off the coast made futile any effort to grapple the cables where the bottom could not be seen through the clear water. . . . We were now within about a hundred feet of the shore-line, and with the eastern end of the rifle-pits about fifty feet farther back. Suddenly the dark patches of coral cropping up from the white sand of the bottom were seen through the clear water, thirty or forty feet in depth. The grapnels were at once thrown overboard and the dragging began.

The cable was a bundle of copper wires, insulation, and lead shielding. It was two inches in diameter, and each foot of it weighed six pounds. Dredging it up from the bottom and draping it over the boats was a back-breaking job. Next the boats were hauled out into the deeper water, underrunning the cable and raising it from a depth of several fathoms. Then there remained the task of cutting it.

It was like cutting an iron bar as thick as a man's wrist. Axes and cold chisels were tried, but hacksaws worked best. It took half an hour to saw through. A 150-foot length was cut out of the cable, and the end was dropped in thirteen fathoms. The boats now rowed to the east, dredging for the second cable. They passed directly in front of the rifle pits and about a hundred feet from them.

The ships, realizing the danger of our position, increased their fire until it became a furious cannonade, the shells passing so close over our heads that the crews instinctively ducked as they went by and burst against the rocks beyond.

The second cable was hooked, and the exhausted sailors dragged it aboard and cut a hundred-foot length from it. Winslow sighted a third, smaller cable lying on the ocean bottom. It was probably the line that ran up the bay to the city of Cienfuegos and was of little importance, but he decided to pull it up and cut it too.

The rifle pits had gone quiet and the ships had ceased firing, but now the Spanish rifle fire resumed, much heavier than before.

We saw the splash of the bullets in the water about us, and I ordered the steam-cutters to open fire again. Now the bullets began dropping so fast that the little sheets of spray where they struck the water could be plainly seen by the ships, and those on board realized that the enemy was in force, and began a terrific cannonade.

The firing continued and increased in intensity. The third cable was pulled aboard the boats, and the cutting commenced. Winslow stood up in the boat and looked around.

> Just then I saw a marine in the *Marblehead*'s steam-cutter fall, shot through the head. Turning in the direction of [Lieutenant] Anderson's boat, I saw one of the men drop, struck by a Mauser bullet. As I faced the shore to look at the trenches, a seaman, Robert Volz, standing in the stern-sheets of my boat, collapsed, then struggled to his feet, and immediately after sank in the bottom of the boat, a gaping wound six inches long in his head, two bulletholes through his body, and a bullet in his shoulder, probably the result of machine-gun fire. . . . This man lived, and ten days later, while the *Nashville* was at Key West, he ran away from the hospital on shore, came off to the ship in one of our boats, and reported.

But there was one dead Marine and another man mortally wounded and six badly wounded, and Winslow had been hit in the hand by a Mauser bullet. The price of the third cable was too high, so he ordered the boats back to the ships. The principal objective had been accomplished.

In Havana, Domingo Villaverde scribbled down the telegraph report of the attack coming over the land line from Cienfuegos. Within the hour a message was placed on the desk of President McKinley at the White House:

> Report received from Havana. Cienfuegos being bombarded, cable between that point and Havana cut. Land line all right yet. Can't get any more as instrument is guarded. Do not give out sources of information as my man will be shot if found out.

· · ·

THE INTELLIGENCE NETWORK that stretched from the governor general's palace at Havana to the White House in Washington had been in place for months, perhaps longer. Its most important node was the two-story brick building that stood beneath an arch of palm trees at 410 Greene Street in Key West and housed the offices of the International Ocean Telegraph Company.

International Ocean owned the four submarine telegraph cables that ran from Punta Rassa on the west coast of Florida, south to Key West, and across the Florida Straits to Havana. All cable traffic between Cuba and the United States was carried by these lines. The company was a wholly owned subsidiary of the Western Union Telegraph Company. The company manager was one of Key West's most respected citizens, Martin Luther Hellings.

Hellings was fifty-seven at the time of the Spanish War. He was a native of Jenkinstown, Pennsylvania. During the Civil War he served in Company G, Seventh Regiment Reserve Corps, and was severely wounded at Antietam. After the war he worked as a telegrapher for Western Union and settled in Key West. In 1888 he was made supervisor of the Cuban cables there.

He married Eleanor Curry, daughter of William Curry, a prominent Key

West merchant and one of the richest men in Florida. In addition to his work for the telegraph company, Hellings took part in his wife's family business, the mercantile house of William Curry's Sons. The Hellings lived in a magnificent house on Duval Street.

Among the cable manager's many friends was Captain Charles D. Sigsbee of the ill-fated *Maine*. Some twenty years earlier, when Sigsbee commanded the Hydrographic Survey ship *Blake* and was mapping the floor of the Gulf of Mexico, he had met Hellings and done some great favor for the telegraph company, probably in some matter concerning the submarine cables lying on the ocean bottom. When Sigsbee returned to Key West in mid-December 1897, he found Hellings "conspicuously courteous" and eager to discharge the "considerable obligation" of Western Union toward him. Sigsbee knew just how the favor could be returned—he wanted to know immediately if there was any sign the Spanish were shutting down the cable from Havana. After the *Maine* went to Havana, Sigsbee arranged to have Hellings notify the local Navy authorities at Key West if the cable was closed.

This modest arrangement expanded as Sigsbee made more confidential arrangements at Key West. Hellings was personally well acquainted with Florida railroad and steamship magnate H. B. Plant, and it was probably through Hellings that Sigsbee met Plant's Key West agent, Robert W. Southwick, a genial and urbane native of Poughkeepsie, New York. Every week the Plant Line's steamship *Olivette* made three round trips between Tampa and Havana, stopping en route each way at Key West. Southwick arranged to have the ship's purser serve as a secret courier between Fitzhugh Lee in Havana and the Navy at Key West.

Far more valuable than any of this, however, were the secret services rendered by several of Hellings's staff of telegraph operators. The International Ocean Company operated both ends of the Havana–Key West cable, and the company's eight-man staff was divided between the telegraph offices in both cities. Two of the telegraphers were Hispanic—probably middle-class Cubans. One of these, Domingo Villaverde, was regarded by Hellings as extremely trustworthy and reliable. He agreed to do the difficult and dangerous extra work Hellings asked of him.

Even before the outbreak of the war Villaverde was in a critically important position. The Havana cable office was in the governor general's palace, a place where the most sensitive local government affairs might be overheard. Official Spanish government telegrams originating from Madrid or elsewhere in the Caribbean passed through his hands, as did consular dispatches to and from European legations at Havana. There hardly could have been a better place for a spy in all of Cuba.

Hellings established his secret intelligence network with the full knowledge and consent of Western Union President Thomas T. Eckert. Eckert was fully aware of the value of communications intelligence, having spent the Civil War as chief of Secretary of War Edwin Stanton's telegraph service. It may have been Eckert who arranged to have Hellings's intelligence reports conveyed to President McKinley by White House telegrapher and cipher clerk Benjamin F. Montgomery. Montgomery, who had been a White House fixture since the administration of Rutherford B. Hayes, was a former Western Union telegrapher.

When the war came, Eckert turned over the Hellings network to the U.S. Army Signal Corps. Eckert and Plant both wrote to McKinley, asking that Hellings be given a commission in the Volunteer Signal Corps. Hellings was made a captain on May 20 and assigned to detached service at Key West. Benjamin F. Montgomery was also commissioned in the Signal Corps as a lieutenant colonel.

The Havana–Key West cable was kept open by the mutual agreement of the Spanish and United States governments. Signal Corps officers were sent to Key West to censor all telegraph traffic found to pertain to military matters. Domingo Villaverde's reports to Hellings from Havana were, of course, excepted.

The existence of the Hellings network was a well-kept secret. It was necessary that the chief of the Signal Corps, General Adolphus W. Greely, be informed, but apparently Secretary of War Alger was not in the secret. he made two fruitless efforts to get Greely to close the Havana cable on the grounds that Spain might be using it to receive valuable information from agents in the United States. Alger was unaware that all the valuable information was moving in the opposite direction, from Villaverde's key in the Havana palace to Montgomery's sounder in the White House and that nothing of any importance happened in Cuba that President McKinley did not know of within an hour.

·   ·   ·

THE SPECTER OF Admiral Cervera continued to terrify the Atlantic coast. The Navy received an unlikely report that the Spanish squadron had been seen off New England and dispatched the cruisers *Columbia* and *Minneapolis* to cruise the waters between Newport, Rhode Island, and Eastport, Maine, calling at different ports to reassure the local inhabitants. The ships were part of the newly formed Flying Squadron, commanded by Commodore Winfield Scott Schley and based at Hampton Roads to protect the Atlantic coast from Cervera. The fast auxiliary cruisers, *Harvard* and *St. Louis*, were sent to cruise east of the Windward Islands and look for the Cape Verde fleet, and the *Yale* was dispatched to Puerto Rican waters on the same errand.

Puerto Rico, which had not been blockaded, seemed the most reasonable destination for Cervera to many naval officers, including Rear Admiral William T. Sampson, commander of the blockading North Atlantic Squadron. On May 4, Sampson took most of the larger warships from the blockade and sailed to San Juan, arriving at the Puerto Rican port on May 12. Cervera was not there. Sampson bombarded some coastal batteries, then headed back to Cuba.

·   ·   ·

PREPARATIONS FOR THE PLANNED Mariel invasion continued. Tampa was to be the staging point, and at concentration points across the country the Army thrashed about trying to free itself from its administrative morass and move thousands of hastily inducted recruits to the Florida port. The experience of the Seventy-first Regiment of New York Volunteers was typical. Chaplain George R. Van Dewater described the scene on the morning of May 12:

> Promptly at the time mentioned in orders the regiment proceeded in heavy marching order, preceded by Squadron A band, to the Long Island Railroad terminus near Camp Black, there to discover that a large supply of ammunition had just arrived and must be transferred to train before its departure. It was seven o'clock before the trains finally moved out and ten o'clock before we reached Long Island City. It was here that we began first to experience the absolute incompetency of Government quartermaster officials. . . . Transport ships of the Ward Line had been engaged to convey the 2nd Massachusetts Infantry and the 71st New York to Tampa. No arrangements whatever had been made for transporting the Seventy-first from the depot at Long Island City to the transport ships. . . . It was not until 3:30 A.M., on Friday the 13th instant, that we were able to secure transportation by a ferry-boat to the transport ships lying off Bedloe Island. The labor of handling all the luggage from train to ferry-boat and subsequently to transfer it all to transport was immense. It was daylight when everyone, absolutely tired out, who possibly could get away to rest, retired for needful slumber.

Charles Johnson Post, formerly an illustrator for Hearst's *Journal* and now a private in the Seventy-first, recalled the situation aboard his transport, the *Seneca*, "a little coastwise steamship, shabby and inadequate." Tiers of short, narrow bunks filled the unventilated space below decks, each "built to the exact size of a man flat on his back—like a coffin." The ship's galley, adequate to feed the crew and a hundred or so passengers, was now required to nourish a regiment of more than a thousand men.

Partly cooked "sowbelly" was served from one large kettle. "As [each man] in the mess line of each battalion reached the galley door and was handed his cube of morbid pig, he would walk to the rail and toss it overboard." And across the bay, there was New York City where the finest restaurant meals were "on the house" for any man in uniform! New Yorkers crowded the railings of excursion boats, which circled the transports all day long, while reporters shouted questions through megaphones from the decks of chartered tugboats. But the Seventy-first, ordered to stay aboard the transports, couldn't enjoy the fruits of its popularity.

> We had two days of that wretched *Seneca*. It seemed like weeks. Then came orders to disembark at Hoboken, there to entrain for Florida. We learned that this was because the fleet of the Spanish Navy, under Admiral Cervera, was abroad somewhere on the high seas, location unknown, and the inland railroad would be safer.

In fact, the same day the Seventy-first went aboard the transports, Cervera had been reported off Sandy Hook at the mouth of New York Bay. The Navy knew better, however. The Cape Verde fleet had shown itself at last, in the Caribbean, at the French island of Martinique.

.   .   .

"GOVERNMENT IS PLEASED to hear of your arrival at Martinique," Minister Bermejo cabled on May 12.

> Nothing new in the Peninsula. Telegram received to-day announcing attack San Juan, Puerto Rico, by hostile fleet composed of *New York, Indiana, Terror, Puritan,* two cruisers, one torpedo boat and two colliers. Island of Puerto Rico is watched by auxiliaries *Paris* and *New York.* Admiral at Havana says four hostile ships in sight yesterday, one at Matanzas and several off Cienfuegos. News of bombardment of Cardenas by a battle ship, monitor, and another vessel; enemy repulsed.

Cervera was perilously short of coal, having just enough left to get the squadron to Cuba or Puerto Rico with empty bunkers. Before leaving Cape Verde, Bermejo had cabled him that a collier with a cargo of five thousand tons was on its way from London to Curacao for the Spanish fleet. Cervera left Martinique and steamed for Curacao.

"I came here in hopes of finding the coal announced in your telegram of April 26," Cervera cabled Bermejo on May 14th. "Collier has not arrived, and I have not been able to obtain here the coal I need. There is a controversy about it, and I must see what I can do. Only two ships have been allowed to enter, and their stay has been limited to forty-eight hours."

Cervera's chief of staff recalled the scene when the squadron arrived at Curacao on the morning of May 14:

> The squadron was detained at the harbor entrance. After lengthy and unpleasant negotiations, the governor stated that the conditions of neutrality permitted him to allow only two ships to enter and that these could not remain more than forty-eight hours; also, that we could ship only a limited amount of coal. . . .
>
> It was with difficulty that we acquired the coal available, which, if I remember right, amounted to only 400 tons, and we proceeded to get it on board, working frantically, shipping also such provisions as we could obtain. Nothing can give an idea of the anxiety of that night of May 14, when we interpreted every noise we heard as an attack upon our comrades, and we could not even go to their assistance, for the harbor of Curacao, which is closed by a bridge, is completely cut off from the outside at sunset.

On the evening of May 15 the Spanish squadron formed up again outside the harbor of Curacao and steamed northward, slowly, to conserve the precious supply of coal. Its destination was Santiago de Cuba.

.   .   .

BERMEJO HAD STARTED to think of recalling the squadron to Cádiz, had even sent a cable to Cervera giving him that option on May 12. The admiral never received the cable, but word of it caused panic in official circles at Havana and San Juan.

"I beg your excellency that you will tell me truly whether the squadron is coming," General Blanco cabled from Havana on May 14. "I assure your excellency that absolutely no one besides myself shall know your reply."

Three days later he cabled again, warning that, should Cervera not come, "I could not prevent bloody revolution in this capital and whole island, feelings being already overmuch excited by delay in arrival of our squadron. If our squadron is defeated, it would increase here determination to vanquish or die; but if it flees, panic and revolution are certain."

At 1:33 P.M. on May 18 a report from Villaverde at Havana was placed on the desk of President McKinley:

> The Spanish in official quarters evidently have news of the coming of their fleet, as their vessels cheer now and display great activity in their preparations.
>   They are looking for large supplies of all kinds of provisions, especially ammunition, of which they are very short.

THE U.S. NAVY ALSO BELIEVED that Cervera was bringing supplies for Havana and concluded that, rather than try to run the blockade of that port, he would put in somewhere along the southern coast of Cuba, there to unload the supplies for transshipment over land. The most likely port at which to do that was Cienfuegos, which was linked to the Cuban capital by rail. Santiago, several hundreds of miles away from Havana near the southeast tip of Cuba, did not seem at all likely as Cervera's destination. On May 18 the Flying Squadron, which had been ordered to Key West from Hampton Roads when the Spanish fleet was reported at Martinique, was ordered to blockade Cienfuegos. Between 7 and 8 A.M. on May 19, the squadron left Key West en route to Cienfuegos.

At the same moment, the squadron of Admiral Cervera was dropping anchor in the harbor of Santiago.

IN THE HAVANA CABLE OFFICE Domingo Villaverde scribbled down the messages coming over the wire from Santiago.

> To the Captain-General of Cuba:
>   Have cast anchor to-day in this harbor, whence whole squadron sends you greeting, desirous of cooperating in the defense of country.
>   Cervera

> To the Commandant-General of the Navy-Yard:
>   Cast anchor in this harbor this morning, and have the pleasure of placing myself at your disposal.
>   Cervera

Villaverde handed the telegrams to a messenger, then turned to his telegraph key and began tapping out a message for Key West.

.   .   .

THE OPERATING ROOM on the second floor of the White House was the prototype of the modern military command and control center. Telephones and telegraph instruments stood on rolltop desks. The walls were covered with maps of the Caribbean, the Philippines, and the world, each bristling with colored pins. Lieutenant Colonel Benjamin Montgomery sat at his desk and studied the paper that had just been handed him by a messenger from the Signal Corps headquarters.

To the President:
    The following cipher messages have just been received from Capt. Allen,* Signal Corps at Key West in the order given:

        1. "Is there any confirmation of report that American ships were at Santiago-de-Cuba yet?"
        2. "Send me quick any confirmation of this:—five Spanish vessels arrived Santiago-de-Cuba have informed the Admiral commanding."†
        3. "The Spanish flagship arrived Santiago-de-Cuba the admiral hastily wired Madrid."

Puzzled, Montgomery looked at another dispatch just brought in by a second messenger.

To B. F. Montgomery, Operating Room, Executive Mansion:
    Can you furnish us with any information that will enable us to reply to the questions asked by Capt. Allen Key West, in the first two translations of cipher messages just sent to you for the President. Captain Allen asked if we could confirm information which had reached him that five Spanish vessels had arrived at Santiago-de-Cuba and asking whether the American fleet was still there.
                                        Acting Chief Signal Officer

Montgomery scratched his head and looked up at the map of Cuba. The pins representing the blockading ships were clustered around the northwest end of the island. No American fleet was anywhere near the southeastern port of Santiago de Cuba, and none recently had been in that area. As to the report of

*The regular Army Signal Corps officer who had been put in charge of the Key West cable office and was Hellings's superior.
†Rear Admiral William T. Sampson, commander of the North Atlantic Squadron. Since the sudden announcement of this startling information by the Signal Corps at Key West must certainly have caused Sampson to demand to know its source, it might be presumed that he was now made aware of the Hellings–Villaverde network. It seems reasonable also to presume that Sampson's subordinate, Commodore W. S. Schley, was not aware of the source of the reports of Cervera at Santiago and so had more reason than Sampson to doubt them. These presumptions, if sustained, seem to stand in Schley's favor in the bitter Sampson–Schley controversy that ensued.

Spanish ships at Santiago, he had heard nothing about that either. He took the dispatches and went to see the president.

Shortly after 4 P.M. the manager of the Western Union office called on General A. W. Greely and showed him a telegram he had just received over a private wire from the company's president in New York City.

> Please go at once to [War] Department and tell them that we have a cipher message from Hellings stating that Spanish fleet is now at Santiago and that the Spanish Admiral at 2 P.M. local time, or 3 P.M. Washington time, was in telegraphic communications with Blanco. Please entreat them not to indicate to any one the source of this information, so as to protect Mr. Hellings' informant. We do not, of course, guarantee it, but we have every reason to believe it's true. He (Hellings) is an intelligent and loyal man, and is in a position to get confidential information of this character. Let us know if it is news to them.

It was news to everyone. And they didn't believe it.

. . .

IT SEEMED TOO GOOD to be true. If Admiral Cervera had taken his squadron into the harbor of Santiago de Cuba, then he had virtually taken it out of the war. With the squadron trapped inside or destroyed outside Santiago, part of the American fleet could be sent across the Atlantic to attack Spanish ports. Madrid would be forced to keep its few remaining warships at Cádiz to protect the coasts and could not dispatch a squadron to threaten Dewey at Manila. Faced with the prospect of losing both Cuba and the Philippines, Spain might come to terms, and the costly and bloody landing at Mariel and siege of Havana would not be necessary. President McKinley wanted to believe Villaverde's report. But the Navy War Board knew several good reasons why it could be untrue.

First, it didn't seem to make sense. The Navy assumed Cervera had left Cape Verde fully coaled and carrying supplies for Havana or Puerto Rico. Both assumptions were reasonable, if false, and it was hard to imagine then why the admiral would have chosen to put into a tiny port hundreds of miles from his presumed destination.

Second, the Navy had a report from the auxiliary cruiser *St. Louis,* which had been off Santiago at eight o'clock on the morning of May 19, the very moment when Cervera was supposed to have been dropping his anchor there, and the *St. Louis* positively stated that the Spanish fleet was nowhere in sight.

Finally, Secretary Long and the Navy War Board apparently were ignorant of the Hellings–Villaverde intelligence network's existence and at first did not know the reports of Cervera's arrival were coming from a source in the palace at Havana.

The immediate dilemma was what to tell Commodore Schley to do with his Flying Squadron: stay in front of Cienfuegos or steam to Santiago. If Villaverde's report were true, Cervera might be recoaling and preparing to sail again, perhaps to threaten the Atlantic coast. But the report might be a ruse designed to decoy the American fleet away from Cienfuegos and permit Cervera to slip in with his presumed cargo of supplies for Havana.

· · ·

THE DAY FOLLOWING Cervera's arrival Villaverde managed to get another telegram off to Key West: "*Pelayo* and four cruisers in Santiago. No destroyer or torpedo boat arrived."*

About midnight he sent a follow-up message: "Only know that all five are battle ships; none destroyers or torpedos. Admiral Cervera surely at Santiago de Cuba today."

The telegram arrived on General Greely's desk in Washington at 1 A.M. He sent a copy to the Navy Department. Later on the twenty-first he sent Secretary Long a confidential memo:

> By direction of the President there will be sent you direct copies of all important telegrams that I may receive from Captain James Allen, Key West. For obvious reasons, it will be advisable in these telegrams to omit the fact that they are from Captain Allen, as the fact suspected would immediately close up all sources of information.
>
> Unless otherwise stated, all dispatches of this character received from me will be understood as originating at Key West and their ultimate source as Havana.

Having let Long into the secret of the Hellings–Villaverde network, Greely tried to unburden himself of some of the responsibility attached to it. He added, "While past dispatches have been remarkably accurate, yet this office cannot vouch for them further than that they are the best obtainable information."

General Greely may have begun to wonder if the hand on the telegraph key in Havana continued to belong to Domingo Villaverde.

· · ·

AT 12:30 A.M. on the twentieth, Admiral Sampson received a dispatch from Long:

> The report of the Spanish fleet being at Santiago de Cuba might very well be correct, so the Department strongly advises that you send word immediately by the *Iowa* to Schley to proceed at once off Santiago de Cuba with his whole command, leaving one small vessel off Cienfuegos,

*The battleship *Pelayo* was still at Cádiz being readied to go to Manila with Admiral Cámara. The torpedo boat flotilla could not make the voyage from Cape Verde and had been sent back to Cádiz. The destroyer *Terror* had developed mechanical problems on the voyage to Martinique and had been left there. The squadron that actually arrived at Santiago on May 19 consisted of the cruisers *Infanta María Teresa*, *Vizcaya*, *Cristobal Colón*, and *Oquendo*, and the destroyers *Furor* and *Plutón*.

Cuba . . . If *Iowa* has gone, send orders to Schley by your fastest dispatch vessel.

But Sampson believed that Cevera would ultimately come to Cienfuegos or Havana with his presumed cargo of supplies. He ordered Schley to stay at Cienfuegos.

.   .   .

"As to the advisability of going to Cienfuegos," Cervera's chief of staff, Captain Victor Concas, later recalled,

> that harbor was a veritable rat trap . . . Schley was stationed off Cienfuegos with the *Brooklyn, Texas, Massachusetts,* and *Iowa,* and it was impossible to enter that port or the Yucatan Channel . . . Sampson was at Havana with the rest of the forces, and consequently there was no other course but to remain where we were or to go to San Juan. And why to San Juan? Certainly not to remain in the harbor, for the disaster would have happened the sooner. Hence the object of going to San Juan could only be to coal more rapidly and put to sea before the arrival of the enemy, in order to make an attempt to go to Havana or to return to Europe.

But Cervera was not able even to move on to Puerto Rico for the moment. The ships were in acute need of maintenance; the *Oquendo* and *Vizcaya* had just been twice across the Atlantic, and the other ships of the squadron had been in continuous operation since March 29. All needed boilers cleaned and engines overhauled. And as Concas remembered, their coal bunkers were almost empty.

> The coal supply of the six ships also had to be renewed, and this work was undertaken with frenzy. What coal there was . . . was on a cay . . . where it was difficult for the lighters to come alongside . . . and we were not able to ship more than 150 tons daily, an insignificant amount for six ships . . . Everything which was required for rapid coaling—lighters, tugs, and even baskets—was lacking, and we had to use the sacks we had bought at Cape Verde . . . which were insufficient for the larger vessels.

Everything, including food, was in short supply at Santiago. There had been no cargo ships in the port since April 25, and the local merchants, afraid of losing their investment in case of a Cuban–American victory, had let their inventories dwindle. Concas recalled:

> Although the city was in reality besieged by the insurgents, it was still able to obtain some vegetables . . . But the city, which like all those of Cuba depended upon imports for its principal supplies, was feeling the effects of being closed in and the poorer classes that of hunger a month before any hostile ship had appeared off the entrance of the harbor.

The day after he arrived, Cervera cabled the new minister of marine, Auñón:* "Intend to refit ships in shortest possible time, because, in my opinion, Santiago will soon be in difficult situation if it does not receive aid."

The next day he cabled again: "If we are blockaded before we can finish taking coal, which is scarce, we shall succumb with the city."

On the twenty-second Cervera received word that the English collier *Restormel*, carrying three thousand tons of Cardiff coal, was en route to Santiago.

The local Spanish authorities gave a banquet for Cervera and his men. The archbishop of Santiago proposed a toast to the admiral's anticipated attack on the capitol at Washington, D.C. Concas remembered that the gesture "was received with feverish enthusiasm by some and with profound sorrow by us who knew that our fate was already decided and that we were irredeemably lost."

·   ·   ·

THE OFFICES OF the United States and Haiti Cable Company were located at 17 William Street, near the tip of Manhattan. The submarine cable that terminated there ran fifteen hundred miles southward along the bottom of the Atlantic to Cape Haitien, Haiti. There it intersected a French cable, which ran from Santiago de Cuba eastward to Puerto Rico and southward to Martinique. The William Street office had been taken over by Lieutenant Colonel Joseph E. Maxfield on behalf of the Signal Corps. The purpose of this occupation was censorship of all cable traffic to stop any military information from being sent, but Maxfield was also out to collect intelligence. The Signal Corps apparently had another agent in the cable office at Cape Haitien with access to traffic going over the French cable between Cuba and Madrid.

Thus it was that, within twenty-four hours of Villaverde's initial report, General Greely knew that dispatches were being exchanged between Cervera at Santiago and the minister of marine at Madrid. Greely went to President McKinley and reported that he had confirmation of Cervera's whereabouts from a separate and independent source.

It was no ruse, he assured the president. Cervera was indeed at Santiago.

·   ·   ·

THE STEAMING DISTANCE from Key West to Cienfuegos is 570 statute miles, a distance that the dispatch boats of Admiral Sampson's squadron required as much as forty-eight hours to cover. Thus it was not until May 23 that Commodore Schley received the dispatch Sampson had sent him two days earlier:

> Spanish squadron probably at Santiago de Cuba. Four ships and three torpedo boat destroyers. If you are satisfied that they are not at Cienfuegos, proceed with all despatch, but cautiously, to Santiago de Cuba, and if the enemy is there blockade him in port.

---

*There had been much political unrest in Spain following reports of Dewey's victory at Manila. Sagasta remained in power but appointed a new cabinet on May 18. The new minister of marine was Captain Ramón Auñón y Villalón.

But Schley was not satisfied Cervera was not at Cienfuegos; in fact, he suspected he was. Unlike Havana and the other major ports on the northwest coast of Cuba, the southwest port of Cienfuegos had not been under continuous blockade; the Spanish fleet might have slipped in unseen. And on the afternoon of May 21, as Schley's squadron approached Cienfuegos from the west, he had heard guns from the direction of the harbor, fired in a cadence suggestive of the salute of a warship newly arrived in port. And two days later he had stopped the British steamer *Adula* as it approached from Jamaica to evacuate neutrals from Cienfuegos. The steamer carried a report received in Jamaica that Cervera had arrived at Santiago on the nineteenth but that he had sailed again on the twentieth, misinformation which was completely consistent with Schley's belief that he had just missed seeing Cervera enter Cienfuegos on the afternoon of the twenty-first. Schley settled down to wait outside Cienfuegos harbor.

·   ·   ·

THE SWIFT ARMORED CRUISER *St. Paul* had been an ocean liner but a few months earlier before being chartered by the Navy and fitted out with guns for wartime service. She was more than one-tenth of a mile long, a fact her new skipper often repeated wonderingly to newcomers. She had spent the weeks of the young war in and near the Windward Passage, which separates Cuba and Haiti, and her mission was to be on the lookout for the Spanish fleet. The assignment must have seemed something of a holiday to her commander, Captain Charles D. Sigsbee, coming as it did on the heels of the grim and anxious days of February and March, when he had buried the *Maine's* dead and waited for the verdict of the Court of Inquiry.

Just before six o'clock on the morning of May 25 the *St. Paul* was off the southeast coast of Cuba when she sighted an unidentified steamer and gave chase, intercepting her just outside Santiago harbor. "She proved to be the British steamer *Restormel*, from Cardiff, Wales, with coal, evidently for the Spanish fleet," Sigsbee reported. "She had been at San Juan, Porto Rico, thence to Curacao, where she was informed that the Spanish fleet had left two days before her arrival. She was then directed to proceed to Santiago de Cuba."

Sigsbee put a prize crew aboard the captured collier and sent her to Key West. The Spanish watched the incident in dismay from Santiago. The second in command of the naval forces in the port, Lieutenant José Müller y Tejeiro, recalled, "Our fleet had taken on board all the Cardiff coal that was at the navy depot, without succeeding . . . in filling its bunkers."

There was some thought of sending the fleet out to rescue the *Restormel*, but, Müller explained:

The capture took place a long distance from the mouth of the harbor; before a ship could weigh anchor, clear the channel, get up full steam and traverse that distance, at least three hours must elapse, and where would have been the captor and the prize by that time? . . . Moreover, from the 22d to the 28th, the swell of the sea prevented the ships from going out; the pilots of the harbor were not willing to take them out.

THE ROUGH SEAS and fresh winds off the south coast of Cuba were also hindering Commodore Schley, who was at this moment steaming slowly westward, en route from Cienfuegos to Santiago. Three white lights had been seen along the shore near Cienfuegos during the night of the twenty-third.

"The only officer who professed to know the significance of these signals did not think them important enough at the time to communicate them," Schley later complained.

"I knew [the lights were] the signal from the insurgents that they wished to communicate," Captain Robley D. Evans of the *Iowa* explained.

> I, of course, took it for granted that the commodore understood this signal as well as I did, otherwise I should have informed him of its significance. It appeared afterward that he did not; and thus much valuable time was lost. On the morning of the 24th the *Marblehead* arrived, and the moment Commander McCalla heard of the three lights he went in and communicated, and in a few hours Schley knew that the Spanish fleet was not in Cienfuegos. . . . At 7.55 that evening the squadron got under way and went to sea, bound for Santiago. During the 25th and 26th we steamed along slowly, at times making as low as five knots in order to allow the *Eagle*, a small converted yacht, to keep company with us.

The waters were no angrier or more troubled than Commodore Schley. He felt like a fool, having waited three days outside Cienfuegos because no one had bothered to explain to him the arrangements that had been made to communicate with the insurgents. But something else was beginning to bother him even more. No matter what the insurgents had reported, he had a hunch he couldn't shake that Cervera was not at Santiago. The fifty-nine-year-old naval officer had spent his life at sea and had learned to trust his own instincts. Perhaps, like many sailors, he was a little superstitious. Whatever the reason, Schley became convinced he was taking the Flying Squadron in the wrong direction.

He was sure that Cervera was behind him, at Cienfuegos.

·   ·   ·

"AT 5:25 P.M., May 26th, we stopped our engines at a point twenty-six to thirty miles to the south of Santiago, and there remained four hours or more in communication with the St. Paul, the Yale, and the Minneapolis," Captain Evans recalled.

Captain Sigsbee came aboard the *Brooklyn*. After his interview on the previous day with the captain of the captured *Restormel*, Sigsbee should have strongly suspected that the Spanish squadron was inside Santiago harbor. But whatever he said, Schley got the impression Sigsbee thought just the opposite.

"They [the Spanish] are not here," Sigsbee reportedly said. "I have been here for a week, and they are not here."

"At 7:50 P.M. the commodore made the following general signal to the squadron," Evans recalled: " 'Destination Key West, via south side of Cuba and Yucatan channel . . . speed nine knots.' "

The Flying Squadron proceeded westward, back toward Cienfuegos.

.   .   .

THE DISPATCH FROM SCHLEY, carried by the *Harvard* to the cable head at Kingston, Jamaica, reached the Navy Department on the afternoon of May 28: "Much to be regretted, can not obey orders of the department; forced to proceed for coal to Key West, by way of the Yucatan passage; can not ascertain anything respecting enemy."

"It is difficult to state the anxiety which this dispatch caused the Department," Secretary Long remembered.

> It was the most anxious day in the naval history of the war and was the only instance in which the Department had to whistle to keep its courage up. . . . The feeling that the Spanish fleet might leave the harbor of Santiago was a heavy weight upon the President's mind. To deal with it was not difficult when its whereabouts were known, but to feel that it might leave the Cuban coast, that its movements might be lost track of, and that it might appear at any time on the coast of the United States, was depressing beyond measure.

.   .   .

"THE MANEUVERS OF the hostile squadron . . . were incomprehensible to us," Captain Concas explained. "It would not explain matters if we were to describe the coming and goings of the hostile ships."

In fact, Cervera believed he had been blockaded on the twenty-fifth, after the *Restormel* was captured. He cabled the new minister of marine: "We are blockaded. I qualified our coming here as disastrous for the interests of country. Events begin to show I was right. With disparity of forces any effective operation absolutely impossible. We have provisions for one month."

But even when the dawn of the twenty-seventh disclosed that the American squadron had vanished, he could not take advantage of the turn of events and make his escape from Santiago. The harbor pilots believed the ships would run aground as they tried to pass over the shoals in the heavy seas still running. Cervera continued to be blockaded, now by the weather.

.   .   .

COMMODORE SCHLEY CONTINUED to struggle with his doubts, his intuition, and his instinctive inclination to obey orders. Two hours after starting back for Cienfuegos he ordered the squadron to halt.

"We drifted about until noon of the following day," Captain Evans recalled, "while some of the vessels took coal from the collier. "Then we stood on to the west again, occasionally stopping, until 1:25 P.M., May 28th, when we were signaled to steer east . . . Thus we headed back in the direction of Santiago."

"The only party who was not at the end of a telegraph line, nor apparently in the secrets of the war, was the commander of the Flying Squadron," Commodore Schley protested. "His conclusions had to be reached through all the doubts and surmises of those sending him messages or orders, but who were in no sense nearly so certain as they pretended to be after everything had been made plain."

. . .

THE FLYING SQUADRON ARRIVED off Santiago for the second time at 7:40 P.M. and steamed back and forth before the harbor during the night. At dawn on the twenty-eighth, Captain Evans stood on the bridge of the *Iowa*, scanning the shore through binoculars. Beside him stood Lieutenant Commander Raymond P. Rodgers, who had served as naval attaché at Madrid and knew every vessel of the Spanish Navy by sight. Rodgers made a sudden exclamation.

"Captain, there's the *Cristobal Colón!*"

"In a moment I caught her with my glasses lying moored in front of the Punta Gorda battery in a position to command the channel," Evans recalled. "The information was quickly flagged to the Brooklyn, and in a second or two the answer came back, "I understand." Then we made out another Spanish ship and a torpedo boat and flagged this information at once."

The captains of the squadron went aboard the *Brooklyn* to confer with Commodore Schley.

"The details of this conference I am not at liberty to give," Evans wrote, "but I may say without impropriety that Commodore Schley was at last satisfied that Cervera's fleet was in Santiago Harbor and not in Cienfuegos."

The squadron of Admiral Cervera was at last bottled up for good.

. . .

A GREAT GRAY SPECTER slowly formed in the ocean haze off Jupiter Inlet, on the west coast of the Florida mainland. The Navy signalmen watching from their station ashore had never seen anything like it. For one terrible moment they may have thought it was Cervera, that he had arrived at last on the Florida coast in this fearsome and magnificent man-of-war. Then, from the top of its towering signal mast, the Stars and Stripes unfurled.

Sixty-six days and sixteen thousand miles from San Francisco, the long odyssey of the U.S.S. *Oregon* was at an end.

CHAPTER EIGHT

THE ARMADAS

As MAY TURNED into June, three great armadas made ready to sail. In the Spanish port of Cádiz, Admiral Manuel de la Cámara worked feverishly to make seaworthy the great battleship *Pelayo,* which had not been ready to sail with Cervera six weeks earlier and which was now still in need of refitting. The task force Cámara was assembling included the armored cruiser *Carlos V,* two auxiliary cruisers, the *Patriota* and *Rápido,* three destroyers, and four colliers. A force of four thousand troops was being assembled to sail along with the fleet in a pair of transports. On May 15, U.S. intelligence sources in Europe reported the unconfirmed rumor that Cámara's destination was to be the Philippines.

General Wesley Merritt began assembling a force of some ten thousand men at San Francisco to capture and hold Manila. At the Mare Island Naval Station, two monitor-type warships, the *Monterey* and the *Monadnock,* were readied to sail for Manila Bay to reinforce the Asiatic Squadron. Like the Civil War ironclad that gave the class its name, the monitors were little more than armed and armored barges, intended more for defending coasts than winning empires. Their ten-inch and twelve-inch guns would make a significant addition to Dewey's firepower, but getting them to the Philippines was a major problem. Their low freeboards, not intended for transoceanic cruises, would mean very slow going across the seven thousand miles of ocean ahead.

An army of 25,000 men was assembling at Tampa under the command of General Rufus Shafter. This force had grown during May as the early plans for an expedition to the southern Cuban coast to supply Gómez had been replaced by the plan for a major landing at Mariel and a siege of Havana. On May 30 the plans were changed again, and Shafter was ordered to take his force to Santiago

and to capture the Spanish garrison there, the harbor, and the fleet of Admiral
Cervera.

.   .   .

IN THE OPERATING ROOM at the White House, President McKinley and his
advisors studied the pin-studded maps and considered their next move in the
two-ocean war. Admiral Sampson and General Blanco stared at each other across
the waters outside Havana. Admiral Cervera sat disconsolately in Santiago harbor
and watched Commodore Schley steam back and forth outside. Admiral Dewey
marked time uneasily at Manila, waiting for General Merritt and the monitors,
wondering whether Admiral Cámara was coming, and watching the increasingly
belligerent comings and goings of the German squadron.

Some of the war plans made years before at the Naval War College called
for naval raids along the Spanish coasts. Such raids would be particularly valuable
at this moment because they would force Madrid to keep Admiral Cámara in
Spanish waters to defend the peninsula and so relieve the threat to Dewey. There
was just one problem: The only fleet that might be used to raid Spanish ports
was the Flying Squadron, now fully occupied outside Santiago harbor.

"Our battle fleet before Santiago was more than powerful enough to crush
the hostile squadron in a very short time if the latter attempted a stand-up fight,"
Admiral Mahan later explained.

> The fact was so evident that it was perfectly clear nothing of the kind
> would be hazarded; but, nevertheless, we could not afford to diminish
> the number of armored vessels on this spot, now become the determin-
> ing center of the conflict. . . . Either the enemy might succeed in an
> effort at evasion, a chance which required us to a maintain a distinctly
> superior force of battleships (outside Santiago] . . . or, by merely remain-
> ing quietly at anchor . . . he might protract a situation which tended
> not only to wear out our ships, but also to keep them there into the
> hurricane season.

Schley had bottled up Cervera, but Cervera had tied down Schley. Impoverished, exhausted, and now trapped in the harbor of Santiago, the sad squadron of Admiral Cervera continued to be the pivot on which turned the Spanish
War.

.   .   .

RICHMOND PEARSON HOBSON WAS a handsome and serious young man of twenty-
seven. He was a graduate of Annapolis and the Ecole d'Application du Génie
Maritime in Paris. He was a naval constructor, i.e., a commissioned officer of the
U.S. Navy whose specialty was naval architecture. He was assigned to Admiral
Sampson's flagship, the *New York,* and on May 29 the admiral sent for him.

"I had set to work on the problem of clearing a channel of torpedoes and
mines," Hobson remembered.

The result was the outline design of a craft specially constructed to be unsinkable . . . by being stowed with air-tight cans a foot long, and made indestructable by special arrangements in construction . . . I had elaborated a plan for the use of five such unsinkable craft, to precede the fleet in entering the harbor of Havana. . . .

After listening with attention to the plans, the admiral said that at the time it was not a question of how to make a vessel unsinkable . . . but how to make a vessel sink in an enemy's harbor, and make her sink swiftly and surely; that it was "not a question of an unsinkable, but a sinkable"; not a question of Havana, but of Santiago . . .

He then confided to me that he was about to start for Santiago, where Admiral Cervera's fleet had taken refuge, and that he intended to sink a collier in the channel.

The entrance to the harbor of Santiago de Cuba was narrow and shallow. A single wreck lying in the middle of that channel could keep a large warship from passing, and a few monitors or cruisers stationed nearby could prevent the Spanish from removing the wreck. Sampson believed he saw a way to replace the Flying Squadron with a single, sunken collier.

Hobson and the admiral studied the charts of Santiago harbor and began working out the details as the New York got underway from Key West and steamed eastward. There was first of all the problem of getting the collier in the desired position before scuttling her; the Spanish were unlikely to let a ship approach the harbor unchallenged, and the coastal batteries might sink her well outside of the entrance channel. They considered a ruse: perhaps the Spanish would regard the sight of a heavily laden supply ship flying the Spanish flag and apparently pursued by the blockading ships as a welcome sight and let her come in unmolested.

"This plan, and various other plans . . . were discarded in favor of the simpler plan of going in alone by moonlight," Hobson recalled.

There were two methods of scuttling the ship quickly: driving off her bottom plates, and exploding a series of charges placed along the outside of the hull. The later method was chosen. A string of ten watertight cans, each containing seventy-eight pounds of gunpowder, would be strung along the port side of the ship twelve feet below the water line. The charges would be detonated electrically from the collier's bridge.

The Merrimac, a collier on station with the Flying Squadron, was chosen for the mission. Its length was 333 feet, and the charts showed the narrow part of the Santiago channel to range from 350 to 450 feet. It would be necessary to enter the channel, swing athwart it, stop dead and anchor her for and aft in that position, and then fire the charges.

The operation would be carried out by a small crew of volunteers, including Hobson. After the charges were fired, the crew would escape in a small boat, or else swim to shore and try to evade capture. Each man would have a rifle, a revolver, and a box of waterproof cartridges.

The final detail was the timetable. The mission was to begin before dawn and just before the moon set; there would be enough darkness to cover the operation, and the tide would be running strong flood; if the anchors tore loose, the ship would have time to settle before the ebb could move her out of the channel. Hobson consulted his tables.

"The moon was then approaching full, and calculations showed that on Thursday, June 2, it would set at Santiago at about half-past three," he recalled. "The special advantage of Thursday was that there would be an interval of darkness of about an hour and a quarter between the time of moonset and daybreak, while on Friday this interval would be reduced to half and hour, and on Saturday day would break before moonset."

The *New York* was now steaming toward Santiago at thirteen knots and would arrive off the harbor early Wednesday morning. Twenty-four hours or less seemed like too little time to get ready, but Hobson knew that seventy-five minutes of darkness was the absolute minimum needed to get the *Merrimac* in place, sink her, and escape.

.　　　.　　　.

"I REALLY DOUBT there ever has been a regiment quite like this," Roosevelt proudly wrote to Cabot Lodge from San Antonio.

> It is as typical an American regiment as ever marched or fought . . . including a score of Indians, and about as many of Mexican origin from New Mexico; then there are some fifty Easterners—almost all graduates of Harvard, Yale, Princeton, etc.,—and almost as many Southerners; the rest are men of the plains and the Rocky Mountains. Three fourths of our men have at one time or another been cowboys or else are small stockmen; certainly two thirds have fathers who fought on one side or the other in the civil war.

Its official designation was the First Volunteer Cavalry, but it would soon be known to the public and to history as the Rough Riders. In the words of Secretary Alger's orders setting it up, it was to be "a regiment of mounted riflemen . . . young, sound, good shots and good riders." Alger offered the command to his friend, Theodore Roosevelt, who declined, surprisingly. Roosevelt had served three years in the New York National Guard, attaining the rank of captain, but he was not under the illusion that this qualified him to command a cavalry regiment.

"I told him that after six weeks' service in the field I would feel competent to handle the regiment," Roosevelt recalled. But he had no intention of spending six precious weeks of the fast-moving war learning to be a colonel. He asked for the post of second in command instead and proposed his friend, Army Surgeon Leonard Wood, to command the regiment. Wood, in addition to having graduated from Harvard Medical School, had earned the Medal of Honor fighting Apaches in Arizona. Wood needed no introduction to the secretary of war; he was the Algers' family doctor.

Wood selected San Antonio as the main mustering point for the regiment. It was good horse country and near to embarkation ports along the Gulf Coast,

and there was an old arsenal and army base nearby. Throughout the first two
weeks in May the recruits arrived.

They were a rare assortment—New York City policemen, Ivy League quar-
terbacks, bronco busters and polo players, Indians and Indian fighters, sheriffs,
deputies, and one former marshal of Dodge City, a national tennis champion, a
few professional gamblers, several Methodist clergymen, one man who had been
both bookkeeper and buffalo hunter, and an ex-mayor of Prescott, Arizona. Men
with Christian names like Dudley, Guy, Hamilton, and Woodbury met men who
went by such handles as Cherokee Bill, Happy Jack, and Rattlesnake Pete.
Members of the Somerset and Knickerbocker clubs bunked with veterans of the
Texas Rangers and constituents of the Cherokee Nation.

An Eastern dude himself, Roosevelt took aside the Ivy League contingent
and explained

> that if they went in they must be prepared not merely to fight, but to
> perform the weary monotonous labor incident to the ordinary routine
> of a soldier's life. . . .
> I warned them that work that was merely irksome and disagreeable
> must be faced as readily as work that was dangerous, and that no
> complaint of any kind must be made; and I told them that they were
> entirely at liberty not to go, but that after they had once signed there
> could then be no backing out.
> Not a man of them backed out; not one of them failed to do his
> whole duty.

There was no shortage of volunteers for the regiment. "Within a day or two
after it was announced that we were to raise the regiment," Roosevelt remembered, "we were literally deluged with applications from every quarter of the
Union." He was given the task of writing the many letters of rejection that were
necessary. One went to an eager young cowboy in Pocatello, Idaho: "I wish I
could take you, in but I am afraid that the chances of our being over-enlisted
forbid my bringing a man from such a distance."

A pity. Roosevelt would probably have found Edgar Rice Burroughs a man
very much after his own heart.

The task of drilling the regiment also fell to Roosevelt, and he welcomed
it as "a piece of great good fortune," for, as he admitted, "I had plenty to learn."
But along with the other recruits he found the military essentials easy to learn.
He later reflected:

> The reason why it takes so long to turn the average civilized man into
> a good infantryman or cavalryman is because it takes a long while to
> teach [him] to shoot, to ride, to march, to take care of himself in the
> open, to be alert, resourceful, cool, daring, and resolute, to obey quickly,
> as well as to be willing, and . . . to act on his own responsibility. "If
> he already possesses these qualities, there is very little difficulty in
> making him a soldier. . . . Parade ground and barrack square maneuvers
> are of no earthly consequence in real war.

On May 25 Roosevelt wrote to President McKinley, "We are in fine shape. . . . We are ready to leave at any moment, and we earnestly hope we will be put into Cuba with the very first troops; the sooner the better."

.   .   .

LIEUTENANT WILLIAM S. SIMS, the young naval attaché at Paris, cabled Washington in cipher May 26:

> Special agent at Paris, retired naval officer, Baron, amicable relations with Spanish Ambassador, is certain Spanish Ambassador informed French Ministry that objective fleet at Cadiz was Philippine Islands; but he believes [new Spanish Ministry] has changed plan. He believes he will be able to ascertain destination when Spanish Ambassador has returned tomorrow evening.
> Shall I send him to Madrid?

The following day Secretary Long replied, "Send agent if deemed best."
Prudently, Long declined to try to run a European secret intelligence operation from his Washington office. Besides, young Sims seemed to have a flair for secret service.* The network of agents he had quickly organized stretched from the Canary Islands, where a cut-rate spy watched for Cervera's return, to Spain, where "an Italian citizen" reported naval movements for three hundred dollars per month, to Port Said, where a "reliable gentleman, lately [a] Swedish Army officer," watched and waited for Admiral Cámara to arrive en route to Manila. None could doubt the thoroughness of Sims's methods who had read his report of May 19 that a letter sent by a French mechanic working on the *Carlos V* at Cádiz, and received the day before by his family at Le Havre, mentioned that the cruiser would be "ready for sea within a few days."

The Office of Naval Intelligence, to which Sims and the other naval attachés reported, was a relative newcomer, having been organized in 1882. In a time when the word "intelligence" simply meant information and did not necessarily connote espionage or, as it was then called, "secret service," ONI began life primarily as a compiler of such statistics of foreign navies as tonnage, coal capacity, armor thickness, number and size of guns, and other details that were no more easily hidden than the men-of-war they described. The Navy's lack, at this time, of anything in the way of a general staff, caused ONI to inherit the additional function of producing operational war plans, a task it shared with the Naval War College.

In April 1898, when ONI found itself in its first war, it was given another responsibility—procuring ships, supplies, and other materials needed by the Navy from European vendors. But on April 26 the attaches in London and Paris were suddenly given new and urgent orders: "Make every effort to obtain reliable information movements Spanish fleet at Cádiz, Spain. Necessary expenditures for this authorized."

*Sims, multitalented, became the Navy's most influential admiral and commanded the U.S. Navy in Europe during the final year of World War I.

ONI rose to the occasion with inspired amateurism, that hallmark of so many successful intelligence operations before and since. Two young ensigns, William H. Buck and Henry Heber Ward, posing as wealthy tourists, cruised aboard yachts in the Atlantic and Mediterranean to watch for movements of the Spanish fleets. Edward Breck, a young naval officer who had attended Heidelberg University and become an accomplished swordsman, was sent by the naval attaché at Berlin to Spain in the guise of a German physician on vacation. But the most effective sources were the paid agents hired by Sims and by his London counterpart, Lieutenant John C. Colwell.

Colwell sent an agent to Spain late in April, a man who was paid $2,500 per month to take risks. Apparently he tried to give ONI its money's worth, for on May 6 Colwell reported, "My agent sent to Cádiz has been wounded," and six days later, "My first man, sent to Cádiz, Spain, has disappeared in Spain."

But Colwell had plenty of replacements and plenty of money to pay them with. Agents "E" and "F," at $1,500 each per month, followed in the vanished man's footsteps, while "G" watched the London waterfront for Spanish cargoes at the bargain-basement rate of $10 per month. Two hundred dollars per month bought "K," an employee at the Spanish Embassy in London, $1,000 per month paid "L" to go to Port Said, while "G" was clever enough to get sent to Paris *and* draw $1,500. Spending money like a sailor, Colwell paid out some $27,000 during the course of the three-and-a-half-month war. But there were no complaints; Colwell's information would have been a bargain at a hundred times the price. On May 27 he reported to Long:

> My best man just returned from Cadiz. . . . He assures me . . . that Camara's fleet will sail for Ceuta, Morocco, and then to the Philippine Islands, before June 14th. Three armored vessels in readiness for sea; two Hamburg-American steamers will be ready for sea June 1st, good armament; seven Compania Transatlantica steamers will be ready for sea June 14th, fair armament, full cargo coal, provisions. . . .
>
> Several thousand troops have been moved to Ceuta, Morocco. Carlos V forward turret not working yet.
>
> They assure me the Spanish policy is after this: Cervera's fleet to hold American fleet in Cuba; the Spanish coast will not be threatened, and Camara will be free to disappear ostensibly for the United States coast, but in fact to attack Dewey, and to recover Manila. . . .
>
> I have good man at Suez canal, two in Spain, one in Lisbon, one shipmaster on the coast of Spain, two in England.
>
> This business is expensive; funds are needed.

In Washington, the members of the Navy War Board, seeing the war to be as much a game of poker as of chess, ordered Lieutenant Sims to plant some disinformation with the Spanish. On June 1 the board cabled:

> Give out the following information; probably false, possibly true. As soon as Cervera's squadron is destroyed, an American fleet of armored vessels and cruisers will be detached against Spanish ports and the coast

of Spain generally. The Americans seem to be especially incensed against Cádiz, and doubtless that place will come in for a taste of actual war.

It was Cádiz, where the wives, children, and sweethearts of the men of Cámara's fleet would wait when the ships sailed away to Manila.

.   .   .

"UNQUESTIONABLY, Tampa was not adapted to the concentration and the effective handling of the vast quantities of supplies necessary for an army of 25,000 men," Secretary Alger acknowledged.

It would hardly have been selected for the purposes of the Santiago expedition had so large a force been under consideration at the time. The city of Tampa was approached by only two lines of railroad, both single-track. . . . Tampa and Port Tampa [where the transport ships waited] are nine miles apart. The intervening country is, for the most part, very swampy and sandy. One single-track railroad connects the two places. At the terminus there was but one wharf, and that capable of accommodating not more than nine transports at a time.

"Reaching Tampa on the 1st of June," General Miles recalled,

I found that place crowded with an indiscriminate accumulation of supplies and war material. The confusion . . . appeared . . . to be utterly inextricable. The sidings from the port of Tampa for perhaps fifty miles into the interior were blocked with cars, and the resulting difficulties of the situation prevented proper embarkation of the troops.

"Up to May 26th, while the work of preparation had been energetically pushed, it had been done quietly," General Shafter's aide, Lieutenant John D. Miley, remembered. "But now there was a change. . . . Working hours were no longer confined to the day, but were prolonged into the night, and for several days before sailing the embarkation was kept up continuously."

Thirty-two transport ships were fitted out with bunks for the men and stalls for the horses, then brought to the wharf in groups of nine for loading. The railroad track where the boxcars stood lay parallel to the wharf and separated from it by fifty feet of loose sand. There were no hoists or cranes; except for the animals, everything had to be carried from the cars to the transports on the backs of stevedores. Sorting and assembling the foodstuffs into rations—that to be consumed by one man in one day—was done at dockside, causing much of the confusion. Miley recalled:

The components of the ration came direct from the contractors in different cars of the same train or on different trains. Therefore, in order to place a given number of rations on a transport, it was necessary to go from car to car on a train or even to some car on another train to complete the cargo. Often the components needed to complete the ration were on trains that could not be brought to the wharf at the time, and the transport then being loaded would have to be pulled out into the stream and another brought into its place. . . . Cars of meat would come to the Port direct from some place in the North, cars of hard bread or flour from another place, cars of other components from still another place, and these cars were scattered along the congested track from the Port to Tampa City, a distance of ten miles.

There were in round numbers about ten million pounds of rations placed on board.

Assembling the arms and ammunition presented an identical problem:

The siege-artillery and ammunition had come from different arsenals and at different times, and much delay arose in gathering all the parts and mounting the guns on the carriages. . . . To add to this congestion of the railroad, passenger trains were continually running between Tampa and the Port, carrying crowds of sightseers and tourists; and the regular freight, passenger, and express business of the Plant System between Tampa and Key West went on without interruption.

"The Army," Alger explained, "had not been mobilized since the Civil War. The problem was in all respects a new one."

The newspaper correspondents and foreign military attachés rocked and fanned themselves on the veranda of the Tampa Bay Hotel, wondering why H. B. Plant had built it there, yet thanking God he had.

"It is a real oasis in the real desert," Richard Harding Davis marveled. "A giant affair of ornamental brick and silver minarets in a city chiefly composed of derilect wooden houses drifting in an ocean of sand."

The immense hotel also provided quarters and office space for the Army. Old friends and former enemies met in the lobby or encountered one another on the stairs. General Wheeler and General Lee marveled at the new blue uniforms they found each other wearing, while General Shafter sweated and waddled between meetings with the exasperated General Miles. Lieutenant Rowan, just returned from his mission to García, was there, as was exreporter Grover Flint, who had served briefly with General Gómez and was now a major in the U.S. Army. Captain Dorst, fresh from the hilarious *Gussie* expedition, was making preparations for another attempt to supply the insurgents. Davis sketched the scene:

Officers who had not met in years, men who had been classmates at West Point, men who had fought together and against each other in the last war, who had parted at army posts all over the West, who had been with Miles after Geronimo, with Forsythe at Wounded Knee . . . were gathered together . . . and were left to dangle and dawdle under the electric lights and silver minarets. Their talk was only of an immediate advance. It was to be "as soon as Sampson smashes the Cape Verde fleet."

Four miles away, at the end of the trolley line to Tampa Heights, the gallant New York Seventy-first was arriving from Lakeland, a town some thirty miles to the west, where the regiment had been encamped for the past two weeks. Reveille had been sounded at 3:30 that morning and the troops broke camp and boarded the trains that would take them on the last land leg of their journey. Chaplain Van Dewater recalled the scene:

> The train conveyed the regiment from Lakeland in two sections. As usual, the management of this one-horse road mixed things up in such a way that men and goods could not be brought together for hours. Mules were found in one section a mile and a half away from the wagons to which they were to be attached; tents and provisions were so confused that nobody could tell where either could be found; horses were miles from their saddles and the hostlers were with neither. . . . The march to Tampa Heights will never be forgotten by those who took it. The day was very hot, the hour of the day its hottest, every man had been up since half-past three, and most of the time on his feet. The road was in such a dry condition that fully eighteen inches of dust finer than powder had to be trudged through along its entire course. . . . Several men were prostrated by the heat on arriving at camp, but were quickly restored. The effects, however, of the march were seen for several days, in cases of general weakness and obstinate diarrhea. It was soon discovered that there was no prospect of procuring tents or provisions to any considerable extent before the following morning.

But by the following afternoon the regiment had sorted itself out and settled in, and Chaplain Van Dewater grudgingly acknowledged that "this camp at Tampa Heights was much superior to the one at Lakeland." A Red Cross official who visited the camps around Tampa described a homely scene:

> As we drove up to the camp, smoke was rising lazily into the warm summer air from a dozen fires in different parts of the grounds; company cooks were putting the knives, forks and dishes that they had just washed into improvised cupboards made by nailing boxes and tomato-crates against the trees; officers in fatigue-uniform were sitting in camp-chairs, here and there, reading the latest New York papers; and thousands of soldiers . . . were . . . lounging and smoking on the ground in the shade of the army wagons, playing hand-ball to pass away the time, or swarming around a big board shanty, just outside the lines, which called itself "Noah's Ark" and announced in big letters its readiness to dispense cooling drinks to all comers at a reasonable price.

"Now that we knew we were destined for Cuba and would be among the first in the actual fighting," Private Post reminisced, "daily after drill the men began to line up before the chaplain's tent."

The newly baptized regiment was now issued live ammunition for its rifles and practiced firing them.

"Each cartridge was as big as your finger, with a .45-caliber slug at its front end," Post recalled. "It could, properly directed, knock down two men, the one it hit and the one who fired it. . . . It had seventy grains of old-fashioned black powder, and, with each discharge, there burst forth a cloud of white smoke somewhat the size of a cow."

As they endured the heat and hardships of Tampa, the troops consoled themselves with the thought that a million other men from Maine to California would gladly have changed places with them.

"We were envied," Private Post recalled. The newspapermen, temporarily without a war to cover and unable to describe the confusion of Port Tampa, wrote upbeat stories about the troops.

"Everybody in Fine Spirits," proclaimed the St. Louis *Post-Dispatch.* "They are a nice lot of good spirited boys and the right sort of men to defend their country."

The story was not written by one of the worldly scribes staying at the Tampa Bay Hotel but by the audacious sixteen-year-old son of the Eleventh Infantry's bandmaster, who had persuaded the paper to pay his way to Tampa in exchange for some articles. But a promising journalistic career was nipped in the bud when the bandmaster was stricken with food poisoning and invalided out of the Army. For young Fiorello La Guardia fame would come at another time and place, in a different line of work.

·   ·   ·

AMONG THE THOUSANDS OF tourists, merchants, sightseers, and would-be recruits who flocked to Tampa was Canadian-born Frank Arthur Mellor. Mellor tried to enlist but was turned down. He stopped at the Almeria Hotel in Tampa, where he received a curiously worded telegram from a "B. Siddall" in Montreal. Shortly thereafter he was arrested by the U.S. Secret Service and charged with being a Spanish spy, which, in fact, he was.

Mellor had been hired some weeks earlier in Kingston, Ontario, by Lieutenant Ramón Carranza, lately the Spanish military attache in Washington, and currently chief of the hastily established Spanish intelligence station that operated out of the Windsor Hotel in Montreal. Following the example of Ambassador Dupuy de Lôme, who had hired the Pinkerton National Detective Agency to spy on the Cuban Junta, Carranza hired a Canadian private detective agency to recruit agents to spy in the United States. The Spanish officer was looking for someone with a military background to recruit other veterans of the Canadian Army who would go to the United States, enlist, and serve as Spanish agents. When the agents landed in Cuba or the Philippines with the American forces, they were to cross the lines, surrender to the Spanish, and identifying themselves with a distinctive ring furnished by Carranza, report on American military plans.

The detective agency provided Carranza with Frank Mellor, a former artilleryman willing to do the sort of work the Spaniard had in mind. Mellor was a pugnacious man with an unsavory background, and he was unsuited to the task Carranza gave him. One of his recruits, an Englishman, reported the scheme to the British consul in Kingston, and the U.S. State Department was informed by the British government. The matter was passed on to the Secret Service, which already knew of Lieutenant Carranza's operations.

The Secret Service was headed by John E. Wilkie, a thirty-eight-year-old former city editor of the Chicago *Tribune* who had specialized in police reporting. When diplomatic relations were broken off with Spain a few days before the declaration of war, Wilkie sent a team of agents to accompany Spanish ambassador Polo to the Canadian border and insure his safe conduct. Lieutenant Carranza had been in Polo's party.

Polo and Carranza remained briefly in Toronto before moving on to Montreal and stopping at the Windsor Hotel. A Secret Service agent followed and checked into a room next to that of the naval attache. Early on May 6 he overheard a conversation between Carranza and a visitor. The visitor was George Downing, a young English-born naturalized American citizen who had served as a petty officer aboard the *Brooklyn*. Downing apparently had come to peddle information to the Spanish, but Carranza engaged him as an agent and sent him to Washington.

Downing was followed by the Secret Service from the Windsor Hotel to the railroad station, and a description was wired ahead to Wilkie, who arranged to have the man followed when he got off the train in Washington. Downing checked into an E Street boardinghouse, then proceeded to the Navy Department, where he apparently knew his way around. (There was much excitement in the department that day, on which the first report from Dewey at Manila was received.) Two hours later he emerged, returned to the boardinghouse, and an hour later mailed a letter at the main post office at Pennsylvania Avenue and Twelfth Street. The letter was intercepted by the Secret Service agents following him.

The envelope was addressed to Frederick W. Dickon, Esq., 1248 Dorchester Street, Montreal, Canada, which apparently was one of Carranza's letter drops. The letter read:

A cipher message has been sent off from the Navy Department to San Francisco, directing the cruiser *Charleston* to proceed to Manila with five hundred men and machinery for repairs for Dewey. A long cipher has been received from Dewey at the Department at 3:30 P.M. They are translating it now. Cannot find it out yet. I heard important news respecting movements of colliers and cruiser *Newark* at Norfolk Navy Yards; also about the new Holland boat,* as to what they intend to do with her and her destination. I shall go to Norfolk to find important news. My address will be Norfolk House, Norfolk, Virginia, but shall not go until Tuesday.

Downing was arrested. Two days later he was found hanging in his cell, apparently a suicide.

Despite the failures of Mellor and Downing, Carranza was able to obtain

*The *Holland,* a prototype submarine invented and built by John R. Holland under Navy contract.

valuable information and transmit it to General Blanco in Havana, evading the Signal Corps censors by sending it via the Direct West India Cable Company's link between Halifax, Nova Scotia, Bermuda, Kingston, Jamaica, and Santiago de Cuba.* On May 23 Blanco received word from Montreal that Schley's Flying Squadron was en route to the southern coast of Cuba, and on May 25 he warned the army commander at Santiago that "private telegrams from the United States say it is intended to close in [Cervera's] squadron [at] Santiago."

Carranza was doing something right, and it became increasingly important to John Wilkie to put him out of business. Late in May, the Spaniard had moved from the Windsor Hotel to a rented house at 42 Tupper Street. Carranza had taken a short lease on the premises—only two months—and so was not surprised when the rental agency sent three prospective tenants to look at the house on the morning of May 27.

The visitors were two American actors and Secret Service agent Ralph Redfern, who had been watching the Tupper Street house from his rented rooms across the way. Redfern and the actors were shown through the house by a maid while Carranza and his assistant were at breakfast. Sticking his head into one of the bedrooms, Redfern saw a letter, apparently due to be posted. Loitering behind the others, he slipped back into the room and grabbed it. Within forty-eight hours the letter had been put in Chief Wilkie's hands, opened, and translated.

It proved to be a long letter Carranza had written to his cousin, Admiral José Gómez Ymay, and it was for the most part gossip about the Spanish Navy and the war, but it contained this admission:

> I have been left here to receive and send telegrams and to look after the spy service which I have established. . . . We have had bad luck because they have captured our two best spies, one in Washington, who hanged himself—or else they did it for him—and the other day before yesterday in Tampa. The Americans are showing the most extraordinary vigilance.

British neutrality precluded Spanish use of Canada for spying on the United States, of course, so the State Department promptly furnished a photocopy of the Carranza letter to Sir Julian Pauncefote, the British ambassador to Washington. Apparently to hasten British action in shutting down the Montreal station and expelling Carranza, Wilkie released the text of the letter to the New York *Herald*, which published it on June 5.

Confronted by the press, Carranza claimed the letter had been doctored by the Secret Service and mistranslated as well, a position officially adopted by the Spanish government. But Sir Julian and the British Embassy's legal advisor were permitted to inspect the original letter in Wilkie's office and reported to London that it had been correctly translated and contained "no erasure of interpolation

---

*Inexplicably, the insurgents did not cut the land line between Havana and Santiago, so communications between Havana and the outside world remained intact even though the submarine cables had been cut at Cienfuegos.

whatever." Faced with the choice of offending either Washington or Madrid, her majesty's government lost little time in advising Lord Aberdeen, the governor general of Canada, that Carranza should be requested to leave British territory.

A new dilemma had arisen, however. Carranza could hardly be asked to leave Canada; the province of Quebec had just forbidden him to do so. He was being sued by a Canadian private detective whom the Spaniard had accused of stealing the letter and had had arrested, and under Quebec law he could not leave the province until the matter was settled. But it no longer mattered; Carranza had been neutralized, and the Spanish espionage network was out of business.

. . .

THE *Merrimac* moved slowly through the moonlit waters off the Cuban coast. Naval Constructor Hobson could make out the dark outlines of the Morro Castle high up on the steep bluffs that rose from the sea, and knew that the narrow mouth of Santiago harbor lay beneath it.

"As we stood on, the outlines of Morro and other shore objects became clearer and clearer," Hobson recalled. "The blockading vessels were miles behind. When we arrived within about two thousand yards there could be no further question of surprise. In the bright moonlight we were in clear view, and our movements must long since have caused suspicion."

Hobson called for full speed ahead. The engine room telegraph clanged, and the throbbing of the engines quickened.

"The vessel responded as if animated. The foam began to fly from our anchors, which, slung over bow and quarter, just trailed in the water, and our bow swung around to the northward and westward."

The *Merrimac* had started her dash into the narrow channel at the mouth of Santiago Bay. It was shortly past 3 A.M., June 3.

There had been furious preparations throughout the day and evening of June 1, and on into the early hours of the second, but the two hundred men who swarmed over the collier, stripping her and placing the charges around her hull, had not finished their work until almost daylight. Admiral Sampson had ordered Hobson to wait until the last hour of moonlight of the following morning.

There had been no lack of volunteers to go along on the mission. The entire crew of six hundred men and all the officers of the *Iowa* wanted to go, but Captain Evans was informed that his battleship could send only one man. The choice was narrowed down to two candidates, who settled the matter by the toss of a coin. The loser then offered the winner fifty dollars for the privilege, a proposition that was immediately declined.

In all, six enlisted men were selected from the squadron to sail with Hobson on what all seemed to regard as a suicide mission. A seventh, Coxswain Rudolph Clausen of the *New York*, included himself in the adventure through the expedient of stowing away aboard the *Merrimac* in the darkness.

The collier was now making nine knots and had approached to within five hundred yards of the channel. "Another ship's length, and a flash darted out from the water's edge at the left side of the entrance. The expected crash through the ship's side did not follow. . . . Another flash—another miss!"

Through his night glasses Hobson made out the source of the fire—a picket boat armed with rapid-fire guns. The Spanish gunners were aiming at the collier's rudder, trying to disable her steering. The shore battery on the left side of the channel now began to fire. The unarmed *Merrimac* kept on coming. Hobson watched Morro Point approach. According to his plan, the collier would stop engines when it reached two ship's lengths from the point, then coast into the channel to the place designated for sinking.

A shell whistled past the bridge and struck something. Hobson anxiously looked around. To his relief the engine telegraph, the helmsman, and the binnacle seemed intact. Now Morro Point was two ship's lengths off. He gave the order to stop engines.

Her engines silent, the seven thousand-ton *Merrimac* surged on, her speed slowly diminishing. The rapid-fire and machine gun batteries ashore now began pouring out a continuous rain of fire. Bullets rang against the collier's sides, and she shook beneath the exploding shells.

The rocky cliffs of Morro Point slipped past only thirty feet away as the ship coasted into the narrow channel. Hobson sighted the small cove that marked the point where he planned to scuttle.

"Hard aport!" he called. The collier must now turn at right angles to block the narrow channel.

"Hard aport, I say!" But the helm *was* hard aport. The steering gear had been shot away. The *Merrimac* coasted on, out of control past the narrow choke-point of the harbor channel. Hobson signaled, the bow anchor was dropped, and one of the charges was detonated, then a second. That was all. The eight other charges refused to explode.

The bow anchor had not held; the stern anchor had been shot away. Sinking slowly—too slowly—the *Merrimac* drifted on. The channel broadened. The collier passed into the harbor of Santiago.

The Spanish detonated a submerged mine as she passed over it, lifting her slightly out of the water, but otherwise having no effect. The shore batteries continued their deafening roar and rain of lead and steel.

All firing was at point-blank range, at a target that could hardly be missed . . . The striking projectiles and flying fragments produced a grinding sound, with a fine ring in it of steel on steel.

The deck vibrated heavily, and we felt the full effect, lying as we were, full-length on our faces. At each instant it seemed that certainly the next would bring a projectile among us. The impulse surged strong to get away from a place where remaining seemed death, and the men suggested taking to the boat and jumping overboard; but I knew that any object leaving the ship would be seen, and to be seen was certain death, and, therefore, I directed all to remain motionless.

The firing continued for ten minutes as the *Merrimac* drifted into the harbor with the tide. The cruiser *Reina Mercedes* and the torpedo boat *Plutón* both fired torpedos at the collier. She began to settle more rapidly.

The *Merrimac* gave a premonitory lurch, then staggered to port in a death-throe. The bow almost fell, it sank so rapidly. . . . The stern rose and heeled heavily; it stood for a moment, shuddering, then started downward, righting as it went.

A great rush of water came up the gangway, seething and gurgling out of the deck . . . it seized us and threw us against the bulwarks, then over the rail.

As the collier settled to the bottom, Hobson and the crew swam amid the floating debris and gathered around the ship's catamaran. Miraculously, all were present and uninjured. The firing had ceased, and the Spanish had come out from shore in boats looking for survivors. Hobson whispered to the men to keep quiet and try to stay out of sight.

The moon was now low. . . . The sunken vessel was bubbling up its last lingering breath. The boats' crews looking for refugees pulled closer, peering with lanterns . . . The air was chilly and the water positively cold. In less than five minutes our teeth were chattering.

Hobson had no hope of escaping, but he did not want to be shot by a trigger-happy sailor in the dark. He waited for daylight, when he believed it would be safe to surrender.

"We remained there probably an hour. Frogs croaked . . . and as dawn broke, the birds began to twitter and chirp in the bushes near at hand along the wooded slopes. Day came bright and beautiful."

Shortly after daybreak Hobson hailed a passing steam launch. The craft stopped and a squad of riflemen appeared on the forecastle. Hobson heard the order to load, the sounds of the rifle bolts drawing back. "They are going to shoot us!" someone exclaimed.

I called out in a strong voice to know if there was not an officer in the boat; if so, an American officer wished to speak with him with a view to surrendering himself and seamen as prisoners of war. The curtain was raised; an officer leaned out and waved his hand, and the rifles came down. I struck out for the launch and climbed on board aft with the assistance of the officer.

The Spaniard was a distinguished-looking middle-aged man with a full white beard. He helped the coal-blackened Hobson into the launch, then stared at him in complete astonishment. Admiration grew in his gentle and intelligent eyes. He drew himself up.

"Valiente!" Admiral Cervera exclaimed.

.   .   .

ON JUNE 1 Lieutenant Sims cabled from Paris that part of Admiral Cervera's squadron was not at Santiago but en route to the Philippines. Schley and Sampson could not disprove the report since the interior of Santiago harbor was hidden from view by the high bluffs of Morro and Socapa points standing to either side of the narrow and twisting entrance channel.

The false report gave voice to the wishes of the new Spanish minister of war, Miguel Correa, who cabled General Blanco in Havana on June 3:

> Very serious situation in Philippines compels us to send there ships and reinforcements of troops as early as possible. . . . The only thing we can do is send all the ships of Cervera's squadron that can get out of Santiago. But before deciding, the Government wishes to know your opinion as to the effect the withdrawal of Cervera's fleet might produce in Cuba.

To which Blanco immediately replied that the departure of the squadron would have a "fatal effect on public opinion." The Spanish volunteers, "already much exercised over inadequacy [of] Cervera's squadron," and only kept in line by the hope that a second squadron would arrive, "would rise in a body upon learning that instead of reenforcements the few ships here are withdrawing." A bloody uprising against the government would ensue, Blanco warned, and the loss of Cuba would be certain.

Blanco in Havana and Correa in Madrid did not fully understand Cervera's situation in Santiago, otherwise they would not have wasted the cable charges for their exchange of telegrams. But from the castellated ramparts above Morro Point it was perfectly obvious that the squadron of Admiral Cervera could go nowhere. To the nine warships of the blockading squadron had been added Sampson's flagship, the *New York* and one other.

The U.S.S. *Oregon*.

.   .   .

AT 7 A.M., June 6, the warships formed two columns and steamed toward the coastal batteries that protected the entrance of Santiago harbor. George Edward Graham of the Associated Press was aboard Schley's flagship, the *Brooklyn*, and described the scene:

> To the west were the Brooklyn, the Marblehead, the Texas, and the Massachusetts. To the east were the New York, the Yankee, the New Orleans, the Iowa, and the Oregon. As flanking vessels enfilading from each side were the Vixen, the Suwanee, the Dolphin, and the Porter. The ships moved in to a range of about 3,500 yards and at 7:41 o'clock the Iowa fired the first shot.

The Spanish returned fire from the smooth-bore, eighteenth-century cannon on Socapa Point, disregarding the American fire and climbing onto the earthworks to service the muzzle-loading pieces. A shell from the *Texas* landed under a parapet, throwing men, earth, and cannon into the air.

Lieutenant José Müller watched the barrage from inside the harbor. "When the American fleet opened fire, it was so intense and the shots followed each other in such quick succession that it . . . seemed like a fusillade . . . During the first moments, the firing was so intense that it resembled one prolonged thunder."

The fleet began firing over the headlands and into the harbor, where the ships of the Spanish squadron lay out of sight.

"Most of [the shells] dropped in the bay in the direction of the *María Teresa* and the *Vizcaya,*" Müller recalled, "and it was a miracle that both of them were not seriously damaged."

The *Reina Mercedes* was hit thirty-five times. Two fires, one in the ship's paint locker, broke out.

> Commander Emilio Acosta y Eyermann was directing the extinguishing of the fire in the forecastle, when a large shell cut off his right leg at the hip and also his right hand, mutilating him horribly. But he lived for half an hour after that and kept on looking after the fire. . . .
> The large projectiles shot through space across the bay . . . some fell on the opposite coast (to the westward), raising, as they exploded, clouds of dust and smoke. . . . They did not only reach the city, but went thousands of meters beyond.

In a cell in Morro Castle, Naval Constructor Hobson heard the bombardment begin and crawled under a table and washstand. "I knew what good marksmen our gunners were, and did not doubt that they would make quick work of the exposed parts of the Morro," he recalled. But Admiral Sampson had been informed of the location of the *Merrimac* prisoners by Cuban scouts, and the castle was not a target. A few stray rounds struck the Morro, but neither Hobson nor the crewmen were injured. The firing continued for two and a half hours.

The following day the Navy Department in Washington received a dispatch from Admiral Sampson:

> Bombarded forts at Santiago 7:30 to 10 A.M. to-day, June 6th. Have silenced works quickly without injury of any kind, though stationed 2,000 yards. If 10,000 men were here, city and fleet would be ours within forty-eight hours. Every consideration demands immediate army movement. If delayed, city will be defended more strongly by guns taken from the fleet.

"Thereupon," recalls Secretary Alger, "General Shafter was directed to 'sail at once, but with not less than 10,000 men.' "

Shafter still had not completed preparations in Tampa, but, Alger wrote, "Haste was absolutely imperative. It was a question of striking a sudden blow, and so, perhaps, ending the war in short order."

Shafter received the order at about 6 P.M., June 7. He replied that he would sail the next morning, it taking that long to get up steam on the transports. Loading would continue through the night, he said, and he would sail in the morning with whatever he had on board.

·   ·   ·

"STRIKING CAMP is a pretty sight," Private Post wrote.

One moment there is a long, wide and orderly array of tents. From in front of the colonel's tent begins the 'general,' one of those bugle calls, six bars with its up-and-down, staccato phrases. Then, the last lingering note, the only half-note in the call. With this final note, three acres of white canvas sink to the ground and 600 men are pouncing upon their folds, bundling them, lashing them, and hurling them upon the company baggage wagons at the end of each company street.

The Gallant Seventy-first struck camp at 6:30, but through the usual confusion—this time a failure of mules and wagons to arrive at camp to pick up the luggage—the regiment did not begin its march to nearby Ybor City until after midnight.

"The night was hot and close," Chaplain Van Dewater recalled, "and the road very dusty for a mile until we reached the sidewalks leading into the city. The march was uneventful enough, but its weirdness in the early morning hours . . . made it memorable."

At 9 A.M., June 8, the trains carrying the Seventy-first reached Port Tampa. Chaplain Van Dewater recalled the scene as

a condition analogous to Bedlam . . . train after train filled with troops and luggage pulled into the long pier. . . . Our entire regiment, like scores of others, had to stand or sit for six or seven hours in hot sand, with no shelter, before the transport ships, which were in the outer bay, sailed up to the dock and were ready to receive troops.

Private Post was not there. He had spent the evening on a work detail, unloading a freight car, then returned to camp to find the mess closed. Hastily he scraped the bottom of a kettle for "fragments of the noon dinner along the bottom and in the corners," and washed it down with some cold coffee. Shortly thereafter he was in the general hospital suffering from stomach cramps.

Post and another gastrointestinal case spent the night trying to overcome their food poisoning and catch up with the regiment. Shortly after midnight they roused a Tampa druggist and managed to get him to give them a dose of morphine. At dawn they awoke to find themselves beside the railroad line running from Tampa to the port. They climbed aboard a freight car.

Then there came a waving and a halloing far up the track. A train was approaching, and in the open door of a boxcar was Teddy, Colonel Theodore Roosevelt, grinning as his car passed our lines of flatcars. His khaki uniform looked as if he had slept in it—as it always did. He wore the polka-dot blue bandanna that was the hallmark of the Rough Riders. The rest of our army wore red bandannas.

Roosevelt was smiling because he had just hijacked the train on which he and the Rough Riders were riding. He and the regiment had arrived in Tampa four days earlier to find "a perfect welter of confusion."

There was no one to meet us or to tell us where to camp, and no one to issue us food for the first twenty-four hours; while the railroad people unloaded us wherever they pleased, or rather wherever the jam of all kinds of trains rendered it possible.

But with his famous administrative ability and sheer resourcefulness, Roosevelt managed to bring order out of the chaos of Tampa, pitching tents, policing the camp, and drilling the troops. He took with good grace the news that, owing to limitations of space aboard the transports, the Rough Riders would have to leave all but the officers' horses in Tampa and go into battle on foot. "We should be glad to go on all fours rather than not to go at all," he told Cabot Lodge. But soon even that seemed a possibility.

It was the evening of June 7th when we suddenly received orders that the expedition was to start from Port Tampa, nine miles distant by rail, at daybreak the following morning; and that if we were not aboard our transport by that time we could not go. We had no intention of getting left, and prepared at once for the scramble which was evidently about to take place. . . .

We were ordered to be at a certain track with all our baggage at midnight, there to take a train for Port Tampa. At the appointed time we turned up, but the train did not. The men slept heavily, while Wood and I and various other officers wandered about in search of information which no one could give. . . . At three o'clock we received orders to march over to an entirely different track, and away we went. No train appeared on this track either; but at six o'clock some coal-cars came by, and these were seized.

Roosevelt ordered the Rough Riders aboard the coal train, ignoring the protests of the engineer and the conductor. The railroad men—"partly under duress and partly in a spirit of friendly helpfulness"—were persuaded to back the train over the nine miles of track to Port Tampa, where the regiment climbed down onto the dock, "covered with coal-dust, but with all our belongings."

Private Post, meanwhile, had also managed to reach the docks and find the rest of the Gallant Seventy-first as it was going aboard the transport *Vigilancia*. An officer told him it was doubtful the ships would even sail that day, so Post went off in search of some nourishment for his now tender stomach.

He stumbled along a row of tents that had been set up during the night by vendors of food and drink and other comforts. Last Chance Street, it was called. In each tent there was a rude counter—a couple of planks laid across a pair of barrels—and behind it a bartender—"a gent in a white shirt and no collar was the general run." Behind him, a woman.

"You could get a drink or a damsel, or both," Post recalled, but he wanted neither at the moment. He wanted some milk to soothe his empty and aching stomach. He saw a raw lumber building with a sign: Restaurant.

"I plodded up the porch steps, not noticing the line of men that paralleled my weak footsteps as I climbed; they were contendedly motionless. A voice called, 'Hey, git in line!' But it made no impression.

Post stumbled across the porch and asked for the dining room. The line of waiting troops roared with laughter.

"And, before I could ask again, a door at the far side of the plank wall opened slightly and a naked feminine arm was thrust out and upward with a beckoning movement. The leading man in the line vanished, and the line closed up one pace!

"I never did get any milk," Private Post recalled.

At the wharf across Last Chance Street, Roosevelt was clambering aboard the *Yucatan,* a transport that had been mistakenly allotted to the Rough Riders, having previously been assigned to the Second Infantry and the Gallant Seventy-first. Roosevelt had run back to the coal train and double-timed the regiment to the wharf,

> just in time to board her as she came into the quay, and then to hold her against the Second Regulars and the Seventy-first, who had arrived a little too late, being a shade less ready than we were in the matter of individual initiative. There was a good deal of expostulation, but we had possession.

The Rough Riders spent the rest of the day loading luggage, food, ammunition, and the officers' horses. As night fell, the transport pulled away from the dock and anchored among the other waiting ships in the channel of Port Tampa.

> We felt we had spent thirty-six tolerably active hours. The transport was overloaded, the men being packed like sardines, not only below but upon the decks; so that at night it was only possible to walk about by continually stepping over the bodies of the sleepers. The travel rations which had been issued to the men for the voyage were not sufficient because the meat was very bad indeed.

It was, Roosevelt recalled, "horrible stuff called 'canned fresh beef' . . . it was nauseating." The troops called it embalmed beef, and it became one of the famous scandals of the war.

> There were no facilities for the men to cook anything. There was no ice for them; the water was not good; and they had no fresh meat or fresh vegetables.
> However, all these things seemed of small importance compared with the fact that we were really embarked, and were with the first expedition to leave our shores.

Army headquarters at the Tampa Bay Hotel had packed up and boarded a special train at 2 A.M. The train managed to cover the nine miles to the port by six o'clock.

"Early in the morning the loaded transports had begun to slip their moorings and move toward the entrance of the bay," Lieutenant Colonel Miley recalled,

> and by two in the afternoon nearly all the transports had left the Port and proceeded down the bay so as to be in a position for an early start the next morning, as it was expected the expedition would sail at that time. About two o'clock in the afternoon General Shafter, while on his way to board the Seguranca, and to order it to join the fleet down the bay, had a telegram handed him.

The telegram was from Secretary of War Alger in Washington, and it read: "Wait until you get further orders before you sail."

· · ·

THE TELEGRAPH SOUNDER at the Navy Department clattered furiously, and the cipher clerk quickly copied down the message coming over the wire from Key West. It was from Commodore George C. Remey, Sampson's second in command, and the senior officer afloat at Key West: "Spanish armored cruiser second class and Spanish torpedo-boat destroyer seen by *Eagle*, Nicholas Channel, Cuba."

On the heels of this, a second dispatch from Remey was received: "Last cipher just come by *Resolute*, just arrived; was pursued by two vessels, Nicholas Channel, Cuba, last night."

Nicholas Channel lies off the north coast of Cuba, between Santa Clara Province and the Bahamas. It is little more than a hundred miles from Key West, and it lay on the route the American armada was to follow. Faced with the specter of some sixteen thousand troops being sunk in the Florida Straits, Alger prudently halted the invasion fleet until the reports of the Spanish warships could be investigated.

"It seems that it is a naval problem yet unsolved," General Miles cabled sardonically from Tampa, proposing that the troops be returned to camp and the Army transports be fitted out with guns to help the Navy deal with the Spanish fleet. "It seems strange to be suggesting that the army assist the navy in this way, but I am sure we would receive the most loyal support when the waters are safe for crossing with the army."

But Alger directed that the troops were to remain aboard the transports and stay ready to sail. By June 10 Admiral Sampson was satisfied that the "Spanish fleet" had, in fact, been five American ships, and observed that the delay in sending the transports "seems to me most unfortunate." But Secretary Long insisted that positive confirmation be made that Cervera was still in Santiago harbor, no doubt remembering Lieutenant Sims's recent report that part of it was elsewhere.

The forlorn squadron of Admiral Cervera, bottled up and bombarded in Santiago harbor, had once again unknowingly done the impossible and changed the course of the Spanish War.

It had blockaded the American armada in Port Tampa.

.   .   .

"WE HAVE BEEN HERE two days now," Roosevelt wrote to Cabot Lodge on June
10,

> the troops jammed together under the tropical sun on these crowded
> troop ships. We are in a sewer; a canal which is festering as if it were
> Havana harbor. The steamer on which we are contains nearly one
> thousand men, there being room for about five hundred comfortably.
> . . . several companies are down in the lower hold, which is unpleasantly
> suggestive of the Black Hole of Calcutta. We are apparently to be kept
> here three or four days more. . . . The officers' horses were embarked
> last Sunday with the artillery horses; they have had to disembark them
> for the simple reason that they began to die. . . .
>   If the people in Washington understood the fearful danger to
> health that lies in keeping these troops on the transports, and under-
> stood that they cannot be disembarked and reembarked under five days'
> time, they would surely make up their minds in advance whether they
> intended to start or not, and when they once did put us on would let
> us go.

Two days later he fumed again to Lodge:

> Now, if this were necessary no one would complain for a moment, and
> the men are perfectly cheerful as it is; but it is absolutely unnecessary;
> the five days's great heat and crowded confinement are telling visibly
> upon the spirits and health of the troops. . . . I doubt if Cuba is much
> more unhealthy than the low coast of Florida now.

.   .   .

MAJOR FRANCISCO H. MASABA Y REYES of the Cuban Revolutionary Army
turned and beckoned silently. Lieutenant Victor Blue of the U.S. Navy crept up
the jungle path and peered over the Cuban's shoulder. An opening in the
undergrowth disclosed that they were atop a hill northwest of Santiago Bay. Blue
pushed forward a few steps and adjusted the knob on his binoculars.

Across the bay the city of Santiago drowsed lazily in the sun. Blue swung
his glasses to the right and counted the Spanish warships. One by one he picked
them out, rocking gently in the harbor: the *María Teresa*, the *Vizcaya*, the
Cristobal Colón, the *Oquendo*, and the torpedo boat destroyers *Plutón* and
Furor. They were all present and accounted for. Blue packed away his binoculars,
turned, and started back for the coast.

.   .   .

"THE *Vigilancia* began to throb, slow and slight," Private Post remembered.
"From the pilothouse the captain waved to the bow. . . . The winch began its
grind; the anchor was coming up. . . . The Tampa Bay dock was changing its
position. . . . We swung round and found ourselves part of a long column of
ships."

It was June 14. After a full week of broiling beneath the Florida sun as the transports swung at anchor in the fetid waters of the channel, the invasion fleet was forming off Quarantine Station at the entrance to Tampa Bay. Some forty-eight transports assembled in three columns, escorted by warships from the North Atlantic Squadron.

> We were off. The invasion of Cuba had begun. Behind us was every-thing familiar and routine. No one could know what tomorrow would bring forth. The aspiration to survive was there, of course, but it was not a condition. The dice would be thrown, but we could not throw them. We were a fragment of destiny.

CHAPTER NINE

TO WAR

"TODAY WE ARE STEAMING southward through a sapphire sea, wind-rippled, under an almost cloudless sky," wrote Theodore Roosevelt on June 15, one day out of Port Tampa.

> There are some forty-eight craft in all, in three columns, the black hulls of the transports setting off the gray hulls of the men-of-war. Last evening we stood up on the bridge and watched the red sun sink and the lights blaze up on the ships, for miles ahead and astern, while the band played piece after piece, from the "Star Spangled Banner" at which we all rose and stood uncovered, to "The Girl I Left Behind Me." But it is a great historical expedition, and I thrill to feel that I am part of it. If we fail, of course we share the fate of all who do fail, but if we are allowed to succeed (for we certainly shall succeed, if allowed) we have scored the first great triumph in what will be a world movement.

The invasion fleet rounded Key West and headed southeast at a sedate six knots in consideration of the heavily laden transports. On the seventeenth, Admiral Sampson, waiting with his ships outside Santiago, cast an expectant glance at the empty waters to the east and a wary eye toward the southern skies.

"I again urge earnestly army move with all possible celerity," he cabled to the Navy Department. "Fine weather may end any day."

The rainy season was due, and the rains would threaten the troops landed in Cuba with malaria and yellow fever. The rains would turn to mud the roads over which the artillery and supply wagons must be pulled. They would give the Army reason to urge again that the invasion be postponed until October. But

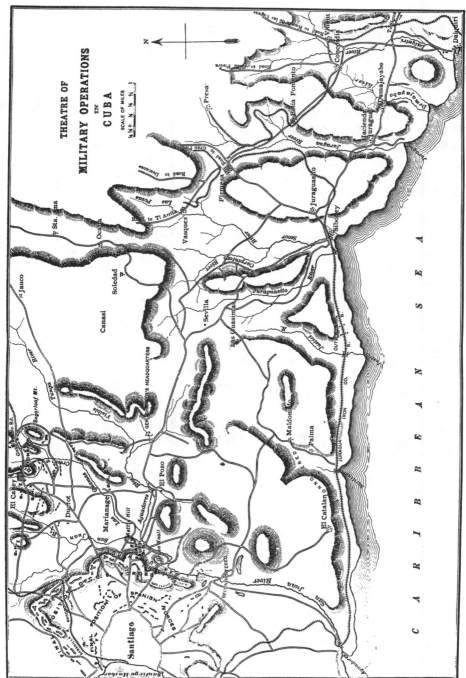

Area of the Daiquiri and Siboney landings and the American advance along the road to Santiago, Cuba.

October would mean the height of the hurricane season, and Sampson did not like to think of the fate of the North Atlantic Squadron if it were caught off the coast of Cuba by a hurricane. And as he glanced at the cloudless sky to the south, he may have remembered that hurricanes sometimes visit the Caribbean as early as June.

.   .   .

STEPHEN CRANE HEARD the rifle fire, recognized the "prut!" of the U.S. Navy Winchester-Lees, and the "pop!" of the Spanish Mausers. He scrambled up the cactus-covered ridge on the heels of C Company, First Marine Battalion. As he reached the crest he heard the Mauser bullets singing overhead, each sounding "as if one string of a most delicate musical instrument had been touched by the wind into a long faint note."

> Then along the top of our particular hill, mingled with the cactus and chaparral, was a long irregular line of men fighting the first part of the first action of the Spanish war. Toiling, sweating marines; shrill, jumping Cubans; officers shouting out the ranges, 200 Lee rifles crashing—these were the essentials. The razor-backed hill seemed to reel with it all.

The hill was in the Cuban countryside beyond Guantánamo Bay, a harbor some forty miles east of Santiago. On June 10, 650 men of the First Marine Division landed at the bay from the U.S.S. *Panther*. The purpose of the expedition was to establish a coaling station for the blockading ships, which previously had to make the eight hundred-mile voyage to Key West to recoal in port.

The Marines at first met no opposition, but on June 11 they came under Spanish sniper fire. For the next three days the firing continued off and on, but on the fourteenth Captain George F. Eliot led a force of some two hundred Marines plus fifty Cuban insurgents to locate and destroy the Spaniards. He found them five miles off, in the steep Cuzco Hills, and the battle ensued.

The Marine assault was augmented by artillery fire from the U.S.S. *Dolphin* just offshore. Crane watched in awe as Sergeant John H. Wick relayed range and bearing instructions to the ship by wig-wag flag signals. The novelist described the scene in a piece for the New York *World* entitled, "The Red Badge of Courage Was His Wig-wag Flag."

> It was necessary that this man should stand at the very top of the ridge in order that his flag might appear in relief against the sky, and the Spaniards must have concentrated a fire of at least twenty rifles upon him. His society was at that moment sought by none. We gave him a wide berth. Presently into the din came the boom of the Dolphin's guns.

The fight continued. Crane saw a black Cuban soldier hit: "He seemed in no pain . . . he made no outcry; he simply toppled over." A Marine lay wounded under a bush: "His expression was of a man weary, weary, weary."

The Spanish broke and ran. Crane watched them scramble across a pair of clearings hundreds of yards distant as the Marine marksmen fired after them in volley.

> Sometimes we could see a whole covey vanish miraculously after the volley. It was impossible to tell whether they were all hit, or whether all or part had plunged headlong for cover. Everybody on our side stood up. It was vastly exciting. "There they go! See 'em! See 'em!"

Marine marksmanship was "splendid"; rifles were reloaded "like lightning"; aim was taken with "a rocklike beautiful poise." By contrast, the Cuban soldier used his rifle "as if it were a squirt-gun."

> The entire function of the [Cuban] lieutenant who commanded them in action was to stand back of the line, frenziedly beat his machete through the air, and with incredible rapidity howl: "Fuego! fuego! fuego! fuego! fuego!" He could not possibly have taken a breath during the action. His men were meanwhile screaming the most horrible language in a babble.
> As for daring, that is another matter. They paid no heed whatever to the Spaniards' volleys, but simply lashed themselves into a delirium that disdained everything. . . .
> At last it was over. . . . A party went out to count the Spanish dead; the daylight began to soften. Save for the low murmur of the men a peace fell upon all the brown wilderness of hills.

The next day the *Texas, Marblehead,* and *Suwanee* shelled the town of Caimanera, where the Spanish were still holding out. Afterward the Marines landed there, and further Spanish resistance in the area was at an end. The Marines established a permanent encampment on a low, flat hill on the eastern shore of the bay, naming it Camp McCalla in honor of the commander of the *Marblehead.*

The Stars and Stripes were raised over Guantánamo Bay.

.   .   .

JUNE 15 was a busy day for spies. From Paris, Lieutenant Sims reported, "Spanish newspaper announces officially Cervera at Santiago; but Spanish government circulates private information that he may be expected daily at Philippine Islands."

Madrid was proving that two could play the disinformation game, but Washington now knew that Lieutenant Blue had actually seen the squadron in Santiago Bay.

In Montreal, Lieutenant Carranza discovered—probably from the newspapers—that the American invasion fleet had sailed from Tampa. He cabled a report to Havana, making a somewhat inaccurate guess about the size and destination of the fleet.

Domingo Villaverde, the Havana telegrapher, brought the process full circle by telegraphing to Washington: "Blanco wires Linares at Santiago that twenty-five thousand Americans had left for Guantánamo. Blanco received this information from Montreal by way of Bermuda."

.   .   .

THE CITY OF MANILA, having been blockaded by Admiral Dewey's squadron for over a month, now found itself besieged as well. The Filipino insurgents had seized the opportunity presented by the blockade to attack the Spanish outposts throughout Luzon. They soon captured Cavite Province, taking 2,800 Spanish prisoners, and pressed the Spanish forces back toward Manila. By mid-June they had nearly surrounded the walled city.

The insurgents were led by Emilio Aguinaldo y Famy, a twenty-nine-year-old Filipino of middle-class background and Tagalog–Chinese ancestry.

"Aguinaldo had been at one time a copyist in the Cavite arsenal under the Spanish regime," Dewey recalled. "He was . . . a soft-spoken, unimpressive little man who had enormous prestige with the Filipino people."

The Filipino leader had been in Singapore, en route to exile in Europe, when the Spanish War began, and on April 24 had met with the American consul there. At Dewey's invitation, Aguinaldo set out for Hong Kong. Dewey was at that moment planning his attack on the Spanish fleet and hoped the Filipino might provide useful intelligence regarding the defenses of Manila Bay.

Aguinaldo missed Dewey at Hong Kong and arrived at Manila Bay on May 19. With Dewey's permission he established himself at the captured Cavite arsenal and began to organize the insurgents. Dewey recalled, "As our purpose was to weaken the Spaniards in every legitimate way, thus hastening the conclusions of hostilities . . . operations by the insurgents in the Philippines under certain restrictions would be welcome."

The "certain restrictions" included Dewey's instructions from Secretary Long "not to have political alliances with the insurgents or any faction in the islands that would incur liability to maintain their cause in the future." Dewey assured Long that he had entered into no such alliance. However, Aguinaldo would later claim that he had already received an American commitment to Philippine independence from E. Spencer Pratt, the U.S. consul-general at Singapore who had persuaded him to follow Dewey to Manila. Whatever understandings or misunderstandings existed, U.S.–Filipino relations were certainly ambiguous, and even a casual observer might have foreseen difficulties on June 12, when Aguinaldo formally proclaimed the independence of the Philippines, or eleven days later, when he announced himself head of a revolutionary government. But Dewey had a more pressing problem on his mind.

"I knew that the intervention of any third power or group of powers while Sampson had yet to engage Cervera . . . might have brought grave consequences for us," Dewey recalled. "The Philippines were a rich prize for any ambitious power."

And the most ambitious power at the moment appeared to be Germany.

On [June] 12th Vice-Admiral von Diedrichs arrived in his flag-ship, the *Kaiserin Augusta*. This made three German cruisers in the harbor. I learned that another was expected. Already, on the 6th, a German transport, the *Darmstadt*, bringing fourteen hundred men as relief crews for the German vessels, had appeared. Such a transfer, for which I readily gave permission, while it might have been unusual in a blockaded harbor, might at the same time be easily explained as a matter of convenience for the German squadron which was absent from its regular base at Kiau Chau. The *Darmstadt*, however, with her force of men nearly equal to the total number of my own crews, remained at anchor for four weeks.

Dewey paid a courtesy call on von Diedrichs. In the course of the conversation he remarked in passing on the size of the large German force at Manila, which he said seemed to him unusual since German interests in the Philippines were limited to a single commercial house in Manila.

"I am here by order of the kaiser, sir!" von Diedrichs snapped. Dewey recalled,

I could only infer that I had expressed myself in a way that excited his displeasure. . . .

Within a week there were five German men-of-war in the port, two of them having a heavier displacement than any of my own ships. The *Kaiser* came in after dark on June 18. She paid no attention to the launch sent to board her. . . .

In the latter part of June and the early days of July the Germans, with the industry with which they aim to make their navy efficient, were keeping very busy. I saw that they did not mean to accept my interpretation of the laws of blockade. German officers frequently landed in Manila, where they were on the most cordial terms with the Spaniards, who paid them marked attention; and, the wish fathering the thought, the talk of the town was that the Germans would intervene in favor of Spain.

·   ·   ·

On June 16 the Spanish task force under Admiral Cámara left Cádiz. Its destination was Manila; its route was eastward, through the Suez Canal.

William Randolph Hearst, perhaps inspired by Hobson's heroic mission, cabled his London correspondent:

I wish you would at once make preparations so that . . . we can buy some big English steamer at the eastern end of the Mediterranean and take her to some part of the Suez Canal where we can then sink her and obstruct the passage of the Spanish warships.

Hearst believed the British government would not permit an English ship to be blown up in order to clear the canal quickly.

·   ·   ·

ON JUNE 18 Secretary Long cabled Sims in Paris that the *Oregon,* the *Iowa,* and the *Massachusetts* were being readied to attack the Spanish coast and would sail as soon as Cámara passed Suez. He told the naval intelligence officer to see that the Spanish government received the information.

"It is true," he added.

.   .   .

THE *Charleston* and three transports carrying 2,500 troops steamed steadily westward across the broad expanses of the Pacific. They left on their month-long voyage from San Francisco to Manila on May 25.

On June 15 a second contingent departed San Francisco for Manila. Aboard were some 3,500 officers and men, including a former reporter for the Pueblo, Colorado, *Evening Post,* now Private Damon Runyon.

.   .   .

THE MARIANAS ISLANDS, lying some 1,500 miles east of the Philippines, had been Spanish since 1668. At 8:30 A.M. on June 20, the *Charleston* steamed into Port San Luis d'Apra on Guam, the principal island of the chain, and proceeded to shell the fortifications ashore. Captain Henry Glass watched the rounds striking through his binoculars. There was no return fire. In fact, the erupting shells were the only activity visible ashore. Glass suspected the place was deserted. He ordered the gunners to cease fire.

Presently two small boats put out from shore. The men aboard them appeared to be wearing Spanish uniforms. Glass held his fire and waited. The boats came alongside, and the Spaniards asked to come aboard.

Lieutenant Guiterrez identified himself as the port captain.

"You will pardon our not immediately replying to your salute, captain," Guiterrez said apologetically, "but we are not accustomed to receiving salutes here, and are not supplied with proper guns for returning them. May I inquire what business brings you to San Luís d'Apra?"

Glass asked the Spaniard when he had last heard any news from the outside world. Guiterrez thought for a moment then replied that no vessel had arrived in the harbor since April 14. Glass invited the Spaniard to sit down while he brought him up to date.

The American ships left the following day, the sixty-man Spanish garrison having been disarmed and taken aboard. The cruiser's flag had been raised above the old fort.

The Stars and Stripes flew over Guam. Almost unnoticed, the United States had acquired its first possession in the Pacific.

.   .   .

"ALL DAY WE HAVE STEAMED close to the Cuban Coast, high barren-looking mountains rising abruptly from the shore," Roosevelt wrote. It was June 20, and the fleet had rounded the eastern tip of Cuba and turned west.

"We are well within the tropics, and at night the Southern Cross shows low above the horizon; it seems strange to see it in the same sky with the friendly Dipper."

They passed Guantánamo. Late in the afternoon they sighted the great gray ships of the Flying Squadron. Beyond the line of breakers and the narrow beach, beyond the steep bluffs rising from the sea, lay Santiago.

CHAPTER TEN

THE ROAD
TO SANTIAGO

IT MAY HAVE SEEMED that a city had risen from the sea during the night, long avenues of black and gray buildings topped by sloping chimneys. The Spanish lookout who climbed to the top of the Morro at dawn murmured pious blasphemies as he swung his glasses along the horizon from east to west, then back again, and gradually understood that this train of ships must run further than a man could see, that both its beginning and its end were hidden from view in the ocean haze.

"Uno . . . dos . . . tres . . . cuatro . . ." he whispered.

There were twenty. No, twenty-five! Even more!

The sun climbed above the headlands to his left and burned the mist from the water. The curtain of haze lifted, revealing a second rank of ships beyond the first, and perhaps a third beyond the second. The lookout turned and hurried down from his perch. Miles away and minutes later a messenger went aboard the *Mariá Teresa*, moored near the top of the bay, and delivered a telegram to Admiral Cervera. There were, it said, seventy hostile ships in sight of the Morro, among them seven modern battleships.

.   .   .

THERE WERE NOW before Santiago, in addition to the blockading warships and an assortment of newspaper tugs, thirty-two troop transports, two water tenders, three lighters, and the dozen naval vessels that had escorted the armada from Port Tampa. Aboard the new arrivals were 819 officers, 15,058 enlisted men, 30 civilian clerks, 89 newspaper correspondents, 11 foreign military observers, 272 teamsters and packers, and 2,295 horses and mules. There were four light artillery batteries, four seven-inch Howitzers, four Gatling guns, and an assortment of other cannon and mortars, including a dynamite gun brought along by the Rough Riders. There were some two hundred wagons, seven ambulances, and one observation balloon. And there were ten million pounds of rations. From the deck of the transport *Seguranca*, General Rufus Shafter surveyed the rugged coastline and considered the question of where to land the expedition.

Admiral Sampson came aboard to welcome the general and advise him that the insurgent leader, Calixto García, was camped near the coast at Aserraderos, about twenty miles to the west. The *Seguranca* steamed west, and Shafter and Sampson landed to confer with the Cuban.

Four boats were required to carry the party ashore. In addition to Sampson and Shafter were their respective staffs, the British and German military attachés, plus Richard Harding Davis, Frederic Remington, and two more newspapermen. They were heartily welcomed by a detachment of Cuban horsemen, who provided mounts for the one-mile trip up a steep trail to the jungle meeting place. The conference was held in the palm-thatched hut of General Jesús Rabí, who, despite the Biblical ring to his name, was one of the few full-blooded Carib Indians surviving in Cuba.

While the attachés and correspondents waited outside, Admiral Sampson introduced Shafter and García. The sixty-two-year-old Shafter had taught school before receiving a lieutenancy in the Seventh Michigan Infantry. Since the Peninsular Campaign of 1862 he had served his time in the Regular Army without much distinction but had reached the rank of brigadier general in 1897 and had been appointed major general of volunteers at the outbreak of the war. Unfortunately, the most striking thing about the spaniel-eyed Shafter—a man of average height—was his weight, which was in excess of three hundred pounds, or, as some of his detractors liked to put it, almost one-sixth of a ton. Shafter was suffering now as only a fat person suffers in the tropics, and the fact that he did not ask to be relieved of his command two months earlier when he encountered the heat of Tampa was a tribute more to his determination than to his prudence.

Calixto García was a tall, elderly man with a snow-white goatee and a deep cleft between his eyebrows, the result of a self-inflicted wound. During the Ten Years' War, when he was about to be taken prisoner by the Spanish, he had tried to kill himself by firing a large-caliber rifle from beneath his lower jaw, the bullet exiting from his forehead between his eyes. A Spanish surgeon pulled him through, and he spent the last four years of the war in prison. Frederick Funston, the American soldier of fortune, recalled him:

> General García was a man of the most undoubted personal courage, and was a courteous and kindly gentlemen. His bearing was dignified, but he was one of the most approachable of men. He seldom smiled . . . With him life had been one long tragedy of war and prison. . . . Those of us Americans who served under Gómez always regarded him with something akin to awe or fear, but all who came in close contact with García had for him a feeling of affection.

García and Gómez were indeed quite different, and Gómez was by far the better commander. García had spent the war in the relatively easy duty of commanding insurgent forces in eastern Cuba, while Gómez had found more Spaniards to fight in the central and western provinces. But the war had followed the squadron of Admiral Cervera into the bay of Santiago, and fortune picked General García to command the Cuban Army in the final and decisive battle for the island.

Sampson, Shafter, and García gathered round a map of Santiago and the Cuban coast. Sampson put his finger on Morro Point at the entrance to the bay. There, he said, were the switchboards controlling the electrically detonated mines in the entrance channel. He pointed to Socapa Point across the harbor entrance. There, he said, were the batteries that defended the bay. Take those points, he told Shafter, and the Navy would enter the bay and take Santiago.

Shafter shook his head. He pointed to the city of Santiago on the northeast side of the bay, five miles from the entrance. That, rather than the heavily defended entrance to the bay, must be his objective.*

Shafter looked at the map and tried to relate it to what he had seen of the coast from the *Seguranca* as she passed from Guantánamo to Santiago. There were three parallel ranges of hills and mountains. The first was a high, flat-topped ridge rising steeply two or three hundred feet above the sea, broken into long terraces by outcropping ledges of limestone. A mile or so beyond this were foothills and jungle valleys. Five or six miles from the sea stood the tall, rocky peaks of the Sierra Maestra.

There was nothing that might be called a harbor. There was not even an anchorage, for the ocean bottom dropped away steeply into the depths of the Caribbean just a little way from the shore. The nearest harbor, other than Santiago itself, was Guantánamo Bay, forty miles to the east.

Guantánamo was tempting. It was already under American control, having been captured by the Marines and the Navy ten days earlier. But the Guantánamo to Santiago route had been tried by an invading army once before, as Shafter knew from the books he had been studying during the voyage. In 1741 a British expeditionary force of five thousand men led by Lord Vernon landed at Guantánamo and marched toward Santiago. When they abandoned their attack sixteen miles short of their goal they had lost two thousand soldiers. The Spanish had not fired a shot; the rains, the heat, the jungle, and tropical fever had done it all. Shafter knew those same adversaries were still waiting along the Guantánamo to Santiago road.

The wall-like bluff that stood above the beaches to the east of Santiago Bay was broken by three V-shaped clefts, the outlets of three small streams. One of these was the Aguadores ravine, about four miles east of Morro Point. A second

*This inferential version of the conference is based on the accounts of García, Shafter, and Shafter's aide, Lieutenant John D. Miley. However, Captain French E. Chadwick, who had discussed the Santiago campaign strategy with Shafter earlier in the day, received the impression that the Army intended to follow the Navy's plan of attacking the harbor fortifications, rather than the city. Chadwick believed that Shafter did not change his plan until some days after the meeting with García. Like the question of which plan was better, the facts of this question can now be matters only of speculation.

TOP: *Troops landing on the dock at Daiquirí. Source: National Archives.*
BOTTOM: *Troops assembling at Daiquirí and beginning the march to Siboney. Source: Library of Congress.*

TOP: *Troops encamped at Siboney while transports wait off-shore. Source: National Archives.* LEFT: *Stephen Crane. Source: Library of Congress.* BOTTOM: *Capron's Battery firing on El Caney, July 1, 1898. Source: Library of Congress.*

TOP: *The stone fort, El Viso, after the fight at El Caney. Source: National Archives.* RIGHT: *Balloon carrying Lieutenant Colonels Maxfield and Derby over the jungle during the attack on San Juan, July 1, 1898. Source: National Archives.* BOTTOM: *Sixteenth Infantry in bottom of San Juan Creek, under Spanish fire from San Juan Hill, July 1, 1898. Source: Library of Congress.*

TOP: *San Juan Hill. Source: Library of Congress.* BOTTOM: *Theodore Roosevelt and the Rough Riders atop a hill overlooking Santiago. Source: Library of Congress.*

ABOVE: *Rear Admiral Pascual Cervera y Topete. Source: Library of Congress.* LEFT: U.S.S. Oregon. *Source: Author's Collection.* BOTTOM: *Burned-out hulk of the Spanish cruiser* Almirante Oquendo *after the sea battle off Santiago. Source: Author's Collection.*

TOP: *Generals Joseph Wheeler, Rufus Shafter, and Nelson Miles (left to right) meeting during Santiago surrender negotiations. Source: Library of Congress.* LEFT: *María Cristina, Queen Regent of Spain, and her son, King Alfonso XIII. Source: Author's Collection.*
BOTTOM: *Generals Miles, Shafter, Wheeler (left to right, front) and aides going to or from Santiago surrender negotiations with the Spanish. Source: Library of Congress.*

TOP: *Formal surrender of Santiago. General Shafter is wearing a helmet; General Toral is to his right. Source: National Archives.* BOTTOM: *American troops cheering news of the surrender of Santiago. Source: National Archives.*

RIGHT: *Emilio Aguinaldo. Source: Author's Collection.* BOTTOM: *Dead Filipino insurgents near Santa Ana. Source: National Archives.*

notch, eleven miles further east, marked the hamlet of Siboney; and a third, seven miles beyond that, enclosed the village of Daiquirí. A road ran along the coast from Daiquirí to Siboney, then turned inland, running some ten miles northwest to the city of Santiago. Shafter pointed to the coastline. If he could land somewhere along there, he said, at Siboney or Daiquirí, he could march up that road to Santiago. But the beach was commanded by the bluff rising above it, and the War Department had advised him that there were seven thousand Spanish troops entrenched above Siboney and Daiquirí.

General García shook his head. There were not seven thousand troops on the heights. There were perhaps one thousand; six hundred men at Siboney and three hundred at Daiquirí. He advised making the landing at Daiquirí.

After an hour's discussion it was agreed that the landing would take place at Daiquirí. Depending on the level of Spanish resistance, it would be extended to Siboney as soon as possible. Prior to the landing, the Navy would shell the coast to drive the Spanish back from the bluff. The coastal points of Aguadores and Cabañas—the latter an inlet two and a half miles west of Santiago Bay—would also be shelled as a feint to confuse the Spanish, and a force of five hundred insurgents under General Rabí would attack Cabañas to create the impression that the landing was actually to take place there. A force of one thousand Cubans under General Demetrio Castillo would help clear the Spanish from the landing zone.

The landing would begin the following day, at dawn.

.   .   .

"ALL NEXT DAY we rolled and wallowed in the seaway," Roosevelt recalled. There were rain squalls and rough seas running in the morning, scattering the transports and delaying the meeting between Shafter and his division and brigade commanders until 4 P.M. The landing was postponed until the following morning.

.   .   .

AT DAYBREAK on the twenty-second the transports stood in toward Daiquirí. Aboard the *Allegheny*, General Joseph Wheeler went on deck for a look at the coast.

> With the aid of our glasses we could see the town of Daiquirí, the place selected for our landing. The place has no harbor, but as it was a shipping-point for iron-ore, General Shafter and the naval officers concluded we could safely land the army by the use of the small-boats belonging to the fleet and the transports. There is a strongly built iron pier extending out some distance from the shore, but we readily saw this could not be used by us. It extended very high above the water, it being constructed for the purpose of dumping iron-ore from the cars into lighters. It was, therefore, evident that we would be obliged to land on the beach, or else at the end of a small dock that extended some twenty yards from the shore.

At 9:40 A.M. the bombardment began. A dozen miles away, Naval Constructor Hobson, recently transferred from his cell in the Morro to an army barracks
in Santiago, heard the guns and knew the invasion was underway. Aboard the
Vigilancia, three miles off the coast, Private Post watched the warships firing.

> Their turrets would burst into a vast billow of smoke as they scanned
> the hills with their fire; and occasionally they would turn one into the
> ancient forts that would burst forth in a blast of shattered brick and
> dust. We could see shells burst in the jungle. The cruisers steamed
> slowly from Daiquirí, past Siboney, and on past the Santiago forts and
> into the west, bombarding as they went, and then came back again.

After thirty minutes the fleet ceased firing. At 10:25 A.M. a troop of cavalry
galloped down the beach at Daiquirí, the Cuban flag flying over their heads.
General Castillo had arrived. The Spanish had evacuated Daiquirí at five o'clock
that morning, permitting the American expedition to land unopposed. The
troops began to disembark.
    "It was delightful to see the fine scorn of the coxswains as the 'dough-boys'
fell and jumped and tumbled from the gangway ladder into the heaving boats,
that dropped from beneath them like a descending elevator or rose suddenly and
threw them on their knees," Richard Harding Davis recalled.

> Soon the sea was dotted with rows of white boats filled with men bound
> about with white blanket-rolls and with muskets at all angles, and as
> they rose and fell on the water and the newspaper yachts and transports
> crept closer and closer, the scene was strangely suggestive of a boat race.

The crowded boats were strung together in convoys and towed to shore by
the Navy's steam launches. Aboard the *Vigilancia* the men of the Gallant
Seventy-first crowded the rails and watched.
    "Great Scott," Private Post remembered, "there wouldn't be any Spaniards
left by the time we got to shore."
    Davis watched the first boat convoy approach the shore.

> A launch turned suddenly and steered for a long pier under the ore-
> docks, the waves lifted it to the level of the pier, and a half-dozen men
> leaped through the air and landed on the pier head, waving their
> muskets above them. At the same moment two of the other boats were
> driven through the surf to the beach itself, and the men tumbled out
> and scrambled to their feet upon the shore of Cuba. In an instant a
> cheer rose faintly from the shore, and more loudly from the war-ships.
> It was caught up by every ship in the transport fleet, and was carried
> for miles over the ocean. Men waved their hats, jumped up and down,
> and shrieked.

The horses and mules could not be landed in the boats; there was only one
way to get them ashore. The animals were led to a cargo port and herded

overboard. The beach was often a half-mile away, and it was sink or swim. Some terrified creatures swam out to sea, while others simply were exhausted before they could reach the shore. The ocean was soon dotted with the bodies of drowned horses and mules. After that orders were given to tether the animals together and tow them ashore, and there were no further losses.

Roosevelt fumed at the delay while the Rough Riders waited their turn. "Who got ashore first largely depended upon individual activity," he recalled.

> Fortunately for us, my former naval aide . . . Lieutenant-Commander Sharp, a first-class fellow, was there in command of a little ship to which I had succeeded in getting him appointed before I left the Navy Department. He gave us a black pilot, who took our transport right in shore . . . and we disembarked with our rifles, ammunition belts, and not much else. In theory it was out of turn, but if we had not disembarked then, Heaven only knows when our turn would have come, and we did not intend to be out of the fighting if we could help it.

He stood on the beach and surveyed the scene. Behind the high iron pier of the Spanish-American Iron Company stood a machine shop, a cluster of zinc shacks, and rows of palm-thatched huts. This was the village of Daiquirí Beyond it rose the steep bluffs, and at the crest stood a Spanish blockhouse.

"The country would have offered very great difficulties to an attacking force," he recalled. "It was little but a mass of rugged and precipitous hills, covered for the most part by dense jungle. Five hundred resolute men could have prevented the disembarkation at very little cost to themselves."

But the Spanish were nowhere in sight. There were instead hundreds of General Castillo's men, whom Roosevelt described as "a crew of as utter tatterdemalions as human eyes ever looked on, armed with every kind of rifle in all stages of dilapidation."

He dismissed the insurgents. "It was evident, at a glance, that they would be no use in serious fighting," he wrote, failing to wonder who it might have been that had kept General Weyler at bay for two years.

He returned to the wooden dock and supervised the unloading of the Rough Riders' equipment, the Colt machine guns that had been purchased by Sergeant William Tiffany and several other New York society men turned soldier, and the regiment's dynamite gun. Getting these heavy items ashore involved much work and some hazard.

One of his horses, Rain-in-the-Face, had been drowned, he was told. The second, Little Texas, made it ashore safely. The sea had become increasingly rough during the afternoon. As he looked on, a boatload of Negro cavalrymen capsized. Stephen Crane saw the accident from the beach. "At last it has happened," he reported.

> Men of the Tenth Cavalry, tied in blanket rolls and weighty cartridge belts are in the water. It is horrible to think of them clasped in the arms of their heavy accoutrements. Wild excitement reigns on the pierhead;

lines are flung; men try to reach down to the water; overboard from launches and cutters go blue-jackets.

Two of the men were dragged under and did not reappear. Roosevelt ran to the end of the pier to help. Rough Rider Captain "Bucky" O'Neill jumped into the water and tried to bring the pair to the surface. But the two men drowned before they could be hauled onto the dock.

Crane wandered down the beach and watched the new arrivals wade from the surf. "Bugles sound the assembly. Men hurry off to join their companies. Sergeants come looking for stragglers. And still the boatloads continue to come."

Crane explored the tiny village. One of the buildings—a shop belonging to the ore company—had been burned by the retreating Spanish and continued to smolder now, late in the afternoon. He looked inside and saw the burned-out hulk of a Baldwin locomotive which had been used to haul ore from the interior over a narrow-gauge railroad.

General Castillo had established his temporary headquarters in one of the huts. Crane saw Cuban scouts arriving every few minutes to report on the enemy's movements. He was told that the Spaniards had retreated several miles and, as yet, there had been no fighting.

About 5 P.M. all attention was directed toward the bluff above the village. Davis recalled:

> Outlined against the sky, we saw four tiny figures scaling the sheer face of the mountain up the narrow trail to the highest blockhouse. For a moment they were grouped together there at the side of the Spanish fort, and then . . . the American flag was thrown out against the sky, and the sailors on the men-of-war, the Cubans, and our soldiers in the village, the soldiers in the longboats, and those still hanging to the sides and ratlines of the troop-ships, shouted and cheered . . . and every steamwhistle on the ocean for miles about shrieked and tooted and roared in a pandemonium of delight.

It was, Crane wrote, a "symbol that our foot is firmly and formidably planted."

The Rough Riders assembled and marched a quarter-mile or so inland and pitched camp, Roosevelt recalled, "on a dusty, brush-covered flat, with jungle on one side, and on the other a shallow, fetid pool fringed with palm trees." He called the roll.

"We had all our men," he remembered, "and were ready for anything that might turn up."

·   ·   ·

AT THE SAME MOMENT four of General Wheeler's cavalrymen were raising the American flag over Daiquirí, a Spanish relief column left Manzanillo and marched eastward into the jungle on the first leg of its route to Santiago. Colonel Federico Escario led the column, which consisted of 3,752 soldiers and 148 horses and mules, loaded with 28,000 rations of food, ammunition, medical supplies, and other material. Ahead lay 160 miles of thick jungle and rugged mountains and the insurgent forces of General García. The column reached Palmas Altas by nightfall and made camp. It rained heavily and steadily throughout the night, and few of the Spanish troops chose to lie down in the wet jungle.

* * *

"AS THE QUESTION is to be decided on land," Admiral Cervera cabled the minister of marine, "I am going to send ashore the crews of the squadron as far as the rifles will hold out. The situation is very critical."

* * *

SIX THOUSAND TROOPS—almost half of the American expedition—landed at Daiquirí on June 22. The following morning the landing resumed. At daylight General Henry W. Lawton led two regiments of his Second Division eastward along the narrow jungle trail to Siboney, seven miles down the coast. Arriving shortly after 9 A.M., he found that the Spanish had evacuated the place during the night, leaving behind a locomotive and several coal-laden cars and some thirty barrels of liquor, wine, and whiskey. General Lawton placed a guard over the beverages and reported back to Shafter that Siboney was his. Around noon some of the boatloads of troops began landing there.

Back at Daiquirí Roosevelt spent the morning supervising the unloading of the regiment's equipment from the *Yucatan*, and in the early afternoon the Rough Riders received orders from General Wheeler to join him at Siboney. Wheeler had arrived there in the morning and ridden three miles past the village, where he overtook General Castillo and a Cuban force. The Cubans had overtaken the retreating Spanish, who stopped, dug in, and turned to fight. Wheeler saw one dead Spaniard and three wounded Cubans. He sent word to Colonel Wood at Daiquirí to bring the Rough Riders.

"It was mid-afternoon and the tropic sun was beating fiercely down when Colonel Wood started our regiment," Roosevelt recalled. "It was a hard march, the hilly jungle trail being so narrow that often we had to go in single file. We marched fast, for Wood was bound to get us ahead of the other regiments. . . . We did not halt until we were at the extreme front."

While the Rough Riders trudged through the jungle, the Gallant Seventy-first marked time aboard the *Vigilancia*, watching desperately as line after line of loaded boats were towed past them to the shore and empty convoys were towed back out to the transports, but never to their ship. It was late in the afternoon, and they had been watching this spectacle since the bombardment ended yesterday morning.

They had been aboard the *Vigilancia* continuously for the past sixteen days. They had suffered patiently in the heat of Port Tampa for seven days; novelty and a spirit of adventure had sustained them during the six days the convoy took to crawl around the Windward Passage to the south coast of Cuba; the two-day wait for the landings to begin was endured through the knowledge that all aboard the other ships were in the same boat. But during the past thirty hours they had suffered the agony of watching nearly twelve thousand of their more fortunate comrades taken ashore, while they languished in their floating prison, strongly suspicious that there would not be enough war to go around and that they were to be denied the joys of combat. So when the *Seguranca* came alongside at 5 P.M. and General Shafter himself called out from the bridge that their colonel was to begin unloading his men, and to unload all night if necessary, a great deafening roar of approval nearly drowned out the rest of the portly commander's words.

A gangway was lowered along the side of the ship—a flight of steps leading down to the water—and the boats were brought to its foot. The bugle blew and the regimental adjutant took his place at the head of the gangway. Private Post and the rest of Company F filed down the steps. At the bottom two sailors grabbed each man as he arrived and steadied him while he stepped into the heaving boat.

> "I got in the boat," Private Post remembered. Men squatted on the floorboards, packed tight. There was room for a few on the seat that ran around the sides. Sailors at bow and stern held the boat to the ship's side. In the stern a coxswain bossed the loading of the soldiers.
>
> The four sailors pulled us away from the transport and hooked us into line with the boats already loaded, and in the next moment we were headed for the beach at Siboney. As we neared the shore the steam launch cast off her line, and the sailors pulled in until the deep-laden lifeboat grounded a hundred feet off the beach.

The men of Company F waded ashore and assembled on the beach. Post was put to work unloading ammunition crates as the afternoon passed into evening. At one point, after dark, he paused and looked up from his labor to see a column marching into the village along the road from Daiquirí. A familiar figure with prominent eyeglasses rode at its head.

"It was long after nightfall when we tramped through the darkness into the squalid coast hamlet of Siboney," Roosevelt recalled. The Rough Riders made camp, cooked a meal of coffee, pork, and hardtack, then endured the drenching of a two-hour thunderstorm. After the rain stopped, the fires were relighted and the troopers gathered round and tried to dry out. Roosevelt chatted with Sergeant Hamilton Fish, scion of a prominent New York family and grandson of President Grant's secretary of state of the same name. Fish, he remembered, was "a huge fellow, of enormous strength and endurance and dauntless courage [who] took naturally to a soldier's life."

Colonel Wood had climbed up the hill to the house recently vacated by the former Spanish commander of Siboney to confer with General Wheeler and General Samuel B. M. Young, one of Wheeler's brigade commanders and Wood's immediate superior. The subject was the entrenched Spanish position Castillo had encountered that morning three miles up the road to Santiago at a tiny placed called Las Guásimas. Richard Harding Davis, who was present at the meeting, explained:

> Guasimas is not a village, nor even a collection of houses; it is the meeting-place of two trails which join at the apex of a V, three miles

from the seaport town of Siboney, and continue merged in a single trail
to Santiago. General Wheeler, accompanied by the Cubans, reconnoi-
tred this trail . . . and returned to Siboney and informed General Young
and Colonel Wood that he would attack the place on the following
morning.

Wheeler was close to exceeding his authority in planning an engagement
with the Spanish at this moment. Shafter's orders to his division commanders
were to dig in at strong defensive positions until the landing was completed. But
Shafter remained aboard the *Seguranca*, and Wheeler, as the senior officer
ashore, had considerable latitude in carrying out Shafter's orders. It may have
been, as Roosevelt approvingly explained, that Wheeler was "anxious . . . to get
first blood, and he was bent upon putting the cavalry division to the front as
quickly as possible." Or it may have been that Wheeler just wanted to keep the
Spanish on the run, falling back toward Santiago.

The conference ended around midnight. Wood and Davis walked back
down to the Rough Riders' camp and explained the plan for tomorrow's action
to Roosevelt.

"No one slept that night," Davis remembered,

for until two o'clock in the morning troops were still being disembarked
in the surf, and two ships of war had their searchlights turned on the
landing-place, and made Siboney light as a ball-room.

Back of the searchlights was an ocean white with moonlight, and
on the shore the red campfires, at which the half-drowned troops were
drying their uniforms . . . Below [the camp] was the beach and the
roaring surf, in which a thousand or so naked men were assisting and
impeding the progress shoreward of their comrades, in pontoons and
shore-boats, which were being hurled at the beach like sleds down a
water-chute.

It was one of the most weird and remarkable scenes of the war,
probably of any war. An army was being landed on an enemy's coast
at the dead of night, but with somewhat more of cheers and shrieks and
laughter than rise from the bathers in the surf at Coney Island on a
hot Sunday. It was a pandemonium of noises. The men still to be
landed from the "prison hulks," as they called the transports, were
singing in chorus, the men already on shore were dancing naked around
the camp-fires on the beach, or shouting with delight as they plunged
into the first bath that had offered in seven days, and those in the
launches as they were pitched head-first at the soil of Cuba, signalized
their arrival by howls of triumph. On either side rose black overhanging
ridges, in the lowland between were white tents and burning fires, and
from the ocean came the blazing, dazzling eyes of the search-lights
shaming the quiet moonlight.

·   ·   ·

THE ROAD TO SANTIAGO leaves the coast at Siboney and runs inland through the
foothills east of the city. General Antero Rubín and a force of about 1,500
Spanish troops had fallen back along this route in the early hours of June 23 and

were overtaken by the Cuban insurgents about three and a half miles from Siboney, near the village of Sevilla. After a brief skirmish the Spanish dug in along the ridge of high hills beside the road. This was the position General Wheeler chose to attack early on the twenty-fourth.

From Siboney a narrow jungle trail ran inland a few hundred yards to the left, or west, of the main Santiago road and rejoined the main road about three miles from the coast, just short of the Spanish position. Wheeler's plan of action called for Wood and Roosevelt to lead five hundred Rough Riders up this trail, while Wheeler and General Young would lead a column of almost five hundred men of the First and Tenth Regular Cavalry up the main road, bringing along three Hotchkiss guns and the Rough Riders' dynamite gun. A force of Cubans under General Castillo was to accompany Wheeler and Young along the main road. At a point near the Spanish positions, the Rough Riders were to leave the trail and advance through the jungle to their right, connecting up with the main column and attacking the Spaniards' right flank, while Wheeler and Young attacked their left.

At 5:40 A.M. on the twenty-fourth, the Rough Riders started up the jungle trail. Five minutes later the main column of regulars began marching along the Santiago road. Three miles ahead, near the point where the road and the trail merged, an advance party of Spanish hid in the jungle. The place was called Las Guásimas, not a town or a village but a fork in the road named after the guacimo trees that grew there in abundance.

At 6 A.M. the Rough Riders were struggling up the steep coastal bluff behind Siboney.

"The trail was so narrow that for the most part the men marched in single file," Roosevelt recalled, "and it was bordered by dense, tangled jungle, through which a man could with difficulty force his way; so that to put out flankers was impossible, for they could not possibly have kept up with the march of the column."

Two Cuban scouts were in the lead, followed by New York socialite Hamilton Fish, Muskogee teamster John Byrne, and three other troopers marching in the advanced "point" position. They were part of an advance troop of sixty men led by Captain Allyn Capron, Brooklyn born, lately of Oklahoma, a fifth-generation soldier, and according to Roosevelt, "the best soldier in the regiment."

The rest of the regiment followed a few hundred yards to the rear, led by Wood and Roosevelt in the company of Richard Harding Davis and another reporter, Edward Marshall of the New York *Journal.*

"After reaching the top of the hill the walk was very pleasant," recalled Roosevelt, who had not, in fact, been walking, but riding his horse, Little Texas.

> Now and then we came to glades or rounded hill-shoulders, when we could look off for some distance. . . . It was very beautiful and very peaceful, and it seemed more as if we were off on some hunting excursion than as if we were about to go into a sharp and bloody little fight.

"At 7:10 our advanced point discovered what they believed to be signs of the immediate presence of the enemy," Wood reported. "The command was halted."

He rode ahead, disappearing around a bend in the trail. The men sat down to wait.

"We had stopped near the end of a beautiful lane," Edward Marshall wrote,

carpeted with grass almost as soft as the turf in the garden of an old English country house. The tropical growth on our right shot up rank and strong for ten or fifteen feet, and then arched over until our resting-place was almost embowered. On the left was a narrow, treeless slope on which tall Cuban grass waved lazily.

"When we halted the men sat down beside the trail and chewed the long blades of grass, or fanned the air with their hats," Davis recalled. "They had no knowledge of the situation."

Roosevelt overheard a group of men gossiping about "a certain cowpuncher" who had quit herding cattle and opened a saloon somewhere in New Mexico. Marshall, who had walked back down the column, heard talk of dogs and ill-fitting army shoes. One man was shooting spitballs at the others.

"Damn!" exclaimed one. "Wouldn't a glass of cold beer taste good?"

After ten minutes Wood returned on foot leading his horse. He placed a finger to his lips and began deploying the men to either side of the trail. Edward Marshall, who had returned from the rear of the column, was approaching Wood and Roosevelt when he heard "a long z-z-z-z-z-eu" overhead and the crack of a rifle.

"There was no more gossip in the ranks," he recalled. "The men sprang to their feet without waiting for an order. As they did so a volley which went over our heads came through the mysterious tangle on our right. A scattering fire was heard from the direction in which the scouts had gone. Then silence."

Heavy firing now resumed. Wood ordered Major Brodie to deploy his men to the left of the trail and told Roosevelt, who had jumped down from his horse, to take his men to the right and, if possible, link up with the regulars on the main road.

"In theory this was excellent," Roosevelt recalled, "but as the jungle was very dense the first troop that deployed to the right vanished forthwith, and I never saw it again until the fight was over—having a frightful feeling meanwhile that I might be court-martialed for losing it."

Resolved to lose no more men in the jungle labyrinth, he did not deploy the next troops but marched them in column through the underbrush toward the firing line.

This sounds simple. But it was not. I did not know when I had gotten on the firing line! I could hear a good deal of firing, some over to my right at a good distance, and the rest to the left and ahead. I pushed on expecting to strike the enemy somewhere between.

He had no time to feel fear. He was experiencing the very unfamiliar feeling of self-doubt.

> "It was a most confusing country," he remembered, and I had an awful time trying to get into the fight and trying to do what was right when in it; and all the while I was thinking that I was the only man who did not know what I was about, and that all the others did— whereas, as I found out later, pretty much everybody else was as much in the dark as I was.

Richard Harding Davis thought there were no Spaniards ahead; he believed all the firing had been Captain Capron's point men. He ran after the troop that had disappeared into the jungle to the right of the trail. When he overtook G Troop the men were trying to break their way through the dense jungle growth.

"It was like forcing the walls of a maze," he recalled. "If each trooper had not kept in touch with the man on either hand he would have been lost in the thicket."

Davis stumbled forward and lost sight of the others, but he could hear them crashing through the jungle, breathing heavily. In a few minutes he broke out of the brush and found the troop in a clearing overlooking the valley that separated them from the main Santiago road. The firing seemed to be coming from the wooded ridge on the other side of the valley, but the Spanish were not visible.

"The effect of the smokeless powder was remarkable," recalled Roosevelt, who had also broken out of the jungle a short way off.*

> The air seemed full of the rustling sound of the Mauser bullets, for the Spaniards knew the trails by which we were advancing, and opened heavily on our position. Moreover, as we advanced we were of course exposed, and they could see us and fire. But they themselves were entirely invisible. The jungle covered everything, and not the faintest trace of smoke was to be seen in any direction to indicate from whence the bullets came.

It was now about 8 A.M. As Roosevelt, Davis, and the others peered at the ridge in search of the Spanish snipers, they heard the booming of the main column's Hotchkiss guns.

"At 7.30 A.M.," General Young reported, "the right column being massed in an open glade, Captain [A. L.] Mills with a patrol of two men advanced and

*Smokeless powder was a new military development, and surprisingly, there was a difference of opinion about it. When Roosevelt and Wood were equipping the regiment they encountered a War Department bureaucrat, "one fine old fellow [who] did his best to persuade us to take black powder rifles, explaining with paternal indulgence that no one yet really knew just what smokeless powder might do, and that there was a good deal to be said in favor of having smoke to conceal us from the enemy." Roosevelt snorted at "this pleasing theory," and demanded the Army's new Krag-Jorgenson rifle, which used smokeless cartridges. The demand was met and the Rough Riders were equipped with the rifles, although most other volunteer troops were issued the black powder Springfield rifles.

discovered the enemy located . . . in a locality called Guasimas, from trees of that name in the vicinity."

Young set up the Hotchkiss guns at a range of nine hundred yards from the Spanish positions and sat down to wait. He had dispatched a Cuban scout to warn Wood's column of the Spanish position, and he knew it would take the Rough Riders some time to work their way along the jungle trail and through the brush. Apparently he had not heard the sounds of the battle, which was now already in progress. As he waited, Wheeler came up the road from Siboney.

"General Young and myself examined the position of the enemy," Wheeler recalled. "The lines were deployed, and I directed him to open fire with the Hotchkiss guns. The enemy replied, and the firing immediately became general. . . . For an hour the fight was very warm, the enemy being very lavish in the expenditure of ammunition, most of their firing being by volleys."

Back on the jungle trail, Edward Marshall had remained with Wood. One of the point men came around the bend. His face was covered with blood, and he was cursing and sobbing. Marshall asked if he was badly hurt.

"I ain't hurt! I'm a goddam fool, an' I set off one of my own cartridges while I was loading. My face and eyes are full of powder and I can't fight."

He threw himself down in the grass and swore loudly.

"Stop that swearing," Colonel Wood called. "I don't want to hear any cursing today."

Marshall watched as Wood wandered slowly about on horseback among the men. The sound of the Mauser bullets whining through the air was no longer novel, and he wondered vaguely how long it would be before Wood fell from his horse. He had already seen several Rough Riders fall.

"Every one went down in a lump without cries, without jumping up in the air, without throwing up hands," he recalled. "They just went down like clods in the grass. . . . Some were only wounded; some were dead."

A moment later he heard a "chug," and he found himself lying beside the others in the grass.

"There was no pain, no surprise. The tremendous shock so dulled my sensibilities that it did not occur to me that anything extraordinary had happened . . . I merely lay perfectly satisfied and entirely comfortable in the long grass."

The battle seemed to move on. He lay where he was, dumbly staring at a dead man a few feet away. Presently some first aid men came by, calling out for the wounded.

"It did not occur to me to answer them. The sun was very hot and I had some vague thoughts of sunstroke, but they were not specially interesting thoughts and I gave them up. It seemed a good notion to go to sleep, but I didn't do it."

A few hundred yards away, on the brink of the deep valley that ran parallel to the road, Roosevelt and his men continued to be pinned down by an invisible enemy. He had tried some volley firing at points in the jungle where he thought the Spanish might be; the result, like the enemy, could not be seen.

Richard Harding Davis squirmed through the grass, clutching his binoculars.

He grabbed Roosevelt's elbow and pointed across the valley.

"There they are colonel! Look over there!"

Roosevelt turned his own glasses in the direction Davis indicated.

"Near that glade," Davis panted. "You can see their hats."

Roosevelt saw the distinctive Spanish hats. He turned and wriggled through the brush until he found four of the best shots in the troop. He showed them the enemy position, made an estimate of the range, and the men began firing their Krag rifles.

"For a minute or two no result followed, and I kept raising the range, at the same time getting more men on the firing line," he remembered.

Then, evidently, the shots told, for the Spaniards suddenly sprang out of the cover through which we had seen their hats, and ran to another spot; and we could now make out a large number of them.

I accordingly got all of my men up in a line and began quick firing. In a very few minutes our bullets began to do damage, for the Spaniards retreated to the left into the jungle, and we lost sight of them.

Roosevelt and his men gave chase and a running battle through the jungle ensued.

At every halt we took advantage of the cover, sinking down behind any mound, bush, or tree-trunk in the neighborhood. The trees, of course, furnished no protection from the Mauser bullets. Once I was standing behind a large palm with my head out to one side, very fortunately; for a bullet passed through the palm, filling my left eye and ear with the dust and splinters.

But the firing diminished as the advance party of Spaniards dropped back toward Sevilla. Roosevelt's men linked up with the regulars, some of whom were coming over from the main road.

"What to do then I had not an idea," Roosevelt explained. The Spanish fire seemed to have stopped, and the Spanish were nowhere in sight. Dense jungle lay in every direction. He was inclined to advance, but he did not know in what direction. Moving his men out of position might open up a gap in the line through which the Spanish could counterattack. But he could still hear firing off to the left from Wood's direction.

"It did not seem to me that I had been doing enough fighting to justify my existence," he recalled. Leaving his men in position he set off at a trot, back toward the jungle trail. As he ran, his sword kept swinging between his legs, threatening to trip him. The refrain of an old fox-hunting song kept running inanely through his head, "Here's to every friend who struggled to the end."

He found the trail and ran in the direction of the firing. Now he passed the dead point men who had fallen in the first seconds of the battle. He saw the body of Allyn Capron. He ran on. A hundred yards beyond the others lay Hamilton Fish, his dead eyes staring into the Cuban sky, apparently the first of the Rough

Riders to die. He ran on. *Here's to every friend who struggled to the end.* He stumbled as the sword slapped at his knees. He ran on.

"Pretty soon I reached Wood and found, much to my pleasure, that I had done the right thing," he recalled. Major Brodie had been wounded; Roosevelt was given charge of the left wing as the troops advanced through the open country beyond the jungle. The men scrambled forward from tree to hillock to bush, keeping their interval, pausing to take careful aim, running forward again. A hail of bullets swept over them. The Spanish marksmen were, again, invisible.

"I know nothing about war," Stephen Crane warned, "but I have been enabled from time to time to see brush fighting, and I want to say here plainly that the behavior of those Rough Riders while marching through the woods shook me with terror as I have never before been shaken."

Crane had arrived at Siboney in time to see the last of the regiment file up the mountain trail. He followed, overtaking the head of the column just as the fighting erupted. Like the hero of *The Red Badge of Courage,* he saw a battle that was confusing, impersonal, absurd, and deadly.

> There was nothing to be seen but men straggling through the under-brush and firing at some part of the landscape. . . .
> The Rough Riders advanced steadily and confidently under the Mauser bullets. They spread across some open ground—tall grass and palms—and there they began to fall, smothering and threshing down in the grass, marking man-shaped places among those luxuriant blades.

Richard Harding Davis had followed Roosevelt back to the jungle trail. He borrowed a carbine from a wounded man and joined the remnant of L Troop—the men who had been in the point position—now commanded by Lieutenant Richard Day.

> He [Day] was walking up and down the line as unconcernedly as though we were at target-practice, and an English sergeant, Byrne, was assisting him by keeping up a continuous flow of comments and criticisms that showed the keenest enjoyment of the situation. Byrne was the only man I noticed who seemed to regard the fight as in any way humorous. I suspect Byrne was Irish.*

Roosevelt thought the fire was coming from a cluster of red-tiled buildings he could see up ahead, apparently part of a ranch. He ordered a halt and concentrated his fire on them. Suddenly he heard cheering off to his right and supposed Wood's men were charging. He recalled:

> I sprang up and ordered the men to rush the buildings ahead of us. They came forward with a will. There was a moment's heavy firing from the Spaniards, which all went over our heads, and then it ceased

*Private (not Sergeant) John Byrne, thirty-four, of Muskogee, Oklahoma Territory, had been born in Dublin, Ireland.

entirely. When we arrived at the buildings, panting and out of breath, they contained nothing but heaps of empty cartridge-shells and two dead Spaniards, shot through the head.

It was suddenly very quiet. He did not know if the Spanish were retreating, or if was merely a lull in the battle. He went looking for Wood. One of the men came and told him that Colonel Wood was dead.

It was now about ten o'clock. At 8:30 a runner had arrived at Siboney bringing a message for General Lawton, the Second Division commander. General Wheeler had the honor to inform him that he was engaged with a larger force of the enemy than was anticipated and asked that Lawton's division be sent forward as quickly as possible.

The Gallant Seventy-first marched double time up the Santiago road, passing the walking wounded as they limped back towards Siboney. Private Post saw a Rough Rider astride a mule, his trouser leg soaked with blood.

"How'd you get yours?" Post called out.

"Damn near stepped on the sonofabitch—then he got me. But I got him. I got mine. Now you go an' git yours."

Another man cried out some advice, the central fact of the morning: "You can't see 'em."

The Seventy-first trotted up the road, double time, quick time, double time again. No halts, no rest. Now they could hear the guns—artillery, rifles. Post heard "a long-drawn, seething whine" overhead.

"We were under fire!" he exulted. "We were veterans!"

But that was to be his day's ration of battle. The order suddenly came down the line: "Rest."

"The popping grew fainter," he remembered. "Then there were no shots at all. We realized that the fight was over."

"Then the heroic rumor arose," Crane reported. "Everybody was wounded. Everybody was dead. There was nobody. Gradually there was somebody. There was the wounded, the important wounded. And the dead."

Roosevelt was still uncertain of anything but that the Spanish firing had stopped. Having been informed Wood had been killed, he believed he was now in command of the regiment. He began moving his men to the right to join the main column on the Santiago road. Then a joyful anticlimax: "I started over toward the main body, but to my delight encountered Wood himself, who told me the fight was over and the Spaniards had retreated."

But there were eight dead Rough Riders, and eight more from the ranks of the First and Tenth Regulars. Roosevelt counted eleven dead Spaniards and guessed there were a few more hidden in the thick underbrush. The vultures had blackened the sky during the battle and had already gotten at the dead. Roosevelt and Captain William "Bucky" O'Neill found the torn body of one Rough Rider.

"Colonel, isn't it Whitman who says of the vultures that 'they pluck the eyes of princes and tear the flesh of kings'?"

Roosevelt shrugged, shook his head and turned away.
Here's to every friend who struggled to the end.

. . .

"THERE'S A CORRESPONDENT up there all shot to hell," said the soldier.

Crane followed him back up the jungle trail to the shady place where they had carried Edward Marshall. A surgeon had examined his shattered spine and advised him he was about to die.

"Hello, Crane!"

"Hello, Marshall! In hard luck old man?"

"Yes, I'm done for."

"Nonsense! You're all right, old boy. What can I do for you?"

"Well, you might file my despatches. I don't mean file 'em ahead of your own, old man—but just file 'em if you find it handy."

Crane and Richard Harding Davis found some soldiers to gather Marshall up on a tent and help carry him to a field hospital—a spot on the road where the wounded were being taken. As Crane waited for the surgeons to get to Marshall, he overheard a pair of walking wounded from Roosevelt's regiment wheedling the medics.

"Say, doctor, this ain't much of a wound. I reckon I can go now back to my troop," said Arizona.

"Thanks, awfully, doctor. Awfully kind of you. I dare say I shall be all right in a moment," said New York.

While they bandaged Marshall, Crane trudged back to Siboney, the reporter's dispatches in his pocket. After he saw to it that they were filed, he returned to the field hospital and arranged for Marshall to be carried to the coast. Just before sundown Private Post and several other soldiers carried him to one of the landing boats so that he could be taken out to the *Olivette,* which was now doing duty as a hospital ship.

Crane had decided that Marshall was done for.

"No man could be so sublime in detail concerning the trade of journalism and not die. There was the solemnity of a funeral song in these absurd and fine sentences about despatches."

Marshall died in 1933 at the age of sixty-four, having outlived Crane by more than three decades.

. . .

GENERAL WHEELER STOOD ATOP a rise a half-mile beyond Sevilla and studied the city of Santiago some seven miles away through his binoculars. The countryside appeared to be deserted. The way was open for an American advance. The Spanish had fallen back to the hills just east of the city. That was where the next battle would be fought. He looked at his map and saw that the place was called San Juan.

. . .

ONE MILE BEYOND the San Juan hills, on the eastern outskirts of Santiago, stood the Reina Mercedes barracks where Hobson and the *Merrimac's* crew were now being kept. From the barred window of his room Hobson had a clear view of the open ground to the east, of the hills, and of some of the country beyond. Throughout the day he had watched Spanish couriers racing back and forth between the city and the distant heights. He had heard much gunfire from the southeast and decided it was coming from the area near a building he could just glimpse in the distance. Details were softened by the tropical haze, but it now seemed to him that the flag flying above that building was the Stars and Stripes.

. . .

ABOARD THE *María Teresa* Admiral Cervera met with his captains. He read them a cable he had received the day before from Madrid ordering him to take the squadron out of Santiago Bay at the "first favorable opportunity."

Next he read them his reply: "As it is absolutely impossible for squadron to escape under these circumstances, intend to resist as long as possible and destroy ships in the last extreme."

The captains expressed their unanimous agreement.

. . .

THE SPANISH RELIEF COLUMN led by Colonel Escario continued to march east-ward. The column had been harassed by the insurgents the day before as it passed through the Don Pedro plain and proceeded to Yara. One man had been killed and three wounded. This night the column reached the Canabacoa River, having fought skirmishes with the insurgents all during the day's march. A second man was killed, another wounded.

. . .

AT MID-MORNING on June 25 the Rough Riders gathered at a quiet place off the Santiago road to bury their dead. Chaplain Henry A. Brown of Prescott, Arizona, led the men through "Rock of Ages," then read the burial service. Afterward trumpeter Emilio Cassi of Jerome, Arizona, played taps.

A great river of men, horses, pack mules, wagons, and artillery now flowed along the nearby road past the battlefield of yesterday, past Sevilla and into the countryside beyond. Tent cities had sprung up in the grassy meadows to either side of the road for three miles, ending at the outpost that had been established within sight of the San Juan hills. Almost all of the sixteen thousand men of the expeditionary force had now been landed, and most of them were in these camps or trudging up the Santiago road on their way to them. The Army was presented with a new task: to move ten million pounds of rations off the ships and up eight miles of the Santiago road faster than sixteen thousand mouths could eat them. And the biggest problem was the road, which Richard Hard-ing Davis recalled:

The trail was a sunken wagon road, where it was possible, in a few places, for two wagons to pass at one time, but the greater distances were so narrow that there was but just room for a wagon, or a loaded mule-train, to make its way. The banks of the trail were three or four feet high, and when it rained it was converted into a huge gutter, with sides of mud, and with liquid mud a foot deep between them.

The expedition's two hundred wagons had been taken apart at Tampa to be packed aboard the transports. Now the task of putting them back together had to be faced. Meanwhile supplies arriving on the beach at Daiquirí and Siboney were loaded on trains of pack mules and sent off toward the front, but as the population of the camps grew, there were not enough mules to carry the needed rations forward.

Priority was given to the matter of the wagons, and the flow of supplies up the Santiago road increased. Since the road was too narrow to permit lines of wagon traffic to move freely in both directions, a system was established: empty wagons moved down the road to Siboney in the morning, and loaded wagons moved up the road to the camps and depots in the afternoon.

"If this scheme for supplying the command had worked as smoothly as might be expected with macadam roads to travel over," explained Lieutenant Miley,

the troops would have had full supplies of every kind and description. But the road to the rear became blocked by wagons stalled in the mud or breaking down, delaying the entire train into the night and some-times so as to interfere with the next day's trip. . . . Then the streams toward the front would often rise after a rain, so they could not be forded until the next day, and loaded trains would have to pass the night on the road. . . .

It was soon very evident that only the coarser components of the rations . . . could be supplied to the troops with any certainty. . . . There were instances where individual regiments were without rations for a day or more.

It soon was apparent to Shafter that he had not escaped the confusion of Tampa. It had followed him to Santiago aboard the transports.

·   ·   ·

LIEUTENANT COLONEL JOSEPH E. MAXFIELD was a determined man. Once given a task he sunk in his teeth and clung tenaciously to it until it stopped fighting him. Thus, when General Greely, chief of the Signal Corps, ordered him to confirm the Hellings–Villaverde report of Cervera's arrival in Santiago, he re-mained at his key in the New York offices of the Haitian cable company until he had the evidence. Yet Maxfield's specialty was not telegraph espionage, but balloons, or, more accurately, *a* balloon, since the U.S. Army owned only one such craft. And because, at this moment, Orville and Wilbur Wright were yet fixing bicycles and reading old copies of the *Scientific American* in Dayton, Ohio,

Lieutenant Colonel Maxfield and his balloon were, in a sense, the U.S. Air Force.

The balloon train consisted of six wagons, which carried the balloon, a gas generator, 180 steel tubes for holding the gas, a telephone system for talking to the ground, ropes, cables, tools, and other assorted equipment and supplies. It had been sent to New York City from Fort Logan, Colorado, early in April, the idea being that Maxfield would float above Sandy Hook and look out over the Atlantic Ocean for Admiral Cervera's ships. But when Maxfield and the Signal Corps located Cervera by more indirect means, he was told to take his balloon to Tampa to help in the invasion of Cuba.

Maxfield arrived at Tampa in the hectic days of early June to discover that the freight cars containing the balloon, the wagons, and all the equipment were lost somewhere out on one of the railroad sidings among the thousands of freight cars that had lately arrived. Undaunted, Maxfield camped in the office of the depot quartermaster and proceeded to examine each of the thousands of bills of lading that had been dumped upon the desk of that wretched man. Eventually he found what he was looking for, a piece of paper with the number of the car containing his balloon. But where among the fifty miles of freight cars that particular car might be the precious scrap did not reveal. Discovering *that* took legwork. Lieutenant Colonel Maxfield set out along the tracks.

To those who knew Maxfield it must have come as no surprise when he turned up on the wharf at Port Tampa as the transports were taking aboard their final consignments and pointed to the car that held the balloon, the wagons, and all the other paraphernalia of nineteenth-century aviation. Only missing was the flat car aboard which he had shipped the gas generator, a twelve-foot cylinder that some of the Plant Line's employees had tried to take beneath a ten-foot railroad trestle. No matter; Maxfield knew a way to fly without it. He was that sort of individual.

Aboard the transport *Rio Grande* Maxfield fretted as the armada made its leisurely way around the Windward Passage. He had the balloon brought up from the hold and spread out on the deck. As he suspected, the Port Tampa heat had softened the varnish on the silk, causing the sides to stick together. Repairs made, the balloon was returned to hold, but he had it on deck again a day or so later.

Just to check.

Since the disembarkation had begun on the twenty-second, Maxfield had waited patiently for transportation to take ashore the balloon and its accessories, but in this he was frustrated by the limited vision of those in charge of the landing who, while they could readily imagine the utility of a infantryman, a horse, a mule, a sack of beans, a wagon, or a Hotchkiss gun, failed to encompass within their ken the military value of a balloon. It is possible that some even demanded to know why the fool thing could not fly itself ashore. No matter; Lieutenant Colonel Maxfield would overcome this obstacle as he had overcome the others.

·   ·   ·

THE MINISTER OF MARINE notified Admiral Cervera that he was now under the direct command of Captain General Blanco in Havana. Minister Auñón explained that he had taken the step "to give perfect unity to conduct of war in

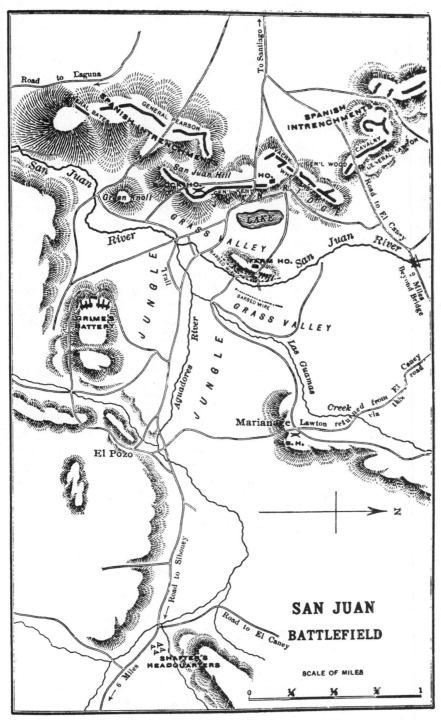

Area of the Battle of San Juan, July 1, 1898. (Top of map is west; north is to the right).

[the] island." This was but a euphemistic reference to the grim controversy that now had come to a crisis. General Blanco believed that sailing out of Santiago to certain destruction was far better than scuttling the squadron in the harbor. Admiral Cervera could not accept the useless sacrifice of two thousand lives on the altar of national honor. Minister Auñón had resolved the question in Blanco's favor.

With dignified irony, Cervera cabled Auñón and thanked him for the orders, which, he said, "will relieve me from taking on my own responsibility extreme measures of the utmost importance." Next he fired off a telegram to Blanco: "Minister of marine commands me to place myself under orders of your excellency. . . . I believe it my duty to set forth conditions of squadron."

He then recited the now familiar catalog of defects, deficiencies, inadequacies, and malfunctions that he had come to know by heart, concluding with the advice that "hence, our sortie [from Santiago Bay] would be positively certain destruction." He stated again his own proposal to resist as long as possible and to sink the squadron if capture threatened.

"I await instructions from your excellency," he said.

Blanco now saw he had been handed a hot potato and gave the matter second thoughts. By putting him in charge of Cervera, Madrid had washed its hands of the squadron's fate. Cervera refused to share any part of the responsibility for sending it out of the harbor. That left Blanco solely responsible for orders Cervera had warned him meant "certain destruction."

Blanco took momentary refuge in wishful thinking. Perhaps matters weren't as bad as Cervera believed, after all. Two Spanish ships had just escaped from Havana harbor and eluded the American blockade at 2 A.M. Why shouldn't Cervera's squadron be able to do the same? And whether or not a successful sortie was possible, why wasn't the man at least willing to try? Why must he, Blanco, be forced to shoulder the full responsibility for sending the squadron on a suicide mission?

Rather than make a direct attempt to change Cervera's mind, Blanco telegraphed General Arsenio Linares, the Spanish army commander at Santiago:

> I beg that your excellency will tell Admiral Cervera that I should like to know his opinion and plans. It is my opinion that he should go out from Santiago as early as possible whenever he may deem best, for the situation in that harbor is, in my judgement, the most dangerous of all. Last night there were only 7 warships there . . . and 9 here, yet the *Santo Domingo* and *Montevideo* had no trouble in running the blockade, going out at 2 A.M. If we should lose the squadron without fighting, the moral effect would be terrible, both in Spain and abroad.

Blanco was probably mistaken in seeking an ally in General Linares. The general had almost as much to lose as did Cervera if the squadron left the bay. There was, first of all, the matter of the two thousand crewmen who were now supplementing Linares's troops; they would have to be withdrawn to man the ships once again. And there were the rapid-fire cannon of the fleet; if Havana and Madrid would finally abandon this madness of a sortie, those guns could be dismounted and placed on the San Juan hills, where they might do some good. As to the idea of steaming out of the harbor at 2 A.M., Linares well knew what Blanco chose to ignore—that at darkness the blockading fleet stood close in near the harbor and played its searchlights on the entrance channel all through the night. The ships were so close to shore that the sentinels on Socapa and Morro points could hear the cries of the watch.

Linares, in any case, chose not to argue Blanco's case to Cervera. He passed along the captain general's message without comment. Cervera read it and with the seething anger of a patient man he sat down to write his reply. Disdaining to make a direct answer to Blanco, he addressed his letter to General Linares:

> The Captain-General is kind enough to want to know my opinion, and I am going to give it as explicitly as I ought to. . . . I have considered the squadron lost ever since it left Cape Verde, for to think anything else seems madness. . . . For that reason I energetically opposed the sailing of the squadron from Cape Verde, and I even thought that I would be relieved by some one of those whose opinions were opposed to mine.
>
> I did not ask to be relieved, because it seems to me that no military man should do so when he receives instructions to march against the enemy. . . .
>
> Today I consider the squadron lost as much as ever, and the dilemma is whether to lose it by destroying it, if Santiago is not able to resist, after having contributed to its defense, or whether to lose it by sacrificing to vanity the majority of its crews and depriving Santiago of their cooperation, thereby precipitating its fall. What is best to be done? I, who am a man without ambitions, without mad passions, believe that whatever is most expedient should be done, and I state most emphatically that I shall *never* be the one to decree the horrible and useless hecatomb which will be the only possible result of the sortie from here by main force, for I should consider myself responsible before God and history for the lives sacrificed on the altar of vanity, and not in the true defense of the country.
>
> As far as I am concerned, the situation has been changed today from a moral standpoint, for I received a telegram this morning which places me under the orders of the Captain-General in everything relating to the operation of the war. It is therefore for him to decide whether I am to go out to suicide, dragging along with me those 2,000 sons of Spain. I . . . trust you will see in this letter only the true and loyal expression of the opinion of an honorable old man who for forty-six years has served his country to the best of his ability.

· · ·

"IT IS A SATISFACTORY THING to be an American," wrote William Randolph Hearst, "and be here on the soil of Cuba at the threshold of what may prove to be the decisive battle of the war."

Hearst had assumed a proprietary attitude toward the war, ecstatically embracing the grand illusion that he had caused it. "How Do You Like the *Journal's* War?" exulted the front-page banners of his newspaper. Having decided the war was his personal property, he wished to go and see it. He had donated his yacht, the *Buccaneer,* to the Navy for conversion to a gunboat, so he chartered the *Sylvia,* a large steamer belonging to the Baltimore Fruit Company, and fitted it out with offices, a printing press, even a darkroom. His idea was to lead his own army of reporters, artists, and photographers to the front to report the war for his New York and San Francisco papers and even to bring out a Cuban edition of the *Journal* to be distributed free of charge to the troops.

The *Sylvia* had arrived off Santiago even before the expedition. Hearst had interviewed Admiral Sampson—"a quiet, conservative man with thin features and almost snow white beard, and melancholy eyes." When the *Seguranca* arrived he went aboard and interviewed General Shafter—"a bold, lion-headed hero, and massive as to body—a sort of human fortress in blue coat and flannel shirt." When he was permitted to land in Siboney he found General García— "a splendid old hero in spotless white linen from head to foot." In a piece dated June 27 he wrote:

> The struggle for the possession of the city of Santiago and the capture of Cervera's fleet seems to be only a few hours away, and from the top of the ridge where I write this we can see dimly on the sea the mon- strous forms of Sampson's fleet lying in a semicircle in front of the entrance to Santiago harbor, while here at our feet masses of American soldiers are pouring from the beach into the scorching valley where the smell of stagnant and fermented vegetation ground under the feet of thousands of fighting men rises in the hot mists through which vultures that have already fed on the corpses of slain Spaniards wheel lazily above the thorny, poisonous jungle.

Near the *Sylvia,* another civilian ship stood offshore from Siboney—the *State of Texas,* which the American Red Cross had chartered to carry food, medicine, and other relief supplies to the Cuban *reconcentrados.* The Red Cross expedition was led by Clara Barton. Author-lecturer George Kennan had been sent along by *Outlook* magazine to report on the war and the Red Cross work.*

Barton and the Red Cross workers had already been to Guantánamo, where they had tried to land some of their cargo for shipment to the interior. They had been waiting for the insurgents to provide some mules to transport the supplies when word of the Las Guásimas fight reached them and they proceeded at once to Siboney. They arrived on the evening of the twenty-sixth, two days after the battle, and immediately landed a team of medical officers to see whether the Red Cross could help.

"They returned in the course of an hour," Kennan recalled,

> and reported that in two of the abandoned Spanish houses on the beach they had found two hastily extemporized and wholly unequipped hospi- tals, one of which was occupied by the Cuban sick and wounded, and the other by our own. No attempt had been made to clean or disinfect

*Kennan was a cousin of the grandfather of the distinguished diplomat George F. Kennan.

either of the buildings, both were extremely dirty, and in both the patients were lying, without blankets or pillows, on the floor.

The Army's medical facilities had fallen victim to the general logistical confusion. The hospital supplies were still aboard the transports waiting to be landed, and the surgeons found they could not cut through the military red tape and get them where they were desperately needed.

The following morning a Red Cross doctor and five trained nurses—all women—landed with a boatload of medical supplies and asked to see Dr. Winter, the Army surgeon in charge of the hospital.

To their great surprise they were informed that the assistance of the Red Cross—or at least their assistance—was not desired. What Dr. Winter's reasons were for declining aid and supplies when both were so urgently needed I do not know. Possibly he is one of the military surgeons . . . who think that women, even if they are trained nurses, have no business with an army, and should be snubbed, if not brow-beaten, until they learn to keep their place. . . .

When told by Dr. Winter that they were not wanted, the nurses went to the Cuban hospital, in a neighboring building, where their services were accepted not only with eagerness, but with grateful appreciation. Before night they had swept, disinfected, and scrubbed out that hospital with soap and water, and had bathed the Cuban patients, fed them, and put them into clean, fresh cot-beds. Our own soldiers, at the same time, were lying, without blankets or pillows, on the floor, in a building which Dr. Winter and his assistants had neither cleaned nor attempted to clean.

But Kennan's resentment of the army surgeon's mulish attitude did not keep him from seeing that the basic problem lay elsewhere.

"The blame should rest . . . upon the officer or department that sent thirty-five loaded transports and sixteen thousand men to the Cuban coast without suitable landing facilities."

. . .

LIEUTENANT COLONEL MAXFIELD STRODE down the beach at Daiquiri and inspected his air force, or that part of it which his characteristic conjuring had managed to get ashore. There was, first of all, the balloon wagon and in it the balloon. There was his assistant, Second Lieutenant Volkmar, and there was Sergeant Baldwin and a dozen enlisted men. The rest of the balloon train consisted of five wagons loaded with 180 tubes of hydrogen gas, a tool wagon containing assorted cables, wires, ropes, rubber patches and glue, and a sufficient number of mules to pull the whole caravan to the front.

Maxfield consulted his map. The way to the front was through Siboney, eleven miles distant. He reckoned it would take all day to get that far. He gave the order and the teamsters cracked their whips. The balloon train started out on the road to Santiago.

.   .   .

IN A LONG CABLE to Admiral Cervera, Governor General Blanco argued his case.

> For my part, I repeat I do not believe that the hostile fleet, no matter how strong, can do so very much damage. . . .
> The eyes of every nation are at present fixed on your squadron, on which the honor of our country depends, as I am sure your excellency realizes. . . .
> I leave entirely to the discretion of your excellency, who are so highly gifted, the route to be followed and the decision as to whether any of the ships should be left behind on account of slow speed. As a favorable item, I will tell your excellency that the captain of German cruiser *Geier* has expressed the opinion that the sortie of the squadron can be effected without running great risks.*

"I have to respect your excellency's opinions without discussing them," Cervera telegraphed in reply,

> especially after having given you my own opinion formed after mature consideration. I have always believed that there are many sailors more able than I am, and it is a pity that one of them can not come to take command of the squadron. . . . I construe your excellency's telegram as an order to go out, and therefore ask General Linares for reembarkation of forces . . . I beg that you will confirm the order of sortie, because it is not explicit, and I should feel very sorry if I did not interpret your excellency's orders correctly.

Blanco was now desperate for any partner to share the responsibility of sending out the squadron. He telegraphed General Linares: "Tell me candidly your opinion of squadron, whether you believe it can go out and what solution seems best to you."

Linares's reply put the whole question in abeyance. He could not spare Cervera's crewmen until Colonel Escario's column arrived from Manzanillo. It was now June 28, and Escario's column, six days out of Manzanillo, had covered about half the distance to Santiago.

.   .   .

THE LAST OF the American troops landed on the evening of June 26. General Shafter estimated that it would take two full days to get all of them up the Santiago road to camps near the front. The twenty-ninth, then, seemed the date for a general advance on Santiago. But on the twenty-seventh the *Yale* arrived at Siboney, bringing 1,200 men of the Michigan Volunteers and word that the *Harvard* was following with 2,800 more of the Michigan brigade. Shafter decided

---

*The *Geier* was the large cruiser sent to join the German school ship fleet in the Caribbean after the Lüders affair in Haiti. It may have been in Havana harbor since before the blockade was put in place April 22, or it may have been granted permission by the State Department to enter the harbor and stand by in case the evacuation of German nationals became necessary.

to delay the advance until the 4,000 reinforcements were ashore. In the meantime he ordered Wheeler to reconnoiter the country along the Santiago road and learn what he could about the Spanish defenses of the city.

. . .

SOME THREE MILES beyond Sevilla, and about an equal distance short of Santiago, the road ran past a hill called El Pozo. Richard Harding Davis and General Adna R. Chaffee climbed to the top of El Pozo and looked westward across the great valley that lay beyond.

To the left the sea was hidden by a range of high hills. There were hills far off to the right, and nested among them was the village of El Caney, a name that every veteran of the Santiago campaign would remember. And straight ahead, a mile and a half across the thickly forested valley, rose the San Juan Heights.

"These hills looked so quiet and sunny and well kept that they reminded one of a New England orchard," Davis wrote.

> There was a blue bungalow on a hill to the right, a red bungalow higher up on the right, and in the centre the block-house of San Juan, which looked like a Chinese pagoda. Three-quarters of a mile behind them, with a dip between them, were the long white walls of the hospital and barracks of Santiago.

These were the Reina Mercedes barracks and hospital, where Hobson and the *Merrimac's* crew were now imprisoned.

Immediately beneath the vantage point of El Pozo the Santiago road disappeared into the thick forest to emerge again about a mile across the valley in the grassy plain at the foot of the San Juan Heights. Chaffee pointed to the map, which showed that a narrow jungle trail departed from the main road in the middle of the woods and branched off to the southwest, emerging on the grassy plan about a thousand feet south of the main road.

"The enemy knows where those two trails leave the wood, Chaffee said. "They have their guns trained on the openings. If our men leave the cover and reach the plain from those trails alone they will be piled up so high that they will block the road."

The Spanish were indeed expecting the American advance to come across the valley along the Santiago road. On June 27, Davis recalled,

> a long, yellow pit opened in the hillside of San Juan, and in it we could see straw sombreros rising and bobbing up and down . . . The rifle-pits were growing in length and number, and . . . in plain sight from the hill of El Poso [sic], the enemy was entrenching himself at San Juan, and at the village of El Caney to the right.

. . .

A TRICKLE OF Cuban refugees emerged from the city and into the countryside. General Wheeler questioned some of them to learn of the conditions in Santiago and the Spanish preparations to defend the city. On June 28 he interviewed a young man who had left the city the day before to join the Cuban forces.

Although a thousand men from Cervera's squadron had been landed, the young man reported, there were no more than twelve thousand Spanish troops in the city, and a part of the force was stationed at the harbor entrance. The troops were suffering from malaria and other diseases. There was a shortage of attendants to care for the cases that had been hospitalized. Food was very scarce. Artillery ammunition was in short supply.

Two parallel lines of barbed wire ran around the city, linked by many criss-cross lines. The trenches that were being dug were intended to give cover to riflemen. Generally, there was little artillery defending the city, and what guns there were were for the most part old smooth-bore muzzle loaders.

San Juan had been reinforced. There were about a thousand men, plus some light mountain artillery on the hills. The trenches that could be seen from El Pozo would probably not be finished for a week.

The most disquieting news Wheeler got from the Cuban was the rumor that a Spanish relief column men was on its way from Manzanillo.

"Late in the afternoon [of June 28]," Secretary Alger wrote,

General Shafter was informed that General Pando, with 8,000 Spanish regulars, was advancing from Manzanillo to relieve the garrison in Santiago. Pando was reported to be within fifty-four miles of the city, and moving at the rate of twelve miles a day, with an abundance of supplies in the way of pack-trains and beef on the hoof. If the Spanish general met with no opposition, this would bring a strong force, with a large quantity of food, for the relief of General Linares, by the 2nd or 3rd of July. General Shafter determined, if possible, to prevent General Pando's entering Santiago, and to make the attack without waiting for the additional reinforcements.

General Shafter would have been heartened had he known that the column —which was not 8,000 men led by General Pando but 3,752 led by Colonel Escario—was facing serious difficulties at this moment. Six days out of Manzanillo, it had reached Baïre, only halfway to Santiago. There it had been ambushed by the insurgents. Four Spaniards were killed and six wounded, including Colonel Manual Ruiz, second in command of the column.

The men of the relief column were exhausted. For the past six days they had been hacking their way through the jungle in suffocating heat while the insurgents constantly harassed them from ambush. Escario recalled:

The frequent rains, which not only soaked the clothing, but also the ground, making it slippery and difficult to walk on for such large numbers; the sickness caused by the inclement weather and the hard work of these operations; the ever increasing convoy of stretchers . . . all these were reasons which the commander of the column took into consideration when he decided to suspend the march and rest during the day of the 29th. It was ordered owing to fatigue; but the enemy kept harassing us and we had three more wounded.

. . .

THE BATTLEFIELD OF Las Guásimas had become a landmark on the road to Santiago, a place the newcomers watched for as they slogged up from Siboney toward the front. George Kennan stopped there and examined the place:

> Evidences and traces of the fight, in the shape of cartridge-shells and -clips, bullet-splintered trees, improvised stretchers, and blood-soaked clothes and bandages, were to be seen almost everywhere, and particularly on the trail along which the Rough Riders had advanced. . . .
> A short distance from the intersection of the trail with the road was a large grave-shaped mound of fresh earth, under which had been buried together eight of the men killed on our side during the fight. There had been no time, apparently, to prepare and put up an inscribed headboard to show who the dead men were, but some of their comrades had carefully collected two or three hundred stones and pebbles . . . and had laid them close together on the burial-mound in the form of a long cross.

But the name of at least one of the dead Rough Riders was known to at least one of the newcomers who marched past, for it was his own name. Captain Allyn Capron, Sr., battery commander of the Fourth Artillery, stopped and spent a moment beside the grave of his son, Captain Allyn Capron, Jr., First Volunteer Cavalry. Then he turned away and continued up the road to Santiago.

. . .

OUT BEYOND THE LAST of the regimental camps along the Santiago road, one battalion of the Gallant Seventy-First was on guard duty. As the sun dropped behind the sierra and darkness filled the valleys, Private Post gazed toward the west and knew that other soldiers had drawn the same duty that night.

> We could see the tiny flickers of Spanish campfires at outposts like ours, far off, and beyond those our minds pictured a city with people passing to and fro. We wondered if the Spaniards drank beer and if there would be any left when we got there.
> The whole battalion was on outpost guard, a picket. One company was posted as an outer line on double guard—two men, back to back; one hour on, two hours off; ball cartridge; challenge and then shoot. Down in the valley by the Aguadores road on which we had come, we heard the regimental bugle blow retreat, and then taps. Far across the rolling jungle below us we could hear the Spanish bugles, lovely in the strange cadences. The stars turned on their lights in the black sky and all was as peaceful as peace itself.

Soon the darkness was filled with exotic choruses of tropical insects and the occasional cry of a night bird. The night wore on.

At 3 A.M. the quiet was suddenly rent by the cry of a New York voice. "Halt! Who's there?"

A shot followed immediately. Private Post recognized the now familiar sound of a .45-caliber Springfield.

"Corporal of the guard!"

A bugle call down in the valley and the regimental camp came alive. Men struggled into their pants, found their rifles.

Again the cry, "Halt! Who's there?"

"The captain, goddammit! Who you shooting?"

"I seen a Spaniard, sir. I seen him—well, I heard him—yeah, I got him— down there—I seen him just as plain—"

Bang!

Post's partner had fired this time. The captain came running up.

"Who fired?"

"I did. I heard him—right there. I seen a Spaniard, captain."

The captain turned to Post.

"Did you see him?"

"No, sir. I wasn't facing that way."

"Maybe you was asleep," suggested the partner unpleasantly.

Bang! This time it came from farther down the line. The captain was off.

"The battle with the land crabs was beginning," Post remembered.

Of all the Cuban fauna, the land crab was the least popular with the Americans. They are scavengers that emerge from their subterranean nests in large numbers at night, but they can also been seen during the day in the vicinity of carrion. At La Guásimas Roosevelt had seen a dying Rough Rider around whom "the big, hideous land-crabs had gathered in a grewsome ring, waiting for life to be extinct." George Kennan recalled the creature:

> It resembles the common marine crab in form, and varies in size from the diameter of a saucer to that of a large dinner plate. . . . The creature has two long fore claws, or pincers; small eyes, mounted like round berries on the ends of short stalks or pedicels; and a mouth that seems to be formed by two horny, beak-like mandibles. It walks or runs with considerable rapidity in any direction . . . If you approach one, it throws itself into what seems to be a defensive attitude, raises aloft its long fore claws, looks at you intently for a moment, and then backs or sidles away . . .
>
> [At night] they come out by the hundred, if not by the thousand . . . and the still atmosphere of the deep, lonely forest is filled with the rustling, crackling noise that they make as they scramble through the bushes.

The stuff of bad dreams, they robbed the Gallant Seventy-first of its slumber, although Private Post knew that "the Spaniards, with but one pair of legs, could never have made such a clatter in the underbrush." But other men along the line were not so confident, and as the night slowly passed the stillness was now and then punctuated by a shouted challenge and a shot.

The sky grew light and a chorus of exotic birdsong prefaced the dawn. The land crabs retreated beneath the moist earth. Post watched as the first rays of the morning illuminated the San Juan hills.

Across the ridges that lay between our outpost and the Spanish lines we could see the distant wisps of blue smoke that marked their early-morning coffee, their *desayuno*. Doubtless they could see the little smoke from our fires where the hardtack and the sowbelly were frying. We had our bugles and reveille, and we could hear theirs. All was peaceful and calm—except that we were at war.

. . .

GOVERNOR GENERAL BLANCO HAD TAKEN refuge in ambiguity. His orders to Admiral Cervera now stood thusly: "The squadron will remain in the harbor . . . it will watch for a favorable opportunity to go out . . . but in case . . . the fall of Santiago is believed near, the squadron will go out immediately as best it can."

But Cervera, who was now becoming very adept at this game, turned to General Linares and said: "I . . . beg that, if at any time you think that the unfortunate situation referred to in [Blanco's orders] may arise, you will kindly advise me in time, so that I may be able to reembark the men I have ashore and put to sea, in compliance with the instructions."

And Linares, feeling that the moment the Americans seemed about to overrun his defenses would be the worst time to pull a thousand men out of the line, responded:

> In reply to your [request] to advise you when the city may be in danger of falling into the hands of the enemy, I have the honor to state that . . . it is not possible to determine the moment when to notify your excellency . . . Nevertheless, I shall endeavor to keep your excellency posted as to the course of the battle.

. . .

GENERAL RUFUS SHAFTER TIPPED BACK his pith helmet and mopped the sweat from his eyes. From the back of the uncomplaining beast that had carried him to the top of El Pozo he surveyed the valley and the San Juan Heights. Lieutenant Colonel George McC. Derby reined alongside him and proffered the hand-drawn map. Derby, Shafter's chief engineering officer, was responsible for updating the Army's maps of the country around Santiago.

Shafter ran a stubby finger along the map as Derby pointed out the corresponding features of the distant terrain. The road to Santiago ran across the valley, through the thick forest, and over the grassy plain beyond. The San Juan Heights lay athwart the route. Lieutenant Miley handed the general his binoculars. Shafter could see the long yellow scars of the Spanish trenches running across the ridge.

It was just as he had thought. The situation demanded no complicated maneuvering. The Army would march down that road and make a frontal assault on the San Juan Heights. After they had been taken, the city, the bay, and the Spanish fleet would be his.

"There was no attempt at strategy," Shafter recalled,

> and no attempt at turning their flanks. It was simply [a matter of] going straight for them. If we had attempted to flank them out or dig them

out by regular parallels to get closer to them, my men would have been sick before it could have been accomplished, and the losses would have been many times greater than they were.

Shafter saw what General Chaffee had seen: that the two roads emerging from the woods offered perfect targets to the Spanish forces entrenched in the hills, but he also saw the specters of Lord Vernon and the two thousand British troops that had died on the road to Santiago in 1741, victims, not of Spanish bullets, but of the heat and tropical fever. A frontal attack might be costly, he realized, but a long siege could be costlier. And there was also the factor of the Spanish relief column of several thousand reinforcements on its way to Santiago. Time was becoming critical.

But there was one obstacle to an immediate advance toward San Juan. Shafter put his finger on a place on the map called El Caney. Derby pointed toward the hills far off to their right.

The village of El Caney lay nestled in the hills six miles northeast of the city of Santiago, and about two and a half miles due north of the spot where Shafter and his staff now stood. Reconnaissance parties had found it to be a strong defensive location with six wooden blockhouses and a stone fort called El Viso and had estimated that a small Spanish force was entrenched there. Troops could move back and forth rapidly between Santiago and El Caney over one of the better roads in the area.

Shafter saw that a force crossing the valley to attack the San Juan Heights would have El Caney on its right flank at first, and then at its rear. It was clear that the place must be taken before the main assault could begin. He and his staff rode down into the valley to examine the roads, then returned to his headquarters at La Redonda about a mile past El Pozo back along the road from Siboney. Around noon he met with his division and brigade commanders to plan the advance.

General Lawton and General Chaffee had just returned from a reconnaissance of the country around El Caney. Lawton estimated he could take the place in two or three hours. Wheeler, who had earlier reconnoitered the position and learned there were only five hundred Spanish troops there, had made a similar estimate and had urged Shafter to permit him to attack the place. At this moment, however, the rugged old ex-Confederate was lying in his tent sick with tropical fever. His attending surgeon advised Shafter not to let Wheeler know the attack was now imminent.

Shafter considered what he had been told. He had been thinking of an attack on El Caney to be followed, perhaps the next day, by a frontal assault on the San Juan Heights. But if Lawton and the others were right, if El Caney could be taken by a small force in two or three hours, then it might be possible to attack both positions at the same time. He detailed the plan.

Lawton would take one division of infantry and one light artillery battery and move up the road that branched off the Santiago road at El Pozo and ran north to El Caney. As the attack began on that point, a second artillery battery at El Pozo would commence bombarding the San Juan Heights across the valley, and the main force—the rest of the infantry under General Kent, and Wheeler's dismounted cavalry—would start to advance toward San Juan. By the time they had crossed the valley and gotten into place for the assault on the heights, Lawton would have taken El Caney and come down the road that linked that village with Santiago, arriving before San Juan in time to take part in the assault. At the same time this two-pronged attack was underway, one regiment of the Michigan reinforcements, still on the beach at Siboney, would advance along the coast and attack the Spanish outpost at Aguadores, providing a diversion and preventing the Spanish force there from marching inland and attacking the left flank of the main force.

There was much to be said for the plan. Attacking San Juan while the assault on El Caney was in progress would prevent the Spanish from rushing reinforcements to El Caney or attacking Lawton's left flank. But the main advantage of the plan was that it saved one day in the advance on Santiago, and a day could make all the difference. In the space of a single day the rains could come in full force, rendering the Army's movements all but impossible; a hurricane could blow in from the Atlantic and scatter the transports and the blockading fleet, cutting the Army off from its supplies; the dreaded yellow fever could break out among the troops; or the Spanish relief column could arrive from Manzanillo; and any one of those things would swing the military balance in favor of the Spanish.

It was agreed, then. The attack would commence early the next day, July 1. Shafter took out his watch. It was nearly three o'clock. There was time for the troops to get into place before dark—Lawton going up the road to El Caney to camp within sight of the Spanish positions, the rest of the main force to move up behind El Pozo, where Captain George Grimes's light artillery battery would be put in place. The officers filed out of Shafter's headquarters tent and stopped, open-mouthed. A great, glistening sphere hung in the sky overhead.

As LIEUTENANT COLONEL MAXFIELD SUPERVISED, four men of the Signal Corps balloon detachment hauled on the ropes depending from the car and brought the balloon slowly back to earth. Maxfield came forward and gave a helping hand to General Castillo as the Cuban climbed over the rim of the basket and dropped to the ground, while Lieutenant Volkmar smiled down from the craft. Castillo's legs may have trembled slightly as he took a few steps on firm ground, then stared up in wonder and admiration at the Yankees' marvelous flying machine.

The balloon train had arrived at La Redonda and Shafter's headquarters earlier in the day, but Maxfield had discovered new holes and rents, and it had taken some time to make repairs and then inflate the silken envelope. Maxfield and Sergeant Baldwin then ascended for a test flight, and when they were convinced the craft was airworthy, Castillo was invited to join Volkmar in an ascent over the Cuban countryside.

Lieutenant Colonel Derby, emerging from the meeting in the headquarters tent, was delighted to see the aircraft. The Army's maps of the country around Santiago were sketchy, reconnaissance had been limited, and there were many features of the terrain that remained mysterious. As General Castillo climbed down from the car, Derby told Maxfield that he wished to make an ascent.

The jungle dropped away beneath them as Maxfield leaned over the rim of the car and signaled to the crew of the balloon wagon, who slowly turned a large reel and paid out the rope that anchored the craft. Derby looked ahead eagerly as the obstructing hills fell away. He could see over the heights of El Pozo, a mile ahead, and down into the valley beyond. But most of the country in back of the San Juan Heights was still hidden. Derby wanted to see it; he asked Maxfield to take the craft higher.

The great reel on the wagon below was turned, paying out more rope, and the balloon climbed higher—five-hundred feet; seven-hundred feet; a thousand feet. Derby clutched the suspension ropes on his side of the car and beheld the astonishing panorama. Far to his left he could see the ocean and the gray ships of the American blockade standing in a long curve about the entrance to the harbor like the floats of a net. Straight ahead, beyond the San Juan Heights, open country dropped away toward the bay. The city of Santiago—rows and columns of red-tiled roofs—drowsed in the late afternoon sun. Beyond, the six ships of Cervera's squadron—the prey that had drawn the American expedition to this remote corner of Cuba—drifted at their moorings. And off to the right Derby could see the stone fort and blockhouses of El Caney.

Some four miles away, from the window of his room in the Reina Mercedes barracks on the eastern outskirts of Santiago, Naval Constructor Hobson saw the balloon and knew that an American attack was imminent.

Derby would have liked Maxfield to have the balloon moved forward to a closer vantage point, but the sun had dropped low in the sky behind Santiago, and much of the terrain was now hidden in the lengthening shadows. But tomorrow, when the battle was getting underway, he would make a second ascent. He looked over the rim of the car as the balloon crew far below began to reel in the anchor rope. He could see troops moving up along the Santiago road and dispatch riders galloping back and forth. Up through the strange stillness came the notes of a bugle.

·   ·   ·

"THE HEADQUARTERS CAMP was crowded," Richard Harding Davis remembered.

> After a week of inaction the army, at a moment's notice, was moving forward, and everyone had ridden in haste to learn why.
>
> There were *attaches*, in strange uniforms, self-important Cuban generals, officers from the flagship *New York*, and an army of photographers. At the side of the camp, double lines of soldiers passed slowly along the two paths of the muddy road, while, between them, aides dashed up and down, splashing them with dirty water, and shouting, "You will come up at once, sir." "You will not attempt to enter the trail yet, sir." "General Sumner's compliments, and why are you not in your place?"
>
> Twelve thousand men, with their eyes fixed on a balloon, and treading on each other's heels in three inches of mud, move slowly, and after three hours, it seemed as though every man in the United States

was under arms and stumbling and slipping down that trail. The lines passed until the moon rose. They seemed endless, interminable; there were cavalry mounted and dismounted, artillery with cracking whips and cursing drivers, Rough Riders in brown, and regulars, both black and white, in blue. Midnight came, and they were still slipping forward.

Roosevelt rode at the head of the regiment. General Young had been put out of action by an attack of tropical fever. Colonel Wood had been given command of Young's brigade.

"This left me in command of the regiment," Roosevelt recalled, "of which I was very glad, for such experience as we had had is a quick teacher."

The Rough Riders had struck camp at noon, then sat down to wait by the side of the road for the order to march. Roosevelt watched impatiently,

> while regiment after regiment passed by, varied by bands of tatterdemalion Cuban insurgents, and by mule trains with ammunition.
> At last, toward mid-afternoon, the First and Tenth Cavalry, ahead of us, marched, and we followed. . . . Every few minutes there would be a stoppage in front, and at the halt I would make the men sit or lie down beside the track, loosening their packs. The heat was intense as we passed through the still, close jungle, which formed a wall on either hand. Occasionally we came to gaps or open spaces, where some regiment was camped, and now and then one of these regiments, which apparently had been left out of its proper place, would file into the road, breaking up our line of march. . . . Once or twice we had to wade streams. Darkness came on, but we still continued to march. It was about eight o'clock when we turned to the left and climbed El Poso [sic] hill. . . . Here I found . . . Wood, who was arranging for the camping of the brigade.

The men dropped their gear where they stood and lay down. Roosevelt and Wood spread their raincoats on the ground.

> We did not talk much, for though we were in ignorance as to precisely what the day would bring forth, we knew that we should see fighting . . . and I suppose that, excepting among hardened veterans, there is always a certain feeling of uneasy excitement the night before the battle.

AROUND MIDNIGHT, Richard Harding Davis wrote a dispatch for the New York *Herald*.

> The attack on Santiago is to begin in a few hours—at four o'clock tomorrow morning. From this ridge we can see the lights of the city street lamps, shining across a sea of mist two miles wide and two miles long, which looks in the moonlight like a great lake in the basin of the hills. . . .
> In the bushes of the basin beneath us twelve-thousand men are sleeping, buried in a sea of mist, waiting for the day.

CHAPTER ELEVEN

WHEN
HEROES MEET

DAYBREAK.

CAPTAIN ARTHUR H. LEE of the British Army crept silently over the grassy ridge and looked down at the thatched and tiled roofs of El Caney. As British attaché he had come along with General Chaffee's brigade to observe the American attack. During the night the Second Division had advanced silently up the trail from El Pozo and gotten into position. Captain Allyn Capron's battery of four light artillery pieces was put in place on a knoll about a mile and a half to the southeast of the village. A brigade of Negro infantry under Colonel Evan Miles advanced across the El Caney–Santiago road and took up positions around the Ducoureaud House, a large deserted French plantation southwest of the village.* General Lawton's brigade made camp near Capron's battery, while Chaffee's force crept to a point within a mile southeast of El Caney.

"Our chief fear throughout the march," Captain Lee remembered, "was that the Spaniards at El Caney would learn of our advance and evacuate the place before we could surround and capture them."

Shortly before dawn, Chaffee's brigade advanced to a ridge a few hundred yards northeast of the village. Lee recalled looking down on the sleeping town:

> In the village . . . profound quiet reigned, and there was no sign of life beyond a few thin wisps of smoke that curled from the cottage chimneys. Beyond lay the fertile valley with a few cattle grazing, and around us on three sides arose, tier upon tier, the beautiful Maestra Mountains, wearing delicate pearly tints in the first rays of the rising sun. . . . Three

*Alger gives the name as "Ducrot."

miles away . . . loomed the long undulating ridge of San Juan, streaked with Spanish trenches, and behind it . . . the city of Santiago.

      .   .   .

LIEUTENANT MILEY RODE OUT of the headquarters camp at La Redonco and up the Santiago road toward El Pozo. A few minutes earlier he had reported to Shafter's tent, where he had found the general lying in bed, unable to rise. Shafter was not a victim of tropical fever; the corpulant sixty-three-year-old man had succumbed to the heat and an attack of gout. Unable to take the field, he had deputized Colonel Edward J. McClernand to go to the observation post atop El Pozo and act in his behalf. A field telephone line had been set up to put Shafter in contact with McClernand. Lieutenant Miley was to serve as Shafter's roving observer.

      .   .   .

IN THE ROUGH RIDERS CAMP at El Pozo, Roosevelt and Wood finished breakfast and went over to the hill to watch as teams of horses dragged the four light field guns of Captain Grimes's battery up the hill. Frederic Remington made some quick sketches of the straining animals and the swearing artillerymen. Six horses pulled each gun, and on the left horse of each pair sat an artilleryman wielding a whip. One of the teamsters was Private Tom Mix, a young rodeo rider from Pennsylvania. A crowd of newspapermen and foreign attachés gathered to watch as the crews put the guns in place. Standing nearby was thirty-seven-year-old Lieutenant John J. Pershing of the Tenth Cavalry, which was camped near El Pozo.* Pershing watched as the fieldpieces were lined up on the distant San Juan Heights, then he turned his gaze toward the target.

    "From the ridge of the hill . . . could be seen . . . the dark lines of masked intrenchments and the mysterious blockhouses of the hills of San Juan," he recalled. "To the left of the first hill, holding a horse, stood one lone Spanish sentinel."

      .   .   .

THREE FOURTHS OF A MILE behind the San Juan Heights, at the intersection of the Santiago road and the road running out to El Caney, stood the Spanish fort of Canosa, and here General Arsenio Linares established his headquarters for the defense of Santiago. As daylight brightened the eastern sky, Linares reviewed his situation.

    There was a total of 10,429 troops available to him at Santiago, but he had established a very long defense perimeter beginning at the village of Dos Caminos, a mile northwest of the city, running eastward through El Sueñc to the San Juan Heights, continuing south along the heights, and finally stretching back several miles to Las Cruces, a point on the bay a mile south of Santiago. Food and water were the reasons why Linares had stretched his forces out over so long a line; there was already famine in the city, and he did not want to be cut off

---

    *The Tenth Cavalry was one of the Army's Negro regiments. Like all such units, the Tenth was made up of black troops but led exclusively by white officers. Pershing's admiration for his men had earned him the nickname "Black Jack" among his white comrades.

from the surrounding farmlands or the aquaduct that supplied water to Santiago. So as July dawned, the two objectives the Americans planned to attack that day were lightly defended.

At El Caney, surrounded at this moment by 5,400 American troops, there were 520 men under General Joaquín Vara del Rey. And on the San Juan Heights, directly in the path of the remaining 10,000 men of Shafter's Fifth Corps, stood 521 Spanish soldiers and two pieces of light artillery.

.   .   .

FOR SEVERAL MILES in back of El Pozo the road to Santiago was filling with lines of marching men. The Gallant Seventy-first, up before dawn, had drawn five days' rations. A rumor ran down the line that the regiment was to march to Havana.

"We were going to march through Cuba to the sea, like Sherman," Private Post recalled. "That sounded rather good—we translated it in terms of sugar cane and cigars."

The regiment formed up and filed out of camp, flowing into the great river of men that was moving west.

6:30 A.M.

A STEEP, CONICAL HILL rose one hundred feet above the southeast corner of the village of El Caney, and on its crest stood a stone fort with the red and gold flag of Spain flying above it. A rifle trench had been dug along its south and east sides. Five wooden blockhouses stood at other points around the village, amid more trenches and barbed wire. From the cover of the tall grass on a ridge a few hundred yards to the west, Captain Lee could see the Spanish soldiers lounging outside the fort "in their light blue pajama uniforms and white straw slouch hats."

> If they were aware of our presence they seemed remarkably indifferent to it, though they watched with apparent interest the movements of Capron's battery, which now showed black in a small green clearing a mile or more to our left.
>
> On the left of the artillery on the south side of the village the remainder of Lawton's division was coming into line, Ludlow's Brigade in front, with [Colonel Evan] Miles's in reserve to guard against any interference from Santiago.
>
> At 6:35 the intense peacefulness of the scene was broken by a white puff from Capron's battery, and before the report reached our ears the Spaniards outside the fort had vanished with the rapidity of prairie dogs. Simultaneously appeared a fresh row of hats that sprouted from the ground like mushrooms and marked the position of the deep rifle-pits and trenches on the glacis of the fort and at various points around the village.
>
> For the next quarter of an hour our battery kept up a leisurely fire upon the stone fort, eliciting no reply, and so little disturbing the white hats that someone suggested they were dummies.

In his cell at the Reina Mercedes barracks, Hobson heard the sound of artillery and jumped to the window. He was surprised to see that the shells were landing far to the northeast of Santiago, near the El Caney blockhouses.

Capron's battery was trying to find the range, but four light guns firing at 2,400 yards could not lay down the heavy concentrated fire needed to dislodge the Spanish from their fortifications.

"Consequently," Lee explained,

> the infantry had to do all the fighting, and the brunt of it fell upon the men of Chaffee's Brigade. Their skirmish line pressed forward, and soon the sharp crackle of musketry was busy along both lines. . . .
> For the next three hours the fight was a continuous infantry duel at about six hundred yards' range.

THE GALLANT SEVENTY FIRST heard the sound of Capron's battery as it marched along the Santiago road three miles to the southeast.

"For the first time it dawned on us that there might be fighting ahead," Private Post recalled.

Beside the road a tall figure in a black business suit sat astride a horse and watched the procession from the shadow of a large straw hat. One of the New Yorkers recognized him.

"Hey, Willie!" he called. The others took up the cry.

"Hey, Willie!" they chorused. William Randolph Hearst looked on impassively and did not reply.

"If he thought we were jeering he was wrong," Post explained. "We were just glad to see someone from home."

Journal correspondent James Creelman rode up.

"Hello, Jimmy!" everyone cried. Journalists were celebrities. He waved and smiled.

"Boys, you're going into battle," he announced. "Good luck!"

Hearst unbent a bit and spoke to the marching men.

"Good luck!" he called stiffly. "Boys, good luck be with you."

The road now sloped downward. Post looked over the heads of those marching in front and saw the battle flags of the Gallant Seventy-first unfurled, floating in the morning breeze. The distant sound of artillery continued.

"Now we knew."

7 A.M.

A FORCE OF FOUR THOUSAND Cuban insurgents under General García arrived at the abandoned Spanish blockhouse at Marianage, a hill about a mile north of El Pozo. García sent two companies to the El Caney–Santiago road, a mile further to the northwest, to occupy the stone bridge over the San Juan River. Pickets were placed at Santa Cruz, a quarter-mile nearer Santiago, and at the Ducoureaud plantation, which commanded the road south from the Spanish outpost at San

Miguel. According to Shafter's plan of attack, García's men were to interdict any Spanish reinforcements sent from Santiago to El Caney.

·   ·   ·

GENERAL JACOB F. KENT, commander of the First Infantry Division, arrived at Grimes's battery on El Pozo. Lieutenant Colonel McClernand, Shafter's deputy, pointed to a green hill across the valley. The First Infantry was to deploy between the leftmost end of that hill and the main road. Kent consulted his map and saw that the place was called San Juan Hill.

8 A.M.

THERE WAS A MOOD of impatient expectancy among the artillerymen and onlookers on El Pozo. Grimes's battery had been in place for an hour, its four guns ready to fire at the San Juan Heights. McClernand looked at his watch. It was nearly ninety minutes since the sound of Capron's battery had signaled the opening of the attack on El Caney. Lawton had said he could take the place in two hours. McClernand guessed he must nearly have done so by now. It was time for the main advance to begin. He told Captain Grimes to open fire.

Grimes chased the crowd of curious newspapermen and attachés away from the battery.

"Number one, ready! Fire!"

The light fieldpiece bucked backward as the shell soared across the valley. Dozens of binoculars were raised and leveled toward the San Juan Heights, but the thick curtain of smoke that had belched out of the gun barrel blocked the view to the west. Among those straining to see the effect of the shot was Lieutenant Colonel John Jacob Astor, a member of General Shafter's staff (Wheeler remarked wonderingly that "a man said to be worth some hundred million dollars" would take up soldiering).

The smoke cleared. Grimes could see the dust settling on the San Juan Heights beyond the target, a Spanish blockhouse. The shot had been too long; Grimes ordered the range shortened by 150 yards.

"Number two, ready! Fire!"

The second gun leaped and filled the air at El Pozo with a new cloud. A few hundred yards away on the Santiago road Private Post heard the roar and saw the gun smoke rising above the palm trees. Then, another blast. And another. And one more. And then a ragged cheer.

Newspaper artist Howard Chandler Christy sat in the branches of a tree behind Grimes's battery and tried to sketch the scene. When he heard the cheering he looked up from his pad and saw that "a shell went through the roof [of the Spanish blockhouse] and exploded, covering itself in a reddish smoke and throwing pieces of tile and cement into the air."

The firing continued. The sweating artillerymen manhandled the guns, tore open smoking breeches and rammed shell and powder in place. *Ready! Fire!* The lanyards were yanked, the guns danced. El Pozo was wreathed in a nimbus of gunsmoke. The attachés discoursed professionally. The correspondents scribbled eagerly. Shutters snapped. Swift pencil strokes limned the scene on sketch pads. It was a bit like a field day.

The Swedish military attaché gestured toward the erupting hills across the valley.

"I should think they would tire of receiving these," he said, meaning the American shells. "Have they, then, no artillery?"

Colonel Wood was thinking the same thing. He turned to Roosevelt and said he wished the brigade hadn't been stationed so close to Grimes s battery. There would be hell to pay if the Spanish returned the fire.

"Hardly had he spoken when there was a peculiar whistling, singing sound in the air, and immediately afterward the noise of something exploding over our heads," Roosevelt recalled. They jumped to their horses as a second shell exploded overhead. A piece of shrapnel hit Roosevelt on the wrist, "raising a bump about as big as a hickory nut." The Rough Riders quickly left the crest of El Pozo and took shelter on the far side of the hill.

As Christy scrambled down from his tree he saw a shell land in one of the abandoned buildings nearby and remembered he had seen some Cuban troops inside. He recalled:

> Instantly another shell came, which burst in front of the building and in the ranks of the troops gathered there. Several men were wounded; one poor fellow had his leg torn off. Another shell penetrated the roof and exploded inside, where several Cubans were hiding. They were literally blown through the windows and door. One shell tore up the ground in front of gun No. 1, and others exploded just back of the building, killing men who were already badly wounded.

"Get out of this hell spot!" General Samuel Sumner roared unnecessarily. Henry L. Stoddard of the New York *Mail and Express* and Lieutenant Colonel Astor ran down toward the Santiago road. Most of the other onlookers, their curiosity gone, stampeded down the far side of the hill. An hysterical reporter clutched the elbow of Richard Harding Davis.

"Isn't this awful?" he cried.

Davis nodded. "Very disturbing; very disturbing."

Lieutenant Colonel Maxfield rode his horse through the rain of shrapnel. His serenity was intact; the bombardment was not nearly as distressing as that moment a few hours earlier when dawn revealed that the winds of a midnight thunderstorm had made new holes in the balloon, partially deflating it. He had quickly rallied his men around the glue and patches, healed the wounded thing, and emptied the last of the precious tubes of gas into it. Now, triumphant and unconcerned with the Spanish artillery, he had come up El Pozo in search of Lieutenant Colonel Derby.

Abruptly Maxfield was pitched to the ground. His horse lay dead, killed by a piece of shrapnel. He got up, dusted himself off, and resumed his search for Derby.

Grimes's gunners were returning the fire, and a full-scale artillery duel was in progress. Spanish appreciation of the virtues of smokeless powder again worked to American disadvantage. Captain Grimes couldn't find where the Spanish guns were positioned, while the smoke from his old-fashioned black powder marked his own position clearly to the artillery on the San Juan Heights.

Down on the Santiago road Private Post heard the loud *plop* of a Spanish shell and knew he was under fire. A pair of Cubans came down from El Pozo carrying a wounded comrade in a hammock. The man had been hit in the groin by a shell fragment and was groaning. A trail of blood marked the procession's passage.

"I felt a tenseness in my throat," he remembered, "a dryness that was not thirst, and little chilly surges in my stomach."

Farther back along the road the Cubans passed Stephen Crane, who was hurrying toward the sound of the guns.

General Wheeler also heard the artillery. It was his first clue that an attack was underway. He rose up in his cot, summoned an orderly, and demanded to know what was going on. When he was told he got to his feet, pulled on his pants, and called for his horse.

General Sumner had been given command of Wheeler's volunteer cavalry. At this moment he was receiving his orders from one of Shafter's aides. He was to take his division down the Santiago road and halt at the edge of the woods.

"What am I to do then?"

"You are to await further orders."

The same word had been given to the infantry. General Hawkins's brigade was moving ahead. The lines of men advanced across the valley under cover of the dense forest, but the forest ended at the bank of the San Juan River.

And what to do then? Wait. Wait for further orders. Wait for General Lawton to finish taking El Caney.

.   .   .

GRIMES'S BATTERY CEASED FIRING, temporarily silenced by the heavy and accurate Spanish response. Deprived of their target, the Spanish gunners ceased firing as well. A sudden silence descended over El Pozo and the valley, but through it came the distant sound of heavy rifle fire from El Caney. Lieutenant Colonel McClernand was surprised. He looked at his watch. It was more than two hours since Capron's battery had opened fire. The capture of El Caney seemed to be taking longer than General Lawton had predicted.

.   .   .

"THROUGHOUT THE MORNING the fire of Capron's battery was kept up," Captain Lee recalled,

> but in such deliberate fashion, five and ten minutes elapsing between successive rounds, that it was little material assistance to the infantry

attack. Meanwhile Ludlow's brigade was closing in on the south and west sides of the village, and his two regular elements (Eighth and Twenty-second Infantry) were hotly engaged with the enemy's riflemen in the block-houses and behind the loop-holed walls.

Lawton's men were creeping forward through the tall grass and bushes, covering their advance with a hail of rifle fire. But the firing had little effect. "There was little target visible," Lee explained, "but the Spanish sharpshooters concealed in the trees, cottages, and block-houses were replying with deadly effect. They knew every range perfectly and picked off our men with distressing accuracy if they showed as much as a head."

It was now obvious to Lawton that he had seriously underestimated the time needed to take El Caney.

9 A.M.

FROM THE BRIDGE of the *New York*, Admiral Sampson watched the line of troops of the Thirty-third Michigan advance along the railroad tracks toward Fort Aguadores. The planned feint against the Spanish force there was also running behind schedule. At 9:20 came the wig-wag signal from shore indicating that the American force was in place. The *New York*, the *Gloucester*, and the *Suwanee* opened fire on the Spanish fort. The handful of Spaniards Sampson had seen before now ran for cover. The bombardment continued for several minutes, then the *New York* hoisted the signal to cease firing. Lieutenant Victor Blue of the *Suwanee* was given permission to fire three more shots to try to knock the Spanish flag off the fort. The third round from the four-inch gun, over a range of thirteen hundred yards, did the job.

The 2,500 Americans advanced toward the fort. When they reached the Aguadores River they discovered that the Spanish had blown up the bridge across it. The troops took positions and began to exchange some desultory firing with the enemy.

      .   .   .

A THOUSAND FEET above the Santiago road Lieutenant Colonel Maxfield gazed serenely toward the distant horizon while Lieutenant Colonel Derby scribbled a dispatch for General Shafter:

> Balloon over river bed to right of road 500 yards from El Posc [sic].
> Capron's battery in position to right of Caney, firing single shots at intervals of several minutes. Active skirmish fire south of Caney. Cannot distinguish troops. Large force of Cubans at Marianage and along road to west and south.
> Troops moving to front from south of El Pozo—also on main road from headquarters towards Santiago. Latter road is blocked with troops at its junction with road from El Poso[sic]. Grimes's battery has not fired since 9 o'clock; nor has the Spanish battery in its front, which

opened fire with shrapnel at 8:30. Cannot make out location of the battery, which had ceased firing before balloon went up.

Only few Spaniards visible at block-house beyond San Juan River. This block-house is south of main road to Santiago. There are also trenches north of road and a short piece between block-house and the road. Country beyond San Juan is open; also field half-mile wide a quarter of mile north of road and west of Marianage.

No troops marching on main road from Santiago to San Juan.

Head of our column halted in main road within 400 yards of San Juan River. Woods on both sides of road, not very dense to right, where there is a skirmish line deployed.

He weighted the message, leaned over the car, and watched it flutter to earth. A dispatch rider waiting below recovered it and set out for the field telephone to relay it to General Shafter's headquarters.

Maxfield beamed as Derby expressed his complete satisfaction with the Signal Corps's aircraft. Of some 26,000 American and Spanish troops taking part in the battle of Santiago, none had a clearer picture than he of the total state of things at this moment, 9:30 A.M., and in a very few minutes General Shafter would share that knowledge.

Maxfield knew the pleasure of a man whose extraordinary efforts are appreciated.

How long would it take, asked Derby, to move the balloon forward to the San Juan River?

Maxfield was startled by the question. He knew that the Spanish riflemen on the heights a mile and a half away were armed with Mausers having an effective range of two miles. The balloon was already a tempting target, dangling high over El Pozo. It must be said that Lieutenant Colonel Maxfield had no great concern with his own personal safety, but the welfare of the great glistening sphere above his head was another matter. He told Derby that in his professional opinion the balloon should be brought no closer to the front.

Derby dismissed the objection. If the balloon had proved so valuable a full mile and a half from the front, how much more valuable might it be when the intervening distance was shortened to a half-mile? His appetite for knowledge of the Spanish defenses had only been whetted. Fly on, he insisted.

A pretty problem was posed. A pair of lieutenant colonels dangled one-fifth of a mile above the nearest superior officer and found that they shared a difference of opinion. But Maxfield finally reflected that his passenger represented the major general commanding the Fifth Corps and saw that he must defer. He cast an anxious, loving glance at the silken envelope overhead, then signaled to the crew below.

The balloon was slowly hauled down to tree-top level, then four of Maxfield's men shouldered the guide ropes and joined the flow of troops marching down the Santiago road.

From the heights of El Pozo Stephen Crane watched the "huge, fat, yellow, quivering" thing floating above the road. Had he lived in another time he might have written something about Broadway on Thanksgiving Day.

. . .

LIEUTENANT MILEY URGED his horse ahead as fast as possible along the congested Santiago road. A line of mounted orderlies followed. They were to be the last links in the chain of command linking General Shafter with the front. Orders were to be transmitted by field telephone from Shafter's headquarters to Lieutenant Colonel McClernand at El Pozo, then sent forward by courier to Miley at the front, who would in turn pass them on to the division and brigade commanders. It was a cumbersome arrangement, but with Shafter prostrated by the heat at his headquarters more than two miles to the rear, it was the best that could be improvised.

Near El Pozo Miley passed the Signal Corps team dragging Maxfield's balloon forward. Overhead the observation car was swinging pendulumlike above the trees, while an eager Derby and a dubious Maxfield watched the San Juan Heights grow larger.

A little farther on Miley passed Lieutenant Colonel Astor. One of the richest men in the world was afoot; his orderly had disappeared with his horse in the bloody confusion of the bombardment on El Pozo.

Farther along the road was almost blocked by four Gatling guns, each drawn by a pair of mules. The Gatling consisted of six .30-caliber rifle barrels in a rotating cylindrical mount. As the gunner turned a crank the cylinder rotated; each barrel fired in turn, ejected the spent cartridge, and was automatically reloaded. The whole affair was mounted on a swivel atop a light artillery caisson. Despite the fact that the gun could spray fifteen rounds a second—nine hundred in a minute—it had been assigned little importance by the Army since its introduction at the end of the Civil War. That any Gatling guns at all had been brought to Santiago was due to the persistence and resourcefulness of Lieutenant John H. Parker, a young officer just six years out of West Point, possessed of a fanatical single-mindedness equal to that of Lieutenant Colonel Maxfield. Parker now rode at the head of the Gatling detachment as Miley and the mounted orderlies went past.

Beyond the Gatlings Miley found the Rough Riders trudging forward, Roosevelt riding at their head. The Gallant Seventy-first, along with the rest of the infantry, had been halted in the road to let the cavalry pass. This worsened the congestion.

"The trail," Richard Harding Davis recalled,

> was as wide as its narrowest part, which was some ten feet across. At places it was as wide as Broadway, but only for such short distances that it was necessary for the men to advance in column, in double file. A maze of underbrush and trees on either side was all but impenetrable, and when the officers and men had once assembled into the basin, they could only guess as to what lay before them, or on either flank

The jungle hid the advancing men from view, but the Spanish riflemen on the heights knew where the trail was and began a random fire.

"Overhead the clicking and buzzing noises had become more definite," Private Post remembered. "The Spaniards were firing blindly through the jungle and going high. . . . The first high bullets had been a thrill. Now the bullets were proof that someone was trying to kill us, each one of us individually, and in a highly impersonal way."

Miley passed Colonel Wood and the rest of the cavalry brigade and came to the place where the Santiago road forded the San Juan River.* There, as ordered, General Sumner was halted, awaiting further orders.

One brigade of regular cavalry had already crossed the river and taken cover in the thinning forest beyond. Beyond them was an open glade of waist-high grass and rising above that were the San Juan Heights, some nine hundred yards away. Miley could see the Spanish trenches. It suddenly occurred to him that if the rapid-fire cannon had been removed from Cervera's ships and mounted on the heights, it would be possible for the Spanish to start lobbing shells down the length of the jammed Santiago road. The possibility seems not to have occurred to General Shafter or any of his commanders before this moment. But not to be outblundered by the Americans, the Spanish had ordered Cervera to stand ready to make a run out of the harbor, thus forcing him to keep the guns aboard.

Miley sent a dispatch back to headquarters suggesting that Grimes's battery resume firing to cover the advance onto the grassy plain.

10 A.M.

AT EL CANEY Chaffee's infantrymen continued to inch forward through the tall grass beneath a hail of Mauser bullets. Their advance was blocked by a barbed wire fence running parallel to the Spanish trenches. Private James W. Smith and Private James L. McMillen crawled forward.

"Two men of the Twelfth Infantry crept forward alone," Captain Lee recalled,

> armed only with pliers, and skilfully taking advantage of the cover afforded by a few bushes and folds in the ground passed along the whole east front of the village, within two hundred yards of the enemy's trenches, cutting the barbed-wire fencing which would have impeded our assault. Both of these gallant fellows returned in safety after completing their work with great deliberation and thoroughness.

While the Twelfth Infantry inched forward toward the trenches along the east of the village, the Seventh and Seventeenth deployed along a ridge to the northeast. The Seventeenth was driven back by withering Spanish fire. The Seventh was pinned down by a cross-fire from the village and several of the

*I have joined with most of the contemporary writers in referring to this stream as the San Juan River, although a glance at the map will reveal that it was actually the Aguadores River, a branch that flowed into the San Juan six hundred yards to the south of the road. Six hundred yards to the west of this ford, the Santiago road crossed the San Juan River at a second ford.

blockhouses. The battle was entering its fifth hour, and the Spanish showed no sign of loosening their hold on El Caney.

. . .

FROM HIS WINDOW in the Reina Mercedes barracks, Naval Constructor Hobson could see Spanish troops pouring out of Santiago and eastward along the road toward the San Juan Heights. General José Toral had assembled a group of some twenty officers for a conference in the courtyard beneath Hobson's window. Abruptly Toral broke off and pointed to the east. Hobson followed his gaze and saw Maxfield's balloon hanging in the sky.

"The officers seemed to have misgivings as to the balloon," he recalled, "and drew over to some buildings about a hundred yards away, where they were screened from its view."

. . .

FROM EL POZO Stephen Crane watched the progress of the balloon along the Santiago road and also a lone figure walking on the San Juan Heights.

In truth, there was a man in a Panama hat strolling to and fro behind one of the Spanish trenches, gesticulating at times with a walking-stick. A man in a Panama hat, walking with a stick! That was the strangest sight of my life—that symbol, that quaint figure of Mars. The battle, the thunderous row, was his possession. He was the master. He mystified us all with his infernal Panama hat and his wretched walking-stick. From near his feet came volleys and from near his side came roaring shells, but he stood there alone, visible, the one tangible thing. . . . But there was one other figure which arose to symbolic dignity. The balloon of our signal corps had swung over the tops of the jungle trees toward the Spanish trenches. Whereat the balloon and the man in the Panama hat with a walking-stick—whereat these two waged tremendous battle.

A balloon, a Panama hat, a walking stick. Badges of courage. Emblems of folly. Symbols of war.

. . .

"A CAPTIVE BALLOON was up in the air at this moment," Roosevelt fumed, "but it was worse than useless."

"Before and above us went a balloon," Chaplain Van Dewater marveled. "What purpose it served . . . nobody has ever discovered."

"A four-man ground crew held its trail rope and kept the balloon under control," Private Post remembered.

Signal Corps men followed with coils of the rope, which they paid out or took in according to the directions from the basket of the balloon above. Two heads peered over the rim of the basket and occasionally a little note would flutter down, to be rescued and brought to General

Kent. . . . The trail rope led directly down into the . . . road; it was a beautiful range marker for the Spanish artillery and infantry, and they promptly used it as such.

"It came blundering down the trail, and stopped the advance of the First and Tenth Cavalry," stormed Richard Harding Davis.

A Spaniard might question if he could hit a man, or a number of men, hidden in the bushes, but had no doubt at all as to his ability to hit a mammoth glistening ball only six hundred yards distant, and so all the trenches fired at it at once, and the men of the First and Tenth, packed together directly behind it, received the full force of the bullets. The men lying directly below it received the shrapnel which was timed to hit it.

The balloon was now above the ford at the San Juan River. Lieutenant Colonel Derby wished to ascend; an altitude of one thousand feet would afford him the desired view of the Spanish positions, as well as diverting the Spanish fire from the men in the road below and making the balloon itself a more difficult target. A fainter heart might have wished the ground crew to tow the craft back to the rear as fast as possible. And a prudent man such as Lieutenant Colonel Maxfield would have wished the balloon be brought to earth immediately so that it could promptly be deflated.

Unfortunately, none of these options was available at the moment. The guide ropes had become tangled in the tree tops. The balloon and its two unhappy passengers were condemned to dangle fifty feet above the jungle while every Spanish gun on the San Juan Heights was turned on the novel target.

·   ·   ·

"REMAINING THERE under this galling fire of exploding shrapnel and deadly mauser volleys the minutes seemed like hours," Black Jack Pershing remembered. At the ford, directly beneath the balloon, Pershing was riding back and forth amid the hail of fire, trying desperately to get his men across the river and into a safer position. Then he saw General Wheeler sitting astride his horse in the midst of the river, calmly observing the action. Pershing rode up to him, saluted, and began to speak. At that instant a Spanish shell landed in the stream, drenching both of them.

Wheeler returned the salute and raised an eyebrow.

"The shelling seems quite lively," he said.

11 A.M.

THE ROUGH RIDERS had reached the San Juan River. Roosevelt was ordered to take the regiment across, march half a mile or so to the right, and await further orders. He had been watching the approach of the balloon and its trail of devastation with fascinated horror, and as it became apparent that the craft's destination was to be the ford, he hurried the regiment across.

The regular cavalry brigade that had crossed earlier had taken cover behind the bushes and trees at the edge of the jungle and was now exchanging fire with the Spanish. Roosevelt led his men slowly to the right through the high grass and eventually came to a sunken lane. He led the regiment into the shelter of its bank. The Rough Riders now formed the rightmost end of an American line stretching northward from the Santiago road and facing the San Juan Heights. He could see some large ranch buildings atop the hill immediately ahead of them and slightly to the right, a place he would later know as Kettle Hill.

"The fight was now on in good earnest," he recalled, "and the Spaniards on the hills were engaged in heavy volley firing. The Mauser bullets drove in sheets through the trees and the tall jungle grass, making a peculiar whirring or rustling sound."

The Rough Riders kept under cover and awaited further orders.

.   .   .

LIEUTENANT COLONEL MAXFIELD CLIMBED out of the observation car and gazed dolefully at the shriveling, hissing yellow envelope. Oblivious to the Mauser bullets that whirred and rustled through the surrounding trees, he made a circuit of the collapsing silken ball and counted the wounds. Eighteen holes were visible. Of course it could be patched, but the last of the precious hydrogen gas was bleeding into the air. Folly had triumphed over ingenuity and resourcefulness. For Maxfield's balloon, the Spanish War was over.

Lieutenant Colonel Derby made his way through the underbrush and found the Santiago road. The fortune of fools continued to favor him; having escaped the Spanish bullets he had invited, he now was spared the American bullets he deserved. Those with the best reason for shooting him lay dead or wounded along the road. Derby pressed along the crowded road to the ford in search of General Kent.

"Lieut.-Colonel Derby . . . met me about this time," Kent reported,

> and informed me that a trail or narrow way had been discovered from the balloon, a short distance back, leading to the left of a ford lower down the stream. I hastened to the forks made by this road, and soon after the 71st New York Regiment of Hawkins' Brigade came up. I turned them into the by-path indicated by Lieut.-Col. Derby.

"This was a most opportune discovery," Lieutenant Miley recalled, "as the main road was congested with troops, and the fire so heavy as to tend to demoralize the men."*

Kent stood in the Santiago road and waved the troops of the Gallant

---

*Apologists for Derby point to the discovery of this trail as justification for his actions, while critics point out that an adequate reconnaissance of the ground before the battle would have turned up the same information at a much lower cost. However, the trail in question seems to have been one of the two trails mentioned by General Chaffee five days before the battle (Davis, *Campaigns*, p. 181); in which case the fault lay with communications rather than reconnaissance.

Seventy-first into the trail as they came up from the rear. *Come on! Move it! Get the lead out!*

"The jungle trail into which we had been ordered was as narrow as a cowpath," Private Post recalled.

> On either side the undergrowth was laced together by vines and branches. The first battalion broke from a column of fours to a column of twos, and then into a column of files; and this slowed up the following companies. Outside, at the entrance to the trail, General Kent was wondering at the delay! . . . We were aware of a coolness and a shadowy dimness freckled with sunshine. Yet this did not lessen the sense of those thin seething sounds that streaked through the jungle. We walked through a light shower of snipped-off twigs and leaves fluttering in lazy spirals to the ground. One instant your eye lighted on a twig and suddenly it was gone. It seemed that if one stuck out his hand the fingers would be clipped off. We huddled within ourselves and bent over to shield our bellies. Overhead a shell burst . . . That shell got twelve men.

What happened then is known but to God.

"Under the galling fire of the enemy the leading battalion . . . was thrown into confusion and recoiled in disorder on the troops in the rear," Kent reported.

> At this critical moment the officers of my staff practically formed a cordon behind the panic-stricken men, and urged them to again go forward. I finally ordered them to lie down in the thicket and clear the way for others of their own regiment, who were coming up behind.

"If any of General Kent's staff made a cordon back of the regiment, in order to force them into action," Henry L. Stoddard wrote, "no one among the dozen or more with whom I stood saw or spoke of such action."

"The regiment did not run away," Richard Harding Davis wrote, "but it certainly did not behave well. The fault was entirely that of some of the officers. They funked the fight and . . . refused to leave the bushes, and as a result the men . . . funked it too."

"The Seventy-first Regiment *obeyed its orders* and was *obeying orders when it halted*," insisted Chaplain Van Dewater.

"There was no panic," wrote Private Post.

The Gallant Seventy-first was strung out along the length of the trail. The lead battalion had reached the river, where it met a withering fire and halted. Back on the Santiago road Kent and his staff continued to jam newcomers into the narrow trail. Post was somewhere in between.

"Just ahead of me a man stumbled and dropped, dead. We stepped over him. The man beside me lurched a little and sank down: 'Je-e-sus!' he grunted. Four bullets had caught him between knee and thigh."

Post stumbled forward past dead and wounded. The body of a young lieutenant lay in the path.

"His glazed eyes were staring at the trees overhead, and ants were already crawling over his eyeballs." A regular army major stood over the body, plucking the sleeves of the men as they pushed past, sobbing and shouting hysterically.

"Cover him up! He's an officer! Cover him up, goddammit!"

"Cover him up yourself, you sonofabitch!" someone answered.

"Over four hundred men were killed or wounded in that trail," Post recalled, "in an area that was, perhaps, a city block in length—some eight hundred feet —in a path not as wide as a city sidewalk."

NOON

A BRIGADE OF INFANTRY pressed past the halted Seventy-first on the narrow trail, forded the San Juan River, and deployed to the left. At 12:10 its commander, Colonel C. A. Wikoff, was killed. Lieutenant Colonel Worth took command and was wounded at 12:15. Lieutenant Colonel Liscum took command and was wounded at 12:20. Lieutenant Colonel Ewers took command and led the men into position along the American line, which now stretched half a mile on either side of the Santiago road and faced the San Juan Heights.

.   .   .

"FOR A TIME it seemed as though every second man was either killed or wounded," Richard Harding Davis recalled. Spanish snipers hidden in the trees along the river and the road added to the fire from the San Juan Heights. Davis remembered that the snipers were especially demoralizing.

> There was no hiding from them. Their bullets came from every side. Their invisible smoke helped to keep their hiding places secret, and in the incessant shriek of shrapnel and the spit of the Mausers, it was difficult to locate the reports of their rifles. They spared neither wounded nor recognized the Red Cross; they killed the surgeons and the stewards carrying the litters, and killed the wounded men on the litters.

"I think that the bulk of the Spanish fire was practically unaimed," Roosevelt recalled, "but they swept the whole field of battle up to the edge of the river, and man after man in our ranks fell dead or wounded, although I had the troopers scattered out far apart, taking advantage of every scrap of cover."

But Captain William O. "Bucky" O'Neill was strolling up and down in front of his men, puffing on a cigarette. The Irish-born ex-mayor of Prescott, Arizona, was an authentic Wild West character—a gambler, miner, and county sheriff. Roosevelt said O'Neill had a theory that an officer ought never to take cover, that daring enemy fire served to encourage the men. But O'Neill's men were now begging him to get down.

"A bullet is sure to hit you," cried a sergeant.

"Sergeant, the Spanish bullet isn't made that will kill me," he answered, and resumed his strolling and smoking.

"As he turned on his heel a bullet struck him in the mouth and came out at the back of his head," Roosevelt remembered, "so that even before he fell his wild and gallant soul had gone out into the darkness."

He was gone, but as Roosevelt looked down on the dead man he could hear O'Neill's voice echoing inside his head.

Colonel, isn't it Whitman who says of the vultures that "they pluck the eyes of princes and tear the flesh of kings?"

Roosevelt covered the dead man.

Here's to every friend . . .

1 P.M.

BEHIND THE RIDGE northeast of El Caney, Captain Lee crawled over to the shelter of a sunken road, where he found more than a hundred men lying prone.

"Are those your reserves?" he asked an officer.

"No, sir, by God, they are casualties."

Lee took a closer look and saw that many of the supine figures were corpses. "A sudden lull in the battle brought into sickening prominence the angry buzzing of the disturbed flies and the creaking of the land crabs, which waited in the bushes."

At exactly one o'clock a shell from Capron's battery hit the flagpole atop the stone fort, knocking the Spanish flag halfway down the hill. A cheer went up from the American lines. The lucky hit was good for morale, but it in no way changed the military situation. The American advance was all but halted by the heavy rifle fire from the trenches and the blockhouses. The battle that was to have been won by ten o'clock was now in its seventh hour.

. . .

FROM EL POZO Lieutenant Colonel McClernand swung his binoculars back and forth between the two battlefields, straining to see Lawton's progress at El Caney and Kent's situation at the San Juan River. Occasionally a mounted orderly rode up with a report from the front, but the most eloquent account of what was happening could be seen at the bottom of the hill, where increasing numbers of wounded were being brought back to the field hospital set up there.

A mile further back, at the headquarters camp, General Shafter put down the field telephone, struggled to his feet, and walked out unsteadily to a vantage point near his tent, from which he could see the distant line of hills. There was little evidence of the battle, but for the sound of distant rifle fire and an occasional puff of smoke from Capron's battery. But he knew the situation had become very unfavorable. Two-thirds of his force was engaged in a costly wait at an untenable position beneath the San Juan Heights, while Lawton struggled to root the Spanish defenders out of El Caney.

·   ·   ·

"THE SITUATION WAS desperate," Richard Harding Davis wrote. "Our troops could not retreat, as the trail for two miles behind them was wedged with men. They could not remain where they were for they were being shot to pieces. There was only one thing they could do—go forward and take the San Juan hills by assault."

"I sent messenger after messenger to try to find General Sumner or [Colonel] Wood to get permission to advance," Roosevelt recalled. Back at the Santiago road the generals and colonels were turning to Lieutenant Miley for orders, and Miley was waiting for a mounted orderly to come forward from El Pozo with some word from Shafter. But no rider appeared on the tightly packed, bullet-swept road. It gradually dawned on Miley that someone on the scene was going to have to take the initiative, and as Shafter's spokesman, the onus seemed to have fallen on him.

Lieutenant Miley took a deep breath, swallowed hard, and turned to the expectant gathering of colonels, brigadiers, and major generals.

"The heights must be taken at all hazards," he said. "A retreat now would be a disastrous defeat."

Lieutenant Miley ordered the attack.

·   ·   ·

"I . . . WAS JUST ABOUT making up my mind that in the absence of orders I had better 'march toward the guns,'" Roosevelt recalled, "when Lieutenant Colonel Dorst came riding up through the storm of bullets with the welcome command 'to move forward and support the regulars in the assault on the hills in front.'"

The hill almost directly in front of the Rough Riders was Kettle Hill. The first brigade of the regular cavalry was deployed along it a hundred yards or so ahead.

> The instant I received the order I sprang on my horse and then my "crowded hour" began. . . .
>
> I started in the rear of the regiment, the position in which the colonel should theoretically stay. . . . I soon found that I could get that line, behind which I personally was, faster forward than the one immediately in front of it, with the result that the two rearmost lines of the regiment began to crowd together; so I rode through them both, the better to move on the one in front. This happened with every line in succession, until I found myself at the head of the regiment.

Roosevelt rode back and forth along the lines of advancing men, shouting orders, urging them forward. He found one man lying in the cover of a bush, either unaware that the advance had been ordered, or too frightened to stand up.

"Are you afraid to stand up when I am on horseback?" Roosevelt demanded.

Before the man could either reply or get up, he collapsed, a bullet having gone through him lengthwise. Roosevelt realized the bullet had probably been aimed at him. "A curious incident," was how he later characterized it.

The Rough Riders reached the line of regulars before the regulars received the order to advance. Roosevelt encountered a confused junior officer and ordered him to take his men ahead. When the man hesitated he snapped, "Then let my men through, sir."

As the Rough Riders passed, the regulars got up and followed.

"I had not enjoyed the Guasimas fight at all," Roosevelt reflected,

> because I had been so uncertain as to what I ought to do. But the San Juan fight was entirely different. The Spaniards had a hard position to attack, it is true, but we could see them, and I knew exactly how to proceed. . . . By the time I had reached the lines of the regulars of the first brigade I had come to the conclusion that it was silly to stay in the valley firing at the hills, because that was really where we were most exposed, and that the thing to do was to try to rush the intrenchments. . . . I waved my hat and we went up the hill with a rush.

I HAVE SEEN MANY illustrations and pictures of this charge on the San Juan hills, but none of them seem to show it just as I remember it," Richard Harding Davis wrote.

> In the picture-papers the men are running up hill swiftly and gallantly, in regular formation, rank after rank, with flags flying, their eyes aflame, and their hair streaming, their bayonets fixed, in long, brilliant lines, an invincible, overpowering weight of numbers. Instead of which I think the thing which impressed one the most, when our men started from cover, was that they were so few. It seemed as if someone had made an awful and terrible mistake. One's instinct was to call to them to come back. You felt that someone had blundered and that these few men were blindly following out some madman's mad order. It was not heroic then, it seemed merely terribly pathetic. The pity of it, the folly of such a sacrifice was what held you.
>
> They had no glittering bayonets, they were not massed in regular array. There were a few men in advance, bunched together, and creeping up a steep, sunny hill, the tops of which roared and flashed with flame. The men held their guns pressed across their breasts and stepped heavily as they climbed. Behind these first few, spreading out like a fan, were single lines of men, slipping and scrambling in the smooth grass, moving forward with difficulty, as though they were wading waist high through water, moving slowly, carefully, with strenuous effort.

"BY GOD, THERE GO our boys up the hill!" someone shouted. Stephen Crane watched the charge from El Pozo, a mile and a half away.

"One saw a thin line of black figures moving across a field," he recalled. A murmur of astonishment spread through the crowd of foreign attachés.

"It is very gallant, but very foolish," said one.

"Why, they're trying to take the position," exclaimed another. "It's impossible. It's plucky, you know! By Gawd, it's plucky! But *they can't do it!* It will simply be a hell of a slaughter with no good coming out of it."

.   .   .

To THE LEFT of the Rough Riders other regiments were charging up Kettle Hill.

"The whole line, tired of waiting and eager to close with the enemy, was straining to go forward," Roosevelt recalled, "and it seems that different parts slipped the leash at almost the same moment."

The black troopers of the Ninth and Tenth Cavalry were charging. Among the white officers was Lieutenant Pershing.

"By this time we were all in the spirit of the thing and greatly excited by the charge," Roosevelt wrote, "the men cheering and running forward between shots."

Urging his horse to a gallop, he raced toward the ranch buildings on the top of the hill.

Some forty yards from the top I ran into a wire fence and jumped off Little Texas, turning him loose. He had been scraped by a couple of bullets, one of which nicked my elbow, and I never expected to see him again. As I ran up to the hill, [Private Henry] Bardshar stopped to shoot, and two Spaniards fell as he emptied his magazine. . . .

Almost immediately afterward the hill was covered by the troops, both Rough Riders and the colored troopers of the Ninth, and some men of the First. . . .

No sooner were we on the crest than the Spaniards from the line of hills in our front, where they were strongly intrenched, opened a very heavy fire upon us with their rifles. They also opened upon us with one or two pieces of artillery, using time fuses which burned very accurately, the shells exploding right over our heads.

On the top of the hill was a huge iron kettle, or something of the kind, probably used for sugar refining. Several of our men took shelter behind this. We had a splendid view of the charge on the San Juan block-house to our left, where the infantry of Kent, led by Hawkins, were climbing the hill. Obviously the proper thing to do was to help them, and I got the men together and started them volley-firing against the Spaniards in the San Juan block-house and in the trenches around it.

The blockhouse stood on San Juan Hill, about a quarter-mile to the southwest of Roosevelt's position, across the grassy valley. An infantry brigade led by General Hamilton S. Hawkins had been advancing across the valley under heavy Spanish fire while the dismounted cavalry was moving up Kettle Hill.*

"We kept up a brisk fire for some five or ten minutes," Roosevelt recalled,

meanwhile we were much cut up ourselves. . . . Suddenly, above the cracking of the carbines, rose a peculiar drumming sound, and some of

*Some may be surprised to read that it was Kettle Hill, and not San Juan Hill, up which Roosevelt and the Rough Riders charged. Nonetheless it is so.

the men cried, "The Spanish machine-guns!" Listening, I made out that it came from the flat ground to the left, and jumped to my feet, smiting my hand on my thigh, and shouting aloud with exultation, "It's the Gatlings, men, our Gatlings!"

Lieutenant Parker had gotten his four Gatling guns across the San Juan River and into position. Spurting jets of dust raced along the Spanish trenches on the crest of San Juan Hill, the four guns pouring sixty rounds each second in combination—thirty-six hundred per minute—into the rifle pits.

In the grassy valley below the hill, Lieutenant Jules Garesche Ord* of the Sixth Infantry ran forward, his saber in one hand, his revolver in the other.

"Come on!" he shouted. "We can't stop here!"

"In the next instant the scraggly undergrowth burst in a ragged fringe of blue-shirted men, crouching and running, with Ord in the lead," Private Post recalled.

There went up what the academic histories call a cheer, but it was nothing more than a hoarse scream of relief from scores of men and the yell that soldiers give those whom they wish to honor. It was Hawkins's brigade, its two regiments, the Sixth and the Sixteenth running in a pack, unleashed from the jungle, and hell-bent for the red tiled roof that crowned San Juan Hill. It was a running spearhead. There was no nice order, no neatly formed companies crossing that plain or mounting the slope. It was more like a football field when the game is over and a mess of people are straggling across it, except that these men were on the run, yelling, and with no time to lose.

The Gatlings and the Rough Riders lifted their covering fire as the infantry reached the crest of the hill. The Spaniards spilled out of their trenches and fled down the far side. But Lieutenant Ord, the first man up San Juan Hill, lay dead.

.   .   .

"WHEN HAWKINS'S SOLDIERS captured the blockhouse," Roosevelt recalled, "I, very much elated, ordered a charge on my own hook to a line of hills still farther on."

He jumped a fence and ran forward a hundred yards. Looking back he discovered that only five Rough Riders had followed. One of them was badly wounded and another was dying. Convinced that the rest of the regiment had boggled before the heavy fire, he stormed back and proceeded to abuse them as a pack of cowards.

"They, of course, were quite innocent," he later admitted, "and even while I taunted them bitterly for not having followed me, it was all I could do not to smile at the look of injury and surprise that came over their faces. . . ."

"We didn't hear you. We didn't see you go, colonel."

General Sumner had arrived on the scene and gave the charge his official

*Son of the distinguished Civil War general Edward O. C. Ord.

blessing. Roosevelt turned and, with almost the entire dismounted cavalry at his heels, charged across the valley toward the line of hills.

There was now little resistance. The Spanish spilled from the trenches and ran back toward Santiago. Most of those remaining behind were dead. But not all.

> I was with Henry Bardshar, running up at the double, and two Spaniards leaped from he trenches and fired at us, not ten yards away. As they turned to run I closed in and fired twice, missing the first and killing the second. My revolver was from the sunken battle-ship Maine.

He pushed on, the cavalry right behind him, past the ranch houses the Spanish had just evacuated, through a grove of palm trees, and to the crest of the hills.

Beneath them lay Santiago.

.   .   .

"THEY DROVE THE yellow silk flags of the cavalry and the Stars and Stripes of their country into the soft earth of the trenches, and then sank down and looked back at the road they had climbed and swung their hats in the air," Richard Harding Davis recalled.

> And from far overhead, from these few figures perched on the Spanish rifle-pits, with their flags planted among the empty cartridges of the enemy, and overlooking the walls of Santiago, came, faintly, the sound of a tired, broken cheer.

2 P.M.

THE BATTLE WAS not finished. The American force had exchanged an impossible situation in the valley for a difficult position, strung thinly along the crests of the San Juan Heights, and this had been done at great cost. An advance beyond this line was, for the moment, impossible; the Spanish were making an orderly retreat, and their fire from the outskirts of Santiago was quite as heavy as it had earlier been from the hills.

"Along the top of each hill were tiny groups of not more than from a dozen to fifteen soldiers," Richard Harding Davis recalled.

> They were sprawled on their backs . . . or sitting with their elbows on their knees and panting for breath. . . . Three hundred yards below them . . . thousands of Spanish rifles were spluttering furiously . . . making the crest of hills behind which our men lay absolutely untenable . . . They could neither retreat nor advance.

And two miles to the northeast, some five thousand American troops were pinned down at El Caney where, Captain Lee recalled, "our situation was extremely serious; we were holding our own and no more, and we were losing far more heavily than the enemy."

Back at his headquarters General Shafter reviewed the situation with dismay. "I was fearful I had made a terrible mistake," he recalled. He sent a dispatch to Lawton at El Caney: "I would not bother with little block-houses; they cannot harm us. Bates's brigade and your division and García should move on the city and form the right of line going on [Santiago] road. Line is now hotly engaged."

But this was more easily said than done. Withdrawing the force from El Caney might prove more costly than persevering. Like everyone else, Lawton found he had a Spanish tiger by the tail.

3 P.M.

"THERE WAS VERY GREAT confusion at this time," Roosevelt wrote, recalling the situation on the San Juan Heights, "the different regiments being completely intermingled—white regulars, colored regulars, and Rough Riders." The immediate and urgent task was to dig in. Lieutenant R. J. Fleming of the Tenth Cavalry sent two of his black troopers to the rear to bring up some entrenching tools. Roosevelt, seeing the two men start down the hill, jumped up and drew his revolver.

"I . . . halted the retreating soldiers, and called out to them that I appreciated the gallantry with which they had fought and would be sorry to hurt them, but that I would shoot the first man who, on any pretence whatever, went to the rear."

Lieutenant Fleming then explained to Roosevelt that he had ordered the men back, and why. Several of the black cavalrymen spoke up, assuring Roosevelt that they would stay on the firing line.

"Everyone who saw the incident knew the Colonel was mistaken about our men trying to shirk duty," Private Presley Holliday recalled, "but . . . no one thought ill of the matter."

The troopers were professionals, "buffalo soldiers," as the Negro veterans of the Indian wars were called. The colonel was an amateur soldier who, but for this lapse, had acquitted himself surprisingly well. There were no hard feelings.*

.   .   .

GENERAL LINARES HAD taken personal command of the Spanish lines as his troops fell back toward the city. At 3:30 P.M. Lieutenant Müller saw him being carried on a stretcher through the Plaza de Dolores. He had been seriously wounded. General Toral had succeeded to command.

*There was, however, understandable resentment at the graceless and distorted way Roosevelt recounted this incident in *The Rough Riders* (pp. 144–145): "Under the strain the colored infantrymen [sic] (who had none of their [white] officers) began to get a little uneasy and drift to the rear, either helping wounded men, or saying that they wished to find their own regiments. This I could not allow."

· · ·

FOR A SECOND TIME that day a lone figure walked the crest of the San Juan Heights, silhouetted against the sky, heedless of bullets, daring heaven, tempting fate. The man wore no Panama hat, carried no walking stick.

"Crane wore a long India rubber rain-coat and was smoking a pipe," Richard Harding Davis remembered. "He appeared as cool as though he were looking down from a box at the theatre."

The Spanish riflemen had not seen so tempting a target since Maxfield's balloon had sunk into the jungle. A torrent of Mauser bullets whined low over the heads of the cavalrymen crouched in the nearby trenches.

"You're drawing fire on these men!" Colonel Wood shouted. "Get down!"

Crane strolled away, taking the fire along. Davis poked his head up.

"You're not impressing any one by doing that, Crane!" he called.

Crane took cover.

"I knew that would fetch you," Davis said.

Crane smiled. "Oh, was that it?"

That was not it. Stephen Crane had performed for a small and select audience—the man with the Panama hat and the walking stick and the two passengers of the yellow balloon.

And himself.

4:15 P.M.

NEARLY TEN HOURS after Lawton began his attack, El Caney was taken.

"Inside the shattered fort the walls were splashed with blood and a dozen dead and wounded were laid out on the floor, or wedged under the debris," Captain Lee recalled.

> The trench around the fort was a grewsome sight, floored with dead Spaniards in horribly contorted attitudes and with sightless, staring eyes. Others were littered about the slope, and these were mostly terribly mutilated by shell fire. Those killed in the trenches were all shot through the forehead, and their brains oozed out like white paint from a color-tube.

The handful of Spanish prisoners seemed to believe they were to be shot. "The Spaniards persisted in preparing for instant death," Lee remembered, "and would not be comforted either by encouraging smiles or the offer of water and hard-tack."

Among the American wounded was *Journal* reporter James Creelman, who was hit while in the midst of a schoolboy stunt—trying to recover the fallen Spanish flag from the hill beneath the fort. Now, as he lay on the grass beside the road, he felt someone put a hand on his head.

Opening my eyes, I saw Mr. Hearst . . . a straw hat with a bright ribbon on his head, a revolver at his belt, and a pencil and note-book in his hand. . . . Slowly he took down my story of the fight.

"I'm sorry you're hurt, but"—and his face was radiant with enthusiasm—"wasn't it a splendid fight? We must beat every paper in the world."

.   .   .

THE DAY HAD COST 420 lives—205 Americans, 215 Spaniards. The Americans suffered 1,180 wounded; the Spanish, 376.

"The Americans, it must be acknowledged, fought that day with truly admirable courage and spirit," Lieutenant José Müller wrote. "[They] resembled moving statues . . . rather than men; but they met heroes."

CHAPTER TWELVE

THUNDER
ON THE SEA

"WE ARE WITHIN measurable distance of a terrible military disaster," Roosevelt warned as he crouched in the Rough Riders' entrenchments on the San Juan Heights and wrote a letter to Cabot Lodge.

The troops were exhausted in body, mind, and spirit. The day before, from dawn to sunset, they had marched, run, crawled, charged, and fought their way across the valley and onto the heights. Then, throughout the night, they had wielded picks and shovels, racing to dig shelters before dawn brought a new rain of Mauser bullets. Had there been time to sleep they would have slept on the ground in their sodden clothes; their bedrolls lay stacked beside the road back down in the valley. Had there been time to eat there would have been no rations; the Army's mules and wagons must first bring ammunition up to the front.

At dawn the Spanish opened fire all along the line. Their main line of entrenchments was six hundred yards away on the outskirts of the city, but some skirmishers and snipers had crept up during the night, concealing themselves in the tall grass and trees near the American trenches. Yet there was no sign of a Spanish counterattack.

"As the day wore on," Roosevelt recalled, "the fight, though raging fitfully at intervals, gradually died away."

But one did not relax.

"The long-range bullets of the Mausers were constantly dropping all day along the road for at least a mile in the rear of the American lines," Lieutenant Miley remembered,

often striking down men who were going to or coming from the front. This led to the belief that the jungle on both sides of the road was infested by sharpshooters, and this belief was very demoralizing. Companies of infantry and a mounted troop of cavalry were detailed to hunt down the sharpshooters, but they never found one. Still the fear of them existed.

Now the rains came. There had already been storms, of course. Nearly every afternoon towering yellow-white thunderheads boiled above the Sierra Maestra to the north, then marched down to the sea, drenching the foothills and jungle valleys. But today came the monsoon rains of summer, opaque curtains of water that swept over the country, drumming relentlessly on the earth. The twelve miles of road from Siboney became a river of mud. The narrow streams it crossed were turned into deep, wide cataracts. The wagons could not move. Some of the mule trains were swept away at the fords.

"It was greatly feared that one or two days' more rain would make it utterly impossible to bring supplies to the front," Miley recalled.

General Wheeler, temporarily recovered from the malaria that had afflicted him for the past few days, made a reconnaissance of the city.

"The defenses of Santiago were certainly constructed with commendable, engineering skill," he recalled.

> With a very powerful glass I viewed them from every possible point, to accomplish which I selected places from which to view them on all sides of the city. This investigation convinced me, and I so reported, that to take the city by assault would cost us at least three thousand men.

If that was not completely out of the question, it was certainly nothing that General Shafter was yet ready to contemplate; nearly 10 percent of the expeditionary force was already dead or wounded.

Hoping there might be another way, he sent a dispatch to Admiral Sampson: "I urge that you make effort immediately to force the entrance to avoid future losses among my men, which are already very heavy. You can now operate with less loss of life than I can."

To which Sampson replied: "Impossible to force entrance until we can clear channel of mines—a work of some time after forts are taken possession of by your troops."

Which was, of course, what he had urged Shafter to do in the first place, when the expedition arrived off Santiago. Shafter now asked Wheeler if it would be possible to capture the Morro and the other forts at the harbor entrance.

"I would like to do it," Wheeler answered, "but the effort would be attended with terrible loss."

Frustrated and angry, Shafter fired off a petulant note to Sampson: "I am at a loss to see why the navy can not work under a destructive fire as well as the army. My loss yesterday was over 500 men.*

*At this moment Shafter had not yet received a complete list of casualties and did not know that his losses were nearly three times that number.

Sampson replied, explaining to Shafter the cold military equations: "It is not so much the loss of men as it is the loss of ships which has until now deterred me from making a direct attack upon the ships within the port."

The ultimate objective was, after all, to force Spain to surrender by threatening a naval attack on her coasts. But there had to be battleships afloat to make that threat credible after Cervera's squadron was captured or destroyed.*

> If it is your earnest desire that we should force the entrance, I will at once prepare to undertake it. I think, however, that our position and yours would be made more difficult if, as is possible, we fail in our attempt.

While Shafter pondered that ominous reply, a rumor began to spread along the American lines that the order to fall back would soon be given. Wheeler visited the Rough Riders' trenches and told Roosevelt to get ready in case the order was issued. Roosevelt recalled:

> I answered, "Well, General, I really don't know whether we would obey an order to fall back. We can take that city by a rush, and if we have to move out of here at all I should be inclined to make the rush in the right direction." The old General, after a moment's pause, expressed his hearty agreement, and said that he would see that there was no falling back.

Wheeler sent a dispatch back to Shafter:

> A number of officers have appealed to me to have the line withdrawn and take up a strong position farther back, and I expect they will appeal to you. I have positively discountenanced this, as it would cost us much prestige.

Lost prestige was the cost of retreat; three thousand casualties, the cost of advance; sunken battleships the cost of forcing the harbor. And the cost of staying in place—rain, disease, and the arrival of the Spanish relief column.

· · ·

THE VIEW FROM within the city of Santiago was different:

"The enemy, during the night of the battle of Caney," Lieutenant José Müller recalled,

> continued to surround our lines with the new reenforcements constantly arriving, and installed modern artillery and machine guns on the

---

*Mahan later explained: "The Navy Department had . . . to keep in mind . . . that we had not a battleship in the home ports that could in six months be made ready to replace one lost or seriously disabled . . . If we lost ten thousand men, the country could replace them; if we lost a battleship, it could not be replaced. The issue of the war, as a whole and in every locality to which it extended, depended upon naval force . . . A million of the best soldiers would have been powerless in the face of hostile control of the sea (*Lessons of the War with Spain*, p. 185).

heights. The insurgents were covering Cuabitas and adjoining points.
. . . We were decidedly surrounded and all our communications by land
cut off, as they had by sea for over a month and a half. Each hour that
elapsed the enemy fortified the circle that enclosed us.

"At daybreak the enemy renewed attack upon city, which is still going on,"
General Toral reported that day in a telegram to Governor General Blanco.*

[I] believe that Escario's column has been held up by [American]
landing forces at Aserraderos. At request [of] Admiral Cervera have
ordered immediately reembarkation troops of squadron, thereby weak-
ening defense by 1,000 men. . . . Situation becoming more and more
untenable.

ESCARIO'S COLUMN had been held up by the Cuban insurgents, who had harassed
it every step of the way from Manzanillo. The day before it had been ambushed
near the Guarinao River—seven men were killed, forty-three wounded. The day
before that it had fought at La Mantonia, a farm near the Contramaestre River,
where it had lost five dead and ten wounded. Today it reached Palma Soriano.
The cost of the day's march was four dead and six wounded. Total losses for the
ten-day, 140-mile march totaled twenty-seven dead, seventy-one wounded. But
the Cubans had paid heavily to slow Escario's advance; in one battle alone
fourteen insurgents were killed.

At 3 P.M. General Toral received word by heliograph from Escario that the
column was twenty miles to the west, a bit more than one day's march from
Santiago. A forced march would get him there within twenty-four hours. Toral
replied, describing the situation. He told Escario to hurry.

·   ·   ·

WORD THAT HELP was near lifted some spirits in Santiago. It was the best news,
the only good news, the city had had in more than a month. In this unfamiliar
mood of optimism some began to transform faint hopes into serious expectations.
Lieutenant José Müller had been watching the preparations aboard the ships of
Cervera's squadron during the day.

"It occurred to me (and nobody could have dissuaded me from it)," he
recalled,

that a fleet from the Peninsula was on its way to Santiago; that it would
pass in sight of the semaphore of Porto Rico; that consequently Admiral Cervera would know . . . when it would reach Santiago; and when
fire was opened on the enemy it would leave the mouth free, he would
go out and the two fleets combined would defeat the enemy. . . . We
had ships and they were coming. No doubt they were quite near, or
perhaps only a few miles distant, but where had the ships come from?
I do not know—from heaven, from earth, from the air, from nothing

*Apparently this was written shortly after daybreak on July 2, when the American lines were
answering the Spanish fire. Of course, the Americans did not renew the attack upon the city.

at all—I do not know. But everything appeared possible to me, except that our fleet should go out alone to fight the ships that were assembled at the Morro.

Throughout the evening he and his comrades talked of it as they sat on the steps of the harbormaster's office. "At times we even thought we could hear firing out there on the sea at a great distance and in a southeasterly direction." A Spanish fleet, coming to the rescue, was doing battle with the blockaders.

"How much desire and imagination can do!" he reflected bitterly.

.   .   .

"Pando," said General Shafter, "is reported to have been sixteen miles out yesterday with 8,000 men."*

He glanced around at the division commanders gathered in the new headquarters on El Pozo for this evening meeting. Turning again to the map he resumed his summary of the situation.

"A large force of troops is at San Luis, twenty-five miles in our rear; 10,000 men are at Holguín; and 7,000 more are in my rear at Guantánamo. If they come down we shall have to get back."

He looked around significantly.

". . . and I want an expression of opinion against anything that might come. If those forces take us in flank, which would not be difficult in our present exposed position, I will be held responsible."

Shafter's greatest enemy was not the Spanish forces that might be on their way to Santiago to lift the American siege but the relentless heat that turned the Cuban jungle into a green, steaming hell. It had crippled him, and then it had humiliated him. He had had to be carried to the meeting lying on a door from an abandoned farmhouse by six strong men. He was acutely aware that the men who now stood looking at him—Lawton, Bates, Kent, Wheeler—had spent the last two days under fire, while he had been forced to remain in the safety of his tent two miles to the rear. Whatever things his soldier's spirit may have aspired to, the crushing, sweltering burden of surplus flesh pressed him down in mind, body, and heart. Had he been fit enough to march to the front, stand shoulder to shoulder with his men, and look the enemy in the eye, he might have seen that desperation was the province of the Spanish, the last thing in Cuba to which they held exclusive claim. Instead, shackled by infirmity, he could see only the precarious situation of his own forces and, beyond them, phantom Spanish armies advancing through the jungle night.

Hold the line or fall back? He polled the commanders.

"Hang on," General Lawton voted.

General Bates agreed.

General Kent said that, while he was not for withdrawal, his brigade commanders advised it. Therefore he was casting his vote for retreat.

General Wheeler voted to hold the line.

*Shafter still believed that Escario's relief column was led by General Pando and was more than double its actual size.

Shafter nodded. "Very well. We shall hold our present position for the next twenty-four hours, and if our condition is not improved, I shall call upon you again."

.   .   .

"CIVILIZED PEOPLE," General Shafter observed, "do not, if they can avoid it, fire on towns filled with women and children." Yet he contemplated doing just that as dawn broke on Sunday, July 3. He wrote a letter to be carried through the lines under a flag of truce and presented to the Spanish commander.

> Sir,
>   I shall be obliged, unless you surrender, to shell Santiago de Cuba. Please inform the citizens of foreign countries and all women and children that they should leave the city before ten o'clock to-morrow morning.

IT WAS A Sunday morning. As it had on each of the preceding thirty-seven days, the blockading fleet stood in an eight-mile-long semicircle, each ship positioned about three miles from the entrance to Santiago harbor. Because it was Sunday there were to be church services aboard the ships, and because it was the first Sunday of the month there was to be general muster. Most of the officers and crewmen had put on dress whites.

"This is pretty slow," Commodore Schley remarked, as he tilted back his chair on the deck of the *Brooklyn*. Schley was at the moment senior officer on the blockade, Admiral Sampson having left to go ashore and confer with General Shafter on the matter of forcing an entrance into the harbor. His flagship, the *New York*, had steamed eastward toward Siboney at 9 A.M. It was now nearly thirty minutes later and the *New York* had almost vanished beyond a headland to the east.

Yesterday afternoon six columns of smoke had been seen rising above the harbor, evidence that the Spanish warships had fired their boilers. Schley could think of only two explanations: either the ships were taking new positions in the harbor from which to bombard the American lines, or else they were finally preparing to come out. This morning the smoke was still visible. From the bridge of the *Brooklyn*, Quartermaster Anderson studied the billowing black clouds through his binoculars.

"That smoke looks as if it was moving toward the entrance, sir," he told Lieutenant Hodgson, the ship's navigator. Hodgson took the glasses, studied the entrance for a moment, then spun around.

"Afterbridge, there! Report to the commodore! The enemy's ships are coming out!"

The boom of a six-pounder thundered over the ocean, and a cloud of gunsmoke burst from the *Iowa*. The officer of the deck, Lieutenant F. K. Hill, had fired it as he caught the first glimpse of a ship in the entrance channel. The sound of the gun reached the *New York*, seven miles to the east, and she began to come about. Up every signal mast of the fleet went the three flags that formed

"250," the signal that meant, "Enemy's ships are coming out."

Gongs rang, bugles sounded, engine room telegraphs jangled. Men who had assembled on deck for inspection broke from line, thundered down ladders and across decks. Watertight doors were slammed and secured. Fire crews wet down decks. Blowers forced air over glowing coals, and the steam pressure in the boilers climbed. In three minutes the fleet had cleared for action.

The Spanish ships came out, one at a time, at intervals of ten minutes and six hundred yards. The *María Teresa* was in the lead, followed by the *Viscaya*, the *Cristobal Colón*, and the *Oquendo*. The two torpedo boat destroyers, *Plutón* and *Furor* brought up the rear. From the bridge of the *Brooklyn*, George Edward Graham of the Associated Press studied them through his binoculars.

> We saw what probably has not been witnessed since the days of the Armada, ships coming out for deadly battle, but dressed as for a regal parade or a festal day. From their shining black hulls, with huge golden figureheads bearing the crest and coat-of-arms of Spain, to the tops of their masts where fluttered proudly the immense silken flags . . . to the brightly colored awnings over their decks, they bespoke luxury and chivalry, and a proud defiance.

The hour had come. Don Pascual, the reluctant Quixote, came forth to do battle.

.   .   .

"WITH THE BATTLE FLAG hoisted the *Infanta María Teresa* advanced ahead of the other large cruisers," Captain Concas remembered.

> It was a solemn moment, capable of making the calmest heart beat faster. . . . I asked leave of the admiral to open fire, and, that received, I gave the order. The bugle gave the signal for the commencement of the battle. . . .
>
> The sound of my bugles was the last echo of those which history tells us were sounded at the capture of Granada. It was the signal that the history of four centuries of grandeur was at an end and that Spain was becoming a nation of the fourth class.

"Poor Spain!" Concas exclaimed. Cervera had neither words nor voice to reply. He made a silent gesture of despair.

.   .   .

CAPTAIN ROBLEY EVANS clambered up to the bridge of the *Iowa*.

> I found the engines set full speed ahead and the ship pointing straight for the entrance of the harbour. In about two minutes the guns of the starboard battery began firing . . . As the leading Spanish ship, the flagship Maria Teresa, swung into the channel leading out from the Punta Gorda, she presented a magnificent appearance with her splen-

did new battle flags and her polished brass work. . . .

As she passed the Diamond Shoal at the entrance to the harbour she swung off to the westward and opened fire smartly with her port broadside and turret guns. From this moment the battle may be said to have been on, and the roaring of the guns became incessant. . . . The speed I judged to be about eight knots as the ships came down the channel, which was increased to thirteen or more as they kept away to the westward in the open sea. They came at us like mad bulls.

"As soon as the *Teresa* went out," Cervera recalled,

she opened fire on the nearest hostile ship, but shaping her course straight for the *Brooklyn,* which was to the southwest, for it was of the utmost importance to us to place this ship in a condition where she would not be able to make use of her superior speed. The rest of our ships engaged in battle with the other hostile ships, which came at once from the different points where they were stationed.

"If I were to live a thousand years and a thousand centuries," Lieutenant Müller declared,

never should I forget that 3d day of July, 1898, nor do I believe that Spain will ever forget it.

It was 8:30. Feeling sure that the ships would not go out, and taking advantage of the chance of getting a horse, for the distance was great, I went to the military hospital to see Mr. Joaquin Bustamente.

Bustamente was captain of Cervera's flagship, the *Infanta María Teresa.* He had commanded some of the sailors sent ashore to reinforce the Spanish Army and had been seriously wounded in the fighting two days before.

"Is the fleet not going out?" Bustamente asked, when he saw Müller.

"Not just now, I believe, though it is ready to go out," Müller answered. "Is it known when the other fleet will arrive?"

Müller still clung to his fantasy of last night.

"What other fleet?"

"The one that is supposed to come from Spain; they probably know at about what time it may be expected at the mouth of the harbor."

"Don't be a fool. There is no other fleet; the ships are going out and that is all there is to it. I have a letter from Don Pascual in which he tells me so."

Bustamente's words were punctuated by the distant sound of a cannon.

"Two or three minutes later," Müller recalled,

a terrific cannonade commenced . . . shaking the building, thundering through the air.

I could not think coherently. I kept looking at Mr. Bustamente like an imbecile, and he looked at me and didn't say a word. . . . Then, suddenly, without taking leave, I went out, got on my horse and rode down the hill at breakneck speed.

The squadron had left the harbor. The headlands at the bottom of the bay hid the drama that had begun out on the sea.

> The noise caused by the gunshots which the mountains and valleys echoed was truly infernal and comparable to nothing. . . . The earth trembled, and very soon Punta Gorda, the Morro, and the Socapa took part in the frightful concert, adding the thunder of their guns to the noise of those of the two fleets.

ABOARD THE *Brooklyn,* Commodore Schley had stationed himself on a wooden platform next to the conning tower, from which he could both view the battle and communicate with the bridge. At this moment his attention was not directed at the Spanish ships but to the east.

"Can you see the flagship?" he called to Lieutenant Hodgson.

"No, sir. The *New York* is out of sight."

Schley flashed a smile of satisfaction. He was not fond of Admiral Sampson, and the admiral had picked the wrong moment to leave the blockade. Commodore Schley considered himself, as senior officer, now to be in command of the combined squadron in what was clearly to be the decisive battle of the Spanish War.

"Commodore," Hodgson yelled, "they are coming right at us!"

"Go right for them!" Schley answered.

.   .   .

ABOARD THE *Oregon* there was disbelief. Lieutenant W. H. Allen, who was officer of the deck at that moment, recalled:

> Although I had many times rehearsed what I would do in case the Spaniards came out, I was momentarily dazed, but recovering quickly, I caused the alarm gongs to be sounded from the pilot house. For a moment or two every one thought the gongs had sounded accidentally, as was often the case, but the order, "To your quarters," convinced the crew that this was no false alarm. A rousing cheer went up from the men as they rushed to their stations.

They had long since come to believe it would never happen. As they rocked idly in the trade wind swells, as days became weeks, as they stared past the barrels of their giant naval guns at the narrow entrance channel, they had ample time to grow fast in the belief that no admiral would engage in such folly. Now it was happening and there was confusion.

There was, first of all, the question of who was in command. Schley said the *New York* was out of sight behind the headland west of Siboney. Captain Evans of the *Iowa* said the *New York* was in plain sight when the battle began, turning around and flying the admiral's flag. Given the relative positions of the ships and the contours of the coast, both men could have been right. Perhaps the significant fact is that the *New York* had left the blockade thirty minutes earlier flying the signal, "Disregard movements of the flagship."

"If the battle . . . had miscarried," Schley later grumbled, "there would have been no difficulty whatever about who was in command, or who would have had to bear the censure."

The situation then, at this moment, some ten to twenty minutes after the first Spanish ship was sighted, was this:

The *María Teresa* had come out of the harbor, run due south until she cleared the shoals, then turned toward the *Brooklyn*, which was some three miles to the southwest. The *Brooklyn* and the other eight blockading ships were converging like the spokes of a wheel on the harbor entrance. The *New York*, some seven miles to the east, had come about and was steaming due west toward the battle. The *Vizcaya* came out of the harbor some ten minutes after the *Teresa*, and the *Cristobal Colón*, the *Oquendo*, the *Plutón* and the *Furor* at equal intervals.

At 10:05 A.M. the *María Teresa* and the *Brooklyn* had closed to within six hundred yards of each other, when the *Brooklyn* began to veer to starboard. Most of the other American ships were, at this moment, turning to port, i.e., from a northerly heading—toward the harbor—to a westerly heading—the direction in which the Spanish squadron was turning to flee along the coast. The *Brooklyn*'s maneuver brought it across the path of the battleship *Texas*, which was immediately to her east, steaming west in hot pursuit of the enemy. To avoid a collision, the *Texas* was forced to stop her engines and come to a halt.

The *Brooklyn* continued to turn to port until she had made nearly a full circle, then headed west, parallel to the course of the Spanish ships. The turn confused both Spanish and American onlookers. Captain Concas of the *Teresa* observed, "The turn was to starboard, although it would seem reasonable for it to have [been] made to port."

Schley would later angrily deny "the silly twaddle that, in turning outward for tactical advantage, [the *Brooklyn*] separated herself to any appreciable extent from the battle line." The reason for the maneuver, he explained, was to avoid being rammed* by the one of the first two Spanish ships. As to the *Texas*, he wrote, "That ship was never for a moment in the least danger from the *Brooklyn*. During the turn, her distance was never nearer than five or six hundred yards from the *Brooklyn*."†

While the *Brooklyn* spun around, trying to avoid being rammed by the *Teresa* or the *Vizcaya*, the *Teresa* turned to the west to avoid being rammed by the *Texas* or the *Iowa*, both of which were in the lead of the American fleet.

---

*Ramming, a vestige of the Civil War ironclads, was regarded as an effective battle tactic at the time. The bows of warships protruded beneath the water line for this purpose.

†Neither the "retrograde turn," as it was called, nor Schley's assumption of command of the squadron made any difference to the outcome of the battle. But they did attract strong criticism and fueled his feud with Sampson. Schley's unshakable belief that Cervera was in Cienfuegos and his temporary refusal of the order to blockade Santiago were still fresh in the minds of many officers. These seemingly insignificant matters eventually led to a bitter public controversy with Sampson and a Court of Inquiry. The dispute damaged the careers of both men, cheated them of the pride and satisfaction they might otherwise have taken in their accomplishments, and poisoned the remainder of their lives, which amounted to eleven years for Schley and four years for Sampson.

"It had been my intention from the first to ram or torpedo the flagship if I could reach her," Captain Evans of the *Iowa* explained.

> I kept the Maria Teresa on my starboard bow, so that the guns could have a chance at her, until it became evident that I could not ram her or even get within torpedo range, when I swung off to port, gave her the full benefit of my starboard broadside, and then swung back quickly and headed across the bows of the second ship, hoping to be able to reach her with my ram. The Maria Teresa passed me at a distance of about twenty-six hundred yards, and, as she crossed my bows, our forward twelve-inch guns were fired and I was confident that I saw both shells strike the Spanish ship.

"One of the first projectiles burst an auxiliary steam pipe on board the *Maria Teresa,*" Admiral Cervera recalled. "A great deal of steam escaped, which made us lose the speed on which we had counted. About the same time another shell burst one of the fire mains. The ship made a valiant defense against the galling hostile fire."

Live steam filled the afterturret and ammunition hoists, scalding men to death. Others suffocated in the thick smoke from the fires that raged out of control. Captain Concas was seriously wounded; Cervera took direct command of the ship.

The battle was turning into a sea chase. The column of Spanish ships raced westward along the coast, with the *Iowa,* the *Texas,* and the *Brooklyn* running parallel to them, about a mile to the south, trying to keep up. The rest of the blockading fleet was far behind. Cervera's squadron had come out ready for the chase with full steam up on each ship, while most of the American fleet had only the steam pressure needed to maneuver at the blockade stations. Thick black smoke now poured from the warships' stacks as the forced-draft blowers worked to bring up the pressure.

Aboard the *Iowa* Captain Evans saw the *Vizcaya* and the *Cristobal Colón* beginning to pull ahead of him. Twice again he swung, first to port to loose a broadside, then back to starboard to fire his massive forward turret.

"At this time the Colon came with a great show of speed," he remembered.

> As she passed she struck me twice—two as beautiful shots as I ever saw made by any ship. . . . The first shell . . . struck on the starboard side a little forward of the bridge, about four feet above the water line, passed through the cellulose belt, and exploded on the berth deck, demolishing the dispensary, breaking almost every medicine bottle in it, and doing great damage otherwise.

The second shot tore a jagged hole at the water line forward of the first one. The cellulose packing, which was supposed to swell up and keep the hull watertight in such situations, washed out and floated astern, a brown streak in the *Iowa*'s foaming wake. The sea poured in through the gaping wound.

.   .   .

FROM A MOUNTAIN PASS some miles to the northwest, Colonel Escario was able to see Santiago and the bay. Cervera's squadron was gone. He heard the sound of the guns and, believing the fighting was on land, near the city, he dispatched part of his force to speed ahead and join the battle.

.   .   .

THE *Iowa*, now limping from the hits she had sustained, closed to within sixteen hundred yards of the *Oquendo* as the Spanish ship came up from behind.

"At this time she was under the concentrated fire of several of our ships," Captain Evans recalled,

> and the effect was most striking.
> She rolled and staggered like a drunken thing, and finally seemed to stop her engines. I thought she was going to strike her colours, and was on the point of ordering the battery to cease firing, when she started ahead again and we redoubled our efforts to sink her. As I looked at her I could see the shot holes come in her sides and our shells explode inside of her, but she pluckily held on her course and fairly smothered us with a shower of shells and machine-gun shots.

"We continued to steam until we left the *Iowa* somewhat behind on the port quarter, but within range of her artillery," Lieutenant Calandria of the *Oquendo* reported.

> The *Brooklyn* was on the bow of the same side and the other ships at a distance astern of the *Iowa*. This was the situation of the hostile fleet when I was notified through the speaking tube that fire had broken out in the after torpedo rooms, and as I came out I saw flames issuing forth from the officers' hatchway in the poop.

The fire was burning out of control. Calandria rushed to the bridge and found the captain preparing to run the ship aground. Calandria warned him the forward torpedos might explode from the shock. The torpedos were quickly jettisoned.

Fire and the danger of a massive explosion of the ammunition was also the situation aboard the *Teresa*.

"I realized that the ship was doomed," Cervera recalled,

> and cast about for a place where I could run her aground without losing many lives and continue the battle as long as possible. . . .
> I steered for a small beach west of Punta Cabrera, where we ran aground just as the engines stopped. . . . In this painful situation, when explosions commenced to be heard in the ammunition rooms, I gave orders to lower the flag and flood all the magazines. . . . The fire was gaining rapidly.

"The Spanish flagship headed for the shore, in flames, fore and aft," Captain Evans recalled,

and soon took the ground about seven miles to the west of the entrance to Santiago Harbour, and a few minutes later the Oquendo followed her, the flames bursting out through the shot holes in her sides and leaping up from the deck as high as the military tops. It was a magnificent, sad sight to see these beautiful ships in their death agonies; but we were doing the work we had been educated for, and we cheered and yelled until our throats were sore.

THE *Vizcaya* and *Colón* continued to run to the west. The *Brooklyn* was now in the lead of the pursuers and nearly abeam of the *Vizcaya*.

"Get in close, Cook, and we'll fix her," Commodore Schley called.

Guns blazing, the *Brooklyn* closed in to a range of 950 yards. There was heavy answering fire from the Spanish ship. A shell ripped through a gun compartment belowdecks, cutting away a four-inch steel stanchion, demolishing an iron staircase, and then exploding. There were twelve men in the compartment, but only one was injured.

On deck Yeoman George Ellis, a twenty-five-year-old sailor from Brooklyn, New York, called off ranges to the gun crews. Then came a dull thud, and the men nearby were splattered with blood and brains.

"It was a shocking scene to those who had never before witnessed such things," Schley recalled. Two men picked up Ellis's headless body and started for the side; in battle, mutilated bodies were to be thrown overboard where they would not demoralize the living.

"Don't throw that body overboard," Schley yelled. "Take it below, and we'll give it a Christian burial."

The gun smoke had become so thick that Schley could no longer see the effect of his firing on the *Vizcaya*. He called to a marine in the *Brooklyn*'s forward military top and asked for a report.

"His reply, that he could see none of the shots striking the water, left the impression that they must then be striking that ship," Schley recalled. "It proved to be correct."

Shuddering beneath the pounding of the *Brooklyn*'s batteries, the *Vizcaya* began to turn to port, her bow swinging toward the American ship. It seemed she was preparing to ram.

"Just at that moment, an eight-inch shell from [the *Brooklyn*'s] starboard turret struck her a slanting blow on the bow," Associated Press reporter Graham recalled,

and there was a terrific explosion. Every one of us who were watching knew it was more of an explosion than an eight-inch shell would make and we held our glasses on her to discover her injury. It became apparent, as the smoke cleared, that the shell had undoubtedly exploded a torpedo placed in her tube to fire at us, and that it had blown out a large section of her bow.

An eight-inch shell struck her next.

We could see men's bodies hurled into the air, and see others dropping over the sides. One end of her bridge tumbled down as though the underpinning was driven out, and then at 11:06 o'clock she turned and ran for shore, hauling down her flag, her deck one mass of flames, and the ammunition, which had been brought up to supply her deck guns, exploding in every direction.

The *Texas* had been coming up quickly from behind, adding her fire to that of the *Brooklyn* and the other ships. From her bridge Captain J. W. Philip watched the burning *Vizcaya* and heard his own men cheering.
"Don't cheer, boys! Those poor devils are dying!"

.   .   .

"WHILE WE WERE hotly engaged with the last ship," Captain Evans recalled,

two dense spots of black smoke and two long white streaks on the water indicated the positions of the Spanish torpedo boats as they made their gallant dash for liberty. We turned our rapid-fire guns and the after guns of the main battery on them, and at the same time other ships concentrated on the little gamecocks. In a very short time—not more than five minutes, I should say—a splendid column of steam mixed with coal dust sprang hundreds of feet in the air, and I knew that the boiler of one of them had blown up.

"One of the projectiles struck one of the hatches of the boiler ventilators," recalled Lieutenant Bustamente of the torpedo boat destroyer *Furor,*

thereby reducing the pressure and consequently the speed of the ship. By this time the projectiles were falling in large numbers. One of the shells struck Boatswain Duenas, cutting him in two; one part fell between the tiller-ropes, interrupting them momentarily, and it was necessary to take it out in pieces. Another projectile destroyed the engine and the servo-motor, so that the ship could neither proceed nor maneuver. Another had struck in the after shell room, exploding and destroying it.

The *Furor* began to sink rapidly. Captain Fernando Villaamil gave the order to abandon ship. The shore was three miles away.
The *Furor* had been sunk by the converted yacht, *Gloucester,* formerly J. P. Morgan's *Corsair.* It was commanded by Lieutenant Commander Richard Wainwright, who had been the *Maine*'s executive officer.
The *Plutón,* also, was sinking. Lieutenant Commander Vasquez rushed to his cabin, retrieved the code book and a packet of confidential documents, and threw them into the sea. Then he lowered his flag and ran the boat onto the rocky shore.

. . .

IT WAS NOW 11:15 A.M., one hundred furious minutes since the first Spanish ship had come out of the harbor. Three cruisers and one torpedo boat were beached and burning; another torpedo boat was sunk. Of the squadron of Admiral Cervera, only the swift *Cristobal Colón* remained, now steaming westward at full speed. The nearest of her pursuers, the *Brooklyn,* was six miles behind. The *Texas,* the *Vixen,* and the *New York* were farther back. But now the great, gray specter of another warship moved up through the pack, past the *Texas,* past the *Brooklyn,* into the lead. There was, as the sailormen of those days said, "a bone in her teeth," a pair of great white foaming waves curling out from her bows as she raced through the ocean. Billows of black smoke poured out of her stacks and blew back over her tumbling wake. Very slowly, she was overhauling the *Colón.*

The U.S.S. *Oregon* had come sixteen thousand miles to do this.

Eager eyes stared ahead; anxious eyes glanced back. The warships were almost equally swift. The chase would be a long one. An hour passed.

At 12:20 a white cloud erupted with a roar from one of the massive thirteen-inch guns in the *Oregon's* forward turret. A half-ton of steel and high explosive screamed into the sky, and seconds later a distant fountain sprang from the ocean astern of the *Colón.*

"The *Oregon* commenced to gain on us," Captain Paredes recalled,

> and soon after opened fire with her heavy bow guns, which I could answer only with gun No.2 of the battery, while the distance grew constantly shorter. . . . I decided to run ashore and lose the ship rather than sacrifice in vain the lives of all these men. . . . I therefore shaped our course for the mouth of the Tarquino River and ran aground on the beach.

It was 1:15 P.M. The squadron of Admiral Cervera was destroyed. In the bitter words of Captain Concas, "The hour foreseen at Cape Verde had arrived."

. . .

"IT WAS ONLY a short time before the boatloads of dead and wounded began to arrive alongside," Captain Evans recalled. The *Iowa* and two other American ships had sent boats in to rescue the Spanish seamen from the *Vizcaya.*

> Presently a boat came alongside bearing Captain Eulate, commander of the *Vizcaya.* . . . In the stern supported by one of our naval cadets, sat the captain covered with blood from three wounds, with a blood-stained hankerchief about his bare head. Around him sat or lay a dozen or more wounded men. In the bottom of the boat, which was leaking, was a foot or so of blood-stained water and the body of a dead Spanish sailor which rolled from side to side as the water swashed about.

Eulate was carried on board the *Iowa.* He got to his feet and presented his sword to Captain Evans. Evans handed it back to the Spaniard, as the American seamen cheered. Then he steadied the wounded man and helped him toward his own cabin.

He stopped for a moment just as we reached the hatch, and drawing himself up to his full height, with his right arm extended above his head, exclaimed, "Adios, Vizcaya!" Just as the words passed his lips the forward magazine of his late command, as if arranged for the purpose, exploded with magnificent effect.

OF THE AMERICAN FLEET, only Yeoman Ellis was killed; 323 Spaniards died, and 151 were wounded. The squadron of Admiral Cervera was no more.

"God and the gunners had had their day," Captain Evans observed.

.   .   .

"IN ORDER TO COMPLETE the outline of the history of this mournful day," Cervera wrote in his report to Governor General Blanco,

there only remains for me to tell your excellency that our enemies have treated and are treating us with the utmost chivalry and kindness. They have clothed us as best they could, giving us not only articles furnished by the Government, but their own personal property. They have even suppressed almost entirely the usual hurrahs out of respect for our bitter grief. We have been and are still receiving enthusiastic congratulations upon our action, and all are vying in making our captivity as light as possible.

Cervera and his surviving crew were picked up from the beach by the *Gloucester* and later transferred to the *Iowa*. Captain Evans welcomed him with elaborate naval ceremony. A full Marine guard was drawn up on the quarterdeck, while the crew massed atop the superstructure and afterturrets.

As the brave old admiral came over the side . . . without shirt or hat, yet an admiral every inch of him, the officers saluted and the marines presented arms, and the buglers sounded the salute for an officer of his rank. As he bowed and extended his hand to me, my men burst into cheers. For an instant it seemed to me that Admiral Cervera misunderstood the demonstration; but then he realized its meaning, that it was the tribute of brave men for a brave and gallant foe, and he stood bowing his acknowledgement while the men behind the guns made him understand what they thought of him.

Cervera was to wait for the end of the war in comfortable captivity at the Naval Academy in Annapolis. There he would discover that he had become nearly as popular a hero to the American people as though he had been a native son.

.   .   .

"I'LL SAY this much f'r him," said the Chicago *Journal*'s Mr. Dooley,

> he's a brave man, a dam brave man. I don't like a Spanyard no more than ye do, Hinnissy. I niver see wan. But, if this here man was a— was a Zulu, I'd say he was a brave man. If I was aboord wan iv them yachts that was converted, I'd go to this here Cervera, an' I'd say: "Manuel," I'd say, "ye're all right, me boy. Ye ought to go to a doctor an' have ye'er eyes re-set, but ye'er a good fellow. Go downstrairs," I'd say, "into th' basemint iv the ship," I'd say, "an' open th' cupboard jus' nex' to th' head iv th' bed, an' find th' bottle marked 'Floridy Wather,' an threat ye'ersilf kindly." That's what I'd say to Cervera. He's all right.

"IF SPAIN WERE as well served by her statesmen and public officials as she is by her sailors," wrote another American, "she might yet be a great country."

CHAPTER THIRTEEN

THE HONOR
OF ARMS

THE MOOD AT the White House was gloomy apprehension. Nothing had been heard from General Shafter since late on the night of July 1, when he reported that his troops had taken the San Juan Heights at the cost of heavy casualties. The next day was Saturday. All day long President McKinley and Secretary of War Alger paced the floors of the Operating Room, waiting for a dispatch, forced to turn to the newspapers for a clue to the situation at Santiago. The press said Shafter was seriously ill. So was Wheeler, it said.

Afternoon passed into evening. Midnight came and went. At 1 A.M. Alger sent a telegram to Shafter: "We are waiting with intense anxiety tidings of yesterday."

No tidings were offered. At 4 A.M. Alger went home. At 11 A.M. he was back in his office. Still no word. Another telegram to Shafter demanding a report on the situation. Silence.

Whatever the reason for Shafter's total silence, it was not lack of a means to reply. The Signal Corps had dredged up the submarine cable to Haiti, tied into it, and run a telegraph line out to the general's headquarters near El Pozo. Shafter was in almost direct telegraphic contact with Washington via Cape Haitien and New York. Alger's exasperated telegram arrived at El Pozo minutes after it was sent from Washington.

Shafter was, at that moment, waiting for General Toral to reply to his surrender demand. He was also waiting for Admiral Sampson to arrive at his headquarters for their scheduled meeting to discuss plans for the Navy to force the harbor. He did not know that Cervera's ships had left the harbor, or that, at that very instant, all but one had been destroyed less than twenty miles from the tent in which he lay suffering from the midday heat.

340

Forty-five minutes later he sent a reply to Alger. The Army had laid siege to Santiago, he reported, but "with a very thin line." The city's defenses were too strong to be stormed by the present force. He was trying to persuade Sampson to force the harbor. General Wheeler was "seriously ill."* So was General Young. Shafter himself was suffering from the weather and could not go out during the heat of the day. The road to the coast was threatening to become impassable. He was seriously considering withdrawing about five miles back toward Siboney.

Alger and McKinley eagerly read the telegram. Somewhere along the line it had been garbled and now seemed to say that the Spanish had flanked the American force on the right and the rear. At the White House suspense gave way to dismay. Much later in the afternoon the message was unscrambled. The good news was that the Army had not been flanked by the Spanish; the bad news was that Shafter, nonetheless, was considering a withdrawal. Then came another dispatch from Shafter—the Spanish squadron had come out of the harbor and escaped. The nightmare of an attack on the Atlantic coast returned. Even in death the squadron of Admiral Cervera had the power to dismay Washington. It was, Alger recalled, "the darkest day of the war." Secretary Long went home and wrote to his wife: "I suppose we all wish that Congress had appreciated what it was undertaking when it forced McKinley into war."

By 7:45 P.M. things had been sorted out. The Signal Corps censor at Playa del Este, the Cuban end of the Haitian cable, forwarded a report that all but one of the Spanish ships had been destroyed. Alger waited at the White House throughout the evening, fearing that this report, too, might be in error. But by 1:15 A.M. there had been enough confirmation to convince him and President McKinley that it was true.

At 2 A.M. Alger left the White House and walked home. He could hear the newsboys crying, "Spanish fleet destroyed!"

He remembered that it was the Fourth of July.

.   .   .

IN SANTIAGO, in Havana, in Cienfuegos, in Manzanillo, and in Holguín, in every Spanish enclave on the island, the *peninsulares* gathered in the public squares and read the captain general's manifesto.

> Inhabitants of the island of Cuba:
> Fortune does not always favor the brave. The Spanish squadron, under the command of Rear-Admiral Cervera, has just performed the greatest deed of heroism that is perhaps recorded in the annals of the navy in the present century, fighting American forces three times as large. It succumbed gloriously, just when we considered it safe from the peril threatening it within the harbor of Santiago de Cuba. It is a hard blow, but it would be unworthy of Spanish hearts to despair. . . .
>
> Blanco

*Wheeler later wrote that he "regretted very much" to learn that Shafter had "overstated" his illness, which did not materially impair his usefulness at any time (Wheeler, pp. 117–119). Judging from his performance, Wheeler was in far better physical condition than Shafter.

The blood sacrifice had been made. National honor had been rescued. The final act of the drama could now begin.

On July 7, Admiral Cámara, having taken his armada through the Suez Canal and into the Red Sea, was ordered to turn around and return to Spain.

.   .   .

"Now THAT THE FLEET is destroyed," Shafter told Wheeler on July 3, "I believe the garrison will surrender, and all we have to do is hang on where we are and very soon starve them out."

As to the relief column, he was confident it could not get into the city:

> If necessary we can . . . let Lawton's whole Division cut loose on Gen.
> Pando, whose men will have to come into the open and charge us. I
> have sent Lawton a battery of Lt. Artillery to play on them. There is
> but one road which they can come in on, which heretofore has been
> under the guns of [the Spanish] fleet.

But Shafter moved too slowly to take advantage of Cervera's absence. Colonel Escario's column was already in Santiago.

"It is my duty to say to you that this city will not surrender," General Toral said in reply to Shafter's ultimatum.

Not able to face the truth that his own lethargy was to blame for the setback, Shafter looked for a scapegoat.

"Through the negligence of our Cuban allies, Pando, with five thousand men, entered Santiago last night," he told Admiral Sampson on July 4, renewing his demand that the Navy force its way into the harbor (to which Sampson could only point out that the mines were still in the channel).

"Lawton says [he] cannot compel General García to obey my instructions," Shafter lamented in a cable to Alger that same day, "and doubts if they intend to place themselves in any position where they will have to fight, and that if we intend to reduce Santiago, we will have to depend alone upon our own troops."

In his own defense García explained to Gómez that he had been ordered to maintain contact with the Americans' right flank, to the northeast of the city, and this left him in a position from which he could not effectively interdict Escario. Nearly a week earlier García had proposed sending two thousand Cubans under General Jesús Rabí to block Escario's advance at one of the mountain passes farther to the west, which was probably a more practical plan. But Shafter, intent on having the largest possible force to hurl at Santiago, had refused.*

But there was much more to this than a dispute over tactics, or even the need to fix blame for a military blunder. Americans had romanticized the Cuban

*Of course, the Cuban insurgents had been harassing Escario's column continually from Manzanillo to Santiago, action that cost the Cubans many casualties and the Spanish, at the very least, one day. Had the relief force been within Santiago on July 2, Blanco quite possibly would not have issued an unconditional order to Cervera to leave the harbor. Mahan reflected that Escario had arrived "too late . . . to take part in the defense of San Juan and El Caney . . . yet not so late but that it gives a shivering suggestion how much more arduous would have been the task of our troops had Escario come up in time."

insurgents for years. Whatever picture they carried in their heads, it in no way resembled the tattered, battle-weary men who met them on the beaches at Daiquirí and Siboney.

"What seems to have caused considerable comment and unjust criticism by many jolly excursionists that accompanied the Shafter expedition," wrote García's son, General Carlos García Velez, was the personal appearance of our soldiers.

> The sad and weary gaze of these unfortunate men . . . so different from the bold, defiant look of the free citizens of the north . . . caused these incipient war-critics to draw an unfair parallel without stopping to consider that the . . . appearance of the first was a logical result of a rough campaign of numberless hardships, as was the optimistic and brilliant disposition of the others, the product of a charming civilized life of liberty, love and relative prosperity.

At first it seemed to the Americans that there was nothing wrong with the Cubans that a few square meals couldn't fix. Rations were handed out freely. The nutritional problem was solved; the moral effect was not what had been expected. Stephen Crane observed the largesse with an insightful eye:

> Everybody knows that the kind of sympathetic charity which loves to be thanked is often grievously disappointed and wounded in tenement districts, where people often accept gifts as if their own property had turned up after a short absence. The Cubans accept our stores in something of this way. If there are any thanks it is because of custom.

And there was a difference in fighting style. The Cubans had, for three years, fought a guerrilla war, the hit and run war of the flea in which the object is never to win battles or capture ground but to exhaust the superior strength of the enemy. They had mastered the tactics of raid and ambush, but they looked upon the Americans' massive frontal assault on fortified and entrenched positions with more awe and admiration than comprehension. Shafter must have seen this and so kept García's men in reserve on July 1, waiting idly in positions along the road between El Caney and Santiago.

"We expected to be utilized in some way," Carlos García explained, "and every Cuban heart was beating for envy and disappointment, being compelled to wait there between the two fights, inactive, while the men who came to aid us in our struggle were being killed in heaps by *our* enemy."

But almost every American at Santiago—officers, men, and correspondents —was already convinced: the Cubans were lazy, ungrateful, and cowardly. It was not difficult to convince them next that García was to blame for Escario's success. It is likely that Shafter soon believed that himself.

·   ·   ·

AT THE REQUEST of the foreign consuls within the city, Shafter agreed to postpone the bombardment for another day, until noon on July 5, to give the civilian population enough time to evacuate. Then he decided to postpone the bombard-ment indefinitely.

"If it were simply a going out of the women and children to outside places where they could be cared for, it would not matter much," he cabled Alger, "but now it means their going out to starve to death or be furnished food by us, and the latter is not possible now."

But around midnight on the fourth the fleet bombarded the Spanish de-fenses at the harbor entrance. The inhabitants of Santiago believed the ships were forcing their way in.

The morning of July 5 found a pitiful procession of women, children, elderly, and a few foreigners trudging out along the road to El Caney. Faced with an American bombardment, the entire civilian population of Santiago was evacua-ting the city to take refuge in the village of El Caney.

The British consul, Frederick W. Ramsden, recorded the exodus in his diary:

> Three hours and a half on the road. The scene was terrible; people flocking out, sick carried on chairs or as they could, children getting lost by the way, etc. . . . The entrance to Caney was stinking with half-buried corpses of men and horses, as three days before there had been a tremendous battle there.

There was no food in El Caney. There were three hundred houses. There were twenty thousand refugees.

.   .   .

THE BAND WAS PLAYING "When Johnny Comes Marching Home Again." Ste-phen Crane looked down from San Juan Hill at the road from Santiago. It was July 6 and he was there to watch the exchange of Naval Constructor Hobson and the crew of the *Merrimac* for a Spanish officer.

"Along the cut roadway, toward the crowded soldiers, rode three men, and it could be seen that the central one wore the undress uniform of an officer of the United States navy."

The soldiers were sprawled on the grass. As Hobson approached they got to their feet, came to attention, and took off their hats.

> Then there was a magnificent silence, broken only by the measured hoof-beats of the little company's horses as they rode through the gap. It was solemn, funereal, this splendid silent welcome of a brave man by brave men who stood on a hill which they had earned out of blood and death—simply, honestly, with no sense of excellence, earned out of blood and death.

Next came the wagon with the crewmen. The Army and the Navy ex-changed banter.

"Well, Jackie, how does it feel?"

"Great! Much obliged to you fellers for comin' here."

"Say, Jackie, what did they arrest ye for anyhow? Stealin' a dawg?"

The navy still grinned. Here was no rubbish. Here was the mere exchange of language between men.

Crane followed the procession to the headquarters camp to hear Shafter congratulate the returned seamen.

The general sat in his chair, his belly sticking ridiculously out before him as if he had adopted some form of artificial inflation. . . . But the words he spoke were proper, clear, quiet, soldierly, the words of one man to others. . . . At the bidding of their officer [the men] aligned themselves before the general, grinned with embarrassment one to the other, made funny attempts to correct the alignment, and—looked sheepish. They looked sheepish. They looked like bad little boys flagrantly caught. They had no sense of excellence. Here was no rubbish.

.   .   .

SHAFTER TRIED AGAIN. On July 6 he wrote to Toral, explaining in detail the complete destruction of Cervera's fleet. The admiral was on board the *Harvard*, he said, waiting to sail to Annapolis. Toral could send an officer under a flag of truce, if he wished, to hear the story from Cervera's lips.

"Our fleet is now perfectly free to act," he continued. It could sail to within easy gun range of Santiago and bombard it. He mentioned eight-inch and thirteen-inch guns. He pointed out that no matter how much Spanish or American blood was to be shed, the final result would be the same. He suggested Toral surrender. He gave him three days to talk it over with Madrid.

To which General Toral replied that the telegraphers—English employees of the cable company—had fled the city and he had no means to confer with Madrid. He asked for their return. British Consul Ramsden persuaded "poor Cavanagh, Frume and Booney" to go back into the city and handle the messages.

The truce had almost expired on the morning of July 9 when Shafter received Toral's counterproposal. The Spaniard pointed out two facts of which Shafter was already painfully aware: that he no longer had to feed the civilian population—now Shafter's problem—and therefore what food he had would last "a reasonably long time"; and that the Spanish troops, unlike the Americans, were fully acclimated to Cuba and not nearly as susceptible to "the rigors of a bad climate and the sickness of the present season." Therefore he proposed a compromise: Shafter could have Santiago if he would permit Toral and his troops, "with all their baggage, arms and munitions," to withdraw to the town of Holguín, about seventy-five miles to the northwest, and if their safe passage en route were guaranteed.

Shafter forwarded the proposition to Washington and offered four good reasons for accepting it:

First, it releases at once the harbor; second, it permits the return of thousands of women, children and old men, who have left the town fearing bombardment and who are now suffering where they are, though I am doing my best to supply them with food; third, it saves the great destruction of property which a bombardment would entail, most of which belongs to Cuban and foreign residents; fourth, it at once relieves the command, while it is in good health, for operations elsewhere.

To underscore the last point he added: "There are now three cases of yellow-fever at Siboney, in Michigan regiment, and if it gets started no one knows where it will stop.

"We lose by this simply some prisoners we do not want and the arms they carry," he argued. "I believe many of them will desert and return to our lines. I was told by sentinel, who deserted last night, that 200 men want to come but were afraid our men would fire upon them."

Alger snapped back: "You will accept nothing but an unconditional surrender." He reminded Shafter that the general, just before receiving Toral's proposal, had stated that the American fortifications were impregnable and that the Spanish would eventually surrender unconditionally. Whatever Shafter needed to take the city, Alger said, he would have—men, ammunition, or supplies. Reinforcements were already on the way, in fact. In the meantime, nothing would be lost by staying in position.. As regards women and children, "The responsibility of destruction and distress to the inhabitants rests entirely with the Spanish commander."

Of course, Alger's response was not made without consulting the president. The gentle and pacific McKinley seemed to have grown more fond of war than he had been in the anxious days of March and April. He sent his own message directly to Shafter: "What you went to Santiago for was the Spanish army. If you allow it to evacuate with its arms you must meet it somewhere else. This is not war."

The memory of dead men piled upon the battlefield at Antietam had dimmed. War was now a matter of colored pins stuck into a map.

Shafter's reply to Alger was brief: "The instructions of the War Department will be carried out to the letter."

.   .   .

"NOT SINCE THE CAMPAIGN of Crassus against the Parthians has there been so criminally incompetent a General as Shafter," thundered Roosevelt in a letter to Lodge on July 5. And to Lodge two days later:

It is criminal to keep Shafter in command. He is utterly inefficient; and now he is panic struck. . . . The mismanagement has been beyond belief. We have a prize fool—who handled a balloon so as to cause us very great loss. We are half starved; and our men are sickening daily. The lack of transportation, food and artillery has brought us to the very verge of disaster; but above all the lack of any leadership, of any system or any executive capacity.

And again on the tenth,

> We on the firing line are crazy just at present because Gen. Shafter is
> tacking and veering as to whether or not he will close with the Span-
> iards' request to allow them to walk out unmolested. It will be a great
> misfortune to accept anything less than unconditional surrender.
> . . . We can surely get the whole Spanish army now, at the cost of
> probably not more than a couple of days' fighting, chiefly bombard-
> ment.

The shooting resumed at 4 P.M. that day. The firing continued through
the following morning. Although it was light on both sides, two Americans and
seven Spaniards were killed. The total wounded on both sides amounted to sixty-
seven.

Neither side gained or lost an inch.

.   .   .

CONSUL RAMSDEN RECORDED the situation at El Caney in his diary:

> The people are starving. The Red Cross Society cannot get provisions
> up in time for want of means of transportation, nor can the army. The
> people, thinking they had come out for but a couple of days and not
> being allowed to bring animals of burden with them, have now no
> provisions left. . . . The place is one big pigsty, and soon there must
> be a frightful epidemic. . . . In some houses you will find fifty in a small
> room.

And a few days later: "Frightful scenes; children crying for food and nothing
to give them; a few provisions arrived this afternoon, but not one-twentieth
enough."

.   .   .

SECRETARY ALGER HAD an idea. He had been giving some thought to the possibility that the Spanish would eventually surrender. Then what to do with them? At
first, Alger thought to ship them off to detention camps in Galveston, Texas.
President McKinley approved of the plan. But then Alger had an inspiration. He
cabled Shafter: "Should the Spaniards surrender unconditionally, and wish to
return to Spain, they will be sent back direct at the expense of the United States
government."

"In addition to avoiding the danger of introducing yellow fever into the
United States," Alger later explained,

> this plan . . . would have a good effect upon the people of Spain; the
> world would regard it as a gracious act on the part of a victorious nation,
> and it would tend to demoralize those Spanish soldiers remaining in
> Cuba, some of whom had been campaigning there three years, and

were anxious to return to their homes. Moreover, it would cost but little more to send them to Spain than to Galveston.

Shafter passed along the proposal to Toral and added the advice that he had lately received reinforcements, troops, and artillery newly arrived from Tampa.

Toral replied, first repeating his proposal that he be permitted to retreat to Holguín, but then following up with a second message in which he emphasized that he desired "conditions honorable for the Spanish arms." He said he trusted Shafter's "chivalry and sentiments as a soldier, and therefore must a solution be found that leaves the honor of my troops intact."

If this language baffled Shafter, it was clear to General Nelson Miles, who had just arrived with the reinforcements.

"The Spanish general to-day asked that some conclusion be reached that shall save his honor," he cabled Alger.

> Offers to surrender Santiago province, force, batteries, munitions of war, etc., all except the men and small-arms. Under ordinary circumstances would not advise acceptance, but this is a great concession and would avoid assaulting intrenching lines with every device for protecting his men and inflicting heavy loss on assaulting lines. The siege may last many weeks, and they have the provisions for two months. There are 20,000 starving people who have fled the city and were not allowed to take any food. . . . I concur with General Shafter and the major-generals, and would request that discretion be granted in view of the importance of other immediate operations. . . . The very serious part of this situation is that there are 100 cases of yellow-fever in this command, and the opinion of the surgeon is that it will spread rapidly.

Alger was indignant. It was enough that Shafter wanted to let the Spanish walk out of Santiago scot-free, but here was Miles (of whom, it may be recalled, Alger was never fond), "fresh from the United States, and had not been subjected to the trying experience of three weeks' campaigning in the tropics," adding his voice to Shafter's. Alger, still in the United States, and with no prospect of campaigning in the tropics or of any other experience more trying than arguing with his generals by telegraph, refused to think in terms of yellow fever, heavy American losses, or twenty thousand starving women and children. He fired off a brisk rejection to Miles. From behind his desk in the War Department, from the map-lined Operating Room in the White House, nothing but unconditional surrender seemed acceptable.

·   ·   ·

FACE-TO-FACE NEGOTIATIONS began on July 13, in the shade of a great ceiba tree down in a little valley midway between the Spanish and American lines. Robert Mason, the British vice consul, came with General Toral and his party to serve as interpreter. The American delegation consisted of Shafter, Miles, Wheeler, Lieutenant Miley, and an interpreter. Courtesies and pleasantries were exchanged, then the meeting got down to business.

General Toral spoke first and at great length. Blanco had authorized him to open negotiations, he said, but only as a spokesman; he could not surrender, capitulate, or evacuate without first obtaining the approval of Madrid. He was ready to hear the American demands and pass them along, but communications were slow, and at least two or three days would be required for an answer.

"That is all very well," Shafter said, "but you have had already time enough to consult with your government." Further delay was impossible. He could only give him until 5 A.M. the next morning.

"If by that time you have not received an answer, or decided, as to what you are going to do, well—I will open fire upon your works with every gun I have."

Toral shrugged. "Very well, I cannot help it." He promised to fight to the bitter end, to block the harbor, to destroy the city.

"You would gain practically nothing, and we both would suffer a terrible loss, for my men can fight."

Shafter wryly agreed that the Spanish soldiers certainly could fight. Wheeler, listening from the sidelines, formed his own impression of the Spanish general:

> I readily saw that the great desire on the part of General Toral was to maintain his honor and prestige as a soldier. . . .
> It was evident to me, from his preoccupied look and manner, that General Toral had constantly looming before him in his mind's eye the events which would follow when he once more stood upon Spanish soil with his conquered troops. It was explained to me by one of the Spanish commissioners that, as general commanding the Spanish forces, he would be held accountable for the surrender; and that he would probably, even though he had received the consent of his Government to capitulate, have to answer for same before a court-martial at Madrid.

Toral repeated his plea for more time.

> It can do you no harm; it will not weaken your position; it will not strengthen mine.
> I appeal to your soldierly feelings. You see, I am in a very bad plight, and my strong desire, my only wish, is to save the honor of the Spanish army. . . . This is all I ask; this is all I can do.

Shafter and Miles walked off a few paces, conferred briefly, then returned. They would extend the deadline by seven hours, until noon of the next day.

·   ·   ·

GENERAL ARSENIO LINARES, the Spanish commander of Santiago who had been severely wounded in the battles of July 1, had been following the course of the negotiations from his hospital bed in Santiago. The day before the meeting between Toral and the Americans he had sent a long message to the minister of war at Madrid:

The situation is fatal; surrender inevitable; we are only prolonging the agony; the sacrifice is useless; the enemy knows it, fully realizing our situation. . . .

These defenders are not just beginning a campaign, full of enthusiasm and energy; they have been fighting for three years with the climate, privations and fatigue; and now that the most critical time has arrived their courage and physical strength are exhausted, and there are no means for building them up again. The ideal is lacking. . . .

There is a limit to the honor of arms, and I appeal to the judgement of the government and the whole nation. . . .

If it should be necessary to consummate the sacrifice for reasons which I ignore, or if there is need of some one to assume the responsibility of the *denouement* anticipated and announced by me in several cablegrams, I offer myself loyally on the altar of my country for the one purpose or the other, and I will take it upon myself to perform the act of signing the surrender, for my humble reputation is worth very little when it comes to a question of national interests.

.   .   .

IT ONLY REMAINED to agree upon the details. Toral continued to be sensitive to matters of form and honor; Shafter and Miles remained cooperative, flexible, and persevering; Alger stayed snappish and impatient; the cable operators and telegraphers were kept busy.

The Spanish insisted upon the term "capitulate," rather than "surrender." The Americans instantly agreed. The Spanish demanded they be permitted to keep their small arms. Alger indignantly refused. Schafter devised a compromise: the arms would be shipped to Spain along with the troops. And so it went for several days, with frequent meetings beneath the giant ceiba, now known to the Americans as the Surrender Tree, the language of the official documents notwithstanding.

On July 17 they held the ceremony.

.   .   .

WITH SOME ASSISTANCE General Shafter mounted his horse. He rode out of the headquarters camp and down the road to Santiago, across the jungle valley and the San Juan River fords, across the grassy plain beyond, beneath the San Juan Heights—places that had until very recently been for him only scribbled lines on a map or flattened images in his binoculars.

Wheeler rode at his side, Lawton and Kent behind him. Next came the rest of the generals and their staffs, an honor guard, and the ubiquitous newspapermen. As they rode into a large open field between the lines they were met by General Toral and the Spanish party.

Wheeler recalled: "The American generals were drawn up in line from right to left according to rank, and their staffs were drawn up in the same manner, forming several successive lines."

James F. J. Archibald of the San Francisco *Post* watched from the sidelines.

One might have thought it was a meeting of old friends and not the acknowledgement of defeat. Smiles everywhere and bright looks from the defeated Spaniards more marked than from our own officers. Intense interest and curiosity was shown on both sides, for this was the first time the opposing forces had been afforded a good look at each other.

General Toral rode forward and smilingly saluted General Shafter, who stretched forth his hand and heartily shook that of the Spanish general. He congratulated General Toral upon the bravery of his men and of their gallant defence of Santiago, and both expressed satisfaction that the campaign had closed. All this was communicated through an interpreter.

There was one small gunboat in the harbor. A Spanish naval officer stepped forward to surrender it formally to Shafter, a gesture that demanded the general dismount. Flushing with embarrassment, Shafter apologized for staying in the saddle, frankly explaining that if he dismounted he would not be able to get back on his horse.

The capitulation ceremony ended, Shafter led the American party into the city.

"Between the lines, and especially as we neared the city, the condition was terrible," Archibald recalled.

Along the road were carcasses of horses, most of which still had the saddle, bridle, and in many cases saddle-bags full of effects . . . Shallow graves along the road had been scratched open by vultures and the odor was horrible . . .

As we rode through the streets toward the Plaza the way was lined by thousands of Spanish soldiers eager to see their conquerors . . . Many companies were drawn up and saluted as we passed.

Americans and Spaniards assembled in the plaza and waited. When the clock on the ancient cathedral struck twelve, the Stars and Stripes were raised over the palace. The band played "Hail Columbia" and "The Stars and Stripes Forever."

·   ·   ·

"WE MOUNTED THE PARAPET of our trench and gave three cheers," Private Post recalled.

Capron's battery had been named for the honor of firing the twenty-one guns of victory. Far down on either side of us stretched the trenches, on back to the blockhouse, Roosevelt's men, and beyond them. On the right they began the encirclement of the Bay of Santiago, and at our extreme right were the Cuban troops in their trenches. Miles of men in tattered and ragged blue; sick and well, waving and cheering and shaking hands.

CONSPICUOUS IN THEIR ABSENCE from the capitulation ceremonies were General García and the other Cuban officers. Shafter had excluded them from the negotiations. Now he added a final, gratuitous insult by denying them any part of the triumph.

.   .   .

"THAT EVENING at sunset," Archibald remembered, "I heard vespers chanted in the old Cathedral and heard an old priest pray for the success of Spanish arms, but the sun set with the American flag floating over the city."

CHAPTER FOURTEEN

PUERTO RICO

"I DID NOT SEE the ceremony of the raising of our flag over Santiago," Richard Harding Davis explained. "The surrender itself had become an accomplished fact, and, as the campaign in Porto Rico promised better things, I left the rifle-pits when General Miles sailed for Juanica."

Miles had sailed to Guantánamo Bay, where he was assembling transports, a naval escort, and a force of 3,314 men for the Puerto Rican expedition. At 3 P.M. on July 21 the flotilla got underway.

Puerto Rico, Spain's other Caribbean colony, had not loomed large in the long Spanish–American dispute that led to the war. The three factors that made Cuba an object of contention—proximity to the United States, long and bitter resistance to Spanish rule, and large American capital investment—were not present. But as the war began, the military value of the island became obvious. As a coaling station, naval base, and supply depot, it might have been a major Spanish asset in a protracted Caribbean war; it was, after all, Cervera's intended destination when he left Cape Verde in April. Now, after the destruction of the Spanish squadron, it was no longer an immediate threat to American operations in Cuba. However, Miles believed the time had come to invade.

"I consider it of the highest importance that we should take and keep that island," Miles advised Alger on July 5, "which is the gateway to the Spanish possessions in the Western Hemisphere, and it is also important that our troops should be landed there as early as possible this month."

In Puerto Rico, the rainy season does not begin until August. And Miles had reason to believe there would be little resistance.

Early in May, Lieutenant Henry H. Whitney of the Fourth Artillery was given a secret mission by the Bureau of Military Information, the Army's fledgling intelligence service. The thirty-one-year-old West Pointer was to visit Puerto Rico under the assumed identity of a British subject and reconnoiter the Spanish defenses. The mission got off to a bad start.

"Certain newspapers," Alger recalled,

> with a criminal disregard for his personal safety, to say nothing of the government's plans, took pains, as soon as he had sailed, to publish, with the utmost attention to detail, not only the fact, but the purpose of his mission. The result was, of course, that when the foreign merchantman, with Whitney on board, touched Puerto Rico, she found the Spanish officials awaiting her. The ship was boarded and carefully searched, but the American officer was hard at work in the furnace-room, "stoking" like a professional, and thoroughly disguised in sweat and coal dust. He landed at last, and, under a different disguise, made a thorough inspection of the southern part of the island.*

Whitney went ashore at Ponce on the southern coast of the island in the guise of H. W. Elias, a British merchant marine officer. "The information thus obtained was of great value to our army," Alger wrote.

What Whitney learned was that there were relatively few Spanish troops on the island—about eight thousand regulars. There were perhaps nine thousand more poorly trained militiamen. There was almost no artillery. There was a handful of small, antiquated naval vessels.

The roughly rectangular island was small—about one hundred miles long (east to west), and forty miles wide (north to south). San Juan, the capital, lay on the northeast coast. Ponce, a city of comparable size, lay on the southeast coast. A fine macadam road connected the two cities.

General Miles's declared destination was Point Fajardo on the northeast coast near San Juan. However, he did not suppose that this information would remain within the War Department. Perhaps recalling the experience of Lieutenant Whitney—now an officer on his staff and, for his pains, a captain—he did not announce his real destination until the flotilla was safely at sea. On July 26 Alger was astonished to read an Associated Press report that the expedition had landed the day before at Guánica, a port near Ponce on the southeastern coast. Caught off balance, Alger at first denied the AP story.

"Why did you change?" he cabled Miles.

*Alger dodges the question of how the newspapers learned of Whitney's mission in the first place; the answer would certainly point to extreme negligence in his own department. Despite the unfortunate initial publicity, there is almost no mention of Whitney's impressive exploit in contemporary accounts of the Spanish War, perhaps in part because he was a man of great modesty and circumspection. However, another reason for the obscurity of the operation may have been the probably considerable involvement of the British government in providing Whitney's cover. It may be noted that Whitney received his orders in person from Secretary Alger, who issued them orally. It seems apparent that in the event Whitney was captured the War Department intended to deny that his mission had official sanction, thus sparing Great Britain the embarrassment of an international incident with Spain.
Whitney also carried out a courier mission to Máximo Gómez, a fact that also nearly escaped published record.

"Circumstances were such that I deemed it advisable," Miles wired back. "Spaniards surprised."*

If surprise could be measured by their lack of resistance, the Spanish were dumbfounded. The *Gloucester* steamed into Guánica harbor at daybreak, fired her three-pound gun at a Spanish blockhouse, and landed a party of sailors armed with a Colt machine gun. The Spanish fled the town after a brief skirmish, leaving four dead behind.

"All the transports are now in the harbor," Miles reported in an afternoon dispatch, "and the infantry and artillery are going ashore. . . . The Spanish flag was lowered and the American flag raised at eleven o'clock to-day. . . . Hope to move on Ponce in a few days."

"Upon opening fire the inhabitants, terror stricken, fled from the town to the hills," Lieutenant Whitney recalled.

> During the day word was sent to them to return to their homes, which, before night, they did and were very demonstrative in their expressions of joy at the arrival of the Americans. It was the policy of the General Commanding to make the best impression upon the natives on the initial landing, knowing how rapidly the news of arrival would travel over the island and the effect his every act would have upon future operations in the interior. . . . At the date of the invasion . . . a large proportion of the illiterate native element were in doubt whether to support the ills they already had or to fly to others that might be worse. The best protection to life and property was what they wanted and what they would fight for.

"At least four-fifths of the people hail with great joy the arrival of the United States troops," Miles reported, "and requests for our national flag to hang over public buildings come in from every direction."

To which he might have added that, in choosing a flag to fly over a town or village, a prudent person would realize that the most important difference between the Spanish and the Americans was that the Americans had all the artillery.

· · ·

AFTER OFFERING LESS THAN token resistance, the Spanish garrison at Ponce left the city and retreated up the road to San Juan. The Americans marched in on July 28. Reinforcements arrived in a few days, and by August 5 the strength of the American expedition had increased to about fifteen thousand men.

"The army in Porto Rico advanced with the precision of a set of chessmen," Richard Harding Davis recalled. "Its moves were carefully considered and followed to success."

---

*Miles later offered a variety of reasons in support of his change of plans, suggesting that the decision was reached while the flotilla was at sea, hence Alger could not be informed. Of course, to have said that he had made the decision before he left Guantánamo would be to offer an unnecessary insult to Alger and his ability to control confidential War Department information.

Miles's plan called for a four-pronged advance on San Juan. The principal thrust was along the good paved highway that ran northeast from Ponce toward the capital. Miles anticipated that the Spanish would dig in along this highway at the town of Coamo, and at Aibonito, a three thousand-foot-high pass through the mountains that run generally east to west across the middle of the island.

A force landed at the southeast port of Arroyo, forty-five miles east of Ponce, was to advance northwest to Cayey, a small town on the Ponce–San Juan road beyond the Aibonito pass. The object was to cut off the Spanish retreat and attack them from the rear.

The large western seaport of Mayagüez was the objective of a third column, which was to advance from Ponce by rail to the town of Yauco, and thence over the road through Sabana Grande and San Germán.

A fourth column was to strike due north from Ponce, cross the island, and capture the town of Arecibo, thirty-five miles west of San Juan.

Miles's guiding principle was to substitute flanking maneuvers for frontal assaults. The memory of the advance on Santiago was still fresh.

. . .

A STRANGE PAIR of figures appeared on the empty highway just beyond the town of Juana Díaz, about ten miles northwest of Ponce. One rode a bicycle, the other a horse. Both were correspondents for the New York *Journal;* the one on the horse was Stephen Crane. They were a couple of miles beyond the Sixteenth Pennsylvania Infantry, which is to say they had passed beyond the spearhead of the American advance. Crane recalled the scene:

> The road, beautifully hard, wound through two thick lines of trees. We circled spurs of mountains, the grass upon them being yellowish green in the afternoon sunlight. We crossed tumbling brooks. . . . There was no man nor beast to be seen ahead on the road nor in the fields. . . . Rounding a corner we came suddenly upon a country store. Chickens and pigs scouted in the road and in the yard of the house across the road. On the steps of the store, on a fence, on boxes and barrels, and leaning against trees were about thirty men dressed in civilian garb. As we appeared they turned their heads, and as we rode slowly up every eye swung to our pace. They preserved an absolute stony silence. Now, here were men between the lines. The Americans were on one side and the Spaniards were on the other. They knew nothing of any American advance. They were, as far as they knew, on strictly independent ground, and could drop on either side of the fence. Americanism was here elective.
>
> We drew up and looked at them. They looked at us. Not a word was said. . . .
>
> This reception was new to our experience. These men were as tongue-tied and sullen as a lot of burglars met in the daytime. Not one of them could endure a straight glance, and if we turned suddenly we were likely to catch two of them whispering.
>
> A half-hour passed as slowly as time in the sick room. . . . A man

talking with another glanced at us, and spat in a way that left a feeling in our minds that perhaps it was not altogether unlikely that he was referring insultingly to us. . . .

Up the cool, shady country road toward Juana Díaz appeared a figure. It was a quarter of a mile away, but no one could mistake the slouched service hat, the blue shirt, the wide cartridge belt, the blue trousers, the brown leggings, the rifle held lightly in the hollow of the left arm. It was the first American scout.

He stood for almost two minutes, looking in our direction. Then he moved on toward us. When he had come ten paces four more men, identical in appearance, showed behind him. . . .

The five soldiers on foot arrived opposite the store. They did not stop, paying little heed to anyone. With their passing the Porto Ricans began to brace up and smile. Then appeared the support of the scouts and flankers, forty men blocked in a solid wall of blue-black up the road. The Porto Ricans looked cheerful. After the support had gone on there was a considerable pause. Then six companies of Pennsylvania infantry marched past, with a rattling of canteens and shuffling of feet. The Porto Ricans looked happy. By the time the general clattered forward with his staff they were happy, excessively polite, overwhelming every one with attentions and shyly confessing their everlasting devotion to the United States. The proprietor of the store dug up a new English and Spanish lexicon and proudly semaphored his desire to learn the new language of Porto Rico. There was not a scowl anywhere; all were suffused with joy. We told them they were a lot of honest men. And, after all, who knows?

.   .   .

HAD THE Spanish regulars not known that the squadron of Admiral Cervera was no more and that Santiago had fallen, they might have resisted the advance more diligently. Had they resisted more diligently, the militia might not have deserted en masse. Had the militia not deserted, the inhabitants of Puerto Rico might not have welcomed the American troops with open arms. All that is theory. The fact is this: the four American columns swept northward almost unopposed. The outcome was a foregone conclusion. The only question remaining was whether they would reach San Juan before the Spanish War was brought to an end.

CHAPTER FIFTEEN

YELLOW JACK

"WE EARNESTLY HOPE that you will send us . . . to Porto Rico," Roosevelt declared in a July 23 letter to Alger.

"If we stay here all summer we shall have yellow fever among us," he told a friend four days later. "I wish they would let us go to Porto Rico."

And to another friend on the thirty-first: "At present I am ardently longing to be out of here before yellow fever knocks us out. I would rather go to Porto Rico; if not that, then to the north."

Yellow Jack, a tardy Spanish ally, arrived at Santiago too late to save the city but in plenty of time to exact a leisurely vengance. There were 639 new cases of fever among the American troops on July 26; the next day there were 822 more, making a total of 3,193 fever cases. Most were suffering from malaria, which was not fatal and generally lasted no more than a few days, but there was a growing number of yellow fever cases.

"Each morning," Private Post recalled, "we would hear bugles blowing taps very shortly after reveille.

First, from off in the hills back of the trench line, a volley—the burial detail. Then the bugle. Taps, those slow, steady, and plaintiff notes that mark the end of a day or the end of a soldier's life. The sickness was striking in harder. The volleys became more frequent and one bugle followed another throughout the day; they followed each other almost as if they were but echoes among the hills about us.

"I am told that at any time an epidemic of yellow fever is liable to occur," Shafter warned the War Department on August 2. "I advise the troops be moved as rapidly as possible while the sickness is of a mild type."

The news came as a shock to Alger. "Up to this time the yellow fever situation was reported constantly 'improving,' and 'not alarming,' " he explained. Shafter's reports had been conflicting. The Army had no experience with tropical disease and tended to confuse yellow fever with malaria.

"The quarantine authorities in the United States were reluctant to advise that an army infected with yellow-fever be brought to any part of the country,' Alger recalled.

In fact, when it was made known that the department proposed to bring this army to some point on the New England coast, several prominent Senators called at the War Department to personally protest against such a course. . . .

Military necessity demanded the presence of the troops at Santiago to guard the Spanish prisoners;* prudence and protection of the country against an epidemic of yellow-fever prevented their return until that supposed danger had passed, or its real condition was determined —every consideration, in fact, of strategy and prudence made it imperative that the Fifth Corps remain in Cuba. Such was the position held by the administration in the light of the information then before it.

Shafter had further confused the issue by encouraging Alger to believe the troops could be sent twenty miles inland by railroad and there on the higher ground would be safe from yellow fever. This was the course Alger and McKinley quite naturally advised after they received Shafter's alarming report on August 2. But the railroad had been damaged in the fighting, had not yet been repaired, and could not carry more than a thousand men per day to the interior after it was put back in working order. Moreover, Lieutenant Miley went and had a look at the high ground at the end of the tracks and saw that the place received even more rainfall than the coast and might actually be worse than the Army's camps around Santiago.

"It was a perfect hotbed of malaria," Roosevelt recalled, "and there was no dry ground whatever in which to camp. To have sent the troops there would have been simple butchery."

"In my opinion there is but one course to take," Shafter cabled on August 3, "and that is to immediately transport the Fifth Corps and the detached regiments that came with it to the United States. If it is not done, I believe the death-rate will be appalling."

While this bombshell was reverberating through the War Department and the White House, another was close behind.

---

*Shafter had warned on July 18: "Feeling between Spaniards and Cubans is very bitter, and care will have to be taken to avoid collision." There was a widespread belief that the Cubans would, if given the chance, slaughter the disarmed Spaniards. In fact, the only Spanish troops that seemed to have had anything to fear in this regard were the "guerillas," the irregular volunteers who had treated the Cubans with exceptional brutality (see Funston, pp. 137–138).

.   .   .

THAT MORNING Shafter had called a meeting of all his medical officers and division and brigade commanders to review the fever situation. Roosevelt was surprised when he was specifically invited to attend. After polling the doctors and hearing each of them urge that the troops be sent back to the United States, Shafter got down to business.

"The General then explained that he could not get the War Department to understand the situation," Roosevelt recalled,

> that he could not get the attention of the public; and that he felt that there should be some authoritative publication which would make the War Department take action before it was too late. . . .
>
> Then the reason for my being present came out. It was explained to me by General Shafter, and by others, that as I was a volunteer officer and intended immediately to return to civilian life, I could afford to take risks which the regular army men could not afford to take and ought not be expected to take.

The scheme, then, was to have Roosevelt write a statement of the fever situation and give it to the press. Shafter calculated that the resultant public outcry would force Alger and McKinley to ship home the troops. Roosevelt agreed to do it. However, Wood, who had also been present, now cautioned him to make his statement in the form of a letter to Shafter, and let Shafter devise some discreet way of leaking it to the press. Roosevelt went back to his tent and composed the letter in his characteristic style:

> To keep us here, in the opinion of every officer commanding a division or a brigade, will simply involve the destruction of thousands. There is no possible reason for not shipping practically the entire command North at once. . . .
>
> In this division there have been 1,500 cases of malarial fever. Hardly a man has yet died from it, but the whole command is so weakened and shattered as to be ripe for dying like rotten sheep, when a real yellow-fever epidemic . . . strikes us, as it is bound to do if we stay here at the height of the sickness season. . . . Quarantine against malarial fever is much like quarantining against a toothache.
>
> All of us are certain that as soon as the authorities at Washington fully appreciate the condition of the army, we shall be sent home. If we are kept here it will in all human possibility mean an appalling disaster, for the surgeons here estimate that over half the army, if kept here during the sickly season, will die. . . .
>
> I write only because I cannot see our men, who have fought so bravely and who have endured extreme hardship and danger so uncomplainingly, go to destruction without striving so far as lies in me to avert a doom as fearful as it is unnecessary and undeserved.

"When I had written my letter," Roosevelt recalled,

the correspondent of the Associated Press, who had been informed by others of what had occurred, accompanied me to General Shafter. I presented the letter to General Shafter, who waved it away and said: "I don't want to take it; do whatever you wish with it." I, however, insisted on handing it to him, whereupon he shoved it toward the correspondent of the Associated Press, who took hold of it, and I released my hold.

Meanwhile, Wood had written an equivalent if less lively letter to Shafter, and the division and brigade commanders and Roosevelt signed it in round robin fashion. Wood presented the letter to Shafter, and it was leaked to the Associated Press in the same manner as was Roosevelt's letter.

"Later," Roosevelt remembered, "I was much amused when General Shafter stated that he could not imagine how my letter and the round robin got out!"*

The Associated Press lost no time in cabling the two letters back to the United States. President McKinley discovered them in his morning newspaper the next day, and in the words of Alger, "he became very much excited and indignant."

"The publication of the 'Round Robin' at that time was one of the most unfortunate and regrettable incidents of the war," Alger recalled.

It threatened, and might have accomplished even, an interruption of the peace negotiations then in progress between the United States and Spain. These negotiations had been inaugurated by Spain on the 26th of July, through M. Cambon, the ambassador of France, and had reached their most delicate stage at the time when the "Round Robin," with all its suggestions of panic and disaster, was made public in the four corners of the earth.

The first peace feelers had actually gone out on July 22 in a form of a letter from María Cristina to McKinley asking him what his terms for peace would be. But when the letter arrived on the desk of Ambassador Jules Cambon of France, who had agreed to act as go-between in the negotiations, it was discovered to be in cipher, and the nearest copy of the Spanish cipher book was at the Spanish consul general's office in Montreal. Thus it was that between the Spanish question and the American reply came Miles's landing in Puerto Rico.

The Spanish were ready to trade Cuba for peace. They still hoped to retain Puerto Rico, the Philippines, and the Marianas. But McKinley's terms were

---

*This version of the leaking of Roosevelt's letter comes from his *Autobiography* (pp. 251–252). However, there may may have been a bit more to the story than he tells. Four days before the date of this episode, Roosevelt wrote to Lodge about the fever situation: "I am determined that my skirts shall be clear of this particular form of murder, and so I have written the enclosed letter" (Roosevelt to Lodge, July 31, 1898, Elting Morison, 2:861–864). The enclosed letter was apparently a draft of the letter he says he wrote at the instigation of the others on August 3.

independence and Spanish evacuation of Cuba, plus the cession of Puerto Rico and one of the Marianas to indemnify the losses suffered by American interests in Cuba. As to the Philippines, the United States would hold Manila pending conclusion of the peace treaty.

Since the war had moved into the bargaining phase and McKinley was, at that moment, trying to force a quick and satisfactory end to hostilities, his anger at the publication of Roosevelt's letter and the round robin is understandable. Publishing the news that the American force at Santiago was "so weakened and shattered as to be ripe for dying like rotten sheep" and that the army surgeons had estimated "that over half the army, if kept here during the sickly season, will die" was more than giving aid and comfort to the enemy; it was a powerful bargaining chip that Spain might have played as events drew to a conclusion.

"We did not suppose that peace was at hand," Roosevelt shrugged, "being ignorant of the negotiations."

Ironically, the entire contretemps had been unnecessary. Even as Roosevelt and Shafter were leaking the letters to the press, Alger was cutting orders to Shafter to bring the troops home. The president and the secretary of war had read Shafter's reports and gotten the point.

·   ·   ·

"THE WAR DEPARTMENT," wrote Secretary Alger, "selected Montauk Point as a place in every way suitable for the return of the troops."

On the extreme tip of Long Island, 125 miles east of New York City, Montauk Point was cool and isolated—requisites of a yellow fever quarantine camp—yet readily supplied by the railroad that linked it with the port of New York. The depot was to be called Camp Wikoff, in honor of an officer who was killed in the assault on the San Juan Heights, and would actually consist of two camps: a small detention camp where new arrivals from Cuba would spend a five-day quarantine, and a larger general camp. But there was nothing there on August 2 when the administration abruptly decided to bring the troops home. Work began immediately and proceeded at a frantic pace to get the camp ready before the first transport arrived.

·   ·   ·

THE TROOPS WENT ABOARD the ships and waited. The Gallant Seventy-first was on a transport named the *Grand Duchesse*. Private Post recalled:

> We swung in the idle waters of Santiago's landlocked bay that first day, and the next, and the next. At night we watched the surface of the bay where the sharks were cutting figure eights or patterns of graceful curves that left brilliant phosphorescent arcs on the dark waters as though some vast hand was striking matches. . . . The night was full of pale blue-green arrows and sudden fountains of soft luminescence. We slept in fitful naps and woke to the bugle's reveille. From there on we waited for the clank of anchor chain that would mean the first leg of the trip home.

Roosevelt passed one afternoon with a visit to the Morro.

> We wandered all through it, among the castellated battlements, and in the dungeons, where we found hideous rusty implements of torture; and looked at the guns, some modern and some very old. It had been little hurt by the bombardment of the ships. Afterward I had a swim, not trusting much to the shark stories.

"THEN EARLY ONE MORNING," Private Post recalled,

> there was the whir of a winch up forward and we could hear the anchor chain clanking in. . . . The ship trembled as we felt the first throb of her engines and saw the red-roofed buildings along the shore start slowly sliding past the stanchions. On the deck above, the regimental band struck up "Home, Sweet Home" and then drifted into "Hail Columbia." Men crawled up the ship's rail and cheered—sickly men and a sickly cheer.

Down the bay, past the wreck of the *Merrimac*, her masts reaching above the tide, through the channel, and into the broad ocean beyond.

"The mountains of Cuba slowly sank into one long, undulating bank of thin blues and purples," Post remembered.

The Rough Riders were on the transport *Miami*. "We were favored by good weather during our nine days voyage," Roosevelt recalled.

> and much of the time when there was little to do we simply sat together and talked, each man contributing from the fund of his own experiences. Voyages around Cape Horn, yacht races for the America's cup, experiences of foot-ball teams which are famous in the annals of college sport; more serious feats of desperate prowess in Indian fighting and in breaking up gangs of white outlaws. . . . General Wheeler joined us and told us about the great war, compared with which ours was such a small war.

But there were still thousands of Spaniards in Cuba. There was still plenty of war remaining to be fought, he believed. He wrote a letter to a friend:

"I am on my way home and I hope to see you at some not distant date before we start off on the great Havana campaign."

CHAPTER SIXTEEN

THE FALL
OF MANILA

THERE WOULD BE no great Havana campaign; the last loose end of the Spanish War dangled at Manila. Admiral Dewey was still there, doing what he had done since early May—blockading the port, warily watching the German squadron, and waiting for the American troops to arrive and capture the city.

The first contingent of General Merritt's expeditionary force—some 115 officers and 2,386 enlisted men—had arrived on June 30. A week or so later came the welcome news that Cervera's fleet had been destroyed and Admiral Cámara's expedition had turned back to Spain. Dewey might then have sat back and enjoyed the long interlude had it not been for the Germans.

Admiral von Diedrichs continued to step on his toes. The German ships steamed in and out of the bay at all hours of the day and night, often ignoring American orders to stop and identify themselves. Without Dewey's permission the Germans landed men at Mariveles, opposite Corregidor at the entrance to the bay, took possession of the quarantine station, and drilled their troops. A German cruiser visited Subic Bay and reportedly interfered with the Filipino siege of the Spanish naval station there. (In fact, the cruiser was on a humanitarian mission, evacuating Spanish women and children from the besieged station and carrying them back to the relative safety of Manila.)

However, the constant irritant was the question of whether the Americans had the right to board German vessels passing the blockade, and this turned upon the interpetation of a fine point of international law. Von Diedrichs acknowledged the right of the blockaders to demand identification of passing warships but denied that this included the right to board. Dewey claimed that boarding was necessary to make proper identification. Captain Edward Chichester of the British cruiser *Immortalite*, which had also come to stay for a while in Manila

Bay, sided with Dewey, but the German stuck to his position.

The question was not simply a matter of military punctilio. There was the question of what so large a German fleet was doing at Manila in the first place, and Dewey could find no innocent explanation for it. The reality of the German menace was magnified in his mind. In fact, the kaiser had no intention of allying Germany with Spain against the United States. Von Diedrichs had been sent to Manila to test the fatuous theory that the Filipinos might like to become Germans and apparently was being kept there in hopes of catching whatever colonial crumbs might fall from the Spanish–American bargaining table. Dewey, of course, knew only that he was outgunned and outtonned by the German fleet. As to German national intentions, he remembered the conversations he had heard at the Metropolitan Club in Washington, where Roosevelt and his fellow expansionists gathered to discuss geopolitics.

Communicating with Washington involved the slow and cumbersome step of sending a dispatch ship back and forth over the six hundred miles of ocean separating Manila from the cable head at Hong Kong. Perhaps for this reason Dewey did not ask the administration for instructions in dealing with the Germans. In fact, he almost completely omitted informing Washington that there even was a problem.

"As I was on the spot and familiar with the situation from day to day," he later explained to McKinley, "it seemed best that I look after it myself, at a time when you had worries enough of your own."

Dewey's style of looking after things consisted of meeting rudeness with belligerence and not giving an inch in the punctilious enforcement of what he saw as the rights of a blockading fleet. The policy brought things to a dangerous head during the second week in July.

It began with an incident involving the German cruiser *Cormoran*—"an old offender," Dewey noted—which was sighted coming up the bay by Lieutenant T. F. Brumby aboard the cutter *McCulloch.*

"When the *Cormoran* saw the *McCulloch* approaching," Dewey recalled,

she turned and steamed toward the northern part of the bay, compelling the *McCulloch* to follow. Brumby first hoisted the international signal, "I wish to communicate." No attention was paid to this by the *Cormoran.* Then Brumby fired a shot across her bows, which had the desired effect.

On the following day Vice-Admiral von Diedrichs sent a capable, tactful young officer of his staff to me with a memorandum of grievances.

Dewey did not write a detailed account of the colloquy, but an unidentified officer of the *Olympia,* who claimed to have overheard it, gave this account to John Barrett of the New York *Journal:*

As soon as the German officer was shown into the presence of the Admiral, the latter began to discuss the situation. The Admiral has a way of working himself up to a state of great earnestness as he thinks out a question. Commencing in a subdued tone, he gradually became querulous and then emphatic as he spoke of the activity of the Germans. Growing more earnest, his voice took a higher pitch until he complained in vigorous terms of what had been done:

"If the German Government has decided to make war on the United States, or has any intention of making war, and has so informed your Admiral, it is his duty to let me know."

Hesitating a moment, he added:

"But whether he intends to fight or not, I am ready."

Then having given vent to his suppressed feelings, he quieted down like a calm after a storm. The German officer made some hurried apologies, and hastened away, remarking to one of the officers of the *Olympia*, "Mein Gott! Mein Gott! What is the matter with your Admiral to-day?"

Of the conversation with the young German officer Dewey only recounted:

"I made the most of the occasion by using him as a third person to state candidly and firmly my attitude in a verbal message which he conveyed to his superior so successfully that Vice-Admiral von Diedrichs was able to understand my point of view.

There was no further interference with the blockade or breach of the etiquette which had been established by the common consent of the other foreign commanders. Thus, as I explained to the President, after the war was over, a difference of opinion about international law had been adjusted amicably, without adding to the sum of his worries.

·   ·   ·

THROUGHOUT JUNE AND JULY the American troop buildup at Manila continued. The second contingent of General Merritt's expedition, consisting of 3,586 officers and men under General Francis Vinton Greene, arrived on July 17. When the third contingent under General Arthur MacArthur* arrived on July 25 and 31, the American troops strength had reached a total of 470 officers and 10,464 men.

"General Merritt found both a difficult and delicate task confronting him on his arrival in Manila Bay," Secretary Alger wrote. It was difficult because the city was defended by a force of some 20,000 Spanish troops—twice the size of the American expedition—in strongly fortified and entrenched positions. It was delicate because it was complicated by the tense and ambiguous relationship of the Filipino insurgents under Emilio Aguinaldo to the American forces.

"The situation was difficult to deal with," Merritt recalled, "owing to the peculiar relations which existed between the American and insurgent leaders as a result of the active operations undertaken by the latter, more or less encouraged by the naval authorities, prior to the arrival of the army reinforcements."

"My policy," Dewey recalled, "was to avoid any entangling alliance with the insurgents, while I appreciated that, pending the arrival of our troops, they might

*Father of Douglas MacArthur.

be of service in clearing the long neck of land that stretches out from Cavite Peninsula to the environs of Manila."

On June 27 Dewey reported the status of his relationship with Aguinaldo to Secretary Long:

> Consistently I have refrained from assisting him in any way with the force under my command, and on several occasions I have declined requests that I should do so, telling him the squadron could not act until the arrival of the United States troops. At the same time I have given him to understand that I consider insurgents as friends, being opposed to a common enemy. . . . My relations with him are cordial, but I am not in his confidence. The United States has not been bound in any way to assist insurgents by any act or promises, and he is not, to my knowledge, committed to assist us. I believe he expects to capture Manila without my assistance, but [I] doubt [the insurgents'] ability, they not yet having many guns.

When the first contingent of Merritt's expedition arrived under General T. M. Anderson, the general found that Aguinaldo had taken advantage of the reduced mobility of the Spanish to surround the city on its land approaches. Anderson hoped for amicable relations with the Filipinos, but this was not to be. Merritt wrote:

> It was found necessary to solicit [Aguinaldo's] aid in obtaining horses, buffaloes, carts, etc. for purposes of transportation, for which the native population was disposed to charge exorbitant prices. Further communications passed between [Anderson and Aguinaldo] on the subject of securing maps and other data concerning the topography of the country about Manila. Aguinaldo, although profuse in promises of assistance in every possible direction, actually rendered very little aid. This correspondence was abruptly terminated by a letter from the Filipino General dated July 24, in which he asserted that he had come from Hong Kong in order to prevent his own countrymen from making common cause with the Spaniards against the Americans and protested against the landing of American troops in places conquered and occupied by the insurgents, without previous notice, in writing, to his "Government."

General Merritt furnished no such notice to Aguinaldo, feeling that Dewey had already gone much too far in tacit recognition of Aguinaldo's claims to legitimacy.

"As General Aguinaldo did not visit me on my arrival nor offer his services as subordinate military leader," Merritt explained,

> and as my instructions from the President fully contemplated the occupation of the islands by the American land forces, and stated that "the powers of the military occupant are absolute and supreme and

immediately operate upon the political conditions of the inhabitants," I did not consider it wise to hold any direct communication with the insurgent leader until I should be in possession of the city of Manila, especially as I would not until then be in a position to issue a proclamation to enforce my authority, in event that his pretensions should clash with my designs.

For these reasons the preparations for the attack on the city were pressed and military operations conducted without reference to the situation of the insurgent forces.

Thus, the two armies that confronted the common Spanish enemy at Manila were not talking to each other.

.   .   .

WHATEVER THE SPANISH COMMANDER may have known or guessed of the tense Filipino–American relations, it could not have encouraged him to believe that the military situation was in any way improved. He remained blockaded by a formidable naval force and besieged by a combined force of 32,000 men who, if they shared nothing else, had in common the intention of conquering the city of Manila.

"Owing to the restriction of the blockade and to the investment of the city on the land side by the insurgents, the people of Manila were in a bad way for supplies," Dewey recalled.

> Soon after the victory of May 1 . . . General Don Basilio Augustin Davila [the Spanish commander], through the British consul, Mr. Rawson-Walker, had intimated to me his willingness to surrender to our squadron. But at that time I could not entertain the proposition because I had no force with which to occupy the city, and I would not for a moment consider the possibility of turning it over to the undisciplined insurgents, who, I feared, might wreak their vengeance upon the Spaniards and indulge in a carnival of loot.

While Dewey waited for the troops to arrive in order to be able to accept the Spanish surrender, Madrid, having sensed Davila's surrendering proclivity in the desperate tone of his dispatches, replaced him with General Firmín Jaudenes. British Consul Rawson-Walker had meanwhile succumbed to illness and passed away, bequeathing the role of go-between to the Belgian consul, Edouard André.

Dewey soon realized that General Jaudenes was only slightly less disposed to surrender than Davila, and he believed that he could soon talk him into it. He got General Merritt's consent to delay taking any step that might precipitate a general engagement. Merritt was not ready to launch a full-scale assault on the city in any case; the landing of MacArthur's troops had been delayed by severe squalls, heavy rains, and a shortage of landing craft.

"However, with two armed forces facing each other in time of war," Dewey explained, "it is difficult to prevent a clash; and it was not long before the inevitable happened."

"The activity of the Americans in pushing forward and constructing trenches aroused the Spaniards," General Merritt recalled, "who made a sharp attack with infantry and artillery on the night of July 31. . . . For about an hour and a half both sides kept up a heavy artillery and infantry fire."

American losses amounted to ten killed and thirty-three wounded. There were more attacks by the Spanish during the next few nights; five more American troops were killed, ten more were wounded.

While Merritt continued to get ready for the final assault on the city, Dewey resumed his informal negotiations with General Jaudenes by way of M. André.

Jaudenes at Manila was in precisely the same predicament as Linares and Toral had been at Santiago. On the one hand, he could see that his position was impossible, defeat inevitable, and he wished to avoid useless bloodshed; and on the other hand he knew that the government in Madrid, refusing to accept responsibility for the disaster, would hold him entirely to blame for the fall of Manila if he surrendered without offering resistance. What he proposed, then, was a formula for honorable surrender.

"Finally," Dewey recalled,

> without making any definite promise, General Jaudenes agreed that, although he would not surrender except in consequence of an attack upon the city, yet, unless the city were bombarded, the Manila batteries would not open on our ships. Moreover, once that attack was begun he would, if willing to surrender, hoist a white flag over a certain point in the walled city from which it could be seen both from Malate and from the bay.
>
> In other words, his attitude differed from that of Don Basilio [Augustín Davila] only in that he wished to show the form of resistance for the sake of Spanish honor; or, as the Chinese say, to "save his face."

The elaborate choreography included an understanding that Dewey would demand surrender as he opened the attack upon the city; the admiral made a sketch of the signal flags he would fly so that the general would be sure to know the demand had been made. This was the only piece of paper involved in the negotiations; all other communications were conveyed orally through the medium of M. André.

By August 7 General Merritt was ready. Everyone took their places, the curtain was raised, and the players began to speak their lines.

"We sent the usual forty-eight hours' notice preparatory to a bombardment to General Jaudenes," Dewey recalled.

> He answered that, being surrounded by insurgent forces, he had no place of refuge for the wounded and sick and the women and children except within the walls of the city. In reply we pointed out how helpless was his position and how clearly it was his duty to save the city from the horrors of bombardment. He demurred and begged time in which to consult his government, a request which was promptly refused.

Silence fell upon Manila as the hours passed. "Great difficulty was experienced during this period," Merritt recalled, "in preventing the insurgents from provoking further outbursts from the Spaniards, and it was necessary to use stringent measures, even force, to keep them from breaking the tacit armistice."

"On the ninth," Dewey recalled,

> the foreign men-of-war and the refugee steamers under their charge were notified to shift their anchorages so as to be out of the line of fire. It was noticeable that while the German and French vessels took up a position to the northward of the city, the English and Japanese came over to Cavite and anchored near our squadron.

Dewey and Merritt had scheduled their token attack for the tenth, but on the morning of that date Merritt came aboard the *Olympia* and reported that his troops were not quite ready. The attack was rescheduled for the thirteenth.

"The 13th dawned as a typical Manila day, after intervals of rain during the night," Dewey recalled.

> The air was lifeless, the thermometer in the 80's, and everything steaming with humid heat. But at eight o'clock the sky partially cleared and a light breeze sprang up. At 8.45 the ships got under way and moved in to their stations . . .
> As we got under way the officers and men of the British ship *Immortalite* crowded on the deck, her guard was paraded, and her band played "Under the Double Eagle," which was known to be my favorite march. Then, as we drew away from the anchorage from which for over three months we had watched the city and bay, Captain Chichester got under way also and with the *Immortalite* and the *Iphigenia* steamed over toward the city and took up a position which placed his vessels between ours and those of the foreign fleet.* We broke our battle flags from the mast-heads with the conviction that we were to see the end of the story which we had begun when they were broken out on May 1.
> At 9.35 the *Olympia, Raleigh, Petrel,* and *Callao* opened fire on Fort San Antonio, on the flank of the Spanish intrenchments, which was continued slowly for about an hour, without any response from the fort. Meanwhile, we could see our troops on shore advancing through the fields and along the beach.

The fleet ceased firing. The troops advanced, meeting light resistance, and found the fort abandoned. At 10:35 A.M. the Spanish flag was hauled down and the Stars and Stripes raised. The *Olympia* arrived off the city flying the signal flags representing the preestablished surrender demand. Dewey and his officers scanned the battlements through their glasses, looking for General Jaudenes's reply.

"The background was so indefinite that for a time nothing was sighted,"

---

*The movement of the English ships gave rise to the enduring myth that Captain Chichester, in placing himself between Dewey and von Diedrichs, supposedly signified that if the Germans should interfere and attack the Americans they should be attacking Great Britain, as well.

Dewey recalled. "Finally, however, it was my fortune to be the first to make out a white flag flying on the appointed place on the southwest bastion of the city wall. Our own signal had been hoisted at 11 A.M., and it was not until 11.20 that we distinguished the answer."

Only the formalities remained. At 5:43 P.M. the American flag replaced the Spanish over Manila. It had not been an entirely bloodless victory, however. While the admirals and generals knew the battle was to be a sham, they did not so inform the privates. On the American side the day's losses amounted to six dead and forty-three wounded.

Filipino–American relations were also a casualty.

"After the battle the insurgent forces gathered outside the American lines endeavoring to gain admission to the town," Merritt recalled, "but strong guards were posted and General Aguinaldo was given to understand that no insurgents would be allowed to enter with arms."

To which Aguinaldo could only reply with the complaint, "My troops are forced by yours, by means of threats of violence, to retire from positions taken." But keeping the insurgents out of the city had been part of the unwritten bargain struck with General Jaudenes.

.   .   .

THE DETAILS OF the surrender were worked out the next day and were recalled by Dewey:

> The Spanish troops surrendered the city and its defenses with the honors of war, laying down their arms and referring the question of their future status and repatriation to the government at Washington; officers were allowed to retain their side-arms, horses, and private property; all public property and public funds were turned over to United States authority; and Manila, with its inhabitants, churches, educational institutions, and private property, was placed under guard of the American army.

Dewey sent off a report of the surrender to be cabled from Hong Kong. Two days later, on August 16, a dispatch ship brought back a message from Washington.

President McKinley had signed a peace protocol with Spain the day before the sham battle of Manila.

The Spanish War had been over since August 12.

CHAPTER SEVENTEEN

VERSIONS
OF PEACE

"Peace came differently to different men," Richard Harding Davis remembered. Davis was with an Army column advancing toward Cayey in Puerto Rico when word of the peace protocol was received.

An artilleryman, on the point of firing a fieldpiece, swore angrily. Another threw his hat in the air and cried, "Thank God! Now I won't get killed."

General Miles was disappointed that he had been denied the chance to capture San Juan. He cabled Alger: "Please notice on map our troops occupy best part of Porto Rico. They are moving in such strong column in concert that nothing could check their progress."

Disappointment was the mood prevailing in dozens of Army camps in the United States, where the eager recruits learned there would not be enough war to go around. Major Hugh Scott, adjutant general of a volunteer infantry division waiting in camp near Lexington, Kentucky, recalled,

> The signing of the protocol with the Spaniards brought us great trouble. The men had volunteered for the war and now that the war was over they could see no reason why they should not lay down their guns anywhere they happened to be and walk home. As many as three hundred men would be reported absent without leave from a single regiment.

But there was no disappointment at the New York *Journal*. William Randolph Hearst was prepared to cover the peace as flamboyantly as he had reported the war. The victorious North Atlantic Squadron was steaming up the East Coast to New York City. Hearst was delighted.

"Make Saturday a Full Holiday, so All the People May See Our Victorious Fleet," the *Journal* urged. Hearst enlisted the mayor, the governors of New York and New Jersey, and several large New York City employers in the plan. The *Journal* arranged to fly an observation balloon over the city to mark the progress of the fleet and signal its progress to those below through showers of red, white, and blue confetti.

The arrival of the fleet would hardly have been ignored in any case, but Hearst's promotional campaign freed thousands of New Yorkers who would otherwise have spent the morning in shops and offices. Even the usually prim New York *Times* was moved to exuberance in its report of the festivities:

> A half-dozen of the best Fourth of Julys that New York ever put itself out to celebrate compressed into one couldn't compare with the rather impromptu welcome that the sailors of the New York, Iowa, Indiana, Brooklyn, Massachusetts, Oregon and Texas received yesterday from the people of New York and its vicinity.
>
> Every pier, every excursion boat . . . every roof of a tenement house fronting the water between the Narrows and Grant's Tomb, held a mass of well-nigh frantic men and women, who cheered until they were hoarse, and then screamed through parched throats, while wildly waving their ten-cent flags.

The seven warships appeared off Sandy Hook at daybreak and steamed into the harbor in majestic column. A flotilla of some four hundred vessels—tugboats, ferries, fishing boats, yachts, even ocean liners, and every one crowded to the gunwales—joined in the parade, and every steam whistle screamed a welcome. Batteries along the harbor thundered salutes that were answered by the heavy guns of the fleet. The column passed before the Statue of Liberty and steamed up the Hudson River.

"Reaching Riverside Drive," Commodore Schley recalled,

> the hillsides from the water to their tops were packed with enthusiastic people, women and children being clad in raiment of every variety of summer colors, which gave to the slopes the appearance of having been padded with flowers. The effect from the ships as they swung past was entrancingly beautiful in the bright sunshine of that beautiful summer day.

The fleet stopped abeam of Grant's Tomb, where Hearst's balloon continued to rain patriotic confetti. A gun battery on the New Jersey bank filled the air with smoke and thunder.

The New York *Times* regretted that the president and the secretary of the Navy were not on hand to witness the spectacle. McKinley was in Washington, and Long had fled the August heat of the capital for his annual retreat to Massachusetts. It may have been hard for the secretary to believe that less than a year had passed since his brash young assistant was having immense fun running the Navy and explaining his war plans to the president.

.   .   .

"I AM AFRAID I am the last of your friends to congratulate you on the brilliant campaign . . . in which you have gained so much experience and glory," wrote Ambassador John Hay from London.

> When the war began I was like the rest; I deplored your place in the Navy where you were so useful and so acceptable. But I knew it was idle to preach to a young man. You obeyed your own demon, and I imagine we older fellows will all have to confess that you were in the right. . . . You have written your name on several pages of your country's history, and they are all honorable to you and comfortable to your friends.

"Yes, I was right to go," Roosevelt replied with obvious pleasure,

> although I suppose, at bottom I was merely following my instinct instead of my reason. . . . At Santiago we had a great fight. . . .
>
> My Regiment will be mustered out in a few days, and then I shall be footloose. Just at the moment there is a vociferous popular demand to have me nominated for Governor, but I very gravely question whether it materializes and I haven't the slightest knack at making it materialize. I wish I were going to be in Washington. . . .

.   .   .

"IN THE SPACE of less than three weeks, twenty thousand soldiers, fully half of whom were suffering from diseases contracted in Cuba, were landed upon the barren fields of Montauk Point," recalled General Wheeler, who had been put in charge of the camp there.

> Notwithstanding that doctors, nurses, hospital stewards, and all neces-sary supplies were in abundance, and that a small army of civilian laborers, carpenters, teamsters, and other workmen were busily engaged in their respective departments; that there were unlimited supplies of delicacies for the sick; and that everything was done which hand could do and brain devise for the well-being of the soldiers . . . numerous had become the newspaper articles concerning what they were pleased to call the maladministration and mismanagement at our military camps, and which according to them had entailed untold hardships and priva-tions upon our brave soldiers.

"Starving Men at Montauk Point," cried the *Journal*. "Sick and Dead at Jacksonville." "Story of Horrors Hourly Grows Worse." "It Is Murder That Is Being Done at Montauk."

A grim cartoon showed a tombstone with the epitaph, "Killed by Spaniards, Two Hundred; Killed by Official Negligence and Incompetence, Two Thou-sand."

"On August 24th, the Secretary of War paid a visit to Montauk Point,"

Wheeler recalled. "He made a thorough investigation of all parts of the camp and was much pleased with what he saw."

"The Secretary walked through each street in a frock coat and a silk hat," Private Post recalled.

> Slightly behind him came his staff, golden and immaculate. . . . The Secretary stopped and looked through the open tent flap.
>
> "Attention!" someone called. Men rose from their cots.
>
> "At ease," said the Secretary. "How are you, men? Can we do anything for you?" . . . I saluted. I have never forgotten that moment.
>
> "Mr. Secretary," I said, "I am speaking for this tent and many other tents. We are dying here without attention, without rations or medicines. Five men were picked up yesterday morning, dead. . . . Every effort has been made to make this place nice for your inspection. And it's a lie. We are dying of neglect."
>
> I could see the official staff, two paces behind stiffen. . . .
>
> "You have been lied to in this inspection, Mr. Secretary," I went on, "this hospital is a lie. Anyone who tells you different is a liar. . . . We will die if we are kept here."
>
> The Secretary listened. "There, there, my man," he said mildly. "We'll fix everything." This was just soothing talk to a sick man. . . .
>
> I dropped back on my cot. From other tents he got the same, I heard. Now and then someone would say that everything was fine, but there were many who told him the truth, and even cursed as they did it.

Even Alger's friends were critical. Roosevelt, now at Camp Wikoff, recalled the administrative disaster of Tampa and told Lodge:

> I am very much afraid that with Alger the trouble is congenital. He simply *can't* do better; he *can not* learn by experience. Now I don't want to grumble, and I am doing my best to keep the "Rough Riders" from grumbling, but we did not have good food on our transport coming back here; we did not have good water; and we were so crowded that if an epidemic had broken out, we should have had literally no place in which to isolate a single patient. . . . I do most earnestly wish that the President would change Alger before election, and change him for some man who would himself begin to uproot the evils in the [War] Department.

One hundred twenty-six men died at Camp Wikoff. No one can say whether they would have lived had they received better care. Alger claimed that 126 dead out of 22,000 men was a creditable record.* Few agreed with him.

---

*The total number of deaths in the Army from disease and other noncombat causes between the end of April and the end of September was 2,565; only 365 men had died in action. The total strength of the Army during this period reached 274,717.

Disease in the Army camps was but one of several sources of contention within and between the Army and Navy. General Miles blamed the sickness on the War Department's canned beef, which he claimed had been treated with chemicals—he used the term "embalmed"—and fed to the troops as an experiment. Commissary General Charles P. Eagan responded with what amounted to the charge that, if Miles had said that, he was a liar. Eagan was court-martialed and cashiered.

General Shafter continued to receive some very severe criticism but survived relatively unscathed. His dispute with Admiral Sampson was eclipsed by Sampson's quarrel with Schley. General Miles interposed his own opinion into the Sampson–Schley controversy and was reprimanded.

There were so many charges made against Secretary Alger that, in the hope of clearing his name, he asked the president to appoint a commission to investigate the War Department. McKinley obliged with the Dodge Commission, named after its chairman, railroad magnate Grenville M. Dodge. The commission found that there had been no corruption or intentional neglect of duty in the department but that it had been poorly managed. Alger had no choice but to be satisfied with this very qualified vindication. After a painful and humiliating year had elapsed, he resigned from the cabinet.

Private Post finally managed to get a pass, a Long Island Railroad ticket, and five dollars. He left Camp Wikoff and went home to New York City. There the cumulative effects of battle, tropical fever, and neglect combined to put him in a hospital.

Later, after he had gotten back on his feet, he had one more battle to fight. While away in Cuba he had been called for jury duty; now he faced a five hundred dollar fine for failing to show up.

"It took a judge to get me off!"

.   •   •   •

LATE IN AUGUST Roosevelt traveled from Camp Wikoff to nearby Oyster Bay for a five-day reunion with his family. The house at Sagamore Hill was besieged by crowds of well-wishers, eager for a glance at the war hero. Reporters asked him about the New York governorship.

"I will not say a word about myself," he protested, "but I will talk about the regiment forever."

The Rough Riders were to be demobilized and disbanded, the troopers to return to civilian life. He returned to Camp Wikoff to see to the details.

"I have been very busy with my Regiment," he told Lodge on September 4, "and have let [the gubernatorial nomination] attend to itself. If I am nominated, well and good. . . . If I am not nominated, I shall take the result with extreme philosophy and with a certain sense of relief."

Nine days later, while working in his tent-office, he was asked to step outside. He found the whole regiment assembled in a hollow square formation, with the officers and color-sergeant in the middle. Private William S. Murphy of Oklahoma led him to the middle of the square, where an army blanket hid a mysterious object standing on a table.

It was, Murphy said, "a very slight token of admiration, love and esteem." The young cowboy stumbled through his prepared speech, at last reaching its merciful conclusion:

"Allow me to say that one and all, from the highest to the lowest . . . will carry back to their hearths a pleasant remembrance of all your acts, for they have always been of the kindest."

With that the blanket was whipped away, revealing a bronze statue of a rider on a bucking horse. It had been done by Frederic Remington and was called, "The Bronco Buster."

For once at a loss for words, Roosevelt ran his hand over the thing while he blinked back the tears. At last he found his voice.

Officers and men, I really do not know what to say. . . . I would have been most deeply touched if the officers had given me this testimonial, but coming from you, my men, I appreciate it tenfold. . . . To have such a gift come from this peculiarly American regiment touches me more than I can say. . . .

There was a momentary silence. He could say no more. One of the troopers lifted his hat in the air and turned to his fellows.

"Three cheers for the next Governor of New York!" he cried, and the cheering began.

It was soon to be a familiar sound. He would hear it throughout the length and breadth of New York State during the next two months. And in November, after the election returns had been counted, he could only look back on the year with mild astonishment.

"I have played it with bull luck this summer," he told a friend.

First, to get into the war; then to get out of it; then to get elected. I have worked hard all my life, and have never been particularly lucky, but this summer I *was* lucky, and I am enjoying it to the full. I know perfectly well that the luck will not continue, and it is not necessary that it should. I am more than contented to be Governor of New York, and shall not care if I never hold another office.

       •   •   •

FOR WILLIAM R. DAY, peace meant a new job. Since April, when John Sherman had resigned in poor health, he had been secretary of state, a job he had held in fact, if not in title, since he was appointed assistant secretary. Now there was to be a peace conference in Paris to draft a treaty with Spain and bring the Spanish War to a formal conclusion. Day was appointed to head the American delegation.

The new secretary of state was to be John Hay, charter member of the Roosevelt–Lodge–Adams "Pleasant Gang." During his sixteen-month tour of duty as American ambassador in London, Hay had become an ardent Anglophile, a sentiment he now suddenly shared with thousands, if not millions, of his countrymen. The fashionable subject of the hour was "the Anglo–American Alliance."

"The war," said General Miles at a dinner given in his honor, "has given us reason and opportunity to appreciate our obligations to the mother country." Lord Alfred Paget, British naval observer during the Santiago campaign, arose and responded, "We shall be proud in the future whenever we see the Stars and Stripes on a warship or a merchantman, for we shall know that on board we have, if not a brother, an ally."

An Anglo-American League had been formed in July, with branches on both sides of the Atlantic. The western branch included such diverse American notables as Whitelaw Reid, Carl Shurz, and Archbishop M. A. Corrigan, leader of New York City's Roman Catholics. The league's charter proclaimed that "the same language and the same principles of ordered liberty should form the basis of an intimate and enduring friendship between these kindred peoples." Even Cleveland's secretary of state, Richard Olney, whose intemperate note at the height of the Venezuelan Boundary Crisis had nearly sparked an Anglo–American war, now reflected:

> Family quarrels there have been heretofore and doubtless will be again, and the two peoples . . . take with each other liberties of speech which only the fondest and dearest relatives indulge in. Nevertheless that they would be found standing together against any alien foe by whom either was menaced . . . it is not permissible to doubt.

British Colonial Secretary Joseph Chamberlain's visit to the United States set off rumors that he had gone to advise McKinley on the matter of the Philippines. Chamberlain denied the report and claimed the sole purpose of the trip was to visit his in-laws (he was married to the daughter of President Cleveland's secretary of war). But while in the United States he set down some thoughts of an Anglo–American alliance for publication in *Scribner's* magazine:

> In the course of the last few months a great and noteworthy change has come over the relations between the United States and Great Britain. . . .
>   No great gift of imagination is required to foresee the far-reaching and beneficent consequences that may result in the future from a cordial understanding between the two great branches of the Anglo-Saxon race. . . .
>   [Until recently] there existed, unfortunately, in the minds of the American people, a deep-rooted conviction that England was unsympathetic and even hostile to the ideals of the United States; and it required the unmistakable evidence afforded by the attitude of Great Britain during the recent war to convince them that this suspicion was unfounded. . . .
>   Great Britain alone [among the European powers] sympathized with the national sentiment in America. . . .
>   The natural sympathies which have thus been proved to exist must tend to bring about that close union which, if accomplished, will be the most important event that the coming century has in store for us. . . .

It can hardly be necessary to say that the British nation will cordially welcome the entrance of the United States into the field of colonial enterprise, so long and so successfully occupied by themselves. There would be no jealousy of the expansion of American enterprise and influence; on the contrary, every Englishman would heartily rejoice in the co-operation of the United States in the great work of tropical civilization.

Like German enmity, British assistance during the war had been more a matter of perception and potential than actuality. Some observers saw that British sympathy sprang more from practical self-interest—fear of Germany and colonial aspirations in China—than from sentiment. But, as Americans now for the first time stepped beyond their shores and borders, it was a comfort to find people who spoke their language and offered moral support. The seeds of the enduring North Atlantic alliance had been planted.

.   .   .

FOR NAVAL CONSTRUCTOR HOBSON peace brought the chance to demonstrate that he was better at raising ships than sinking them. He supervised the salvage of the burned-out hulks of Cervera's ships from the Cuban beaches where they had been abandoned. The Admiral's flagship, the *María Teresa,* thus resurrected, was towed north but broke loose in the midst of one of the several hurricanes that finally arrived in the Caribbean in September. She drifted for several days, then broke apart on a coral reef in the Bahamas, on Cat Island. It was a strange coincidence, because the only living creature aboard was Admiral Cervera's cat, which had somehow survived unnoticed since the sea battle off Santiago. The cat was eventually rescued and adopted by Hobson. Hobson, Cervera, and the cat seemed to share a quality that transcended language, allegiance, and species— an uncanny ability to survive.

.   .   .

THE SPANISH MONARCHY survived. Spain counted bloody defeat less shameful than peaceful acquiescence, and so the discontent that followed did not cost the nation its throne. For María Cristina this was enough. An Austrian princess, widowed in her pregnancy, alone in a strange land, she sought above all else to preserve her dead husband's legacy so that it could be passed on to her son, and this, at least, was granted her. Alfonso XIII came of age and ascended the throne in 1902.

.   .   .

"THERE IS ONE THING relating to the Spanish evacuation of Havana," wrote Steven Crane,

of which, surely, the less said the better, and yet the exquisite mournfulness of it comes to one here at all times. . . .
A friend and myself went on board the Alfonso XIII a few days

ago as she was about to sail for Spain with an enormous passenger list of sick soldiers, officers, Spanish families, even some priests—all people who, by long odds, would never again set their eyes on the island of Cuba.

The steamer was ready to sail. We slid down the gangway and into our small boat. There were many small boats crowding about the big ship. Most contained people who waved handkerchiefs and shouted "Adios!" quite cheerfully in a way suggesting that they themselves were intending to take the next steamer, or the next again, for Spain. But from a boat near to ours we heard the sound of sobbing. Under the comic matting sun shelter was a woman, holding in her arms a boy about four years old. Her eyes were fastened upon the deck of the ship, where stood an officer in the uniform of a Spanish captain of infantry. He was making no sign. He simply stood immovable, staring at the boat. Sometimes men express great emotion by merely standing still for a long time. It seemed as if he was never again going to move a muscle.

The woman tried to get the child to look at its father, but the boy's eyes wandered over the bright bay with maddening serenity. He knew nothing; his mouth was open vacuously. The crisis in his life was lowering an eternal shadow upon him, and he only minded the scintillant water and the funny ships.

She was not a pretty woman and she was—old. If she had been beautiful, one could have developed the familiar and easy cynicism which, despite its barbarity, is some consolation at least. But this to her was the end, the end of a successful love. The heart of a man to whom she at any rate was always a reminiscence of her girlish graces was probably her only chance of happiness, and the man was on the Alfonso XIII, bound for Spain.

The woman's boatman had a face like a floor. Evidently he had thought of other fares. One couldn't spend the afternoon or three pesetas just because a woman yowled. He began to propel the boat toward the far landing. As the distance from the steamer widened and widened, the wail of the woman rang out louder.

Our boatman spat disdainfully into the water. "Serves her right. Why didn't she take up with a man of her own people instead of with a Spaniard?" But that is of small consequence. The woman's heart was broken. That is the point.

.　　　.　　　.

"FUTURE GENERATIONS will hardly believe it possible that the recent events actually occurred," Captain Victor Concas reflected bitterly.

The war was not desired, and yet nothing was done to ward it off. Peace was desired, but nothing was done to preserve it. With a loud voice our statesmen declared that they wanted peace at any cost, and yet they wanted it to cost nothing. . . .

Instead of making terms while the squadron was yet intact at Santiago, and when that city and Manila could keep up the defense for some time, they waited until all was lost, although they knew beforehand that all must thus be lost. . . .

The political idea which ruled our destinies was one fearful denial, and by denials nothing can be attained. Was the object of our policy war?—No. Was it peace?—No. Resistance?—No. The relinquishment of Cuba?—No. Was it determination to defend ourselves?—Not either. To allow ourselves to be killed?—Still less. Was it believed that Cervera would be victorious in the West Indies?—No. Was it believed that he would be defeated?—No. Would he be relieved from his command on account of his opposition to everything that was being done?—No. Finally, did we want battles?—No, and a thousand times no. For we have been assured . . . that Señor Moret, minister of colonies, had said that the war would not be of any importance, because as soon as the Americans had sunk three or four of our ships peace would be concluded. . . .

It may be said that all this is already a matter of history, although the wounds of all who feel themselves Spanish are still shedding blood, and their eyes tears.

.　　.　　.

GENERAL MÁXIMO GÓMEZ CAME aboard the *Dellie,* a filibuster boat about to leave Punta Alegre to take home some American *expeditionarios.* His aide was carrying a package, and Gómez took it and unwrapped it. It was a stained and faded Cuban flag, the relic of an old and illustrious battle in the long war. He presented it to the captain to honor the man's many services to the insurgent cause. The flag was fastened to the ship's signal halyards, but before the captain could raise it aloft, Gómez stopped him and told him to get an American flag. Narcisco Gonzales, a South Carolina newspaper editor who spent the war fighting beside Gómez, recalled the scene:

> Old Glory was attached to the halyards and the two flags were raised together, the American above the Cuban, the cornets on the wharf sounding the *Himno de Bayamo,* the Cuban "Marseillaise."
>
> The "Old Man" took off his black slouch hat, and watched the flags go up the line and ripple out in the morning breeze. He continued for fully a minute to gaze up at them there with a solemn, rapt expression on his grim features. Standing a few feet away, by the mainmast, I could see every working of his lean, brown face and could well divine the thoughts that passed through his mind. After many years of hardship and struggle and sacrifice, after ten years of one war and three of another unparalleled in privation, after failure and exile and the bitterness of hope deferred, he looked at last upon the flag of Free Cuba, floating over the blue waters, under the kindly, protecting egis of the Stars and Stripes. It was a great moment for Máximo Gómez.

He was seventy-five years old. He had given nearly half of his life to the Cuban cause, and as he gazed up at the flags, he must have remembered those who had given all of theirs. He must have remembered Martí, the Maceo brothers, his own beloved Panchito, and a thousand more. And he must have remembered Flint and Funston and all the other Americans who had made the Cuban struggle their own.

Withdrawing his gaze slowly from the flags, and bringing himself from the things of the past and the future to those of the present, General Gómez straightened himself with a quick movement suggesting the click of a trigger, lifted his big black hat at arm's length above him, and said, with a sudden, dynamic energy in his sharp voice:

Viva Cuba!

The officers and men on the schooner and on the wharf, their hats off, too, echoed, *Viva!*

Viva Libertad! said Gómez.

Viva! shouted the little crowd.

Viva los Americanos!

Viva!

CHAPTER EIGHTEEN

THE WHITE MAN'S
BURDEN

THE FATE OF the Philippines was in the hands of President McKinley. According to the terms of the peace protocol that had ended the fighting, "the control, disposition, and government" of the islands were to be determined by the final peace treaty between the United States and Spain, but this amounted to saying little else than that America had not yet made up her mind whether to take them or give them back. When the American Peace Commission sailed for France in mid-September, McKinley had not yet decided what he was going to do.

An expansionist mood was sweeping the country. The Hawaiian Islands had been annexed in July, the culmination of a long process unrelated to the Spanish War. The terms of the peace protocol had already settled the matter of Puerto Rico. America seemed suddenly to have acquired an appetite for overseas acquisitions. As Cabot Lodge put it, "Where the flag once goes up it must never come down."

Mr. Dooley and his friend, Mr. Hennessy, thrashed out the question in the pages of the Chicago *Journal:*

> "I know what I'd do if I was Mack," said Mr. Hennessy. "I'd hist a flag over th' Ph'lippeens, an' I'd take in th' whole lot iv thim."
>
> "An' yet," said Mr. Dooley, "tis not more thin two months since ye larned whether they were islands or canned goods. . . . If yer son Packy was to ask ye where th' Ph'lippeens is, cud ye give him anny good idea whether they was in Rooshia or jus' west iv th' tracks?"
>
> "Mebbe I cudden't," said Mr. Hennessy, haughtily, "but I'm f'r taking thim in, annyhow."

Only a small minority seemed to have no opinion. "I dinnaw what to do about th' Ph'lippeens," Mr. Dooley lamented, "an' I'm alone in th' wurruld. Ivrybody else has made up his mind."

McKinley went on a speaking tour through the Midwest in October. Audiences seemed to favor expansion. References to "duty," "destiny," and "Dewey" triggered loud applause.

"We want to preserve carefully all the old life of the nation,—the dear old life of the nation and our cherished institutions," he told an Iowa crowd. There was a flurry of polite clapping. "But we do not want to shirk a single responsibility that has been put upon us by the results of the war." There was thunderous applause.

"Shall we deny to ourselves what the rest of the world so freely and so justly accords us?" he demanded of the audience at the Trans-Mississippi Exposition in Omaha, and the crowd roared back the answer with a single voice, "No!"

The country's largest and most influential dailies favored annexing the Philippines; in mid-September the *Literary Digest* listed eighty-four major newspapers that had gone on record in favor of it. The prospect of foreign markets interested businessmen. A prominent financier pointed out in a *Century* magazine article that half of the people of the earth lived within easy reach of the Philippines. The *Wall Street Journal* urged that a naval base be established in the Philippines so that the United States might share in "the breaking up of China," a reference to the European scramble for Chinese territories in the wake of the kaiser's land grab at Kaichow Bay. The *American Banker* saw the opportunity to get a foothold in the Pacific at this moment as "a coincidence which has a providential air."

"If it is commercialism," orated McKinley's friend, Senator Mark Hanna, "to want the possession of a strategic point giving the American people an opportunity to maintain a foothold in the markets of that great Eastern country [China], for God's sake let us have commercialism."

God was invoked literally by many Protestant clergymen who saw a divinely imposed national duty to Christianize the Filipinos. The fact that they had already been Christianized most forcibly by Catholic Spain did not count. Episcopal Bishop Henry C. Potter of New York visited the islands and reported that the Spanish priests charged the natives between five and eight dollars to perform a marriage, an unaffordable fee that caused thousands of people to live "in a state of concubinage." American dominion would bring the blessings of legitimacy.

Not everyone was on the bandwagon. Prominent among the naysayers was Senator George F. Hoar, Cabot Lodge's Republican colleague from Massachusetts. Hoar had expressed some qualms in July when the Senate was ratifying the Hawaiian annexation treaty:

> If this be the first step in the acquisition of dominion over barbarous archipelagoes in distant seas; if we are to enter into competition with the great powers of Europe in the plundering of China, in the division of Africa . . . if our commerce is hereafter to be forced upon unwilling peoples at the cannon's mouth; if we are to govern subjects and vassal

States, trampling as we do it on our own great Charter which recognizes alike the liberty and dignity of individual manhood, then let us resist this thing in the beginning, and let us resist it to the death.

Compromises were proposed by Secretary Long, former Secretary of State Day, and others: take only Manila, or the whole island of Luzon, just enough territory for a naval base or coaling station. The plan pleased only Germany, Japan, and Great Britain, which were prepared to take any islands that Uncle Sam didn't want.

Late in October one of the peace commissioners in Paris sounded a warning. Senator George Gray, Democrat of Delaware, stated his reasons for counseling against the acquisition in a long telegram to the new secretary of state:*

> The undersigned cannot agree that it is wise to take Philippine Islands in whole or in part. To do so would be to reverse accepted continental policy of the country, declared and acted upon throughout our history. . . . Policy proposed introduces into European politics and the entangling alliances against which Washington and all American statesmen have protested. It will make necessary a navy equal to largest of powers; a greatly increased military establishment; immense sums for fortifications and harbors; multiply occasions for dangerous complications with foreign nations, and increase burdens of taxation. . . .
>
> Our declaration of war upon Spain was accompanied by a solemn and deliberate definition of our purpose. Now that we have achieved all and more than our object, let us simply keep our word. . . .
>
> At the very least . . . if conditions require the keeping of Luzon forego the material advantages claimed in annexing other islands.

If Senator Gray's jeremiad was passed along by Secretary Hay to the president it had no effect. The telegram had hardly reached the State Department before McKinley was issuing a new directive to the Peace Commission:

> The information which had come to the President since your departure convinces him that the acceptance of the cession of Luzon alone, leaving the rest of the islands subject to Spanish rule, or to be the subject of future contention, can not be justified on political, commercial, or humanitarian grounds. The cession must be of the whole archipelago or none. The later is wholly inadmissible, and the former must therefore be required.

The information that convinced McKinley may have been furnished by Generals Merritt and Greene, who had stopped in Washington en route to Paris to brief the commissioners. But in one of his rare reminiscences, McKinley implied that he had tapped a higher source:

*The other four commissioners were former Secretary of State William R. Day; Senator Cushman K. Davis, Republican of Minnesota and chairman of the Foreign Relations Committee; Senator William P. Frye, Republican of Maine; and Whitelaw Reid, editor of the New York *Tribune*. Davis, Frye, and Reid were expansionists.

The truth is I didn't want the Philippines and when they came to us as a gift from the gods, I did not know what to do about them. . . . I sought counsel from all sides—Democrats as well as Republicans—but got little help. I thought first we would take only Manila; then Luzon; then other islands, perhaps, also. I walked the floor of the White House night after night until midnight; and I am not ashamed to tell you, gentlemen, that I went down on my knees and prayed Almighty God for light and guidance more than one night.

And one night late it came to me this way—I don't know how it was, but it came: (1) that we could not give them back to Spain—that would be cowardly and dishonorable; (2) that we could not turn them over to France or Germany—our commercial rivals in the Orient—that would be bad business and discreditable; (3) that we could not leave them to themselves—they were unfit for self-government—and they would soon have anarchy and misrule over there worse than Spain's was; and (4) that there was nothing left for us to do but to take them all, and to educate the Filipinos, and uplift and civilize and Christianize them, and by God's grace do the very best we could by them, as our fellow-men for whom Christ also died. And then I went to bed, and went to sleep and slept soundly, and the next morning I sent for the chief engineer of the War Department (our mapmaker), and I told him to put the Philippines on the map of the United States, and there they are, and there they will stay while I am President!

When the Spanish peace commissioners in Paris were advised by their American counterparts that the United States intended to keep the Philippines they objected on the grounds that the surrender of Manila had actually taken place after the official cessation of hostilities on August 12. There followed some days of wrangling over fine points of legal language, then the Americans announced that the United States would pay Spain twenty million dollars for the islands. That was their best offer, they said, in effect; take it or leave it. The Spanish took it. The peace treaty was signed December 10. There remained one more hurdle, however: obtaining Senate ratification. There the treaty met opposition.

In November the Anti-Imperialist League was formed in the Boston office of retired textile manufacturer Edward Atkinson. "We hold that the policy known as imperialism is hostile to liberty and tends toward militarism," stated the league's platform.

We regret that it has become necessary in the land of Washington and Lincoln to reaffirm that all men, of whatever race or color, are entitled to life, liberty, and the pursuit of happiness. We maintain that governments derive their just powers from the consent of the governed. We insist that the subjugation of any people is "criminal aggression" and open disloyalty to the distinctive principles of our Government.

Prominent among the league's members were Senator Hoar, Boston attorney and political reformer Moorfield Storey, journalist Carl Schurz, and, surprisingly, steel magnate Andrew Carnegie.

"Andrew Carnegie really seems to be off his head," confided Secretary Hay to Peace Commissioner Reid.

> He writes me frantic letters signing them "Your Bitterest Opponent." He threatens the President, not only with the vengence of the voters, but with the practical punishment at the hands of the mob. He says henceforth the entire labor vote of America will be cast against us, and he will see that it is done. He says the Administration will fall in irretrievable ruin the moment it shoots down one insurgent Filipino. He does not seem to reflect that the Government is in a somewhat robust condition even after shooting down several American citizens in his interest at Homestead. But all this confusion of tongues will go its way. The country will applaud the resolution that has been reached.

The league's most prestigious voice in the Congress was Senator Hoar, who delivered an antiratification speech to packed galleries on January 9 in which he declared, paraphrasing Lincoln on slavery, "No nation was every created good enough to own another."

"It is difficult for me to speak with moderation of such men as Hoar," Roosevelt told Lodge on January 26. (Roosevelt had, thus far, been too preoccupied with the New York State gubernatorial campaign and his new duties in Albany to have taken an active part in the national debate over the Philippines.)

> They are little better than traitors. . . . It must be *really* a matter of regret that any American should go wrong at a time like this. . . . This huge materialistic community is at bottom, either wrong or halfhearted on the Philippine question.

Voices were heard from abroad, chiefly from Great Britain, which welcomed the prospect of an Anglo-Saxon partner joining John Bull on the road to empire. Early in February words of encouragement came in the form of a poem by Rudyard Kipling entitled, "The White Man's Burden," and meaningfully subtitled, "The United States and the Philippine Islands":

> Take up the White Man's burden—
>   Send forth the best ye breed—
> Go bind your sons to exile
>   To serve your captives' need;
> To wait in heavy harness
>   On fluttered folk and wild—
> Your new-caught, sullen peoples,
>   Half devil and half child.

>   .   .   .

"THE DIVISION OF OPINION in this country regarding the question of acquiring sovereignty over the Philippines," Secretary Alger recalled,

> together with the encouragement received from certain individuals in the United States . . . all conspired to give Aguinaldo what Admiral

Dewey described at the time in a personal letter as the "big head." His own arrogance and that of his troops increased rapidly and expressed itself in repeated insults to our officers and men guarding Manila, where the insurgent troops were allowed to freely pass, if unarmed. . . .

Finally, on the night of February 4th, growing bolder and more persistent in their efforts to bring on a conflict, a strong detail of Filipino soldiers again appeared at one of our outposts on the east of the city . . . The detachment was led by one of Aguinaldo's officers who attempted to pass and push back our picket, then a hundred yards or more within our lines. Private Grayson, Company D, 1st Nebraska Volunteers, challenged the Filipino and his detachment.

"About eight o'clock," Private Willie Grayson recalled,

something rose slowly up not twenty feet in front of us. It was a Filipino. I yelled "Halt!" . . . He immediately shouted "Halto" at me. Well, I thought the best thing to do was to shoot him. He dropped. . . . Then two Filipinos sprang out of a gateway about fifteen feet from us. I called "Halt," and Miller fired and dropped one. I saw that another was left. Well, I think I got my second Filipino that time. We retreated to where our six other fellows were, and I said, "Line up, fellows, the niggers are in here all through these yards."

"Aguinaldo had accomplished that which he had so long conspired to bring about," Alger wrote.* "By an overt act he had succeeded in drawing the fire of our picket. The Americans had 'fired the first shot.' And this was their signal for assaulting us along the entire line of their works."

"I am more grateful than I can say," Governor Roosevelt told Lodge three days later, "partly to the Senate, partly to Providence, and partly to the Filipinos. They just pulled the treaty through for us."

The day before the Senate had ratified the treaty with the necessary two-thirds vote.

"My nation," Aguinaldo declared,

cannot remain indifferent in view of such a violent and aggressive seizure of a portion of its territory by a nation which has arrogated to itself the title: champion of oppressed nations. Thus it is that my government is disposed to open hostilities if the American troops attempt to take forcible possession.

Upon their heads will be all the blood which may be shed.

·   ·   ·

THE UNITED STATES now found itself embroiled in a war of counterinsurgency in the jungles of Southeast Asia. The Spanish War had been chivalrous and gallant. The Philippine War was not.

"The Filipino troops have frequently fired upon our men from under the

---

*The anti-imperialists charged that the conspiracy to provoke the clash had been on the part of the U.S. Army in order to unify American public opinion in favor of ratifying the treaty (Schirmer, pp. 127–129).

protection of flags of truce," Elihu Root, the new secretary of war told Congress,

> tortured to death American prisoners who have fallen into their hands, buried alive both American prisoners and friendly natives, and horribly mutilated the bodies of the American dead. That the soldiers fighting against such an enemy and with their own eyes witnessing such deeds, should occasionally be regardless of their orders and retaliate by unjustifiable severities, is not incredible.

It was said that the unwritten policy of the American troops was to take no prisoners. The anti-imperialists pointed to the Filipino battle casualty ratio of five killed to one wounded as evidence that this was true. The distinction between combatants and civilians became obscure. To the Americans all Filipinos looked alike, although many smiled and cried, "Amigo!" But the troops suspected that many of the shots fired at them in the night came from rifles held by the young boys and old men they saw by day in the Filipino villages. They were probably right.

"There are no more amigos," said the Americans.

There was the so-called water cure, a brutal interrogation technique. One instance of its use was described to a congressional committee by Sergeant Charles S. Riley of the Twenty-sixth Infantry:

> The [prisoner] was tied and placed on his back under a water tank holding probably one hundred gallons.
> The faucet was opened and a stream of water was forced down or allowed to run down his throat. His throat was held so he could not prevent swallowing the water, so that he had to allow the water to run into his stomach. He was directly under the faucet, with his mouth held wide open. When he was filled with water it was forced out of him by pressing a foot on his stomach or else with the hands; and this continued from five to fifteen minutes. A native interpreter stood immediately over this man as he lay on the floor and kept saying some word which I should judge meant "confess" or "answer."

The man did not provide all the information wanted, so the process was repeated. This time a syringe was used to pump water from a five-gallon can.

> The syringe did not have the desired effect and the doctor [Dr. Palmer Lyons, an Army contract surgeon] ordered a second one. The man got a second syringe and that was inserted in his nose. Then the doctor ordered some salt and a handful of salt was procured and thrown into the water. Two syringes were then in operation. The interpreter stood over him in the meantime asking for this second information that was desired. Finally, he gave in and gave the information they sought, and then he was allowed to rise.

Back home, the average American knew little of such things, nor wished to know. There was first of all strict military censorship in the Philippines. And the press had far less appetite for war stories than it had had a year before. The action in the Philippines seemed somehow anticlimactic. The Spanish War had been short, glorious, and easily understood. The Philippine War was long and ugly, and it baffled everyone except the generals and the men in Washington. But some soldiers wrote home and told of the water cure and said that there were no prisoners and no amigos. Some of the letters fell into the hands of the Anti-Imperialist League and were published as a collection called *Soldiers' Letters*.

> With my own hand [I] set fire to over fifty houses of Filipinos after the victory at Caloocan. Women and children were wounded by our fire.
> . . .

> Caloocan was supposed to contain seventeen thousand inhabitants. The Twentieth Kansas swept through it, and now Caloocan contains not one living native. Of the buildings, the battered walls of the great church and dismal prison alone remain. . . .

> With an enemy like this to fight, it is not surprising that the boys should soon adopt "no quarter" as a motto, and fill the blacks full of lead before finding out whether they are friends or enemies.

The league's vocal opposition to the war drew the charge of treason from some quarters. The New York *Times* declared that the league should "send rifles, Maxim guns, and stores of ammunition to the Filipinos," a policy the paper said would "be more openly and frankly treasonable." The expansionists charged the peace movement with prolonging the war by lending encouragement to Aguinaldo and the insurgents. Antiwar agitation, they said, amounted to stabbing the American fighting man in the back. They laid the mounting American casualty list at the door of the Anti-Imperialist League.

There had to be some reason why the war dragged on. The generals kept reporting that the rebels were on the point of utter defeat. They said so every year.

                    .   .   .

NINETEEN HUNDRED WAS an election year. It was also the second year of the Philippine War.

"In America there is a great party that insists on the United States government recognizing Filipino independence," Aguinaldo told his comrades. "The great Democratic party of the United States will win the next fall election. . . . Imperialism will fail in its mad attempts to subjugate us by force of arms."

The Democratic presidential candidate once again was William Jennings Bryan. Aguinaldo may have known that Bryan had often espoused anti-imperialism. He may not have known that Bryan had been instrumental in marshaling the Republican vote in the Senate needed to ratify the peace treaty, a move made for political reasons; but many American anti-imperialists knew it and refused to support Bryan's candidacy. In any case, the Democrats estimated that the Philippine issue had little popular appeal, or, as one of Bryan's campaign managers put it, "We have failed to waken the lethargic American conscience." The only prominent politician who seemed inclined to disturb the American conscience was Senator Hoar. And he was a Republican.

The Philippine War was not a major issue of the campaign of 1900. McKinley was reelected. His campaign may have benefited from the popularity of his vice presidential running mate, Governor Theodore Roosevelt of New York.

.   .   .

THE OLD MAN IN the white suit, with the flowing white moustache and the luxuriant tangle of white hair, drew on his cigar, put it down, and arose. Glancing at those assembled at the banquet table, he tapped a spoon against a water glass until the murmur of dinner conversation died away.

Mark Twain was one of the most outspoken and bitterest critics of the Philippine War. Tonight he was supposed to introduce a young Englishman who was touring the United States and lecturing about his exploits in the Boer War.

"I think that England sinned when she got herself into a war in South Africa which she could have avoided," he began, "just as we have sinned in getting into a similar war in the Philippines."

There was a ripple of nervous anticipation around the table. The young Englishman smiled uneasily.

"Mr. Churchill by his father is an Englishman," Twain continued.

By his mother he is an American, no doubt a blend that makes the perfect man. England and America; we are kin. And now that we are also kin in sin, there is nothing more to be desired. The harmony is perfect—like Mr. Churchill himself, whom I now have the honor to present to you.

But Churchill, perhaps remembering the controversy in England that followed his public remarks about the Cuban revolution five years earlier, did not rise to the bait. He avoided commenting on the Philippines and confined himself to the firmer ground of South Africa. It was a doubly prudent choice, for this audience seemed to share the anti-imperialist views of the toastmaster.

"There is a strong pro-Boer feeling," he reported in a letter to his mother, "particularly in New York."

.   .   .

ON MARCH 23, 1901, Emilio Aguinaldo was in the village of Palanan in the remote and mountainous northeast Luzon. He was waiting for the arrival of guerrilla replacements who were not expected to arrive in a single force but to drift in in small groups over a period of several days. He had received a message that a group of guerrillas were on their way with some American prisoners.

Late in the afternoon three of the party, marching in advance of the others, reached Palanan and Aguinaldo's headquarters and reported to the general's office on the second floor of the building. Suddenly there was shooting in the street below. Aguinaldo, believing his men were firing their weapons to celebrate the arrival of the replacements, went to the window.

"Stop that foolishness," he called. "Don't waste your ammunition."

But now there was shooting inside the room. One of his bodyguards went down; the other fled. One of the newcomers grabbed the general and threw him to the floor. There were footsteps running up the stairs. The door flew open and an American burst into the room.

"General Aguinaldo, I am Frederick Funston, brigadier general of U.S. Volunteers. These are my troops, not yours, and you are a prisoner of war."

Aguinaldo appeared dazed. "Is this not some joke?" he asked.

"I assure you that it is not," the American replied.

Funston spoke to Aguinaldo in fluent Spanish. He had learned it when he had served in Cuba as Máximo Gómez's chief of artillery.

.   .   .

THE CAPTURE OF Aguinaldo did not end the Philippine War. On September 28 a detachment of the Ninth Infantry stationed at the town of Balangiga was surprised while at breakfast, when most of the troops were at an outdoor mess about a hundred feet from where they had stacked their rifles. The local Filipino police chief—he was considered a loyal "amigo"—approached an American guard, grabbed his rifle away from him, and smashed his skull with the butt. Instantly several hundred Filipino laborers waiting nearby produced huge bolo knives from beneath their clothing and fell upon the breakfasting Americans. Most of the troops were cut to pieces before they could get to their feet. Some forty-eight were killed. A few escaped to tell the tale.

The scene that met the eyes of the Americans who arrived at Balangiga the next day was one of unmitigated horror. What had been done to the dead was revolting.

"All of the dead had been mutilated and treated with indescribable indignities," the secretary of war reported to the president.

The president whose unhappy duty it was to receive the report was Theodore Roosevelt. Three weeks earlier McKinley had visited the Pan-American Exposition at Buffalo, New York, and had been cut down by an anarchist's bullet.

.   .   .

"IT IS A DREADFUL THING to come into the presidency this way," Roosevelt told Lodge, "but it would be a far worse thing to be morbid about it. Here is the task, and I have got to do it to the best of my ability; and that is all there is about it."

"Thou hast it now: King, Cawdor, Glamis," Brooks Adams effused in a letter to the new president.

The world can give no more. You hold a place greater than Trajan's, for you are the embodiment of a power not only vaster than the power of empire, but vaster than men have ever known. You have too the last and rarest prize, for you have an opportunity. You will always stand as

the President who began the contest for supremacy of America against
the eastern continent.

In other words, Hail Caesar! The forty-three-year-old Roosevelt found this
heady wine. Perhaps he had misjudged the gloomy philosopher. He took a closer
look and found the philosopher was no longer gloomy. Since the Spanish War
Adams had abandoned his theory that the relentless forces of history were beyond
the power of individuals to influence. Roosevelt and the recent series of astonishing events proved that the law of decay was not irresistible. Adams new thesis:
America must now pursue a policy of expansion and militarism to take this new
tide of history at the flood.

"If it be conceded that war is a form of economic competition," he wrote
in the *Atlantic Monthly,*

> war must be regarded as a speculation; a hazardous one, it is true, but
> one deserving to be tried, where the chance of gain outweighs the risk
> of loss. . . . If the American people, after due deliberation, feel aggres-
> sion to be for their best interest, there is little to be urged by way of
> precedent against the logic of their decision. . . . [But] America enjoys
> no immunity from natural laws. She can pay for what she takes, or she
> can fight for it, but she cannot have the earth for nothing.

Roosevelt was beguiled. Four years earlier he had struggled against Adams's
pessimistic theories, too awed by the man's intellect simply to dismiss them. But
now that powerful mind was endorsing what Roosevelt had always believed, or
longed to believe.

"Your letter . . . pleased me particularly," he told Adams. "Before I finish
my message [to Congress] I would like to see you, for I intend (although in rather
guarded phrase) to put in one or two ideas of your Atlantic Monthly article."

The Roosevelt–Brooks Adams relationship had entered a new phase. "I do
not know whether you want either reward or recognition," Henry Adams told his
brother, "[but] you will have a better chance of it between now and May, 1904
than you ever had before in your life."[*] Adams was soon a frequent caller at the
White House, where the president proved to be a most attentive listener.

"The game is ours," Adams now told Cabot Lodge. "The fruit is ripe and
only needs picking. If the President is ably advised and well supported I tell you
frankly I see no reason why the present administration should not go down as
the turning point in our history, as the moment when we won the great prize."

At this moment the Philippine question was at the top of the national
agenda, of course. Adams's able advice on that subject was elegantly simple: "We
have the Philippines, therefore in my judgment it is necessary we should have
them."

Roosevelt would probably not have listened to contrary advice, even from
the impressive Adams. He already believed the islands an American necessity.

---

[*]In fact Brooks Adams's new influence with Roosevelt was to last through his second term and
long afterward.

But the undeclared war against the Filipinos was now near the end of its third year. The stream of grim reports from the Far Pacific was eroding the popularity of expansionism at home. And now there was the appalling news of the massacre on Samar.

He ordered General Chaffee, now in the islands, to adopt "the most stern measures to pacify Samar."

.			.			.

"I HAVE PROMISED to end this campaign by December 25th," General Smith told his commanders.

Brigadier General Jacob Smith, or "Hell Roaring Jake," was a grizzled sixty-two-year-old veteran of the Civil War and the Indian Wars. He had been given the job of pacifying the island of Samar. A brigade of Marines under Major Littleton Waller was assigned to help him.

"I want no prisoners," he told Waller. "I wish you to kill and burn. The more you kill and burn the better you will please me. I want all persons killed who are capable of bearing arms in actual hostilities against the United States."

Waller was shocked into silence. Finally he spoke.

"I would like to know the limit of age to respect, sir," he said.

"Ten years."

"Persons of ten years and older are those designated as being capable of bearing arms?"

"Yes."

These were not written orders. General Smith's written orders advised his commanders that "short, severe wars are the most humane in the end. No civilized war, however civilized, can be carried out on a humane basis." He ordered them to "create in the minds of all the people a burning desire for the war to cease; a desire or longing so intense, so personal . . . and so real that it will impel them to devote themselves in earnest to bringing about a state of real peace."

He told his men to turn the island of Samar into "a howling wilderness."

And they did.

.			.			.

"IN THE PHILIPPINES our men have done well," President Roosevelt told a friend several months later,

> and on the whole have been exceedingly merciful; but there have been some blots on the record. Certain of the superior officers got to talking with loose and violent brutality, only about one-fourth meant, but which had a very bad effect upon their subordinates. . . . I have bestowed rewards and praise liberally for all the good deeds that have been done there. But it was necessary to call some of those who were guilty of shortcomings to sharp account. Brigadier General Smith was an offender of high rank.

Smith had been court-martialed and convicted on the charge of "conduct to the prejudice of good order and military discipline." With Roosevelt's approval he was treated leniently and simply forced to retire.

.   .   .

ON THE FOURTH OF JULY, 1902, President Roosevelt declared the Philippine War ended. For all practical purposes it was. It had cost 4,200 American dead, 2,800 wounded. Some 20,000 insurgents had been killed; 200,000 Filipinos died from disease, famine and other indirect effects of the war.

In the end, the insurgents had been crushed, not by shooting prisoners or killing everyone over the age of ten or turning the land into a howling wilderness, although all of these things were done. It was accomplished when General J. Franklin Bell, the American commander in the province of Batangas, saw that the guerrilla was the fish, and the people the ocean in which he swims; when he realized that the insurgents could be beaten only by cutting them off from the aid and shelter provided by the Filipino people.

In his order of December 8, 1901, to all his station commanders Bell proclaimed:

> In order to put an end to enforced contributions now levied by insurgents upon the inhabitants of sparsely settled and outlying barrios and districts by means of intimidation and assassination, commanding officers . . . will immediately specify and establish plainly marked limits surrounding each town bounding a zone within which it may be practicable . . . to exercise efficient supervision over and furnish protection to inhabitants (who desire to be peaceful) against the depredations of armed insurgents. . . .
>
> Commanding officers will also see that orders are at once given and distributed to all the inhabitants . . . informing them of the danger or remaining outside of these limits, and that unless they move by December 25 from outlying barrios and districts with all their movable food supplies, including rice, palany, chicken, live stock, etc., to within the limits of the zone established at their own or nearest town, their property (found outside of said zone at said date) will become liable to confiscation or destruction.

The following day Bell issued a second order which, in part, observed:

> Natural and commendable sympathy for suffering and loss and for those with whom friendly relations may have been maintained should . . . [be relegated] to a place subordinate to the doing of whatever may be necessary to bring a people who have not as yet felt the distressing effect of war to a realizing sense of the advantages of peace.

"Within a comparatively few weeks after this policy was inaugurated the guerrilla warfare . . . ended," the War Department reported.

The long and ugly anticlimax to the Spanish War had finally been brought to a close through a policy of reconcentration. That which Americans had once despised, they now had embraced.

General Valeriano Weyler y Nicolau, "the Butcher," had the last ironic laugh.

THE WAKE OF
THE *MAINE*

THE RUSTING WRECK of the *Maine* lay on the muddy bottom of Havana harbor for many years, all but forgotten. In 1911 Congress appropriated funds to remove her and recover the bodies believed still to be trapped in her hull. The work was carried out by the Army Corps of Engineers.

A large steel cofferdam was constructed around the wreck and the water was pumped out, exposing an eerie sight. Barnacles encrusted the hull and silt covered the decks. For the first time the form and extent of the damage were visible. The remains of sixty-four men were removed and shipped to Arlington Cemetery, where their graves are marked by the battleship's mast.

Because questions remained regarding the cause of the explosion, the Navy appointed a board of inspection to examine the exposed wreck and review the conclusions of the 1898 Court of Inquiry. After two weeks on the salvage site the board members returned to Washington and wrote their report. The board disagreed with the court only regarding the location of the initial explosion. It confirmed that the explosion had been set off by a submerged mine

The wreck was to be disposed of by refloating her, towing her out to sea, and sinking her. A concrete and wooden bulkhead was constructed to seal the gaping wound in her hull. On February 13, 1912, the water was let into the cofferdam and the *Maine* floated free of the harbor mud. March 16 was set as the date for the ceremony.

.   .   .

THE REMARKABLE FIGURE of a man dressed in formal black morning clothes climbed from the pilot boat and onto the flower-draped hulk floating beside the cofferdam. "Dynamite Johnny" O'Brien was chief of the Havana harbor pilots, a position granted the old filibuster captain by the Republic of Cuba in recognition of his gallant service during the war of independence. Today he had been chosen to guide the tugs that were to tow the *Maine* out to sea, a duty both professional and ceremonial.

The officials and dignitaries were aboard the navy tug *Osceola*, which was linked to the hulk by a seven-inch manila cable. Two smaller tugs were to follow on either quarter of the *Maine*, steering the wreck according to the signals O'Brien would make from his post atop what once had been the aft superstructure. At 2:15 P.M. the procession got underway.

"The harbor was smooth and there was not enough wind to bother," O'Brien recalled.

> From the masthead floated the Stars and Stripes, the biggest and handsomest navy ensign I think I ever saw. . . . As I stood alone under the colors there came to me a sudden realization of the wonder of this ceremony in which I was taking part, the like of which the world had never seen nor was likely to see again. I looked across that desolate deck, and there rose in my mind a picture of it bristling with cannon and crowded with strong sailormen, and I never felt so much like crying in my life.
>
> We passed slowly down the line of warships, rails lined with sailors and marines standing at attention, waiting to fall in behind us. . . . To starboard the gray walls of the great Cabana fortress, its ramparts lined with soldiers and its cannon firing minute-guns. A little farther was the historic Morro swarming with spectators. To port was the city of Havana, whose whole population seemed to be thronging the roofs and sea walls. Astern was the escort fleet falling into line, the warships leading, and everywhere the flags were at half-mast.

The procession passed out of the harbor and into the ocean. Four miles out the *Osceola* stopped.

> At last came the three whistles from the *North Carolina*, signaling that the voyage was over, and only the last sad rites remained to be performed. These were delayed a little while to permit all of the vessels of the escort fleet to arrive and group themselves around the grave of the *Maine*.
>
> A tug put the working crew aboard again, and at a signal from the *Osceola* they opened the sea-cocks in the ship's bottom and raised the sluiceways in the bulkhead and returned to the boat, leaving me again alone. I took one last look around to see that nothing had been forgotten and then signaled the pilot boat to come alongside, dropped into her, and stood by to wait for the end.

THE WORLD WAS much changed since that morning fourteen years before when the battleship steamed into Havana harbor.

Roosevelt had served out his term as president and was reelected for another one. He had been succeeded by his protégé and disciple, William Howard Taft, who now occupied the White House. But Roosevelt disliked the sidelines and was at this moment preparing to run in the 1912 presidential election. It was one campaign he was not destined to win. The next president would be Governor Woodrow Wilson of New Jersey.

Cuba was free—more or less. After two years under Military Governor Leonard Wood the country was permitted to elect an assembly and draft a constitution. Máximo Gómez declined the presidency with the words, "Men of war, for war . . . and those of peace, for peace." Tomás Estrada Palma was the first Cuban president. As a condition of American withdrawal the Cuban assembly was required to incorporate into its constitution the so-called Platt Amendment. The amendment forced Cuba to recognize the right of the United States to intervene to protect Cuban independence, maintain a stable government, or protect life and property; it restricted the right of Cuba to enter into a treaty with any foreign government without American approval; and it granted the United States coaling stations and naval bases. Thus Cuba had become an American client state. The United States had invoked the powers of the amendment in 1906 in order to establish a provisional government after a rebellion and the resignation of Estrada Palma.

The long voyage of the *Oregon* in 1898 had underscored to Roosevelt and the Mahanites the need for a canal across the Central American isthmus, and American expansion into the Pacific made it a military necessity. In 1903, with Roosevelt's encouragement, Panama broke off from Colombia and granted the United States rights to a zone of land for the canal. Construction was well on the way to completion; the canal would be in operation in 1914.

In 1902 British and German warships bombarded Venezuelan ports for nonpayment of debts. Two years later Roosevelt enunciated the "Roosevelt Corollary" to the Monroe Doctrine, which stated that the United States would act as an international peace force in such cases. In 1905 the United States took over management of the debt payments of the Dominican Republic.

In 1909 Nicaragua, bankrupt and in a state of near anarchy, appealed to President Taft for assistance. Taft appointed an American collector of customs to supervise the payment of foreign debts along the lines of the Dominican Republic's plan and arranged with a group of New York bankers for a loan. The intervention was resented by many Nicaraguans, and the cry "Down with Yankee Imperialists" had already been heard. But Nicaraguan unrest imperiled American interests in nearby Panama. Within a few months, in August 1912, the Marines would be sent to pacify and occupy Nicaragua. They would stay there, almost continuously, until 1933, and their presence would be long remembered.

Japan had begun expansion in the Pacific, taking Korea and part of China. There had been friction with the United States and a war scare in 1907. Roosevelt now saw the Philippines as a potential problem. In the event of war with Japan, he said, the islands would "form our heel of Achilles."

In Hawaii construction of a naval base was underway at a place called Pearl Harbor.

· · ·

You could see that with every plunge she was settling deeper and deeper by the bulkhead and rising higher and higher at the stern. Soon the waves began to wash across her decks. Then a few more plunges and the stern was heaved high in the air until all the keel was in plain view and the hulk stood almost perpendicular, the jury-mast struck the water flat, and Old Glory vanished under the foam with a flash of red, white and blue as vivid as a flame. Down she went, smoothly and with an almost incredible velocity, her decks exploding under the air pressure and hurling masses of flowers and clouds of spray into the air. In a moment she was gone. Then over the spot where the *Maine* had disappeared a moment before there appeared a glistening area, probably of fifty yards radius, of perfectly smooth water. . . . In this area there floated quantities of flowers, and now and then there shot to the surface a bit of loose timber or a rope end from the wreck. A moment later the heavy rollers came boiling over the smooth surface and there remained no trace of the grave of the *Maine*.

IN 1976 Rear Admiral Hyman G. Rickover published the results of a study he had undertaken of the cause of the destruction of the *Maine*. He had enlisted the aid of some of the U.S. Navy's technical specialists, including an engineer from the Naval Ship Research and Development Center and a physicist from the Naval Surface Weapons Center. Using the testimony of the 1898 Court of Inquiry, the photographs and other data compiled by the 1911 board of investigation, and the advancements in the technical knowledge of the effects of explosives upon hulls gained during the ensuing eighty years and two world wars, the Rickover team reached its conclusion:

We have found no technical evidence in the records examined that an external explosion initiated the destruction of the *Maine*. The available evidence is consistent with an internal explosion alone. We therefore conclude that an internal source was the cause of the explosion. The most likely source was heat from a fire in the coal bunker adjacent to the 6-inch reserve magazine. However, since there is no way of proving this, other internal causes cannot be eliminated as possibilities.

SPONTANEOUS COMBUSTION, as Captain Sigsbee pointed out, is a gradual process. The explosion that destroyed the *Maine* could as easily have happened when she was at Key West, or after she went to New Orleans, which was to have been her next port of call. It is reasonable to ask, then, why the coal reached the point of ignition in Havana harbor, and why, of the more than twenty cases of coal bunker fires aboard warships of the U.S. Navy in this period, the only one resulting in an explosion occurred at a time and in a place where it would blow America from her traditional and cherished isolation. The answer to such questions lies beyond the realm of chemistry, physics, or naval architecture. Each must find it within his own personal understanding of the universe. However, there seem to be but three answers to choose among:

God, chance, or the impatient hand of destiny.

NOTES

Sources cited in the notes can be found in the Bibliography with full bibliographic details.

Abbreviations: DAB—*Dictionary of American Biography;* WAMB—*Webster's American Military Biographies.*

CHAPTER ONE. "THIS MEANS WAR!"

19–20

Telegraphers on duty: Adams, "First Man to Hear About the *Maine* Disaster." Meriwether's message to Burgin, Meriwether's background: Meriwether, "Remembering the *Maine.*"

21

Corporal Newton plays taps, Sigsbee writes to wife: Sigsbee, 63.

21–22

Sigsbee's background: WAMB.

22

History and description of *Maine:* Rickover, 1–3; Sigsbee, 6–9.

22–24

"In certain events . . .": Rickover, 33. "It was an intuition . . .": Sigsbee, 20–21. "I did not desire to reach Havana at early daylight . . . ," *Maine's* arrival: ibid., 24–31.

24

Fitzhugh Lee's background: WAMB. Decision to send *Maine* to Havana is treated at length in Chapter 4, "Marching As To War."

24–25

"Ship quietly arrived . . .": Lee to Day, January 25, 1898, *Foreign Relations,* 1898. "I am so happy . . .": Lee to Day, January 26, 1898, *Despatches,* Reel 131. Courtesies exchanged: Sigsbee, 31–32.

25–26

Spanish circular, Sigsbee attends bullfights: Sigsbee, 32–39, 41–42.

26

Security aboard *Maine:* Sigsbee, 42–43; Sigsbee's testimony in *Court of Inquiry.*

26

Maine to go to New Orleans: Long to Sicard, January 22, 1898, *Area File,* Reel 225.

"We are the masters of the situation . . .": Lee to Day, February 5, 1898, *Despatches*, Reel 132.

26–27

Clara Barton. Working late night of explosion: Epler, 286–287. State Department arranges for duty-free import of aid: Chadwick, *Diplomacy*, 529. Arrives Havana February 9; confers with authorities regarding *reconcentrados:* Epler, 284–286. Visits *Maine:* Epler, 286.

27–28

Chidwick reads Rea's book: Weems, 69. Rea's and Scovel's adventures in covering Cuban revolution: Brown, chs. 3 and 4, *passim.*

28–32

Accounts of Explosion. Meriwether in cafe: Meriwether, "Remembering the *Maine.*" Clara Barton hears blast: Epler, 286–287. Rea and Scovels see harbor "lit up with an intense light . . .": Brown, 115. Domingo Villaverde sees smoke: Adams, "First Man to Hear About the *Maine* Disaster." Rea and Scovel go to harbor, join Paglieri in boat: Brown, 115. Captain Teasdale's story: his testimony in *Court of Inquiry.* Sigmund Rothchild's story, screams from water: his testimony in *Court of Inquiry.* Rescue delayed by damaged boats: ibid. Sigsbee finds his way to the deck: Sigsbee, 64–71. Paglieri beats boatmen: Brown, 115. "Great masses of twisted and bent iron . . .": ibid., 116. "The superstructure alone loomed up . . .": ibid. Clara Barton at San Ambrosia Hospital: Epler, 287–288. Meriwether at city hospital: Brown, 119. Sigsbee leaves *Maine:* Sigsbee, 71–73.

32–33

Key West. Gleaves's account of the scene at the dock and the telegraph office is quoted in Chadwick, *The Spanish American War,* 1:9; substantially the same account is in an unpublished manuscript by Gleaves in the Gleaves Papers. Hellings and Villaverde are treated at length in Chapter 7, "A Dream of Spring."

33–34

Sigsbee writes telegram, meets Spanish official, gives telegram to Rea: Sigsbee, 75–79. Scene in Key West telegraph office: Chadwick, *Spanish American War,* 1:9; Gleaves's manuscript in Gleaves Papers.

34

Washington and New York. Helen Long finds messenger, "It was almost impossible to believe . . .": *American-Spanish War,* 341–342. Dickens notifies White House: ibid.; Leech, 166. Hearst hears news: Coblentz, 59.

CHAPTER TWO. THE PEARL

35–36

Early Cuba. "Everything is green . . .": Halstead, *Story of Cuba,* 24. Colba: Samuel Eliot Morison, 44. Avan: ibid., 153, n.12. "Boulevard of the New World": Thomas, 12. British conquest: ibid., 1–11. New fortifications bring slaves: ibid., 63. Slave population: ibid., 169. Prosperity and sugar: ibid., 27–41.

36–37

Thoughts of Annexation. Slave trade ended: ibid., 94. "These islands . . . are natural appendages . . .": LaFeber, *John Quincy Adams,* 129. "The transfer of Cuba to Great Britain . . .": ibid., 130. ". . . in looking to the probable course of events . . .": ibid., 129.

37–38

American Apprehensions. French fleet: Chadwick, *Diplomacy,* 208. Henry Clay on European designs on Cuba: Bailey, 304. "You are authorized to assure the Spanish government . . .": ibid., 305.

38
American Efforts. Polk authorizes purchase: ibid., 306–307. Lopez expedition: Chadwick, *Diplomacy*, 237. Ostend Manifesto: ibid., 262–267. Buchanan presses for purchase: ibid., 272.

39
Ten Years' War: Thomas, 245–263.

39–44
Virginius Incident. Chase and capture: Halstead, *Story of Cuba*, 36–37; Chadwick, *Diplomacy*, 317. *Virginius* and *Tornado* in the Civil War: Walker, 214–215. Invalid registry: Chadwick, *Diplomacy*, 314–315. Court-martial: ibid., 317. Schmidt's telegrams embargoed: ibid., 317–318. Executions, Sherman imprisoned: Halstead, *Story of Cuba*, 38. *Times* dispatch: N.Y. *Times*, November 7, 1873. Castelar's order: Chadwick, *Diplomacy*, 319–320. Fry's letter: Halstead, *Story of Cuba*, 43. "The capture on the high seas of a vessel bearing the American flag . . .": Chadwick, *Diplomacy*, 320. British subjects: ibid., 317. *Niobe* arrives, Burriel's reply to Lorraine: ibid., 318. "If the report be confirmed, you will protest . . .": ibid., 323. Sickles's background: Swanberg, *Sickles the Incredible*, 37–67. Sickles conciliatory: Chadwick, *Diplomacy*, 320–321. Indignation meetings: ibid., 325. *Times* report of cabinet meeting: N.Y. *Times*, November 15, 1873. Fish's ultimatum: Chadwick, *Diplomacy*, 329. Carvajal's angry rejection, Sickles's angry response: ibid., 330–333. Carvajal's long-winded note: ibid., 334–338. Sickles proposes to close legation: ibid., 340. Successful negotiations in Washington: ibid., 341–347. Sickles resigns: Swanberg, *Sickles the Incredible*, 349–350. Naval unpreparedness; Davis, *A Navy Second to None*, 16. "The force assembled at Key West was the best . . .": Robley D. Evans, 171.

44–45
Ten Years' War ends. Thomas, 263–266.

CHAPTER THREE. CUBA LIBRE

45–49
Gómez in New York. Arrives in New York: Manach, 226–230. "a stern, hard-hearted man . . . ," Funston, 31. "He is a gray little man . . .": Flint, 119. Gómez biographical details: Murat Halstead, "Our Cuban Neighbors and Their Struggle for Liberty." Cuban depression following Ten Years' War: Thomas, 271–273. Gómez and Maceo travel to New York: Martí, 15. Martí at Delmonico's: Manach, 225. Martí's biography: Manach, *passim;* Martí. Marti–Gómez clash: Manach, 229–230; Martí, 16–17. Martí's letter to Gómez: Martí, 16. Gómez note on letter: Manach, 230. Failure of Gómez's visit: Manach, 227–228.

49–50
Cuban Revolutionary party: Martí, *passim;* Manach, ch. 25, *passim.* Estrada Palma: Foner, 1:164–165; Rubens, 101.

50–51
New Uprising. Landing in Cuba: Manach, 346–348; Martí, 56; Foner, 1:7–9; Thomas, 316. Martí–Gómez reconciliation: Manach, 304. Hard times delay uprising: Martí, 49–50. "I called up the war . . . ,": Foner, 1:8–9. "Radiant with pride . . . ,": Manach, 347–348.

52–54
Churchill in Cuba. "There was a low mist . . . ,": Winston S. Churchill, 83. Churchill to Cuba: ibid., 75–82; Randolph S. Churchill, 225–264. "A long distance away . . .": Murat Halstead, *The Story of Cuba*, 610. Shot at while bathing: Randolph S. Churchill,

265. "The General, a very brave man . . .": ibid., 266. Churchill's opinions, controversy over mission: ibid., 266–270; Foner, 1:194n.

54–55

Gómez Moves West. Gómez's strategy: Foner, 1:ch. 2, *passim.* "The chains of Cuba . . .": ibid., 1:21. Orders to destroy plantations: ibid., 1:22. "They ride incessantly . . .": ibid., 1:31–32. Campaign in Matanzas and Pinar del Río: ibid., 1:ch. 4, *passim;* Thomas, 321. "Blessed be the torch!": Foner, 1:23.

55–58

Weyler and Reconcentrado Policy. Policy proposed: Thomas, 320–321. Martínez Campos arrives in Cuba: ibid., 316; Foner, 1:14–15. "The misery and hunger would be horrible . . .": Payne, 71. "How do they want me to wage war?": Carr, 385. Weyler biographical details: Payne, 73. Policy put in effect: Foner, 1:77–78, 77n, 111. Results of policy: ibid., 1:115–116.

58–59

Pro-Cuban Feeling in United States. Cuban-American Fair at Madison Square Garden: Foner, 1:166n; N.Y. *Times,* May 31, June 4, 1896. Sickles speaks: Funston, 3. Gompers: Foner, 1:174–175. Knights of Labor: Foner, 1:174. McDowell, Cuban League: ibid., 1:164, 164n. Chicago rally: May, 71–73.

59–64

Funston hears Sickles and applies to Estrada Palma: Funston, 3–5. *Horsa* case: Chadwick, *Diplomacy,* 412–415. Funston to Cuba: Funston, 5–30. Background of Johnny O'Brien: Horace Smith, *passim.* Junta's Washington office: Rubens, 107. Olney meets with Estrada Palma: Atkins, 213–214.

64–65

Congress Debates Belligerency. Senate Foreign Relations Committee resolution of January 28: *Congressional Record,* 54th Cong., 1st sess., 1065–1066. Cameron's minority resolution: ibid., 2281. Lodge's speech: ibid., 1971–1972. Morgan–Cameron resolution passed: ibid., 2679–2685.

65–66

United States Offers Good Offices. Olney–Dupuy de Lôme meeting: Ferrara, 16. Note predated: Foner, 1:192–193. April 4 note: Chadwick, *Diplomacy,* 452–458. O'Donnell background: Ferrara, 14. Anti-American riots: Chadwick, *Diplomacy,* 439, 439n. O'Donnell's reply of June 4: ibid., 460–465.

66–69

European Alliances. Hazeltine's article, entitled "Possible Complications of the Cuban Question," was excerpted by the *Review of Reviews* from the *North American Review* of April 1896. The origin of the Anglo–American crisis in the Venezuelan Boundary Dispute is traced in detail in Forrest Davis, 29–67, and Perkins, ch. 2. Olney's July 1895 note: *Foreign Relations, 1895.* The Jameson Raid and the Kruger telegram: Benson, 118. Victoria's letter to the kaiser: Victoria, 3: 8–9. British foreign minister's speech: Forrest Davis, 58. "The sudden appearance of Germany as the grizzly terror . . .": Henry Adams, 362–363. "It is no affair of ours . . .": James, 244.

70–72

O'Donnell's Proposed Joint Memorandum: Ferrara, chs. 1–3. O'Donnell's instructions to London envoy: ibid., 29. Demands made in the proposed memorandum: ibid., 44–45. O'Donnell's meeting with Taylor: ibid., 58–62.

73

Presidential Campaign of 1897. Cuba not an issue: Foner, 1: 201–202; LaFeber, *New Empire,* 333–334.

73

Conditions in Cienfuegos: Atkins, 199. Weyler's regard for Negro soldiers: Halstead, *Story of Cuba*, 110.

73–75

Trochas. Weyler builds Mariel to Majana *trocha:* Foner, 1:81. Description of Jucaro to Moron *trocha:* Davis, *A Year from a Reporter's Note-book*, 113–116, 124–129. Maceo trapped in Pinar del Río: Foner, 1: 81, 89–90.

75–76

Death of Maceo. Dissension among insurgents: Foner, 1: 85–87. Maceo crosses *trocha:* ibid., 1:87–91. Maceo killed: ibid., 1: 92. Gómez's general order of December 28: ibid., 1: 97. Gómez's letter to Maceo's widow: ibid., 1: 97n.

76

Cleveland's address to Congress: *Foreign Relations, 1897.*

77–78

Yellow Journals. Peanut Club: Rubens, 195; Swanberg, *Citizen Hearst*, 129–130. Hearst's background, early career, and competition with Pulitzer: Swanberg, *Citizen Hearst*, 3–107; Winkler, 3–145. Hearst sincerely sympathetic toward Cubans: Swanberg, *Citizen Hearst*, 128. Sword for Gómez: ibid., 122.

78–79

Stephen Crane Shipwrecked. Excerpts from "The Open Boat," Crane, 215–241. Crane sent to Cuba by Bacheller Syndicate: Beer, 142. Accounts of the sinking by Crane and others: Crane, 242–265.

79–82

Richard Harding Davis in Cuba. Davis tries to cross to Santa Clara: Brown, 77–78. Davis's background: Downey, chs. 1–8. Five hundred dollars to cover Harvard–Yale game: Swanberg, *Citizen Hearst*, 124. Payments for Cuban assignment: ibid.; Brown, 78. *Journal* says Davis with rebels: Brown 79. "I always imagined that houses were destroyed . . ." ibid. "The Death of Rodriguez": Davis, *A Year from a Reporter's Note-book*, 99–113. *Olivette* incident, including Davis's February 10 *Journal* story: Brown, 81–82. Alleged Remington–Hearst exchange: Creelman, 177–178. Hearst's denial: Winkler, 144.

82–83

Situation After Maceo's Death. 160,000 Spanish troops sent to Cuba by end of 1896: Chadwick, *Diplomacy*, 487. Weyler's report of pacification of western provinces: Thomas, 245; Foner, 1:119. Military situation in Cuba early in 1897: ibid., 1:119–120. Cánovas announces constitutional reforms: Chadwick, *Diplomacy*, 487. Lee's report that rebels not interested in autonomy: Foner, 1:207.

83–84

McKinley Inaugurated. Arrival in Washington: Leech, 111–115. Dinner at White House, ibid., 115–116. ". . . if I can only go out of office . . .": Rhodes, 41. McKinley's background and character: DAB. ". . . settled sadness and sincerity": Leech, 115.

84–85

McKinley Selects Cabinet. McCook offered Interior: Leech, 107–108. "I do not understand Col. McCook's interest . . .": LaFeber, *New Empire*, 346. McKenna attorney general: Leech, 106–107. Sherman secretary of state to make room in Senate for Hanna: ibid., 99–101; Rhodes, 31. Day to run State Department: Leech, 152; Rhodes, 41–42. Alger unsuited as secretary of war: Leech, 102–103. Long's views on role of secretary of the navy: Mayo, 157. Lodge proposes Roosevelt for Navy post: Leech, 137. Davis sponsors Roosevelt: Beringause, 157–158. "The only . . . thing . . . adverse . . ." Lodge, 1:253. "If he becomes Assistant Secretary . . .": Morris, 560. Platt's endorsement: ibid. See also May, 121–122.

85–87
Relief appropriation: Chadwick, *Diplomacy*, 495. Sherman's note and O'Donnell's reply: ibid., 496–502. Siege and capture of Las Tunas: Funston, 116–141.

87–88
Assassination of Cánovas. Assassination: Tuchman, *Proud Tower*, 114–115; Foner, 1: 127, 127n.; Thomas, 350.

88–89
Sagasta Takes Power. "The situation at our entry to power.": Levy and Peterson, 2: 165. "The administration has reached the last stage of disarray . . .": ibid. "Understand this well . . .": ibid., 167.

CHAPTER FOUR. MARCHING AS TO WAR

90–91
Roosevelt Comes to Washington. For Roosevelt's early life: Morris, *passim*. Dakota barroom incident: Roosevelt, *Autobiography*, 124–125. Lodge background: Schriftgiesser, *passim*. Lodge–Cameron salons: ibid., 130; Morris, 414–418; Josephson, 65–67. "Pleasant gang": Morris, 417.

91–93
Expansionism. Roosevelt's definition: Roosevelt, *Works*, 14: 336–339. "I think you have struck on some first class ideas . . .": Elting Morison, 1: 363. For an analysis of the influence of Turner and Josiah Strong on the Expansionists: LaFeber, *New Empire*, ch. 2. "It is a *very* good book . . .": Elting Morison, 1: 221. Roosevelt's review of *Influence of Sea Power: Atlantic Monthly*, October 1890. Lucid summaries of Mahan's views can be found in LaFeber, *New Empire*, 85–101; and George T. Davis, chs. 5, 8. The Mahan work which offers the most direct application of his principles to American global strategy of the Spanish War period is his *Interest of America in Sea Power*. For the post-Civil War reconstruction of the Navy, see George T. Davis, chs. 2, 3, 6. The mutual influence of Roosevelt and Mahan: Morris, 574–575.

93–97
Brooks Adams. Roosevelt's daily lunches with Adams and Lodge: Beringause, 157–160. Adams's background: ibid., *passim*. "I would have written my review very much more brutally . . .": Elting Morison, 1: 620. "I have watched your career with deep interest . . .": Beringause, 208–209. For an analysis of Adams's influence on Roosevelt: ibid., *passim*; Josephson, 25–27, 60–62. Roosevelt's Naval War College speech: Roosevelt, *Works*, 13:182–199.

97–99
War Plans. Origins of Naval War College: Nathan Miller, 198–201; Rickover, 10–11. Development of Spanish War plans at the Naval War College and by the Office of Naval Intelligence: Rickover, 10–13; Trask, 73–78; Grenville, "Diplomacy and War Plans in the United States, 1896–1898."

99–100
Roosevelt and Germany. "I suppose I need not tell you . . .": Elting Morison, 1: 607. "At the moment Japan is a more dangerous opponent . . .": ibid., 1: 636. ". . . keeping our Navy at a pitch . . .": ibid., 1: 645. "I am just now not reading but devouring Captain Mahan's book . . .": Tuchman, *Proud Tower*, 153. Mahan meets the kaiser: ibid., 152. German legislator's speech in Reichstag: N.Y. *Times*, December 10, 1897. "Germany shows a tendency to stretch out for colonial possessions . . .": Elting Morison, 1: 662. For examples of similar views on Germany held by others in Roosevelt's circle: Ford, 129; Thayer, 2: 275–279; Mahan, *Interest of America in Sea Power*, *passim*.

100–103

Roosevelt Acting Secretary of the Navy. Roosevelt made acting secretary: Morris, 580. "I am having immense fun . . .": Elting Morison, 1: 655. "Now stay there just exactly as long as you want to.": ibid., 1: 662. Carriage rides and dinner with McKinley: ibid., 1:676, 685–686. ". . . before you commit yourself definitely to Commodore Howell . . .": ibid., 1: 691. "I was already watching him . . .": Roosevelt, *Autobiography,* 215–216. Proctor's endorsement of Dewey: ibid., 216–217; Dewey, 167–169.

103–104

Taylor in Spain. Woodford presents his credentials: Chadwick, *Diplomacy,* 508. Woodford meets with O'Donnell on September 18: Ferrara, 79–80; Chadwick, *Diplomacy,* 513. ". . . before the first of November next . . .": ibid. O'Donnell briefs cabinet: Ferrara, 81. Weyler recalled, Blanco replaces him: Chadwick, *Diplomacy,* 521. Weyler's farewell speech, his arrival in Barcelona: ibid., 521–522. Weyler's popularity in Spain: Payne, 80.

104–108

German Adventures in China and Haiti. For a brief profile of Kaiser Wilhelm II and a sketch of his eccentricities: Tuchman, *Zimmerman Telegram,* ch. 2. "I believe it is now high time that we other monarchs . . .": May, 196–197. Von Bülow's subterfuge: ibid., 197–200; Ferrara, 86–89. Kaichow Bay incident: Steinberg, 154–155; Forrest Davis, 62–63. Kaiser's instructions to Diedrichs: ibid., 63. Lüders incident: Heinl, 324–325. November 30 Haitian note to Germany: N.Y. *Times,* December 1, 1897. *Marblehead* dispatched to Haiti: ibid. Leger calls at State Department, *Stein* and *Charlotte* sent to Haiti: ibid., December 4, 1897. North Atlantic Squadron to go on winter maneuvers off Florida coast: ibid., December 5, 1897; Chadwick, *Diplomacy,* 532. German ships at Port-au-Prince, Thiele demands indemnity, etc.: Heinl, 324–325; N.Y *Times,* December 8, 1897. Powell's advisories to Washington, "This is the first time in my life . . .": Heinl, 324–325. "They are a contemptible crowd of negroes . . .": N.Y. *Times,* December 8, 1897. Statement of Haitian president: ibid., December 9, 1897. American "designs on Cuba and Spain . . .": *Revue des deux mondes,* December 15, 1897. *Marblehead* arrives Port-au-Prince: N.Y. *Times,* December 10, 1897. "I doubt if those Spaniards can really pacify Cuba . . .": Elting Morison, 1: 743.

108–109

Maine to Key West. Leaves Norfolk: Rickover, 23. Lee asked for warship: Foner, 1: 225n. Detached from North Atlantic Squadron: Rickover, 22. Lee reports anti-American plot: Lee to Day, December 1, 1897, *Despatches,* Reel 131. Code to summon *Maine* established: Day to Lee, December 2, 1897, ibid. "A large national steamer . . .": Lee to Day, December 22, 1897, ibid. "I wish there were a chance that the *Maine* was going to be used against some foreign power . . .": Elting Morison, 1: 747. "As I said before, if there is trouble . . .": ibid., 1: 748.

109

Weyler Maneuvers. Military Club of Palma luncheon, "So long as their Majesties are heads of the State . . .": N.Y. *Times,* December 5, 1897. Left, Right, and Carlists rally to Weyler: Payne, 79–80. Carlists in "substantial agreement": ibid. Planned meeting with Don Carlos: ibid; also see reports of Weyler's political activities in the N.Y. *Times,* December 10, 12, 16, 1897.

109–112

Naval Movements, Riots. Roosevelt assigns warships to maneuvers: Rickover, 23. Largest fleet since Civil War: N.Y. *Times,* December 5, 1897. "On the Continent . . . ill will towards the United States . . .": Ferrara, 97. *Geier* arrives Port-au-Prince: Powell to Sherman, January 9, 1898 (copy), *Area File,* Reel 225. Specifications of *Geier: Jane's*

Fighting Ships. "I learn on inquiry . . . this port has not been left without a German ship . . .": Todd to Navy Department, January 10, 1898, *Area File*, Reel 225. Long orders European Squadron to retain men: Rickover, 28. "The German Consul-General informed me . . . ships were coming here . . . I am sure the majority of all classes . . . welcome . . .": Lee to Day, January 12, 1898, *Despatches*, Reel 131. "There was a lull during the midday . . .": Pepper, 90. *Maine* prepares to sail, Sigsbee conceals preparations: Sigsbee, 11–12. "During the days of rioting . . .": Pepper, 93. "If American interests are further imperiled . . ." N.Y. *Herald,* January 15, 1898.

    112–113

Roosevelt's Preparations. Memorandum of several thousand words: Elting Morison, 1: 759–763. Roosevelt's personal preparations: ibid., 1: 758.

    113–114

Woodford's meetings with the queen, minister of colonies: Woodford to McKinley, January 17, 1898, No. 24, Moore Papers.

    114–115

Naval Visits Proposed to Spain. Dupuy de Lôme's meeting with Reick: Dupuy de Lôme to Gullon, January 16, 1898, No. 42, *Spanish Diplomatic Correspondence.* Dupuy de Lôme does not mention Reick by name but as "the head of staff of the *Herald.*" For Reick's role at the *Herald,* in New York City Republican politics, and as an intimate of the McKinley administration: DAB; Seitz, 228–230; LaFeber, *New Empire,* 392–393. Dupuy de Lôme's visit to Day: Dupuy de Lôme to Gullon, January 20, 1898, No. 46, *Spanish Diplomatic Correspondence.* Gullon's response to report of Reick meeting: Gullon to Dupuy de Lôme, January 17, 1898, No. 43, ibid. Day's account of meeting with Dupuy de Lôme: Interview with the Spanish Minister, January 1898, Day Papers.

    115–116

McKinley Watches German Fleet. Long's note to McKinley regarding German ships at Havana: Long to McKinley (handwritten), January 21, 1898, Day Papers. Powell reports departure of *Geier:* Powell to Sherman, January 18, 1898 (copy), *Area File,* Reel 225. Day's inquiry regarding foreign vessels at Havana: Day to Lee, January 22, 1898, *Foreign Relations, 1898.* Lee's report that German warships expected: Lee to Day, January 22, 1898, *Foreign Relations, 1898.* Powell's report of German fleet at Haiti: Powell to Sherman, January 23, 1898 (copy), *Area File,* Reel 225.

    116–120

Maine Sent to Havana. "Generally speaking, President McKinley did not write letters . . .": *Index to the McKinley Papers,* introduction. Meeting between Day and Dupuy de Lôme, Day version: "Memorandum of Interview with the Spanish Minister," January 24, 1898, Day Papers; Dupuy de Lôme version: Dupuy de Lôme to Gullon, January 24, 1898, No. 48, *Spanish Diplomatic Correspondence.* "The most significant conference of the day at the White House . . .": Washington *Evening Star,* January 24, 1898. Long's diary entry: Mayo, 153–155. Cable to Woodford: Day to Woodford, January 24, 1898, *Foreign Relations, 1898. Times* report: N.Y. *Times,* January 25, 1898. Second meeting between Day and Dupuy de Lôme; Day's version: "Memorandum of Interview with the Spanish Minister," January 24, 1898, Day Papers; Dupuy de Lôme version: Dupuy de Lôme to Gullón, January 24, 1898, No. 49, *Spanish Diplomatic Correspondence.* Lee's cable advising postponement: Lee to Day, January 24, 1898, *Foreign Relations, 1898;* the State Department's copy of this cable, bearing the time of receipt, is in *Despatches,* Reel 131. "*Maine* has been ordered . . .": Day to Lee, January 25, 1898, *Foreign Relations, 1898.*

A careful reading of the official diplomatic correspondence leaves little doubt that the *Maine* reached Havana before the Spanish government had given its permission or even had been notified of the visit. Woodford's dispatch to Day acknowledging receipt of Day's cable and reporting that he had "this day" informed the Spanish Ministry of the proposed visit is dated the twenty-fifth (Woodford to Sherman, January 25, 1898, *Foreign Relations, 1898.*) Minister Gullón's note to Woodford, acknowledging the latter's note of the twenty-fifth announcing the visit, is dated the twenty-sixth, the day after the *Maine* arrived, and refers to the fact that the battleship was already at Havana (The Minister of State to the Minister Plenipotentiary of the United States, January 26, 1898, *Spanish Diplomatic Correspondence*).

Captain Sigsbee's statement that the *Maine* had been unexpected, even by Consul General Lee, is in Sigsbee to Long, January 26, 1898, *Area File,* Reel 225. Lee made a point of putting on record at the *Maine* Court of Inquiry that he had not expected the battleship to arrive that morning (*Court of Inquiry,* pp. 246–247).

Lee's report of German ship's arrival: Lee to Day, January 24, 1898, *Foreign Relations, 1898.* The State Department's copy bearing the time of receipt is in *Despatches,* Reel 131. The German ships are identified by name in Sigsbee, 26–27.

120–121

Cervera Prepares. Cervera's background: Dierks, 44–45. Letter to cousin: Cervera, 12–13. Letter to minister of marine requesting intelligence: ibid., 22–23.

121–122

Woodford reports ministry will make no more concessions: Woodford to McKinley, February 7, 1898, Moore Papers.

122–123

Dupuy de Lôme Letter. Rubens and McCook visit Day: Rubens, 290–291; LaFeber, *New Empire,* 347, 347n. There are several slightly different translations of the text of the letter; the one used here was that published in Hearst's *Journal* and is quoted in Foner, 1:232. Day's confrontation of Dupuy de Lôme: Chadwick, *Diplomacy,* 540. Spanish apology, ibid., 540–541.

CHAPTER FIVE. SIXTY-SIX DAYS

124–126

February 16. Regular and special editions of *World:* Brown, 120–121. Dawn at White House: Leech, 166–167. Lee's telegram: Lee to Day, February 16, 1898, *Foreign Relations, 1898.* "There is an intense difference of opinion . . .": Mayo, 162–164. "I don't propose to be swept off my feet . . .": Leech, 168. Long orders survivors kept at Key West: Long to Sicard, February 16, 1898, *Area File,* Reel 226. Moret's instructions "to gather every fact": Rickover, 45. Spanish Board established: ibid., 50. Sigsbee on board *City of Washington,* his description of wreckage: Sigsbee, 99–101. Casualty totals: *Lives Lost by Sinking of U.S. Battle Ship Maine,* Document 231. *Olivette* takes back survivors, Lee reports sympathy: Sigsbee, 103–104. "The *Maine* was sunk by an act of dirty treachery . . .": Elting Morison, 1 775.

126–127

February 17. Funeral: Sigsbee, 106–111. "The cause of the blowing up of the ship . . .": Brown, 124. *Evening Star* survey, other coal bunker fires, statements by Admiral Bradford and others: Rickover, 20–21, 45–46. *Journal's* diagram and story: Brown, 123. "Probably the *Maine* destroyed by mine . . .": Rickover, 45.

128

February 18. Vultures over wreck, bodies at seawall: Sigsbee, 143, 158. Sigsbee and divers turned back at wreck, meeting with Blanco: ibid., 115–119.

128–130

February 19. Roosevelt's advice against joint investigation: Elting Morison, 1:779–780. Cable to Lee regarding separate investigations: Sigsbee, 145. Sicard names Court: Rickover, 48–50. Chadwick's background: WAMB. Duties of the court: *Court of Inquiry,* 285–287. Spanish Board of Inquiry, Rickover, 50. Sigsbee–Manterola interview: Sigsbee, 129–131. Sigsbee reports burials: ibid., 145.

131

February 20. Sigsbee visits crewmen in hospital: Sigsbee, 121–123. Captain Peral's report: Rickover, 52.

131–133

February 21. Sigsbee's testimony: *Court of Inquiry.* Diver recovers keys and other items: Sigsbee, 148–150, 156–157.

133–134

February 22. Testimony of Holman, Wainwright, Cluverius, and Holden: *Court of Inquiry.* Lee reports intact ammunition, concludes a mine: Rickover, 62.

134–136

February 23. Testimony of Howell, Sigsbee, Powelson: *Court of Inquiry.* For Powelson's background and an analysis of the influence of his testimony on the Court of Inquiry: Rickover, 57, 60, 67–70, 95–97.

136

February 24. Testimony of eyewitnesses: *Court of Inquiry.* For a recent analysis of the eyewitness testimony: Rickover, 116–118.

136–137

February 25. "Whenever I was left as Acting Secretary . . .": Roosevelt *Autobiography,* 218. Roosevelt's orders to Navy Yard, squadron commanders: Rickover, 62–63. "All that was needed with Dewey . . .": Roosevelt, *Autobiography,* 219. Dewey took flagship to Hong Kong: Dewey, 178. "It was evident that in case of emergency Hong Kong was . . .": ibid. Roosevelt's orders to Dewey: Elting Morison, 1: 784–785. Long's diary entry: Long, 216–217. Powelson's testimony: *Court of Inquiry;* Rickover, 60.

137–138

February 26. Proctor arrives in Havana: Sigsbee, 159. "We must not indulge in any illusions . . .": Cervera, 29. "Do we not owe our country not only our life . . .": ibid., 30. Powelson's testimony: *Court of Inquiry;* Rickover, 60.

138–140

February 28. "Never in the history of similar proceedings . . .": Brown, 127. White House meeting, Lee's theory of makeshift mine: Rickover, 63–64; Leech, 171. Long's diary entry: Long, 220. Alger interview: Rickover, 46–47. Roosevelt's snappish letter: Elting Morison, 1: 785–786.

140

March 2. Court at Key West: *Court of Inquiry.*

140–141

March 4. Bermejo's letter: Cervera, 31–33.

141

March 6. "We are certainly drifting towards . . . war": Elting Morison, 1: 789. McKinley authorizes purchase of ammunition: Rickover, 66. "I must have money to get ready. . . . It may be more than war with Spain": May, 149.

141–142

March 7. Reply to Bermejo: Cervera, 34. Spain renews appeal to great powers: Ferrara, 93–97.

142

March 9. "If there is a war . . .": Elting Morison, 1: 791. "I have been in a great quandary . . .": ibid., 1: 792. Psychological effect of congressional appropriation: *Foreign Relations, 1898,* 684.

142

March 10. Court at wreck: *Court of Inquiry.*

142–143

March 11. María Cristina's meeting with Dubsky: Levy and Peterson, 2:181–182. Woodford approached regarding sale of Cuba: May, 166–167. Court at wreck site, hears Converse testimony: *Court of Inquiry;* Rickover, 67–68.

143–144

March 12. Woodford told that Cuban sale off: May, 166–167.

144

March 13. Woodford reports dispatch of torpedo boats: Woodford to Sherman, March 13, 14, 1898, Day Papers.

144

March 14. "We should fight this minute . . .": Elting Morison, 1:793–794. For a contemporary view of torpedo boats: Spears, "Torpedo-boats in the War with Spain."

144–145

March 15. Sigsbee's letter to his wife: Rickover, 68–69. "I don't want to be in an office . . .": Elting Morison, 1: 794–795. Roosevelt offers to go in any capacity: ibid., 1: 795. Wood's background: WAMB.

145–146

March 16. Cervera's plea: Cervera, 38–39. Naval War Board: Trask, 88. Roosevelt and board call for court's report: Rickover, 67. "McKinley is bent on peace . . .": Elting Morison, 1: 958.

146–148

March 17. Senator Proctor's speech: *Congressional Record,* 55th Cong., 2d sess., 2916–2919. Effect of speech on business community: Pratt, 246–247. María Cristina's letter to Victoria: Victoria, 3: 236.

148

March 19. *Oregon* departs San Francisco for Caribbean: Sternlicht, 55–56. Battleship's background, specifications: ibid., chs. 2, 3, app. A.

148–149

March 20. "He appeared to me careworn . . .": Leech, 173. Day's cable: Day to Woodford, March 20, 1898, *Foreign Relations, 1898.*

149–150

March 23. Meeting between Woodford and Spanish officials: Woodford to McKinley, March 23, 1898, *Foreign Relations, 1898.*

150

March 24. Roosevelt meets with Shoemaker: Stephen H. Evans, 164–165. "These craft will be from one-half to two-thirds as fast . . .": Elting Morison, 1: 798–799. Naval officers bring court's report to Washington: Leech, 174; Rickover, 69.

150–159

March 25. McKinley meets with cabinet, walks in park: Leech, 175; Rickover, 70. Woodford's proposal: LaFeber, *New Empire,* 394–395.

159–160

March 26. President's response, Day to Woodford, March 26, 1898, *Foreign Relations, 1898.* Gullón's cable to London: Ferrara, 107–108. Von Bülow's cable to German minister at Vatican: ibid., 114. Roosevelt's report regarding Spanish torpedo gunboat: Elting Morison, 1:800. "Things look as if they were coming to a head . . .": ibid. Speech at Gridiron Club, remark to Hanna: Morris, 607–608. Cortelyou types report: Rickover, 70.

160–161

March 27. Cables between Day and Woodford: *Foreign Relations, 1898,* 712–713. Russia agrees to joint action: May, 171. Drinking water on *Oregon* cut: Sternlicht, 56–57. Bunker fire on *Oregon:* Offley, "The Oregon's Long Voyage."

161

March 28. Report obtained by Associated Press: Leech, 177–178; Brown, 143–144. Angry reaction in Congress, fear of "Cuban outbreak": Leech, 178–179. Spanish Board of Inquiry report presented to State Department: Chadwick, *Diplomacy,* 561–562.

161–162

March 29. Prowar hysteria: Leech, 178–181. Cables between Day and Woodford: *Foreign Relations, 1898,* 718–721. "I have not felt the loss of the *Maine* nearly as much . . .": Elting Morison, 1:785. Illness of wife and son: Morris, 601, 604. Letter to Bigelow: Elting Morison, 2:801–803.

163–164

March 31. Sigsbee's testimony before Senate Committee: *Report of the Committee on Foreign Relations, United States Senate, Relative to Affairs in Cuba,* 55th Cong., 2d sess., April 13, 1898, Senate Report 885, p. 484. "Spanish pride will not permit . . .": Woodford to Day, March 31, 1898, *Foreign Relations, 1898.* Spanish Foreign Ministry's dispatch: *Spanish Diplomatic Correspondence,* 108.

164

April 1. Salisbury's note to Victoria: Victoria, 3:239. Roosevelt asks to blockade Havana: Elting Morison, 2: 810–811.

164

April 2. Pope's offer to request armistice unwelcome in Madrid: May, 172.

165

April 3. Public enthusiasm for the war: Swanberg, *Citizen Hearst,* 170. Ireland's report to Vatican, misunderstanding: Chadwick, *Diplomacy,* 569–570; May, 174. Cables between Day and Woodford: *Foreign Relations, 1898,* 732.

165–166

April 4. Oregon arrives Callao, receives warning of *Temerario:* Sternlicht, 57–58, 69; Offley, "The Oregon's Long Voyage." "I would give a large sum . . .": Elting Morison, 2: 810. Lee warns of danger to Americans in Cuba: Leech, 183; May, 154.

166

April 5. "I have no advice to give you . . .": Ferrara, 126–127. Hay's letter: Thayer, 2:165. Long's cable to Dewey: Dewey, 188.

166–167

April 6. Hay's meeting with Balfour: Ferrara, 131–132. Note presented at Blue Room meeting, Pauncefote clears with White House and State Department: Ferrara, 129–130; Leech, 186. Bermejo's claim that "nothing can be decided": Cervera, 42. Cervera's reply: ibid., 42–43.

167–168

April 8. Cervera ordered to rendezvous with flotilla: Cervera, 43. No time to explain: ibid., 44. "I regret very much to have to sail . . .": ibid. Sails at 5 P.M.: ibid.

168

April 9. Oregon fires fourth boiler: Offley, "The Oregon's Long Voyage." Pope asks

Spain for armistice, ambassadors call on Gullón: Ferrara, 121–122. Woodford's report: Woodford to McKinley, April 9, 1898, *Foreign Relations, 1898.*

168–169

April 10. Cabinet meetings, American conditions not met: May, 156–158; Chadwick, *Diplomacy,* 574–576. Lee departs Havana: Rickover, 73.

169–170

April 11. McKinley's message: *Foreign Relations, 1898,* 750–760. Congressional outrage over question of independence: Foner, 1:263ff. "We talk about liberty . . .": quoted in ibid., 1:267. Foraker's statement: ibid., 1:268. "I am perfectly willing to follow the policy of intervening . . .": Elting Morison, 2: 814.

170–171

April 14. Engines and boilers of two Spanish warships not working well, nine hundred tons of coal consumed: Cervera, 47. U.S. consul bought up all the coal: Concas, 24. Reports arrival: Cervera, 46. "I earnestly hope that it will not be passed . . .": Elting Morison, 2: 815.

171

April 16. Senate passes Teller Amendment: Foner, 1:270. Gullón asks Pope for naval intervention: Ferrara, 122–123. *Oregon* reaches Straits of Magellan: Sternlicht, 59.

171

April 19. Congress passes joint resolution: *Congressional Record,* 55th Cong., 2d sess., vol. 31, pt. 4, pp. 3699–3702.

172

April 20. Deficiencies in Cervera's squadron: Cervera, 35, 48–49, 57, 65. Meeting aboard *Colón:* ibid., 50–54.

172–173

April 21. Oregon heads into Atlantic: Offley, "The Oregon's Long Voyage." "War seems hopelessly declared . . .": Victoria, 3:244.

173

April 22. Blanco's cable: Cervera, 55. Bermejo orders Cervera to proceed: ibid., 54. "Though I persist in my opinion . . .": ibid., 55. North Atlantic Squadron forms, blockade put in place: *American-Spanish War,* 353; Millis, 145.

CHAPTER SIX. MANILA

174–178

Hong Kong and Mirs Bay. Governor Black orders fleet to leave colony: Dewey, 193. "God knows, my dear Commodore . . .": Healy, 167. Squadron to Mirs Bay, tugboat *Fame* chartered, "War has commenced between the United States and Spain": Dewey, 194–195; Healy, 168. Ships of the squadron: Healy, 170. "The English crews . . . agreed to stand by their ships . . .": Dewey, 191–192. "The prevailing impression among even the military class . . . that our squadron was going to certain destruction . . .": ibid., 192. Dewey buys charts of Philippines: *American-Spanish War,* 104. Dewey's makeshift spy system: Healy, 156–157. Strength of Spanish fleet: Dewey, 203, 295; Healy, 170. Coastal defenses: Dewey, 198, 200; *American-Spanish War,* 110. Reports of mines in channel: Dewey, 198–199. "A specious bluff": Healy, 157. Waits for Williams: Dewey, 194–195. Departs Mirs Bay: ibid., 196; *American-Spanish War,* 108–109; Spears, *Our Navy,* 157; Stickney, 30. Band plays "El Capitan": Stickney, 30.

178–179

En Route to the Philippines. Williams brings reports Spanish at Subic: Dewey, 204. Dewey's estimate of the strategic value of Subic: ibid., 200–201. Spanish commander realizes Subic's importance at last moment: ibid., 204–205. Battle drills: ibid., 204. Midnight drill: Stickney, 31–32. Wood jettisoned: *American-Spanish War*, 109. "Essential to comfort in time of peace": Dewey, 204. Spanish proclamation: Young, 66–67; Stickney, 27–30. Band serenades: Young, 32–33.

179–180

Montojo Prepares. Montojo asks for help, is refused: Trask, 69–70. Montojo goes to Subic and returns to Manila: Dewey, 301–303.

180–181

Off the Luzon Coast. "The presence of the squadron on the waters . . .": Dewey, 204. "A dark mass and a rank tropical odor . . .": *American-Spanish War*, 109. Fishermen questioned: Dewey, 205; Young, 70. *Boston* and *Concord* sent ahead: Dewey, 205. Gunfire heard, *Baltimore* sent ahead: ibid. Arrives at Subic, "Now we have them": ibid. Meeting of captains, "We shall enter Manila Bay to-night . . .": ibid., 206. Conversation between Lieutenant Winder and Dewey: Healy, 174–175. "If the guns commanding the entrance were well served . . .": Dewey, 208.

182–183

Into Manila Bay. "No local knowledge was needed . . .": *American-Spanish War*, 110. Best artillery on El Fraile: ibid. Signal light, rocket seen: ibid., 111. "As we watched the walls of darkness for the first gun-flash . . .": Dewey, 209. Swings to NEN heading: *American-Spanish War*, 111. Fire in *McCulloch*'s stack: Stephen H. Evans, 168; Sears, 161. Shore batteries silenced: Dewey, 210. "The moon set shortly after the firing ceased . . .": *American-Spanish War*, 112. "I did not wish to reach our destination before we had sufficient daylight . . .": Dewey, 211. White glow of city, electric lights, breakfast: *American-Spanish War*, 113. "Just Before the Battle, Mother": Young, 72. "Dawn came out behind Manila . . .": *American-Spanish War*, 113.

183–189

Battle. Enemy sighted: *American-Spanish War*, 114. "Take her close along the 5-fathom line . . .": Stickney, 42. "A white cloud with a heart of fire . . .": *American-Spanish War*, 114. Firing from shore batteries returned: ibid., 114–115. "All the guns were pointed constantly at the enemy . . .": Dewey, 213–214. "You may fire when you are ready . . .": ibid., 214. "The Americans fired most rapidly . . .": ibid., 304. Montojo receives telegram from Subic, hears fire from Corregidor, receives telegram about Boca Grande fight, signals prepare for action: ibid., 303–304. Accounts of events during battle: Dewey, 214–225; Young, 73–81; *American-Spanish War*, 115–120; Stickney, 44–65. "They climbed on the ramparts of the very battery that had fired on us in the morning . . .": Dewey, 225.

189–191

American and European Reaction. Spanish report of battle: Healy, 192. Proctor reminds McKinley he recommended Dewey: Dewey, 228. Headlines of May 7: Brown, 199. Dispatch received at *World:* Sullivan, 1:321. Harden's dispatch: Brown, 198. News received at Navy Department: ibid., 199; Leech, 205–206. Roosevelt releases report to press: Leech, 206; Millis, 196–197. Dewey song: Spector, 65. Mr. Dooley: Dunne, 20. Roosevelt's cable: Dewey, 229. Long's cable: Healy, 195. "The state of feeling here is the best I have ever known . . .": Thayer, 2:168–169. Chamberlain's speech: ibid., 169n. For an analysis of the speech and British, European and American reaction: Reuter, 153ff. Victoria's birthday celebrated, "Their colors never run": Wilcox, 132.

191–193

German Activity. Irene incident, *Cormoran* incident: Dewey, 254–256. Dewey's conversations with Prince Henry: ibid., 185. Henry's farewell comments: Healy, 168. Assessments of Philippine situation by Henry and German consul: Spector, 73. Kaiser's designs: ibid. Dewey estimates five thousand troops needed, advised *Charleston* and troops on way: Trask, 369–370. Naval Intelligence report of Spanish task force for Manila: Spector, 69.

CHAPTER SEVEN. A DREAM OF SPRING

194–195
Anxiety Over Cervera. Squadron at Cape Verde: Concas, 24. Portugal declares neutrality: Alger, 46; Wilcox, 93–94. Squadron sails: Concas, 42–43. "Am going north" code phrase: Cervera, 54. Code phrase sent: ibid., 68. Squadron followed by correspondent: Brown, 235–236. "The Governor of one State actually announced . . .": Roosevelt, *Autobiography*, 220–221.

195
Roosevelt Departs. Orders uniform: Elting Morison, 2: 822. "My Assistant Secretary, Roosevelt, has determined upon resigning . . .": Long, 223–224.

195–199
Military Plans and Preparations. McKinley calls for volunteers: Alger, 7. Thirteen dollars per month: Post, 4. A million volunteers: Alger, 7. Recruiting stations: Post, 5. Physical exam: ibid., 4. Attempts to pass physical: Alger, 31–32. Percent rejected: ibid., 16, 31. McKinley appoints ex-Confederates: Cosmas, 149. Background of Joseph Wheeler: WAMB. Wheeler meets with McKinley: Wheeler, 3–4. (For a slightly different account of this meeting, see Post, 214–215.) Remarks of old comrade at funeral: Fleming, 269. Size of Army on April 1: Alger, 7. Confusion as Army expands: Alger, chs. 2–4; Cosmas, chs. 4–6. April 20 White House meeting: Trask, 153; Cosmas, 107. "The sanitary objections to a campaign in Cuba . . .": *American-Spanish War,* 517. McKinley adopts Miles's plan: Cosmas, 107. Tunas landing planned, canceled on news of Cervera: Alger, 44–46; Cosmas, 111–112; Trask, 162–163. Mahan's analysis and definition: Mahan, *Lessons of the War with Spain,* 75–85, 101. Miles's background: WAMB. Organizational problems of Miles–Alger relationship: White, 142–144. May 2, meeting, plans for Mariel landing: Alger, 46–47; Trask, 163; Cosmas, 123. Long–Alger clash: Trask, 165; White, 148; Mayo, 189. Alger forces postponement of Mariel landing: Trask, 165–166; Mayo, 192.

200–202
Reporters and the Blockade. Stephen Crane writing aboard *Three Friends:* Stallman, 123. "A day on the Cuban blockade . . .": ibid., 120–123. First shot of the war: Davis, *Campaigns,* 7–11; Spears, *Our Navy,* 122–124. Shelling of Cabañas and fight between *New York* and cavalry: Davis, *Campaigns,* 35–38. Thrall's exploits and rescue: Stallman, 124–130; Brown, 174–179.

203–204
Early Landings in Cuba. Rowan's trip to Cuba: Foner, 2:340–342; *American-Spanish War,* 55–56; Trask, 174. Hubbard's *A Message to Garcia* and its success: Pizer, 468–472. Somerford and Blue visit Gómez: *American-Spanish War,* 57–58; Brown, 180. *Gussie* expedition: Trask, 163; Brown, 212–220, Freidel, 47–48.

204–205
Battle at Cárdenas. Bernadou, "The 'Winslow' at Cardenas"; Spears, *Our Navy,* 145–153.

205–207
Battle at Cienfuegos. Winslow, "Cable-Cutting at Cienfuegos"; Spears, *Our Navy,* 141–144. Villaverde's report: Chief Signal Officer to the President, May 11, 1898, Greely Papers.

207–209

Hellings–Villaverde Intelligence Network. Background of International Ocean Telegraph Company: Harlow, 300–301. Telegraph cable links to Cuba: James Rankin Young, 188. Hellings's background: Chapin, 498–499; records of Captain Martin L. Hellings in Military Records of Spanish-American War Volunteers, especially Thomas T. Eckert to the President (McKinley), May 12, 1898; H. B. Plant to Thompson & Slater, May 12, 1898; Thompson & Slater to the President (McKinley), May 16, 1898. Other background information on Hellings in records of Local and State History Department, Monroe County Public Library, Key West, Florida.

Sigsbee's earlier connection with Hellings: Sigsbee to Long, January 16, 1898, and Sigsbee to commander of the torpedo boat *Cushing,* January 21, 1898, in *Area File,* Reel 225. Hellings's acquaintance with Plant: Plant to Thompson & Slater, May 12, 1898, in Hellings's Spanish-American War military records. Sigsbee's arrangements with Southwick and purser of the *Olivette:* Sigsbee to commander of the *Cushing,* January 21, 1898, *Area File,* Reel 225. Southwick's background: *Daily Equator-Democrat,* Trade Edition, Key West, March 1889 (holdings of Local and State History Department, Monroe County Public Library).

Hellings's telegrapher staff: photo and letter to author from Mrs. Betty Bruce, Local and State History Division, Monroe County Public Library, December 14, 1982.

Benjamin F. Montgomery's obscure but important role as founder of the White House telegraph office under President Hayes and subsequent career as a White House fixture: "One of the 'Old Guard,' " *The Telegraph Age* 19, no. 11, June 1, 1902, p. 225 (copy found in library of Western Union Corporation, Upper Saddle River, N.J.). Some additional background on Montgomery's role as "chief intelligence officer" at White House under McKinley and Roosevelt: Willets, 180–181. Montgomery's birth and death dates were not found in any biographic dictionary consulted, but a "Dear Comrade" letter to members of the U.S. Veteran Signal Corps Association, Spanish War Division, from Herbert F. Tomlinson, Commander, January 22, 1927, reports Montgomery had died in December 1926 (letter found in the association's records in the U.S. Army Communications Systems Center Electronics Museum, Myer Hall, Fort Monmouth, N.J.).

Roles of General A. W. Greely and the Signal Corps in the Hellings–Villaverde network: Greely, *Reminiscences,* Ch. 19; Greely, "Signal Corps in War Time"; *Report of the Chief Signal Officer.* Alger's attempt to close Havana–Key West cable: Greely, *Reminiscences,* 181.

209–211

Cervera Disrupts Invasion Plans. Cruisers sent to New England coast: *American-Spanish War,* 353–354. Auxiliary cruisers look for Cervera: ibid., 354–355. Sampson to Puerto Rico: ibid., 355. Van Dewater's account of the Seventy-first: New York State Historian, 163–164. Post's account of situation aboard *Seneca:* Post, 28–32. Cervera reported off Sandy Hook: Alger, 37. Report of Cervera at Martinique: *American-Spanish War,* 355.

211–212

Cervera in the Caribbean. "Government is pleased to hear of your arrival . . .": Cervera, 72–73. "I came here in hopes of finding coal . . .": ibid., 74. Squadron detained at harbor entrance: Concas, 49. Departs for Santiago de Cuba: ibid., 50. Bermejo's cable giving option of returning not received: Cervera, 73, 73n. "I beg your excellency to tell me truly . . .": ibid., 74. "I could not prevent bloody revolution . . .": ibid., 78. "The Spanish in official quarters evidently have news of the coming of their fleet . . .": Chief Signal Officer to the President, May 18, 1898, Letterbooks, Greely Papers.

212–221

Cervera, Schley and the Flying Squadron. Navy believed Cervera bringing supplies to Cienfuegos: Schley, 266–267. Flying squadron departs Key West: ibid., 263. "Have cast anchor today . . .": Cervera, 80. White House Operating Room: Trask, 169. "The following cipher messages have just been received from Capt. Allen . . .": Acting Chief Signal Officer to the President, May 19, 1898, Letterbooks, Greely Papers. 'Can you furnish us with any information . . .": Acting Chief Signal Officer to B. F. Montgomery, May 19, 1898, Letterbooks, Greely Papers. Telegram from Western Union president: J. C. Willever to M. Marean, May 19, 1898, *Area File*, Reel 230.

Skepticism of McKinley and Navy War Board: Greely, *Reminiscences,* 182–185. *St. Louis* reports Cervera not at Santiago: *American-Spanish War,* 358. "*Pelayo* and four cruisers at Santiago . . .": Chief Signal Officer to the President, May 20, 1898, Letterbooks, Greely Papers. "Only know that all five are battle ships . . ."; copy sent to Navy: Chief Signal Officer to the President, May 21, 1898, Letterbooks, Greely Papers. "By direction of the President . . .": Chief Signal Officer to the Secretary of the Navy, May 21, 1898, Letterbooks, Greely Papers. Long's dispatch to Sampson, Sampson's orders to Schley: Schley, 269–270.

"As to the advisability of going to Cienfuegos . . .": Concas, 55. "The coal supply of the six ships also had to be renewed . . .": ibid., 54. "Although the city was in reality besieged by the insurgents . . .": ibid., 52. "Intend to refit ships . . .": Cervera, 81. "If we are blockaded before we can finish taking coal . . .": ibid., 83. *Restormel* en route to Santiago: ibid., 86. Archbishop's toast: Concas, 52–53.

Lieutenant Colonel Maxfield confirms Cervera report: Greely, *Reminiscences,* 183; *Report of the Chief Signal Officer;* Greely, "The Signal Corps in War Time." Maxfield takes possession of Haiti cable office: *Report of the Chief Signal Officer.*

"Spanish squadron probably at Santiago . . .": Schley, 270. Schley heard guns from Cienfuegos: ibid., 265. Steamer *Adula* stopped: ibid., 268. Sigsbee remarks on length of *St. Paul:* ibid., 276. Sigsbee reports capture of *Restormel:* Graham, 124. Lieutenant José Müller's account of the capture, reasons for not interfering: Müller, 43–44.

"The only officer who professed to know the significance of these signals . . .": Schley, 268. "I knew . . . the signal from the insurgents that they wished to communicate . . .": Robley Evans, 427–428. "At 5.25 P.M., May 26th, we stopped our engines . . .": ibid., 428. Sigsbee says the Spanish fleet not at Santiago: Graham, 134–135; Schley, 276–277. "At 7.50 P.M. the commodore made the following general signal . . .": Robley Evans, 428. "Much to be regretted, cannot obey orders . . .": Schley, 279. "It is difficult to state the anxiety which this dispatch caused . . .": *American-Spanish War,* 360.

"The maneuvers of the hostile squadron . . . were incomprehensible . . .": Concas, 57. We are blockaded . . .": Cervera, 91. Harbor pilots fear ships run aground: Cervera, 98; Müller, 44.

"We drifted about until noon of the following day . . .": Robley Evans, 429. Flying Squadron back at Santiago, Evans and Rogers see *Cristobal Colón,* Schley at last satisfied Cervera at Santiago: ibid., 430–431.

Oregon arrives off Jupiter Inlet: *American-Spanish War,* 174–175.

CHAPTER EIGHT. THE ARMADAS

222–223

Cámara's squadron: Trask, 270. Ten thousand men at San Francisco: *American-Spanish War,* 264. Monitors at Mare Island: Trask, 374–375. Mahan's analysis: Mahan, *Lessons,* 184.

223–225

Hobson's account of plans: Hobson, pt. 1.

225–227

Rough Riders. "I really doubt there has ever been a regiment quite like this": Elting Morison, 2:832–833. Alger's orders: Roosevelt, *Autobiography*, 224. Roosevelt declines command: ibid., 223. Wood's background: WAMB. Wood Alger family doctor: Roosevelt, *Autobiography*, 223. Types of recruits: Roosevelt, *Rough Riders*, 9–29. Roosevelt's warning to the Ivy Leaguers: ibid., 14. Deluged with applications: ibid., 7. Burroughs rejected: Porges, 1:126–127. Roosevelt drills the regiment: Roosevelt, *Autobiography*, 233. "The reason why it takes so long . . .": ibid., 233–234. "We are in fine shape . . .": Elting Morison, 2:832.

227–229

ONI. "Special agent at Paris . . .": Sims to Bureau of Navigation, May 26, 1898, *Naval Operations*, Entry 100. Long's reply: ibid. Sims background: WAMB. Agent in Canary Islands: Sims to Bureau of Navigation, May 29, 1898, *Naval Operations*, Entry 100. "Italian citizen": Sims to Bureau of Navigation, May 2, 1898, ibid. ". . . Swedish Army officer": Sims to Bureau of Navigation, May 22, 1898; ibid. Letter from French mechanic: Sims to Bureau of Navigation: May 19, 1898, ibid. Background of ONI: Dorwart, *passim.* Attachés ordered to obtain information on Cádiz fleet: Long to Alusna, Paris and London, April 26, 1898, *Naval Operations*, Entry 100. Buck and Ward cruise aboard yachts, Breck goes to Spain: Dorwart, 64–65. Colwell pays agent $2,500: ibid., 64. Agent wounded, disappears: Colwell to Long, May 6, 12, 1898, *Naval Operations*, Entry 100. Payments to agents, assignments: Dorwart, 64–65. Report of Cádiz agent on Cámara's fleet: Colwell to Secretary of the Navy, May 27, 1898, *Naval Operations*, Entry 100. Orders to plant disinformation: Allen to Alusna, Paris, June 1, 1898; ibid.

229–232

Tampa. "Unquestionably, Tampa was not adapted to the concentration . . .": Alger, 65. "Reaching Tampa on the 1st of June . . .": *American-Spanish War*, 522–523. "Up to May 26th . . .": Miley, 19–24. "The Army had not been mobilized since the Civil War . . .": Alger, 70. Tampa Bay Hotel: Davis, *Campaigns*, 46–60. "The train conveyed the regiment from Lakeland in two sections . . .": New York State Historian, 184–187. "As we drove up to the camp . . .": Kennan, 4. Men line up to be baptized, ammunition issued: Post, 75–77.

232–235

Montreal Spy Ring. Details from Wilkie, ch. 2; *American-Spanish War*, 423–436; Young, ch. 29; Jeffreys-Jones, ch. 3. Information passed on to Havana and Madrid by Carranza ring: Cervera, 74, 81, 87, 91. Bermuda cable route: Chief Signal Officer to the President, June 15, 1898, Letterbooks, Greely Papers.

235–237

Sinking of Merrimac and Hobson's Rescue by Cervera: Hobson, pt. 2.

237–238

Cervera to the Philippines? Sims reports part of squadron not at Santiago: Sims to Bureau of Navigation, June 1, 1898, *Naval Operations*, Entry 100. "Very serious situation in Philippines . . .": Cervera, 100. Blanco's reply: ibid., 100–101.

238–239

Bombardment of Santiago. Schley, 289–290. Graham's account, Spanish return fire: Graham, 216–217. Müller's account: Müller, 58–61. Hobson's account: Hobson, 193–205. Sampson's report to Navy Department: Alger, 71. Shafter ordered to Santiago: ibid., 71–72.

239–243

Embarkation at Tampa. Seventy-first strikes camp: Post, 77; New York State Historian, 193–198. Post sick, sees Roosevelt in boxcar: Post, 77–83. Roosevelt arrives in Tampa: Roosevelt, *Rough Riders,* 53; *Autobiography,* 237. "We should be glad to go on all fours . . .": Elting Morison, 2:835. "It was the evening of June 7th when we suddenly received orders . . .": Roosevelt, *Rough Riders,* 57–58. "Partly under duress . . .": Roosevelt, *Autobiography,* 238. Post goes in search of milk, finds line: Post, 84–87. Roosevelt seizes ship, Rough Riders board: Roosevelt, *Rough Riders,* 59–61; *Autobiography,* 238–239. Transports begin to slip moorings, Shafter gets telegram: Miley, 30–33.

243–245

Transports Halted. Reports of Spanish ships: Alger, 72. Miles's dispatch: ibid., 73. Sampson identifies ships, finds delay "most unfortunate": Trask, 187. "We have been here two days now . . .": Elting Morison, 2:837–838. "Now if this were necessary no one would complain . . .": ibid., 2:841–843. Lieutenant Blue sees fleet: Trask, 138. Post's account of departure from Tampa: Post, 95–96.

CHAPTER NINE. TO WAR

246

Fleet Underway. "Today we are steaming southward . . .": Elting Morison, 2:-843–844. Sampson urges Army to hurry: Trask, 141.

248–249

Crane's account of Guantánamo action: Stallman, 140–148.

249–250

Spies. Sims reports Cervera goes to Philippines: Sims to Bureau of Navigation, June 15, 1898, *Naval Operations,* Entry 100. Villaverde's report of Blanco's telegram: Chief Signal Officer to the President, June 15, 1898, Letterbooks, Greely Papers.

250–251

Manila. Siege: Dewey, 248. Aguinaldo: ibid., 245–247. Long's instructions: Trask, 404–405. Aguinaldo declares independence: ibid., 407. "I knew that the intervention of any third power . . .": Dewey, 251. "On the 12th Vice-Admiral von Diedrichs arrived . . .": ibid., 256–257. Dewey's visit: ibid., 257. "Within a week there were five German men-of-war . . .": ibid., 258, 262. Hearst proposes blocking canal: ibid., 260; Swanberg, *Citizen Hearst,* 173–174.

252

Long says ships to attack Spain: Long to Alusna, Paris, June 18, 1898, *Naval Operations,* Entry 100.

252

Expeditions to the Philippines: *American-Spanish War,* 263–264.

252

Capture of Guam: Wilcox, 236–239; Titherington, 354–355; Trask, 385–386.

252–253

"All day we have steamed close to the Cuban Coast . . .": Elting Morison, 2:844.

CHAPTER TEN: THE ROAD TO SANTIAGO

254–265

Armada Arrives at Santiago. Spanish report of seventy hostile ships: Cervera, 107. Armada inventory: Miley, 43–45. Sampson meets with Shafter: ibid., 52. Landing at

Aserados, meeting with García: ibid., 53–59; Davis, *Campaigns*, 102–112; *American-Spanish War*, 58–59, 180; Shafter, "The Land Fight at Santiago." Shafter's background: WAMB. García described, background: Funston, 63–64. Description of coast based on Kennan, 77–78; large foldout map of Santiago de Cuba and vicinity in Miley. García reports on Spanish strength at Daiquirí: Miley, 56. Shafter studies Lord Vernon's plan: Alger, 83–84. Plans for landing: Miley, 57–58. "All next day we rolled and wallowed in the seaway": Roosevelt, *Rough Riders*, 69–70. Weather delays meetings, landing: Miley, 59.

265–269
Landing at Daiquirí. Wheeler examines landing site: Wheeler, 13. Bombardment begins: Miley, 66. Hobson hears guns: Hobson, 260. Post watches bombardment: Post, 107. Castillo arrives: Miley, 66. Spanish left at 5 A.M.: ibid., 66–67. "It was delightful to see the fine scorn of the coxswains . . .": Davis, *Campaigns*, 116. "Great Scott, there wouldn't be any Spaniards left . . .": Post, 109. Davis watches first boats land: Davis, *Campaigns*, 117–118. Horses swim ashore, drown: Miley, 69–70; Post, 109–110. "Who got ashore first largely depended on individual activity . . .": Roosevelt, *Autobiography*, 239. "The country would have offered very great difficulties to an attacking force . . .": Roosevelt, *Rough Riders:* 74–75. TR's opinion of insurgents: ibid., 75. "Rain-in-the-face": ibid., 60; drowned: ibid., 71. Crane sees troopers drown: Stallman, 140. O'Neill dives in: Roosevelt, *Rough Riders*, 71. Crane tours Siboney: Stallman, 137–140. Davis sees flag raised: Davis, *Campaigns*, 119. Rough Riders make camp, "We had all our men . . .": Roosevelt, *Rough Riders*, 72. Escario's relief column: Müller, 116–117. "As the question is to be decided on land . . ." Cervera, 107.

269–271
Landing at Siboney. Six thousand troops landed on twenty-second: Miley, 69–70. Lawton pushes on to Siboney, finds Spanish left during night, posts guard over alcohol, boats begin landing at noon: ibid., 70–76. Wheeler advances, sends for Rough Riders: Wheeler, 16–17, 241–242. "It was mid-afternoon and the tropical sun was beating fiercely down . . .": Roosevelt, *Rough Riders*, 77. Seventy-first gets orders to land: New York State Historian, 212; Post, 112. Post lands: Post, 112–114. Post sees Roosevelt ride into Siboney: ibid., 115. "It was long after nightfall . . .": Roosevelt, *Rough Riders*, 78. Meal, thunderstorm, TR chats with Fish: ibid., 78–79. Wood meets with Wheeler, Young: ibid., 79; Davis, *Campaigns*, 136. "Guásimas is not a village . . .": ibid., 135–136. Wheeler close to exceeding orders: Trask, 219–220. Wheeler "anxious to get first blood . . .": Roosevelt, *Rough Riders*, 76. "No one slept that night . . .": Davis, *Campaigns*, 136–138.

271–279
Las Guásimas Fight. Roosevelt, *Rough Riders*, 81–105; *Autiobiography*, 240–245; Davis, *Campaigns*, 138–170; Wheeler, 16–39; Marshall, "A Wounded Correspondent's Recollections of Guásimas." Wood's and Young's reports are in Wheeler, 24–38. Crane's account is in Stallman, 154–159. Wheeler requests reinforcements from Lawton: Alger, 110. Post's march up from Siboney: Post, 119–124. Background of Sergeant Byrne: Jones, 288. Roosevelt and O'Neill find body: Roosevelt, *Rough Riders*, 105. "Here's to every friend . . .": Roosevelt, *Autobiography*, 242.

279
Crane takes Marshall to hospital, dispatches to Siboney: Stallman, 157–159. Post carries Marshall to boat: Post, 134–135.

279–280
Wheeler sees Santiago: Wheeler, 243–244. Hobson sees flag: Hobson, 261. Cervera meets with captains: Cervera, 109. Escario's column: Müller, 117.

280–281
Advance up the Road. Burial of Rough Riders: Roosevelt, *Rough Riders,* 108–109; Jones, 143–145. All the troops landed: Miley, 96. Trail described: Davis, *Campaigns,* 174–175. Wagons unloaded and assembled, Miley, 85–86. "If this scheme for supplying the command had worked as smoothly . . .": Miley, 87–89.

281–282
Maxfield's balloon: Giddings, 49–57.

282–285
Cervera's Squadron. Cervera placed under Blanco: Cervera, 110. Cervera says he is relieved of responsibility: ibid. Cervera reports squadron's status to Blanco: ibid., 110–111. Blanco asks Linares to intercede with Cervera: ibid., 111. Blockading fleet so close cries of watch could be heard: Concas, 59. Cervera's angry reply: Cervera, 111–112.

285–286
Hearst in Cuba. "It is a satisfactory thing to be an American . . .": Swanberg, *Citizen Hearst,* 182. "How do you like the Journal's war": ibid., 173. Donates *Buccaneer,* charters *Sylvia,* leads expedition to Cuba: ibid., 179–182. Interviews Sampson, García, Shafter: Brown, 330–331. "The struggle for the possession of the city of Santiago . . .": ibid., 330; Swanberg, *Citizen Hearst,* 182.

286–287
Red Cross. Barton at Guantánamo: Kennan, 66–69. Barton arrives at Siboney: ibid., 83; Epler, 295. Army surgeons refuse Red Cross help: Kennan, 84–87.

287
Maxfield lands at Daiquirí, takes one day to reach Siboney: Giddings, 57–58.

288
Cervera's Squadron. Blanco argues his case: Cervera, 113. Cervera replies, asks for clarification of orders: ibid., 114. Blanco asks Linares's opinion: ibid. Linares says he cannot release crewmen: ibid., 115. Escario's progress: Müller, 119.

288–289
Shafter's Plans. All troops ashore on twenty-sixth, Shafter estimates two days to get them to front, plans advance on twenty-ninth: Miley 96–97. *Yale* arrives on twenty-seventh with 1,200 men, Shafter delays for reinforcements: Alger, 126–127. Wheeler ordered to reconnoiter: Wheeler, 41–42, 254–255.

289–290
Santiago's Defenses. "These hills looked so quiet and sunny . . .": Davis, *Campaigns,* 178–179. "The enemy knows where those trails leave the wood . . .": ibid., 182. Rifle pits dug on twenty-seventh: ibid., 180. Wheeler gets Santiago information from young Cuban refugee: Wheeler, 257–261. "Late in the afternoon . . .": Alger, 127. Escario calls a halt: Müller, 120.

291
Graves at Las Guásimas. Description: Kennan, 100–101. Capron visits son's grave: Jones, 153.

291–293
Post on Guard. "We could see the tiny flickers of Spanish campfires . . .": Post, 149–150. Battle of the land crabs: ibid., 151–155; New York State Historian, 223–224. Land crabs at Las Guásimas: Roosevelt, *Rough Riders,* 104. Kennan's description: Kennan, 101–102. Post says Spanish "with but one pair of legs could never have made such a clatter": Post, 155. "Across the ridges that lay between our outpost and the Spanish lines . . .": ibid.

293
Cervera's Squadron. Blanco's orders: Cervera, 115. Cervera asks to be informed when Santiago to fall: ibid., 116. Linares says advice impossible: ibid.

293–295

Shafter Plans Attack. Shafter visits El Pozo: Miley, 101–102; *American-Spanish War,* 185. "There was no attempt at strategy . . .": Shafter, "The Land Fight at Santiago," 76. El Caney an obstacle to attack: *American-Spanish War,* 185. Shafter meets with division commanders: Miley, 102; *American-Spanish War,* 185. Plan of attack: Miley, 102–106; *American-Spanish War,* 185–186. Shafter feels time critical factor: ibid., 186.

295–296

Maxfield's Balloon. Balloon train arrives, repairs, test flight, Castillo ascends, Derby ascends: Giddings, 58–59.

296–297

Eve of Battle. "The headquarters camp was crowded . . .": Davis, *Campaigns,* 189–190. Wood takes brigade, Roosevelt takes regiment: ibid., 188; Roosevelt, *Rough Riders,* 109. "At last . . . the First and Tenth Cavalry marched . . . and we followed . . .": ibid., 113–114. "We did not talk much . . .": ibid., 115. Davis's dispatch: quoted in Brown, 338–339. Note: The quoted dispatch reads, "In the bushes of the basin beneath us *twenty-two thousand* men are sleeping" (emphasis added), which was probably a cable error. A parallel passage in Davis's *Cuban and Porto Rican Campaigns* (193) reads, "Near us, drowned under the mist, seven thousand men were sleeping, and, farther to the right, General Chaffee's five thousand men were lying under the bushes along the trails to El Caney. . . ." Davis's original dispatch must have read, "twelve thousand men were sleeping . . ."

CHAPTER ELEVEN. WHEN HEROES MEET

298–299

Lee at El Caney: Lee, "The Regulars at El Caney."

299

Miley. Miley dispatched to El Pozo: Miley, 106. McClernand at El Pozo, field telephone: ibid., 107. Shafter's illness, command arrangements: Trask, 234.

299

El Pozo. Roosevelt and Wood at breakfast: Roosevelt, *Rough Riders,* 115–117. Remington sketches: Brown, 351. Pershing, "From the ridge of the hill . . .": Vandiver, 1:199–200.

299–300

Linares headquarters, Spanish strength, Spanish defense perimeter: Trask, 230. Seventy-first expects to march through Cuba: Post, 159.

300–301

Shelling of El Caney. El Caney described: Lee, "The Regulars at El Caney." Bombardment begins: ibid. Hobson sees bombardment: Hobson, 265–266. Post sees Hearst: Post, 162–163.

301–302

7 A.M. Cubans take position: *American-Spanish War,* 70, 525. Kent at El Pozo: Wheeler, 60.

302–304

Grimes's Battery. Firing described: Christy, "An Artist at El Poso." Wheeler remarks on Astor: Wheeler, 200–201. Swedish military attaché: Azoy, 113. Wood's warning, Spanish fire: Roosevelt, *Rough Riders,* 117–118. Christy sees Cubans hit: Christy, "An artist at El Poso." Davis and reporter: ibid. Sumner's warning, Stoddard and Astor: Stoddard, 308–309. Maxfield on hill, balloon damaged and repaired, horse killed: Giddings, 59–61. Post sees wounded Cubans: Post 165–166. Crane sees wounded Cubans:

Stallman, 174. Wheeler hears guns, joins battle: Miley, 102. Sumner gets orders from aide: Davis, *Campaigns*, 200.

304–305
Battle continues at El Caney: Lee, "The Regulars at El Caney."

305
Feint at Aguadores. Firing begins at 9:20: Trask, 235. Lieutenant Blue knocks down flag: Titherington, 260.

305–306
Balloon Over El Pozo. Derby's dispatch to Shafter: Alger, 154–155. Dispute with Maxfield: Giddings, 59–61. Crane sees balloon moving forward: Stallman, 176, 282–283.

307–308
Miley Rides to Front. Miley to front: Miley, 107–108. Astor afoot: New York State Historian, 262. Parker and the Gatling detachment: Azoy, 40–42, and *passim*; Miley, 113–114. Seventy-first halted to let Rough Riders past: New York State Historian, 228; Wheeler, 60. The trail described: Davis, *Campaigns*, 203. Post hears bullets: Post, 166–167. Miley reaches river, meets with generals: Miley, 108. Report of situation at front, warns of rapid-fire guns: ibid.; Alger, 154.

308–310
10 A.M. Wire-cutting at El Caney: Alger, 140; Lee, "The Regulars at El Caney." Hobson sees Toral and officers see balloon: Hobson, 271. Crane sees man in Panama hat and balloon: Stallman, 282–283. Roosevelt sees balloon: Roosevelt, *Rough Riders*, 119–120. Chaplain Van Dewater sees balloon: New York State Historian, 230. Post sees balloon: Post, 169–170. Davis sees balloon: Davis, *Campaigns*, 211–212. Derby hopes to ascend to one thousand feet, balloon lines caught in trees: Alger, 155. "Remaining there under this galling fire . . .": Vandiver, 1:201–202. Pershing encounters Wheeler: ibid., 202.

310–313
11 A.M. Rough Riders cross river, take position, under fire: Roosevelt, *Rough Riders*, 119–122. Maxfield finds eighteen holes in balloon: Giddings, 61. Derby reports side road to Kent: Wheeler, 61; Miley, 109–110; Alger, 155–156. Post describes trail: Post, 170–171. Kent says troops panic-stricken: Wheeler, 61–62. Stoddard says no cordon was formed: New York State Historian, 263. Davis says regiment did not run: Davis, *Campaigns*, 238. Chaplain Van Dewater says regiment obeyed orders: New York State Historian, 232. Post says no panic: Post, 172. Post sees casualties on trail: ibid., 176–179.

313–314
12 Noon. Infantry commanders killed and wounded: Wheeler, 53, 62–63. Davis thinks every second man a casualty: Davis, *Campaigns*, 209. Snipers in trees: ibid., 208–209. Roosevelt thinks Spanish fire unaimed: Roosevelt, *Rough Riders*, 122. O'Neill killed: ibid., 123–124.

314–319
1 P.M. Lee sees casualties at El Caney, stone fort hit: Lee, "The Regulars at El Caney." Shafter watches battle: Miley, 111. Davis says situation desperate: Davis, *Campaigns*, 213–214. Roosevelt sends messengers for orders: Roosevelt, *Rough Riders*, 125. Miley orders attack: ibid.; Trask, 241. Note that Alger (pp. 156–157) says the order to attack came from Shafter. Roosevelt gets orders, starts attack, curious incident: Roosevelt, *Rough Riders*, 125–127. "I had not enjoyed the Guasimas fight at all . . ." Roosevelt, *Autobiography*, 247–248. Davis describes charge: Davis, *Campaigns*, 218–220. Crane sees charge, hears attachés' remarks: Stallman, 176–177, 283. "The whole line . . . was straining to go forward . . .": Roosevelt, *Rough Riders*, 131. Pershing on Kettle Hill: Vandiver, 1:204. "By this time we were all in the spirit of the thing . . . ," charge to top of hill, hears Gatlings: Roosevelt, *Rough Riders*, 131–135. Ord leads charge, Post describes charge: Post, 182–186.

Roosevelt charges next hill, returns for regiment, shoots Spaniard: Roosevelt, *Rough Riders*, 136–139. Davis describes scene on heights: Davis, *Campaigns*, 223.

319–320

2 P.M. Davis describes thin line of troops on heights: Davis, *Campaigns*, 224–227. Lee says situation at El Caney extremely serious: Lee, "The Regulars at El Caney." Shafter fears he made terrible mistake: Trask, 237; Alger, 143. Dispatch to Lawton: Alger, 143; Miley, 111–112.

320–321

3 P.M. "There was great confusion at this time . . .": Roosevelt, *Rough Riders*, 139. Roosevelt's version of this incident is in ibid., 144–145; Private Holliday's is in Gatewood, 92–97. Müller sees Linares on stretcher: Müller, 88. Davis and Crane on San Juan Heights: Davis, *Notes of a War Correspondent*, 125.

321–322

4:15 P.M. Lee describes inside of fort, Spaniards expect to be shot: Lee, "The Regulars at El Caney." Hearst takes story from wounded Creelman: Swanberg, *Citizen Hearst*, 184–185. Spanish and American casualties: Trask, 245. "The Americans . . . fought that day . . .": Müller, 86.

CHAPTER TWELVE. THUNDER ON THE SEA

323–328

Situation After San Juan Battle. "We are within measurable distance of a terrible military disaster": Elting Morison, 2: 846. Troops exhausted, entrenchments, ammunition a supply priority: Roosevelt, *Rough Riders*, 150, 154, 161; Miley, 114–115, 119, 123; Alger, 170. Spanish open fire at dawn: Alger, 170; Miley, 119. Snipers crept up during night: Roosevelt, *Rough Riders*, 170. "As the day wore on . . .": ibid., 169. Mauser bullets dropping a mile in the rear lead to belief in sharpshooters: Miley, 123–124. Rains immobilize supply trains: ibid., 124; Alger, 170. Wheeler's reconnaissance: Wheeler, 87. Shafter urges Sampson to force the harbor: Alger, 227. Sampson's reply: ibid., 228. Shafter asks Wheeler about capturing Morro, Wheeler's reply: Wheeler, 286–287. "I am at a loss to see why the navy cannot work under a destructive fire . . .": Alger, 228. "It is not so much the loss of men . . .": ibid., 229. "If it is your earnest desire . . .": ibid. Rumor of fall back order, Wheeler visits trenches, Roosevelt tells him he might disobey fall back order: Roosevelt, *Autobiography*, 249. Wheeler's dispatch to Shafter regarding withdrawal: Wheeler, 277. "The enemy during the night of the battle of Caney . . . continued to surround our lines . . .": Müller, 93. "At daybreak the enemy renewed attack upon city . . ." Cervera, 120. Escario's column harassed by insurgents: Müller, 120–123. Escario reports to Toral by heliograph: ibid., 123. "It occurred to me that a fleet from the Peninsula was on its way . . .": Müller, 94. Shafter meets with his commanders: Alger, 175–176; Miley, 124–125; Davis, *Campaigns*, 248; Post, 218–224.

328–331

The Spanish Fleet Comes Out. "Civilized people do not . . . fire on towns . . .": Shafter, "The Land Fight at Santiago." Shafter threatens Toral with bombardment: Alger, 182. "This is pretty slow": Graham, 284. Smoke seen above harbor: ibid., 275. Anderson tells Hodgson smoke approaching harbor entrance: ibid., 287–288. Lieutenant Hill fires signal gun on *Iowa*: *American-Spanish War*, 156. *New York* comes about, signal through the fleet: ibid., 156–157. Graham watches fleet from the *Brooklyn*: Graham, 293. Concas's account: Concas, 73–74. Evans on the *Iowa*'s bridge, opens fire: Robley Evans, 444–445. Cervera tries to ram the *Brooklyn*: Cervera, 123. Lieutenant Müller visits Bustamente, hears guns, sounds of battle: Müller, 96–97.

331–337
Accounts of the Battle. Sampson, "Destruction of Admiral Cervera's Fleet"; Graham, 287–330; Robley Evans, 443–450; *American-Spanish War*, 155–164, 176–178, 145–154; Schley, 298–309, 323–331; Cervera, 123–134; Concas, 71–84. Excellent reconstructions of the battle are in Dierks, ch. 5 and 6; and Trask, ch. 11.

337–339
After the Battle. Eulate brought aboard the *Iowa:* Robley Evans, 450–452. "God and the gunners . . .": ibid., 449. "In order to complete the outline of the history of this mournful day . . .": Cervera, 126. Cervera welcomed aboard *Iowa:* Robley Evans, 456. Mr. Dooley on Cervera: Dunne, 70. "If Spain were as well served by her statesmen . . ." Concas, 113, 117.

CHAPTER THIRTEEN. THE HONOR OF ARMS

340–341
White House Awaits Word. No messages from Shafter: Alger, 172–173. Telegrams to Shafter: ibid., 173–174. Direct telegraphic link between White House and Shafter: Miley, 94. Shafter's reply, garbled en route, later clarified: Alger, 174–175. Long writes to his wife: Long, 227. Report from Signal Corps at Playa del Este: Alger, 179. Confirmation, Alger walks home, hears newsboys: Alger, 179–180.

341–342
Reaction to Cervera's Defeat. Blanco's manifesto: Cervera, 134. Cámara ordered home: Trask, 276.

342–343
Shafter and García. "Now that the fleet is destroyed . . .": Wheeler, 291–292. "It is my duty to say to you that this city will not surrender": Alger, 183. "Through the negligence of our Cuban allies . . .": ibid., 87. "Lawton says [he] cannot compel García . . .": ibid., 187. García's defense: Trask, 256; Foner, 2:350, 363–364. "What seems to have caused considerable comment . . .": *American-Spanish War*, 69. "Everybody knows the kind of sympathetic charity which loves to be thanked . . .": Stallman, 163. "We expected to be utilized in some way": *American-Spanish War*, 71.

343–344
Noncombatants. Bombardment postponed: Alger, 187–188. "If it were simply a going out of the women and children . . .": ibid., 188. Fleet bombards Santiago, population flees: Miley, 133. British consul describes exodus: quoted in Watterson, "The Fall of Santiago." Three hundred houses, twenty thousand refugees: ibid.

344–345
Crane describes Hobson exchange: Stallman, 289–291.

345–350
Siege and Negotiations. Shafter tells Toral of Cervera's defeat: Alger, 190–191. Toral requests telegraphers: ibid., 191–192. British Consul Ramsden persuades telegraphers: Watterson, "The Fall of Santiago." Toral's counterproposal: Alger, 192–193. Shafter recommends acceptance: ibid., 194. Alger demands unconditional surrender: ibid., 194–195. McKinley's message to Shafter: Leech, 266. Shafter's reply to Alger: Alger, 195. "Not since the campaign of Crassus against the Parthians . . .": Elting Morison, 2:849. "We on the firing line are crazy just at present . . .": ibid., 2:850. Firing resumes, casualties: Alger, 196–197. Ramsden describes situation at El Caney: Watterson, "The Fall of Santiago." Alger proposes repatriating Spanish, Toral's reply: Alger, 197–199. Miles's cable to Alger, Alger's indignation: Alger, 200–201. Face-to-face negotiations begin, first meeting: ibid., 204–210. Wheeler's impression of Toral: Wheeler, 128–129. Toral granted

more time: Alger, 209–210. Linares's cable to minister of war: ibid., 202–203. Agreement on details of surrender: ibid., 211–220; Wheeler 128–180; Miley, 160–184.

350–352
Capitulation ceremony: Miley, 185–186; Wheeler, 180–182; Archibald, "The Day of the Surrender of Santiago"; Post, 248.

CHAPTER FOURTEEN. PUERTO RICO

353
Miles Sails for Puerto Rico. "I did not see the ceremony . . .": Davis, *Campaigns*, 291. Flotilla underway 3 P.M., July 21: Trask, 352. "I consider it of the highest importance that we should take and keep that island . . .": Alger, 300.

353–354
Whitney's Reconnaissance. Whitney's mission: Alger, 42; Wilcox, 99–101. Whitney's biographic details, use of pseudonym "H. W. Elias": *Who's Who, 1899–1900*. Spanish troop strength: Trask, 338. Roads, terrain: ibid., 336–337.

354–355
Landings. Change of landing site: Alger, 304–307; *American-Spanish War*, 201 (Whitney says the change of plan was made at sea). War Department denies AP report: Brown, 410. *Gloucester* lands a party in Guánica: *American-Spanish War*, 202; Davis, *Campaigns*, 305–306. "All the transports are now in the harbor . . .": Alger, 305–306. "Upon opening fire the inhabitants . . . fled . . .": *American-Spanish War*, 202. "At least four-fifths of the people . . .": Alger, 307.

355–356
Advance Across Island. Troop strength fifteen thousand: Alger, 308. "The army . . . advanced with the precision of a set of chessmen": Davis, *Campaigns*, 303. Four-pronged advance: Trask, 358–359.

356–357
Crane's account of advance at Juana Diaz: Stallman, 193–196.

CHAPTER FIFTEEN. YELLOW JACK

358
Roosevelt Wants to Leave Cuba. "We earnestly hope that you will send us . . .": Elting Morison, 2: 859. "If we stay here all summer we shall have yellow fever . . .": ibid., 2:860. "At present I am ardently longing to be out of here . . .": ibid., 2:861.

358–359
Yellow Fever Danger. Numbers of fever cases: Trask, 329. "Each morning we would hear bugles blowing taps . . .": Post, 260. "I am told that at any time an epidemic of yellow fever is liable to occur . . .": Alger, 262. Alger shocked; "Up to this time the yellow fever situation was reported . . . 'improving' ": ibid. "The quarantine authorities in the United States . . .": ibid., 258. Shafter proposes sending troops twenty miles inland: ibid. Alger and McKinley advising sending troops inland: ibid., 262. Railroad inadequate, Miley found camp inadequate: ibid., 262–263. "It was a perfect hotbed of malaria . . .": Roosevelt, *Rough Riders*, 207. "In my opinion there is but one course to take . . .": Alger, 263.

360–362
Round Robin Incident. Shafter calls meeting; "The General then explained . . .": Roosevelt, *Autobiography*, 250–252. "To keep us here . . . will simply mean the destruction of thousands . . .": Elting Morison, 2:864–865. "When I had written my letter . . .": Roosevelt, *Autobiography*, 252. Round Robin letter: Alger, 266. Letters leaked, published,

McKinley indignant: Alger, 269–271. Peace negotiations threatened: ibid., 270. Peace feelers: Trask, 428. "We did not suppose that peace was at hand": Roosevelt, *Rough Riders*, 209. Alger already ordered troops home: Alger, 264–265.

362–363

Departure. War Department selected Montauk Point, work begins on camp: Alger, 261, 424–429. "We swung in the idle waters . . .": Post, 297. "We wandered all through it . . .": Roosevelt, *Rough Riders*, 214. "Then early one morning there was a whir of a winch . . .": Post, 299. "The mountains of Cuba . . .": ibid., 301. "We were favored by good weather during our nine days' voyage . . .": Roosevelt, *Rough Riders*, 218. "I am on my way home . . .": Elting Morison, 2:866.

CHAPTER SIXTEEN. THE FALL OF MANILA

364–366

Dewey and the Germans. First contingent of expeditionary force arrives: *American-Spanish War*, 263. Germans land at Mariveles: Dewey, 263–264. Subic Bay incident: ibid., 264–265; Spector, 76–78. Blockaders' rights: Dewey, 265–266; Trask, 380–381. Kaiser's intentions: Spector, 73. "As I was on the spot . . .": Dewey, 252. *Cormoran* incident: ibid., 266–267. Barrett's account of Dewey's interview with German officer: Barrett, 115. Dewey's recollection of incident: Dewey, 267.

366–368

The Americans and Aguinaldo. Second and third contingent of expeditionary force arrive: *American-Spanish War*, 263–264. "General Merritt found both a difficult and a delicate task confronting him . . .": Alger, 331. "The situation was difficult to deal with . . .": *American-Spanish War*, 265. "My policy was to avoid any entangling alliance . . .": Dewey, 247. "Consistently I have refrained from assisting him in any way . . .": ibid., 312. Merritt's relationship with Aguinaldo: *American-Spanish War*, 266; Alger, 333.

368–371

Fall of Manila. "Owing to the restrictions of the blockade . . .": Dewey, 272–273. Jaudenes replaces Davila, Rawson-Walker dies, André becomes go-between: ibid., 273–274. Jaudenes inclined to surrender: ibid., 274–275. Dewey persuades Merritt to delay attack during negotiations: ibid., 269, 273. "However, with two armed forces facing each other . . .": ibid., 269–270. "The activity of the Americans in pushing forward . . .": *American-Spanish War*, 267. Losses: ibid., 267–268. "Finally, without making any definite promise . . .": Dewey, 274–275. Dewey sketches signal flag: ibid., 275. 'We sent the usual forty-eight hours notice . . .": ibid. "Great difficulty was experienced during this period . . .": *American-Spanish War*, 268. "On the 9th the foreign men-of-war . . . were notified . . .": Dewey, 276. Attack rescheduled for the thirteenth: ibid. "The 13th dawned as a typical Manila day . . .": ibid., 276–278. Spanish raise white flag, Manila surrenders: ibid., 278–281. "After the battle the insurgent forces gathered outside . . .": *American-Spanish War*, 277. "My troops are forced by yours . . .": Trask, 419–420. Details of surrender, word of peace protocol received on the sixteenth: Dewey, 280–282.

CHAPTER SEVENTEEN. VERSIONS OF PEACE

372–373

Reactions. "Peace came differently to different men": Davis, *Campaigns*, 359. "Please notice on map our troops occupy best part of Porto Rico . . .": Trask, 365. "The signing of the protocol with the Spaniards brought us great trouble . . .": Scott, 226. Hearst organizes celebration: Swanberg, *Citizen Hearst*, 195–198. *Times*'s report of naval parade:

N.Y. *Times*, August 21, 1898. Schley's account of welcome: Schley, 341–342. Long in Massachusetts: Long, 227–228.

374
Roosevelt. "I am afraid I am the last of your friends to congratulate you . . .": Thayer, 2: 337. "Yes, I was right to go . . .": Elting Morison, 2: 870.

374–376
Camp Wikoff. "In the space of less than three weeks . . .": Wheeler, 207, 214. *Journal's* criticism: Swanberg, *Citizen Hearst*, 199–200. Alger's visit to camp: Wheeler, 219; Post, 327–329. "I am very much afraid that with Alger the trouble is congenital . . .": Elting Morison, 2: 871. One hundred twenty-six dead at Camp Wikoff: Alger, 438. Total deaths, total strength: ibid., 454. Miles's "embalmed beef" charge, Eagan court-martial: ibid., 376ff. Dodge Commission: Trask, 484–485. Post returns to New York, jury duty: Post, 332–340, 243.

376–377
Roosevelt. At Sagamore Hill: Morris, 668–669. "I have been very busy with my Regiment . . .": Elting Morison, 2:872. Presented with Remington statue: Morris, 672–674. "I have played it with bull luck . . .": Elting Morison, 2:888.

378–379
Anglo-American Alliance. General Miles says war opportunity to appreciate Britain, Paget says British proud of Stars and Stripes: Reuter, 177–178. Anglo-American League: ibid., 160–161. Olney's reflection: ibid., 158. Chamberlain's visit to United States: Perkins, 58–60. Chamberlain's thoughts on alliance: Chamberlain, "Recent Developments of Policy in the United States."

379
Hobson and Cervera's cat: Halliburton, 47–58.
379–380
Crane sees Spanish-Cuban family separate: Stallman, 218–219.
380–381
Concas's bitter reflections: Concas, 114–116.
381–382
Gómez's triumphant moment: Gonzales, 332–334.

CHAPTER EIGHTEEN. THE WHITE MAN'S BURDEN

383–387
Keeping the Philippines. McKinley undecided: Trask, 440–442. Mr. Dooley: Dunne, 43–47. McKinley's speaking tour: May, 258–259; Trask, 452–453. Newspapers favor annexation: May, 256; Pratt, 268–269. Clergy favors annexation: Welch, ch. 6. Bishop Potter: Potter, "Religious Situation in the Philippines." Hoar's qualms regarding Hawaiian annexation: Hoar, 2:311. Long's proposal: Pratt, 329. Gray's long telegram: Hoar, 2:313–315. McKinley's new directive: May, 252. McKinley's rare reminiscence: Olcott, 2:108–111. Negotiations with Spanish commissioners: *American-Spanish War*, 478–483. Platform of Anti-Imperialist League: Commager, 2:11–12. "Andrew Carnegie really seems to be off his head . . .": Thayer, 2:199. "No nation was ever created good enough . . .": Schirmer, 116. "It is difficult for me to speak with moderation . . .": Elting Morison, 2:923–924. "White Man's Burden": Kipling, 321–323.

387–388
Philippine War Begins. "The division of opinion in this country . . .": Alger, 355–357. Private Grayson's recollection: Schirmer, 129. "Aguinaldo had accomplished

that . . .": Alger, 357. "I am more grateful than I can say . . .": Elting Morison, 2:935. "My nation cannot remain indifferent . . .": Wolff, 201.

388–391
Controversy Over War. Elihu Root's statement: Schott, 162. Sergeant Riley describes "water cure": ibid., 163–164. Soldiers' descriptions of atrocities: Schirmer, 142. N.Y. Times attacks Anti-Imperialism League: Welch, 52. "In America there is a great party . . .": Wolff, 252. Anti-imperialists fail to support Bryan, "We have failed to waken the lethargic American conscience": Koenig, 330–331. Mark Twain introduces Winston Churchill: Randolph S. Churchill, 524–525.

391–392
Capture of Aguinaldo: Funston, 384–426.

392
Balangiga massacre: Schott, ch. 2. "All of the dead had been mutilated . . .": ibid., 54.

392–394
Roosevelt President. "It is a dreadful thing to come into the Presidency this way . . .": Lodge, 1:506. "Thou hast it now . . .": Beringause, 204. Adams's Atlantic article: Adams, "Reciprocity or the Alternative." "Your letter pleased me . . .": Elting Morison, 3:152–153. "I do not know whether you want either reward or recognition . . .": Beringause, 217. Adams's new influence with Roosevelt: ibid., ch. 8 and passim. "The game is ours . . .": ibid., 224. "We have the Philippines . . .": ibid., 223. Roosevelt orders stern measures on Samar: Miller, 206.

394
Pacification of Samar. Smith's orders to Waller: Schott, 71–72, 76. Smith's written orders: ibid., 285–289. "In the Philippines our men have done well . . .": Elting Morison, 3:297–298.

395
Reconcentration. Dead and wounded in Philippine War: Welch, 42. Bell's orders of December 8 and 9, 1901, their effect: U.S. Senate, "Issuance of Certain Orders in the Philippines."

EPILOGUE: THE WAKE OF THE MAINE

397
Maine refloated and towed out to sea: Rickover, 79–86.

397–400
"Dynamite" Johnny O'Brien's account of the burial of the Maine: Caldwell, "Most Mournful of Sea Pageants."

400
Rickover investigation: Rickover, chs. 7, 8, app. A. "We have found no technical evidence . . . that an external explosion initiated the destruction of the Maine: ibid., 127–128.

BIBLIOGRAPHY

ARTICLES

Adams, Brooks. "Reciprocity or the Alternative." *Atlantic Monthly* 88 (August 1901).

Adams, Earl R. "First Man to Hear About the *Maine* Disaster." *The Key West Citizen,* February 15, 1974.

Archibald, James F. J. "The Day of the Surrender of Santiago." *Scribner's Magazine* 24 (1898), 413–416.

Bernadou, J. B. "The 'Winslow' at Cardenas." *Century Magazine* 57 (1899), 698–706.

Caldwell, J. R. "Most Mournful of Sea Pageants." *Harper's Weekly,* May 11, 1912.

Chamberlain, Joseph. "Recent Developments of Policy in the United States." *Scribner's Magazine* 24 (1898), 674–682.

Christy, Howard Chandler. "An Artist at El Pozo." *Scribner's Magazine* 24 (1898), 283–284.

Greely, A. W. "The Signal Corps in War Time." *Century Magazine* 66 (1903), 811–826.

Grenville, John A. S. "American Naval Preparations for War With Spain, 1896–1898." *Journal of American Studies* (April 1968).

Halstead, Murat. "Our Cuban Neighbors and Their Struggle for Liberty." *Review of Reviews* 13 (1896), 419–438.

Hazeltine, Mayo et al. "What if Spain Should Declare War?" *Review of Reviews* 13 (1896), 577–579.

Lee, Arthur H. "The Regulars at El Caney." *Scribner's Magazine* 24 (1898), 403–413.

Marshall, Edward. "A Wounded Correspondent's Recollections of Guasimas." *Scribner's Magazine* 24 (1898), 273–282.

Meriwether, Walter Scott. "Remembering the *Maine.*" *United States Naval Institute Proceedings* (May 1948).

Offley, C. N. "The Oregon's Long Voyage," 64–71. In *The Great Republic.* Vol. 4. New York: Lippincott, 1901.

Potter, Henry C. "Religious Situation in the Philippines," 327–329. In *Men and Issues of 1900,* ed. James P. Boyd. Philadelphia: Ziegler, 1900.

Sampson, W. T. "Destruction of Admiral Cervera's Fleet" (Copy of Sampson's report of the battle to the Secretary of the Navy, July 15, 1898), 55–64. In *The Great Republic.* Vol. 4. New York: Lippincott, 1901.

Shafter, W. R. "The Land Fight at Santiago," 71–82. In *The Great Republic*. Vol. 4. New York: Lippincott, 1901.

Spears, John R. "Torpedo-boats in the War with Spain." *Scribner's Magazine* 24 (1898), 614–619.

Watterson, Henry. "Significance of the Fall of Santiago," 83–102. In *The Great Republic*. Vol. 4. New York: Lippincott, 1901.

Winslow, Cameron McR. "Cable-cutting at Cienfuegos." *Century Magazine* 57 (1899), 708–717.

UNPUBLISHED DOCUMENTS

Adolphus Washington Greely Papers. Library of Congress, Manuscript Division.

Albert Gleaves Papers. Library of Congress, Manuscript Division.

Area File of the Naval Records Collection, 1775–1910. Microcopy M625. U.S. National Archives.

Despatches from U.S. Consuls in Havana, 1783–1906. Microcopy T20. U.S. National Archives.

Hellings, Martin L., Captain, 6 Co., Signal Corps, U.S. Volunteers. Military Records of Spanish-American War Volunteers. U.S. National Archives.

John Bassett Moore Papers. Library of Congress, Manuscript Division.

Records of the Office of the Chief of Naval Operations. Records Group 38. U.S. National Archives.

U.S. Veteran Signal Corps Association, Spanish War Division. Records, U.S. Army Communication Systems Center Electronics Museum. Myer Hall, Fort Monmouth, N.J.

William R. Day Papers. Library of Congress, Manuscript Division.

U.S. GOVERNMENT DOCUMENTS

Congressional Record.

Lives Lost by Sinking of U.S. Battle Ship Maine. 55th Congress, 2d session, April 8, 1898. Senate Document 231.

Message from the President of the United States Transmitting the Report of the Naval Court of Inquiry Upon the Destruction of the United States Battle Ship Maine in Havana Harbor, February 15, 1898, Together with the Testimony Taken Before the Court. 55th Congress, 2d session, 1898. Senate Document 207.

Papers Relating to the Foreign Relations of the United States . . . [year]. Washington, D.C.: Government Printing Office.

Report of the Chief Signal Officer to the Secretary of War for the Fiscal Year Ending June 30, 1898.

The Issuance of Certain Orders in the Philippines. 57th Congress, 1st session. Senate Document 347.

U.S. Library of Congress. *Index to the McKinley Papers*. Washington, D.C.: Government Printing Office, 1963.

SPANISH DOCUMENTS:

Cervera y Topete, Pascual, *The Spanish American War: A Collection of Documents Relative to the Squadron Operations in the West Indies*. Washington, D.C.: Government Printing Office, 1899. (Translation of *Guerra hispano-americana. Colección de documentos referentes á la escuadra de operaciones de las Antillas*, El Ferrol, 1899).

Concas y Palau, Victor M., *The Squadron of Admiral Cervera*. Washington, D.C.: Government Printing Office, 1900. (Translation of *La escuadra del Almirante Cervera*, Madrid, n.d.)

Müller y Tejeiro, José, *Battles and Capitulation of Santiago de Cuba*. Washington, D.C.: Government Printing Office, 1899. (Translation of *Combates y capitulación de Santiago de Cuba*, Madrid, 1898.)

Spanish Diplomatic Correspondence and Documents, 1896–1900, Presented to the Cortes by the Minister of State. Washington, D.C.: Government Printing Office, 1905. (Translation of *Negociones generales con los Estados Unidos desde 10 de Abril de 1896 hasta la declaración de guerra*, Madrid, 1898; *Negociones diplomáticas desde el principio de la guerra con los Estados Unidos hasta la firma del protocolo de Washington*, Madrid, 1898; and *Conferencia de París y tratado de paz de 10 Diciembre de 1899*, Madrid, 1899.)

BOOKS

Adams, Henry. *The Education of Henry Adams*. New York: Modern Library, 1931.

Alger, R. A. *The Spanish-American War*. New York, 1901.

The American-Spanish War. Norwich, Conn., 1899.

Atkins, Edwin F. *Sixty Years in Cuba*. Cambridge: Harvard University Press, 1926.

Azoy, A.C.M. *Charge! The Story of the Battle of San Juan Hill*. New York: Longmans, Green, 1961.

Bailey, Thomas A. *A Diplomatic History of the American People*. New York: Crofts, 1940.

Barrett, John. *Admiral George Dewey*. New York, 1899.

Beer, Thomas. *Stephen Crane*. New York: Knopf, 1923.

Benson, E. F. *The Kaiser and English Relations*. New York: Longmans, Green, 1936.

Beringause, Arthur F. *Brooks Adams*. New York: Knopf, 1955.

Brown, Charles H. *The Correspondent's War*. New York: Scribners, 1967.

Carr, Raymond. *Spain, 1808–1939*. London: Oxford University Press, 1966.

Chadwick, French Ensor. *The Relations of the United States and Spain: Diplomacy*. New York, 1909.

Chadwick, French Ensor. *The Relations of the United States and Spain: The Spanish American War*. 2 vols. New York, 1911.

Chapin, George M. *Florida, 1513–1913: Past, Present and Future*. Chicago, 1914.

Churchill, Randolph S. *Winston S. Churchill: Youth, 1874–1900*, Boston: Houghton Mifflin, 1966.

Churchill, Winston S. *My Early Life*. New York: Scribners, 1930.

Coblentz, Edmond D. *William Randolph Hearst, a Portrait in His Own Words*. New York: Simon & Schuster, 1952.

Commager, Henry Steele. *Documents of American History*. 2 vols. New York: Appleton-Century-Crofts, 1968.

Cosmas, Graham A. *An Army for Empire*. Columbia: University of Missouri Press, 1971.

Crane, Stephen. *Stephen Crane: Stories and Tales*. Edited by Robert Wooster Stallman. New York: Vintage, 1955.

Creelman, James. *On the Great Highway*. Boston, 1901.

Davis, Forrest. *The Atlantic System*. New York: Reynal Hitchcock, 1941.

Davis, George T. *A Navy Second to None*. New York: Harcourt, Brace, 1940.

Davis, Richard Harding. *The Cuban and Porto Rican Campaigns.* New York, 1898.
————. *A Year from a Reporter's Note-Book.* New York, 1897.
Dewey, George. *Autobiography.* New York, 1913.
Dierks, Jack Cameron. *A Leap to Arms.* Philadelphia: Lippincott, 1970.
Dorwart, Jeffery M. *The Office of Naval Intelligence.* Annapolis: Naval Institute Press, 1979.
Downey, Fairfax. *Richard Harding Davis and His Day.* New York: Scribners, 1933.
Dunne, Finley Peter. *Mr. Dooley in Peace and in War.* Boston, 1898.
Epler, Percy H. *The Life of Clara Barton.* New York: Macmillan, 1930.
Evans, Robley D. *A Sailor's Log.* New York, 1908.
Evans, Stephen H. *The United States Coast Guard, 1790–1915.* Annapolis: Naval Institute Press, 1949.
Ferrara, Orestes, *The Last Spanish War.* Translated by William E. Shea. New York: Paisley Press, 1937.
Fleming, Thomas J. *West Point.* New York: Morrow, 1969.
Flint, Grover. *Marching with Gomez.* New York, 1898.
Foner, Philip S. *The Spanish-Cuban-American War and the Birth of American Imperialism.* 2 vols. New York: Monthly Review Press, 1972.
Ford, Worthington Chauncey, ed. *Letters of Henry Adams, 1892–1918.* New York: Houghton Mifflin, 1938.
Freidel, Frank. *The Splendid Little War.* Boston: Little, Brown, 1958.
Funston, Frederick. *Memories of Two Wars.* New York, 1914.
Gatewood, Willard B., Jr. *Smoked Yankees.* Urbana: University of Illinois Press, 1971.
Giddings, Howard A. *Exploits of the Signal Corps in the War with Spain.* Kansas City, Mo., 1900.
Gonzales, N. G. *In Darkest Cuba.* Columbia, S.C.: State Company, 1922.
Graham, George Edward. *Schley and Santiago.* Chicago, 1902.
Greely, A. W. *Reminiscences of Adventure and Service.* New York: Scribners, 1927.
Halliburton, Richard. *Seven League Boots.* Indianapolis: Bobbs-Merrill, 1935.
Halstead, Murat. *The Story of Cuba.* New York, 1898.
Harlow, Alvin F. *Old Wires and New Waves.* New York: Appleton-Century, 1936.
Healy, Laurin Hall and Luis Kutner. *The Admiral.* New York: Ziff-Davis, 1944.
Heinl, Robert Debs and Nancy Gordon Heinl. *Written in Blood: The Story of the Haitian People, 1492–1971.* Boston: Houghton Mifflin, 1978.
Hoar, George F. *Autobiography of Seventy Years.* 2 vols. New York, 1903.
Hobson, Richmond Pearson. *The Sinking of the "Merrimac."* New York, 1899.
James, Henry. *Richard Olney and His Public Service.* New York: Houghton Mifflin, 1923.
Jane's Fighting Ships. London, 1898, 1901.
Jeffreys-Jones, Rhodri. *American Espionage.* New York: Free Press, 1977.
Jones, Virgil Carrington. *Roosevelt's Rough Riders.* New York: Doubleday, 1971.
Josephson, Matthew. *The President Makers.* New York: Putnams, 1940.
Kennan, George. *Campaigning in Cuba.* Port Washington, N.Y.: Kennikat Press, 1971.
Kipling, Rudyard. *Rudyard Kipling's Verse.* New York: Doubleday, 1940.
Koenig, Louis P. *Bryan.* New York: Putnams, 1971.
LaFeber, Walter, *The New Empire,* Ithaca: Cornell University Press, 1963.
————, ed. *John Quincy Adams and American Continental Empire.* Chicago: Quadrangle, 1965.
Latimer, Elizabeth Wormeley. *Spain in the Nineteenth Century.* Chicago, 1897.
Leech, Margaret. *In the Days of McKinley.* New York: Harper, 1959.

Levy, Leonard W. and Merrill D. Peterson. *Major Crises in American History.* 2 vols. New York: Harcourt, Brace, 1962.

Lodge, Henry Cabot, ed. *Selections from the Correspondence of Theodore Roosevelt and Henry Cabot Lodge, 1884–1918.* 2 vols. New York: Scribner's, 1925.

Long, Margaret, *The Journal of John D. Long.* Rindge, N.H.: Richard Smith, 1956.

Mahan, Alfred Thayer. *The Interest of America in Sea Power, Present and Future.* New York, 1897.

————. *Lessons of the War with Spain.* New York, 1899.

Manach, Jorge. *Marti, Apostle of Freedom.* Translated by Coley Taylor. New York: Devin-Adair, 1950.

Martí, José. *Our America: Writings on Latin America and the Struggle for Cuban Independence.* Edited with an introduction by Philip S. Foner. New York: Monthly Review Press, 1977.

May, Ernest R. *Imperial Democracy.* New York: Harcourt, Brace, 1961.

Mayo, Lawrence S. *America of Yesterday as Reflected in the Journal of John Davis Long.* Boston: Atlantic Monthly Press, 1923.

Miley, John D. *In Cuba with Shafter.* New York, 1899.

Miller, Nathan. *The U.S. Navy.* New York: American Heritage Press, 1977.

Miller, Stuart Creighton. *"Benevolent Assimilation."* New Haven: Yale University Press, 1982.

Millis, Walter. *The Martial Spirit.* Boston: Houghton Mifflin, 1931.

Morison, Elting E., ed. *The Letters of Theodore Roosevelt.* 8 vols. Cambridge, Mass.: Harvard U. Press, 1951–54.

Morison, Samuel Eliot. *Christopher Columbus, Mariner.* Boston: Atlantic Monthly Press, 1955.

Morris, Edmund. *The Rise of Theodore Roosevelt.* New York: Coward, McCann, 1979.

New York State Historian. *New York and the War with Spain.* Albany, 1903.

Olcott, Charles S. *The Life of William McKinley.* 2 vols. Boston, 1916.

Payne, Stanley G. *Politics and the Military in Modern Spain.* Stanford: Stanford University Press, 1967.

Pepper, Charles M. *Tomorrow in Cuba.* New York, 1910.

Perkins, Bradford. *The Great Rapprochement.* New York: Atheneum, 1968.

Pizer, Donald, ed. *American Thought and Writing: The 1890's.* New York: Houghton Mifflin, 1972.

Porges, Irwin. *Edgar Rice Burroughs.* 2 vols. New York: Ballantine, 1976.

Post, Charles Johnson. *The Little War of Private Post.* Boston: Little, Brown, 1960.

Pratt, Julius W. *Expansionists of 1898.* Baltimore: Johns Hopkins Press, 1936.

Rea, George Bronson. *Facts and Fakes About Cuba.* New York, 1897.

Reuter, Bertha Ann. *Anglo-American Relations During the Spanish-American War.* New York: Macmillan, 1924.

Rhodes, James Ford. *The McKinley and Roosevelt Administrations, 1897–1909.* New York: Macmillan, 1922.

Rickover, H. G. *How the Battleship Maine Was Destroyed.* Washington, D.C.: Government Printing Office, 1976.

Roosevelt, Theodore. *An Autobiography.* New York, 1913.

————. *The Rough Riders.* New York, 1899.

————. *The Works of Theodore Roosevelt.* National Edition. 20 vols. New York: Scribners, 1926.

Rubens, Horatio S. *Liberty: The Story of Cuba.* New York: Brewer, Warren and Putnam, 1932.

Schirmer, Daniel B. *Republic or Empire.* Cambridge, Mass.: Schenkman, 1972.

Schley, Winfield Scott. *Forty-five Years Under the Flag.* New York, 1904.

Schott, Joseph L. *The Ordeal of Samar.* Indianapolis: Bobbs-Merrill, 1964.

Schriftgiesser, Karl. *The Gentleman from Massachusetts.* Boston: Little, Brown, 1944.

Scott, Hugh Lenox. *Some Memories of a Soldier.* New York: Century, 1928.

Seitz, Don C. *The James Gordon Bennetts.* Indianapolis: Bobbs-Merrill, 1928.

Sigsbee, Charles D. *The Maine.* New York, 1899.

Smith, Horace. *A Captain Unafraid.* New York, 1912.

Spears, John R. *Our Navy in the War with Spain.* New York, 1898.

Spector, Ronald. *Admiral of the New Empire.* Baton Rouge: Louisiana State University Press, 1974.

Stallman, R. W. and E. R. Hagemann, eds. *The War Dispatches of Stephen Crane.* Westport, Conn.: Greenwood Press, 1977.

Sternlicht, Sanford. *McKinley's Bulldog: The Battleship Oregon.* Chicago: Nelson-Hall, 1977.

Stickney, Joseph L. *Life and Glorious Deeds of Admiral Dewey.* n.p., 1899.

Stoddard, Henry L. *As I Knew Them.* New York: Harper, 1927.

Sullivan, Mark. *Our Times.* 6 vols. New York: Scribners, 1926.

Swanberg, W. A. *Citizen Hearst.* New York: Scribners, 1961.

————. *Sickles the Incredible.* New York: Scribners, 1956.

Thayer, William Roscoe. *Life and Letters of John Hay.* 2 vols. Boston, 1915.

Thomas, Hugh. *Cuba.* New York: Harper & Row, 1971.

Titherington, Richard H. *A History of the Spanish-American War.* New York, 1900.

Trask, David F. *The War with Spain in 1898.* New York: Macmillan, 1981.

Tuchman, Barbara. *The Proud Tower.* New York: Macmillan, 1966.

————. *The Zimmerman Telegram.* New York: Macmillan, 1958.

Vandiver, Frank E. *Black Jack: The Life and Times of John J. Pershing.* 2 vols. College Station, Tx.: Texas A & M Press, 1977.

Victoria. *The Letters of Queen Victoria, third series, 1886–1901.* Edited by George Earle Buckle. 3 vols. London: John Murray, 1930.

Walker, Jeanie Mort. *Life of Capt. Joseph Fry, the Cuban Martyr.* Hartford, 1874.

Watterson, Henry. *History of the Spanish-American War.* Hartford, 1898.

Webster's American Military Biographies. Springfield, Mass.: Merriam, 1978.

Weems, John Edward. *The Fate of the Maine.* New York: Holt, 1958.

Welch, Richard E., Jr. *Response to Imperialism.* Chapel Hill: University of North Carolina Press, 1979.

Who's Who in America: 1899–1900. Chicago, 1899.

Wheeler, Joseph. *The Santiago Campaign, 1898.* Port Washington, N.Y.: Kennikat, 1971.

White, Leonard D. *The Republican Era.* New York: Macmillan, 1958.

Wilcox, Marrion. *A Short History of the War with Spain.* New York, 1898.

Wilkie, Don. *American Secret Service Agent.* New York: Stokes, 1934.

Willets, Gilson. *Inside Story of the White House.* New York, 1908.

Winkler, John K. *Hearst.* New York: Simon & Schuster, 1928.

Wolff, Leon. *Little Brown Brother.* New York: Simon & Schuster, 1961.

Young, James Rankin. *History of Our War with Spain.* n.p., 1898.

Young, Louis Stanley. *Life and Heroic Deeds of Admiral Dewey.* Springfield, Mass., 1899.

INDEX

Aberdeen, Lord (Geroge Hamilton-Gordon, 4th Earl of Aberdeen), 235
Acosta y Eyermann, Cmdr. Emilio, 239
Adams, Brooks, 17, 91, 93–96, 377, 392–93, 393n
Adams, Henry, 69, 91, 93, 393
Adams, John Quincy, 36–37, 39
Adee, Alvee, 122
Adula, 218
Aguadores, Cuba, 264, 265, 291, 295
Aguadores River, Cuba, 308n
Aguadores, Fort, 305
Aguinaldo y Famy, Emilio, 13, 250, 366–68, 371, 387–88, 390, 391–92
Aibonita, P.R., 356
Alfonso XII, 44, 65, 88
Alfonso XII, 20, 24, 30, 202
Alfonso XIII, 65, 109, 379
Alfonso XIII, 379–80
Alger, Lt. Philip, 139–40
Alger, Russell A., 225, 229, 230, 239, 290, 298n, 342, 344, 350, 353, 358, 366, 372, 376, 387–88
  appointed secretary of war, 85
  awaits Santiago battle report, 340–41
  background, 198
  demands unconditional surrender of Santiago, 346, 348
  and disease in Army, 359, 360, 362, 374–75
  halts Santiago invasion fleet, 243
  and Mariel invasion plan, 199
  and Puerto Rican reconnaissance and landings, 354, 354n, 355n
  proposes Spanish repatriation, 347–48
  tries to close Havana cable, 209
Allegheny, 265
Allen, Capt. James, 213, 215
Allen, Lt. W. H., 331
Almeria Hotel, 232
Almirante Oquendo, 164, 172
American Banker, 384
American Federation of Labor, 58
American National Red Cross, 27, 286–87, 347
"A Message to Garcia," 203n
Anderson, Lt. E. A., 207
Anderson, Quartermaster, 328
Anderson, Gen. Thomas M., 367
André, Edouard, 368, 369
Angiolillo, Miguel, 88
Angle, Dr. A. Sidney, 58
Anglo-American League, 378
Anthony, Pvt. William, 30
Anti-Imperialist League, 386, 390

Arango, Clemencia, 81–82
Archibald, James F. J., 204, 350–51, 352
Arecibo, P.R., 356
Ariete, 172
Arlington Cemetery, 397
Arroyo, P.R., 356
Arroyo Blanco, Cuba, 52
Arthur, Pres. Chester, 92, 102
Aserraderos, Cuba, 255, 326
Associated Press, 124, 161, 238, 329, 335, 354, 361
Astor, Lt. Col. John Jacob, 302, 303, 307
Atkins, Edwin F., 63–64, 65, 73
Atkinson, Edward, 386
Atlantic Monthly, 92, 393
Augustín Davila, Gen. Don Basilio, 368, 369
Auñon y Villalón, Capt. Ramón, 217, 282–84
Austria, 68, 97, 105, 141, 167
Azor, 172

Bache, 128
Bacheller Syndicate, 78
Bagley, Ens. Worth, 204–5
Bahía Honda, Cuba, 38, 200
Baire, Cuba, 51, 290
Balangiga, P.I., 392
Baldwin, Sgt., 287, 295
Balfour, Arthur, 166–67
Balino, Carlos, 50
Baltimore, 176, 177, 181, 183, 186, 188
Baltimore Fruit Company, 286
Baracoa, Cuba, 51
Barberes, John, 205
Bardshar, Pvt. Henry, 317
Barker, Capt. Albert S., 145
Barnegat, N.J., 60
Barrett, John, 365–66
Barton, Clara, 26–27, 29, 30, 286
Bataan, P.I., 188
Batabanó, Cuba, 205
Batangas, P.I., 395
Bates, Gen. John C., 320, 327
Bayamo, Cuba, 39, 47, 203
Bell, Gen. J. Franklin, 395
Bennett, James Gordon, Jr., 20, 114
Bermejo, Segismundo, 137–38, 140–41, 145, 167, 170, 172, 173, 180, 194, 211, 212
Bermuda, 234, 250
Bernadou, Lt. John B., 204
Bigelow, William Sturgis, 161
Black, Gen. Wilsone, 174
Blaine, James G., 91

437

Blake, 21, 208
Blanco, Ramón, 11, 25n, 33, 111, 113, 114, 119,
    120, 125, 214, 223, 234, 250, 326, 338, 349
  announces that Cervera's fleet was destroyed, 341
  orders Cervera to run blockade, 282–85, 288, 293,
    342n
  proposes joint investigation of *Maine* explosion,
    128
  replaces Weyler, 104
  urges Cervera's fleet to Cuba, 173, 212, 238
Blue, Lt. Victor, 203, 244, 249, 305
Boca Chica, P.I., 177, 181
Boca Grande, P.I., 177, 181–82, 184, 188
Boers, 68
Boer War, 391
Bolívar, Simón, 47
Bonaparte, Charles, 91
Bonaparte, Joseph, 36
Bonaparte, Napoleon, 36
Boston, 176, 177, 180, 181, 182, 184, 186
Bradford, Adm. Royal B., 127
Breck, Edward, 228
British Guiana, 67–69
British War Office, 68
"Bronze Titan," *see* Maceo, Gen. Antonio
Brodie, Major Alexander O., 273, 277
Brooklyn, 216, 219, 221, 233, 238, 328, 329, 330,
    331, 332, 333, 334, 335, 336, 337, 373
Brooklyn National Guard Cavalry, 58
Brooklyn Navy Yard, 22
Brooks Brothers, 195
Brown, Chaplain Henry A., 280
Brumby, Lt. T. F., 186, 365
Bryan, William Jennings, 66, 72, 73, 83, 84, 91, 390
Buccaneer, 286
Buchanan, Pres. James, 38
Buck, Ens. William H., 228
Buenaventura, 200–1
Bülow, Prince Bernhard von, 104–5, 159, 166, 192
Burgin, 19
Burriel, Gen. Juan, 40, 41, 42, 43, 44, 44n
Burroughs, Edgar Rice, 225
Bustamente, Capt. Joaquín, 330
Bustamente, Lt., 336
Byrne, Pvt. John, 272, 277, 277n

Cabañas, Cuba, 201, 204, 265
Cadarso, Don Luís, 187
Cádiz, Spain, 35, 97, 120, 144, 167, 193, 212, 214,
    215n, 222, 227, 228, 229, 251
Caimanera, Cuba, 249
Calandria, Lt., 334
Caldwell, Lt. H. H., 174
Calkins, Lt. C. G., 180, 182, 183–84, 186, 188
Callao, 370
Callao, Peru, 160, 165, 168
Caloocan, P.I., 73, 390
Camagüey Province, Cuba, 45, 47, 75
Cámara, Adm. Manuel de la, 193, 215n, 222, 223,
    227, 228, 229, 251–52, 342, 364
Cambon, Jules, 361
Cameron, Sen. Donald, 64, 91
Cameron, Elizabeth, 91, 92
Camp Black, 210
Camp McCalla, 249
Camp Wikoff, 362, 374–75, 376
Canada, 99, 109, 197, 232–35
Canalejas, Don José, 122
Canary Islands, 67, 144, 167, 172, 173, 227
Cannon, Rep. Joseph G., 141
Canosa, Cuba, 299
Cánovas del Castillo, Antonio, 11, 44–45, 56, 65, 66,
    83, 87–88, 103, 104, 109
Cape Bolinao, P.I., 180
Cape Hatien, Haiti, 217, 340
Cape Tunas, Cuba, 197
Cape Verde Islands, 167–168, 170, 172, 194, 197,
    211, 214, 215n, 216, 285, 337, 353
Capron, Capt. Allyn, Jr., 272, 274, 276, 291

Capron, Capt. Allyn, Sr., 291, 298, 300–1, 305, 314,
    351
Cárdenas, Cuba, 12, 200, 204–5, 211
Carlists, 37, 88, 89, 109, 113
Carlist Wars, 37
Carlos, Don (Charles VII), 66, 88, 109
Carlos, Infante Don (Carlos V), 37
Carlos V, 193, 222, 227, 228
Carnegie, Andrew, 386–87
Caroline Islands, 67
Carranza, Lt. Ramón, 232–35, 249
Cartagena, Spain, 137, 145
Carvajal, Foreign Minister, 43
Cascorra, Cuba, 86
Cassi, Emilio, 280
Castelar, Emilio, 41
Castilla, 177, 180
Castillo, Capt., 40
Castillo, Gen. Demetrio, 265, 266, 267, 268, 269,
    272, 295–96
Cavite, P.I., 177, 183, 184, 185, 186, 187, 188, 189,
    189n, 250, 367, 370
Cayey, P.R., 356, 372
Central Valley, N.Y., 50
Century, The, 80, 384
Cervera y Topete, Adm. Pascual, 12, 13, 140–41,
    173, 179, 195, 199, 201, 209, 212, 214, 215,
    216, 217, 218, 219, 222, 224, 227, 228, 264,
    281, 286, 293, 296, 332n, 379, 381
  advises against running blockade, 280, 282–85, 288
  advises against voyage to West Indies, 172, 173
  arrives at Cape Verde Islands 170
  arrives at Santiago, 213, 213n
  arrives in West Indies, 211
  background, 120
  blockaded in Santiago, 220, 221
  causes panic on Eastern seaboard, 194–95, 209,
    210, 341
  counsels against war, 121, 137–38, 141, 145
  disrupts American war plans, 197–98, 210–11,
    223, 243, 250, 325
  lends crewmen to Spanish Army, 269, 290
  ordered to run blockade, 282–85, 288, 293, 308,
    326–27, 342n
  popular with Americans, 338–39
  as prisoner of war, 338
  reported en route to Philippines, 249
  requests intelligence information, 121
  rescues Hobson, 237
  sails for West Indies, 194, 353
  and sea battle off Santiago, 329, 330, 333, 334,
    337
  squadron destroyed, 337, 340, 341, 345, 357, 364
  urges planning for war, 167, 170
Ceuta, Morocco, 228
Chadwick, Capt. French E., 129, 264n
Chaffee, Gen. Adna R., 289, 294, 298, 301, 308,
    311n, 394
Chamberlain, Joseph, 191, 378–79
Chandler, Sen. William E., 102, 103
Chanler, Rep. William Astor, 145, 160
Chapman, Gen. E. F., 52
Charleston, S.C., 61, 62
Charleston, 193, 233, 252
Charlotte, 106, 107, 110, 116, 120
Chicago, Ill., 59
Chicago *Journal,* 190, 339, 383
Chicago Trades Assembly, 59
Chicago *Tribune,* 190, 233
Chichester, Capt. Edward, 364–65, 370, 370n
Chidwick, Chaplain John P., 27, 28, 126
Chile, 102
China, 35, 56, 97, 105, 107, 110, 384, 399
Christy, Howard Chandler, 302–3
Churchill, Winston S., 52–54, 391
Cienfuegos, Cuba, 12, 73, 197, 200, 206, 207, 211,
    212, 214–16, 217–18, 219–20, 221, 332n, 341
Cienfuegos Bay, 205
Cigar Makers' International Union, 58

Cincinnati, Ohio, 59
Cincinnati, 127
Cisneros Betancourt, Salvador, 75, 86
City of Pekin, 193
City of Washington, 20, 29, 30, 32, 33, 125, 131
Civil Service Reform Association, 59
Clark, Capt. Charles E., 148, 166, 171
Clausen, Coxswain Rudolph, 235
Clay, Henry, 37
Cleveland, Ohio, 59
Cleveland, Pres. Grover, 11, 24, 60, 64, 65, 66, 68, 72, 76, 80, 83, 84, 198, 378
Cluverius, Cadet W. T., 133
coal bunker fires,
  frequency aboard U.S. warships, 127, 400
  on *Oregon,* 160–61
  suspected cause of *Maine* explosion, 127, 134, 139, 161, 400
Coamo, P.R., 356
Coaster's Harbor Island, R.I., 97
Cody, William, 165
Colon Cemetery, Cuba, 126
Colombia, 399
Columbia, 209
Columbus, Christopher, 35
Colwell, Lt. John C., 228
Commodore, 62, 78
Compania Transatlantica, 228
Concas, Capt. Victor, 216, 220, 329, 332, 333, 337, 380–81
Concord, 176, 177, 180, 181, 182, 184
Congosto, Secretary General, 33, 128
Contramaestre River, Cuba, 326
Converse, Cmdr. George A., 143
Corinto, Nicaragua, 67
Cormoran, 191–92, 365
Correa, Miguel, 238
Corregidor, P.I., 177, 178, 181–82, 184, 188, 364
Corrigan, Archbishop M. A., 378
Corsair, 336
Cortelyou, George, 148–49, 150
Costa Rica, 47
Cowles, Lt. Cmdr. W. S., 32–33, 34
Cox, Jennings, 79
Crane, Stephen,
  and Battle of San Juan, 304, 306, 309, 316, 321
  on Cuban insurgents, 343
  reports Hobson's return, 344–45
  reports on Battle of Las Guásimas, 277, 278, 279
  reports on blockade of Cuba, 200
  reports on Daiquirí landing, 267–68
  reports on Puerto Rican civilians, 356–57
  reports Spanish evacuation of Havana, 379–80
  shipwrecked en route to Cuba, 78–79
  with Marines at Guantánamo, 248–49
Creelman, James, 301, 321–22
Crimean War, 38
Cristina, Queen Regent, 66
Cristobal Colón, 167, 170, 172, 215n, 221, 244, 328, 332, 333, 335, 337
Crittenden, W. S., 38
Crowninshield, Capt. Arent S., 145
Cuabitas, Cuba, 326
Cuban Junta, 39, 40, 59–60, 60–64, 71, 77, 82n, 84, 115, 122, 232
Cuban League of the United States, 58–59
Curacao, 211, 218
Curry, Eleanor, 207
Curry, William, 207–8
Cushing, 32
Cuzco Hills, Cuba, 248

Daiquirí, Cuba, 265–68, 269, 270, 280, 287, 343
Dana, Charles A., 49, 58
Danish West Indies, 110
Darmstadt, 251
Dauntless, 62, 86
Davis, Adm. Charles H., 85, 93, 142
Davis, Sen. Cushman K., 385n

Davis, Richard Harding, 255, 311n
  background, 79
  and Battle of Las Guásimas, 270–71, 272–77, 279
  and Battle of San Juan, 303, 307, 310, 312, 313, 315, 316, 319, 321,
  describes road to Santiago, 280–81
  describes San Juan Heights, 289
  and Puerto Rican campaign, 353, 355, 372
  reports eve of Battle of San Juan, 296–97,
  reports on Army at Tampa, 230
  reports on Daiquirí landing, 266, 268
  reports on Cuban revolution, 79–82
  reports on shelling of Matanzas, 201
  reports on Siboney landing, 271
Day, Lt. Richard, 277
Day, William R., 84, 114–15, 116–19, 122, 128, 139, 149, 159, 160, 161, 165, 167, 168. 377, 385n
Dellie, 381
Deneefe, G., 205
Derby, Lt. Col. George McC., 293, 295–96, 303–4, 305–7, 310, 311, 311n
Deva, 29
Dewey, Adm. George, 12, 13, 112, 166, 199, 217n, 233, 384
  and Aguinaldo, 250, 366–67, 387–88
  appointed commander of Asiatic Squadron, 102–3, 137
  and Battle of Manila Bay, 174–90
  and Cámara's squadron, 193, 214, 223, 228
  and German squadron, 191–92, 223, 250–51, 364–66
  ordered to bring squadron to Hong Kong, 136–37
  ordered to retain seamen, 120
  negotiates surrender of Manila, 368–71
Díaz, Gen. Pedro, 203
Dickens, Cmdr. Francis W., 34
Dickon, Frederick W., 233
Diedrichs, Adm. Otto von, 105, 251, 364–66, 370n
Dinsmore, Rep. Hugh A., 170
Direct West India Cable Company, 234
Doddridge, Ens. J. S., 186
Dodge, Grenville M., 376
Dodge Commission, 376
Dolphin, 238, 248
Dominican Republic, 399
Don Antonio de Ulloa, 188
Dorst, Lt. Col. Joseph H., 203, 230, 315
Dos Caminos, Cuba, 299
Dos Rios, Cuba, 51
Downing, George, 233
Dry Tortugas, 20, 21, 119
Dubsky, Count Viktor, 142
Ducoureaud House, 298, 301
Dumont, 22
Dupuy de Lôme, Enrique, 65, 114–15, 116, 118–19, 120, 122–23, 232

Eagan, Gen. Charles P., 376
Eagle, 219, 243
East Shantung Province, China, 105
Ebbitt House, 83
Eckert, Thomas T., 208–9, 214
Eighth U.S. Infantry, 305
El Caney, Cuba, 13, 289, 294–95, 296, 298, 300, 301–2, 304–5, 308–9, 314, 319–20, 321, 325, 342n, 343, 344, 347
Eleventh U.S. Infantry, 232
El Fraile, P.I., 177, 182
"Elias, H. W.," *see* Whitney, Lt. Henry H.
Ellis, Yeoman Geroge, 335, 338
Elliot, Capt. George F., 248
El Nacional, 143
El Pozo, Cuba, 289, 290, 293, 294, 295, 296, 297, 298, 299, 300, 301, 302–4, 305, 306, 307, 309, 314, 315, 316, 327, 340
El Sueño, Cuba, 299
El Viso, Cuba, 294
Escario, Col. Federico, 268, 280, 288, 290. 326, 334, 342, 342n, 343

Esmeralda, 177
Estrada Palma, Tomas, 49–50, 59, 60, 64, 78, 399
Eulate, Capt. Antonio, 337–38
Evans, Capt. Robley D., 101, 219–21, 235, 329–30, 331, 333, 334, 335, 336, 337–38
Ewers, Lt. Col. E. P., 313
expansionism, 91, 92, 99, 170, 365, 393, 394
Facts and Fakes About Cuba, 27
Fame, 174–77
Farragut, Adm. David, 177
Fern, 32, 135, 146
Ferdinand VII, 36, 37
Fifth Army Corps, 300, 306, 359
filibustering, 39–40, 60, 62, 71
First Marine Battalion, 248
First Marine Division, 248
First Nebraska Volunteer Infantry, 388
First U.S. Infantry, 203, 302
First U.S. Regular Cavalry, 272, 278, 297, 310, 317
First U.S. Volunteer Cavalry (Rough Riders), 12, 190, 255
    advance toward Santiago, 297
    at Battle of Las Guásimas, 272–80, 291, 292
    at Battle of San Juan, 299, 303, 307, 310–11, 313–14, 315–19, 320,
    at Camp Wikoff, 374, 375, 376–77
    composition, 225–26
    at Daiquirí, 267–69
    leaves Santiago, 363
    at San Antonio, 225–27
    at Siboney, 270–71
    and siege of Santiago, 323, 325, 351,
    at Tampa, 240–42, 244
Fish, Secretary of State Hamilton, 41–42
Fish, Sgt. Hamilton, 270, 272, 276
Fleming, Lt. R. J., 320
Flint, Maj. Grover, 230, 381
Flying Squadron, 12, 209, 212, 214, 219–21, 223, 224, 234, 253
Foraker, Sen. Joseph, 170
Forsyth, John, 37
Fort San Antonio, P.I., 370
Fort Zachary Taylor, 140
Forum, The, 94
Fourth Artillery, 291, 353
Fourth U.S. Cavalry, 203
France, 37, 38, 67, 71, 72–73, 103, 105, 141, 143, 166, 191, 361, 370, 386
Franz-Joseph, 71, 142, 147
Fritot, Mr., 61
Fry, Capt. Joseph, 40, 41, 43
Frye, Sen. William P., 163, 385
Funston, Gen. Frederick, 59, 60–63, 86–87, 255, 359n, 381, 392
Furor, 172, 215n, 244, 328, 332, 336

Galacia, 62
García, Gen. Calixto, 86, 203, 230, 255, 264–65, 269, 286, 301, 320, 342, 343, 352
García Velez, Gen. Carlos, 343
Geier, 107, 110, 115, 116, 288, 288n
German-American Committee, 59
German Asiatic Squadron, 191–92, 364–66, 370
Germany, 66–68, 72–73, 99, 103, 104, 108, 141, 143, 167, 191, 385, 386, 399
    American fears of, 66–67, 99–100, 106, 107–8, 110, 115, 120, 141
    British fears of, 68–69, 379
    and China, 105, 107, 110
    expansionist plans of, 100, 105, 107, 110
    and Haiti, 105–7, 108, 110, 116
    sends ships to Havana, 108, 110–11, 115–16, 120
    and the Philippines, 191–92, 223, 250–51, 364
Gibson, Charles Dana, 79
Glass, Capt. Henry, 252
Gleaves, Lt. Albert, 32–33, 34
Gloucester, 305, 336, 338, 355
Gniesenau, 116n, 120
Gómez, Juan Gualberto, 50

Gómez, Gen. Máximo, 28, 52, 53, 64, 73, 78, 79, 83, 97, 98, 109, 197, 222, 230, 255, 264, 342
    attacks western provinces, 54–55, 56
    background 47
    and Cisneros, 75
    contacted by American agents, 203, 354n
    and death of Maceo, 76
    declines Cuban presidency, 399
    described, 46
    and Funston, 62–63, 86, 392
    lands in Cuba, 50, 51
    and Martí, 48–49, 50–51
    in New York, 46–49
    salutes comrades and allies, 381–82
Gómez Toro, Francisco "Panchito," 75–76, 381
Gómez Ymay, Adm. José, 234
Gompers, Samuel, 49, 58
Gonzales, Narcisco, 381–82
Gould, Jay, 77
Graham, George Edward, 238, 329, 335–36
Grand Army of the Republic, 59
Grand Duchesse, 362
Grant, Pres. Ulysses S., 39, 42–43, 44
Gray, Sen. George, 385
Grayson, Pvt. Willie, 388
Great Britain, 35–36, 37, 42, 72–73, 99, 103, 105, 142, 191, 385, 387, 391, 399
    fears of Germany, 68–69, 379
    relations with U.S., 37, 67–69, 166, 378–79
    sabotages European coalition, 11, 70–73
Great Cuban-American Fair, 58, 59
Greely, Gen. Adolphus W., 209, 214, 215, 217, 281
Greene, Gen. Francis Vinton, 113, 144, 366, 385
Gridiron Club, 160
Gridley, Capt. Charles V., 183, 184, 187
Grimes, Capt. George S., 295, 299, 302–3, 304, 305, 308
Guaimaro, Cuba, 86
Guam, 13, 252
Guanabacoa, Cuba, 201, 202
Guánica, P.R., 354, 355
Guantánamo, Cuba, 250, 253, 264, 286, 327, 355n
Guantánamo Bay, Cuba, 248–49, 264, 353
Guarinao River, Cuba, 326
Guatemala, 48
Guitterrez, Lt., 252
Gulf of Mexico, 20, 21, 36, 98, 106, 109, 116n, 119
Gullón, Pío, 149–50, 159, 160, 164, 165, 168, 171
Gussie, 203, 204, 230

Haiti, 36, 38, 106–7, 108, 109, 110, 115, 116, 218, 288n, 340
Halifax, N.S., 234
Hamburg-American Line, 228
Hampton Roads, Va., 62, 97, 114, 209, 212
Hankow, China, 105
Hanna, Marcus, 84, 160, 384
Hardin, Edwin, 189–90
Harding, Rebecca, 79
Harper's Weekly, 79, 80, 204
Hartley and Graham, 60
Harvard, 209, 220, 288, 345
Havana, Cuba,
    blockade of, 173, 174, 195, 213
    riots in, 12, 19, 20, 24, 111–12, 113, 114
    telegraph office, 19, 27, 29, 32–33, 34, 80, 130, 207–9, 212–13
Havana City Hospital, 31–32
Hawaiian Islands, 99, 101, 140, 383, 384, 399
Hawkins, Gen. Hamilton S., 304, 311, 317, 318
Hay, John, 91, 93, 166, 191, 374, 377, 385, 387
Hayes, Pres. Rutherford B., 83, 209
Hazeltine, Mayo B., 66–67, 69
Hearst, William Randolph, 34, 77, 78, 79, 82, 251, 285, 301, 322, 372–73
Hellings, Martin Luther, 32–33, 34, 207–9, 213n, 214, 281
Henry, Prince (of Prussia), 192
Hill, Lt. F. K., 328

Hill, Mrs. Leo Villard, 58
Hoar, Sen. George F., 384–85, 386, 387, 391
Hobson, Naval Constructor Richmond P., 223–25,
    235–37, 239, 266, 280, 289, 296, 301, 309,
    344–45, 379
Hodgson, Lt., 328, 331
Hohenzollern, 100
Holden, Cadet J. H., 133
Holguín, Cuba, 39, 327, 341, 345
Holland, John R., 233n
Holland, 233, 233n
Holliday, Pvt. Presley, 320
Holmon, Lt. George F. M., 133
Holzer, Frederick C., 131
Homestead, Pa., 387
Hong Kong, 102, 136, 137, 166, 174, 176, 180, 188,
    189, 190, 192, 250, 365, 367
Hood, Lt. John, 150
Horsa, 60
Houghton, Mr., 70
Howell, Charles P., 134
Howell, Commo. John A., 102, 103
Howells, William Dean, 91
Hubbard, Elbert, 203n
Hudson, 204

Iguara, Cuba, 52, 53
Illinois Federation of Labor, 59
Immortalité, 364, 370
Inagua, Haiti, 50
Indiana, 109, 173, 211, 373
Infanta María Teresa, 167, 170, 172, 215n, 239, 244,
    254, 280, 328, 332–33, 334, 379
Influence of Sea Power Upon History, 92, 93
Inglaterra Hotel, 27, 28–29, 80, 130
intelligence operations,
    American, 32–33, 176, 203, 207–9, 213, 213n, 214,
    217, 222, 227, 249–50, 252, 281, 353–54, 354n
    British, 52
    Spanish, 232–35, 249
International Ocean Telegraph Company, 19, 33–34,
    207, 208
Iowa, 110, 129, 135, 148, 173, 215–16, 219, 221,
    235, 238, 251, 328, 329, 331, 332–33, 334, 337,
    338, 373
Iphigenia, 370
Ireland, Archbishop John, 165
Irene, 191
Irish Volunteers, 58
Isabella II, 37
Isla de Cuba, 187
Isla de Luzon, 187
Isle of Pines, Cuba, 98
Italy, 68, 97, 141, 167

Jacomel, Haiti, 116
Jamaica, 39, 40, 41, 42, 218, 353
James, Frank, 165
Jameson, Dr. Leander Starr, 68
Japan, 35, 97, 99, 101, 370, 385, 399
Jaramillo, Gen. Paez, 109
Jaudenes, Gen. Firmin, 368, 369, 370, 371
Jekyll Island, Ga., 195
Jiguaní, Cuba, 86
Jimaguayú, Cuba, 75
Journal of the Knights of Labor, 58
Juana Díaz, P.R., 356, 357
Júcaro, Cuba, 73
Júcaro-Morón *trocha*, 74–75, 80
Jupiter Inlet, Fla., 221

Kaichow Bay, China, 105, 192, 251, 384
Kaiser, 251
Kaiserin Augusta, 251
Kansas City, 59
Kennan, George, 286–87, 291, 292
Kennan, George F., 286n
Kent, Gen. Jacob F., 295, 302, 309–10, 311–12, 314,
    316, 327, 350

Kettle Hill, Cuba, 13, 311, 315–17, 317, 317n
Key, Francis Scott, 42n
Key, Philip, 42n
Key West, Fla., 19, 22, 24, 32, 44, 47, 79, 80, 101,
    106, 108, 111, 112, 118, 119, 125, 126, 129,
    130, 132, 133, 144, 148, 149, 150, 165, 173,
    201, 204, 207, 208, 209, 212–13, 217, 220, 224,
    230, 243, 400
    cable office, 19, 32–34, 207–9, 212–13, 213n, 243
    naval station, 32, 119
Kimball, Lt. William W., 98, 108
Kingston, Jamaica, 41, 220, 234
Kipling, Rudyard, 91, 387
Koebler, George, 131
Kruger, Pres. Paul, 68

labor unions, 58, 59
La Guardia, Fiorello, 232
Lakeland, Fla., 231
Lamberton, Cmdr. B. P., 181, 186
La Mantonia, Cuba, 326
La Redonda, Cuba, 294, 295, 299
Las Cruces, Cuba, 299
Las Guásimas, Cuba, 12, 270–71, 272–79, 286, 291,
    292, 316
Las Tunas, Cuba, 28
Las Villas, Cuba, 203
Law of Civilization and Decay, The, 93–94, 96
Lawton, Gen. Henry W., 269, 278, 294–95, 298,
    300, 304–5, 314, 320, 321, 327, 342, 350
Lazarraga, Capt., 200–1
Leahy, Adm., William D., 148
Lee, Capt. Arthur H., 298–99, 300, 301, 304–5, 308,
    314, 319–20, 321
Lee, Gen. Fitzhugh, 25, 26, 32, 80, 82, 115, 126,
    128, 129, 130, 133, 208, 230
    advised that *Maine* en route to Havana, 117–18,
    119
    advises *Maine* visit be postponed, 119, 120
    background, 24,
    believes *Maine* disaster caused by mine, 134, 139
    commissioned as general of volunteers, 196
    departs Havana, 169
    and Havana riots, 112
    hears reports of anti-American plot, 108
    reports German warships en route to Havana, 110,
    120
    reports destruction of *Maine*, 124
    urges *Maine* stay at Havana, 26
    urges warship be sent to Havana, 21, 24, 108,
    110–11, 116
    warns of danger to Americans in Cuba, 166
Leger, Jacques Nicolas, 106
Leo XIII, Pope, 164, 165, 168, 171
Lessons of the War with Spain, 325n
Linares, Gen. Arsenio, 250, 284–85, 288, 290, 293,
    299, 320, 349–50, 369
Lincoln, Pres. Abraham, 67, 93, 386, 387
Liscum, Lt. Col. E. H., 313
Lissa, Battle of, 97
Literary Digest, 384
Lodge, Henry Cabot, 64, 85, 90–91, 92, 93, 95, 101,
    161, 166, 171, 191, 225, 241, 244, 323, 346–47,
    361n, 375, 376, 383, 387, 388, 392, 393
Lodge, Nannie, 90, 91, 92
London *Daily Graphic*, 52
London *Standard*, 70
Long, Helen, 34
Long, John D., 102, 103, 112, 113, 124, 127, 128,
    141, 148, 164, 228, 367, 373
    announces the *Maine* to go to Havana, 118
    announces victory at Manila Bay, 190
    anxious over Schley's dispatch, 220
    appoints Roosevelt to war planning panel, 145
    approves ONI agent's mission to Madrid, 227
    on cause of *Maine* disaster, 125, 139
    conflict with Alger, 199
    has no information on German ships at Havana,
    115–16

Long (continued)
    and Havana intelligence source, 214–15
    insists on confirmation of Cervera's whereabouts,
        243
    intends attack on Spanish coasts, 252
    learns of Maine disaster, 34
    leaves Roosevelt in charge, 100–1, 136
    named secretary of navy, 85
    orders Dewey to forego alliances with Filipino
        insurgents, 250
    orders European Squadron to retain seamen, 110
    proposes compromise on Philippine acquisition,
        385
    recalls decision to send Maine to Havana, 117
    regrets McKinley forced to war, 341
    on Roosevelt, 137, 195
    stations Maine at Port Royal, 108
    warns Dewey war near, 166
Long, Margaret, 117n
Lopez, Narcisco, 38
Lorraine, Sir Lambton, 42
L'Overture, Toussaint, 36
Loyal Legion, 59
Luce, Adm. Stephen B., 97
Lüders, Emile, 105–7, 120, 288n
Ludlow, Gen. William, 300, 305
Luque, Gen. Augustín, 109
Luzon, P.I., 180, 181, 250, 385, 386, 391
Lyons, Dr. Palmer, 389

MacArthur, Gen. Arthur, 366, 368
McCalla, Cmdr. Bowman H., 219
McClernand, Col. Edward J., 299, 302, 304, 307,
    314
McCook, John J., 84, 122
McCulloch, 176, 177, 182, 188, 189, 190, 365
McDowell, William O., 58
Maceo, Gen. Antonio, 47, 48, 51, 53, 55, 73, 75–76,
    83, 381
Maceo, José, 51, 75, 381
Maceo, María, 76
McKenna, Justice Joseph, 84, 117
McKinley, Ida, 83
McKinley, Pres. William, 11, 13, 21, 66, 82n, 91,
    93, 96, 102, 113, 114, 122, 124, 137, 143, 160,
    164, 167, 197, 215, 223, 227, 347, 365, 373,
    378
    administration, 21, 114, 119–20
    advocates invasion of Cuba, 199
    appoints cabinet, 84–85, 198
    appoints Dodge Commission, 376
    appoints ex-Confederates, 198
    asks Barton to manage Cuban relief, 27
    asks for volunteers, 195
    asks for war appropriation, 141
    assassinated, 392
    awaits Santiago battle report, 340–41
    background, 83–84
    demands Spanish apology, 122–23
    demands unconditional surrender of Santiago, 346
    and disease in Army, 359, 360, 361
    elected president, 73
    hopes to avoid war, 83, 125, 146, 159, 161,
        168–69, 171
    inquires about German fleet in Caribbean,
        115–116
    listens to Roosevelt's war plans, 101
    and Maine investigation, 125, 133–34, 139,
        148–49, 150, 161
    orders Maine to Havana, 24, 116–20
    and peace negotiations, 361–62, 371, 383
    and Philippine question, 383–84, 385–86
    receives intelligence reports, 207–9, 212, 214, 217
    recommends Dewey, 103, 189
    reelected, 391
    seldom wrote official letters, 116
    sends Cuban message to congress, 163, 166,
        168–70
    signs Cuban intervention resolution, 172

    told of Dewey's victory, 190
    told of Maine disaster, 34
    and Vatican, 165
McMillen, Pvt. James L., 308
Madison Square Garden, 58, 59
Madrid Heraldo, 122
Mahan, Adm. Alfred Thayer, 92, 93, 94, 99, 100,
    144, 145, 150, 197, 223, 325n, 342n
Maine, 12, 20, 21, 22, 25, 26, 27, 29, 110, 111,
    117n, 150, 162, 169, 189, 190, 208, 218, 319,
    336, 397–98, 400
    damage to, 30–31, 125–26, 135, 137, 138, 143
    explosion and casualties, 12, 28–32, 33, 123,
        124–26, 130–31, 133
    eyewitness accounts of explosion, 29–32, 136
    history and specifications, 22, 92
    sent to Havana, 12, 21, 22–24, 116, 116n,
        118–120, 131, 208
    sent to Key West, 22, 106, 108, 133
    theories of sinking, 124–25, 126, 127, 128–29,
        130, 132, 134, 135, 138, 139–40, 161, 163, 397,
        400
Majana, Cuba, 74
Majorca, Spain, 109
Malate, P.I., 369
Mangrove, 131, 133, 134, 137, 138, 139
Manila, P.I., 12, 13, 98, 99, 101, 136, 199, 222, 223,
    227, 228, 233, 250–52, 362, 380, 385, 386, 388,
    ch.6, and 16
Manila Bay, P.I., 12, 222, 250, ch.6
Manila Bay, Battle of, 12, 194, 199, ch.6
Manning, 204
Manterola, Adm. Vincente, 125, 129–30, 131
Mantua, Cuba, 55
Manzanillo, Cuba, 268, 288, 290, 295, 326, 341,
    342n
Mao Tse-tung, 56
Marblehead, 106, 107, 108, 205, 207, 219, 238, 249
Mare Island Naval Station, 222
María Cristina, 65–66, 72, 105, 109, 113, 114, 138,
    142–44, 147, 159, 160, 164, 361, 379
Marianage, Cuba, 301, 305–6
Marianao, Cuba, 76, 202
Marianas Islands, 252, 361, 362
Mariel, Cuba, 74, 75, 199, 203, 209, 214, 222
Mariel-Majana trocha, 74, 75
Marietta, 159
Mariveles, P.I., 364
Marix, Lt. Cmdr. Adolph, 129, 131–33, 134,
    135–36, 140, 150
Marshall, Edward, 272–73, 275, 279
Martí, José, 48–49, 50–51, 55, 58, 59, 75, 381
Martínez Campos, Gen. Arsenio, 45, 55–56
Martinique, 211, 212, 215n, 217
Masaba y Reyes, Maj. Francisco, 244
Masó, Gen. Bartolomé, 86
Mason, Robert, 348
Massachusetts, 110, 216, 238, 251, 373
Matanzas Province, Cuba, 54, 55, 83, 108, 201, 211
Maxfield, Lt. Col. Joseph E., 217, 281–82, 287,
    295–96, 303–4, 305–7, 309–11, 321
Mayagüez, P.R., 356
Meek, George B., 205
Mella, Vasquez de, 109
Mellor, Frank Arthur, 232–33
Meriwether, Walter Scott, 19–20, 21, 28–29, 31–32
Merrimac, 224–25, 235–37, 239, 280, 289, 344–45,
    363
Merritt, Gen. Wesley, 13, 222, 223, 364, 366,
    367–70, 371, 385
Metropolitan Club, 365
Mexico, 48
Miami, 363
Michigan Volunteers, 288, 295, 305, 346
Miles, Col. Evan, 298, 300
Miles, Gen. Nelson A.,
    advises Cuban invasion be postponed, 197
    background, 198
    and Alger, 198

and Anglo-American relations, 378
and disease in Army, 376
and dispatch of *Maine* to Havana, 117
finds confusion in Tampa, 229, 230
proposes aid to Navy, 243
and Puerto Rican campaign, 353, 354–55, 355n, 356, 361, 372
sends Rowan to García, 203
and surrender of Santiago, 348, 349, 350
Miley, Lt. John D., 229–30, 242–43, 264n, 281, 293, 299, 307, 308, 311, 315, 320–21, 359
Military Club of Palma, 109
Mills, Capt. A. L., 274
Minneapolis, 209, 219
Mirs Bay, China, 174, 178, 180
Mix, Tom, 299
Monadnock, 222
Monocacy, 137
Monroe Doctrine, 67, 68, 71, 100, 399
Montauk Point, N.Y., 362, 374–75
Monterey, 222
Montevideo, 284
Montgomery, Benjamin F., 208–9, 213–14
Montojo y Pasarón, Adm. Patricio, 179–80, 184, 185, 186–87, 189n
Montserrat, 104
Montecristi, Santo Domingo, 47
Montjuich Prison, 88
Moret, Segismundo, 113–14, 125, 149, 381
Morgan, J. P., 336
Morgan, Sen. John T., 64, 72
Morgan-Cameron resolution, 64–65
Morón-Júcaro *trocha*, 74–75, 80
Morgen, Charles, 135–36
Morón, Cuba, 73
Morro Castle (Havana), 200, 398
Morro Castle (Santiago), 235, 239, 254, 266, 324, 331, 363
Morro Point, Cuba, 236, 238, 264, 285, 327
"Mr. Dooley," 190, 339, 383–84
Müller y Tejeiro, Lt. José, 218–219, 238–39, 320, 322, 325–27, 330–31
Murphy, Pvt. William S., 376–77

Nagasaki, Japan, 136
Nanshan, 176, 177, 180
Nashville, 201, 205
Nation, The, 88
Naval Observatory, 85
Naval Ship Research and Development Center, 400
Naval Surface Weapons Center, 400
naval technology and tactics, 97, 144, 148
Naval War Board, 145–46, 214, 228–29
Naval War College, 92–93, 96, 97, 223, 227
Naval War of 1812, The, 90, 93
Newark, 233
Newcastle *Leader*, 54
New Orleans, 238
Newport News, Va., 134
New Smyrna, Fla., 78
Newton, Corp. C. H., 21
New York, 109, 127, 129, 135, 173, 200, 201, 202, 211, 223, 224, 225, 235, 238, 296, 305, 328, 331–32, 337, 373
New York Central Railroad, 203n
New York City, 46, 47–49, 58, 59, 82n
New York *Evening Journal*, 126
New York *Herald*, 19, 20, 27, 41, 112, 114, 115, 121, 139, 189, 194, 203, 234, 297
New York *Journal*, 34, 56, 77–78, 80, 81–82, 122, 127, 142, 165, 189, 210, 272, 285–86, 301, 321, 356, 365, 372–73, 374
New York *Mail and Express*, 303
New York National Guard, 108, 113, 142, 144, 145, 225
New York State Assembly, 90
New York *Sun*, 49, 52, 58, 66, 79
New York *Times*, 20, 41, 42, 58, 118, 373, 390
New York *Tribune*, 67, 189, 385n

New York *World*, 28, 77, 78, 82, 83, 124, 127, 165, 189, 200, 202, 203, 248
Nicaragua, 67, 99, 399
Nicholas II, 71, 105
Nicholas Channel, 243
Ninth U.S. Regular Cavalry, 317
Ninth U.S. Infantry, 392
Niobe, 42
Nordstrand, 50
Norfolk Navy Yards, 233
North American Review, 91
North Carolina, 398
Nuevitas, Cuba, 62

O'Brien, Fisher, 62
O'Brien, Capt. "Dynamite Johnny," 49, 62, 398, 400
O'Brien, Mrs. John, 62
O'Donnell y Abreau, Carlos, duke of Tetuán, 65, 66, 70–72, 76, 86, 103
Office of Naval Intelligence, 85, 98, 108, 115, 129, 227–28
Olivette, 52, 80, 81–82, 126, 130, 137, 208, 279
Olney, Richard B., 64, 65, 66, 67–68, 72, 83, 378
Olympia, 136, 137, 174, 177, 178, 179, 180, 181, 182, 183, 184, 186, 187, 188, 189, 191, 192, 365, 370
O'Neil, Adm. Charles, 139, 141
O'Neill, Capt. William O. "Bucky," 268, 278, 313–14
Open Boat, The, 78–79
Operating Room, 213, 223, 340, 348
Oquendo, 215n, 216, 244, 328, 332, 334, 335
Ord, Gen. Edward O. C., 318n
Ord, Lt. Jules Garesche, 318
Oregon, 140, 148, 159, 160–61, 165, 168, 171, 172, 221, 238, 252, 331, 337, 373, 399
Oriente Province, Cuba, 39, 47, 55, 74, 75, 86, 97
Osceola, 398
Ostend Manifesto, 38
Our America, 92
Oyster Bay, N.Y., 90, 376

pacificos, 56
Paget, Lord Alfred, 378
Paglieri, Col. José, 29, 30
Palanan, P.I., 391
Palmas Atlas, Cuba, 269
Palma Soriano, Cuba, 326
Panama, 62, 399
Pan-American Exposition, 392
Pando, Gen. 290, 327, 327n, 342
Panther, 248
Paredes, Capt. Jose de, 337
Paris, 211
Parker, Lt. John H., 307, 318
Parrado, Gen., 25, 26
Patriota, 222
Patterson, John F., 40
Pauncefote, Sir Julian, 167, 234
Peace Commission, 383, 385, 385n, 336
Peanut Club, The, 77, 78
Pearl Harbor, H.I., 18, 178, 399
Pelayo, 193, 215, 215n, 222
peninsulares, 47, 104, 341
    conspiracies, 108
    oppose insurgents, 64
    riot over autonomy, 111–12, 114
Pepper, Charles M., 111–12
Peral y Cabellero, Capt. Don Pedro del, 129, 131
Pershing, Lt. John J. ("Black Jack"), 299, 299n, 310, 317
Petrel, 176, 177, 188, 370
Philadelphia, Pa., 59
Philistine, 203n
Philip, Capt. J. W., 336
Philippines, 11, 12, 13, 73, 88, 112, 136–37, 140, 222, 227, 228, 238, 249, 250–52, 361, 362, ch.6, 16 and 18.

Pierce, Pres. Franklin, 38
Pinar del Río Province, Cuba, 54, 55, 74, 83, 203
Pinkerton National Detective Agency, 61, 62, 232
Plant, Henry B., 61, 208, 209, 230
Plant Line, 52, 61, 126, 130, 132, 208, 230, 282
Platt, Sen. Thomas C., 85
Platt Amendment, 399
Playa del Este, Cuba, 341
Pleasant Gang, The, 91, 92, 377
Plutón, 172, 215n, 236, 244, 328, 332, 336
Point Abolitas, Cuba, 203
Point Fajardo, P.R., 354
Polk, Pres. James K., 38
Polo de Bernabe, Luís, 123, 161, 168, 233
Ponce, P.R., 354, 355, 356
Port Antonio, Jamaica, 60
Port-au-Prince, Haiti, 106, 107, 108, 110, 115, 116,
    120
Port de Pax, Haiti, 116
Porter, 238
Port Royal, S.C., 22, 108
Port San Luís d'Apra, Guam, 252
Port Tampa, Fla., 229–30, 232, 240–43, 254, 269,
    282
Portugal, 37, 194
Post, Pvt. Charles Johnson, 210, 231–32, 239–40,
    241–42, 244–45, 266, 270, 278, 279, 291–93,
    300, 301, 302, 304, 308, 309–10, 312–13, 318,
    351, 358, 362, 363, 375, 376
Potter, Bishop Henry C., 384
Potter, William P., 129
Powell, William F., 107, 115
Powelson, Wilfred Van Nest, 135–36, 137, 138, 142
Pratt, E. Spencer, 250
Proctor, Sen. Redfield, 12, 103, 137, 146–147, 149,
    189
Providence, R.I., 59
Pueblo (Colorado) Evening Post, 252
Puerto Rico, 13, 36, 99, 172, 173, 194, 209, 216,
    217, 358, 361, 362, 372, 383, ch.14
Pulitzer, Joseph, 77, 78
Punta Alegre, Cuba, 381
Punta Cabrera, Cuba, 334
Punta de la Colorados, Cuba, 205
Punta Gorda, Cuba, 329, 331
Punta Rassa, Fla., 207
Puritan, 211

Quesada, Gonzalo de, 50, 63, 64

Rabí, Gen. Jesús, 255, 342
Raleigh, 176, 177, 182, 192, 370
Ramsden, Frederick W., 344, 345, 347
Rápido, 222
Rawson-Walker, E. H., 368
Rayo, 172
Rea, George Bronson, 27–28, 29, 30–31, 33
reconcentrados, 11–12, 20, 27, 56, 57–58, 58n, 59,
    137, 146–47, 202, 286
    death toll of, 11, 20, 57–58, 58n, 83, 146–47
    sufferings of, 20, 27, 56, 57, 85–86, 88, 146–47
reconcentration policy, 11–12, 20, 27, 56, 57–58,
    58n, 59, 83, 86, 109, 146, 160, 163, 168, 169
Red Badge of Courage, The, 79, 277
Redfern, Ralph, 234
Regla, Cuba, 25, 28, 29
Reick, William C., 114, 115
Reid, Whitelaw, 378, 385n, 387
Reina Cristina, 177, 184, 185, 186–87
Reina Mercedes, 236, 239
Reina Mercedes barracks, 280, 289, 296, 301, 309
Remey, Commo. George C., 243
Remington, Frederic, 79, 80, 82, 255, 299, 377
Resolute, 243
Restormel, 217, 218, 219, 220
Review of Reviews, 66, 69
Revue de deux mondes, 89, 107
Rhodes, Cecil, 68
Rickover, Adm. Hyman G., 400

Riley, Sgt. Charles S., 389
Rio Grande, 282
Robeson, George, 44
Robledo, Romero, 113, 143
Rodgers, Lt. Cmdr. Raymond P., 221
Rodriguez, Adolfo, 80–81
Rodriguez, Gen. José María, 83
Rohan, Berthe de, 109
Roloff, Carlos, 50
Romero, Matias, 63
Roosevelt, Alice, 162
Roosevelt, Edith, 90, 101, 162
Roosevelt, Pres. Franklin, 148
Roosevelt, Pres. Theodore, 11, 13, 32n 106, 109, 171, 190,
    194, 274n, 363, 398–99
    acting secretary of navy, 100–3, 136–37, 162
    and advance on Santiago, 269, 270, 297
    appointed assistant secretary of navy, 85
    attitude toward Germany, 99–100, 108
    briefs McKinley on war plans, 101–2
    Brooks Adams's influence on, 93–97, 392–93
    contrives Dewey's appointment, 102–3
    and disease in Army, 358, 359, 360–62, 375
    early career, 90
    elected vice-president, 391
    en route to Santiago, 246, 252–53, 265
    expansionist views, 91, 92, 99, 170, 365
    gubernatorial campaign, 374, 376–77, 387
    joins Rough Riders, 190, 195, 374
    and Las Guásimas battle, 271, 272–79, 292
    lands with Rough Riders at Daiquirí, 267–268
    and Maine explosion, 126, 128–29, 139–40, 141,
        146, 162
    and Philippines, 387, 388, 393–94, 394–95, 399
    and Rough Riders in Tampa, 240–42, 244
    and San Juan battle, 299, 303, 307, 309, 310–11,
        313–14, 315–19, 320
    seeks combat role, 109, 113, 142, 144–45, 160,
        162, 190,
    and siege of Santiago, 323, 325, 346–47, 351
    succeeds to presidency, 392–93
    trains Rough Riders, 12, 225–27
    urges war preparations, 112–13, 144, 145–46, 150,
        159–60, 164, 166
Roosevelt Corollary, 399
Root, Elihu, 388–89
Rothschild, Sigmund, 29–30
Rough Riders, see First U.S. Volunteer Cavalry
Rough Riders, The, 320n
"Round Robin," 361
Rowan, Lt. Andrew S., 203, 203n, 230
Rubens, Horatio S., 50, 77, 122
Rubín, Gen. Antero, 271
Ruiz, Felipe, 28
Ruíz, Col. Manuel, 290
Runyon, Damon, 252
Russia, 67, 105, 141, 160, 167
Ryan, William A. C., 39, 41

Sabana Grande, P.R., 356
Sagamore Hill, 376
Sagasta, Práxedas Mateo, 11, 88, 104, 109, 111, 114,
    120, 121, 217n
St. Louis, 209, 214
St. Louis Post-Dispatch, 232
St. Paul, 218, 219
St. Thomas, Danish West Indies, 110
St. Vincent, Cape Verde Islands, 170, 172, 194
Salas y Gonzales, Lt. Don Francisco Javier de, 129
Salisbury, Lord Robert Cecil, 69, 164
Samar, P. I., 394
Sampson, Adm. William T., 202, 230, 250, 286,
    305, 376
    bombards Puerto Rico, 209
    bombards Santiago, 239
    and Cervera's whereabouts, 213n, 215–16, 217,
        237, 243
    and Havana blockade, 173, 223
    on Maine Court of Inquiry, 129, 133, 145

and Santiago blockade, 238–39
and Santiago campaign plans, 255, 264, 324
and Santiago sea battle, 331, 332n,
and sinking of *Merrimac*, 223–24, 235
and siege of Santiago, 324–325, 328, 340–41, 342
urges troops to Santiago, 239, 243, 246–48
San Ambrosio Hospital, 31, 131
San Antonio, Tx, 12, 195, 225
Sancti Spíritus, Cuba, 52
San Francisco *Examiner*, 77
San Francisco *Post*, 204, 350
San Germán, P.R., 356
San Juan Hill, Cuba, 12, 279–80, 285, 289–90, 292,
293, 294–96, 299, 300, 302, 307, 308–9, 310,
311, 313, 314–15, 316, 317, 317n, 318, 319,
320, 321, 323, 340, 342n, 344, 350, 362
San Juan River, Cuba, 301, 304, 306, 308, 308n,
310, 314, 318, 350
San Juan, P.R., 209, 211, 212, 216, 218, 354,
355–56, 357, 372
San Juan del Monte, P.I., 73
San Luís, Cuba, 327
San Miguel, Cuba, 301–2
San Pedro de Hernandez, Cuba, 76
San Sebastian, Spain, 69, 71, 87, 103
Santa Agueda, Spain, 87
Santa Clara Province, Cuba, 52, 79, 80–81, 243
Santa Cruz, Cuba, 301
Santa María, 35
Santiago de Cuba, 12, 13, 40–42, 43. 51, 79, 83,
205, 211–21, 222, 223, 224–25, 229, 234,
235–39, 243, 244, 249, 250, 253, 353, 356, 357,
358, 359, 362, 369, 374, 378, 379, 380, ch.10,
12 and 13.
Santo Domingo, 47, 49, 50
Santo Domingo, 284
Schley, Commo. Winfield Scot, 209, 213n, 214,
215–16, 217–18, 219–21, 223, 234, 237, 238,
328, 331–32, 335, 373, 376
Schmidt, E. G., 41
Schurz, Carl, 378, 386
Schwerin, Count Kurt Christoph von, 106, 107,
115
Scott, Maj. Hugh, 372
Scovel, Sylvester, 28, 29, 30–31, 33, 83, 127
Scribner's, 378
Second Division, 269, 278, 298
Second Massachusetts Volunteer Infantry, 210
Second U.S. Infantry, 242
Seguranca, 243, 255, 264, 270, 271, 286
Seneca, 210
Seventh U.S. Infantry, 308
Seventeenth U.S. Infantry, 308
Seventy-first Regiment of New York Volunteers, 210,
231, 240, 241, 242, 266, 269–70, 278, 291–92,
300, 301, 307, 311–13, 362
Seven Years' War, 35
Sevilla, Cuba, 272, 275, 279, 280, 289
Shafter, Gen. W. Rufus, 197, 229, 286, 300, 304,
376
assembles force at Tampa, 222, 230, 239, 243
blames Cubans, 342, 352
commanding during battles of El Caney and San
Juan, 299, 305–6, 307
and disease in army, 358–61, 362,
fears Spanish reinforcements, 290, 327
incapacitated, 299
and landings, 269, 270, 271, 281
plans Santiago campaign, 255, 264–65, 288–89,
293–95, 302, 308, 314–15, 320
and siege of Santiago, 324–25, 327–28, 340–41,
342–44, 345–50
and surrender of Santiago, 350–52
Shantung Province, China, 105
Sharp, Lt. Cmdr., 267
Sherman, George W., 41
Sherman, John, 24, 84, 85–86, 377
Sherman, Gen. William T., 24, 57, 86, 300
Shoemaker, Capt. Charles F., 150

Siboney, Cuba, 265, 266, 269, 270, 270–72, 275,
277, 278, 279, 281, 286, 288, 291, 294, 295,
324, 328, 331, 341, 343, 346
Sicard, Adm. Montgomery, 101, 125, 129, 145, 199
Sickles, Gen. Daniel E., 42, 43–44, 49. 58, 59
Siddall, B., 232
Sierra Maestra, 264, 324
Sigsbee, Capt. Charles D., 27, 108, 111, 124, 130,
144, 400
actions night of *Maine* disaster, 30, 32, 33, 34,
125
background, 21–22
believes *Maine* destroyed by mine, 127, 130, 139,
163
commands *St. Paul*, 218, 219
describes damage to *Maine*, 125–26
and Hellings, 208
oversees salvage and burial operations, 126, 128
relations with Spaniards at Havana, 25–26, 128,
130
takes *Maine* to Havana, 22–24, 120
testifies at Naval Court of Inquiry, 131–33,
134–35
Sigsbee Deep, 21
Sims, Lt. William S., 227, 227n, 228, 237, 243, 249,
252
Singapore, 250
Sixth U.S. Infantry, 318
Sixteenth Pennsylvania Infantry, 356, 357
Sixteenth U.S. Infantry, 318
Smith, Gen. Jacob, 394–95
Smith, Pvt. James W., 308
Socapa Point, Cuba, 238, 264, 285, 331
Social Darwinism, 91, 93
Soldiers' Letters, 390
Soldiers of Fortune, 79
Somerford, Fred O., 203
Sons of the Colonial Wars, 59
Sousa, John Philip, 178, 179
South African Company, 68
South African Republic, 68, 391
South China Sea, 178
Southwick, Robert W., 208
Spanish-American Iron Company, 267
Spanish monarchy,
preserved, 379
restored, 65
threatened by Cuban crisis, 65, 66, 70–71, 114,
121–22, 163
Spanish Naval Board of Inquiry, 125, 129–30, 131,
161
Spring-Rice, Cecil Arthur, 99
Stanton, Edwin, 208
State of Texas, 286
Stein, 106, 107, 116
Stevens, Capt. Frank, 30, 132
Stickney, Joseph, 185, 186
Stoddard, Henry L., 303, 312
Storey, Moorfield, 386
Strong, Josiah, 91–92, 93
Subic Bay, P.I., 178, 180, 181, 184, 364
Suez Canal, 251–52, 342
Sumner, Gen. Samuel S., 296, 303, 304, 308, 315, 318
Supreme Court, 60
Suwanee, 238, 249, 305
Sylvia, 286

Taft, Pres. William Howard, 399
Tainos Indians, 35
Tamar Island, 171
Tampa Bay Hotel, 230, 232, 242
Tampa, Fla., 99, 203, 208, 209–10, 222, 229–32,
234, 239–45, 281, 282, 348, 375
Tampa Heights, Fla., 231
Tapia Valley, Cuba, 75
Tarquino River, Cuba, 337
Taylor, Hannis, 69–72
Taylor, Capt. Henry C., 98
Teasdale, Capt. Frederick G., 29

Tejera, Diego Vincente, 50
Teller, Sen. Henry M., 171
Teller Amendment, 171
Temerario, 159, 166
Tenth Regular Cavalry, 267–68, 272, 278, 297, 299, 299n, 310, 317, 320
Ten Years' War, 39–45, 47, 48, 50, 55, 63, 73, 75, 255
Terror (Spanish), 172, 215n
Terror (U.S.), 110, 211
Texas, 92, 110, 216, 238, 249, 332, 333, 336, 337, 373
Theile, Kapitan-zur-See August, 107
Thirty-third Michigan Volunteers, 305
The Three Friends, 200
Thrall, Charles, 201–2
Tiffany, Sgt. William, 267
Tillinghast, C. Whitney II, 108, 113, 142
Todd, Cmdr. Chapman C., 110, 201, 204
Toral, Gen. Jose, 309, 320, 326, 340, 342, 345–46, 348–51, 369
Tornado, 39, 40
Train, Lt. Cmdr. Charles J., 97–98
Trans-Mississippi Exposition, 384
Transvaal, 68
Treaty of Paris, 13, 386–88
trocha, 73–75, 80, 82–83, 146
Tunnell, E. B., 205
Turner, Frederick Jackson, 91
Twain, Mark, 391
Twelfth U.S. Infantry, 308
Twelfth Kansas, 390
Twenty-second Infantry, 305
Twenty-sixth Infantry, 389
Twenty-third Infantry Regiment, 58

Union Iron Works, 148
Union League Club, 59
United States and Haiti Cable Company, 217, 281
U.S. Army Corps of Engineers, 397
U.S. Army Military Information Division, 203, 353–54
U.S. Army Signal Corps, 209, 213, 213n, 217, 234, 281–82, 287, 295–96, 306, 307, 309–10, 340
U.S. Asiatic Squadron, 12, 98, 99, 101–2, 103, 112, 120, 136–37, 222, 250, ch.6
U.S. Coast Guard, 150n
   see also U.S. Revenue Cutter Service
U.S. Coast Survey, 112
U.S. Code, 60
U.S. Congress
   House of Representatives,
      Appropriations Committee, 141
      Foreign Affairs Committee, 171
      Ways and Means Committee, 196
   and *Maine* investigation report, 161
   Senate Foreign Relations Committee, 64, 163, 385n
U.S. European Squadron, 110
U.S. Naval Academy, 338
U.S. Navy Court of Inquiry on *Maine* disaster, 125, 126, 139, 140, 145–46, 397, 400
   appointed, 129
   conclusions, 12, 148, 149
   considers coal bunker fire evidence, 134–35
   delivers its report, 148, 149, 150, 163
   final deliberations, 144, 148
   hears testimony, 131–36, 137–38, 139, 142, 143
   report of, 146, 160, 161
U.S. North Atlantic Squadron, 12, 68, 101, 125, 128, 145, 150, 164, 165, 173, 180, 200, 209, 245, 248, 372
   winter exercises, 20, 21, 22, 106, 108, 109–10, 114, 115, 116n, 119
U.S. Revenue Cutter Service, 86, 112, 150, 176
   see also U.S. Coast Guard
U.S. Secret Service, 232–33, 234
U.S. Volunteers, 392
Upham, Ensn. F. B., 176

Valdés, Gen. Suáres, 52, 53, 54
Vamoose, 79, 80
Van Dewater, Chaplain George R., 210, 231, 240, 309, 312
Vara del Rey, Gen. Joaquín, 300
Varona, Gen. Oscar, 39, 41
Vasquez, Lt. Cmdr. 336
Vatican, 159, 164, 165, 168, 171
Venezuela, 48, 79
Venezuela Boundary Dispute, 67–69, 94, 378
Vera Cruz, Mexico, 35
Vernon, Lord Edward, 264, 294
Victoria, 68–69, 71, 147, 159, 164, 173, 191
Victoria de las Tunas, Cuba, 86
Vigilancia, 241, 244, 266, 269
Villaamil, Captain Fernando, 144, 336
Villaverde, Domingo, 19, 29, 32, 33, 207, 208, 209, 212–13, 213n, 214–15, 217, 249, 281
Virginius incident, 39–44, 58, 92
Vixen, 238, 337
Vizcaya, 164, 172, 215n, 216, 239, 244, 328, 332, 333, 335–36, 337–38
Volkmar, 2nd Lt., 287, 295
Volunteer Signal Corps, 209
Volz, Robert, 207

Wainwright, Lt. Cmdr. Richard, 30, 32, 108, 133, 336
Walker, Adm. John G., 101, 101n
Waller, Maj. Littleton, 394
Wall Street Journal, 147, 384
Ward, Henry Heber, 228
Ward Line, 20, 33, 125, 210
war plans, 117
   development of, 97–99, 108
   Office of Naval Intelligence and, 98
   Naval War College and, 97–99
   Roosevelt and, 99, 101–2, 136–37
Warren, Tom, 19, 33–34
Washington, George, 96, 386
Washington *Evening Star*, 117, 127, 139
Washington Navy Yard, 136
Washington *Post*, 68
Washington *Star*, 111, 127
Wasp, 204
Western Union Telegraph Company, 207, 208, 213
Weyler y Nicolau, Gen. Valeriano, 11, 20, 25, 25n, 56–57, 59, 62, 73–74, 75, 80, 83, 86, 98, 104, 109, 111, 113–14, 122, 147, 267, 396
Wheeler, Gen. Joseph, 230, 295, 302, 363
   background, 196
   and Daiquirí landing, 265
   and disease in army, 374–75
   illness, 294, 324, 340, 341, 341n
   and Las Guásimas battle, 269, 270–71, 272, 275, 278, 279
   learns of relief column, 289–90
   reconnoiters El Caney, 294
   reconnoiters Santiago, 279, 324
   and San Juan battle, 304, 310
   and siege of Santiago, 325, 327, 340, 342, 348–49
   and surrender of Santiago, 350
"White Man's Burden, The," 387
Whitman, Walt, 278, 314
Whitney, Lt. Henry H., 353–54, 354n, 355
Wick, Sgt. John H., 248
Wikoff, Col. C. A., 313, 362
Wildes, Capt., 186
Wilhelm II, 67, 68–69, 71, 100, 104–5, 107, 192, 365, 384
Wilkie, John E., 233, 234
Wilmington, 110, 201–2, 204
William Curry's Sons, 208
Williams, O. F., 176, 178
Wilson, Pres. Woodrow, 399
Wilson-Gorman tariff, 51
Wilmington, 108, 110
Winder, Lt. William, 181

Windom, 205
Windsor Hotel, 232, 233, 234
Winning of the West, 91
Winslow, 204
Winslow, Lt. Cameron, 205–7
Winter, Dr. Francis A., 287
Wolff, Sir Henry Drummond, 70–72
Wood, Leonard, 145, 225, 269–73, 274n, 275,
    277–78, 297, 299, 303, 308, 315. 321, 360, 361,
    399
Woodbine, Ga., 61
Woodford, Gen. Stewart L., 103, 104, 113–14, 118,
    119, 121–22, 123, 142, 143–44, 149–50, 159,
    160, 161, 163, 165, 168
Worth, Lt. Col. William, 313
Wright, Orville, 281
Wright, Wilbur, 281

Yale, 209, 219, 288
Yalu, Battle of, 97
Yankee, 238
Yara, Cuba, 280
Yauco, P.R., 356
Ybor City, Fla., 240
yellow journalism, 20, 77–78, 82, 82n, 147
Yokahama, Japan, 102, 120
Young, James Rankin, 116n
Young, John Russell, 116n
Young, Gen. Samuel B. M., 270–71, 272, 274–75,
    297, 341
Yucatan, 242, 269
Yucatan Channel, 216, 220

Zafiro, 176, 177, 181, 188
Zanjón, Cuba, 45, 47, 55